FARM HOLIDAY
BUREAU

Stay on a farm

JARROLD
PUBLISHING

English
Tourist Board

SCOTLAND

BWRDD CROESO CYMRU
WALES TOURIST BOARD

Northern Ireland
Tourist Board

1/95
Published by Jarrold Publishing, Whitefriars, Norwich NR3 1TR
in association with the Farm Holiday Bureau (UK) Ltd, the English Tourist Board and the
National Tourist Boards of Scotland, Wales and Northern Ireland
© Farm Holiday Bureau UK 1995
National Agricultural Centre, Stoneleigh, Warwickshire CV8 2LZ

ISBN 0 7117 0838 X

The information contained in this Guide has been published in good faith on the basis of
the details submitted by the proprietors of the premises listed. These proprietors are
current members of the Farm Holiday Bureau and have paid for their entries in this
Guide. Whilst every effort has been made to ensure accuracy in this publication, neither
the publisher, the Farm Holiday Bureau nor the National Tourist Boards can guarantee
the accuracy of the information in this Guide and accept no responsibility for any error
or misrepresentation. All liability for loss, disappointment, negligence or other damage
caused by reliance on the information contained in this Guide, or in the event of
bankruptcy, or liquidation, or cessation of trade of any company, individual or firm
mentioned is hereby excluded.

The Farm Holiday Bureau of the United Kingdom gratefully acknowledges the
continuing assistance and advice offered by the National Tourist Boards, the Agricultural
Development Advisory Service of the Ministry of Agriculture, the Scottish Agricultural
Organisations Society Ltd, and all those who seek to maintain a balance in the rural
community.

Produced by The Pen and Ink Book Company Limited, Huntingdon, Cambridgeshire

Colour maps provided by Lovell Johns Ltd., Oxford

Printed and bound in Great Britain

Contents

Stay on a Farm –
with The Archers

Each year millions of listeners to The Archers on BBC Radio Four hear Phil Archer's wife Jill making bookings for her 'bed and breakfast' guests. (They also hear her preparing for them, pulling out all the stops to make sure they're made welcome and comfortable, and also, inevitably, sinking back exhausted when they've gone!)

Truth and fiction often overlap in *The Archers:* that must surely be one of the many reasons for its long run – I first played the part of Phil forty-five years ago in May 1950, and I've got a personal entry in the *Guinness Book of Records* to prove it! In the early days some of us had the greatest difficulty in convincing our listeners that we weren't really farmers, and that Brookfield Farm and the village of Ambridge didn't exist. And it's the same with Jill's guests: they are as real as Phil's pigs or Eddie Grundy's dreadful hat. That is to say very real indeed… but only in the minds of our listeners.

Like hundreds of other farming folk, the Archers are finding life far from feather-bedded. Times are hard. Many farmers are turning to other ways of using their assets. And what assets they are! Many farmhouses are of considerable architectural interest. Most of them have idyllic views over charming countryside. From a farmhouse window you can see today the beginning of a resurgence in the growth of our woods and valleys, our wild flowers and our wildlife, which only so recently were under threat. You can see for yourself how the work of all those environmental enthusiasts is proceeding.

The mind-soothing peace of the countryside lies within a couple of minutes' walk from most of our farmhouses. Birds sing undisturbed. Of course there may be sounds of farm-machinery on occasions; but most of their work is done far away from the farmhouse in the surrounding fields. If you happen to be staying on a dairy farm, then twice a day you may hear the throb-

throb-throb of the milking-parlour. I personally find that a rather comforting, reassuring sound and so – would you believe – do the cows.

Don't think that by staying on a farm you'll be out in the wilds, miles from civilization. Some, it is true, are more tucked away than others, though many people are amazed to find how near to the centre of some towns the wild open spaces are: as little as five or ten minutes in the car. In this age of the motorway many farmhouses have suddenly found themselves only a few miles from a motorway exit, near enough for convenience, but far enough away not to be disturbed by the traffic noise. Many farmhouses are on coastal areas, offering sea-views, surfing, sailing, cliff walks and even a private beach.

You can stay on a farm for a short break or a single night; or stay for a week or more and make a full holiday of it. Those in business can not only enjoy farmhouse fare in the calm of the country after a busy day on the road, but can also book a meeting room to get together with colleagues away from the

distractions of the office.

Mention of farm food reminds me that one of the greatest joys of staying on a farm is the quality of the food and cooking. Most offer dinner and a full, very English, (or Welsh, Scottish or Irish!), cooked breakfast, often with home-produced fresh fruit and vegetables.

Check that the farm where you are going is a member of the Farm Holiday

Bureau. You'll then have the satisfaction of knowing that every aspect of the accommodation, from the bathroom to the kitchen has been inspected and quality graded by the National Tourist Boards. Over one thousand independent farmers offer this type of accommodation. Most farmers are only too keen to show you over the farm and some have created 'farm trails'. Some of the accommodation may be in converted farm buildings, some of which offer self-catering. Not too long ago I stayed myself in such a conversion: I had an airy bedroom, with tea and coffee-making facilities, a large en suite bathroom and a country view – with delicious farmhouse food only a few yards away. What more could one ask?

Self-catering accommodation on farms is becoming increasingly popular. At Brookfield Phil and Jill have Rickyard Cottage while the Aldridges at Home Farm go one better (of course!). Jennifer has three cottages, all self-contained and self-catering.

You may be wondering why it is I who am telling you all this. Let me explain. When the Farm Holiday Bureau was set up under the auspices of the Royal Agricultural Society of England (RASE), the Ministry of Agriculture, the English Tourist Board and *Farmers Weekly*, a launch was held at a farm museum in Oxfordshire. Various representatives of the organisations concerned made short speeches, and so did I, not of course as P. Archer 'farmer' but as the honorary Life Governor of RASE (an honour bestowed on me to mark the first quarter-century of *The Archers*). I am extremely proud of it: and so you can imagine my discomfiture a few years later when wearing my other hat as Phil Archer, I had to play the irritated husband who felt his wife was giving more time to her holiday guests than she was to him. All quite untrue of course, and it quickly blew over.

Those who are members of the Farm Holiday Bureau set very great store on producing the highest possible standards in the services they offer. That's because they are real country people. They do their utmost to give you a warm welcome, with the best they can afford at a fair price. Real country people are like that.

If you are reading these words then you are holding in your hand the best guide to farmhouse accommodation available. It's a fascinating read in itself, even for the armchair traveller. Here, taken at random are a few extracts: "Georgian farmhouse… well-behaved pets welcome… babysitter… swimming in our own pool… riding… close to golf course … coastal walks and fishing… en suite rooms suitable for disabled guests… ducks on the pond and badgers in the wood… thatched farmhouse… four-poster beds… oak beams… children may search for eggs, milk the goat, ride the pony, feed the lambs, pigs, chickens, ducks and geese, or play in our games room… inglenook… modern bungalow in glorious surroundings… all the usual extras, including hairdryer, remote control colour teletext TV plus trouser press, direct dial telephone…" and on and on and on.

There is, though, one final thing: Jill and Phil Archer, the Aldridges, Ambridge and Brookfield Farm may be more real than real to our listeners, but you won't find them in this guide. They are all the creations of the imagination. But don't despair: there are hundreds of other real 'Brookfields' to choose from; whether on your own or with a family, whether you're on business or travelling for pleasure; whether you're less abled or fit enough for the most strenuous of holidays, I know from experience that you'll receive a very warm welcome if you decide to STAY ON A FARM.

by Norman Painting OBE, 'Philip' in BBC Radio 4's The Archers.

How to use the guide

Selecting your farm...

The guide lists all the members of the Farm Holiday Bureau (UK) Ltd in the countries of England, Scotland, Wales and Northern Ireland. Members belong to one of 92 Farm Holiday Bureau Groups: key maps in the section entitled, Where to Go on pages 10–12 will tell you which counties and areas the individual FHB Groups cover. Arranged within countries, each Group has a numbered section in this guide which opens with a description of the area and an outline map showing the location of each farm. The Group contacts can help you find suitable accommodation if you wish.

Properties in each Group section are listed alphabetically under Bed and Breakfast, Self-Catering, and Camping and Caravanning. All entries feature a brief description and a line illustration, along with an indication of prices for bed and breakfast, self-catering and for evening meals where available. Clear symbols (see page 15) indicate what further facilities are provided.

An Index at the back of the guide (page 383) shows all members who offer facilities for camping and caravanning and those who welcome business travellers (with meeting room capacity where provided). The Index also lists those farms who welcome disabled guests (indicated in the entries by the wheelchair symbol). Facilities provided will vary so we recommend you check any special needs before booking. The Accessible Symbol (explained on page 14) identifies those farms who have invited the Tourist Board to check the facilities they offer to wheelchair users or those who have difficulty walking.

How to book...

All you have to do is telephone the farm of your choice. If the accommodation you want is not available, the owner will be happy to refer you to similar alternative FHB accommodation. **Alternatively, the Group Contact will be happy to help you find the right accommodation, and can usually provide you with a local group leaflet.**

Many members also offer a 'book a bed ahead' service to their guests. If you are touring, just tell your host where you wish to visit next, and he or she can make the booking for you.

PLEASE REMEMBER TO MENTION *STAY ON A FARM* WHEN MAKING A BOOKING

When making a booking...

- Mention the guide.

- Specify your planned arrival and departure dates.

- Specify accommodation needed and any particular requirements, eg twin beds, family room, private bath, ground floor, cot.

- Specify terms required, eg B&B, evening meal etc. Evening meal times vary and high tea may be available for children. Farms offering evening meals do not necessarily do so all year round so do check.

- Specify special requirements, eg special diets, facilities for disabled people, arrangements for children, dogs.

- Check prices and any reductions that may be offered.

- Check whether a deposit is payable and, if so, what charges will apply if the booking is cancelled (see 'Cancellations' opposite).

- Check method and date of payment.

- Check whether B&B access is restricted through the day. Many farms are happy for visitors to stay in the house all day, but on some farms this is not practical and guests are asked to be out of the farmhouse between 10.30am and 4.30pm. Remember, it is essential that children are carefully supervised at all times on and around the farm.

• Check the best time to arrive and ask for directions to the farm. When you are near your destination, look out for the Farm Holiday Bureau member sign at the end of the drive. Your host will be glad to direct you by phone if you get lost.

• Give your name, address and telephone number.

NB We recommend that, time permitting, all telephone bookings are confirmed in writing, specifying exactly what you have booked and the price you expect to pay.

Payment and deposits
For reservations made in advance a deposit is usually payable and this will be deducted from the total bill. When you book please check when and how payment should be made.

Cancellations
Once a booking has been agreed, on the telephone or by letter, a legally binding contract has been made with the host. If you cancel a reservation, fail to take up the accommodation or leave prematurely (regardless of the reasons), the host may be entitled to compensation if it cannot be relet for all or a good part of the booked period. If a deposit has been paid it is likely to be forfeited and an additional payment may be demanded.

Insurance
Travel and holiday insurance protection policies can be taken out to safeguard visitors in the event of cancellation or curtailment. Insurance of personal property can also be sought. Hosts cannot accept liability for any loss or damage to visitors' property, however caused. Do make sure that your valuables are covered by your household insurance before you take them away.

Compliments and complaints

Many visitors write to the Farm Holiday Bureau saying how much they have enjoyed their stay. If you feel that something or someone deserves acknowledgement, or if you have a suggestion on how to improve the guide, please write to the Farm Holiday Bureau (UK) Ltd, National Agricultural Centre, Stoneleigh, Warwickshire CV8 2LZ, or ring (01203) 696909.

If you are dissatisfied, please make your complaint to the host there and then. This gives an opportunity for rectifying action to be taken at once. It is usually difficult to deal with a complaint if it is reported at a later date. If the host fails to resolve the problem, please write to the Farm Holiday Bureau who will be happy to help.

Where to go

The Farm Holiday Bureau has 92 local Groups, each of which has a section in this guide. The maps show the location of each Group and their position in the countries. Page numbers are indicated in *italic*; Group numbers are in red.

Scotland

England

Wales

Northern Ireland

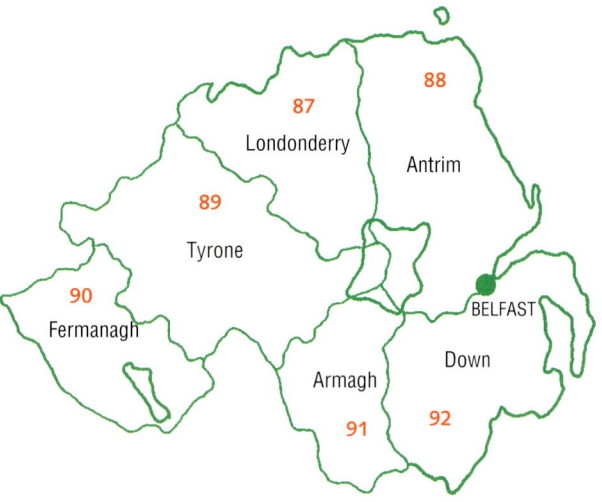

Accommodation classification and grading

Farm Holiday Bureau members are inspected by their Groups to ensure that a high standard of cleanliness, courtesy and service is maintained. All members must also be inspected by their National Tourist Board, agree to meet the Tourist Board's Minimum Standards and observe the Tourist Board's Code of Conduct.

Listed

Crown classification and grading scheme for serviced accommodation

The National Tourist Boards for England, Scotland and Wales operate a common classification and grading scheme for serviced accommodation including farmhouses. Each member has a thorough annual inspection by the Tourist Board and is classified, according to the range of facilities provided, within 6 bands from '**Listed**' and then from **1–5 Crowns**. The more Crowns, the more extensive the range of facilities.

Quality grading

Classified establishments can apply to be assessed for a separate quality commendation of '**Approved**', '**Commended**', '**Highly Commended**' or '**De Luxe**'. When granted, the quality commendation appears alongside the classification. In Wales, members who offer superior standards and have completed a tourism training course also have the 'Award' sign indicating that they are in receipt of the Wales Tourist Board's Farmhouse Award.

Self-catering holiday homes

All Bureau members who offer self-catering accommodation must have been inspected by the Tourist Boards or have applied for an inspection.

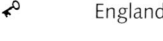

England

Scotland

Wales

Those inspected in England and Scotland are classified according to the range of facilities they provide (**1–5 Keys** in England, **1–5 Crowns** in Scotland). Holiday Homes with higher quality standards have the term 'Approved', 'Commended', 'Highly Commended'or 'De Luxe' alongside the classification. In Wales quality standards are indicated on a scale of **1–5 Dragons**.

Northern Ireland

The Northern Ireland Tourist Board registers and grades all accommodation under a statutory system. All the farms listed offer a high standard and are inspected annually.

✓
✓ ✓
✓ ✓ ✓
✓ ✓ ✓ ✓
✓ ✓ ✓ ✓ ✓

British graded holiday parks scheme

The National Tourist Boards for England, Scotland and Wales operate a common quality grading scheme for holiday caravan, camping and chalet parks. The scheme grades parks according to the relative quality of what is offered, in a range of 1–5 ✓s. The more ✓s the higher the quality.

Wheelchair accessibility symbols

All the places that display one of the symbols shown here have been checked by a Tourist Board Inspector against standard criteria that reflect the practical needs of wheelchair users.There are three categories of accessibility:

 Category 1:
Accessible to all wheelchair users including those travelling independently.

 Category 2:
Accessible to a wheelchair user travelling with a helper.

 Category 3:
Accessible to a wheelchair user able to walk short distances and up three steps.

Please check at the time of booking if you have special needs.

Inspected accessible schemes have been developed throughout the UK as part of the nationwide Tourism for All campaign in conjunction with the Hotel and Holiday Consortium and are designed to provide disabled travellers with reliable information on standards and facilities. Additional help and guidance on finding suitable holiday accommodation for those with special needs can be obtained from: Holiday Care Service on (01293) 774535.

Welcome Host

The National Tourist Boards recently launched a Welcome Host scheme. Service and hospitality are as important as good accommodation and good food. The Welcome Host training programme places the emphasis on warm hospitality and first-class service. Recipients of the Welcome Host certificate or badge are part of a fine tradition – a tradition for friendliness.

Look at the entries to find those farms participating in the Welcome Host scheme.

 Wales   *England* W *Scotland*

Taste of Wales

The Taste of Wales Hospitality Scheme promotes the use of fresh local food produce, and where better to find the freshest, most local food than down on the farm. Farmhouses have always played a great part in the Taste of Wales scheme, and in many regions they are the backbone of the local economy. The Farm Holiday Bureau promotes the best of farmhouses, and many Taste of Wales members are included in this guide.

Symbols

Symbol	Explanation	French	German
☎(3)	Children welcome (minimum age)	Enfants bienvenus (âge minimum)	Kinder willkommen (Mindestalter)
🐕	Dogs by arrangement	Chiens autorisés sous réserve d'accord préalable	Hunde nach Vereinbarung
♿	Accommodation for disabled/less able people (check for full details)	Hébergement pour les handicappés (demandez les détails)	Unterkunft behindertengerecht (weitere Information auf akzeptiert)
✼	No smoking	Non fumeurs de préférence	Nichtraucher bevorzugt
💳	Credit cards accepted	Cartes de crédit acceptées	Kreditkarten werden akzeptiert
♟	Business people welcome	Facilités pour hommes d'affaires	Geschäftsreisende willkommen
🌲	Waymarked walks on farm	Visite de fermes avec indication d'itinèncuies	Wanderwege gezeichnet
♞	Foreign language(s) spoken	Langues étrangères parlées	Hier werden Fremdsprachen gesprochen
🐎	Riding on farm	Randonnée à poney ou équitation	Reiten auf Ponys oder Pferden
🎣	Fishing on farm	La pêche à la ligne	Angeln
⊜	Country house, not a working farm	Manoir (pas une) exploitation agricole)	Landhaus, kein aktiver Bauernhof
⛺	Camping facilities	Camping	Camping – Einrichtungen
🚐	Caravanning facilities	Caravaning	Caravan – Einrichtungen
Prices		**Prix**	**Preise**
B&B	price per person per night for bed and breakfast	Prix par personne par nuit pour chambre + petit déjeuner	Preis pro Person pro Nacht für Bett und Frühstück
EM	price per person for evening meal	Prix par personne pour repas du soir	Preis pro Person für Abendessen
SC	price per unit per week self-catering	Prix par location par semaine	Preis pro Einheit pro Woche bei Selbstversorgung
Tents	price per tent pitch per night	Prix par tente par nuit	Preis pro Zeltaufstellung pro Nacht
Caravans	price per caravan pitch per night	Prix par caravane par nuit	Preis pro Caravanaufstellung pro Nacht
	All prices include VAT and service charge if any.	Tous les prix tiennent compete de la TVA et du service, le cas échéant.	Alle Preise inklusive MWSt und Bedienungsgeld, wenn überhaupt

Further information

These official Tourist Boards will be happy to supply you with further general information on their areas.

National Tourist Boards

English Tourist Board
Thames Tower, Black's Road, Hammersmith, London W6 9EL
☎ (0181) 846 9000

Northern Ireland Tourist Board
59 North Street
Belfast
BT1 1ND
☎ (01232) 231221

Scottish Tourist Board
23 Ravelston Terrace, Edinburgh EH4 3EU
☎ (0131) 332 2433

Wales Tourist Board
Brunel House, 2 Fitzalan Road, Cardiff CF2 1UY
☎ (01222) 499909

Regional Tourist Boards

Cumbria Tourist Board
(covering the county of Cumbria)
Ashleigh, Holly Road, Windermere, Cumbria LA23 2AQ
☎ (015394) 44444

Northumbria Tourist Board
(covering the counties of Cleveland, Durham, Northumberland, Tyne & Wear)
Aykley Heads, Durham DH1 5UX
☎ (0191) 384 6905

North West Tourist Board
(covering the counties of Cheshire, Greater Manchester, Lancashire, Merseyside and the High Peak District of Derbyshire)
Swan House, Swan Meadow Road,
Wigan Pier, Wigan WN3 5BB
☎ (01942) 821222

Yorkshire and Humberside Tourist Board
(covering the counties of North Yorkshire, South Yorkshire, West Yorkshire and Humberside)
312 Tadcaster Road, York, North Yorkshire YO2 2HF
☎ (01904) 707961

Heart of England Tourist Board
(covering the counties of Gloucestershire, Hereford & Worcester, Shropshire, Staffordshire, Warwickshire and West Midlands)
Woodside, Larkhill, Worcester, Hereford & Worcester WR5 2EF
☎ (01905) 763436

East Midlands Tourist Board
(covering the counties of Derbyshire, Leicestershire, Lincolnshire, Northamptonshire and Nottinghamshire)
Exchequergate, Lincoln, Lincolnshire LN2 1PZ
☎ (01522) 531521

East Anglia Tourist Board
(covering the counties of Bedfordshire, Cambridgeshire, Essex, Hertfordshire, Norfolk and Suffolk)
Toppesfield Hall, Hadleigh, Suffolk IP7 5DN
☎ (01473) 822922

London Tourist Board
(covering the Greater London area)
26 Grosvenor Gardens, London SW1W 0DU
Written enquiries only.

West Country Tourist Board
(covering the counties of Avon, Cornwall, Devon, Dorset (parts of), Somerset, Wiltshire and Isles of Scilly)
60 St Davids Hill, Exeter EX4 4SY
☎ (01392) 76351

Southern Tourist Board
(covering the counties of Berkshire, Buckinghamshire, Eastern and Northern Dorset, Hampshire, Oxfordshire and Isle of Wight)
40 Chamberlayne Road, Eastleigh, Hampshire SO5 5JH
☎ (01703) 620006

South East England Tourist Board
(covering the counties of Kent, Surrey and East, West Sussex)
The Old Brew House, Warwick Park, Tunbridge Wells, Kent TN2 5TU
☎ (01892) 540766

Tourist Information Centres

There are over 800 Tourist Information Centres throughout the United Kingdom and they are there for you to use both before your holiday and during it. Look in your local telephone directory under 'Tourist Information' to find your nearest centre. TICs can give you details about local attractions, events and accommodation and many will even be able to book it for you. Look out for the information sign.

MAP OF GREAT BRITAIN

KEY TO MAP SECTIONS

Map pages 18-32   **Scale 1:2 000 000**

Scotland
Highlands & Islands

Group Contact: 📖 *Margaret Pottie* ☎/Fax 01667 462213
📖 *Jessie Masheter* ☎ 01463 782423/782942

'Ceud mìle fàilte', – a hundred thousand welcomes – to the Highlands and Islands, the last great open space in Europe, a spectacular land mass and myriad islands covering nearly 15,000 square miles of unsurpassed scenic beauty. Mountains, glens, lochs, lonely sandy beaches and rugged unspoilt coastline.

Contrasting Highland landscapes provide an unrivalled backdrop for holiday activities. Enthusiasts of boating, fishing, golf, walking, birdwatching and geology are well catered for. In the land where deer and eagle roam free, wildlife lovers can also observe seals, ospreys and otters in their natural habitat. Old castles, battlefield monuments and folk museums testify to a past rich in history, culture and folklore. Land use ranges from small west coast crofts to larger hill sheep farms and to beef and grain producing units further east.

Easily accessible by road, rail and aeroplane from the south. You are assured of the clean air, peace and freedom and the traditional Highland welcome famed throughout the world. 'Haste ye back.'

[Map of Scotland Highlands & Islands showing numbered locations. Places labelled include: Lochranza, Brodick, Kilmory, ISLE OF ARRAN, Dornoch, Tain, Invergordon, Alness, Cromarty, Lossiemouth, Burghead, Buckie, Fortrose, Forres, Elgin, Nairn, Inverness, Rothes, Charlestown of Aberlour, Dufftown, Grantown-on-Spey, Newtonmore. Roads labelled: A838, A837, A835, A836, A837, A832, A896, A832, A890, A87, A82, A9, A939, A95, A96, A941, A895, A841. Numbered markers 1–17.]

BED AND BREAKFAST

(and evening meal)

---

(1) Balaggan Farm, Culloden Moor, By Inverness, Inverness-shire IV1 2EL

Mrs Phyllis Alexander
☎ 01463 790213
🅱 From £15
EM From £9
Sleeps 5
🛏 🐕 ⬠
Listed *Commended*

A warm welcome awaits you on our small stock rearing farm set in peaceful surroundings. Good home cooking and baking is served. Log fires burn in lounge and dining room. 1 family and 1 twin bedroom, with electric blankets and tea/coffee-making facilities. Ideal for touring Highlands with Culloden battlefield and Cawdor Castle. Many places of interest close by. Open April–Nov.

---

(2) Daviot Mains Farm, Daviot, Nr Inverness, Inverness-shire IV1 2ER

Margaret & Alex Hutcheson
☎/Fax 01463 772215
🅱 From £16–£22
EM From £10
Sleeps 8
🛏 🐕 🧒(3) ⬠ 🏺
🐄🐄
Highly Commended

Comfortable early 19th century listed farmhouse in quiet situation near Inverness. Relax in the warm atmosphere of this friendly home where delicious meals are thoughtfully prepared for you and where log fires burn in both sitting and dining rooms. En suite/private facilities available. The perfect base for exploring the Scottish Highlands. Selected by "Taste of Scotland" and recommended by Elizabeth Grundrey's S.O.T.B.T. Open all year.

---

(3) Drumbuie Farm, Drumbuie, Drumnadrochit, Inverness-shire IV3 6XP

Mrs Caroline Urquhart
☎/Fax 01456 450634
🅱 From £16–£17.50
EM From £8
Sleeps 6
🧒(12) 🍴 🎋
🐄🐄🐄 *Highly Commended*

Custom-built farmhouse with en suite accomodation overlooking Loch Ness and sorrounding hills. Farm is mostly cattle including several Highland (hairy) cows and calves. Drumnadrochit is the perfect base when visiting the Highlands. Skye, Ullapool and the North all within easy reach. You are assured of a Scottish welcome at Drumbuie. Open all year.

---

(4) Easter Dalziel Farm, Dalcross, Inverness, Inverness-shire IV1 2JL

Bob & Margaret Pottie
☎/Fax 01667 462213
🅱 From £15–£17
EM From £10
Sleeps 6
🛏 🐕 ⬠ 🦎
🐄 *Highly Commended*

Scottish farming family offers friendly hospitality on stock/arable farm. Delightful accommodation in early Victorian farmhouse, log fire, colour TV. Delicious home cooking and baking, choice of breakfasts. Superb central location east of Inverness between A96/B9039, panoramic views. Many recommendations including Elizabeth Gundrey and The Best Bed and Breakfast, AA QQQ Recommended. Open all year.

---

(5) Glen Cloy Farmhouse, Brodick, Isle of Arran KA27 8DA

Mr and Mrs Padfield
☎ 01770 302351
🅱 From £20–£26
EM From £10
Sleeps 9
🧒(3) 🛏 🐴 🎋 🐎 🦎
🐄🐄 *Commended*

Glen Cloy farmhouse is a century-old farmhouse set in a quiet glen just outside Brodick. The house is surrounded by a mixed farm and offers warm, cosy rooms and excellent cooking using homegrown produce. A log fire burns cheerily in the drawing room. Taste of Scotland selected member. Close to golf, pony trekking, castle and mountains. Open Mar–Nov.

"Taransay", Lower Muckovie Farm, Inverness, Inverness-shire IV1 2BB

Mrs Aileen Munro
☎ **01463 231880**
[BB] **From £16–£18**
Sleeps 4
✄ ☜ ☂
☙☙ *Commended*

A warm and friendly welcome awaits you at this comfortable, well-appointed bungalow on a quiet dairy farm. 2 miles south of Inverness, on the old A9, close to Drumossie Hotel. Magnificent views. 1 twin bedroom (en suite facilities) and 1 double bedroom. Close to Culloden battlefield, Cawdor Castle and golf courses. Good restaurants nearby. AA Selected. Open all year.

Thistle-Doo, Kilchrenan, by Taynuilt, Oban, Argyll PA35 1HF

K.Lambie
☎ **01866 833339**
[BB] **From £16–£20**
EM from £10
Sleeps 6
✄ ☜ ⚘ ☂ ☂
☙☙☙ *Commended*

Awe-inspiring view of Loch Awe from our friendly family-run establishment. Ideal for all outdoor activities. Very peaceful and relaxing. 20 miles east of Oban, taking the B845 off the A85 at Taynuilt to the shore of Loch Awe. Open all year.

Upper Latheron Farm, Latheron, Caithness KW5 6DT   ⑧

Mrs Camilla Sinclair
☎ **01593 741224**
[BB] **From £14–£16**
Sleeps 6
☜ ☂ ⚘ ❦
Listed *Highly Commended*

This attractive farm is idyllically situated with breathtaking views of the coastline. Ideal centre for touring northern Highlands, Visit John O'Groats, viewing seals and puffins, day trip to Orkney Islands, castles, Highland gatherings or ancient cairns. Friendly farm animals include Sarah the Jersey cow and frolicsome newborn foals. Open May–Sept.

SELF-CATERING

Borlum Farm Cottage, Borlum Farm, Drumnadrochit, Inverness, Inverness-shire IV3 6XN

Mrs Vanessa MacDonald-Haig
☎ **01456 450358**
Fax 01456 450358
[SC] **From £185–£440**
 ♿ ☂ (by arrangement)
☜ ⊞ ⚘ ❦ ☂
☙☙☙ *Commended*

Borlum Farm is a working hill farm with its own BHS-approved riding centre. The self-catering cottage is spacious, comfortable, and tastefully furnished, with splendid views overlooking Loch Ness. Excellently equipped, including microwave cooker, hair dryer and even hot water bottle! Oil-fired central heating also available if required in colder periods. Open all year.

Culligran Cottages, Glen Strathfarrar, Struy, Nr Beauly, Inverness-shire IV4 7JX

Frank & Juliet Spencer-Nairn
☎/**Fax 01463 761285**
[SC] **From £99–£359**
Sleeps 5/7
❦ ☜ ☂
☙☙☙ *Commended to Highly Commended*

A regular? You soon could be. So don't delay – send for a brochure! This is your opportunity to stay on a deer farm within the beautiful Strathfarrar Nature Reserve. Watch the wild deer from your window and feed the farm deer during a conducted tour. Choice of chalet or cottage. Bikes for hire. Salmon and trout fishing. Hotel and inn nearby. Open late Mar–mid Nov.

⑪ Easter Dalziel Farm, Dalcross, Inverness, Inverness-shire IV1 2JL

Bob & Margaret Pottie
☎/Fax 01667 462213
sc From £120–£350
Sleeps 4/6
♿ 🛏 🖼 ♉

Commended to Highly Commended

Enjoy a relaxing holiday in our cosy, traditional stonebuilt cottages. Between Inverness and Nairn on our stock/arable farm. A truly central location from which to explore the Highlands. The local area offers a wide range of activities to suit the sports-minded, tourer or walker alike. Look out for dolphins, badgers and buzzards, visit Cawdor, Culloden, Fort George and Loch Ness. Short breaks or Long Stays welcome all year. Brochure. Open all year.

⑫ Greenhill Farmhouse, Mid-Clyth, Lybster, Caithness, Highland KW3 6BA

Mrs Camilla Sinclair
☎ 01593 741224
sc From £175–£375
Sleeps 6
♿ 🛏 ♉

Highly Commended

Farmhouse overlooking the sea (½ mile away), tastefully decorated, exceptionally well-equipped with all home comforts including dishwasher, washing machine, tumble dryer, fridge/freezer, payphone, microwave, hair dryer, all linen. Ideal for country walks/picnics. Archaeological cairn in farm. Golf, fishing, pony trekking nearby. Perfect centre for touring North of Scotland. Open all year.

⑬ Lochletter Lodges, Lochletter Farm, Balnain, Drumnadrochit, Inverness-shire IV3 6TJ

Miss M Brook/Mrs Bowden
☎ 01456 476313
Fax 01456 476301
sc From £140–£400
EM £10 max
Sleeps 4/6
♿ ♿ ♉ 🧺 ♉

Highly Commended

Four pine lodges situated on farm by Loch Meiklie, all equipped to a high standard, and all accessible to disabled people. Ideal for touring Highlands, hillwalking, golf, fishing. Indoor tennis and badminton on site. Home cooked bread and meals available daily. Open all year.

⑭ Mains of Aigas, By Beauly, Inverness-shire IV4 7AD

Mrs Jessie Masheter
☎/Fax 01463 782423
sc From £150–£390
♿ ♉ ♉ **Guide dogs only**

Commended to Highly Commended

Unique setting beside the peaceful River Beauly at the foot of beautiful Strathglass. Enjoy special guest rates on our own 9-hole golf course, tour the Highland beauty spots from this perfect base or simply "stay at home" and relax. House, courtyard apartments attractively furnished and fully equipped for your comfort. Open Feb–Nov.

⑮ Scatwell Farm, Comrie, Contin, Strathpeffer, Ross-shire IV14 9EN

Margaret Cuthbert
☎ 01997 466234
sc From £100–£260
♿ ♉ ♿

Approved to Commended

Three comfortable cottages in a quiet location in beautiful Strathconon. Ideal for fishing, hill walking, bird-watching and as a touring base yet only 25 miles north of Inverness. Come and see the Red deer, salmon, eagles and abundant wildlife. Electric heating, well equipped kitchens, TV's, cot available. Prices include linen, electricity on meter, laundry on site. Fishing arranged. Illustrated brochure on request. Open Apr–Oct.

⑯ Strone Cottage, c/o Lochbuie Croft, Newtonmore, Inverness-shire PH20 1BA

Mary Mackenzie
☎ 01540 673504
sc From £180–£390
Sleeps 6
♿ ♉ ♿ 🧺

Commended

You'll be welcome at our croft on the outskirts of our lovely Highland village. Cosy renovated cottage has open fire, double glazing and CH. Downstairs en suite bedroom, upstairs 2 bedrooms and bathroom with small drying area. Electricity & coal incl. Enjoy peace and scenery, visit local attractions or take part in varied activities. Central for touring and 3 ski areas. Edinburgh 2 hours, Loch Ness 1 hour, Aviemore 15 mins. Brochure. Open all year.

Tomich Holidays, Guisachan Farm, Tomich, by Beauly, Inverness-shire IV4 7LY   17

Mr & Mrs D J Fraser
☎ **01456 415332**
Fax 01456 415499
SC **From £130–£395**
Sleeps 4–6
🐎 🐕 🐈 ♨
🛏 🛏 🛏 *Commended*
to Highly Commended

Our magnificent farm steading now houses three luxury cottages and a heated indoor swimming pool. Other accommodation is in spacious chalets set in woodland and a Victorian dairy. All have central heating, hot water and electricity included in the price. Tomich, in the depths of the Highlands near Glen Affric, is an ideal base for walking, touring or just relaxing. Open all year.

THE 1000+ BUREAU MEMBERS OFFER A UNIQUE LINK TO CUSTOMERS ACROSS THE UK

All Bureau members belong to a local Group. Each member can refer you to an equally high quality member within his Group... or across the UK: England, Northern Ireland, Scotland, Wales.

DISABLED VISITORS

Many members offer a welcome to disabled/less able visitors. Please do check the extent of the facilities before booking.

THOSE LITTLE EXTRAS

For advice on farms that can offer 'extras' such as four-poster beds, special diets, farm trails, fishing rights – even stabling and trekking arrangements if you are bringing your own horse – ring the Farm Holiday Bureau on (01203) 696909.

Scotland

Angus

Group Contact: *Mrs Deanna Lindsay* ☎ *01307 462887*

Whatever you seek in Scotland, you'll find in Angus, where the Braes of Angus meet the valley of Strathmore. From the glens with their gushing waterfalls to the numerous sandy beaches and bays along the east coast.

Visit Glamis Castle, former home of Queen Elizabeth the Queen Mother and birthplace of Princess Margaret, or Kirriemuir, birthplace of poet J.M. Barrie (Peter Pan). National Trust places of interest include the House of Dun (Adam), the Angus Folk Museum and many others.

Many sports are available, including hill-walking, birdwatching, riding, bowls, swimming, sailing and leisure centre sports. You can fish on the shores and banks of rivers and lochs, or hire a boat and fish the sea. Golf is Angus' most famous sport and can be enjoyed on a wide variety of courses: you can play a different course each day!

The Heritage Trail is a must for the visitor to our area, and Arbroath Abbey, Brechin Cathedral, Restenneth Priory and various Pictish standing stones and hill forts should be seen.

Angus is also an ideal touring base for a day visit to either Aberdeen, Dundee, Perth, St Andrews, Edinburgh or Balmoral. All Group hold Food Hygiene Certificates.

BED AND BREAKFAST

(and evening meal)

Blibberhill Farm, Brechin, Angus, Tayside DD9 6TH

Margaret Stewart
☎ 01307 830225
🅱 From £14.50–£17.50
EM From £8.50
Sleeps 6
✄
🐾🐾🐾 *Highly Commended*

Situated in peaceful surroundings, between Angus Glens and coast, near Glamis Castle, 1 hour's drive from Royal Deeside and St Andrews and central to many golf courses, fishing and hill-walking. 1 twin/double room with bath en suite, 2 twin with shower en suite. All bedrooms tastefully decorated and furnished, with tea/coffee-making facilities. A warm welcome is extended to all guests, with home cooking, baking, marmalade and jams. Evening dinner optional. AA selected. Open all year.

Purgavie Farm, Lintrathen, Kirriemuir DD8 5HZ

Mrs Moira Clark
☎/Fax 01575 560213
🅱 From £15.50–£16.50
EM From £9
Sleeps 6
🐴🐎🏕🐾🕯
🐾🐾🐾 *Highly Commended*

A warm welcome in homely accommodation on our farm set in peaceful countryside and providing traditional Scottish fayre. All rooms have private bathroom, TV and tea-making facilities. Fishing on Lintrathen loch, pony trekking and hill-walking in Glen Isla. Glamis Castle 10 miles. Located 7 miles from Kirriemuir, follow the B951 to Glen Isla; farm signposted at roadside. Open all year.

Wemyss Farm, Montrose Road, Forfar, Angus DD8 2TB

Mrs Deanna Lindsay
☎/Fax 01307 462887
🅱 From £14
EM From £8
Sleeps 6
🐎🐴🕯🅿
Listed *Commended*

190-acre mixed farm situated on the B9113 with a wide variety of animals. Ideal for touring Angus Glens, St Andrews, Royal Deeside, Aberdeen, Edinburgh, east coast resorts. Glamis Castle nearby. Shooting, fishing, golf, swimming, all in the area. Bedrooms overlooking beautiful countryside. Children made welcome, reduced rates. Evening dinner optional, packed lunches. Quiet and peaceful, yet within easy reach of all amenities. Food hygiene certificate held. Open all year.

Wood of Auldbar, Aberlemno, By Brechin, Angus, Tayside DD9 6SZ

Jean Stewart
☎ 01307 830218
🅱 From £14.50
EM From £9
Sleeps 6
🐴🐎✄
Listed *Commended*

Wood of Auldbar is a family farm of 187 acres with lovely farmhouse in first class condition. Very central for touring the Angus Glens, Royal Deeside, Balmoral, Glamis; many more castles within easy reach. Beaches, nature walks, birdwatching, fishing, golf, leisure facilities all near at hand. Standing stones and lovely churches. Excellent farmhouse cooking in award-winning farmhouse. Food hygiene certificate held. Tea facilities in all bedrooms. A warm welcome awaits you. Open all year.

LET THE TELEPHONE RING!

Some farmhouses are big places. Let the telephone ring long enough to give the owner time to answer it.

SELF-CATERING

---

⑤ Purgavie Farm, Lintrathen, Kirriemuir DD8 5HZ

Mrs Moira Clark
☎/Fax **01575 560213**
🆂🅲 **From £150–£350**
Sleep 4/6
🅗 🐂 🏃 🖭 🛍

♛♛♛♛ – ♛♛♛♛♛♛
*Commended to Highly
Commended*

Swedish log house also bungalow in lovely Angus glen. Wonderful views of the Valley of Strathmore. Pony trekking in Glen Isla and fishing in Lintrathen loch. Log house sleeps 6, bungalow 4. All linen supplied. Loghouse has 3 bedrooms, dishwasher and shower. Both properties have fridge freezer, washer, dryer, payphone and microwave. Located 7 miles from Kirriemuir, follow B951 signposted at roadside. Open all year.

GOOD FOOD

Nearly all Bureau members now hold a certificate in Essential Food Hygiene.

FINDING YOUR ACCOMMODATION

The Group contacts at the beginning of each section can always help you find a vacancy in your chosen area.

FOLLOW THE COUNTRY CODE

Leave nothing but footprints,
Take nothing but photographs,
Kill nothing but time!

Scotland

Perthshire

Group Contacts: 🆎 *Jo Andrew* ☎ *01350 724254*
🆂🅲 *Nigel Bruges* ☎ *01350 724208/724241*

Perthshire lies in the very centre of Scotland. For centuries the area has been the crossroads of the nation, and today's modern road, rail and coach service networks maintain that tradition, making it the ideal base for your Scottish holiday.

Here you'll find an area of outstanding beauty, the grandeur of mountains and glens, home of the native deer and other wild animals and flowers, the glimmer of lochs, hunting ground of the rare Osprey, and the River Tay, Scotland's greatest river – a true Angler's paradise.

See Perthshire at work producing top quality glass, pottery, hand-knitted woollens, leather goods, hornware and of course "the water of life". In Perthshire 4 malt whisky distilleries invite visitors to see (and taste) this unique product.

Perthshire is famed for its agriculture from quality cattle and sheep, barley for whisky and other arable crops to field vegetables and soft fruit.

There's something for everyone here – historic castles, houses and gardens, the world's highest beech hedge, Europe's oldest living tree, Perth's ultra modern leisure pool, 25 golf courses, Perth and Pitlochry theatres and of course numerous highland nights and ceilidhs.

BED AND BREAKFAST

(and evening meal)

1　Blackcraigs Farm, Scone, Perthshire PH2 7PJ

Irene Millar
☎ 01821 640254
🅱 From £15–£18
Sleeps 6
🐾
Listed *Commended*

Blackcraigs is a 269 acre farm where a warm welcome awaits you. Quiet and peaceful surroundings but only 5 minutes' drive from the tourist city of Perth. The farmhouse is tastefully decorated and has a homely atmosphere. Many attractions both north and south, this area being an ideal tourist area. Open all year.

2　Letter Farm, Loch of Lowes, By Dunkeld, Perthshire PH8 0HH

Jo Andrew
☎ 01350 724254
🅱 From £18–£25
Sleeps 6
🐾🐕✂🎠
🐝🐛 *Commended*

This tastefully renovated farmhouse offers a warm, friendly welcome to all ages. En suite facilities, king size beds, log fires and good home baking. The farm is central to Perthshire's attractions, but exudes peace and tranquillity, nestled next to the Scottish Wildlife Trust's Loch of Lowes Reserve, home of the osprey. Open all year except Christmas & New Year .

3　Pitmurthly, Redgorton, Nr. Luncarty, Perth PH1 3HY

Mrs Christine Smith
☎ 01738 828363
Fax 01738 828053
🅱 From £15–£18
Sleeps 5
🐾🐕✂🎠
Listed *Highly Commended*

Quiet, comfortable farmhouse in ideal touring location set amidst lovely countryside yet only 5 minutes from historic Perth with its unique shops and excellent restaurants. Log fires and full CH. Working farm with plenty to watch. Golf, fishing, riding and swimming can be arranged. Warm welcome assured. Open all year.

SELF-CATERING

4　Milton of Duchally Cottage, Millhill Farm, Auchterarder PH3 1PQ

Jennifer Davidson
☎ 01764 662227
🆂🅲 From £200–£450
Sleeps 4 + cot
🐾🐕✂

🌼🌼🌼 *Highly Commended*

Very comfortable, well equipped, two bedroomed detached cottage. Tumble drier, auto washing machine, coffee maker, colour TV, living room with open fire. Cot, high chair, play pen, stairgates available. Fenced garden with furniture. Ideal for golfing and touring central Scotland. Three miles from shops. If you like peace and quiet this is the cottage for you. Open Apr–Oct.

Wester Riechip, Laighwood, Butterstone, Dunkeld, Perthshire PH8 0HB

W & WI Bruges
☎ **01350 724241**
sc **From £320–£500**
Sleeps 8

De Luxe

Wester Riechip has been constructed from the west wing of a 19th century shooting lodge to create a luxurious detached holiday house with superb modern facilities. Comfortably accommodates 8. Spectacular views over surrounding hills and lochs. An ideal base for touring, golfing and birdwatching. Shooting and fishing available on our family-run hill farm. Open all year.

BUREAU ACCOMMODATION MEANS QUALITY

All Bureau members are inspected and quality graded by the National Tourist Board each year, as well as by fellow members.

DISABLED VISITORS

Many members offer a welcome to disabled/less able visitors. Please do check the extent of the facilities before booking.

FINDING YOUR ACCOMMODATION

The Group contacts at the beginning of each section can always help you find a vacancy in your chosen area.

Scotland

Fife

Group Contact: *Mrs Isobel Steven* ☎/Fax *01337 828414*

The Kingdom of Fife, a unique corner of Scotland, has many attractions for visitors.

Visit Dunfermline Palace and Abbey, Falkland with its Royal Palace, St Andrews with its wonderful clean beaches and historic buildings.

Rural Fife is dominated by the Lomond Hills and the region's patchwork of fields, forests, well-kept farming communities and enchanting fishing villages.

There are many towns and places, catering for all interests – Auchtermuchty location of television's most recent 'Dr Finlay' drama series; the Scottish Centre for Falconry and Scottish Fisheries Museum; the Scottish Deer Centre near Cupar; Fife Folk Museum in Ceres; Kellie Castle near Pittenweem; St Andrews with its many golf courses including the famous Old Course, venue for the British Open Golf Championship in 1995.

North Fife is blessed with a mild, sunny climate, a coastline which complements its fertile hinterland and a great range of holiday activities including gliding, bird-watching, golf, sailing, cycling and sightseeing.

The farming families of Fife warmly welcome you to this enchanting corner of Scotland.

[Map showing Fife and surrounding areas of Scotland, including Loch Tay, Perth, Dundee, Arbroath, Carnoustie, Newport-on-Tay, Tayport, Cupar, St Andrews, Crieff, Auchterarder, Auchtermuchty, Ladybank, Anstruther, Callander, Doune, Dunblane, Alva, Tillicoultry, Falkland, Leslie, Markinch, Bridge of Allan, Alloa, Glenrothes, Lochgelly, Cowdenbeath, Kirkcaldy, Kylsyth, Cumbernauld, North Berwick, Dunbar, Armadale, Bathgate, Queensferry, Edinburgh, East Linton, Glasgow, Dalkeith, Eyemouth, Motherwell, Peniculk, Lauder, Berwick-on-tweed, with various road numbers including A826, A822, A9, A923, A94, A929, A92, A85, A94, A914, A91, A915, A823, A917, M90, M80, M9, M8, A80, A71, A70, A702, A701, A703, A7, A68, A6105, M74]

BED AND BREAKFAST

(and evening meal)

Ardchoille Farmhouse, Dunshalt, Nr Auchtermuchty, Fife KY14 7EY

Isobel Steven
☎/Fax **01337 828414**
Mobile **0589 988174**
[BB] **From £25–£35**
EM **From £15**
Sleeps 6
🐴 🍴 🐕 🎄 📷

🐾 🐾 🐾 *Highly Commended*

Relax and enjoy the warm comfort, delicious 'Taste of Scotland' food and excellent hospitality. 3 en suite twin rooms, tastefully furnished with colour TV and tea/coffee trays with homemade butter shortbread. Large comfortable lounge, elegant dining room, 4 course dinners. Near Royal Palace of Falkland, 20 mins. St. Andrews, 1hr. Edinburgh. Ideal base for golfing & touring. Open all year. AA Premier selected 5Qs. RAC Highly acclaimed. Holder of REHIS diploma in advanced food hygiene.

Cambo House, Kingsbarns, St Andrews, Fife KY16 8QD

Peter Erskine
☎ **01333 450054**
Fax **01333 450987**
[BB] **From £35–£55**
EM **From £18**
Sleeps 6
🅲🅽 🐴 🍴 ⛳ 🎄 📷 ✂

🐾 🐾 🐾 *Commended*

Come and lose yourself in a glorious four-poster bed in our magnificent Victorian family home, set in parkland and woods that meander down to an unspoilt coastline with a fine sweeping beach. Only 10 minutes from St. Andrews. Open mid-Jan to mid-Dec.

Dunbog Farm, Newburgh, Cupar, Fife KY14 6JF

Arianne Harvey
☎ **01337 840393**
[BB] **From £20**
Sleeps 6
🐴 🐕 🍴 🎄 📷 ✂

Applied

Ideally situated in beautiful rolling countryside, this working arable farm offers spacious, comfortable bedrooms with en suite and private facilities, each with TV, tea/coffee and home baking. Lovely walks and gardens, tennis court and stabling. Cots available. Every effort will be made to ensure you enjoy your stay. Enquiries welcome. Open Apr–Oct.

Easter Clunie Farmhouse, Easter Clunie, Newburgh, Fife KY14 6EJ

Mrs Kathleen Baird
☎ **01337 840218**
[BB] **From £14–£16**
Sleeps 6
🐴(3)

🐾 🐾 *Commended*

David and Kathleen Baird warmly welcome you to their 18th century centrally heated farmhouse on a working farm. Home baking and tea on arrival. Relax in splendid walled garden, enjoy panoramic views of the River Tay. Surrounding countryside provides a wealth of scenic walks. Ideal touring base for Fife and Perthshire. Golf courses nearby. Open Apr–Oct.

SELF-CATERING

---

5 **Cambo House,** Kingsbarns, St Andrews, Fife KY16 8QD

Peter Erskine
☎ 01333 450054
Fax 01333 450987
SC From £150–£550
Sleeps 30
👶 🎠 🐕 🎣 ⛵ 🎾 💼 🎿
♨ ♨ ♨ Commended

We offer the perfect family holiday in self contained self-catering apartments and cottages on a beautiful, traditional wooded coastal estate, only 10 minutes from St. Andrews. At the heart of the estate is a magnificent Victorian mansion with plenty of facilities for all the family from a tennis court to a sauna. Open all year.

---

6 **Mountquhanie Holiday Homes,** Mountquhanie, Cupar by St Andrews, Fife KY15 4QJ

Mrs Andrew Wedderburn
☎ 01382 330252
Fax 01382 330480
SC From £185–£750
Sleeps 6/12
🐎 🐕 🎣 👶 🎣 🎾 💼 🎿
♨ ♨ ♨ ♨ – ♨ ♨ ♨ ♨ ♨
Highly Commended
De Luxe

Quality cottages and farmhouses in tranquil traditional countryside, or quality apartments in Georgian mansion, with all the ambience of country house living. Set in hundreds of acres of parkland with mature ancient trees. Experience harmonious integration of farming, forestry and conservation in action. Super for families, kids and pets. Magic for golfers – packages arranged. Open all year.

FARM HOLIDAY BUREAU

GOOD FOOD

Nearly all Bureau members now hold a certificate in Essential Food Hygiene.

PRICES

Prices include VAT and service charge (if any) and are:
B&B per person per night
EM per person
SC per unit per week
Tents and caravans per pitch per night

FARM HOLIDAY BUREAU

5

Scotland

Heart of Scotland

Group Contact: *Mrs Elsie Hunter* ☎ *01236 830243*

Discover the Heart of Scotland, with its wealth of contrasting scenery and interesting places to visit – plus the friendliness of the people. The area lies between the main towns of Edinburgh, Glasgow and Stirling, with easy access from the motorways.

Visit Edinburgh Castle, Prince's Street Gardens, the Royal Mile and Palace of Holyrood House, the Scottish residence of the royal family; Glasgow's museums and art galleries, plus the world famous Burrell Collection and People's Palace.

The historic town of Stirling, 'the Gateway to the Highlands', with its magnificent castle is a must – also Doune Motor Museum and Castle nearby, Summerlee Industrial Museum, Coatbridge, and Bo'ness and Kinneil Steam Railway Museum.

Explore the beautiful hills and lochs of the 'Trossachs', sail on Loch Lomond, or visit Callendar House and park, Falkirk, Linlithgow Palace (birthplace of Mary, Queen of Scots), also Hopetoun House near the famous Forth Bridges. Outdoor and indoor enthusiasts are all well catered for in the area.

A warm welcome awaits you. Do come and enjoy good food, comfortable farmhouses and Scottish hospitality at its best.

BED AND BREAKFAST

(and evening meal)

---

① Allanfauld Farm, Kilsyth, Glasgow G65 9DF

Libby MacGregor
☎ 01236 822155
🅱 From £15
Sleeps 4
🛏 🐕 ⅋ 🏕 ☂ ♨ ▬
Listed *Commended*

A working family farm situated close to the town of Kilsyth at the foot of the Kilsyth Hills, a great base to explore central Scotland. Located near A803 with easy access to M8 and M9. Golf, fishing, hill walking and a swimming pool are all within half a mile. Glasgow, Stirling 20 minutes. 1 twin/family room, 1 single room, both with TV and tea/coffee facilities. Open all year.

---

② Bandominie Farm, Walton Road, Bonnybridge FK4 2HP

Jean Forrester
☎ 01324 840284
🅱 From £15–£16
Sleeps 5
🛏 🅆
Listed *Commended*

A working farm located 2 miles from the A80 at Castlecary (B816). Easy access from Glasgow and Edinburgh. Lovely view with a homely atmosphere. Central heating, TV lounge. Ample parking. Open all year.

---

③ Belsyde Farm, Lanark Road, Linlithgow, West Lothian EH49 6QE

Mrs Nan Hay
☎ 01506 842098
Fax 01506 847611
🅱 From £16–£20
Sleeps 6
🛏 🐕 ☂ ♨ ▬
🍴🍴 *Commended*

An 18th century farmhouse located in large, secluded gardens with panoramic views over the Forth estuary. Golfing and fishing available locally. All bedrooms have washbasin (hot & cold), tea/coffee-making facilities, colour TV, central heating, 1 bedroom en suite. AA listed. Located close to M8, M9 and M90 and to Edinburgh airport. Follow A706 south-west from Linlithgow (1½ miles); first entrance on left after crossing Union Canal. Open all year except Christmas.

---

④ Easter Glentore Farm, Greengairs, Airdrie, Lanarkshire ML6 7TJ

Elsie Hunter
☎ 01236 830243
🅱 From £18
EM From £10
Sleeps 6
🛏 ⅋ 📺 ▬ 🅆
🍴🍴 *Highly Commended*

240 acre working farm dates back to 1705, located in scenic setting on the B803, mid-way between Greengairs and Slamannan. Panoramic views. All bedrooms on ground floor, 1 double en suite, 2 with washbasin, tea/coffee facilities and radio alarms. CH throughout. Lounge with colour TV. Warm friendly atmosphere with home baking and cooking. Best B&B award winner. Excellent touring base, 25 minutes Glasgow or Stirling. Open all year.

---

⑤ Inchie Farm, Port of Menteith, Stirling FK8 3JZ

Mrs Norma Erskine
☎ 01877 385233
🅱 From £13–£14
EM From £8
Sleeps 5
🛏 🐕 ⅋
🍴 *Commended*

Family farm on the shores of Lake of Menteith where ospreys nest between April and Sept. Featured in 'Wish You Were Here' TV programme. Comfortable twin/family rooms both with washbasins and tea-making facilities, also guests' own bathroom and lounge with colour TV. Central heating throughout. Ideal for trout fishing or hill walking in nearby Trossachs. Open Mar–Oct.

Lochend Farm, Carronbridge, Denny, Stirlingshire FK6 5JJ   6

Jean Morton
☎ 01324 822778
BB From £16.50
Sleeps 4
⌂(3) ⌖
☞ *Highly Commended*

Peace, panoramic view and good wholesome food – all may be enjoyed at Lochend. Delightfully situated over-looking Loch Coulter in unspoiled countryside, yet only 5 miles from M9/M80 (jct 9). A perfect base for exploring this beautiful part of Scotland. Farmhouse centrally-heated, traditionally furnished. 2 double bedrooms with washbasin, radio, tea-making facilities; also guests' own bathroom, dining room and lounge with colour TV. Open Easter till October or by arrangement.

Lochend Farm, Port of Menteith, Stirling FK8 3JZ   7

Mrs Rhona Millar
☎ 01877 385235
BB From £17
EM From £8
Sleeps 4
⌂ ⌖
☞☞ *Commended*

Enjoy a peaceful stay at Lochend, a mixed arable stock farm next to Scotland's only Lake in the heart of the Trossachs. Farmhouse dates back to 1726 being the former dower house of the estate. Spacious accommodation with en suite bedrooms. A warm friendly atmosphere and good home cooking await. Open April–Oct.

Lower Tarr Farm, Ruskie, Port of Menteith, Stirling FK8 3LG   8

Mrs Effie Bain
☎ 01786 850202
BB From £17
EM From £8
Sleeps 6 + cot
⌂ ⌖ ▪
☞☞ *Commended*

A mixed arable farm with clear panoramic views, peaceful situation and pretty garden, with Ruskie burn running past. There are cattle, sheep and hens to be seen, plus lots of interesting wildlife. Good home cooking and baking using fresh local produce where possible. Central for touring the Trossachs, Loch Lomond, Stirling and Edinburgh. En suite room. Open Feb–Nov.

Monachyle Mhor, Balquhidder, Lochearnhead, Perthshire FK19 8PQ   9

Robert & Jean Lewis
☎ 01877 384622
Fax 01877 384305
BB From £27–£35
EM From £18–£22
Sleeps 10
⌂(10) ⊞ &⌖ ♞ ▪ ⁑
☞☞ *Commended*

Monachyle Mhor is an award winning 18th century hotel located in its own 2000 acre estate. All rooms are en suite and have magnificent views over Lochs Voil and Doine. The hotel is delightfully furnished with family antiques and country fabrics. Fully licensed restaurant serving interesting dishes including game and herbs from our own estate. Taste of Scotland and AA featured, private fishing and stalking to guests. Open all year.

Overshiel Farm, East Calder, West Lothian EH53 OHT   10

Mrs Jan Dick
☎ 01506 880469
BB From £16–£25
Sleeps 6
⌂ ✂ ▪
☞☞ *Commended*

A traditional, stone-built farmhouse situated in beautiful surroundings yet only 10 miles from Edinburgh city centre. Near airport, Livingston, M8 and M9 motorways. The bedrooms look onto a large, attractive garden and acres of farmland. En suite bedrooms, central heating, safe parking. Open all year.

Shantron Farm Cottage, Shantron Farm, Luss, Alexandria, Dumbartonshire G83 8RH   11

Anne M Lennox
☎/Fax 01389 850231
BB From £14–£20
Sleeps 6
⌂ ⌖ ⁑
Listed *Commended*

Enjoy a relaxing break in a spacious bungalow with outstanding views of Loch Lomond. The farm is Morag's croft in 'High Road' and other scenes. 3 miles south of Luss. Ideal for touring, hillwalking, fishing, watersports and golf on the new Loch Lomond Golf Course. En suite available. Open Easter–Oct.

12 Shaw of Touch Farm, Stirling FK8 3AE

Cherylene Campbell
☎ 01786 471147
BB From £15–£20
EM From £9.95
Sleeps 6
☼ ♞ ⚰ ☞
♨ *Commended*

Welcome to our delightful turreted farmhouse on family-run mixed arable/stock farm set in lovely countryside with splendid views to Loch Lomond, Trossachs and the Ochils. We offer comfortable accommodation and good home cooking. Food hygiene Scottish cuisine and 'Welcome Host' certified. Excellent touring base for central Scotland 'Home from Home'. Completely non-smoking. Open Mar–Nov.

13 The Topps, Fintry Road, Denny, Stirlingshire FK6 5JF

Mrs Jennifer Steel
☎ 01324 822471
Fax 01324 823099
BB From £18
EM From £12
Sleeps 14
☼ ♞ ⚰ ⊞ ♿ ☞ ☎
♨♨♨ *Commended*

A chalet farmhouse in a beautiful hillside location with stunning, panoramic views. Family, double or twin-bedded rooms available, all en suite with tea/coffee, shortbread, TV, radio, telephone. Food a speciality ("Taste of Scotland" listed). Easy access to all major tourist attractions, or spend your day on the farm with Alistair and Angus (the dog). Your enjoyment is our aim and pleasure! Open all year.

14 Trean Farm, Leny Feus, Callander, Perthshire FK17 8AS

Janette Donald
☎ 01877 331160
BB From £16–£18
Sleeps 6
☼ ⚰
♨♨ *Commended*

A working farm situated in open parkland beside Callander with a 15 minute walk to shops. Outstanding views of Ben Ledi. An ideal base for touring and hill walking. 2 en suite rooms with TV and 1 with washbasin. Tea/coffee facilities. Residents' lounge. Open May–Oct.

15 Wester Carmuirs Farm, Larbert, By Falkirk, Stirlingshire FK5 3NW

Mrs Sheila Taylor
☎ 01324 812459
BB From £16
Sleeps 6
☼ ☀
♨ *Commended*

Relax and enjoy friendly hospitality and good food in our comfortable home on mixed farm on A803 near Falkirk (M9/A80). Comfortable twin/double/family rooms all with washbasins and tea/coffee. Guests' own bathroom, shower room, dining room and TV room with log fire. Ideal centre to visit local attractions, eg. Mariner Centre with swimming pool; also Trossachs, Loch Lomond, Stirling, Glasgow and Edinburgh. Open Jan–Nov.

16 Wester Dullatur Farm, Dullatur, Glasgow G68 0AA

Mrs Eleanor Duncan
☎ 01236 723218
BB From £15
EM From £10
Sleeps 4
♞ ☼
Listed *Commended*

Easily accessible, in a peaceful setting, overlooking the Forth and Clyde canal to the Kilsyth hills, offering comfortable accommodation in a friendly atmosphere. 2 miles from motorway routes to Stirling, Glasgow and Edinburgh. An ideal base for scenic tours of surrounding villages or to see the 'city sights'. Open all year.

17 West Plean, Denny Road, Stirling FK7 8HA

Mrs Moira Johnston
☎ 01786 812208
BB From £18–£25
Sleeps 6
♞ ☼ ⚰ ☞ ⚒ ☎ ♟ W
♨♨ *Commended*

Enjoy warm Scottish farming hospitality in an oasis of peace, with sweeping lawns, walled garden, extensive woodland walks, surrounded by our mixed farm. We offer quality food, spacious comfort, bedrooms en suite, hot drink facilities and attentive hosts. Riding and fishing can be arranged locally. Located on the A872 Denny road, 2 minutes from M9/M80 (jct 9). Open Feb–Nov.

SELF-CATERING

Crosswoodhill, By West Calder, West Lothian EH55 8LP

Mrs Geraldine Hamilton
☎ 01501 785205
⑤ᶜ From £150–£370
Sleeps 4/6
🛏 🐴 ♿ ♨

🐤🐤🐤🐤 – 🐤🐤🐤🐤
Commended to Highly Commended

Choose between an attractively restored cottage on the Pentland Hills or a self-contained wing of our elegant 18th century farmhouse nearby. Both offer rural seclusion just ½ hour's drive from the heart of historic Edinburgh. Easy access from our 1700 acre beef and sheep farm to the Borders, Trossachs, Glasgow, New Lanark and Fife. Lots to see and do. Both properties very well equipped, CH, phone. Lovely atmosphere. Brochure. Open all year.

Shemore Cottage, Shantron Farm, Luss, Alexandria, Dumbartonshire G83 8RH

Mrs Anne M Lennox
☎/Fax 01389 850231
⑤ᶜ From £130–£280
Sleeps 6
🐴 ⚘

🐤🐤🐤
Commended

Regulars often return to this traditional stone cottage attractively situated on a hill sheep farm, 300 ft above Loch Lomond, over which the cottage has magnificent views. The farm has often been filmed for 'High Road' TV series. 3 miles south of picturesque village of Luss. Edinburgh, Oban, Fort William, Ayr – 1½ hours. Ideal for hillwalking, fishing, watersports. Children love to feed lambs. Short breaks available. Open all year.

Scotland

Clyde Valley

Group Contact: *Mrs Margaret Kirby* ☎ *01899 810338*

The Romans were the first to cultivate 'Y Strad Cluyd' – the warm valley – where even today the Clyde Valley's many garden centres show the area to be one of Scotland's most fertile. In all, the valley boasts 23 golf courses, including Scotland's highest at 1,400ft in the Lowther Hills at Leadhills, and where gold and lead mines first worked by the Romans have been restored and serve as a unique museum to the industry.

Then 'Follow the Wallace' through Biggar, with its wide, sweeping main street, its four museums, and home to the internationally-famous Purves Puppets. It was here, in 1297, that Scottish patriot William Wallace, disguised as a beggar, hid from the English troops. Moving on to Lanark, pass Tinto Hill, Clyde Valley's highest point at 2320ft, and topped by a large Bronze Age cairn where Druids once held fertility rites. A most rewarding view for the very fit! Nestling in a gorge by the famous 'Falls of Clyde' is the cotton mill village of New Lanark, built in the 18th century, but now a living museum with working spinning looms, visitors' centre and magical history tour.

The Clyde Valley is steeped in history, from Blantre's David Livingstone Centre, which traces the explorer's journeys through Africa, to Chatelherault Country Park, a William Adam 18th century hunting lodge of the Dukes of Hamilton.

BED AND BREAKFAST
(and evening meal)

Dunsyre Mains, Dunsyre, Carnwath, Lanark ML11 8NG

Mrs M Armstrong
☎ 0189 981 338
BB £14
EM From £9
Sleeps 6
🐕 🐄 🏇 🐈 🐓 🐑
🦆 *Commended*

If you want a holiday to remember, Dunsyre Mains is the place. You can relax in quiet pleasant countryside, admire the animals and become friends with the border collies, yet be close enough to visit the holiday attractions of Edinburgh, Scottish borders and New Lanark. Numerous golf courses. End the day with an evening meal made from home produce, then finish with coffee around the log fire. Make your holiday a lasting memory. Open all year.

Walston Mansion Farmhouse, Walston, Carnwath, Lanark ML11 8NF

Mrs Margaret Kirby
☎ 01899 810338
BB £13–£15
EM From £7
Sleeps 6
🐕 🐄 🦆 🐓
🦆 🦆 *Commended*

A very pleasant family home situated 5 miles from Bigger. A friendly and relaxed atmosphere; children most welcome. Good home cooking with home-produced meat, eggs and organic vegetables.Guest lounge with log fire, TV/video and children's games. An ideal base for touring Strathclyde, Lothian and the Borders; Lanark, Edinburgh and Glasgow only a short drive away. Open all year.

SELF CATERING

Carmichael Country Cottages, Estate Office, Westmains, Carmichael, Biggar, Lanarkshire ML12 6PG

Richard Carmichael of Carmichael
☎ 01899 308336
Fax 01899 308481
SC From £160–£430
EM From £7.50
Sleeps 2/7
🐕 🐎 🐄 🦆 🏊 🐈 🐓 🦮 🛏 🐑 🦆
🦆🦆🦆 🦆🦆🦆🦆🦆 *Commended*
to Highly Commended

Ten 200-year-old stone cottages nestle among the woods and fields of our 700-year-old family estate. You will enjoy our private tennis court and fishing loch. We guarantee comfort, warmth and a friendly welcome in an accessible, unique rural and historic time capsule. We farm deer, cattle and sheep and sell meats and tartan – Carmichael, of course. Breakfast and evening meal available. Visitor centre. Open all year.

LET THE TELEPHONE RING!
Some farmhouses are big places. Let the telephone ring long enough to give the owner time to answer it.

Scotland

S,outh West Scotland

Group Contact: *Mrs Vera Dunlop* ☎ *01465 861220*

You will find plenty of space on our quiet roads and wide rolling countryside. With lush farmlands and miles of beautiful coastline the scenery is enhanced by golden sunsets.

Thanks to our mild climate, many subtropical plants bloom around Port Logan (just one of the many gardens in the area). South-West Scotland is a golfer's paradise, with courses wherever you go, both links and inland.

Fishermen will find plenty of opportunities for river, loch and sea fishing, while the hill climber or gentle walker may even be lucky enough to see the golden eagle, an inhabitant of the area for many years.

The area is also rich in historical and Christian heritage. A visit to the archaeological dig at Whithorn, where St Ninian founded the first Christian church, is a must.

Nearby, Culzean Castle with its famous Adam ceilings and superb furnishings is just one of the many castles to be explored in the area. Only the most discerning visitors choose this area of Scotland, and they are always amply rewarded.

BED AND BREAKFAST
(and evening meal)

Airds Farm, Crossmichael, Castle Douglas, Kirkcudbrightshire DG7 3BG

Barbara McBride
☎ **01556 670418**
🄑 **From £15–£18**
Sleeps 8
🐾 🐕 ☕
🐌🐌 *Commended*

Airds farmhouse overlooks lovely Loch Ken, 4 miles from Castle Douglas on the A713. All bedrooms tastefully decorated, heated, with wash handbasins, family en suite, electric blankets and tea and coffee facilities. Private lounge and dining room with colour TV. Smoking allowed in the sun lounge only. Fire certificate held. Payphone available. Guests are assured a comfortable stay with good home baking. Open all year.

Blair Farm, Barrhill, Girvan, Ayrshire KA26 0RD

Mrs Elizabeth Hughes
☎ **01465 821247**
🄑 **From £14.50–£18**
EM From £8
Sleeps 6
🐕 🐾 ☕ 🅂 🄦
🐌 *Commended*

Blair is a family run beef and sheep farm situated on the A714, 1 mile south of the village of Barrhill. Guests are assured of a warm friendly welcome, comfortable spacious rooms and a high standard of home cooking and baking. Central heating throughout, 1 double en-suite, 1 double and 1 twin with wash basin, electric blankets and tea/coffee facilities. Lounge with colour TV. Fishing available. Open Easter–Nov.

Glengennet Farm, Barr, Girvan, Ayrshire KA26 9TY

Vera Dunlop
☎ **01465 861220**
🄑 **From £18**
Sleeps 4
🐾 ✂ ☕ 🄦
🐌🐌 *Commended*

Original Victorian shooting lodge with lovely views over the Stinchar valley and neighbouring Galloway Forest Park. One double and one twin, both en-suite with tea trays. Guests lounge/ dining room with colour TV. Two miles from Barr village where good meals are available. Good base for forest walking/cycling, golf, Ayrshire coast, Burns country, Culzean Castle and Glentrool National Park. Open Apr–Oct.

Hawkhill Farm, Old Dailly, Girvan, Ayrshire KA26 9RD

Mrs Isobel Kyle
☎ **01465 871232**
🄑 **From £17.50–£18**
EM From £8
Sleeps 6
🐾 🐕 🐎
🐌🐌 *Highly Commended*

Superb farmhouse hospitality in spacious 17th-century former coaching inn where the emphasis is on comfort and good, fresh food. Three delightful bedrooms with private facilities. Visitors' lounge, central heating, log fires, tea tray. Peaceful setting perfect for exploring south west Scotland, Culzean Castle, etc. Golf, fishing, pony trekking, walking and cycling. Brochure. Open Mar–Oct.

Rascarrel Cottage, Rascarrel Farm, Auchencairn, Castle Douglas, Kirkcudbrightshire DG7 1RJ

Ellice Hendry
☎ **01556 640214**
🄑 **From £15–£17**
Sleeps 6
✂
🐌🐌 *Highly Commended*

You will find peace, comfort and wonderful views at our attractive, well-appointed cottage. Situated on an 18th century smuggling route overlooking our 400 acre farm and the Solway Firth, it is 500 yards from the sea and 2 miles from village where good meals are available. 1 double en suite and 1 twin with H & C on ground floor, 1 twin en suite on first floor. Tea trays, CH, bright spacious lounge, sunroom/dining room. Open Mar–Oct.

SELF-CATERING

---

6 **Glengennet Cottage,** Glengennet Farm, Barr, Girvan, Ayrshire KA26 9TY

Vera Dunlop
☎ **01465 861220**
SC **From £140–£290**
Sleeps 6 + cot
⚘ ☏ ☜ Ⓦ
☙☙☙☙ *Commended*

Situated on working farm in quiet River Stinchar valley near Galloway Forest Park, Burns Country, Culzean. Ideal for walking, golf, cycling, visiting coast. Glengennet offers accommodation for 6 and baby in wing, ground floor bedroom and bathroom. Linen provided. Open for short breaks off-season, brochure available. Open all year.

PRICES

Prices include VAT and service charge (if any) and are:
B&B per person per night
EM per person
SC per unit per week
Tents and caravans per pitch per night

CONFIRM BOOKINGS

Disappointments can arise from misunderstandings over the telephone.
Please write to confirm your booking.

FINDING YOUR ACCOMMODATION

The Group contacts at the beginning of each section can always help you find a vacancy in your chosen area.

Scotland

Dumfriesshire (Annandale)

Group Contact: *Mrs Kate Miller* ☎/Fax 01683 300320

A peaceful, undiscovered, easily accessible part of south-west Scotland. Take time to explore the countryside and sample the tranquility.

From the beaches of the Solway coast to the rugged Moffat Hills, with the spectacular 'Grey Mare's Tail' and the striking 'Devil's Beef Tub', here is a variety of scenery unmatched in Britain. Quiet lanes winding through lush green countryside, busy small towns with a variety of interesting shops, numerous challenging golf courses, excellent fishing and much, much more. The county town of Dumfries contains the excellent Robert Burns Centre which documents the many links Scotland's foremost poet has with the area. Moffat is a most attractive town with tennis courts, bowling green, woollen mill and many craft shops. Lockerbie, with its bustling cattle market, is well worth a visit. So, whether you enjoy birdwatching or hill walking, swimming or horseriding, sailing or just relaxing with friendly people, you will find everything you want in Dumfriesshire.

BED AND BREAKFAST

(and evening meal)

---

1 **Broomlands Farm,** Beattock, Moffat, Dumfriesshire DG10 9PQ

Kate Miller
☎/Fax 01683 300320
🛏 From £17–£19
Sleeps 5
🐕(8) 🚶 🐾 🎣
🌺🌺 *Highly Commended*

A lovely spacious farmhouse situated in the Annandale Valley and 2 miles from Moffat, a wonderful area to tour, walk, play golf, etc. High standard accommodation offering double, twin and single rooms, all with beautiful en suite facilities, colour TV, tea/coffee-making facilities. Choice farmhouse breakfast. Personal attention. Safe private parking. Convenient for A/M74. AA selected QQQQ. Brochure available. Open Easter–Oct.

---

2 **Ericstane,** Moffat, Dumfriesshire DG10 9LT

Robert Jackson
☎ 01683 220127
🛏 From £16
Sleeps 4
🐕 🚶 🎣 🌿
🌺🌺 *Commended*

Tastefully renovated period farmhouse in attractive grounds by the Annan Water. 4 miles from Moffat in a peaceful valley. Twin and double-bedded rooms with en-suite facilities, TV, tea/coffee-making facilities. Central heating. Open all year.

---

3 **Nether Boreland Farm,** Boreland, Lockerbie, Dumfriesshire DG11 2LL

Mrs Marjorie Rae
☎/Fax 01576 610248
🛏 From £19–£21
Sleeps 6
🐕(12) 💷
🌺🌺 *Highly Commended*

Sample Scottish hospitality, peaceful friendly surroundings and hearty breakfasts with our free range eggs and homemade preserves. The spacious, comfortable farmhouse has two en suite bedrooms and one with private bathroom, all with TV, tea/coffee-making facilities, hairdryers and clock radios. Enjoy golf, fishing, pony trekking or leisurely sightseeing. Farmhouse Award winner. Brochure. Open Mar–Nov.

BUREAU ACCOMMODATION MEANS QUALITY

FARM HOLIDAY BUREAU

All Bureau members are inspected and quality graded by the National Tourist Board each year, as well as by fellow members.

FARM HOLIDAY BUREAU

Please mention **Stay on a Farm** when booking

Scotland

East Lothian

Group Contact: *Zoë Peace* ☎ *01620 822 131*

The beautiful, unspoilt countryside of East Lothian unfolds from Edinburgh's eastern edge along the Firth of Forth. Nestling under the heather-covered Lammermuir hills are many historic towns and picturesque villages – the county town of Haddington is one of the best preserved traditional market burghs in Scotland.

The area combines an extraordinary blend of scenery, antiquity and culture, with ancient castles, fine country houses, fascinating museums, National Trust properties, sports and leisure centres, and our own working Lowland whisky distillery, Glenkinchie. The choice of outdoor pursuits is endless – 40 miles of sandy beaches, the famous Bass Rock seabird and seal sanctuary, several country parks, racing at Musselburgh, as well as hill walking, pony trekking, fishing and the ubiquitous golf! East Lothian boasts 14 courses including the championship course at Muirfield.

There are numerous pubs, restaurants and bistros to suit all palates and purses. We look forward to seeing you.

BED AND BREAKFAST

(and evening meal)

① Barney Mains, Haddington, East Lothian EH41 3SA

Katie Kerr
☎ 01620 880310
Fax 01620 880639
[BB] From £15–£23
Sleeps 6
🐴 🎌 ⬛
Listed *Commended*

Beautiful farmhouse in quiet location with spectacular views of open countryside. Rooms are spacious, warm and comfortable. Lovely walks on farm to ruined castle and remains of ancient fort. Ideally situated for golfing holidays, touring and sightseeing. Edinburgh 20 minutes drive. Delicious breakfast with homemade bread. Open Mar–Nov.

② Coates Farm, Longniddry, East Lothian EH32 0PL

Zoë Peace
☎/Fax 01620 822131
[BB] From £19.50
Sleeps 4
🐴 🎌 🐴
🌸🌸 *Highly Commended*

Spacious Georgian farmhouse tastefully decorated and furnished throughout. Ideally situated for exploring countryside, coastline or visiting Edinburgh. Train station nearby. Comfortable bedrooms with private facilities. Separate lounge and dining room for guests. Large, well tended, interesting garden. Excellent local pubs and restaurants. Coates is 1¾ miles from the A1. Open Apr–Sept.

③ Eaglescairnie Mains, Gifford, Haddington, East Lothian EH41 4HN

Mrs Barbara Williams
☎/Fax 01620 810491
[BB] From £16–£20
Sleeps 6
🐴 🕯 ⬛ 🎌 🆆
🌸🌸 *Commended*

Join us at Eaglescairnie Mains, a beautifully furnished Georgian house on our 350-acre arable/sheep farm which recently won a National Conservation Award. Near A1, ideal for the coast, golf courses, the Borders or Edinburgh. Double, twin and single rooms – some en suite, full CH, basins, tea/coffee trays. Conservatory, tennis court and games room. Open all year (closed Christmas and New Year).

④ Rowan Park, Longnewton Farm, Gifford, East Lothian EH41 4JW

Mrs Margaret Whiteford
☎ 01620 810327
[BB] From £16–£18
Sleeps 4
🐴(3) 🎌 🎌 ⬛
Listed *Highly Commended*

Our family farm of 450 acres consists of cattle, cereals and ponies. Situated at the foot of the Lammermuir Hills, with magnificent views to the Forth. Only 30 minutes from Edinburgh and near to the Border Country with its stately homes. Golf, fishing, tennis, swimming and pony trekking all nearby. Furnished to a high standard, central heating, guests' lounge and dining room, also welcome tray. A warm welcome awaits you. Open Mar–Nov.

⑤ Whitekirk Mains, Whitekirk, North Berwick, East Lothian EH42 1XS

Mrs J Tuer
☎ 01620 870245
Fax 01620 870330
[BB] From £18
Sleeps 6
🐴 🎌
🌸🌸 *Highly Commended*

Spacious Georgian farmhouse on a 600-acre mixed farm at the edge of a historic village. Large en suite rooms with tea/coffee facilities and colour TV. Oak panelled dining/drawing rooms, log fires, superb views. Country and beach walks. 20 miles Edinburgh/Lammermuir Hills. Adjoining our new Whitekirk Golf Course and club house, restaurant/bar. Open Mar–Nov.

Scotland

Scottish Borders

Group Contact: *Sheila Bergius* ☎ *01896 860 244*

This is an area of great beauty renowned for its abbeys at Kelso, Melrose, Jedburgh, and Dryburgh. Some of the loveliest of Scotland's great houses are to be found at Bowhill, Abbotsford, Floors and Traquair, to mention but a few.

The lowlands contain some of the best farming land in Britain and this rises to the Cheviot Hills. The Pennine Way runs along the top of the Cheviots or there is the Southern Upland Way stretching from coast to coast for those who wish to have a walking holiday.

For the fisherman there is fine fishing to be had in the waters of the Tweed or sea fishing on the east coast. Golfers can plan a trip in the region where they can play a different course every day! Rugby is a popular sport here and in the spring and autumn you can watch the 'sevens'.

Horseriding is a passion in this region – trekking through this lovely area is very popular with visitors and, for those who wish only to observe, the larger Border towns have their 'common ridings' during the summer which are supported by hundreds of riders. A magnificent sight; only one of many in this lovely land.

BED AND BREAKFAST

(and evening meal)

---

① Cliftonhill Farm, Kelso, Roxburghshire TD5 7QE

Archie & Maggie Stewart
☎ 01573 225028
Fax 01573 226416
🅱 From £18.50–£20
EM From £11
Sleeps 4
🛏 🐕 🧒 ☂ ♠ 🎿
🌸🌸 *Commended*

A warm welcome is assured at Cliftonhill. A traditional farmhouse set in the beautiful unspoiled Border country, the farm is 2 miles from Kelso, and an ideal centre for exploring, walking or just relaxing. The River Eden meanders through the farm attracting interesting wildlife. Pools for fishing and swimming/tennis court. Home-made bread. Beautiful double en suite, and 1 twin with private bathroom. Seaside ½ hour's drive, Edinburgh 1 hour. Brochure available. Open all year.

---

② Cockburn Mill, Duns, Berwickshire TD11 3TL

Mrs A M Prentice
☎ 01361 882811
🅱 From £17–£19
EM £11
Sleeps 4
🛏 ✄ 🧒
🌸🌸 *Commended*

A comfortable riverside farmhouse offering 2 twin bedrooms with luxurious en suite bathrooms, within sight and sound of River Whiteadder. Electric blankets and tea/coffee-making facilities. Home baking and farm produce. Water from hillside spring. Trout fishing included. Abundant plant and bird life. Ideal for hill-walking, birdwatching, cycling or just relaxing. Hens, ducks, donkeys and pet lambs. Open Mar–Nov.

---

③ Lyne Farm, Peebles EH45 8NR

Mrs Arran Waddell
☎ 01721 740255
🅱 From £15–£17
Sleeps 6
🧒 🛏(5) ♠ 🎿
Listed *Commended*

Spacious Georgian farmhouse situated on 1300 acre arable/stock farm with outstanding panoramic views. Tastefully decorated rooms, tea/coffee-making facilities. Walled garden. Hillwalking and picnic areas to enjoy. Excellent pubs and restaurants in picturesque town of Peebles. Ideal base for castles, historic houses, museums and outdoor pursuits. A warm welcome awaits you. Peebles 4 miles, Edinburgh 20 miles. Open March–Nov.

---

④ Morebattle Tofts, Kelso, Roxburghshire TD5 8AD

Mrs Debbie Playfair
☎ 01573 440364
Fax 01573 420750
🅱 From £14–£16
EM from £10
Sleeps 6
🧒 🛏 ♠ 🧍 🐕‍🦺 ✄ 🎿 Ⓦ
🌸🌸 *Commended*

Large, elegant 18th century farmhouse set in 3 acres of garden beside the River Kale. Area of Outstanding Natural Beauty, ideal for touring, walking, fishing, golf. Beautifully appointed rooms, 2 double rooms en suite, twin room with private bathroom. Tea and coffee-making facilities. Tennis court, croquet lawn. Brochure available. Open Mar–Oct.

---

⑤ Overlangshaw Farm, Langshaw, Galashiels, Selkirkshire TD1 2PE

Sheila Bergius
☎ 01896 860244
🅱 From £16–£19
Sleeps 6
🧒 🛏 ✄ ♿
🌸 *Commended*

Situated only 4 miles from Galashiels and Melrose. A welcoming, centrally heated home amidst rolling hills and shady woods. Delicious Scottish cooking with emphasis on quality home produce and preserves. Children welcome, cot available. Also dogs by arrangement. Roomy bedrooms, 1 family with private bathroom, 1 double with en suite shower room. Southern Upland Way nearby. Open all year.

Wiltonburn Farm, Hawick, Roxburghshire TD9 7LL

Mrs Sheila Shell
☎ 01450 372414
Mobile 0374 192551
BB From £16–£17
EM From £10
Sleeps 6
⛺ 🐴 ♿ 🎣 🏇 🎿 🏌
Listed *Commended*

Wiltonburn is a friendly working mixed farm situated in a beautiful sheltered valley 2 miles from Hawick. An ideal base for walking, riding, fishing, golf, castles or stately homes. Our new showroom stocks designer cashmere knitwear, paintings, jewellery and small gifts. Log fires, cosy rooms, warm welcome. Open all year.

SELF-CATERING

Bailey Mill, Bailey, Newcastleton, Roxburghshire TD9 0TR

Pamela Copeland
☎/Fax 016977 48617
SC From £78–£428
EM From £8
Sleeps 2/10
⛺ ♿ 🎣 🏇 🏌 🏸
🐾 🐾 🐾 *Commended*

A warm welcome awaits you from Pam and Ian on this small farm holiday complex nestling on the Roxburgh/Cumbria border. The four superior self-contained courtyard apartments include heating (oil), electricity and linen in rent. Colour TV and microwave in each apartment. On-site sauna, solarium, multi-gym, games room, laundry, farm kitchen and horse riding. Baby sitting service. Breakfast and evening meal available. Brochure. Open all year.

The Cottage, Cockburn Mill, Duns, Berwickshire TD11 3TL

Ann Prentice
☎ 01361 882811
SC From £125–£210
Sleeps 5 + cot
⛺ 🐴 🎣
🏵 🏵 🏵 *Approved*

Stone-built cottage within sight and sound of River Whiteadder. Children welcome. Barbecue, colour TV. Overnight storage heating included. Trout fishing included. Water from hillside spring. Abundant plant and bird life. Chicks, donkeys, ducklings and pet lambs. Coast, beaches, Edinburgh, Border keeps and abbeys within easy reach on quiet roads. Pets by arrangement only. Open all year.

Cherry Tree Cottage and Rowan Tree Cottage, Lochton, Coldstream, Berwickshire TD12 4NH

Mrs Rosalind Aitchison
☎ 01890 830205
Fax 01890 830210
SC From £110–£320
Sleeps 4/6
♿ ⛺ 🎣 🏌 🏸
🏵 🏵 🏵 *Highly Commended*

Relax in tranquil surroundings, stay in charming cottages on our farm beside River Tweed. Rowan Tree, beautifully appointed with wood-burning stove, CH, shower/bath, 3 bedrooms and Cherry Tree, 2 bedrooms, log fire, cosy, clean and comfy, wait to welcome you. Fishing, golf, farm walks. Easy motoring to historic homes, abbeys, hills and beaches. Kelso/Coldstream 4½ miles, Edinburgh 1 hour. Open all year.

Craggs Cottage, Cliftonhill Farm, Kelso, Roxburghshire TD5 7QE

Archie & Maggie Stewart
☎ 01573 225028
Fax 01573 226416
SC From £75–£340
Sleeps 7
♿ 🎣 🏸 ☕
🏵 🏵 🏵 *Commended*

A terraced sandstone cottage, lovingly restored, maintaining its character and charm. One double room – large and luxurious, 1 bedroom with 3 single beds and 1 with bunks. Large comfortable kitchen with Rayburn cooker and electric cooker. Central heating. Sitting room with log fire and colour TV. Enclosed colourful garden, garden furniture. Delightful restaurant 3 miles. Coast 18 miles, Edinburgh 35 miles. Short breaks and special winter break offer. Open all year.

11 Kerchesters, Kelso, Roxburghshire TD5 8HR

Mrs J. Clark
☎ 01573 224321
Fax 01573 226609
⌨ From £110–£300
Sleeps 5/7
🐕 ⛱ ✄ ❀
😊 😊 😊 *Commended*

Cockerlaw and Todrig cottages are warm, welcoming terraced cottages on a working farm. Well appointed and peacefully situated with good views and ample play areas. Cockerlaw has separate sitting room and shower room. Three miles east of Kelso. Well placed for touring Borders and Northumbria. Edinburgh 1 hour, beach 30 minutes. Local golf, swimming, fishing, riding. Linen included. Brochure on request. Open all year.

12 Little Swinton Cottages, Little Swinton, Coldstream, Berwickshire TD12 4HH

Sue Brewis
☎ 01890 860280
⌨ From £180–£300
Sleeps 4–7
🐕 ⛱ ♿
😊 😊 😊 *Commended*

A row of quiet refurbished, well equipped one storey stone cottages all with open fires, night store heating, colour TV, washing machine, etc. Electricity and linen included. Large enclosed grass play area. Ample parking. Children and pets welcome. Beaches, hills, historic houses, Edinburgh, Newcastle, all within reach. Open all year.

13 Thirlestane Farm Cottages, Thirlestane, Lauder, Berwickshire TD2 6SF

Mrs Caroline Barr
☎ 01578 722216
⌨ From £150–£300
Sleeps 6
🐕 ⛱ ☂
😊 😊 😊 *Commended*

Renovated to retain their original charm and character, these cottages each provide 3 bedrooms (to sleep 6), large sitting room with open fire and panoramic view, pine kitchen/dining area. Rent includes bedlinen and fuel. Ideal for touring, walking, fishing, riding, easy access to all border towns, only 28 miles from Edinburgh. Pets by arrangement. Open all year.

England's North Country

Hadrian's Wall, North Cumbria and The Borders

Group Contact: *Mrs Harriet Sykes* ☎ *016977 3435*

Discover the Border Country, a wild wonderland of moors, tarns and loughs, wooded river valleys and rich pastureland. Wildlife abounds with peace and quiet for all who seek it. This is an exciting area for the heritage enthusiast with Roman sites and the world famous Hadrian's Wall, Lanercost Priory, Hexham Abbey, Carlisle, and Hermitage Castle. The historic city of Carlisle with its gem of a cathedral has an excellent Lanes shopping centre of large and small shops.

Whether walking, golfing, fishing, birdwatching or gently touring our quiet roads you will find this area has so much to offer – lots of country inns, market towns, woollen and tweed mills, local craft and agricultural shows and, most important of all, friendly people. Kielder Water is on our doorstep offering many water activities, birdwatching and magnificent forest surroundings. Once you have enjoyed the peace, freedom and our North Country hospitality, you will most certainly wish to return to this unspoilt area.

BED AND BREAKFAST

(and evening meal)

---

① **Ald White Craig Farm,** Nr Hadrian's Wall, Haltwhistle, Northumberland NE49 9NW

Isobel Laidlow
☎/Fax 01434 320565
🛏 From £19–£26
Sleeps 6
✂ 🔔 ☕
🌸🌸 *Highly Commended*

17th century croft-style farmhouse, on western edge of Northumberland's National Park, 1 mile Hadrian's Wall, ½ mile A69. Small working sheep farm with other interesting animals. Magnificent touring/walking area. 1 hr Metro Centre and Lakes. Nearby inn (food highly recommended). 1 twin, 2 doubles, (all en suite), hospitality tray, colour TV, CH, etc. AA selected. Customer Choice Award Winner 1994 and '95. Brochure. Open all year.

---

② **Cracrop Farm,** Kirkcambeck, Brampton, Cumbria CA8 2BW

Marjorie Stobart
☎ 016977 48245
Fax 016977 48333
🛏 From £19–£22
EM From £14.50
Sleeps 6
☕ 🖼 ✂ 🎿 🔔
🌸🌸 *Highly Commended*

Looking for somewhere special? Then try our superbly appointed large (1847) farmhouse. Set in peaceful countryside with super views, excellent for birdwatching and walking. Spacious en suite bedrooms, hostess tray, colour TV, fresh flowers. Relax in spa bath or sauna. Games room. Near Roman Wall, Borders, 1 mile from B6318. Excellent pubs nearby. AA selected QQQQ. Every effort has been made to ensure a memorable stay. Open all year.

---

③ **High Rigg,** Walton, Brampton, Cumbria CA8 2AZ

Margaret Mounsey
☎ 016977 2117
🛏 From £14–£15
EM From £9
Sleeps 4
✂ ☕ ☕ 🎿 🍴
🌸 *Approved*

Working dairy/sheep farm with attractive 18th century listed comfortable farmhouse, on the roadside near Walton and Roman Wall. Friendly welcome, excellent home cooking, panoramic views. Convenient for the Lakes, Pennines, Northumbria and Scottish Borders. Patio, childrens play area, pool/snooker table. Follow the farm trail to the waterfall, help to feed the animals or relax in the garden. Open all year (closed Christmas and New Year).

---

④ **Howard House Farm,** Gilsland, Carlisle, Cumbria CA6 7AN

Elizabeth Woodmass
☎ 016977 47285
🛏 From £17–£20
EM From £9.50
Sleeps 6
☕ 🧍 ☕ 🔔
🌸🌸 *Highly Commended*

A warm welcome and comfortable accommodation await you on beef/sheep farm. Situated on an elevated site enjoying magnificent views over 2 counties in the heart of Roman wall country. Guests lounge, colour TV, tea/coffee-making facilities. Dinner by arrangement or bar meals nearby. Discount on 3 night stay. Open all year, except Christmas.

---

⑤ **New Pallyards,** Hethersgill, Carlisle, Cumbria CA6 6HZ

Mrs Georgina Elwen
☎/Fax 01228 577308
🛏 From £19–£20
EM From £12
Sleeps 6
☕ 🧍🔔 🖼 🏇 ☕ 🍴
🌸🌸🌸 *Commended*

Friendly hospitality, warmth and comfort await you in this modernised 18th century farmhouse. Situated in the peaceful countryside, surrounded by nature yet easily accessible from M6, A7, M74. All bedrooms en suite, tea/coffee facilities, disabled people welcome. A wide range of leisure and recreational activities are within a few minutes' drive from the farm. National Gold Award winner. Open all year.

SELF-CATERING

Ald White Craig Farm Cottages, Nr.Hadrian's Wall, Haltwhistle, Northumberland NE49 9NW

Isobel Laidlow
☎/Fax 01434 320565
SC From £115–£400
Sleeps 3/8 + cot
🐕 🐎 🍴
🐾 🐾 🐾 – 🐾 🐾 🐾 🐾
Highly Commended

Comfortable 1 and 3 bedroomed farm cottages, very well furnished and equipped to be your holiday home from home. Personally maintained. Inn/restaurant ½ mile; heated pool, and Leisure Centre 1 mile, golf 3½ miles. Central section Hadrian's Wall nearby. Excellent area for country pursuits. Dogs by arrangement only. Brochure available on request. Open all year.

Bailey Mill, Bailey, Newcastleton, Roxburghshire TD9 0TR

Pamela Copeland
☎/Fax 016977 48617
SC From £78–£428
EM From £8
Sleeps 2/10
🐎 ♿ 🐕 🍴 ♨ 🔫 ■
🐾 🐾 🐾 *Commended*

A warm welcome awaits you from Pam and Ian on this small farm holiday complex nestling on the Roxburgh/Cumbria border. The four superior self-contained courtyard apartments include heating (oil), electricity and linen in rent. Full board riding holidays. On-site sauna, solarium, multi-gym, games room, laundry, farm kitchen and horse riding. Baby sitting service. Breakfast and evening meal available. Brochure. Open all year.

Burn and Meadow View, New Pallyards, Hethersgill, Carlisle, Cumbria CA6 6HZ

Georgina Elwen
☎/Fax 01228 577308
SC From £80–£360
EM From £12
Sleeps 2/10
🐎 ♿ 🐕 ⊞ 🔫 🍴 ♨ ■
🐾 🐾 🐾 – 🐾 🐾 🐾 🐾
Commended

Set amidst beautiful countryside close to the Scottish Borders, our fully centrally heated cottages offer a high standard of accommodation with all modern-day facilities. A wide range of leisure and recreational activities are within a few minutes' drive from the farm. Our on-site games and dining room will make your stay more enjoyable. Open all year.

Long Byres, Talkin Head Farm, Talkin, Brampton, Cumbria CA8 1LT

Mrs Harriet Sykes
☎ 016977 3435
SC From £90–£250
Sleeps 2–5
🐎 🐕 🍴 ⚘
🐾 🐾 – 🐾 🐾 🐾 🐾
Commended

Situated on a small North Pennine hill farm, close to RSPB Geltsdale reserve. 1 mile from Talkin village (Post Office and eating out). Specialist, fully equipped holiday accommodation; five 2-bedroom houselets (sleep 4/5); two single bedroom (sleep 2/3). Freshly home-cooked meals. Facilities for golf, boating, fishing within 2 miles. Open all year.

Please mention **Stay on a Farm** when booking

England's North Country

Carlisle's Border Country

Group Contact: *Dorothy Downer* ☎ *016977 48644*

The country to the north east of Carlisle is one of the last truly peaceful places in England. Here in the Debateable Land where the Border Reivers once rode; your only debate today will be which of the many beautiful and historic places will you visit. Will it be Carlisle with its cathedral, castle, city walls, pedestrianised shopping centre and award winning museum, the Tullie House; or the north to Scotland and wild Liddesdale, Hermitage Castle and the Border Abbeys and historic houses; or the west and the Solway coast and its world renowned birdlife; or will you just walk or cycle on the peaceful tracks of the Border Forest Park basking in tranquility, perhaps catching sight of a deer?

A short drive from the M6 this area is ideal for a stopover for Scotland and Northern Ireland is within easy distance of the Lake District, Hadrian's Wall, Northumberland and Kielder Water, and the Eden Valley: whilst only a step from romantic Gretna Green. A haven of peace with enough to keep you involved for many more holidays because once you have been welcomed for the first time in one of Carlisle's Border Country farms you will certainly want to come back ...

BED AND BREAKFAST

(and evening meal)

Bank End Farm, Roadhead, Bewcastle, Carlisle, Cumbria CA6 6NU

Boy & Dorothy Downer
☎/Fax 016977 48644
BB From £20–£22
EM From £13
Sleeps 2
⚜ ☕ ⌷
⚘ ⚘ ⚘ *Commended*

Relax in peace in your own luxurious self-contained suite (including a private sitting room) on small hill sheep farm close to Scottish border. Friendly atmosphere, delicious home cooking, using fresh local produce by a cook of distinction. Marvellous centre for walking and touring; naturalist's paradise. Close to B6318. Phone for brochure with colour photo and sample menus. Ask for travel directions. Open Apr–Nov.

Bessiestown Farm, Catlowdy, Longtown, Carlisle, Cumbria CA6 5QP

Margaret Sisson
☎/Fax 01228 577219
BB From £19.50–£22
EM From £10
Sleeps 8
⌂ ⌷ ▮
⚘ ⚘ ⚘ *Highly Commended*

One of the nicest B&Bs to be found, peaceful and quiet. Warm, pretty en suite bedrooms. TV lounge, bar lounge. Delicious food. Indoor heated swimming pool (May–Sept). Ideal touring base. Stop off Scotland and Northern Ireland. M6 exit 44, then A7 to Longtown; right at Bush Hotel 7 miles to T-junction,1½ miles to Bessiestown. Open all year.

Craigburn Farm, Catlowdy, Penton, Carlisle, Cumbria CA6 5QP

Jane & Jack Lawson
☎/Fax 01228 577214
BB From £19–£20
EM From £10
Sleeps 14
⌂ ⌂ ♿ ⚘ ⌷
⚘ ⚘ ⚘ *Commended*

Enjoy the delights of beautiful Cumbrian countryside and life on our 250-acre working farm. Relax in the peace and quiet of the farmhouse, with delicious farmhouse cooking. Distinction in cookery held. 28 years in the business. Special breeds animals. Stay here en-route to/from Scotland. Four-poster bed. Colour TV in bedrooms. 20% off weekly bookings. Weekend break, 10% discount. Midweek break, 15% discount. Open all year.

SELF-CATERING

Bank End Farm, Roadhead, Bewcastle, Carlisle, Cumbria CA6 6NU

Dorothy & Boy Downer
☎/Fax 016977 48644
SC From £130–£330
Sleeps 6 + cot
⌂ ⌂ ☕ ⌷
⚘ ⚘ ⚘ ⚘ *Commended*

Come and try our warm, cosy cottages providing all you need for a relaxing holiday. Enjoy the wildlife, flowers and birdsong, walking by our river, basking in the tranquillity. Discover the delights of this little known area. Enjoy a local bar snack or one of Dorothy's freshly made meals. Open all year.

England's North Country

North Northumberland

Group Contact: *Mrs Sally Lee ☎/Fax 01665 574 277*

North Northumberland is an area of great beauty still little known to many people. There are miles of heritage coastline dotted with castles such as Lindisfarne, Bamburgh and Dunstanburgh and further inland a wealth of historic homes including Alnwick Castle and Cragside. Holy Island (Lindisfarne) is accessible by car at low tide and boats run daily in the summer months to the Farne Islands, famous for their colonies of seals and seabirds.

The Northumberland National Park offers wonderful opportunities for those wishing to walk and explore in peace and solitude. Berwick-upon-Tweed and Alnwick are two busy country towns which still have weekly street markets. Scotland's capital city, Edinburgh to the north and Newcastle with its much acclaimed Metro Shopping Centre to the south are within easy reach by car, train or bus.

Our group offers a wide variety of holiday accommodation of a high standard based on working farms in this unspoilt corner of England's most northerly county.

BED AND BREAKFAST

(and evening meal)

Bilton Barns, Alnmouth, Alnwick, Northumberland NE66 2TB

Dorothy Jackson
☎ **01665 830427**
🅱 **From £18.50–£21**
EM From £10.50
Sleeps 6
🐂
Applied

Spacious farmhouse in lovely countryside with magnificent views over Alnmouth and Warkworth bays. Many splendid walks, beaches and castles nearby. Full central heating, guests' lounge and dining room. All with en suite bedrooms, TV and tea/coffee-making facilities. Brian is pleased to take interested guests on a farm walk. Recommended in *Best Bed and Breakfast in the World*. Open Easter–mid Oct.

Burton Hall, Bamburgh, Northumberland NE69 7AR

Eve Humphreys
☎ **01668 214213**
Fax 01668 214538
🅱 **From £18–£25**
Sleeps 16
🐂(4) 🐴 ♿ 🎎 🐾
Listed *Commended*

A traditional farmhouse offering a friendly atmosphere with a high standard of service only 1½ miles from Bamburgh Castle. All bedrooms are spacious with tea/coffee facilities, en suites with colour TV. Ground floor bedrooms available as well as an elegant residents' lounge and dining room. Open all year.

Doxford Farmhouse, Doxford Farm, Chathill, Northumberland NE67 5DY

A & D Turnbull
☎ **01665 579235**
Fax 01665 579215
🅱 **From £16–£25**
EM From £10
Sleeps 10
🐴🍴🐂🈂🏇🎏🎎🛢🐾
🐞🦋 *Commended*

A peaceful, listed Georgian farmhouse with large garden set in wooded countryside between the hills and the award-winning beaches. Guests are welcome to come on our farm walk and follow the newly created nature trail. Trout fishing on nearby lake, and a squash court. Delicious home cooking and homemade bread. We happily welcome children and pets. Open all year (closed Christmas and New Year).

Earle Hill Head Farm, Wooler, Northumberland NE71 6RH

Sylvia Armstrong
☎/Fax 01668 281243
🅱 **From £18–£24**
Sleeps 6
🐂 🏇 🎏 🎎 🛢
Listed *Applied*

Earle Hill Farm is 2 miles from Wooler at the foot of the Cheviot Hills. We have a 4,000-acre stock farm in the National Park. Lovely walks and a warm welcome will await you in our comfortable farmhouse. Wooler is a perfect centre for the coast, castles and Scottish Borders. Household and Farming Museum. Local nature trails and conducted tours. Open Jan–Nov.

Elford Farmhouse, Elford, Seahouses, Northumberland NE68 7UT

Mrs M. Robinson
☎ **01665 720244**
🅱 **From £17–£18**
Sleeps 6
🐂(12) 🎎 🛢 🐾
Listed *Highly Commended*

An old stone farmhouse of great character on an arable farm near the villages of Bamburgh and Seahouses, 1½ miles from the sea. Nearby are beautiful beaches, castles, golf, riding and boat trips to the Farnes and Holy Island. Good local restaurants. Comfortable bedrooms with central heating, colour TV, hair dryers and tea/coffee making facilities. Elegant dining room. Some use of outdoor heated swimming pool and lawn tennis court in summer. Open Mar–Nov.

6 Fenham-le-Moor Farmhouse, Belford, Northumberland NE70 7PN

Mrs K Burn
☎ 01668 213247
BB From £18
Sleeps 2
⚘(12) ✕
🐾 *Applied*

A comfortable stone-built farmhouse in a peaceful situation with magnificent views overlooking farmland and the bay of Lindisfarne Nature Reserve. An area of outstanding natural beauty and excellent centre for birdwatching, golf, good beaches and visiting many castles. One twin room en suite. Open Easter–Oct.

7 Hipsburn Farm, Lesbury, Alnmouth, Northumberland NE66 3PY

Hilda Tulip
☎ 01665 830206
BB From £18–£20
Sleeps 6
✕
🐾 *Highly Commended*

A spacious farmhouse situated ½ mile from Alnmouth, overlooking the Aln estuary. Rooms comfortably furnished, one double en suite, one twin en suite and one double with private bathroom. TV, tea/coffee-making facilities in all bedrooms. All rooms are centrally heated, dining room – lounge. Ideal area for golfers, walkers and birdwatchers. Private parking. Open Easter–Oct.

8 Howick Scar Farm, Craster, Alnwick, Northumberland NE66 3SU

Mrs Celia Curry
☎ 01665 576665
BB From £14
Sleeps 4
⚘(5) ☂
Listed *Applied*

Comfortable farmhouse accommodation on mixed farm situated on the coast between the villages of Craster and Howick. Ideal base for walking or exploring the coast, moors and historic castles. Guests have their own television lounge/dining room with coal fire and full central heating. Open May–Dec.

9 The Lee Farm, Longframlington, Morpeth, Northumberland NE65 8JQ

Mrs Susan Aynsley
☎ 01665 570257
BB From £15
Sleeps 5
⚘ 🐕
🐾 *Highly Commended*

Large traditional farmhouse on 1,200 acre farm. Spacious bedrooms with tea/coffee-making facilities and washbasins. Guests' lounge with log fire and dining room. Central heating throughout. Excellent central location for walking or exploring Northumberland's many attractions. Fishing, riding and golf available nearby. Open Mar–Nov.

10 Lumbylaw Farm, Edlingham, Alnwick, Northumberland NE66 2BW

Mrs Sally Lee
☎/Fax 01665 574277
BB From £18
Sleeps 6
✕ ⚘(8) ☂ ✗
🐾 *Highly Commended*

Friendly hospitality in a comfortable stone farmhouse on a beef and sheep farm. 6 miles between Alnwick and Rothbury. Outstanding views of the 13th century Edlingham Castle and Victorian railway viaduct in the farm grounds. Two twin bedrooms, 1 double bedroom (all with washbasins; one with en suite shower). Guests' bathroom, central heating throughout. Excellent local eating places available. Open May–Oct.

11 Middle Ord Manor House, Middle Ord Farm, Berwick-on-Tweed TD15 2XQ

Joan Gray
☎ 01289 306323
BB From £19
Sleeps 6
⚙
🐾🐾 *De Luxe*

Award-winning accommodation with spacious en suite rooms (four poster if desired). Two residents' lounges. Secluded gardens. NTB Best Bed and Breakfast Award 1993 and 1994, ETB Silver Award 1994. Sorry no children, no pets. Open Apr–Nov.

Tosson Tower Farm, Great Tosson, Rothbury, Morpeth, Northumberland NE65 7NW

Mrs Ann Foggin
☎ **01669 620228**
🅱 **From £15–£17.50**
Sleeps 6
🐾 🐎 🐕 🏕
🍂 🍂 *Highly Commended*

Large, comfortable farmhouse formerly a coaching inn at the foot of the Simonside Hills beside the ruined pele from which it takes its name. 2½ miles from Rothbury with superb views over Coquet Valley and Cheviot Hills. Perfect base for exploring Northumberland's many attractions. Spacious bedroons with tea/coffee, one twin en suite, two double en suite. Guests' lounge, TV, full CH. Open Mar–Nov.

SELF-CATERING

East Burton Farm Holiday Cottages, East Burton, Bamburgh, Northumberland NE69 7AR

Eve Humphreys
☎ **01668 214213/214458**
Fax 01668 214538
🆂🅲 **From £200–£420**
Sleeps 4–6
🐾(4) 🐎 🏕 ✂
🔑 🔑 🔑 🔑 *Up to Highly Commended*

Six comfortable cottages on a working farm 1½ miles from Bamburgh, all well equipped and furnished. Heat, light, sheets and towels included in rent. Ideal base for birdwatching, golf, sightseeing or relaxing. Open all year.

Farm Cottage, Bilton Barns, Alnmouth, Alnwick, Northumberland NE66 2TB

Mrs Dorothy Jackson
☎ **01665 830427**
🆂🅲 **From £150–£350**
Sleeps 7
🐎

Applied

Ideally situated for exploring the beautiful Northumbrian coastline with its castles and magnificent walks. Our farm cottage has been recently modernised to a very high standard with a new and fully equipped kitchen, central heating and an open fire with fuel provided. Bed linen is also included in rental. Open all year.

Firwood Bungalow and Humphreys House, Earle Hill Head Farm, Wooler, Northumberland NE71 6RH

S. E. Armstrong
☎/Fax **01668 281243**
🆂🅲 **From £180–£550**
Sleeps 6–12
🐕 🐾 🐎 🐕 🏕
🔑 🔑 🔑 – 🔑 🔑 🔑
Up to Highly Commended

Firwood and Humphreys, a choice of two beautiful homes offering a unique and private situation. Standing in 1.5 acres of well maintained gardens on 4,000 acre farm within the National Park at the foot of the Cheviots. Ideal throughout the year. Every comfort, open fires, central heating. Open all year.

Keepers Cottages, Great Tosson, Rothbury, Morpeth, Northumberland NE65 7NW

Mrs Ann Foggin
☎ **01669 620228**
🆂🅲 **From £130–£385**
Sleeps 4–6
🐾 🐎 🐕 🏕
🔑 🔑 🔑 *Up to Highly Commended*

Four delightful cottages situated in the Coquet Valley enjoying panoramic views of the Cheviot Hills. Cosy, comfortable, centrally heated, well equipped and all with enclosed gardens. Set in National Park with many forest and moorland walks clearly marked. Private fishing. 2 miles from Rothbury and the NT property of Cragside. Very central for touring all Northumberland. Bedlinen provided. Log fires during winter. Open all year.

---

17 **Lumbylaw Cottage & Garden Cottage,** Edlingham, Alnwick, Northumberland NE66 2BW

Mrs Sally Lee
☎/Fax 01665 574277
SC From £112–£399
Sleeps 6 + cot, and 2
🦌 🐎 🎠 🐾
🐾 🐾 🐾 – 🐾 🐾 🐾 🐾
Highly Commended

Non smokers. Extensive hill views. The two cottages are situated on our working farm with its own ruined castle and viaduct, providing easy walking along the disused railway line. Both cottages centrally heated. Recently renovated, they are prettily decorated, furnished and equipped to a high standard. No stairs. All fuel and power, bed linen and towels included in rent. Sorry no pets. Brochure available. Open all year.

---

18 **The Old Smithy,** Brackenside, Bowsden, Berwick-upon-Tweed, Northumberland TD15 2TQ

John & Mary Barber
☎ 01289 388293
SC From £170–£375
Sleeps 6 + cot
🐓 🐕 ♿
🐾 🐾 🐾 – 🐾 🐾 🐾 🐾
Up to Highly Commended

The high standards of this attractive conversion of a smithy and stable to a comfortable home makes an ideal setting for a peaceful and relaxing holiday. Explore the farm, discover the woodland and conservation areas. See the cows and calves, sheep, lambs and crops. Table tennis. Bike hire, riding, fishing and golf nearby. Gas central heating makes for a perfect winter break. Open all year.

---

19 **Shepherd's Cottage,** Ingram Farm, Powburn, Alnwick, Northumberland NE66 4LT

Sarah Wilson
☎ 01665 578243
SC From £200–£375
Sleeps 7
🐕 🐓 🐈 🐎
🐾 🐾 🐾 🐾 *Commended*

On a working family farm in the beautiful Breamish Valley, the cottage has superb scenery on the doorstep. Explore the unspoilt Cheviot Hills or the coast and castles. Most mod cons are provided and there are no extras – fuel, linen and towels all included. Central heating from open fire. Night storage heating. Short breaks available. Open all year.

---

20 **No. 2 and 3 Cottages,** Titlington Hall Farm, Alnwick, Northumberland NE66 2EB

Mrs Vera Purvis
☎/Fax 01665 578253
SC From £155–£295
Sleeps 10
🐓 🐕 ♿ 🐈 ▪
🐾 🐾 🐾 🐾 *Commended*

Two lovely country cottages available for holiday lets all year round. They are situated in a beautiful area with many interesting places close by. Facilities include central heating, TV, fridge, washing machine, microwave, tumble dryer and all linen. Children and pets welcome. Stabling for horses and lovely well marked rides. Open all year.

England's North Country
Northumberland and Durham

Group Contact: *Mrs L Vickers* ☎ *01388 527248*

Northumbria covers the four most northerly counties of England – Cleveland, Durham, Northumberland and Tyne and Wear. Visitors can escape on traffic-free roads to open countryside and vast, deserted beaches; a great contrast to the modern cities where shopping and entertainment are of a high standard. Old and new complement each other with some of Britain's finest heritage such as Hadrian's Wall, Durham Cathedral, Beamish Museum, Holy Island and new developments like Newcastle upon Tyne's Eldon Square and the Metro Centre at Gateshead.

The region also boasts some of England's finest countryside – the North Pennines designated as an 'Area of Outstanding Natural Beauty' and the Northumberland National Park – retreats from the pressures of modern life.

Visitors to Northumbria can be assured of a warm and hospitable welcome seldom equalled.

Kielder
Reservoir

A696
A68 15 2
Bellingham

Morpeth   Newbiggin-
           by-the-Sea
Bedlington   Blyth

A69

Haydon
Bridge   Corbridge
A686   A69   Whitley Bay
    Hexham
              Prudhoe   Newcastle UponTyne
10   3   A694 Gateshead
       5 9   A692
                              Sunderland
    11 13   Consett A692
16 Allenheads 8 7
A689   Stanley 18 17
    Chester-Le-Street
              A691
       1   Seaham
    14 Tow law   Durham
6
    12 Crook Brandon
  4   Peterlee
    Willington
              A1(M)
    Spennymoor   Hartlepool
Bishop Auckland
    A19
Shildon

BED AND BREAKFAST

(and evening meal)

---

① Bee Cottage Farm, Castleside, Consett, Co Durham DH8 9HW

Liz Lawson
☎ 01207 508224
BB From £20
EM £12
Sleeps 22
🦮 🐕 ⚡ 🚗 ⚱ ◎
🏆 🏆 *Highly Commended*

A working farm in lovely surroundings with unspoilt views, situated 1½ miles west A68 between Tow Law and Castleside. Visitors may participate in all farm activities, feeding calves, milking goats, bottle feeding lambs, etc. Tea room open daily. Quiet country walks. Fire certificate. No smoking in farmhouse. Ideally located for Beamish Museum, Metro Centre, Durham Cathedral or a break on a journey between England and Scotland. Open all year.

---

② Cornhills, Kirkwhelpington, Northumberland NE19 2RE

Lorna Thornton
☎ 01830 540232
BB From £17.50
Sleeps 6
⚡ 🐕 ⚱
Listed *Highly Commended*

A large Victorian farmhouse complete with mosaic tiled hall, spacious beautifully decorated and furnished bedrooms (one en suite), all with outstanding views. Our stock farm is in the centre of Northumberland, ideal for visiting Cragside, Wallington and Belsay Hall. 1 mile from the A696, 3½ miles from the A68, makes this very convenient for travelling to Scotland. Closed April.

---

③ Flothers Farm, Slaley, Hexham, Northumberland NE47 0BJ

Susan Dart
☎ 01434 673240
BB From £15–£20
Sleeps 5
🐕 🦮 ⚱
🏆 🏆 *Applied*

We are a typical Northumbrian dairy farm, set in beautiful countryside. Accommodation in self-contained area. Full central heating, all rooms en suite, tea/coffee and colour TV. Country pubs within walking distance. Taxi service available. Excellent breakfasts provided. Open all year.

---

④ Friarside Farm, Wolsingham, Weardale, Co Durham DL13 3BH

Mrs Marjorie Anderson
☎ 01388 527361
BB From £15
Sleeps 4
🦮 🐕(5) ⚡ ⚱ ◎
🏆 *Commended*

Relax, enjoy the Friarside experience. A serene, welcoming atmosphere awaits the discerning visitor to our hill farm. We offer home-made bread (hot cross buns at Easter) for breakfast which is served in the conservatory. Enjoy pleasant easy walks on the farm and perhaps an old fashioned musical evening. Good choice of food within easy reach in Wolsingham. Open all year.

---

⑤ Gairshield Farm, Whitley Chapel, Hexham, Northumberland NE47 0HS

Mrs Hilary Kristensen
☎ 01434 673562
BB From £15
Sleeps 4
⚡ 🐕(6) ⚱ 🅰
Listed *Highly Commended*

A comfortable 17th century farmhouse on a quiet hill farm (1,000 ft above sea level), with superb views over open countryside. 20 mins south of Hexham. Ideal for exploring this beautiful historic region. Perfect walking and horse-riding area; horses very welcome. Large attractive family bedroom. Guests' dining room/lounge with TV and tea/coffee making facilities. Open Apr–Oct.

Greenwell Farm, Nr Wolsingham, Tow Law, Bishop Auckland, Co Durham DL13 4PH   6

Mike & Linda Vickers
☎ 01388 527248
BB £18.50
EM From £8.50
Sleeps 6
🌿 🐕 🚷 🐓 ☂ ☎ ☂ ✻ 🅿
♟ ♟ ♟ *Commended*

Enjoy a warm welcome in our charming farmhouse dating back 300 years. On the 280-acre mixed stock and arable farm we have developed our own walks and nature reserve with a wide variety of wildlife. Comfortable and attractive rooms, quality food. Bedrooms with private bathrooms. An excellent base for touring, county cricket and visiting the numerous attractions of the North Pennines and Durham City. Open all year (closed Christmas and New Year).

Low Urpeth Farm, Ouston, Chester Le Street, Co Durham DH2 1BD   7

Hilary Johnson
☎ 0191 410 2901
Fax 0191 410 0081
BB From £16.50–£20
Sleeps 6
🐕 🌿 🅿
Listed *Highly Commended*

Traditional farmhouse accommodation in spacious and comfortably furnished rooms with TV/beverage facilities, one double with washbasin, 2 twin en suite. Within easy reach of Beamish Open Air Museum, Durham and castles and coast of Northumberland. Directions – leave A1(M) at Chester Le Street, follow A693, at 2nd roundabout fork right to Ouston, down hill, over roundabout, turn left at 'Trees Please' sign. Open all year.

Mount Escob Farm, Beamish Woods, Stanley, Co Durham DH9 0SA   8

Mrs Pamela Bovill
☎ 0191 370 0289
BB From £15–£17
Sleeps 6
🐕 🐓 🌿 ☂ ▪ ✻ 🅿
Listed *Applied*

A 12-acre grassland holding with that 'heart of the country' feel, yet less than 10 mins from the A1(M)! Close to Beamish Open Air Museum. The house is on the site of a former paper mill, beside Beamish Burn, with the surrounding hills and woods bearing much evidence of small industries of a byegone age. Our horses and youngstock thrive on their visitors' attention! A short drive takes you to either Durham city or to the Metro Centre. Open all year.

Rye Hill Farm, Slaley, Nr Hexham, Northumberland NE47 0AH   9

Elizabeth Courage
☎ 01434 673259
BB From £18.50–£22
EM From £10
Sleeps 15
🐕 🎣 🏕 🐓 ☂ ▪ 🅿
♟ ♟ ♟ *Commended*

We are a small family-run livestock farm set in beautiful countryside with 360-degree panoramic views. We have recently converted some of the old byres into superb modern guest accommodation. We aim for high standards with a homely atmosphere, ideal for your 'get away from it all' break or holiday. Good, fresh, homemade cooking. All rooms en suite. Well mannered children and pets welcome. Open all year.

Struthers Farm, Allendale, Hexham, Northumberland NE47 9LP   10

Mrs Ruby Keenleyside
☎ 01434 683580
BB From £16.50–£17.50
EM From £8.50
Sleeps 5
🐕 🐓 ☂
♟ ♟ *Commended*

A small working livestock farm situated in a designated area of natural beauty. Quiet country walks, ample safe parking. Children and pets by arrangement. We offer spacious double/twin en suite rooms, Guests' lounge/dining/TV room. Fresh home cooking. Come and enjoy our countryside. Open all year.

SELF-CATERING

---

(11) **Bail Hill,** Allenshields, Blanchland, Consett, Co Durham DH8 9PP

Jennifer Graham
☎ 01434 675274
🆂🅲 From £120–£220
Sleeps 5
🐾 🎦 🎋
🔑 🔑 🔑 *Commended*

Centrally heated, 2-bedroomed farmhouse with breath-taking views to Derwent Reservoir near Blanchland. Enjoy the peaceful surroundings of a typical hill farm or use as a central location for Tynedale, Durham and N E Coast. Blanchland is one of the most picturesque of Northumbrian historic villages with Abbey, pub and post office. Open fire and well-equipped kitchen. Enclosed garden and parking outside the house. Open all year.

---

(12) **Bradley Burn Holiday Cottages,** Wolsingham, Weardale, Co Durham DL13 3JH

Mrs Judith Stephenson
☎/Fax 01388 527285
🆂🅲 From £130–£320
Sleeps 18
♿ 🐾 🐎 🏹 📺 ♨ ◎
🔑 🔑 🔑 – 🔑 🔑 🔑 🔑
Up to Highly Commended

Four cottages, well-designed conversions of redundant farm buildings, preserving the traditional stone exteriors but incorporating all modern comforts indoors. Rural situation, close to a pretty stream. 2 miles east of former market town of Wolsingham. Centrally placed for sightseeing in Durham, Northumberland and North Yorkshire. Send for brochure. Open all year.

---

(13) **Buckshott Farm Cottage,** Blanchland, Consett, Co Durham DH8 9PL

Lorraine & Irene Bainbridge
☎ 01434 675227/ 675296
🆂🅲 From £120–£235
Sleeps 6
🐎 🎋
🔑 🔑 🔑 *Commended*

Attractive 2-bedroom cottage which adjoins the farmhouse and overlooks the beautiful Derwent Valley. Central heating, fitted kitchen, private garden, ample parking. Blanchlands historic village has a shop, post office, pub and a 12th century abbey. Hexham, Durham, Beamish Open Air Museum, Gateshead Metro Centre and the Northumberland coast are all within an easy day's outing. Open Apr–Oct.

---

(14) **Greenwell Hill Stables & Byre,** c/o Greenwell Farm, Nr Wolsingham, Tow Law, Co Durham DL13 4PH

Linda Vickers
☎ 01388 527248
🆂🅲 From £160–£350
Sleeps 5/7
🐾 🏹 ♿ 🎦 🎋 ♨ 🍴
🔑 🔑 🔑 🔑 *Highly Commended*

Enjoy a relaxing stay in one of two quality cottages. This is a traditional farm in peaceful countryside. Marvellous views, pleasant walks and our own nature trail with conservation area. The larger cottage has a four poster bed, dishwasher and en suite bedrooms. Both are well equipped with gas central heating, double glazing, natural beams, pine furniture, fitted carpets, comfy chintzy suites and woodburing stoves. Evening meals available. Open all year.

---

(15) **The Herdsman Cottage,** Cornhills, Kirkwhelpington, Northumberland NE19 2RE

Lorna Thornton
☎ 01830 540232
🆂🅲 From £130–£280
Sleeps 5
✂ 🐎 🎋
🔑 🔑 🔑 🔑 *Commended*

A beamed 19th century farm cottage, provides comfortable accommodation for 5 people (double, twin, single). The fully fitted kitchen is equipped with fridge, washing machine, night storage heaters, open fire in winter. Bed linen provided. Enjoy the peace on our stock farm, in the centre of Northumberland. Open all year.

"Isaac's Cottage", c/o Allenheads Farm, Allenheads, Hexham, Northumberland NE4 9HJ

Heather M Robson
☎ 01434 685312
SC From £150–£280
Sleeps 7
🐕 🐎 ✂ 🐎 ← 🎣
🐾 🐾 🐾 🐾 *Highly Commended*

Cosy character cottage with beamed ceilings and log fire, adjoining farmhouse and overlooking meadow and moorland. Fully equipped to a high standard, 3 bedrooms plus cot/high chair. Own garden with picnic table. Perfect for a peaceful break with lovely walks, also pony trekking and golf nearby. Prices include bed linen, electricity and fuel. Please ring for brochure or further information. Open all year.

Katie's Cottage, c/o Low Urpeth Farm, Ouston, Chester Le Street, Co.Durham DH2 1BD

Hilary Johnson
☎ 0191 410 2901
Fax 0191 410 0081
SC From £200–£225
Sleeps 4
🐕 ✂
🐾 🐾 🐾 🐾
Highly Commended

Relax in our newly converted stone cottage, tastefully furnished. Two en suite bedrooms, cosy living area with timber beams. Three miles A1M, excellent base for Durham, Beamish Museum and easy access to Northumberland and Hadrian's Wall. Open all year.

Papermill Cottages, Mount Escob Farm, Beamish Woods, Stanley, Co Durham DH9 0SA 18

Mrs Pamela Bovill
☎ 0191 370 0289
SC From £130–£280
Sleeps 2/8
🐕 🐎 ✂ 🎣 ■ 🧵
🐾 🐾 🐾 *Commended*

Near Beamish Museum. Two workers' cottages from Urpeth Paper Mill (circa 1792) have recently been renovated to a high standard, retaining traditional features of open fire ranges, beams and stonework whilst updating with modern kitchens and central heating. Set in an idyllic, peaceful situation beside the river, surrounded by woods yet only 6 minutes from A1M at Chester le Street. Open all year.

PRICES

Prices include VAT and service charge (if any) and are:
B&B per person per night
EM per person
SC per unit per week
Tents and caravans per pitch per night

THE 1000+ BUREAU MEMBERS OFFER A UNIQUE LINK TO CUSTOMERS ACROSS THE UK

All Bureau members belong to a local Group. Each member can refer you to an equally high quality member within his Group… or across the UK: England, Northern Ireland, Scotland, Wales.

England's North Country

Teesdale

Group Contact: *Mrs June Dent* ☎ *01833 640349*

Teesdale with its wealth of history and outstanding scenery lies south-west of Durham city. Its gentle dales and rolling moorland abound with features of geological and historical interest. The River Tees itself rises at Cross Fell and courses down the valley and includes the impressive 'High Force', England's highest waterfall with a dramatic 70ft drop over Great Whin Sill. Ancient stone quarries and disused lead mines in the upper dale mark industries dating back to Roman times and the many public footpaths in the dale include a magnificent scenic stretch of the well known Pennine Way.

Teesdale makes an excellent base for exploring the nearby Yorkshire Dales, the Roman wall, Northumberland and the Lake District, all of which are within an hour's drive. For the holidaymaker interested in castles and museums, there are plenty to choose from: Barnard Castle dating back to the 12th century, the famous French-style Bowes Museum and the historic Raby Castle, seat of Lord Barnard. A little further across the county is the now famous Beamish Open Air Museum and many other interesting places too numerous to list.

Visit Teesdale to discover its scenic beauty and historic sights for yourself.

BED AND BREAKFAST

(and evening meal)

East Mellwaters Farm, Bowes, Barnard Castle, Co Durham DL12 9RH

Patricia Milner
☎ **01833 628269**
ᴮᴮ **From £17.50–£20**
EM From £10
Sleeps 10
☜ ♞ ⚥ ☂ ⚘ ⏚ ⚞ ☎ ▣ ▦
⊛
♣ ♣ *Commended*

Come and meet Dolly, our highland cow, watch the dippers and golden plovers or glimpse badgers. Learn about the Bronze Age on our waymarked walks. Fish for brown trout, we'll show you the best pools. Visit Beamish, Bowes Museum, ancient castles, market towns or the Metro Centre for shopping (Christmas?). Then relax with a cup of tea, log fire and delicious food in best farmhouse tradition. Holidays and special break rates. Open mid Jan–mid Dec.

Wilson House, Barningham, Richmond, North Yorkshire DL11 7EB

Mrs Helen Lowes
☎ **01833 621218**
ᴮᴮ **From £16**
EM From £10
Sleeps 6
☜ ♞ ⚥ ⚘ ⚐
♣ ♣ *Commended*

475-acre working family farm in a picturesque and peaceful setting yet only 1 mile from A66. Ideally situated for touring Yorkshire or Durham Dales. Comfortable, spacious en suite bedrooms with colour TV and tea/coffee facilities. Kitchenette for guests' use equipped with fridge and microwave. Good home cooking with choice of menu. Children welcome. Open Mar–Nov.

Wythes Hill Farm, Lunedale, Middleton-in-Teesdale, Co Durham DL12 0NX

Mrs June Dent
☎ **01833 640349**
ᴮᴮ **From £16**
EM From £8
Sleeps 5
☜ ♞ ⚘ ☂ ⊛
♣ *Commended*

Wythes Hill is a working stock-rearing farm with panoramic views from all rooms. Situated on the Pennine Way route with many picturesque walks in Teesdale. Visit the Bowes Museum, Raby Castle and High Force Waterfall. Good plain cooking. One family room with H&C, one twin en suite. All rooms with tea/coffee-making facilities. Lounge with coal fire. Open Mar–Nov.

FARM HOLIDAY
BUREAU

FOLLOW THE COUNTRY CODE

Leave nothing but footprints,
Take nothing but photographs,
Kill nothing but time!

England's North Country
Cleveland and
North Yorkshire Borders

Group Contacts: BB *Mrs P. Fanthorpe* ☎ *01642 710431*
SC *Heather Addison* ☎ *01642 590121*

Cleveland & North Yorkshire is an Area of Outstanding Natural Beauty bordering the north-western edges of the North Yorkshire Moors, the largest expanse of heather moorland in England, familiar from the television series 'Heartbeat'. The name Cleveland comes from the Norse word 'Klifland' meaning land of cliffs and the picturesque Cleveland hills offer many good walks with spectacular views. The area gives its name to the 'Cleveland Way', the long distance walk from Helmsley to Filey, and also to the local breed of horse, the 'Cleveland Bay'.

Tucked beneath the northern edge of the moors lies Great Ayton where the famous explorer Captain Cook was educated and the 50ft monument on Easby Moor can be seen from miles around.

When staying on a farm in this area, tourists have access not only to the beauty of the moors and Yorkshire Dales but also to Teesside with its industry and commerce. Businessmen will be offered the warmth of Yorkshire hospitality within easy reach of Middlesbrough and Stockton.

BED AND BREAKFAST

(and evening meal)

Dromonby Hall Farm, Busby Lane, Kirkby-in-Cleveland, Stokesley, Middlesbrough, Cleveland TS9 7AP

Mrs Patricia Weighell
☎ **01642 712312**
BB **From £15–£17.50**
EM From £8
Sleeps 6
☺(2) 🐴 ✕ ▲ ♿ ☂
👄 *Commended*

Modern farmhouse on 170-acre working farm with superb views of Cleveland Hills. Ideal for walking or touring by car. Easy access from A19 and B1257, 8 miles south of Middlesbrough. ½ hr drive from coast and from Teesside. A warm welcome and good food. Horse riding available locally. Enjoy the peace and beautiful surroundings. Open all year.

Harker Hill Farm, Harker Hill, Seamer, Stokesley, Nr Middlesbrough, North Yorkshire TS9 5NF

Pam & John Fanthorpe
☎ **01642 710431**
BB **From £16**
EM From £7
Sleeps 6
☺ 🐴 ✕ ⛺
Listed *Commended*

Harker Hill is a two hundred year old farm offering warmth and comfort. The cosy accommodation includes full central heating, log fires, lounge and television. Home cooked food is served at times to suit you so businessmen visiting Teesside can enjoy early cooked breakfasts and late evening meals. Open all year except Christmas.

Maltby Farm, Maltby, Middlesbrough, Cleveland TS8 0BP

Clive & Heather Addison
☎ **01642 590121**
BB **From £15–£16**
EM From £8
Sleeps 6
☺(1) 🐴 ✕
👄 *Approved*

Welcome to our working farm which is over 200 years old and looks south onto the Cleveland Hills. Ideally situated on the edge of the North Yorkshire Moors and Captain Cook Country. Within easy distance of the coast or pretty market towns of Stokesley and Yarm. Open Apr–Nov.

FARM HOLIDAY BUREAU

THOSE LITTLE EXTRAS

For advice on farms that can offer 'extras' such as four-poster beds, special diets, farm trails, fishing rights – even stabling and trekking arrangements if you are bringing your own horse – ring the Farm Holiday Bureau on (01203) 696909.

England's North Country

North Pennines

Group Contact: *Pat Dent* ☎ *01434 381383*

The North Pennines – Area of Outstanding Natural Beauty – is truly 'England's Last Wilderness'.

The upland moors and valleys of Cumbria, Durham and Northumberland are encompassed by this area of remote moorland, famed for wild flowers and birds.

Three famous rivers rise here, the Tyne, the Tees and the Wear, fast-flowing streams growing to mighty torrents. In Teesdale, High Force shows the power of the water as does the river Wear harnessed by the lead miners at Killhope Wheel.

Landscapes have been formed by generations of hill farmers, a patchwork separated by stone walls and grazed by sheep and cattle, with heather moors and, from long ago, the remains of Roman occupation.

This area is criss-crossed with footpaths, the most well known being the Pennine Way, but there is something for everyone, from the gentle stroll to the energetic journey to the top of Cross Fell at 2,930 ft. The scenery is varied, with many panoramic views and a different scene around every corner.

Alston with its narrow cobbled street and market cross nestles amongst these hills, as do Allendale town where New Year is celebrated with a procession of blazing tar barrels. St John's Chapel, host to one of the many agricultural shows held in this area. Stanhope boasts a fossilised tree. Nearby are the market towns of Barnard Castle, Appleby, Hexham and Penrith.

Easily accessible, yet far from the hustle and bustle of modern life, this area is excellent for touring, but most people find that once here, they do not want to leave.

BED AND BREAKFAST

(and evening meal)

Ivy House Farm, Garrigill, Alston, Cumbria CA9 3DU

Helen Dent
☎ 01434 382079
🅱 From £13–£15
EM From £8.50
Sleeps 6
🕊 🐕 🐄
Listed *Commended*

A warm welcome awaits you when you visit our 256-acre hill farm with grazing cattle and sheep. Situated in the picturesque village of Garrigill on the Pennine Way. Ideal for walking/touring – our 17th century listed farmhouse has 2 bedrooms with handbasins and tea making facilities. Good farmhouse breakfast and excellent food available in village. Open all year (closed Christmas & April).

Lands Farm, Westgate-in-Weardale, Co Durham DL13 1SN

Mrs Barbara Reed
☎ 01388 517210
🅱 From £17–£18
Sleeps 5
🐕 🕊 🌲
🌷🌷 *Highly Commended*

A friendly welcome awaits you on our 280 acre beef and sheep farm peacefully situated in beautiful Weardale. All bedrooms have luxury en suite facilities, TV and tea/coffee. Conveniently located for Durham City, Beamish Museum, Hadrian's Wall, High Force and walking in the North Pennines. Open Apr–Nov.

Low Cornriggs Farm, Cowshill-in-Weardale, Bishop Auckland, Co Durham DL13 1AQ

Mrs Janet Ellis
☎ 01388 537600
🅱 From £17.50–£18
EM From £9
Sleeps 6
🐕 🕊 🐄 🌲 🛢
🌷🌷🌷 *Applied*

Low Cornriggs has wonderful views over the High Pennines. Luxury 200-year-old farmhouse with en suite rooms, electric blankets, tea trays. Log fires, full central heating, warm and cosy – a real old world place with a warm welcome for every guest. TV lounge, video. Licensed dining room overlooking gardens. Riding centre (fell ponies) and good walks as we are on the Weardale Way. Easy reach of Alston, Hexham and Durham on the A689. Special Christmas/New Year breaks. Open all year.

Middle Bayles Farm, Alston, Cumbria CA9 3BS

Mrs Pat Dent
☎ 01434 381383
🅱 From £15–£18
EM £9
Sleeps 6
🐕 🕊 🌲 🛢
🌷🌷 *Commended*

A 300-acre hill farm where visitors are welcome to wander. Ideal walking/touring area. Warm, comfortable 17th century farmhouse, tastefully furnished, with superb views overlooking South Tyne Valley. 1 double/ twin and 1 family room, both en suite, electric blankets. Tea-making facilities, full CH. Good home cooking including our own bread, warm welcome. Recommended in Good Weekend Guide. Reductions under 14s. Closed Christmas & April.

SELF-CATERING

---

⑤ Ghyll Burn Cottage, Hartside Nursery Garden, Nr Alston, Cumbria CA9 3BL

Mrs Susan Huntley
☎ 01434 381372/381428
⑤⑥ From £140–£330
Sleeps 4/6 + cot
🛏 🐕 ⌨ 🎋 🍴
🔑 🔑 🔑 *Commended*

Recently renovated farm buildings dating back to 1630 offer spacious and comfortable accommodation for 4/6 people. Kitchen/diner, large lounge with oak beams and wood burning stove on first floor. Attractive twin and double bedrooms, bathroom, are downstairs. Full gas central heating. The cottage is set in a secluded valley with small nursery garden. Ideal for bird wildlife and gardening enthusiasts. Open all year.

---

⑥ Grey Croft, The Raise, Alston, c/o Middle Bayles Farm, Alston, Cumbria CA9 3BS

Mrs Pat Dent
☎ 01434 381383
⑤⑥ From £160–£325
Sleeps 2–6
🛏 🐕 ⌨ 📺 🍴 ♿
🔑 🔑 🔑 🔑 *Highly Commended*

Luxury bungalow with open views south towards Crossfell on the fringe of The Raise hamlet, one mile from Alston. Fully equipped and furnished to a very high standard. Two bedrooms with double and single beds, linen provided. Fitted kitchen, dishwasher, microwave, washer/dryer. Gas CH, open fire, TV, video, telephone. Open all year.

FARM HOLIDAY BUREAU

FINDING YOUR ACCOMMODATION

The Group contacts at the beginning of each section can always help you find a vacancy in your chosen area.

Eden Valley & North Pennines

Group Contacts: 📧 *Ruth Tuer* ☎/*Fax 01931 715205*
📠 *Anne Ivinson* ☎ *016974 76230(24hr answerphone/Fax 76523)*

The River Eden rises in Mallerstang, an isolated corner of the old County of Westmorland, and, rushing through the alpine flowers of the still untamed North Pennines, gradually descends, gathering strength from its many tributaries, until it reaches Appleby, a sleepy market town straddling the Eden. The broad tree lined street linking the Castle and the Church make it one of the loveliest towns in the valley. For two weeks every year Appleby awakes from its slumber to host the largest gipsy gathering and horse fair in the country, a sight not to be missed!

On to the attractive town of Penrith, Gateway to the Lakes, a focus for travellers since Roman times the Eden meanders through picturesque villages built of local red sandstone until it reaches the historic City of Carlisle and the Solway Plain. This area is truly a 'Garden of Eden' with its lush vegetation and wide variety of wildlife. The visitor can enjoy a variety of walks, climbing Cross Fell or Wild Boar Fell in the Pennines or take an easier route along one of the many woodland and riverside footpaths signposted through the area.

For the less energetic there are tours around historic houses and sites travelling on the local minibus, the Fellrunner and last but by no means least, the famous Carlisle to Settle railway runs right through Eden with stations at Armathwaite, Lazonby, Langwathby and Appleby: what better way to enjoy the magnificent scenery of the Eden Valley and the North Pennines?

Carlisle

A596

A595

Maryport

7 11

M6

A686

8

A689

Workington

Cockermouth

41

13

Penrith

Whitehaven

A66

40

3

9 10

A5086

Keswick

5

2

M6

6

Appleby-in-
Westmoorland

A591

A66

1 12

A592

39

4

A66

Ambleside

A6

38

A685

A593

Windermere

M6

A683

Kendal

37

BED AND BREAKFAST

(and evening meal)

---

① Augill House Farm, Brough, Kirkby Stephen, Cumbria CA17 4DX

Jeanette Atkinson
☎ **017683 41305**
BB From £18–£20
EM From £8
Sleeps 6
☺(12) ⚥ ✗
♨ ♨ ♨
Highly Commended

Enjoy super breakfasts and delicious 4 course dinners served in our lovely conservatory overlooking the garden. Double and twin en suite bedrooms with colour TV, tea and coffee-making facilities. Ideal for the Lakes, Dales and North Pennines. RAC highly acclaimed. AA. QQQQ selected. Closed Christmas and New Year.

---

② Bridge End Farm, Kirkby Thore, Penrith, Cumbria CA10 1UZ

Mrs Yvonne Dent
☎ **01768 361362**
BB From £18–£20
EM From £9
Sleeps 6
⚥ ♞ ☺ ☞
♨ ♨ *Highly Commended*

Relax in 18th century farmhouse on a dairy farm in the Eden Valley near Appleby. Spacious antique furnished en suite rooms overlooking Pennine Hills. Interesting craftwork. Open fire in guests' lounge. Delicious homemade breakfast: teas and dinners served in dining room. Finish with lovely evening walk along the River Eden. Open all year except Christmas.

---

③ Hornby Hall, Brougham, Penrith, Cumbria CA10 2AR

Ros Sanders
☎ **01768 891114/0831 482108**
Fax 01768 88248
BB From £19–£29.50
EM from £13.50
Sleeps 8
☺ ♞ ▦ ▟
Listed *Highly Commended*

16th century farmhouse situated three miles from Penrith, one mile off A66 in tranquillity of Eden Valley. Two en suite, three double, two single rooms. Evening meals served in original Hall. All food freshly cooked from local produce. Trout fishing available on River Eamont. River paths are a profusion of wild flowers. Open all year except Christmas.

---

④ Meaburn Hill Farm, Maulds Meaburn, Penrith, Cumbria CA10 3HN

Ruth Tuer
☎/Fax **01931 715205**
BB From £19–£24
Sleeps 6
⚷ ⏚ ⚥ ☺ ♞ ☞ ⛺ ▟ ✿
Listed *Highly Commended*

Relax at our beautifully restored 16th century farmhouse, quietly situated in a hidden valley near Appleby. Lovely antique furnished rooms overlooking tranquil river and village green. 2 double rooms and 1 twin room, all with private facilities. Enjoy an award-winning farmhouse breakfast or afternoon tea beside a roaring fire. Explore nearby lakes & dales or roam the quiet footpaths & bridleways around our 200 acre beef and sheep farm. Open Mar–Dec.

---

⑤ Park House Farm, Dalemain, Penrith, Cumbria CA11 0HB

Mrs Mary Milburn
☎ **017684 86212**
BB From £15–£17
Sleeps 6
☺ ⛺
♨ *Commended*

Peace and tranquillity in our valley – you can relax and enjoy stunning views of Lakeland fells. 3 miles from Lake Ullswater or M6 (J40) on A592 entering via Dalemain Mansion ignoring the 'no cars' sign. Cumbrian hospitality is assured with a welcome cup, home baking and generous breakfast. Evening meals available locally. 2 family bedrooms (1 en suite), electric blanket, heater, tea/coffee facilities. Bathroom and shower room. TV lounge with open fire. Open Apr–Oct.

Slakes Farm, Milburn, Appleby in Westmorland, Cumbria CA16 6DP **6**

Mrs C Braithwaite
☎ 017683 61385
BB From £13
EM from £8
Sleeps 6
🐕 🐎
Listed *Applied*

Slakes Farm was built in 1734 and is situated between the villages of Milburn and Knock 6 miles from Appleby. The farm is approx 40 acres rearing cattle and sheep. It makes an ideal base for walking and touring, returning to good farmhouse cooking using fresh local produce. Open March–Oct.

Streethead Farm, Ivegill, Carlisle, Cumbria CA4 0NG **7**

Mrs J Wilson
☎ 016974 73327
BB From £15–£18
Sleeps 4
🐎(7) 🐕 ▪
🐛🐛 *Commended*

Stroll by our ornamental waterfowl ponds. Relax in an antique-filled TV lounge with woodburner. Sleep in spacious bedrooms, one en suite, one with H&C and own bathroom, both hospitality trays, electric blankets, radio alarm, hair drier and many little extra comforts. Choice of breakfasts with homemade preserves. Lakes within 20 minutes' drive. Brochure with pleasure. Open Mar–Nov.

SELF-CATERING

Green View Lodges & Well Cottage, Green View, Welton, Nr Dalston, Carlisle, Cumbria CA5 7ES

Anne Ivinson
☎ 016974 76230
Fax 016974 76523
SC From £140–£440
Sleeps 2/7
📧 🐕 ♿ 🐎 🎿 ▪
🔑🔑🔑🔑 – 🔑🔑🔑🔑🔑
Up to Highly Commended

Superb Scandinavian lodges, surprisingly spacious in peaceful garden setting. 17th century oak-beamed cottages, 1 with open fire, also a tastefully converted Wesleyan chapel for 2. Own gardens. In tiny, picturesque hamlet with unspoilt views to Caldbeck Fells 3 miles. Every home comfort provided for a relaxing country holiday. CH, telephones. Within ½ hr's drive of Keswick, Lake Ullswater or Gretna Green. Golf 5 miles, fishing 3 miles. Open all year.

Skirwith Hall Cottage, Skirwith Hall, Skirwith, Penrith, Cumbria CA10 1RH

Mrs Laura Wilson
☎/Fax 01768 88241
SC From £160–£350
Sleeps 4–9
🐕 🐎 ▪
🔑🔑🔑 – 🔑🔑🔑🔑
Up to Commended

Georgian farmhouse wing built of local red sandstone overlooking large pleasant garden and stream on 400-acre mixed dairy farm. Exposed beams and open fire in lounge, nightstore heaters, washing machine, colour TV. Two double rooms and one with twin beds and bunks. Cot and high chair. Handy for Lakes or north Pennines. Ideal fishing, walking or simply enjoying idyllic rural surroundings. Open all year, short breaks available in low season.

Smithy Cottage, c/o Skirwith Hall, Skirwith, Penrith, Cumbria CA10 1RH

Mrs Laura Wilson
☎/Fax 01768 88241
SC From £115–£250
Sleeps 4
🐕 🐎 ▪
🔑🔑🔑 – 🔑🔑🔑🔑
Up to Commended

Originally the home of the village blacksmith. Situated on the outskirts of an unspoilt village in the shadow of Crossfell. Equipped to a high standard, 1 twin bedded and 1 double room. Nightstore heaters and open fire (coal provided). Colour TV, telephone, washing machine. Shop 2 miles. Handy for Lakes, Yorkshire Dales and Scottish Borders. Golf, riding, fishing nearby. Ideal fell walking, birdwatching or touring. Open all year.

11   **Stable Cottage,** Streethead Farm, Ivegill, Carlisle, Cumbria CA4 0NG

Mrs J. Wilson
☎ **016974 73327**
⬛SC **From £150–£250**
Sleeps 4
🐕(12) ✖
🔑 🔑 🔑 🔑 *Commended*

We invite you to our mixed farm. Watch sunsets over distant hills. Our hobby is ornamental waterfowl which can be viewed from upstairs lounge, the former hayloft with open beams, wood panelling, sandstone walls and cosy woodburner. Kitchen downstairs has a dishwasher, microwave, washing machine, dryer. Lakes and Scotland close by. Brochure with colour photos. Open all year.

---

12   **Swallows Barn,** Augill House Farm, Brough, Kirkby Stephen, Cumbria CA17 4DX

Jeanette Atkinson
☎ **017683 41305**
⬛SC **From £100–£250**
Sleeps 5
🐕 ✖ ✖
🔑 🔑 🔑 *Commended*

This super cottage situated on our working farm has everything. Two double bedrooms and two bathrooms, large lounge with open fire and colour TV and video, modern kitchen, all electric, dishwasher, microwave, etc. Lovely conservatory. Also one bedroomed flat. Both properties have CH and DG. We are handy for the Lakes, Dales and Northern Pennines. Open all year.

---

13   **West View Cottages,** West View Farm, Winskill, Penrith, Cumbria CA10 1PD

Alan and Susan Grave
☎ **01768 881356**
⬛SC **From £130–£320**
Sleeps 2–5
🐕 ✖ 🏕
🔑 🔑 🔑 🔑 *Commended*

A roomy cottage and 2 barn conversions on a mixed working farm. All units have central heating, TV, modern kitchen, washing facilities, and linen provided. Ideally situated for touring and within easy reach of the lakes, North Pennines and Scotland. Local facilities include children's play area, open air swimming pool, walking. Sleeps 2/4/5. Short breaks available in low season. Brochure sent on request. Open all year.

FARM HOLIDAY BUREAU

FOLLOW THE COUNTRY CODE

Leave nothing but footprints,
Take nothing but photographs,
Kill nothing but time!

England's North Country
Central Lakeland

Group Contact: *Margaret Beaty* ☎ *017687 78278*

Stay on a farm in the heart of Cumbria and enjoy the peace and quiet of our valleys. Central Lakeland, with its mountains, lakes and woods is well-known and loved.

For over 200 years travellers have come to this most beautiful corner of England to walk the fells and wander the by-ways. Wonderful at any time of year, certainly in the spring, definitely in the autumn, this is the ideal base for touring.

The Keswick area offers the Pencil Museum, home of the first pencil; the Druid's Stone Circle; Lingholm Gardens; Mirehouse, built 1666, and the 10th century Church of St Bega nearby; or England's only mountain forest park at Whinlatter.

In Grasmere, there are Heaton Coopers Studio and 'Dove Cottage', William Wordsworth's home, now an award winning museum. Ambleside has Hayes marvellous garden centre. See the Beatrix Potter exhibition at Bowness, gallery at Hawkshead or her home 'Hill Top', at Near Sawrey.

Attend local shows, see local crafts, Cumberland wrestling, fell running and hound trailing.

We warmly welcome you to our homely, comfortable and traditional farmhouses.

BED AND BREAKFAST

(and evening meal)

---

1 Birkrigg Farm, Newlands, Keswick, Cumbria CA12 5TS

M M Beaty
☎ **017687 78278**
📖 **From £15–£16**
Sleeps 12
🐕 ⚲
Listed *Approved*

Birkrigg is a dairy and sheep farm very pleasantly situated with excellent outlook in the peaceful Newlands Valley, 5 miles from Keswick. Surrounded by mountains, this is an ideal place to walk and climb. Central for touring. Clean, comfortable accommodation. The breakfasts are good too! Meals available at inns nearby. Packed lunches provided. Open Mar–Dec.

---

2 Fell Foot Farm, Little Langdale, Ambleside, Cumbria LA22 9PE

Mrs S. Harryman
☎ **015394 37294**
📖 **From £15**
EM From £9.50
Sleeps 6
🐕(10) ✕ 🖾 ☕ ♞
Listed *Commended*

Nestling at the foot of the famous Wrynose Pass, this 17th century farmhouse was once a coaching Inn. Owned by the National Trust, it contains fine oak beams and panelling. The house offers warm, comfortable accommodation with beautiful views and excellent home cooking. Three rooms, 1 en suite, tea/coffee-making facilities. Open Easter–Nov.

---

3 Keskadale Farm, Newlands, Keswick, Cumbria CA12 5TS

Mrs M Harryman
☎ **017687 78544**
📖 **From £15–£17**
Sleeps 6
🐕 ✕ ⚲ ☕ ♞ ▪
Listed *Applied*

A working farm pleasantly situated at the head of the Newlands Valley, 6 miles from Keswick, 2½ miles from Buttermere. Traditional Lakeland farmhouse with all home comforts. Relax by real open fire on chilly evenings, colour TV. All rooms with central heating, H&C, tea/coffee-making facilities. Magnificent views. Ideal for walking or touring base. Packed lunches available. A warm welcome awaits you. Open Mar–Dec.

---

4 Tymparon Hall, Newbiggin, Stainton, Penrith, Cumbria CA11 0HS

Mrs Margaret Taylor
☎ **017684 83236**
📖 **From £18–£21**
EM From £10.50
Sleeps 9
🐕 ♞ ☕ ▪
♕♕♕ *Commended*

A spacious farmhouse and colourful summer garden situated on a 150 acre sheep farm in a peaceful rural area. Good home cooking. Tea/coffee-making facilities, electric blankets in bedrooms. Open fire in lounge. Lake Ullswater 10 minutes away. Reduction for under 12s; no charge for cot. 4 miles from M6 (jct.40). Open March–Nov.

Please mention **Stay on a Farm** when booking

England's North Country

West Lakeland

Group Contact: *Mrs Carolyn Heslop* ☎ *01900 824222*

Our hospitality and the warmth of our welcome are renowned. If it is home comforts and peace and tranquillity you are after, then this is the place for you.

To most people the Lakes begin and end at Windermere but just venture a little further and you will discover a whole new experience. See the Border City of Carlisle with its chequered history of Romans, Picts and Scots, or the wild, untamed fells of Wasdale. View the hunting grounds of John Peel at Caldbeck, walk around Cockermouth, home of John Dalton, Fletcher Christian and William Wordsworth. Visit Whitehaven, the site of the last invasion of Britain by John Paul Jones, founder of the American Navy. Take the whole family for a ride on 'laal ratty', the miniature steam railway at Ravenglass. Trace the footsteps of the 'Maid of Buttermere' with the help of Melvyn Bragg, son of Wigton, or take the road to the future and spend a day at the British Nuclear Fuels Exhibition Centre at Sellafield. The energetic may like to discover the secrets of our lakes – Ennerdale, Crummock and Buttermere – and enjoy walking, boating, sea, river or lake fishing.

We are the ideal base for touring anywhere in Cumbria – then it's home to the relaxing atmosphere of your friendly farmhouse hosts.

BED AND BREAKFAST

(and evening meal)

---

① Cragend Farm, Rogerscale, Cockermouth, Cumbria CA13 0RG

Mrs Margaret Ann Steel
☎ 01900 85658
[BB] From £16
EM From £8
Sleeps 4–6
🦮 ♉
Listed *Approved*

Friendly family farmhouse accommodation in comfortable old oak-beamed house dated 1732. Log fire in separate lounge. Good home cooking in guests' own dining room. We are a 250-acre farm looking up Lorton Valley. 4 bedrooms with handbasins, 2 bathrooms (1 with shower), 2 toilets. Easy reach of the Lakes. Open Mar–Nov.

---

② East Farm, Crosscanonby, Maryport, Cumbria CA15 6SJ

Mrs Barbara Carruthers
☎ 01900 812153
[BB] From £14–£15
Sleeps 6
🦮(2) ♉
Listed *Commended*

Welcome to our 236-acre dairy farm on the fringe of the Lake District situated between Maryport and Allonby with beautiful views over the Solway Firth to Scotland. Golf course, windsurfing, pony rides and leisure centre with swimming pool nearby. TV lounge, tea-making facilities, central heating and traditional farmhouse breakfast. Open all year.

---

③ Nook Farm, Belk Foot, Silloth, Cumbria CA5 4LG

Mrs M Greenup
☎ 01900 881279
[BB] From £14–£16
Sleeps 5
🦮 ♉
Listed *Approved*

A warm welcome greets you at Nook Farm situated on Cumbrian Cycle Way, ½ mile from Solway coast between Silloth and Allonby where there is golf, pony rides and leisure centre with swimming pool. Guests have their own sitting/dining room where there are tea-making facilities. A traditional farmhouse breakfast is served with free range eggs. Children welcome. Open March–Nov.

---

④ Stanger Farm, Cockermouth, Cumbria CA13 9TS

Mrs Carolyn Heslop
☎ 01900 824222
[BB] From £16
Sleeps 4
🦮 ♉ ⚭ ⚑ ▪
♥ *Commended*

At the entrance to the magnificent Lorton and Buttermere valleys lies Stanger Farm with its sheep, cows, cats, dogs, beautiful walks, a river to fish in and much more. Bedrooms are centrally heated with tea-making facilities and there are separate dining room and lounge with log fires. A traditional farmhouse breakfast and good old-fashioned hospitality await you. Open all year except Christmas.

NO ANSWER?

Farmers are mostly out and about during the day.
Try to telephone before 9.30am or after 4pm.

FARM HOLIDAY BUREAU

SELF-CATERING

Jenkin Farm Cottage, Embleton, Cockermouth, Cumbria CA13 9TN

Mrs Margaret Teasdale
☎ **017687 76387**
⌗ From £220–£350
Sleeps 6
🐴 ⚺
🔑 🔑 🔑 🔑 *Commended*

Jenkin Cottage has a spectacular outlook over open countryside extending to the Solway Firth and Scottish Lowlands. We are a working family hill farm in a beautiful quiet part of the Lake District. The cottage is fully equipped with all fuel, bed linen, towels provided. Open fire. Ideal base for fell walking or touring the Lakes by car. Sorry no pets. Open all year.

Stanger Farm, Cockermouth, Cumbria CA13 9TS

Mrs Carolyn Heslop
☎ **01900 824222**
⌗ From £180–£325
Sleeps 4
🐴 ✗ 🐕 🐈 ▪
🔑 🔑 🔑 🔑 *Commended*

Set amidst magnificent fell views this is an ideal base for exploring the whole of the Lake District. The Stable is a recently converted 17th century barn adjoining the farmhouse. The open plan lounge with log fire and dining and fully equipped kitchen areas are "upstairs" to benefit from view across the River Cocker and open fields. Fishing, central heating, logs, bed linen all included. Open all year.

CONFIRM BOOKINGS

Disappointments can arise from misunderstandings over the telephone.
Please write to confirm your booking.

FARM HOLIDAY BUREAU

PRICES

Prices include VAT and service charge (if any) and are:
B&B per person per night
EM per person
SC per unit per week
Tents and caravans per pitch per night

England's North Country

South Lakeland

Group Contact: *Mrs Olive Simpson* ☎ *01539 823682*

Find true country hospitality on a farm in this most beautiful corner of England. South Lakeland centres on the town of Kendal, which, in time, has developed into the focal point of the local community and the 'southern gateway' to the Lake District.

There's plenty to do – you can visit the award-winning Abbot Hall art gallery and Museums of Lakeland Life and Industry and Natural History and Archeology – or even the 'K' Village! There are also many National Trust properties and, especially for the children, the new Beatrix Potter exhibition!

If you're feeling active, Windermere and Bowness – where you can stroll by the lakeside, take a cruise on the 'Teal' or 'Swan', or ride on the steam train to Haverthwaite – are only a few minutes drive away. The fell walking is great too – whether in the valleys of Longsleddale or Kentmere, or on Scout Scar.

The seasons come and go in South Lakeland. Springtime here is a photographer's delight, with rhododendrons, azaleas, and daffodils – so immortalised by Wordsworth – while new-born lambs frolic in the pastures. Yet in autumn, the rich golds of the bracken and leaves contrast with the blue sky – a sightseer's delight.

BED AND BREAKFAST
(and evening meal)

Garnett House Farm, Burneside, Kendal, Cumbria LA9 5SF

Mrs Sylvia Beaty
☎ 01539 724542
BB From £14
EM From £7.50
Sleeps 10
🐕 🐎 ▪
👑 👄 *Commended*

AA/RAC acclaimed 15th century farmhouse, just ½ mile from A591 Windermere Road, village inn, shops and public transport. Bedrooms have colour TV, washbasins and tea-making facilities, most en suite. Oak panelled lounge, dining room with choice of breakfast and 5 course dinners. Lovely views of our countryside. During Jan, Feb and Mar, 3 nights B&B £42, en suite £48. Open all year.

Gateside Farm, Windermere Road, Kendal, Cumbria LA9 5SE

Mrs June Ellis
☎ 01539 722036
BB From £15–£19
EM £7.50
Sleeps 10
🐎🐕🐎🐈 🐎 ▪
Listed *Commended*

AA/RAC acclaimed. Traditional Lakeland farm, 2 miles north of Kendal on A591 main tourist route through Lakes. Easily accessible from M6 (jct 36). Ideally situated for touring all Lakes and Yorkshire Dales. All bedrooms have colour TV, tea/coffee-making facilities and heating, some en suite. Short or weekly stays welcome. Good home cooked breakfasts and evening meals served at separate tables. Good parking facilities. Open all year (closed Christmas and New Year).

Riverbank House, Garnett Bridge, Kendal, Cumbria LA8 9AZ

Julia Thom
☎ 01539 823254
BB From £14–£15
Sleeps 6
🆑 🐎🐕🐈
👄 *Commended*

Lovely Victorian family-built house situated at the foot of the beautiful Longsleddale Valley with 20 acres of pasture land. Bordered by river providing private fishing. 4 miles from Kendal. ½ mile off A6. Comfortable bedrooms with handbasins and tea/coffee-making facilities. Guests' bath/shower room, downstairs cloakroom. Guests' sitting room, TV, log fire, background CH. Excellent breakfasts. Open all year.

Stock Bridge Farm, Staveley, Kendal, Cumbria LA8 9LP

Mrs Betty Fishwick
☎ 01539 821580
BB From £14.50–£15.50
Sleeps 11
🐎🐕 🐎
Listed *Commended*

A comfortable, modernised 17th century farmhouse on edge of bypassed village just off A591 Kendal-Windermere road, 15 minutes M6 (jct 36). All bedrooms have fitted washbasins and shaver points, bath/shower room, separate WC. Fire certificate. Full central heating. Separate tables, English breakfast, bedtime drink. Friendly, personal service. Good parking facilities. On Dalesway Footpath. Open Mar–Oct.

Tranthwaite Hall, Underbarrow, Nr Kendal, Cumbria LA8 8HG

Mrs D Swindlehurst
☎ 015395 68285
BB From £16
Sleeps 4
✂ 🐎 🏊 🐎 🐎
Listed *Commended*

This magnificent olde worlde farmhouse dates back to the 11th century. Beautiful oak beams, doors and rare antique fire range. Tastefully modernised with full central heating, en suite available, colour TV lounge, separate dining room. This dairy/sheep farm has an idyllic setting in a small, picturesque village between Kendal and Windermere. Walking, golf, pony trekking. Many good pubs and inns nearby. SAE for brochure. Open all year.

SELF-CATERING

---

⑥ Birchbank Cottage, Birchbank, Blawith, Ulverston, Cumbria LA12 8EW

Mrs Linda Nicholson
☎ **01229 885277**
⌂ **From £125–£225**
Sleeps 4+ cot
🐕 🐎 Å 🛦 🛆
♞ ♞ ♞ ♞ *Commended*

Relax and unwind in this comfortable beamed cottage on a secluded Lakeland sheep farm only 5 miles from Coniston Water. Enjoy marvellous views of the Duddon estuary and Coniston Old Man while walking on the fells around the farm. Ideal base for seeing the many attractions of the southern lakes. Open all year.

---

⑦ High Swinklebank Farm, Longsleddale, Nr Kendal, Cumbria LA8 9BD

Mrs Olive Simpson
☎ **01539 823682**
⌂ **From £100–£190**
Sleeps 4
🐕 🐎 🛆
♞ ♞ ♞ *Commended*

High Swinklebank is near the head of the beautiful Longsleddale Valley with lovely views and walking. A recent conversion which is well appointed includes fitted carpets throughout. Comprising lounge with electric fire, bed settee, TV, lovely kitchen, shower room, 2 bedrooms – double and bunk. Children welcome. Linen provided. Weekends available. Cleanliness and personal attention assured. Open all year.

---

⑧ Preston Patrick Hall Cottage, Preston Patrick Hall, Crooklands, Milnthorpe, Cumbria LA7 7NY

Stephen & Jennifer Armitage
☎/Fax **015395 67200**
⌂ **From £100–£270**
Sleeps 2/6
🐎 🛆 💼
♞ ♞ ♞ *Commended*

Cosy wing of 14th century farmhouse near Crooklands, ideal centre for Lakes and Dales. Oak beamed rooms taste-fully modernised to sleep 2 or 3 (further bedroom sleeping 3 optional extra). Fitted kitchen with dishwasher and fridge. Sitting room with log fire and colour TV. Bedroom with antique brass beds and additional 2' 6" bed (linen, electric blankets and cot available). Use of swimming pool and table tennis table. Brochure available. Open all year.

England's North Country
Yorkshire Dales and Brontë Country

Group Contact: *Anne Pearson* ☎ *01756 791579*

This beautiful region extends from picturesque Kettlewell in the north of the Dales down to Bradford in the south with the National Photographic Museum, the recently refurbished Alhambra Theatre and Mill Shops to explore. Those keen to do their exploring on foot will head for the footpaths in and around the National Park, the Pennine Way and the Dales with their lovely valleys, deep woods, clear streams and waterfalls.

For history and heritage the Brontë Parsonage at Haworth, Harwood House and Skipton with its castle and enchanting Tudor courtyard are a must, as are the semi-ruined abbeys at Bolton and Fountains (reputed to be the most beautiful and certainly the largest of the ruined abbeys in Britain). For a real touch of nostalgia take a ride on the Keighley and Worth Valley or the Yorkshire Dales Railways, or visit Five Rise Locks on the Leeds/Liverpool Canal near Bingley.

Or simply enjoy the beautiful Dales and their villages – Kettlewell, Burnsall, Lothersdale or Malham with its Cove, limestone 'pavements' and Gordale Scar, a ravine with a magnificent succession of waterfalls.

Northallerton, A1, A684, M6, Kirkby Lonsdale, Ingleton, A683, A65, Starbotton (2), A6108, Kettlewell (4), Pateley Bridge, Ripon, A168, Lancaster, Malham, Grassington (10), A61, Hellifield (5), (6), Skipton (8), A59, Knaresborough, M6, Barnoldswick, Ilkley, Harrogate, Clitheroe, Earby, A65, Otley, A658, A1, A59, Longridge, A59, (3)(12)(7), A650, Wetherby, A64, Preston, Padiham, Keighley (11), Bramhope, (12), (9), Haworth, Burnley, Blackburn, Hebden Bridge, Bradford (1), Leeds, Garforth, A666, Halifax, Rothwell, M61

BED AND BREAKFAST

(and evening meal)

---

① Brow Top Farm, Baldwin Lane, Clayton, Bradford, West Yorkshire BD14 6PS

Margaret Priestley
☎ **01274 882178**
🅱🅱 **From £15–£20**
Sleeps 4
🐄 ⬛
🐾🐾 *Highly Commended*

Visitors are most welcome to our family dairy and beef farm. The farmhouse has recently been modernised to a very high standard with central heating throughout. 1 double, 1 twin and 1 family room all with private bathroom, colour TV and tea/coffee-making facilities. Conveniently situated for visiting the Dales and Brontë Country. Plenty of good eating places in the area. Open all year (closed Christmas).

---

② Bushey Lodge Farm, Starbotton, Skipton, North Yorkshire BD23 5HY

Rosie Lister
☎ **01756 760424**
🅱🅱 **From £18–£20**
Sleeps 4
🐄(10) ✳ ✂ 🐾 🌲
🐾🐾 *Highly Commended*

Traditional Dales farmhouse in quiet position in Upper Wharfedale village, with extensive views along the valley, much of which is owned and protected by the National Trust. Superb walking and sightseeing area. Local inns provide excellent evening meals. Each bedroom has en suite bathroom, TV, and tea/coffee-making facilities. Open all year except Christmas.

---

③ Far Laithe Farm, Laycock, Keighley, West Yorkshire BD22 0PU

Sylvia Lee
☎ **01535 661993**
🅱🅱 **From £15**
Sleeps 5
🐄 £
Listed *Commended*

Traditional Yorkshire farmhouse situated 5 minutes from Haworth, 20 minutes from Skipton, offering quality accommodation at realistic prices. We are surrounded by open countryside with beautiful views looking towards the Haworth moors. We pride ourselves on the hospitality we provide and look forward to welcoming you to our home. Open all year.

---

④ Fold Farm, Kettlewell, Skipton, North Yorkshire BD23 5RH

Barbara Lambert
☎ **01756 760886**
Fax **01756 760464**
🅱🅱 **From £17–£19.50**
Sleeps 6
🐄(10) 🌲 ✂
🐾🐾 *Highly Commended*

Fold Farm is a hill sheep farm situated in a quiet part of Kettlewell, within easy walking distance of all village amenities. The house dates back to the 15th century and some of its original beams are still in evidence. There are tea-making facilities in all bedrooms, each of which has a private bathroom and TV, and there is a separate guests' sitting room. Ample private parking. Open Apr–Oct.

---

⑤ Manor House, Rylstone, Skipton, North Yorkshire BD23 6LH

Mary Caygill
☎ **01756 730226**
🅱🅱 **From £20**
Sleeps 4
🐄(12) ✂ 🌲
🐾🐾 *De Luxe*

YHTB White Rose Award Bed & Breakfast of the year 1994. In Rylstone village, halfway between Skipton and Grassington (B6265). Dairy and sheep farm in Yorkshire Dales National Park. Country house in beautiful surroundings with panoramic views. Spacious en suite rooms. Central heating, TV, hot drinks facilities. Excellent food served at the village Inn. Open all year.

Wenningber Farm, Hellifield, Nr Skipton, North Yorkshire BD23 4JR

Mrs Barbara Phillip
☎ **01729 850856**
🅱 **From £16–£19**
Sleeps 4
🎠 🏕 ⊕ 🏕
☙ *Highly Commended*

Wenningber Farm is situated in a picturesque location just 4 miles from Malham in the heart of the Yorkshire Dales. Furnished to a very high standard with oak beams and inglenook fireplace. Full central heating, H&C in both rooms, tea and coffee-making facilities. Warm welcome assured. Open all year.

SELF-CATERING

Bottoms Farm Cottages, Bottoms Farm, Laycock, nr Keighley, West Yorkshire BD22 0QD

Mrs J. Parr
☎ **01535 607720**
🆂🅲 **From £130–£260**
Sleeps 2/5
🎠 🏕 ▣
🔑 🔑 🔑 🔑 *Highly Commended*

Bottoms Farm is a rural 35-acre sheep farm situated on the south side of a beautiful valley with spectacular views. Howarth 4 miles, Skipton 7 miles. These luxury cottages have been recently converted to the highest standard from 200 years mistal/barn. Fully equipped. Heating and linen included. Sorry no pets. Open all year.

Cawder Hall Cottages, c/o Cawder Hall, Cawder Lane, Skipton, North Yorkshire BD23 2QQ

Anne Pearson
☎ **01756 791579**
Fax 01756 797036
🆂🅲 **From £130–£310**
Sleeps 2/6
♿ 🎠 ▣ 🏕 ▪ 🐾
🔑 🔑 🔑 – 🔑 🔑 🔑 🔑
Up to Highly Commended

Enjoy the peace and quiet of our luxury cottages, yet only be 1 mile from the medieval castle and market town of Skipton. Each cottage has been newly converted and is suitable for disabled guests. The cottages are heated and have colour TV, video, fridge and microwave. There is a garden, barbecue, payphone and laundry room. All linen, gas and electricity are included as are cots and high chairs if required. Welcome Host. Open all year.

Heather & Bilberry Cottages, Hole Farm, Dimples Lane, Haworth, Bradford, West Yorkshire BD22 8QS

Mrs Janet Milner
☎ **01535 644755**
🆂🅲 **From £150–£450**
Sleeps 4/8 + cot
🎠 🏕
🔑 🔑 🔑 🔑 *Highly Commended*

The old barn has been carefully converted to make two cottages with most bedrooms en suite. We are a small working farm, the sort that appears in children's Ladybird books. Gloria the sow, Gilbert the turkey, foals and calves. Ideal for children. A short walk to the village to see the Brontë Museum or a walk on the moors 2 minutes from our door. Sorry no pets. Open all year.

Maypole Cottage, Thorpe, Skipton, North Yorkshire BD23 6BJ   🔟

Liz Gamble
☎ **01756 720609**
🆂🅲 **From £190–£320**
Sleeps 4
🎠 🐕 🏕
🔑 🔑 🔑 🔑 *Commended*

An 18th century stable converted to a particularly high standard in the tiny hamlet of Thorpe near Burnsall. This well equipped cottage has full central heating, exposed beams and stonework open fire. Colour TV, microwave, washer/dryer. Bathroom with shower. Linen provided. Large walled garden, ample parking. Open all year.

Meadow & Field Cottages, The Coach House, Spring Head, Tim Lane, Haworth, West Yorks BD22 7RX

David and Hilary Freeman
☎ 01535 644140
[SC] From £130–£270
Sleeps 2/4

Highly Commended

A warm Yorkshire welcome is assured at our two cosy cottages, converted from a 200-year-old barn, ½ mile from the Brontë sisters' Haworth and within easy reach of the Yorkshire Dales. We pride ourselves on our high standard of cleanliness and comfort. Each cottage has full CH, with colour TV, cooker, fridge, microwave, washer, dryer. Gas, electricity, linen and towels, cot, highchair inclusive. Sorry no pets. Open all year.

 Westfield Farm Cottages, c/o Westfield Farm, Tim Lane, Haworth, West Yorkshire BD22 7SA

Wendy Carr
☎ 01535 644568
Fax 01535 646686
[SC] From £130–£320
Sleeps 2/6

Highly Commended

Enjoy the comforts of home in one of our delightful cottages. 100-acre hill farm with suckler cows and sheep. ½ mile from Haworth. Cottages to sleep 2 to 6 people. Cottage for 2 disabled people. Beautiful south-facing aspect. Colour TV, automatic washer, microwave in each. Dogs by arrangement. Farm-trail and safe river for fishing or play. Open all year.

FOLLOW THE COUNTRY CODE

Leave nothing but footprints,
Take nothing but photographs,
Kill nothing but time!

CONFIRM BOOKINGS

Disappointments can arise from misunderstandings over the telephone.
Please write to confirm your booking.

England's North Country
Harrogate & Nidderdale

Group Contacts: *Christine Ryder* ☎ *01943 880354*
Sheila Smith ☎ *01423 771040*

Harrogate has a reputation as one of the most attractive towns in Britain, with acres of immaculate parks and gardens, shops and elegant architecture.

Nidderdale has captured the attention of many by means of films, television, literary works and the personalities of their people.

Imagination becomes reality where sheep and cattle safely graze amongst the seemingly endless green fields divided by dry stone walls. The gentle rise and fall of hills and vales, sparkling streams and rushing rivers interplay with wide expanses of moorland and reservoirs. Picturesque towns, villages and traditional country pubs abound amidst a rarefied atmosphere of peace and tranquillity. A designated Area of outstanding Natural Beauty.

Ideally situated for visiting York, Skipton, The Yorkshire Dales, Herriot Country, Emmerdale, Fountains Abbey, Brimham Rocks (Natural Rock Sculptures), Stump Cross Caverns (Show Caves), Ripley Castle, Lightwater Valley Theme Park and Factory Shops.

Come Spring, Summer, Autumn and Winter the welcome and warmth remains the same.

BED AND BREAKFAST

(and evening meal)

---

① Bowes Green Farm, Bishop Thornton, Ripley, Harrogate, North Yorkshire HG3 3JX

Mrs Bridget Sowray
☎ **01423 770114**
📖 From £18–£19
EM From £9
Sleeps 6
🛏(12) ✂ ☂ ■
🌺🌺 *Highly Commended*

Let us help you to unwind and relax and enjoy the peace and tranquillity of the large cottage garden and surrounding open countryside at our listed 17th century secluded farmhouse, set on a 350-acre family-run working farm. All modern comforts including CH, electric blankets, tea/coffee making and washbasins in each bedroom, one with en suite shower/WC. Guests' separate colour TV, sitting room and dining room with own tables. Delicious and plentiful Aga home cooking. Open Easter–Oct.

---

② Clough House Farm, Summerbridge, Harrogate, North Yorkshire HG3 4JR

Mrs Brenda Walmsley
☎/Fax 01423 780823
📖 From £20–25
EM From £9.50
Sleeps 18
🛏 🐎 ■
Applied

17th century farmhouse/attached farm building converted into eight delightful en suite bedrooms tastefully decorated with CH and tea/coffee-making facilities. Three ground floor rooms. Peaceful position with far-reaching views over the open countryside. Private guests' sitting and dining room. Clough House offers private horse riding lessons or hack around beautiful countryside. Open all year.

---

③ Graystone View Farm, Graystone Plain Lane, Hampsthwaite, Harrogate, North Yorkshire HG3 2LY

Gloria Metcalfe
☎ **01423 770324**
📖 From £16–18
Sleeps 6
🛏 🐎
Listed *Commended*

18th century farmhouse in tranquil setting with comfortable rooms to come back to after a lovely day seeing the wonderful sights that Yorkshire has to offer. We are a mixed farm set in 100 acres and located ¼ mile from the A59 west of Harrogate. Open all year except Christmas and New Year.

---

④ Hatton House Farm, Colber Lane, Bishop Thornton, Nr Harrogate, North Yorkshire HG3 3JA

Mrs Joyce Kellett
☎ **01423 770315**
📖 From £18–18.50
EM from £9
Sleeps 6
🛏(10) ✂ ☂ ■
Listed *Highly Commended*

Farmhouse accommodation at its best on a dairy mixed farm in Nidderdale, close to Harrogate. Quiet and peaceful area. Emphasis on home cooking, beautifully presented. Wash basins, tea-making facilities in all rooms. Luxury bathroom. Separate tables in dining room, large comfortable lounge. Parking no problem. Open all year.

---

⑤ Knabbs Ash, Skipton Road, Felliscliffe, Nr Harrogate, North Yorkshire HG3 2LT

Sheila Smith
☎ **01423 771040**
Fax 01423 771515
📖 From £19–£20
Sleeps 6
🛏(10) ✂ 🍴 ■
🌺🌺 *Highly Commended*

Knabbs Ash is a smallholding where you will find a relaxing and friendly atmosphere. Situated 6 miles west of Harrogate set back off the A59 in a tranquil position with delightful views over the countryside. En suite rooms enhanced by quality furnishings, colour TV, hair dryer, tea/coffee-making facilities, CH, private guest sitting and dining room with separate tables. Ideal area for walking and exploring the Yorkshire Dales. Open all year. White Rose Award for tourism. B&B of the year 1995 runner up.

North Pasture Farm, Brimham Rocks, Summerbridge, Harrogate, North Yorkshire

Eileen Payne
☎ 01423 711470
BB From £19.50
EM from £9.50
Sleeps 4
🐎(14) ⊁ ⚑ ♨ ▥
😊😊😊 *Highly Commended*

North Pasture Farm, a 14th century listed farmhouse, beamed and mullioned and oozing with character, awaits discerning guests. Warm and cosy with central heating throughout, together with en suite bedrooms and separate dining room and separate TV lounge. Peaceful and quiet, sheltered by Brimham Rocks. Within easy reach of Harrogate, Ripon, Skipton, York and Fountains Abbey. Open Mar–Nov.

Scaife Hall Farm, Blubberhouses, Otley, West Yorkshire LS21 2PL

Christine Ryder
☎ 01943 880354
BB From £19
Sleeps 6
🐎 🐎 ⊁ ⚑ ▥
😊😊 *Highly Commended*

Scaife Hall is a working farm set in peaceful countryside, halfway between Harrogate and Skipton (just off A59). Two double bedrooms and one twin bedded room, each tastefully decorated with en suite facilities, central heating, beverage tray. Guests sitting room with log fires on chilly nights. Local inns provide excellent evening meals. Open all year except Christmas.

SELF-CATERING

Clough House Farm, Summerbridge, Harrogate, North Yorkshire HG3 4JR

Mrs Brenda Walmsley
☎/Fax 01423 780823
SC From £125–£280
EM from £9.50
5 cottages + flat
🐎 🐦 ▥
Applied

Clough House Farm offers five delightful small stone cottages and one 2-bedroom flat. Tastefully decorated, fully equipped, heating and linen included. Breakfast and evening meals also available. Village of Summerbridge 5-minute walk. Brimham Rocks and Fountains Abbey close by. Open all year.

Dukes Place, Fountains Abbey Road, Bishop Thornton, Harrogate, North Yorkshire HG3 3JY

Jaki Moorhouse
☎ 01765 620229
Fax 01765 620454
SC From £125–£265
Sleeps 2–6
🐎 🐎 🐦 🐎
🔑 🔑 🔑 *Up to Highly Commended*

Situated in the heart of Nidderdale yet close to Harrogate, Dukes Place is a well-maintained property comprising the owners' 18th century farmhouse and cottage-style apartments developed from the original farm buildings. Working stables from which riding can be arranged. Pets welcome. Open all year.

LET THE TELEPHONE RING!
Some farmhouses are big places. Let the telephone ring long enough to give the owner time to answer it.

England's North Country
Herriot's Yorkshire Moors and Dales

Group Contacts: 🅱🅱 *Mrs Mary Pearson* ☎ *01609 772311*
🆂🅲 *Lady Mary Furness* ☎ *01609 772061/748614*

Take a trip around North Yorkshire and sample for yourself the delights of this area as portrayed in James Herriot's 'All Creatures Great and Small'.

Start with the ancient city of York and wander through narrow streets to the Minster, ride upriver to the Bishop's Palace or visit the Railway Museum and Jorvik Centre. Or drive from Helmsley, over Sutton Bank – a favourite for hang-gliders – to the market town of Thirsk where James Herriot still practises. A day all the family will enjoy is a visit to the Lightwater Valley Theme Park where modern farming exhibits combine with an adventure play area. Or maybe you prefer the peace and tranquillity of the romantic abbeys, stately homes, gardens and deer parks found here.

In Wensleydale, home of the famous cheese, you can fish or picnic by the waterfalls and enjoy real ale in friendly village pubs. Locally, many craftsmen display their skills, the most famous being the Mouseman of Kilburn.

Walkers can follow the Pennine Way past the Buttertubs, through panoramic Swaledale where shepherd and sheepdog work the hills, to the cobbled streets and Norman castle of Richmond, towering over the river below.

Whatever the weather, whatever your interest, you are spoilt for choice. There is something for everyone in North Yorkshire!

Barnard Castle
A67
A66
Darlington
A1(M) ④
Middlesbrough
Guisborough
Loftus
A171
⑱ ⑮ Richmond
⑬
⑫
Whitby
A167
A19
A172
⑦
A684
⑭
⑤ ⑪
A684
①
⑲
㉑
⑩
Northallerton
A171
⑰
Bedale
⑥
A6108
Masham
A1
Thirsk
A170
⑨ ⑯
Scalby
Scarborough
⑧
Pickering
② ⑳
Ripon
③
Malton
A64
Norton
A61
Knaresborough
A19
A59
Harrogate
A166
Ilkley
Otley
York
Gt.Driffield
Keighley
A64

BED AND BREAKFAST

(and evening meal)

Ainderby Myers Farm, Nr Hackforth, Bedale, North Yorkshire DL8 1PF

Mrs Valerie Anderson
☎ 01609 748668/748424
▣ From £16–£17
EM From £9.50
Sleeps 6
✄ ⛺ ⚔ ♨ ✗
♨ Commended

Historical manor house set amidst moors and dales with origins going back to the 10th century. Terrific atmosphere. Once farmed by the monks of Jervaulx Abbey. Sheep, crops, pastures and a stream. Walk the fields and discover the wildlife. Visit castles and abbeys. Excellent base for walkers. Pony trekking and fishing by arrangement. Traditional Yorkshire breakfasts. Picnic facilities. Open all year.

Bay Tree Farm, Aldfield, Nr Fountains Abbey, Ripon, North Yorkshire HG4 3BE

Valerie Leeming
☎ 01765 620394
▣ From £18.50–£19.50
EM From £10.50
Sleeps 12
⛺ ⚔ ▣ ⚘ ♨ ✗
♛ ♛
Highly Commended

17th century farmhouse and converted stone hay barn combining character with comfort in peaceful village setting overlooking Fountains Abbey, ½ mile. York, Harrogate and Dales all in easy reach or explore our fields and footpaths returning to real fires and super cooking (HE trained). All rooms en suite, CH, beverages, overlooking cattle and horses grazing and our resident little owls. Kettle always on the boil. Colour brochure. Open all year.

Carr House Farm, Shallowdales, Ampleforth, York, North Yorkshire YO6 4ED

Anna Lupton
☎ 01347 868526
▣ From £15
EM From £10
Sleeps 6
✄ ⛺(7) ⚘ ⚔ ♨ ■ ✗
♨ ♨ Commended

16th century farmhouse filled with memorabilia. Part of 400-acre family farm for 5 generations. Internationally recommended, "fresh air fiend's dream! Good food, walking, warm welcome". Romantic four-poster bedroom en suite. Relaxing, peaceful, informal – "heartbeat country". ½ hour York. Make your holiday memorable – Highland cattle, north country sheep, ponds, orchards, green fields, wild flowers. Open all year (closed Christmas and New Year).

Clow Beck House, Monk End Farm, Croft-on-Tees, Darlington, Co Durham DL2 2SW

Heather & David Armstrong
☎ 01325 721075
Fax 01325 720419
▣ From £19–£34
Sleeps 10
⛺ ▣ ⚘ ♨
♨ ♨ *Highly Commended*

Elegant country residence set in an acre of garden by the River Tees. Exceptional accommodation, each of the rooms tastefully furnished in an individual style including one with a tented ceiling. Elegant dining room features hand crafted furniture – the perfect setting for a hearty Yorkshire Breakfast. A charming home convenient for Herriot Country, York, Durham and the east coast. Open all year.

Elmfield Country House, Arrathorne, Bedale, North Yorkshire DL8 1NE

Edith & Jim Lillie
☎ 01677 450558
Fax 01677 450557
▣ From £19.50–£29.50
EM From £11.50
Sleeps 20
⊛ ⚘ ⛺ ▣ ■
♨ ♨ ♨ Commended

Situated between Richmond and Bedale. Superb views of surrounding countryside, relaxed friendly atmosphere in luxurious country home. 9 spacious bedrooms (all en suite) including a four-poster bed, twin and family rooms. 2 bedrooms equipped for disabled. All with colour TV (satellite channel), radio, phone, tea/coffee-making facilities, CH. Lounge and bar (residential licence), dining room, games room, large conservatory and solarium. Excellent home cooking. Open all year.

6 Haregill Lodge, Ellingstring, Masham, Ripon, North Yorkshire HG4 4PW

Mrs Rachel Greensit
☎ 01677 460272
BB From £17–£19
EM From £9.50
Sleeps 6
🐓 🐄 🏠
🏆 *Commended*

Wanting a peaceful break? Then come and join us in our 18th century farmhouse set on a mixed farm. Secluded garden with play area overlooking Hambleton Hills, Vale of York. Ideal for Dales, moors and Herriot Country. Two rooms en suite, radio, tea/coffee. Log fire, CH, satellite TV lounge, games room. Excellent home cooking with supper tray. Fishing and trekking nearby. A warm welcome awaits you. Open all year except Christmas.

7 High Force Farm, Bainbridge, Leyburn, North Yorkshire DL8 3DL

Margaret Iveson
☎ 01969 650379
BB From £13–£15
Sleeps 6
🐄 ✄

Listed *Approved*

Working hill farm used in James Herriot TV programme. Ideal centre for exploring the Dales offering guests a warm welcome in a relaxed atmosphere. A non-smoking establishment. Open Jan–Nov.

8 Lamb Hill Farm, Lamb Hill, Masham, Ripon, North Yorkshire HG4 4DJ

Mrs Rosemary Robinson
☎ 01765 689274
BB £16
Sleeps 6
🐄(8) ✄ 🏠 ❀
🏆 *Commended*

A warm welcome awaits you in our genuine old farmhouse on a working farm. Large, comfortable bedrooms with private bathrooms. We are centrally situated for exploring 'Herriot' and 'Heartbeat' country. Many National Trust properties in easy reach. Excellent opportunities for eating out within a two mile radius. York 45 mins, Durham 1 hour. Situated off A6108 between West Tanfield and Masham. Open all year.

9 Laskill Farm, Hawnby, Nr Helmsley, North Yorkshire YO6 5NB

Sue Smith
☎ 01439 798268
BB From £18–£22.50
EM From £11
Sleeps 13
🐓🐄🐕🛁🍴☕🎾🏠
🏆🏆 *Applied*

Amidst beautiful North Yorkshire Moors, in heart of James Herriot Country. Attractive farmhouse with own lake/large walled garden. Own natural spring water. High standard of food and comfort. 2 double rooms en suite, 2 twins en suite, 1 double and 1 twin each with shower and H/C, 1 single; all with colour TV and beverage tray. Ideal for nearby places of interest and scenic beauty, or simply enjoy peaceful and tranquil surroundings. Open all year except Christmas Day.

10 Lovesome Hill Farm, Lovesome Hill, Northallerton, North Yorkshire DL6 2PB

Mrs Mary Pearson
☎ 01609 772311
BB From £17–£20
EM From £8.95
Sleeps 8
🐄🛁☕🐕
🏆 *Commended*

19th century farmhouse on working farm with lovely views of Hambleton Hills. On arrival enjoy tea and homemade biscuits. Our tastefully converted granary adjoins house with spacious, well furnished en suite rooms overlooking patio, croquet lawn. Central for exploring Dales, Moors, Durham and York. A warm welcome and delicious homemade meals await you. You'll love it.

11 Mill Close Farm, Patrick Brompton, Bedale, North Yorkshire DL8 1JY

Mrs Patricia Knox
☎ 01677 450257
Fax 01677 450585
BB From £17–£20
EM From £10
Sleeps 4
🐓🐄🎾🏃🏠
🏆 *Commended*

Mill Close is a 17th century working farm surrounded by beautiful rolling countryside at the foothills of the Yorkshire Dales and Herriot Country. Situated 2 miles from the A1(M). Spacious rooms, furnished to high standard. Guests' private bathrooms, dining and sitting room with colour TV. A relaxing, peaceful atmosphere with large walled garden and open fires. Please send for full colour brochure. Open Mar–Nov.

Mount Pleasant Farm, Whashton, Richmond, North Yorkshire DL11 7JP

Christine Chilton
☎ 01748 822784
BB From £17
EM From £9
Sleeps 14
♿ ✝ 🐴 🎾 ♨
🌺🌺 *Commended*

The business man, a couple touring, or the family with children can all enjoy Mount Pleasant, a working farm in the peaceful countryside. Renovated farm buildings offer comfortable en suite rooms each with their own front door. We are well known for our excellent food. Table licence. A pleasant place to stay for your special holiday or short break. Open all year.

Oxnop Hall, Low Oxnop, Gunnerside, Richmond, North Yorkshire DL11 6JJ

Annie Porter
☎ 01748 886253
BB From £21
EM From £12
Sleeps 11
🐕(7) 🎾 ✄
🌺🌺🌺 *Commended*

Stay with us on our working hill farm with beef cattle and Swaledale sheep. Oxnop Hall is of historical interest and has recently been extended with all en suite rooms. Ideal walking and touring. We are in the Yorkshire Dales National Park, Herriot Country, an Environmentally Sensitive Area which is renowned for its stone walls, barns and flora. Good farmhouse food. Tea/coffee-making facilities. Open Mar–Nov.

Walburn Hall, Downholme, Richmond, North Yorkshire DL11 6AF

Diana Greenwood
☎/Fax 01748 822152
BB From £20
Sleeps 5
✄ 🐕
🌺🌺 *Commended*

Walburn Hall is one of the few remaining working farms with a fortified farmhouse, an enclosed cobbled courtyard and terraced garden. For guests' comfort there is a separate lounge and dining room with beamed ceilings, stone fireplaces and log fires (when required). Centrally heated. Double/twin or family rooms (en suite) with tea/coffee-making facilities. Ideally situated between Richmond and Leyburn for exploring the Dales. Open Mar–Nov.

Whashton Springs Farm, Richmond, North Yorkshire DL11 7LS

Fairlie Turnbull
☎ 01748 822884
BB From £22–£28
EM From £12
Sleeps 16
🐕(5)
🌺🌺🌺 *Highly Commended*

400-acre beef/sheep, family working farm in heart of Herriot Country. Delightful Georgian farmhouse, featured on 'Wish You Were Here', 1988 AA 'Farmhouse of the North' Award, unusual bay windows, overlooking lawns sloping to a sparkling stream. Real Yorkshire breakfast. Home cooking using local produce. All 8 bedrooms have en suite baths/showers, TV, phone. One 4-poster bedroom. Historic Richmond 3 miles away. Open all year (closed Christmas & New Year).

SELF-CATERING

Ceadda Cottages, Keldholme, c/o Laskill Farm, Hawnby, Nr Helmsley, North Yorkshire YO6 5NB

Mrs Sue Smith
☎ 01439 798268
SC From £180–£250
Sleeps 4/5
🐕 ✝ ✄
Applied

Ceadda Cottages offer luxury yet cosy accommodation. These warm, spacious cottages sleep 4–5 people with lovely views all around. Good walking areas in North Yorkshire Moors National Park and yet near to York and coast. Cleanliness assured and personally supervised. A real rural retreat. All cottages have their own garden, CH, colour TV, microwave. Linen included. Open all year.

17 Clematis & Well Cottage, c/o Mile House Farm, Hawes, Wensleydale, North Yorkshire DL8 3PT

Anne Fawcett
☎ 01969 667481
[SC] From £145–£350
Sleeps 4/8

Highly Commended

Two lovely old Dales stone cottages of character with open fires, exposed beams and Laura Ashley prints. Both cottages are peacefully situated with spectacular views over Wensleydale. Fully renovated to a high standard, these cottages provide charming, spacious accommodation with lovely, old fashioned walled gardens. Free trout fishing on farm. Open all year.

18 The Coach House, Whashton Springs Farm, Richmond, North Yorkshire DL11 7LS

Fairlie Turnbull
☎ 01748 822884
[SC] From £150–£270
Sleeps 4–5

Highly Commended

The Coach House offers luxury accommodation on our 400-acre working family farm near Richmond, gateway to the Dales. This warm spacious house sleeps 4–5 in double and twin bedrooms. Beamed lounge and well equipped kitchen with washer, freezer, microwave, etc. Heating and bed linen included in tariff. Good local hospitality. Open all year.

19 Stanhow Farm Bungalow, c/o Stanhow Farm, Great Langton, Northallerton, North Yorks DL7 0TJ

Lady Mary Furness
☎ 01609 748614
Mobile 0378 417625
[SC] From £150–£320
Sleeps 6

Commended

Enjoy our homely, comfortable, detached bungalow and garden. Warm and peaceful, lovely views, well appointed, economy 7 heating, CTV, open fire, automatic washer, tumble dryer, microwave, fridge/freezer. 3 bedrooms, personally maintained to a high standard. Enjoy the 230-acre farm with conservation areas. Central, ideal for relaxing. Good local hospitality and recreations. Family and business guests welcome. Open all year.

20 Trips Cottage, Bay Tree Farm, Aldfield, Nr Fountains Abbey, Ripon, North Yorkshire HG4 3BE

Valerie Leeming
☎ 01765 620394
[SC] From £95–£185
Sleeps 2

Commended

A newly-converted stable which sleeps 2, to the left of the farmhouse. Fine panoramic views over Fountains Abbey. Tasteful conversion consists of lobby, shower, toilet, fitted kitchen (microwave/electric cooker), lounge/ diner (with colour TV). Double bedroom, bed linen and storage heater included in the rent. Pay–phone available. Shops at Ripon (3 miles), eating 2 miles. Private parking and gardens. Ideal for touring Dales, Moors and York. Local walks. Open all year.

21 Wren Cottage, c/o Street House Farm, Little Holtby, Northallerton, North Yorkshire DL7 9LN

Mrs Jennifer Pybus
☎ 01609 748622
[SC] From £105–£225
Sleeps 4

Commended

This cosy cottage in Kirkby Fleetham overlooks the village green, with pub serving food and shop/PO nearby. Ideal centre for exploring Yorkshire Dales and North Yorkshire Moors and within easy reach of York and Durham. The cottage with its traditional oak beams and open fire in the lounge has a fully equipped kitchen with electric cooker and microwave. Also night storage heaters and telephone. Electricity included. Open all year.

FARM HOLIDAY BUREAU

NO ANSWER?
Farmers are mostly out and about during the day.
Try to telephone before 9.30am or after 4pm.

England's North Country
Ryedale, North Yorkshire

Group Contacts: BB *Brenda Johnson* ☎ *01439 798278*
SC *Mrs Susan Garbutt* ☎ *01439 798264*

Upper Ryedale is the western part of the North Yorkshire Moors National Park, where the efforts of man to wring a living from the hillsides has enhanced the natural beauty of the classical glacial valleys. It is a place which appeals particularly to the walker.

There are two nationally famous walks passing through the area, the Lyke Wake Walk and the Cleveland Way, but, for those who want to see the abundant wildlife, the network of unnamed footpaths, through woods and over wild moorland, will be more inviting. There is also trout fishing in the Rye.

The area also has three well known monastery ruins and several stately homes, headed by Castle Howard. York, with its magnificent selection of museums, historic Minster and its encircling walls, is an hour away by car. Literary pilgrimages can be made to Coxwold, where Lawrence Sterne preached, or to Thirsk, where James Herriot has his practice. Music lovers can take advantage of Ryedale Festival in Helmsley for the first week in August.

The seaside towns of Scarborough, Whitby and Filey are within reach. Close by are Lightwater Valley and Flamingoland, plus the slightly more sedate pleasures of a ride on the North Yorkshire Moors Steam Railway.

Barnard Castle
A67
A66
Darlington
Middlesbrough
A1(M)
Guisborough
Loftus
A171
Richmond
A167
A19
A172
Stokesley
Whitby
A684
A684
Northallerton
3
A684
A6108
A1
2
1
A170 5
6 7
Thirsk
4
Helmsley
Pickering
Scalby
Scarborough
A171
Ripon
Malton
A64
A61
Norton
A59
Knaresborough
A19
Harrogate
Ilkley
A166
Otley
York
Gt.Driffield
Keighley
A64

BED AND BREAKFAST
(and evening meal)

---

1 Barn Close Farm, Rievaulx, Helmsley, North Yorkshire YO6 5HL

Joan Milburn
☎ **01439 798321**
⟨BB⟩ **From £18–£20**
EM From £10
Sleeps 6
🐕 🐈 ♿ 🏇 ☕ 🎣 💼
♛ ♛ ♛ *Applied*

Comfortable, relaxed atmosphere at Barn Close Farm set in an idyllic wooded valley of outstanding beauty close to Rievaulx Abbey and Old Byland. Farmhouse cooking recommended by the Daily Telegraph. Speciality home baked bread. Riding, walking from farmyard. Central for touring countryside, 1 hour from York or coast. 1 en suite, 1 family with private bathroom, tea/coffee-making facilities. Open all year.

---

2 Easterside Farm, Hawnby, Helmsley, North Yorkshire YO6 5QT

Mrs Sarah Wood
☎ **01439 798277**
⟨BB⟩ **From £18–£20**
EM From £12
Sleeps 7
🐈 🎣
♛ ♛ *Commended*

A large 18th century Grade II listed farmhouse, nestling on Easterside Hill and enjoying panoramic views. Ideal base for walking, touring, the coast and the city of York. Enjoy good food and a warm welcome in comfortable surroundings. All rooms have en suite facilities. Open all year (closed Christmas).

---

3 Hill End Farm, Chop Gate, Bilsdale, North Yorkshire TS9 7JR

Brenda Johnson
☎ **01439 798278**
⟨BB⟩ **From £16–£18**
EM From £10.50
Sleeps 5
🐈 🐕 🎣 💼
♛ ♛ *Applied*

Looking for a comfortable, peaceful break? Then come and join us in our 17th century farmhouse in picturesque Bilsdale. Eight miles from the market town of Helmsley. Guests are welcome to wander around our family run farm. Two comfortable bedrooms, one bathroom en suite, one with washbasin. Tea/coffee making facilities. Comfortable lounge. Good home cooking with generous helpings. Open Easter–Nov.

---

4 Low Northolme Farm, Salton, York, North Yorkshire YO6 6RP

Diane Peirson
☎ **01751 432321**
⟨BB⟩ **From £17.50–£20**
EM From £10
Sleeps 5
🐈(5) ☕
♛ ♛ *Highly Commended*

Georgian farmhouse, 4 miles from Kirkbymoorside, close to North Yorkshire moors. Arable farm with breeding sheep. Bedrooms en suite, TV lounge, snug and kitchenette with tea/coffee-making facilities. Central heating, log fires in winter. Enjoy excellent home cooking and hospitality. Private fishing, golf nearby. Ancient city of York within easy reach. Evening meal by arrangement. Open Mar–Oct.

---

5 Mount Grace Farm, Cold Kirby, Thirsk, North Yorkshire YO7 2HL

Joyce Ashbridge
☎ **01845 597389**
⟨BB⟩ **From £18–£22**
EM From £9.50
Sleeps 6
🐈 ✂ 💼
♛ ♛ *Commended*

A warm welcome awaits you on working farm surrounded by beautiful open countryside with magnificent views. Ideal location for touring, or exploring the many walks in the area. Luxury en suite bedrooms with tea/coffee facilities. Spacious guests' lounge with colour TV. Garden. Enjoy delicious, generous helpings of farmhouse fayre cooked in our Aga. Weekly rates. Open all year except Christmas.

Valley View Farm, Old Byland, Helmsley, York, North Yorkshire YO6 5LG

Sally Robinson
☎ **01439 798221**
🆎 **From £23–£27**
EM From £12
Sleeps 10
🛉 🐾 ⊞ 🏃 ⛺ ♿ ⛺ 💼
🌣🌣 *Highly Commended*

Friendly relaxed Yorkshire hospitality in our well appointed, tastefully furnished home with open fire. Pretty en suite bedrooms, tea and coffee, TV, etc. Peaceful cottage garden with beautiful views. Hearty country breakfasts, delicious traditional farmhouse fayre, wine list. Way marked walks from the farm. The North York Moors is the driest national park! Open all year.

SELF-CATERING

Valley View Farm, Old Byland, Helmsley, York, North Yorkshire YO6 5LG ⑦

Sally Robinson
☎ **01439 798221**
🆒 **From £110–£400**
Sleeps 2–10
🛉 🐾 ⊞ 🏃 ⛺ ♿ ⛺ 💼
Applied

A beef, sheep and pig farm set on the edge of small village. Newly converted barn furnished with traditional farm theme. The cottages have TV, video, dishwasher, washer/dryer, open fires, CH. All bedrooms are en suite, beds double or twin. Delicious farmhouse meals available (see B&B listing). Phone for colour brochure. Open all year.

BUREAU ACCOMMODATION MEANS QUALITY

FARM HOLIDAY BUREAU

All Bureau members are inspected and quality graded by the National Tourist Board each year, as well as by fellow members.

DISABLED VISITORS

FARM HOLIDAY BUREAU

Many members offer a welcome to disabled/less able visitors. Please do check the extent of the facilities before booking.

England's North Country
Yorkshire Moors, National Park and Coast

Group Contact: *Mrs Gillian Rhys* ☎ *01287 660352*

When you come to stay with us on our farms you have the opportunity to visit the seaside and enjoy the countryside inland as well.

The coast offers sandy beaches, secret caves, pretty fishing villages and 30 miles of Heritage Coast with bird sanctuaries and wildlife. The resorts of Scarborough, Whitby and Bridlington offer lively entertainment in the evenings for all tastes.

There are over 1,000 miles of public footpaths and bridleways in the area and recognised walks like the White Rose Walk, the Cleveland Way and the Lyke Wake Walk. Or perhaps pony trekking through the National Park appeals to you. The North Yorkshire Moors steam railway provides superb nostalgia for railway enthusiasts and spectacular scenery for all who travel on it between Grosmont and Pickering.

Those interested in historic heritage will find much to enjoy. At Pickering the parish church is famous for its unique 15th-century wall painting of St George and the Dragon. Whitby and Rievaulx Abbeys are examples of the magnificent religious architecture of the area. Ancient castles can also be explored at Helmsley, Pickering and Scarborough.

BED AND BREAKFAST

(and evening meal)

Croft Farm, Fylingthorpe, Whitby, North Yorkshire YO22 4PW

Pauline Featherstone
☎ 01947 880231
🅱 From £16.50–£20
Sleeps 6
✂ ☙(5)
👄👄 *Commended*

18th century farmhouse in lawned garden on small working farm overlooking Robin Hood's Bay. Tastefully furnished in the 'olde worlde' charm with open beams, staircase and fireplaces. Rooms with washbasins (1 en suite) all with tea-making facilities and panoramic views of the sea, moors and country-side. Guests' lounge, bathroom. Ideal base for coastal resorts, walking and touring the beauty spots of North Yorkshire. Our speciality is a good hearty breakfast. Open Easter–mid-Oct.

The Grange, Bempton Lane, Flamborough, Bridlington, Humberside YO15 1AS

Joan Thompson
☎ 01262 850207
Fax 01262 851359
🅱 From £13–£14.50
Sleeps 6
🐴 ☙ ⬥ 🐎 🐾
Listed *Commended*

For a relaxing holiday come and stay in our Georgian farmhouse situated in 450 acres of stock and arable land on the outskirts of Flamborough village. Ideally situated for birdwatching at RSPB Sanctuary at Bempton, sandy beaches, cliffs and coves on our 'Heritage Coast'. Golf and sea fishing nearby. Open all year (closed Christmas & New Year).

Island Farm, Staintondale, Scarborough, North Yorkshire YO13 0EB

Mary Clarke
☎ 01723 870249
🅱 From £17–£20
Sleeps 6
🐴 ✂ 🐎 🐾 ▪
👄👄 *Commended*

Relax in our spacious and comfortable farmhouse and garden. All bedrooms have en suite facilities. Being close to coast and in open countryside, it is ideal for walking or visiting many places of interest. Visitors appreciate our large games room with toys, full size snooker table and tennis court. Brochure on request. Open Easter–Nov.

Killerby Cottage Farm, Cayton, Scarborough, North Yorkshire YO11 3TP

Valerie Green
☎ 01723 581236
Fax 01723 585465
🅱 From £14
Sleeps 6
☙(5) ⊞
Applied

Horse/sheep farm with stained glass craft centre in pleasant countryside between Scarborough and Filey. Beautiful Cayton Bay is only 1½ miles away. Tastefully decorated double and twin bedded rooms. Unique split level lounge with colour television. Sun room overlooking lovely garden and water garden. Open March–Nov.

Newgate Foot, Saltersgate, Pickering, North Yorkshire YO18 7NR

Alison Johnson
☎ 01751 460215
🅱 From £15–£20
EM From £10
Sleeps 5
☙ ⊞ ⬥ 🐾 ▪ 🍴
👄👄 *Highly Commended*

Just 1 mile off the A169, but in a world of its own in the middle of the moors with no neighbours in sight! Enjoy walking on the moors, through the forest, or trout fishing in our own lake. See the ewes and lambs and thorough-bred mares and foals. Whitby 14 miles, York 35 miles, "Aidensfield" 6 miles. One en suite bedroom, 1 twin/3 bedded, 1 single. Open all year except Christmas.

---

6 **Plane Tree Cottage Farm,** Staintondale, Scarborough, North Yorkshire YO13 0EY

Mrs Marjorie Edmondson
☎ **01723 870796**
BB **From £16**
EM From £9
Sleeps 4
🐕 🍴 🛡 ♟
Listed *Approved*

This 60-acre mixed farm is situated off the beaten track, between Scarborough and Whitby. We have rare breeds of sheep, pigs and free range hens. Also a very friendly cat called 'Danny'. This small, homely cottage has character with its beams and low ceilings, and beautiful open views. Good wholesome home cooking. Open March–Oct.

---

7 **Rains Farm,** Allerston, Pickering, North Yorkshire YO18 7PQ

Jean or Lorraine Allanson
☎ **01723 859333**
BB **From £16–£19**
EM From £10
Sleeps 11
🐕 🐴 🍴 📺 ♨ ♿
🌺🌺 *Approved*

Rains Farm nestles quietly in the Ryedale's pastoral countryside. Historic York, the coast and moors are all within a few minutes drive. The farm has excellent food, full English breakfast and a varied evening menu. Double/twin en suite rooms including one on ground floor. A warm welcome awaits our guests. Open all year.

---

8 **Seavy Slack,** Stape, Pickering, North Yorkshire YO18 8HZ

Anne Barrett
☎ **01751 473131**
BB **From £13–£16**
EM From £10
Sleeps 6
🐕 🐴
Listed *Approved*

Relax in our comfortable farmhouse on this working dairy/beef farm situated on the edge of the moors and enjoy good home cooking with generous portions. Close to market town of Pickering and North Yorkshire Moors Railway and within easy reach of the coast and historic city of York. Open Easter–October.

SELF-CATERING

---

9 **Asp House Farm Cottage,** Asp House Farm, Stainsacre, Nr Whitby, North Yorkshire YO22 4LR

Patricia Ward
☎ **01947 603997**
SC **From £150–£320**
Sleeps 6 + cot
🐴
🏠 🏠 🏠 🏠 *Commended*

Asp House is a spacious, beamed cottage in an open rural position. Sleeps 6 comfortably. Beautiful views and delightful garden. Situated between the coast, moors and dales; many wonderful walks available. Storage heaters and log fire available for winter breaks. Whitby 3 miles. Open all year.

---

10 **Blackmires Farm,** Danby Head, Danby, Whitby, North Yorkshire YO21 2NN

Gillian & Lewis Rhys
☎ **01287 660352**
SC **From £150–£325**
Sleeps 2/6
🐕 🐴 🛡 ♟
🏠 🏠 🏠 🏠 *Approved*

Self-catering cottage for six with storage heaters. Garden, swing and sandpit. Adjacent to moors in an area of outstanding natural beauty. Our small working farm is in Danby Dale, 3 miles from Danby, Castleton and the North York Moors National Park Information Centre. Good walking and Fishing. Visit Flamingo Park, Castle Howard, Rievaulx and Whitby. Open Mar–Nov.

Croft Farm Cottage, Croft Farm, Fylingthorpe, Whitby, North Yorkshire YO22 4PW

Pauline Featherstone
☎ **01947 880231**
🆂🅲 From £130–£260
Sleeps 4
🐕
🐎 🐎 🐎 *Commended*

Forget the pressures of everyday living! Come and relax in the cottage attached to our 18th century farmhouse on a working farm, offering spectacular views, home comforts, peace and tranquillity. Overlooking Robin Hood's Bay, within easy reach of coastal resorts, Moors Railway and termination of well-known walks. 2 bedrooms, 1 double and 1 with built-in bunk beds. Fully equipped including linen. Colour TV and sun lounge. Open all year.

Rains Farm, Allerston, Pickering, North Yorkshire YO18 7PQ

Jean or Lorraine Allanson
☎ **01723 859333**
🆂🅲 From £125–£350
Sleeps 2/6
🐕 🐎 🖽 🐪 ♿
Applied

Newly renovated for 1996 barns in a sunny courtyard, nestling in peaceful countryside enjoying spectacular views to moors and wolds. Furnished, decorated and equipped to the resident owners' exacting standards, retaining many of the original features. Deft touches enhance the charm of these cottages. Excellent base for North York Moors, forest, steam railway and coast. Five cottages sleeping 2–6 people. Open all year.

CAMPING AND CARAVANNING

Pond Farm, Fylingdales, Whitby, North Yorkshire YO22 4QJ

Grace Cromack
☎ **01947 880441**
🆂🅲 From £110–£190
Sleeps 6
🐎 🐕 🐪 🏕
Tourist Board Inspected

We offer one 6-berth luxury caravan, situated on 400-acre mixed stock farm edging the North Yorkshire Moors and near to Robin Hood's Bay. It is situated in a walled garden with pleasing views and has all mains services including shower, toilet. TV, fridge, double and bunk-bedded rooms. Ideal for visiting historic towns, coastal resorts. Forest and moorland walks, pony trekking and clay pigeon shooting. Short breaks out of season. Open Mar–Nov.

PRICES

Prices include VAT and service charge (if any) and are:
B&B per person per night
EM per person
SC per unit per week
Tents and caravans per pitch per night

England's North Country

Vale of York and the Wolds

Group Contact: *Mrs C. Firby* ☎ *01653 628403*

When you come to stay with us on our farms you are within easy reach of Yorkshire's capital city with its beautiful Minster and a wealth of history; visit the Railway Museum and Jorvik Centre. Whilst in the area see Castle Howard where 'Brideshead Revisited' was filmed and the abbeys of Rievaulx, Byland and Selby.

The area is rich in market towns: Driffield, the capital of the Wolds where reputedly King Alfred is buried, and Beverley, described as the most perfect of county towns with its cobbled streets and 'bars' or town gates. Beverley Minster is one of the finest churches. Explore the many country houses all rich in history and full of beautiful furniture.

Hull is a major port where sailing ships have given way to modern ferries and some of its docks to a yacht marina.

Horse racing takes place at York, Beverley, Ripon and Thirsk, all providing an exciting day out.

A684 • Northallerton
A19
A6108 A1 A170
Thirsk Helmsley ❼ Pickering A171 Scalby ● Scarborough
Ripon ❶ ❽ Malton A64 ● Filey
A61 ● Norton
A19
Knaresborough
Harrogate A166 A166 ● Bridlington
York ❾ ❹ ❸ Gt.Driffield
A64 A19 ❺
A1 A165 ❷ ● Hornsea
Leeds A1079 Beverley
● Garforth
● Rothwell ❶❶ ● Selby A614
Castleford ❻ A63 ● Cottingham **Kingston**
❿ **upon Hull**
31 32 33 34 35 36 37 38 A63
M1 M62 Goole

BED AND BREAKFAST
(and evening meal)

Church Farm, Scackleton, York, North Yorkshire YO6 4NB

Mrs Cynthia Firby
☎/Fax 01653 628403
[BB] From £15–£18
EM From £10
Sleeps 6
🐕 ⚄ 🐎 ♨
Listed *Highly Commended*

A spacious, comfortable stone farmhouse on our sheep and arable farm in a quiet hamlet in the Howardian Hills designated Area of Outstanding Natural Beauty. 2 guest bathrooms, 1 en suite. Family suite. Tea/coffee-making facilities in all bedrooms. Central heating, good home cooking, wonderful views. Ideal base for walking or visiting York, the moors and coast. Open all year except Christmas and New Year.

Crow Tree Farm, Arram, Beverley, Humberside HU17 7NR

Mrs Margaret Hart
☎/Fax 01964 550167
[BB] From £16–£17.50
EM From £7
Sleeps 3
🐕 🐎 🐖 ♨ 🐾
Listed *Approved*

A family smallholding bursting with friendly animals, very child friendly. Traditional Jubilee farmhouse with antique furniture, full central heating, large sunny conservatory leading to tranquil gardens. Situated in secure, undiscovered hamlet close to Beverley, Hull, York and the Heritage Coastline of East Yorkshire. Home cooking with local specialities. Open all year except Christmas.

High Belthorpe, Bishop Wilton, Nr. York, Humberside YO4 1SB

Meg Abu Hamdan
☎ 01759 368238
[BB] From £15
Sleeps 6
🐕 🐎 🧍 ⛵ ♨ 🐾
🐾 *Approved*

Set on an ancient moated site in the Yorkshire Wolds, this large Victorian farmhouse has spacious bedrooms with uninterrupted panoramic views. The centre of a working livery yard, the house has own private fishing lake and access to fabulous country walks. Croquet, small snooker table available. York 12 miles, coast 20 miles. Open all year.

High Catton Grange, High Catton, near Stamford Bridge, York YO4 1EP

Sheila Foster
☎ 01759 371374
[BB] £15–£20
Sleeps 6
🐕 🐎 ♨ 🐾
🐾 🐾 *Commended*

Only 8 miles east of York, High Catton Grange is a 300-acre mixed farm with comfortable 18th century farmhouse. Friendly, relaxed atmosphere and attractive bedrooms, 2 with washbasin, 1 en suite, guest bathroom, central heating, tea/coffee-making facilities. Within 2 miles, local country inns providing excellent meals. Ample private parking. Open all year except Christmas and New Year.

Kelleythorpe Farm, Kelleythorpe, Great Driffield, East Yorkshire YO25 9DW

Mrs Tiffy Hopper
☎ 01377 252297
[BB] From £15
EM From £10
Sleeps 6
🐎 🐕 ♨ 🐾
Listed *Commended*

Imagine peacocks strutting, ducks swimming and trout rising. Enjoy tea on the sun terrace overlooking a crystal clear shallow river, the friendly atmosphere of our lovely Georgian farmhouse with its mellow antique furniture, pretty chintz and new bathrooms, 1 en suite, is sure to captivate you. Delicious country cooking. Children very welcome. Ideally placed for touring. Open all year (closed Christmas & New Year).

---

6 Lund Farm, Gateforth, Selby, North Yorkshire YO8 9LE

Chris & Helen Middleton
☎/Fax 01757 228775
BB From £18–£25
EM From £5
Sleeps 6
🐕 ⌿ ⏚ ⌂ 🛏 ☕
Listed *Applied*

Convenient for York, the Dales and Moors, our peaceful 18th century farmhouse has 2 large en-suite family rooms, pine beams and log fires. Children welcome; 200-acre farm with lambs, hens, donkeys, games, bicycles and baby listening. Evening meals on request. Lambing breaks Dec–Apr. Business people welcome; fax available. Open all year.

7 Sunley Court, Nunnington, York, North Yorkshire YO6 5XQ

Mrs Joan Brown
☎ 01439 748233
BB From £15
EM £10
Sleeps 6
🐕 🐕
🌸 🌸 *Commended*

Sunley Court is a comfortable modern farmhouse with open views in a quiet secluded area. The farm is arable with sheep and horses. All bedrooms have tea/coffee-making facilities, washbasins, electric blankets, 2 have shower/toilet en suite, 2 single bedrooms. Good home cooking. Central for York, moors and coast. Open all year except Christmas.

8 Winifred Farm, Amotherby, Malton, North Yorkshire YO17 0TG

Carolyn Timm
☎ 01653 698165
BB From £14
EM From £10
Sleeps 2
🐕 ⌿ 🜊 🌲
Listed *Commended*

Nestling in between the Howardian Hills, moors and the coast in the heart of Ryedale, 25 miles from York. A traditional, comfortable farmhouse on an arable and stock farm. Large garden with private parking. Situated on the B1257 between Malton and Helmsley. Good variety of attractions in the area. Open Jan–Dec.

SELF-CATERING

9 The Cottage, High Catton Grange, High Catton, near Stamford Bridge, York YO4 1EP

Sheila Foster
☎ 01759 371374
SC From £140–£280
Sleeps 2–6
🐕 🐕 ⌂ ☕
⚘ ⚘ ⚘ ⚘ *Commended*

This former gig shed and stable has been converted to a high standard yet retains many original features. Comfortable and tastefully furnished with colour TV, automatic washer/dryer, fridge, microwave, storage heaters,etc. Patio doors onto large private patio and garden furniture. Glorious views across green meadows. Working farm in peaceful, rural setting, ideally situated for York or touring. Open all year.

10 1 & 2 Dove Cottages, Primrose Hill Farm, c/o Staynor Hall, Selby, North Yorkshire YO8 8EE

Jenny Webster
☎ 01757 708931
Fax 01757 704386
SC From £130–£295
Sleeps Up to 5
🐕 ⌿ ⌂ ☕
⚘ ⚘ ⚘ *Highly Commended*

Our restored 19th century farm cottages on a mixed farm are well equipped with central heating, open log fires and fitted kitchens. Dove cottages offer a quiet retreat in comfortable accommodation. Set in peaceful surroundings with open views only 20 minutes south of historic York. Linen included as are cots and high chair. Open all year.

Lund Farm Cottage, Lund Farm, Gateforth, Selby, North Yorkshire YO8 9LE

Chris & Helen Middleton
☎/Fax 01757 228775
[SC] From £180–£350
Sleeps 7
🐴 ✂ 🐕 🦌 🧺 🎿
🔑 🔑 🔑
Highly Commended

Convenient for York, the Dales and Moors, our peaceful 18th century cottage has 3 bedrooms, beams, fireside range, enclosed private patio and lawn, and friendly owners just next door. Children welcome. Peaceful 200-acre farm with lambs, donkeys, hens, games and bicycles. Evening meals on request. Winter lambing breaks. Prices fully inclusive. Open all year.

FINDING YOUR ACCOMMODATION

The Group contacts at the beginning of each section can always help you find a vacancy in your chosen area.

GOOD FOOD

Nearly all Bureau members now hold a certificate in Essential Food Hygiene.

THE 1000+ BUREAU MEMBERS OFFER A UNIQUE LINK TO CUSTOMERS ACROSS THE UK

All Bureau members belong to a local Group. Each member can refer you to an equally high quality member within his Group... or across the UK: England, Northern Ireland, Scotland, Wales.

England's North Country

South and West Yorkshire

Group Contact: *Mrs Marie Gill ☎ 01924 848339*

We extend a warm welcome to you to visit the gently rolling countryside of South and West Yorkshire.

On the edge of the Peak District National Park is the small town of Holmfirth 'Last of the Summer Wine Country'. Surrounded by hills and moors, it is perfect for walkers who may like to try the Kirklees Way which is a circular walk of 75 miles.

The open air markets of Dewsbury, Leeds and Barnsley are very popular and the area abounds with mill shops. Beside the M1 is Meadowhall Shopping Mall which has 200 shops under one roof.

Within easy access are the Yorkshire Sculpture Park, the Yorkshire Mining Museum and Kirklees Light Steam Railway.

Why not visit Sheffield with its parks and gardens or Leeds with the Henry Moore Gallery or Wakefield's Chantry Chapel?

For water sports enthusiasts there are three water parks in the area.

BED AND BREAKFAST

(and evening meal)

Birch Laithes Farm, Bretton Lane, Bretton, Wakefield, West Yorkshire WF4 4LF

Pat Hoyland
☎ **01924 252129**
🅱 **From £15–£17**
Sleeps 6
🐾 🐕 ☂ ⬛
🍮 *Commended*

A mixed working farm with 18th century house. Comfortable bedrooms, tea/coffee-making facilities, TV, separate dining room and TV lounge, central heating. Ideally situated for Yorkshire towns and countryside, Yorkshire Sculpture Park nearby. 1½ mile J38/39 M1. Open all year.

White Cross Farm, Ash Lane, Emley, Nr Huddersfield, West Yorkshire HD8 9QU

Marie Gill
☎ **01924 848339**
🅱 **From £16–£18**
Sleeps 5
🐕 🐾 ☂
Listed *Approved*

Mixed working farm with listed farmhouse. Some buildings date from 12th century when monks from Byland Abbey lived here and dug for iron ore and kept sheep. Set in rolling Pennine countryside. Tea/coffee-making facilities, TV, central heating in all bedrooms. Close to Yorkshire Mining Museum, Yorkshire Sculpture Park and Holmfirth (Last of Summer Wine country). 3 miles from M1 (jct. 38/39). Open all year (closed Christmas).

FARM HOLIDAY BUREAU

FOLLOW THE COUNTRY CODE

Leave nothing but footprints,
Take nothing but photographs,
Kill nothing but time!

England's North Country

Vale of Lune, Morecambe Bay to Pennine Way

Group Contact: *Mrs Gillian Burrow* ☎ *015242 71446*

Rising in the hills of Cumbria, the Lune flows through richly pastoral countryside. One of its first ports of call is Kirkby Lonsdale, an attractive market town with its 13th century church and Devils Bridge. To the south east lies the busy moorland market town of High Bentham with its Wednesday cattle market and Ingleton, famous for its show caves and spectacular waterfall glens. To the north west lie the unique Limestone Crags of Arnside and Silverdale with its many splendid coastal walks, together with the RSPB bird sanctuary at Leighton Moss and for railway enthusiasts 'Steam Town' at Carnforth will take you back in time. The Lune then flows down to the Roman city of Lancaster with its castle and museums including the Maritime Museum, Museum of Childhood and the Judges Lodgings. At the end of the Lune Valley lies Morecambe Bay.

The River Wyre starts its journey to the sea high in the fells of the ancient hunting Forest of Bowland and flows down through unspoilt villages such as Marshaw, Abbeystead and Dolphinholme to the market town of Garstang. Beacon Fell Country Park is nearby and well worth a visit. The River Lune and the Wyre offer plenty of opportunities for coarse fishing.

THE PENNINES

- Windermere
- M6
- A593
- A683
- A684
- Millom
- Ulverston
- A590
- Dalton-in-Furness
- Grange-over-Sands 8
- Kirkby Lonsdale
- Carnforth 36
- 35 9
- A683
- Morecambe 34
- Lancaster
- A65
- 3 1 4
- 2 6
- 5
- 33
- Fleetwood
- M6
- Garstang 7
- Skipton A59
- Barnoldswick
- Clitheroe
- Earby
- Ilkley
- Blackpool
- Longridge A59
- Keighley A650
- Lytham St.Anne's
- Kirkham M55
- 4 3 32
- Preston
- Padiham 11 12
- 10
- Burnley
- 31
- Blackburn 7 8 9
- 6
- 30
- 29 9
- Hebden Bridge
- Bradford
- Southport
- M61

BED AND BREAKFAST

(and evening meal)

Collingholme Farm, Cowan Bridge, Carnforth, Lancashire LA6 2JL

Anne & Peter Burrow
☎ 015242 71775
[BB] From £13–£16
Sleeps 4
☜(3) ✗
Listed *Highly Commended*

'Quiet luxury and homely excellence' were words used to describe Collingholme. An old and beautifully furnished farmhouse nestling by a pretty stream. We serve breakfasts you won't forget with all the little touches that make a holiday special. Dales, Lakes, historic market towns and unsurpassed scenery plus a football crazy sheepdog called Ted await you. Open Mar–Oct.

Fowgill Park Farm, High Bentham, Nr Lancaster, North Yorkshire LA2 7AH

Shirley Metcalfe
☎ 015242 61630
[BB] From £13–£16
EM From £8
Sleeps 6
♘ ☜ ✗
🐾 🐾 *Commended*

Fowgill is a stock rearing farm, ideal for those who wish to stay where it is quiet. Guests enjoy panoramic views of the Dales and Fells. A good centre for visiting the Lakes, Dales, coast, waterfalls and caves. Beamed bedrooms have washbasins, shaver points and tea/coffee-making facilities; two bedrooms en suite. Comfortable beamed lounge with television. Separate dining room. Bedtime drink included. Open Easter–Oct.

Garghyll Dyke, Cowan Bridge, Kirkby Lonsdale, Cumbria LA6 2HT

Mrs Gillian Burrow
☎ 015242 71446
[BB] From £16–£18
Sleeps 4
☜ ♘ ✗
🐾 *Highly Commended*

We offer a warm, friendly welcome with super breakfasts in our comfortable ivy-clad farmhouse where guests can feel at home. A working dairy farm 3 miles from Kirkby Lonsdale, an ideal base to explore coast, Lakes and Dales. Double and twin room tastefully furnished, each with washbasins and tea/coffee facilities. Country pubs and excellent eating places nearby. Reductions for children. Open Mar–Nov.

Gatehouse Farm, Far Westhouse, Ingleton, Carnforth, Lancashire LA6 3NR

Nancy Lund
☎ 015242 41458/41307
[BB] From £16–£18
EM From £9
Sleeps 6
♘ ☜ ◉
🐾 🐾 *Commended*

Bryan and Nancy welcome you to our dairy and sheep farm built in 1740, rooms with old oak beams in elevated position enjoying panoramic views over open countryside in the YORKSHIRE DALES NATIONAL PARK. Guests dining room, and lounge with colour TV. Bedroom with private facilities and tea trays. Welcome drink on arrival. 15 miles exit 34 M6, 1½ miles west of Ingleton just off A65. Open all year (closed Christmas and New Year).

NO ANSWER?

Farmers are mostly out and about during the day.
Try to telephone before 9.30am or after 4pm.

---

5 Lane House Farm, High Bentham, Lancaster, North Yorkshire LA2 7DJ

Betty Clapham
☎ 015242 61479
BB From £15.50
EM From £8.50
Sleeps 6
🛏 🧍 🐂 💺 🍴 🎋 💼
♨ ♨ *Commended*

Enjoy a relaxing break at our 17th century beamed farmhouse, within ½ mile of the Forest of Bowland, with beautiful views of the Yorkshire Dales. 1 mile from the market town of High Bentham, ½ hour from M6. Ideal for caves, waterfalls, touring the Lakes. Bedrooms have washbasins and tea-making trays. En suite facilities. Guests' lounge with colour TV. Separate dining room. Open Mar–Nov.

6 Nutstile Farm, Ingleton, Carnforth, North Yorkshire LA6 3DT

Carol Brennand
☎ 015242 41752
BB From £14
Sleeps 6
🐂 🎋 🍴
Listed *Commended*

Surrounded by the outstanding beauty of the Yorkshire Dales, Nutstile is a typical working farm providing first class accommodation. The mountains, caves and waterfalls of Ingleton are immediately accessible, the Lake District also close by. Try a leisurely ride on the scenic Settle-Carlisle railway. Three bedrooms (all with views) with wash basin and tea/coffee facilites, en suite available. Guests' lounge with TV. Open all year.

7 Stirzakers Farm, Barnacre, Garstang, Preston, Lancashire PR3 1GE

Ruth Wrathall
☎ 01995 603335
BB From £14–£16
Sleeps 6
🐂 🧍 🍴 💼 🐎
Listed *Highly Commended*

Welcome to our dairy farm where you can relax in the peace and quiet of the beautiful countryside. We have double, family and single rooms in our old stone, beamed farmhouse. CH, separate lounge with colour TV. Two visitors' bathrooms and showers. Tea-making facilities. Children half price. Open all year (closed Christmas and New Year).

SELF-CATERING

8 Brackenthwaite Cottages, Brackenthwaite Farm, Yealand Redmayne, Carnforth, LA5 9TE

Susan Clarke
☎ 015395 63276
SC From £90–£315
Sleeps 4/6
🧍 🐂 🧍 💺 🎋 💼
🔑 🔑 🔑 – 🔑 🔑 🔑 🔑
Commended

Brackenthwaite is situated between Lancaster and Kendal with good access to coast, Lakes and Dales. Lovely walks near nature reserves. Access to farm and woodland with nature trail. The Old Stables are a recent conversion with many features retained. Newly modernised Keepers Cottage has all rooms on a single level. Laundry facilities available. Adventure playground. Open all year. Short lets Nov–Easter.

9 Garden Cottage, High Snab, Gressingham, Lancaster LA2 8LS

Mrs Margaret Burrow
☎ 015242 21347
SC From £160–£260
Sleeps 4 + cot
🐂
🔑 🔑 🔑 *Commended*

Garden cottage, with its own private drive and garden, adjoins our farmhouse on a working dairy and sheep farm in a quiet location. Ideal for touring lakes, dales and coast. Winner of Lancashire Farm Landscape Trophy and NWTB 'Place to stay 93'. Well equipped kitchen/oak beamed lounge. Two bedrooms, 1 double, 1 twin, snooker table, bathroom with shower. CH from farmhouse, cot/high chair available. Electric and linen included. 5 miles jct 35 M6. Brochure.

30

England's North Country
Lancashire Coast and Country

Group Contact: *Mrs Maureen Smith* ☎ *01253 882537*

Contrasting scenery beckons you to the Lancashire Coast and Country where the bracing coastline with its dunes, a National Nature Reserve at Lytham St. Annes, offers sanctuary for wildlife. Travel up the coast to the hustle and bustle of Blackpool with its famous illuminations. Then on through Cleveleys finally resting at Fleetwood, an ancient fishing port, where the River Wyre meets the sea.

Travel east to Poulton-le-Fylde, an ancient market town with its stocks and beautiful Norman church.

Inland from the coast the acres of rich farm land dotted with villages, some with weekly street markets, all have an individual character and charm of their own.

Move up to the hill country, excellent for walkers and explorers: Bleasdale Fell and Beacon Fell, adjoining the rolling hills of the Forest of Bowland, or enjoy a picnic at Brock, an area of outstanding beauty.

We have lots to offer everyone – including excellent theatres at both Preston and Blackpool.

BED AND BREAKFAST

(and evening meal)

---

(1) Stirzakers Farm, Barnacre, Garstang, Preston, Lancashire PR3 1GE

Ruth Wrathall
☎ 01995 603335
BB **From £14–£16**
Sleeps 6
☺ ✕ ✄ ▪ ⚘
Listed *Highly Commended*

Welcome to our dairy farm where you can relax in the peace and quiet of the beautiful countryside. We have double, family and single rooms in our old stone, beamed farmhouse. CH, separate lounge with colour TV. Two visitors' bathrooms and showers. Tea-making facilities. Children half price. Open all year (closed Christmas and New Year).

---

(2) Todderstaffe Hall Farm, off Fairfield Road, Singleton, Poulton-le-Fylde, Lancashire FY6 8LF

Mrs Maureen Smith
☎/Fax 01253 882537
BB **From £15–£25**
Sleeps 4
☺ ✄ ⛶ ⚘
☘ ☘ *Commended*

Enjoy a friendly welcome at our 260-acre arable farm situated 4 miles from the attractions of Blackpool in a peaceful corner of the Fylde and within easy reach of Lake District. Oak beams and open fires maintain the charm of the old farmhouse but modern comforts, like central heating have been added. One twin/family room with en suite bathroom, colour TV, and tea making facilities. Reduced terms early season. Open Jan–Nov.

DISABLED VISITORS

Many members offer a welcome to disabled/less able visitors. Please do check the extent of the facilities before booking.

THOSE LITTLE EXTRAS

For advice on farms that can offer 'extras' such as four-poster beds, special diets, farm trails, fishing rights – even stabling and trekking arrangements if you are bringing your own horse – ring the Farm Holiday Bureau on (01203) 696909.

31

England's North Country

West Lancashire

Group Contact: *Mrs Wendy Core* ☎ *01704 880337*

A vast marshland until the early 18th century, West Lancashire is now one of the most fertile areas in Britain, the main industry being agriculture. In the middle of this 'garden' lies the ancient town of Ormskirk, where the market was first chartered in the 13th century. Henry VIII was responsible for the Parish Church's unusual appearance – after Burscough Prior was dissolved, a bell tower was built alongside the steeple to house the bells of the Priory.

People with an interest in history will find a visit to 15th-century Rufford Old Hall and its collection of Tudor furniture fascinating, and railway enthusiasts will enjoy Steamport Museum at Southport with its collection of railway memorabilia. Nearby, the Cedar Farm Gallery at Mawdsley has farm animals and a children's play area which enables mum and dad to enjoy the Craft Centre.

Bird lovers should head for the Wildfowl Trust Centre at Martin Mere where rare and exotic species come and go in an unspoilt area of natural wetland.

Both the Leeds and Liverpool Canal and the River Douglas are pleasant and intriguing to traverse whether you are walking along the banks or boating on the water. Whatever your pleasure, you can find it in West Lancashire.

[Map of West Lancashire region showing towns including Fleetwood, Blackpool, Lytham St. Anne's, Kirkham, Preston, Poulton-Le-Fylde, Longridge, Clitheroe, Barnoldswick, Skipton, Earby, Ilkley, Keighley, Padiham, Blackburn, Burnley, Bradford, Hebden Bridge, Halifax, Southport, Littleborough, Huddersfield, Wigan, Bolton, Oldham, Crosby, Bootle, St.Helens, Manchester, Liverpool, with road references M6, M55, M61, M62, M56, A59, A565, A570, A565, A666, A646, A650, A635, A628, A57]

BED AND BREAKFAST

(and evening meal)

---

① Brandreth Barn, Brandreth Farm, Tarlscough Lane, Burscough, Nr Ormskirk, Lancashire L40 0RJ

Mrs M Wilson
☎ 01704 893510
🆒 From £20–£27.50
EM From £5.95
Sleeps 14
☺ 🐴 ⊡ ᕕ ⚔ 🏕 ⛺ 💼
Applied

Situated alongside the wildfowl trust Martin Mere, an 18th century brick-built barn conversion dated 1774. 5 minutes from A59, 15 mins from M6. All rooms fully centrally heated, with tea/coffee-making facilities. All rooms en suite plus colour TV. Licensed restaurant. Also disabled facilities. Arable farm. Room only from £17.50, with continental breakfast from £18. Open all year except Christmas.

---

② Sandy Brook Farm, Wyke Cop Road, Scarisbrick, Southport, Lancashire PR8 5LR

Mrs W E Core
☎ 01704 880337
🆒 From £15.50
Sleeps 15
☺ 🐴 ᕕ
🐛 🐛 *Approved*

This small, comfortable arable farm is situated in the rural area of Scarisbrick, midway between the seaside town of Southport and the ancient town of Ormskirk. The A570 is only ½ mile away. The converted farm buildings are attractively furnished, and all bedrooms have en suite facilities, colour TV and tea/coffee-making facilities. Disabled facilities available. Open all year except Christmas.

SELF-CATERING

---

③ Martin Lane Farmhouse Cottages, Martin Lane, Burscough, Lancs L40 8JH

Elaine Stubbs
☎/Fax 01704 893527
🆒 From £200–£350
Sleeps 5/7
☺ ᚷ 🐴 ⚔ 🏕
🗝 🗝 🗝 🗝 *Highly Commended*

These award-winning cosy, comfortable, 'family friendly' cottages are situated in the heart of the peaceful West Lancashire countryside yet only 5 miles from the seaside resort of Southport. The 'Shippon' sleeping 4/5 and the Granary sleeping 7 are both superbly furnished and equipped. Large, safe play area for children. Sheep and free range hens on farm. Open all year.

Please mention **Stay on a Farm** when booking

England's North Country

Lancashire Pennines

Group Contact: *Mrs Carole Mitson* ☎ *01282 865301*

The Forest of Bowland, the largest area of unspoilt countryside in Lancashire, 1,827ft high Pendle Hill and the Pennines afford the visitor to the area a chance to appreciate Lancashire at its most beautiful. Complementing such countryside are a number of towns and villages, all with their own individual character: Clitheroe with its castle and museum; Whalley with its Cistercian Abbey (founded in 1296) and Georgian and Tudor houses; the old market towns of Colne, Skipton and Ribchester, with its Roman Museum; Barley, at the foot of Pendle Hill, with its connections with the Witch Trials of 1612; and Slaidburn, the gateway to the Forest of Bowland, once a royal hunting ground.

There is something here to suit all tastes. For example, places of historic interest, such as Browsholme Hall, the home of the Parker family, which houses a display of 13th century domestic articles, can be contrasted with the new Preston Guild Hall with facilities for many social, cultural and educational activities. If you prefer a quiet, more sedate pace, you can enjoy one of the several country parks and picnic areas, such as Beacon Fell, Spring Wood, Barley or Wycoller. A holiday in the farms of the Lancashire Pennines will also leave you within easy reach of the Yorkshire Dales, the Lake District, Haworth and Brontë Country.

Fleetwood
Poulton-Le-Fylde
M6
Skipton
A59
Barnoldswick
Blackpool
Clitheroe
Earby
Longridge
Ilkley
A650
M55
Keighley
Lytham St.Anne's Kirkham **Preston**
Padiham
Blackburn
Burnley
A59
Bradford
Southport
A565
A59
A646
Hebden Bridge Halifax
M61
Littleborough
A565
A666
M62
Huddersfield
Wigan Bolton
A570
Oldham
A635
Crosby
Bootle
St.Helens
Manchester
A628
Liverpool
M62
M56
A57

BED AND BREAKFAST

(and evening meal)

---

1 Blakey Hall Farm, Red Lane, Colne, Lancashire BB8 9TD

Mrs R Boothman
☎ 01282 863121
▣ From £17–£22
EM From £7.50
Sleeps 6
🐾 🍴 ⛺ ⚓
Listed *Applied*

Pretty and comfortable accommadation on working dairy farm along Leeds Liverpool canal. Fishing available. Own TV lounge. 3 bedrooms, 1 en suite, tea/coffee facilities. Open all year.

---

2 Eaves Barn Farm, Hapton, Burnley, Lancashire BB12 7LP

Mrs M Butler
☎ 01282 771591/
770478
▣ From £18.50–£22.50
EM From £9
Sleeps 5
🐾(10) 🍴 ⛺ ⚓ 🎋
Listed *Highly Commended*

Eaves Barn Farm is a mixed working farm. The accommodation comprises a spacious cottage attached to the main house, furnished to a high standard and offering luxury facilities. Excellent English breakfasts are served in the newly constructed conservatory. Delicious evening meals and homemade preserves a speciality. Ideally situated for all Lancashire's tourist attractions. Open all year.

---

3 Higher Wanless Farm, Red Lane, Colne, Lancashire BB8 7JP

Carole Mitson
☎ 01282 865301
▣ From £18–£22
EM From £10
Sleeps 4
🐾(3) 🛏 🍴 🎋
🌼 🌼 *Highly Commended*

Ideally situated for visiting 'Pendle Witch' country, Haworth or Yorkshire Dales – the farm nestles peacefully alongside the Leeds/Liverpool Canal. Shire horses and sheep are reared on the farm, where the warmest of welcomes awaits you. Spacious and luxurious bedrooms (1 en suite) offer every comfort for our guests. Several country inns nearby offering wide range of meal facilities. AA selected establishment. Open Jan–Nov.

---

4 Lower White Lee Farm, Fence, Burnley, Lancashire BB12 9ER

Helen Boothman
☎ 01282 613563
▣ From £17
EM From £8.50
Sleeps 4
🍴 🐾
🌼 *Commended*

A 200-acre dairy farm, offering accommodation in beautifully furnished 18th century farmhouse. 2 bedrooms, each with tea/coffee-making facilities, central heating. Lounge and separate dining room. Good food a speciality. 25 mins from M6. Ideally situated for Brontë Country, Yorkshire Dales and the Lakes. Many cultural and scenic attractions nearby. Closed Christmas and New Year.

---

5 Parson Lee Farm, Wycoller, Colne, Lancashire BB8 8SU

Patricia Hodgson
☎ 01282 864747
▣ From £14–£17
EM £6
Sleeps 6
🍴 🐾 ⛺
🌼 *Approved*

There's a warm welcome at our 110-acre sheep farm on the edge of beautiful Wycoller Country Park. The 250-year old farmhouse, with exposed beams and mullion windows, is peacefully located and perfect for walking, being on the Brontë and Pendle Ways. Easy access to Lancashire or Yorkshire. Pendle Way walking breaks with transport. Both en suite bedrooms, furnished in country style, have tea/coffee-making facilities. Open all year except Christmas & New Year.

Pasture Bottom Farm, Bacup, Lancashire OL13 9UZ

Ann Isherwood
☎ 01706 873790
🆑 From £14
EM From £7
Sleeps 4
🦮 🐓 🏕 🛋 🔥
🐾 *Approved*

We offer farmhouse accommodation in a quiet rural area on a true working beef farm in a relaxed away-from-it-all atmosphere. Magnificent country views. Centrally located for Pennines and Yorkshire moors, Lancashire hill country and within easy reach of Manchester by M66, making it ideal for business people. Closed Christmas and New Year.

SELF-CATERING

Dove Cottage, Hartley Royd, Bluebell Lane, Shore, Nr Todmorden, Yorkshire OL14 8SE (7)

Mr & Mrs D J Pilling
☎ 01706 816111
Fax 01706 878343
🆑 From £180–£350
Sleeps 4 +cot
🦮 🏕 🛋 🎿
🐾 🐾 🐾 🐾 *De Luxe*

Wuthering Heights with all mod cons. Detached, luxuriously refurbished 17th century cottage adjacent to the owners' Jacobean farmhouse. Warm and cosy with log fire, fully fitted kitchen with dishwasher and beams galore. Wander around our gardens, fields, moors, woods, streams and rocks. Within ½hr of Brontë Country, 1 hour Lancashire coast, York and near to lots of things to do. Open all year.

FARM HOLIDAY BUREAU

THOSE LITTLE EXTRAS

For advice on farms that can offer 'extras' such as four-poster beds, special diets, farm trails, fishing rights – even stabling and trekking arrangements if you are bringing your own horse – ring the Farm Holiday Bureau on (01203) 696909.

England's North Country
South Pennines

Group Contacts: *Mrs Annis Heathcote* ☎ *01457 872424*
Mrs Jean Mayall ☎ *01457 873040*

A warm and friendly welcome awaits visitors to this beautiful and dramatic countryside, still remarkably untouched by tourism. Holiday-makers will find unusual and interesting places to visit close by, with Blackpool, York and the Peak District less than an hour away. The Lake District and the North Yorkshire Moors are an easy two hours, whilst businessmen are well placed for work in Manchester, Liverpool, Leeds and Bradford and close to Manchester Airport and Intercity rail.

Walkers on the Pennine Way will experience stark moorland scenery blending with attractive valley towns like Delph, Uppermill, Marsden and Hebden Bridge and there are equally interesting routes over Blackstone Edge with the Roman Road, the Rossendale Way, the Calderdale Way and the Colne Valley Circular. There are canal trips at Uppermill, Sowerby Bridge and Littleborough, and water sports at Hollingworth Lake and Scammanden Dam, where flocks of wild fowl can be seen. The South Pennine textile heritage is magnificently illustrated in the Colne Valley Museum, Golcar, the Helmshore Museum at Haslingden, and the Saddleworth Museum at Uppermill. Craft centres and mill shops abound and traditional handweaving, clog and slipper making and dyeing and printing can be studied here.

BED AND BREAKFAST

(and evening meal)

Boothstead Farm, Rochdale Road, Denshaw, Oldham, Greater Manchester OL3 5UE

Mrs Norma Hall
☎ **01457 878622**
🅱 **From £18**
Sleeps 4
🚭(4) ⌦
Listed *Commended*

An 18th century hill farm catering for people in the area on business or taking a relaxing break. Ideally situated within 3½ miles of M62 Junctions 21 and 22 (A640). Cosy lounge with open fire, TV, tea/coffee-making facilities, wash basins in rooms. Good base for touring neighbouring counties and beauty spots. Close to Saddleworth leisure amenities, ie. golf, swimming, walking, sailing. Open 2 Jan–22 Dec.

Globe Farm, Huddersfield Road, Standedge, Delph, Nr Oldham, Greater Manchester OL3 5LU

Jean Mayall
☎ **01457 873040**
🅱 **From £18**
EM from £6.50
Sleeps 11
🚭 🅔 🛇 ⚛ 🎿 📂 🏇
🐝 *Commended*

Overlooking the picturesque valleys of Saddleworth but within easy reach of M62 junction 22, Manchester Airport, Yorkshire Dales and Peak District. Only ¼ mile from Pennine Way. All rooms en suite. Evening meal can be provided if required. Colour TV, CH, drying room, tea/coffee-making facilities. Good home cooking and real northern hospitality. Open all year (closed Christmas & New Year).

Higher Quick Farm, Lydgate, Saddleworth, Greater Manchester OL4 4JJ

Annis Heathcote
☎ **01457 872424**
🅱 **From £18–£20**
Sleeps 6
🚭 ⌦ 🎿
Listed *Highly*
Commended

Higher Quick Farm is a grade II listed farmhouse on a 40 acre beef farm, with magnificent views from all rooms. Warm and comfortable house, colour TV and tea-making facilities in each bedroom. 1 twin, 1 double with adjoining private bathroom, 1 double en suite. Ideal area for walking, easy distance M62, 10 miles Manchester Airport, close to Uppermill with a craft centre, museum, golf, canal boat, swimming pool. Open all year except 25/26 Dec.

Needhams Farm, Uplands Road, Werneth Low, Gee Cross, near Hyde, Cheshire SK14 3AQ

Mrs Charlotte Walsh
☎ **0161 368 4610**
Fax 0161 367 9106
🅱 **From £17–£19**
EM From £7
Sleeps 15
🚭 🐎 🅔 🎿 📂
🐝🐝🐝 *Commended*

Farmhouse accommodation dating back to the 16th century, offering 5 en suite rooms. Evening meals available each evening. Residential licence. Surrounded by lovely views. Ideal for Manchester Airport and city centre. Courtesy service from airport and Piccadilly station for a small charge. Six bedrooms in all. Open all year.

Shire Cottage Farmhouse, Benches Lane, Chisworth, Hyde, Cheshire SK14 6RY

Monica Sidebottom
☎ **01457 866536**
or 0161 427 2377
🅱 **From £18–£24**
Sleeps 6
🐎 🚭 ♿ 🚵 ⌂ 🎿 📂
🐝 🐝 *Commended*

Real home from home accommodation in peaceful location. Magnificent views overlooking Etheroe Country Park. Convenient for Manchester Airport, city centre, Peak District, stately homes and numerous places of interest. Ground floor bedrooms and bathroom. All rooms have vanity units/shaver points/tea-making facilities/TV. Family room has own shower and toilet. Bathroom has shower and bidet. Early breakfast for businessmen and travellers. Open all year.

SELF-CATERING

6 **Lake View,** Ernocroft Farm, Marple Bridge, Stockport, Cheshire SK6 5NT

Monica Sidebottom
☎ **01457 866536**
SC From **£150–£275**
Sleeps 6 + cot
⌂ ♿ 🐾 ✿ ♨ ▪
♟ ♟ ♟ *Commended*

A new, self-catering farm bungalow, 2 miles Marple Bridge, 4 miles Glossop. Overlooking Etherow Country Park. Ideal base for exploring Peak District, Marple locks and waterways, country parks and stately homes. Peaceful location. Accommodates 6 with all mod cons. TV. Cot available. Open all year.

BUREAU ACCOMMODATION MEANS QUALITY

All Bureau members are inspected and quality graded by the National Tourist Board each year, as well as by fellow members.

LET THE TELEPHONE RING!

Some farmhouses are big places. Let the telephone ring long enough to give the owner time to answer it.

FOLLOW THE COUNTRY CODE

Leave nothing but footprints,

Take nothing but photographs,

Kill nothing but time!

England's Heartland

Cheshire

Group Contact: *Mrs Hilary Bennion* ☎ *01270 811324*

Cheshire is one of England's undiscovered counties. Renowned for lovely black and white architecture and its superb cheese, it is a county of contrasts. From the majesty of the Peak District across the Cheshire Plain to the Dee estuary, from North Wales to Manchester, from the Shropshire Hills to Liverpool, Cheshire has something for everyone. The county has a rich history, well-documented for visitors, with Roman remains in Chester, Elizabethan towns like Nantwich, fine castles and country mansions and museums about the industrial revolution such as Styal Museum at Northwich or Paradise Silk Mill at Macclesfield.

Cheshire offers many peaceful country pursuits: there are canals, wonderful walking (from the Sandstone Trail to shorter farm walks), cycling and fishing. The county has many charming villages and towns, fine old churches, numerous antique shops. There are beautiful gardens in Cheshire – country house, botanical and municipal – plus two of Europe's largest garden centres, Bridgemere Garden World and Stapley Water Gardens.

Chester, the county town, is one of Britain's top tourist destinations. Situated on the River Dee with a splendid cathedral and unique Rows, it offers sophisticated shopping facilities as well as a fine heritage.

BED AND BREAKFAST

(and evening meal)

---

① Adderley Green Farm, Heighley Castle Lane, Betley, Nr Crewe, Cheshire CW3 9BA

Mrs Sheila Berrisford
☎ 01270 820203
Fax 01782 722422
BB From £15–£18
Sleeps 6
🐴🐂🐎🐕🐈🐖🐑
🌸🌸
Highly Commended

Relax in our lovely Georgian farmhouse on a 250-acre dairy farm. Set in large garden along a pretty country lane near an old ruined castle. Full CH. Colour TV, radio, washbasin and tea tray in all bedrooms. En suites available, draped and 4-poster beds. Beautifully decorated in the Laura Ashley style. Ideally situated for Stapeley Water Gardens, Alton Towers and Chester. Near Keele University and Potteries, 10 mins M6 J16. Fishing and riding. Open all year.

---

② Ford Farm, Nenton Lane, Tattenhall, Chester, Cheshire CH3 9NE

Audrey Charmley
☎ 01829 770307
BB £15
Sleeps 4
🐂🐕🐎
Listed Commended

A friendly welcome to our dairy farm set in beautiful countryside with views of Beeston and Peckforton Castles. Close to ice cream farm and Cheshire workshops and many tourist attractions. Chester 7 miles, Oulton Park 8 miles. Guests' own lounge and dining room with TV. One double and one twin room, tea/coffee making facilities, bathroom with shower. Open all year.

---

③ Goose Green Farm, Oak Road, Mottram St Andrew, Nr Macclesfield, Cheshire SK10 4RA

Dyllis Hatch
☎ 01625 828814
BB From £18–£20
Sleeps 6
🚷🐎(5)🐕🐎🖤
🌸🌸 *Commended*

Welcome to our beef farm set in beautiful countryside with panoramic views. Just off A538 between Wilmslow and Prestbury, in easy reach of M6, M56 and Manchester Airport. Own fishing, horse riding nearby. Comfortable, homely with log fire in guests' lounge. Separate dining room. Pay phone. Double en suite, twin and single rooms, all with washbasin, TV, CH and tea/coffee-making facilities. Open all year (closed Christmas).

---

④ Henhull Hall, Welshmans Lane, Nantwich, Cheshire CW5 6AD

Philip and Joyce Percival
☎ 01270 624158 or
0374 885305
BB From £20–£22
Sleeps 5
🐎🐎🖤
🌸🌸 *Applied*

Choose our attractive and spacious farmhouse on a 300-acre dairy farm bordering the canal. A short walk from the historic town of Nantwich, famous for its Elizabethan architecture, antique shops and restaurants. Each en suite bedroom is warm and welcoming with delicious breakfasts to make your stay memorable. Open Jan–Nov.

---

⑤ Lea Farm, Wrinehill Road, Wybunbury, Nantwich, Cheshire CW5 7NS

Allen & Jean Callwood
☎ 01270 841429
BB From £14
EM From £8
Sleeps 6
🐴🐎🐕🐎🖤
🌸🌸 *Commended*

A charming farmhouse set in landscaped gardens where peacocks roam a 150-acre dairy farm. Spacious, attractive bedrooms with washbasins, TV and tea/coffee-making facilities, two en suite. Luxurious lounge with open log fire, with dining room overlooking garden. Snooker, pool table, fishing available. Near to Stapeley Water Gardens and Bridgemere Garden World. M6 J16, Chester and Alton Towers. Open all year (closed Christmas & New Year).

Little Heath Farm, Audlem, Nantwich, Crewe, Cheshire CW3 0HE   (6)

Hilary Bennion
☎ 01270 811324
[BB] From £15–£20
EM From £8.50
Sleeps 6
Commended

Looking for a comfortable, peaceful break on the edge of picturesque canalside village with shops, pubs and village trails? Come and join us in our 17th century beamed farmhouse. Warm, spacious bedrooms with all facilities, one en suite. Beamed lounge and dining room traditionally furnished. Close to Bridgemere Garden World, Stapeley Water Gardens. We are a working diary farm on the A529, 6 miles Nantwich. Open all year.

Newton Hall, Tattenhall, Chester, Cheshire CH3 9AY   (7)

Mrs Anne Arden
☎ 01829 770153
[BB] From £15–£20
Sleeps 4
Highly Commended

Part 16th century oak-beamed farmhouse set in large well kept grounds, with fine views of historic Beeston and Peckforton Castles and close to the Sandstone Trail. Six miles south of Chester off A41 and ideal for Welsh Hills. Rooms are en suite or have adjacent bathroom. Fully centrally heated. See our rare Shropshire Down sheep and Pedigree Cattle. Open all year.

Poole Bank Farm, Wettenhall Road, Poole, Nantwich, Cheshire CW5 6AL   (8)

Caroline Hocknell
☎ 01270 625169
[BB] From £13.50–£18
Sleeps 6
Commended

A charming 17th century timbered farmhouse on 260-acre dairy farm set in quiet countryside 2 miles from the historic town of Nantwich. Ideal base for discovering the beautiful Cheshire countryside. Central for Chester and the Potteries. Comfortable and attractive rooms, all with period furnishings. TV and tea/coffee making facilities. A warm welcome and an excellent breakfast are assured. Open all year.

Sandhole Farm, Hulme Walfield, Congleton, Cheshire CW12 2JH   (9)

Veronica Worth
☎ 01260 224419
Fax 01260 224766
[BB] From £21–£33
Sleeps 38
Highly Commended

The comfortable traditional farmhouse and delightful converted stable block are situated 2 miles north of Congleton on A34, 15 mins from M6 and 30 mins from Manchester airport. Most of our rooms have modern en suite facilities and all have the usual extras, including hairdryer, remote control teletext TV plus trouser press and direct dial telephone. Large comfortable lounge, separate newly built conservatory/dining room. Cheshire Tourism Award Winner. Now approved for Civil Marriages. Open all year.

Sandpit Farm, Messuage Lane, Marton, Macclesfield, Cheshire SK11 9HS   (10)

Mrs I H Kennerley
☎ 01260 224254
[BB] From £15–£18.50
Sleeps 6
(3)
Commended

A friendly welcome to our 300 year old farmhouse surrounded by 100 acres of grassland. Traditional farmhouse with oak timber features and heated throughout. H&C in T/S, en suite facilities in double and twin, all with tea/coffee and TV. Excellent touring centre for Peak District, Potteries, Chester. Manchester Airport 14 miles, NT properties, stately homes and Jodrell Bank Science Centre nearby. Closed Christmas.

LET THE TELEPHONE RING!
Some farmhouses are big places. Let the telephone ring long enough to give the owner time to answer it.

11 Snape Farm, Snape Lane, Weston, Nr Crewe, Cheshire CW2 5NB

Mrs Jean Williamson
☎/Fax 01270 820208
[BB] From £13.50–£16
EM From £7
Sleeps 6
� 🐕 🥄 📶

🌼 *Applied*

Enjoy a warm welcome to our centrally heated farmhouse on a 150-acre beef/arable farm set in rolling countrside. 3 miles from Crewe. A good centre for visiting Nantwich, Chester or the Potteries. Guests' lounge and snooker room. 1 twin (en suite), 1 twin, 1 double room, each with colour TV and tea/coffee-making facilities. 4 miles from M6 (jct. 16). Open all year.

12 Stoke Grange Farm, Chester Road, Nantwich, Cheshire CW5 6BT

Georgina West
☎ 01270 625525
[BB] From £17.50–£20
Sleeps 6
🐕 🐄 📶 🥄 🎋

🌼🌼 *Commended*

In a picturesque setting, a canalside farmhouse dating from 1838 on a working dairy farm, with large car park and attractive garden. Spacious en suite bedrooms with colour TV and hot drink facilities. Comfortable guest lounge with TV, solarium, games and reading room. Relax on the verandah to watch the canal boats. Vegetarians are catered for. Cheshire Tourism Development Award winner 91/92. Open all year.

SELF-CATERING

13 Stoke Grange Mews, Stoke Grange Farm, Chester Road, Nantwich, Cheshire CW5 6BT

Georgina West
☎ 01270 625525
[SC] From £150–£350
Sleeps 2–6 + cot
🐄 🥄 🎋 📶
🐾 🐾 🐾 *Highly Commended*

Holiday home created from a fine old barn near the owner's canalside farmhouse and dairy farm in lush heritage rich countryside some 15 miles south of the Roman town of Chester. Each has exposed beams, quality furniture, and offers fully equipped accommodation with all mod cons. Small rear patio, large shared garden with canal access. Children's play area and farm pets corner. Barbeque area. Cheshire Tourism Development Award winner 91/92. Open all year.

PRICES

Prices include VAT and service charge (if any) and are:
B&B per person per night
EM per person
SC per unit per week
Tents and caravans per pitch per night

FARM HOLIDAY BUREAU

England's Heartland

Staffordshire

Group Contacts: 🅱🅱 *Mrs Christine Shaw* ☎ *01538 702830*
🆂🅲 *Mr John Myatt* ☎ *01889 22269*

The varied landscape of Staffordshire ranges from that of the Peak District National Park through the moorlands in the north to the fertile valleys of the Trent and its tributaries in the south. In the heart of the county is the extensive Cannock Chase, an area of outstanding natural beauty which offers scope for varied leisure pursuits.

A popular target for visitors to the county are its two leisure parks: Alton Towers, with its exciting rides, is the premier leisure park in the country, while Drayton Manor Park offers an open-plan zoological garden, lakes and an amusement park.

In the county town of Stafford the impressive timber-framed Ancient High House has to be seen. Tamworth, with its Norman Castle, was once the capital of the ancient kingdom of Mercia, while Burton on Trent is famous as the home of the brewing industry. Of particular attraction is the cathedral city of Lichfield, birthplace of Dr Samuel Johnson and host to international music and folk festivals. But of equal antiquity is the town of Tutbury with its fine castle and its glass making tradition.

Many visitors seek out the potteries and visitor centres which offer the chance to see craftsmen at work and perhaps to make purchases at the factory shops.

Whatever your particular interest you can be sure of a warm welcome in Staffordshire!

BED AND BREAKFAST
(and evening meal)

---

1 **Ribden Farm,** Nr Oakamoor, Stoke-on-Trent, Staffordshire ST10 3BW

Christine Shaw
☎/Fax 01538 702830
🅱🅱 From £18–£22
Sleeps 11
🏃 ☂ 🌳
♨ ♨ *Highly Commended*

Ribden Farm is an 18th Century farmhouse c1748 which is situated 1,000 ft high in the Weaver Hills yet is only 5 minutes from Alton Towers. Plenty of underused footpaths. Local inns. All rooms en suite with colour TV, coffee/tea-making facilities. Separate TV lounge and dining room. Secure off road parking. RAC Acclaimed. AA QQQQ selected. Open all year.

SELF-CATERING

---

2 **Priory Farm Fishing House,** c/o Priory Farm, Blithbury, Rugeley, Staffordshire WS15 3JA

Mr John Myatt
☎ 01889 504269
🆂🅲 From £65–£110
Sleeps 4
☂ 🐑
🔑 🔑 *Approved*

Converted 18th century fishing house overlooking River Blithe, offering unique accommodation for up to 4 persons on secluded dairy farm. Ideal for lovers of the countryside and wildlife. Convenient for Abbots Bromley, Lichfield, Cannock Chase, Alton Towers and the Peak District. Comfortable, tastefully furnished accommodation includes large bed-sitting room with colour TV, modern kitchen and shower room. Brochure on request. Open all year.

FARM HOLIDAY
BUREAU

FINDING YOUR ACCOMMODATION

The Group contacts at the beginning of each section can always help you find a vacancy in your chosen area.

England's Heartland

Peak District

Group Contacts: ⒷⒷ *Joy Lomas* ☎ *0162 985 250*

Britain's first National Park offers variety and spectacular scenery, from the exhilaration of the wide, windswept moorlands in the north to the softer south where the Manifold and Dove rivers run parallel through water meadows, woodlands and rocky gorges.

As well as some of the best walking in the country, the Peak District offers numerous stately homes such as Chatsworth, Haddon and Hardwick, as well as the thrills of Alton Towers and Water World, and Water Sports at Carsington Water.

Find a bargain in the Potteries seconds shops and at Gladstone Pottery Museum go back in time amongst the bottle kilns. Wedgwood shows a complete contrast by demonstrating modern production of fine china.

Leek and Bakewell markets transform sleepy country towns when farmers from miles around descend on them. At Matlock cable cars glide majestically across an awe-inspiring gorge to the Heights of Abraham. Castleton is famous for its show caves and Blue John stone. So, whether having afternoon tea at a stately home, admiring the Well Dressings or picnicking amongst the heather, you can be sure that the Peak District has something for you.

BED AND BREAKFAST

(and evening meal)

---

① Beechenhill Farm, Ilam, Ashbourne, Derbyshire DE6 2BD

Sue Prince
☎ **01335 310274**
BB **From £17.50–£23**
Sleeps 5
⚞☐☐☐
☐☐ *Highly
Commended*

Wake up to wonderful views over a pretty garden, grazing cows and sheep, walkable hills and explorable valleys, at our warm old farmhouse near Dovedale. We've two delightful rooms; family en suite and double with private shower room, tea/coffee trays, own lounge, all beautifully decorated (stencils, etc). Fruit, yoghurts and famous Beechenhill porridge feature as well as traditional carefully cooked breakfasts. Open Feb–Dec.

---

② Brook House Farm, Cheddleton, Leek, Staffordshire ST13 7DF

Elizabeth Winterton
☎ **01538 360296**
BB **From £16–£17**
EM From £9
Sleeps 10
☐☐☐
☐☐ *Commended*

A dairy farm in a picturesque and peaceful valley. Central for Peak District, Potteries, Churnet Valley steam railway, Cauldron Canal, Coombes Valley RSPB Reserve and Alton Towers. 3 spacious rooms in a tastefully converted cowshed and 2 in the farmhouse, all en suite with tea/coffee-makers and colour TV. Dine in our attractive conservatory with magnificent country views. Open all year.

---

③ Cote Bank Farm, Buxworth, Whaley Bridge, Derbyshire SK12 7NP

Pamela Broadhurst
☎ **01663 750566**
BB **From £19**
Sleeps 5
☐(6)☐☐☐☐
☐☐ *Commended*

Good old fashioned hospitality, a kettle always on the boil and a breakfast worth waking for! Treat yourself to a relaxing stay on our peaceful sheep farm with stunning views across the hills and excellent walks. A home from home for business travellers (1 mile Chinley, 3 miles A6) and a welcoming base for holidaymakers. Guest lounge with log fire; 1 double, 1 family, both en suite, with TV, radio, tea/coffee. Open Mar–Dec.

---

④ Henmore Grange, Hopton, Carsington, Wirksworth, Derbyshire DE4 4DF

*John & Elizabeth
Brassington*
☎ **01629 540420**
BB **From £25–£27.50**
EM From £6–£12.50
Sleeps 31
☐☐☐☐☐
☐☐ *Commended*

Between Ashbourne and Matlock by Peak National Park overlooking Carsington Water, offering good old-fashioned hospitality in a beautifully converted barn in a garden planted to attract butterflies. Most rooms have private bath/shower rooms. All have tea/coffee-making facilities. Choice of menu. Fire certificate. Visited by HRH Duke of Gloucester. Certificate of Merit in Come to Britain Award. Open all year.

---

⑤ Lane End Farm, Abney, Hathersage, via Sheffield, S30 1AA

Mrs Jill Salisbury
☎/Fax **01433 650371**
BB **From £16–£25**
Sleeps 6
☐☐☐☐
Listed *Highly
Commended*

Award-winning farmhouse on working hill farm above the Hope Valley. Tourist Board Bed & Breakfast of the Year – Commended. Share our enthusiasm for our lovely surroundings. Stunning views, off the beaten track, walks from the door. Traditional farmhouse, beautifully decorated. 3 bedrooms (1 en suite) with hot drink facilities, washbasins, CH. TV lounge. Hearty breakfasts. Own horse welcome. Farm nature trail. Open all year (closed Christmas).

Ley Fields Farm, Leek Road, Cheadle, Stoke-on-Trent, Staffordshire ST10 2EF

Mrs Kathryn Clowes
☎ 01538 752875
🅱 From £16–£17
EM From £8.50
Sleeps 6
�av ⅊ ♞
♥♥♥ *Applied*

Listed Georgian farmhouse amidst beautiful countryside with local walks offering abundant wildlife. Convenient for Alton Towers, Pottery museums and Peak District. Spacious, traditionally furnished accommodation includes guests' lounge and dining room. Luxury bedrooms with hot drink facilities, family suite, family en suite, double en suite. CH. Excellent home cooking and a warm welcome to our family home. Open all year except Christmas.

Middlehills Farm, Grange Mill, Matlock, Derbyshire DE4 4HY

Mrs Linda Lomas
☎/Fax 01629 650368
🅱 From £15
Sleeps 6
☡ ⅄ ⚓ ☗
♥♥ *Applied*

Five miles west of Matlock on the A5012, this small working farm with new limestone farmhouse and large garden is set amidst beautiful scenery. Ideal for touring Peak District, close to Chatsworth House, Dovedale and other places of interest. Spacious accommodation. All bedrooms with washbasins and tea/coffee facilities. Family rooms en suite. Visitors lounge with colour TV/pool table. Open all year.

The Old Bake & Brewhouse, Blackwell Hall, Blackwell in the Peak, Taddington, nr Buxton, Derbys SK17 9TQ

Mrs Christine Gregory
☎ 01298 85271
🅱 From £16–£17
Sleeps 4
☡ ⅄ ⅊ ⚓ ♞
♥♥ *Applied*

Early 18th century much loved farmhouse set in peaceful mature 2 acre garden. Footpath to lovely Cheedale Monsal Dale from our door. A warm welcome awaits you on our busy 300 acre dairy farm. Private oak beamed lounge/dining room furnished with antiques. Delicious traditional breakfasts or your own requirements. All rooms en suite with colour TV, tea/coffee-making facilities, CH. Open all year.

Wolfscote Grange Farm, Hartington, Nr Buxton, Derbyshire SK17 0AX

Jane Gibbs
☎ 01298 84342
🅱 From £16.50–£17
Sleeps 6
☡ ▦ ♞
Listed *Commended*

'Peaceful and away from it all' describes perfectly our 15th century farmstead nestling under Wolfscote Hill with beautiful views over the Dove Valley. 2 miles from pretty Hartington village. Always a warm welcome to our ancient farmhouse; spiral staircase, oak beams, mullion windows and comfortable antique furnishings. Guests' lounge, dining room, tea/coffee facilities. Breakfast then enjoy the views and explore the farm and many footpaths leading to the Dales below. Open all year.

Yew Tree Farm, North Rode, Congleton, Cheshire CW12 2PF

Mrs Sheila Kidd
☎ 01260 223569
🅱 From £16
EM £10
Sleeps 6
☡ ⅄ ⇐ ♞ ⚘ ♣
Listed *Commended*

You can be assured of a warm welcome, a cosy atmosphere and good food at this farm which is set in wooded parkland. Central for the Peak District, Potteries, Alton Towers and the historic houses of Cheshire. Guests are invited to look around the farm and are introduced to the animals which include a wide range of pets. One double en suite and two twin rooms. Open all year.

Please mention **Stay on a Farm** when booking

SELF-CATERING

---

(11) Archway Cottage, Lane End Farm, Abney, Hathersage, Via Sheffield, S30 1AA

Jill Salisbury
☎/Fax 01433 650371
[SC] From £140–£255
Sleeps 2/4
☼ 火 ◑ ☂ 木
ᕈ ᕈ ᕈ *Commended*

Beams, pine furniture, lovely decor make our well-equipped cottage a must for the discerning visitor to the Peak District. Tucked away on our working hill farm in a small hamlet. Superb views, many fabulous walks. Ideally situated for all Derbyshire attractions. 1 double bedroom, sofa bed in lounge. Linen, electricity included. No pets. Own horse welcome. Open all year.

---

(12) Chapelgate Cottage, c/o Lydgate Farm, Aldwark, Grange Mill, Matlock, Derbyshire DE4 4HW

Joy Lomas
☎ 01629 540250
[SC] From £200–£270
Sleeps 5 + cot
☼ 火
ᕈ ᕈ ᕈ ᕈ *Highly Commended*

Beautiful oak beamed, stone mullioned cottage with lovely views and garden, set in the peaceful hamlet of Aldwark. Well appointed open plan kitchen/living area with log fire and colour TV. Two bedrooms and bathroom/shower room. The cottage is centrally heated, double glazed and fully carpeted throughout. Towels, fresh linen and electricity are included. Chapelgate Cottage will give you a wonderful holiday in the heart of the Peak District. Open all year.

---

(13) Cote Bank Farm Cottages, Buxworth, Whaley Bridge, Derbyshire SK12 7NP

Pamela Broadhurst
☎ 01663 750566
[SC] From £140–£420
Sleeps 2/6 +cot
☼ 木
ᕈ ᕈ ᕈ ᕈ *Highly Commended*

Two warm, welcoming cottages on peaceful sheep farm with magnificent views and excellent walks. Chinley 1 mile, Buxton 7 miles. Children can feed the hens with farmer Nic and see happy animals reared naturally. Each cottage has 3 bedrooms (double, twin, bunks), lounge with logfire, TV and video, dining room, modern kitchen, full CH. 'Amongst the best farm cottages we know' – *Good Holiday Cottage Guide 1995*. Short breaks Nov–March. Open all year.

---

(14) Cruck Cottage, Wolfscote Grange Farm, Hartington, Nr Buxton, Derbyshire SK17 0AX

Jane Gibbs
☎ 01298 84342
[SC] From £140–£270
Sleeps 4 + cot
☼ 木 ☂ 木 ▮
ᕈ ᕈ ᕈ *Up to Highly Commended*

This fine old 15th century cottage is an ideal country hideaway, completely on its own overlooking Wolfscote and Berrisford Dales. No neighbours, only cows and sheep! Cosy and warm with massive beamed interior, galley, double plus one twin bedroom. Walled garden, many footpaths to explore that lead from the cottage to the limestone Dales below. Fully equipped, linen inclusive. Ring for details. Open all year.

---

(15) The Hayloft, Stanley House Farm, Great Hucklow, Derbyshire SK17 8RL

Margot Darcey
☎ 01298 871044
[SC] From £135
Sleeps 4
木 ☼(5) ✦ ◑ ☂ 木
ᕈ ᕈ ᕈ ᕈ *Highly Commended*

The accommodation is skilfully converted from the original hayloft and the interior is comfortably furnished, mainly with antiques. Comprises a lounge with open fire, colour TV and cottage suite, two twin-bedded rooms, kitchen/diner. The Hayloft offers an ideal centre for exploring the Peak District. All linen/towels at no extra charge. Electricity by 50p meter. Open all year.

Honeysuckle & Jasmine Cottages, Middlehills Farm, Grange Mill, Matlock, Derbyshire DE4 4HY

Linda Lomas
☎/Fax 01629 650368
[sc] From £120–£350
Sleeps 4/8
Applied

Enjoy a break in our comfortable, secluded 2/3-bedroomed cottages boasting stone mullions, wooden beams, fitted pine bedrooms and kitchens and beautiful oak parquet floors. Both cottages are superbly equipped, have full CH, double glazing and enclosed suntrap patios with magnificent views. Space for children, parking outside door, pub within walking distance. Heating, electricity, linen inclusive. Static caravan available. Open all year.

Limestone View Farm Cottage,   Limestone View Farm, Stoney Lane, Cauldon, Waterhouses, Staffs. ST10 3JP

Mrs Wendy Webster
☎ 01538 308288
[sc] From £100–£200
Sleeps 6+cot
🐴🐕
🦮🦮🦮 Commended

A warm welcome, fresh flowers, open fire and a tea tray await your arrival at Limestone View Cottage, on a typical Staffordshire dairy farm with sheep and poultry. Ideal holiday for two or a family any season, a place where guests keep returning. The cottage is comfortable and peaceful, overlooking open hay meadows; secluded from main roads, with pretty garden and large lawn. Unique pub nearby ideal on a winter's evening. Open all year.

Lower Berkhamsytch Farm, Bottom House, Nr Leek, Staffordshire ST13 7QP

Edith & Alwyn Mycock
☎ 01538 308213
[sc] From £100–£200
Sleeps 2/6 + cot
🐴🐕🦽 ■
🦮🦮🦮 Approved

Two self-contained flats converted from stone farm building on stock rearing farm. Each flat has its own private entrance and is within walking distance of 2 pubs serving meals. Lounge/diner with colour TV and double bed-settee. Well equipped kitchen area, 1 double bedroom, 1 twin, shower room with toilet and washbasin. Ideal for Alton Towers, Potteries, Peak District and moorland beauty spots. Electricity, heating, linen included. Open all year.

The Old Byre, Pye Ash Farm, Leek Road, Bosley, Macclesfield, Cheshire SK11 0PN

Dorothy Gilman
☎ 01260 273650
[sc] From £200–£400
Sleeps 10 + cot
🐕🦽
Applied

The Old Byre is near the Peak District and Staffordshire's moorlands. Shop and pubs are short walk away. In beautiful countryside farmed with beef and sheep. Many National Trust properties close by including Biddulph Grange Gardens. Alton Towers 15 miles. Ideal for two families. All heating, linen, etc inclusive. Open all year.

Old House Farm Cottage, Old House Farm, Newhaven, Hartington, Buxton, Derbyshire SK17 0DY

Sue Flower
☎ 01629 636268
[sc] From £150–£280
Sleeps 6 + cot
🐴🐕🐾 ■
🦮🦮🦮🦮 Commended

Charming cottage conversion on 400-acre working dairy/sheep farm in the heart of the Peak District. Opportunity to watch farm activities. Highly recommended accommodation with storage heaters and fitted carpets throughout, lounge/dining with colour TV, kitchen (electric cooker, fridge, microwave, washer and tumble dryer), bathroom with shower. 1 double bedroom, 1 family with twin beds and full size bunks both with H&C. Cot and highchair. Brochure. Open all year.

The Old Stables, Northfield Farm, Flash, Nr Buxton, Derbyshire SK17 0SW

David & Elizabeth Andrews
☎/Fax 01298 22543
[sc] From £80–£270
Sleeps 2/6
🐴🦽🐕🦓🦌
🦮🦮🦮 Commended

Situated in England's highest village. An ideal centre for outdoor activities or for the more leisurely holiday, close to the many attractions of the Peak Park and Potteries. The farm is also a BHS approved riding centre. Well-appointed flat with all facilities and CH. Linen and electricity inclusive. Games and laundry rooms. Ground floor flat suitable for the less able. Open all year.

22 Shatton Hall Farm Cottages, Bamford, Nr Sheffield, Derbyshire S30 2BG

Angela Kellie
☎/Fax 01433 620635
Sℂ From £150–£275
Sleeps 2/6 + cot
🐓 🐄 ⅍ 🎾 ⌨
🐾 🐾 🐾 *Up to Highly Commended*

Our comfortable, well equipped cottages are stone barn conversions around the Elizabethan farmstead in a peaceful setting. Streamside and woodland walks. Fishing, riding, cycle hire nearby. Each cottage has terrace/garden. Ample car parking. Open plan living room, open fires, CH, colour TV, well equipped kitchen. 2 double bedrooms, linen included. Put-u-up and cot available. Laundry facilities. Hard tennis court. Open all year.

23 Shaw Farm, New Mills, near Stockport, Derbyshire SK12 4QE

Mrs Nicky Burgess
☎ 0161 427 1841
Sℂ From £170–£320
Sleeps 8
🐄 🐓 🎾 🐎
🐾 🐾 🐾 *Commended*

Come and enjoy our working dairy farm. Stay in an old stone built farmhouse with lovely views. Entrance hall leads to fully equipped kitchen diner. Large beamed sitting room. Upstairs 2 bedrooms with third by prior arrangement. Full carpeting and central heating throughout. South facing, pleasant gardens. Pets by arrangement. Open all year.

LET THE TELEPHONE RING!

Some farmhouses are big places. Let the telephone ring long enough to give the owner time to answer it.

THOSE LITTLE EXTRAS

For advice on farms that can offer 'extras' such as four-poster beds, special diets, farm trails, fishing rights – even stabling and trekking arrangements if you are bringing your own horse – ring the Farm Holiday Bureau on (01203) 696909.

THE 1000+ BUREAU MEMBERS OFFER A UNIQUE LINK TO CUSTOMERS ACROSS THE UK

All Bureau members belong to a local Group. Each member can refer you to an equally high quality member within his Group… or across the UK: England, Northern Ireland, Scotland, Wales.

England's Heartland

Derbyshire Dales and Dovedale

Group Contacts: BB *Carl Postles* ☎ *01773 822328*
SC *Linda Adams* ☎ *01335 360352*

Discover the wealth of delights which makes this county of character and contrast the ideal choice for your short, or long, break destination. From the mellow lowlands of the south to the rugged peaks of the north – from picturesque villages to busy market towns – from historic houses and museums to the excitement of Alton Towers and the American Adventure – a warm and friendly welcome awaits you in every corner.

The countryside around the delightful old market town of Ashbourne, at the southern end of the Pennine Range in Derbyshire, is among the most beautiful in the whole of England. The spectacular scenery of Dovedale and the Manifold Valley, the rolling uplands with their scattered copses and stone walls and isolated traditional farmsteads are well known. Less dramatic but no less rewarding is the tranquil beauty of the unspoilt countryside and villages of the area.

Ashbourne itself is a small, historic country town of distinction, with shops, hotels, restaurants– its speciality Ashbourne gingerbread – a delight not to be missed!

Numerous footpaths provide ideal conditions for walking and there are ample facilities for pony trekking, cycle hire and fishing. Within easy access are many places of interest, great country mansions, the National Tramway Museum, Heritage Centres, Factory Shops, the Heights of Abraham and many more attractions for you to enjoy.

[Map showing the Derbyshire region with towns including New Mills, Knutsford, Chaple-en-le-Frith, Macclesfield, Buxton, Sheffield, Dronfield, Worksop, Chesterfield, Staveley, Bakewell, Bolsover, Warsop, Biddulph, Clay Cross, Kidsgrove, Leek, Matlock, Mansfield, Stoke-on-Trent, Wirksworth, Alfreton, Ashbourne, Ripley, Belper, Uttoxeter, Derby, Nottingham, Stafford, Burton-Upon-Trent, Ashby-De-La-Zouch. Roads shown include A6, A623, A537, A54, A53, A515, A6, A5012, A523, A52, A517, A50, A51, M6, A518, A41, A5, A513, A38, A444, A57, A1, A617, A6097, A52, A46, A606.]

BED AND BREAKFAST

(and evening meal)

---

① The Beeches Farmhouse, Waldley, Doveridge, Nr Ashbourne, Derbyshire DE6 5LR

Barbara Tunnicliffe
☎/Fax 01889 590288
🛏 From £23–£38.50
EM From £9.50
🐕 ♿ 🅿
♨ ♨ ♨ *Highly Commended*

Winners of top national award for farm based catering. Enjoy dining in our oak beamed licensed restaurant – after exploring the Derbyshire countryside or the thrills of Alton Towers. Ten rooms including excellent en suite family rooms which retain the character of our 18th century farmhouse. Children love feeding the animals on our working dairy farm. A warm welcome awaits you. Open all year except New Year.

---

② Chevin Green Farm, Chevin Road, Belper, Derbyshire DE56 2UN

Carl & Joan Postles
☎ 01773 822328
🛏 From £14–£20
Sleeps 12
🍴 🐕 ♿ 🔥
♨ ♨ *Commended*

Relax in peaceful picturesque countryside. Our extended and refurbished beamed farmhouse offers single, twin, double and family en suite rooms. Enjoy generous breakfasts. Guests own lounge and dining room. Within easy reach of Dales, Peak District, stately homes (6) and Alton Towers. Pleasant walks, riding and golf nearby. Reductions for children sharing and weekly terms. Open all year except Christmas.

---

③ Dannah Farm Country Guest House, Bowmans Lane, Shottle, Belper, Derbyshire DE56 2DR

Joan Slack
☎ 01773 550273/550630
Fax 01773 550590
🛏 From £27–£37.50
EM From £14.95
Sleeps 18
♿ 🐕 ♿ 🐖 🔥 🛍 ◎
♨ ♨ ♨ *Highly Commended*

Winners 1994 Best of Tourism award. Lovely Georgian farmhouse on mixed working farm. All rooms etc. Colour TVs, etc. 1992 & 93 national award farm catering. Fully licensed. AA Premier Selected, RAC Highly Acclaimed. Johansens recommended. Current fire certificate. Hopefully we have it all, from pot-bellied pigs to award-winning food and, above all, the warmest of welcomes! Open all year.

---

④ Denstone Hall Farm, Denstone, Uttoxeter, Staffordshire ST14 5HF

Mrs Joyce Boden
☎ 01889 590253
Fax 01889 590603
🛏 From £14–£16
Sleeps 6
🐕 ♿

Listed *Applied*

Stay on our dairy farm in the beautiful Churnet Valley. We are only ten minutes from Alton Towers and within easy reach of the Peak District and many stately homes. Absorb the rural atmosphere of market day at Ashbourne or Uttoxeter and visit the many pottery factory shops and museums. Trout fishing available. Open Mar–Nov.

---

⑤ Homefields, Dove Street, Ellastone, Ashbourne, Derbyshire DE6 2GY

Gillyan Prince
☎ 01335 324284/6
🛏 From £16–£18
Sleeps 6
🐕(3) 🍴 🍴
♨ ♨ *Highly Commended*

Tea and homemade cake await you at this delightful small holding on Derbyshire Stafordshire border close to Alton Towers, Dales and stately homes. Relax and watch TV, play piano or sit in beautiful garden overlooking fields. Sleeps 6 people. Walking distance to 2 pubs providing evening meals. Non smoking. No pets. Open Mar–Nov.

Manor House Farm, Prestwood, Denstone, Uttoxeter, Staffs ST14 5DD

Chris Ball
☎ 01889 590415
Fax 01335 342198
BB From £16–£24
Sleeps 6
🐎 ▪
🐌🐌 *Highly Commended*

A beautiful Grade II listed farmhouse set amid rolling hills and rivers. Three bedrooms, two with four-poster beds, tastefully furnished with antiques and traditional features including oak-beamed ceilings and an oak panelled breakfast room. Guests may relax in the extensive gardens with grass tennis court and Victorian summer house. Alton Towers 3 miles. Open all year except Christmas.

Mercaston Hall, Mercaston, Brailsford, Ashbourne, Derbyshire DE6 3BL

Angus & Vicki Haddon
☎ 01335 360263
BB From £15–£17.50
Sleeps 6
🐌(8) 🐎 🏃 🛏 🎋 ▪ 🍴
🐌🐌 *Applied*

Timber-framed, historic, listed building in a quiet countryside location. Situated off the A52 halfway between Derby and Ashbourne. An ideal centre for visits to the Peak District, many tourist attractions and the commercial towns and cities of the Midlands. Kedleston Hall (NT) 1 mile. Hard tennis court. Open all year except Christmas.

New Park Farm, Moorend, Bradley, Ashbourne, Derbyshire DE6 1LQ

Carol Akers
☎ 01335 343425
Fax 01335 300865
BB From £14–£20
EM From £10
Sleeps 12
👍 🍴 🐌 ▪
🐌🐌 *Highly Commended*

A very warm welcome to our comfortable farmhouse in quiet surroundings. Good home cooking with varied menu using wholesome local produce. Children can feed the hens and ducks, collect the eggs. Well situated for all Derbyshire attractions and beautiful countryside. We offer guests en suite double, twin, family rooms, guests' own lounge and dining room. Open all year except Christmas.

Park View Farm, Weston Underwood, Ashbourne, Derbyshire DE6 4PA

Mrs Linda Adams
☎ 01335 360352
BB From £19–£25
Sleeps 6
🍴 🐌 ▪
🐌🐌 *Highly Commended*

Enjoy country house hospitality in our elegant farmhouse set in large gardens with lovely views overlooking the National Trust's magnificent Kedleston Hall and Park, hence the farm's name. All rooms are beautifully furnished and have washbasins and tea/coffee-making facilities. Guests' own bathroom, shower room, sitting room and delightful dining room. Country pubs and restaurants close by. 1 twin and 2 doubles with antique four-poster beds.

Shirley Hall Farm, Shirley, Ashbourne, Derbyshire DE6 3AS

Mrs Sylvia Foster
☎ 01335 360346
BB From £15–£19
Sleeps 6
🍴 🐌(10) ☕ 🍴
🐌🐌 *Highly Commended*

Our 200-acre family-run dairy/arable/sheep farm 4 miles from Ashbourne has a lovely old, part moated, timbered farmhouse in peaceful countryside. Excellent walks and private coarse fishing. Many stately homes, the Dales, Alton Towers nearby. One twin with handbasins and guests' bathroom, 2 double bedrooms en suite. Guests' sitting room, TV, CH and drinks facilities all rooms. Superb English breakfasts. Local pubs, 1 within walking distance, for excellent evening meals. Open all year (closed Christmas).

Waldley Manor, Marston Montgomery, Nr Doveridge, Derbyshire DE6 5LR

Anita Whitfield
☎ 01889 590287
BB From £17–£18
Sleeps 6
🐎
🐌🐌 *Highly Commended*

A warm welcome awaits you in this delightful 16th century Manor farmhouse, with characteristic oak beamed rooms and inglenook fire. Come and help feed the animals and milk the cows on our working dairy and sheep farm, which is within easy reach of the Peak District. Traditional full English breakfast served every day. One family room en suite (double bed and bunk), 1 double en suite (double bed). Open all year except Christmas & New Year.

12 Yeldersley Old Hall Farm, Yeldersley Lane, Bradley, Ashbourne, Derbyshire DE6 1PH

Mrs Janet Hinds
☎ 01335 344504
BB From £15–£18.50
Sleeps 6

Listed *Commended*

Yeldersley Old Hall Farm is a family-run dairy farm of 70 acres. The Grade II listed farmhouse is situated in pleasant and quiet rural surroundings just 3 miles from the market town of Ashbourne and within easy reach of Dovedale, Alton Towers, Matlock and many stately homes. Farmhouse breakfast provided. Lounge with log fire. En suite rooms available. Non-smokers only please. Open Mar–Nov.

SELF-CATERING

13 Briar, Bluebell & Primrose Cottages, c/o Yeldersley Old Hall Farm, Yeldersley Lane, Bradley, Ashbourne, Derbyshire DE6 1PH

Mrs Janet Hinds
☎ 01335 344504
SC From £120–£275
Sleep 5/6

Commended

Situated on a working family dairy farm in rural surroundings, our Grade II listed barn has been converted into 3 self-catering cottages. Two accommodate 5 people (maximum), one 6 people. Each has three bedrooms with bathroom containing bath and shower, fitted kitchen, colour TV. Ample parking area. Ideal spot for touring Derbyshire. Ashbourne 3 miles. Short breaks. Open all year.

14 Chevin Green Farm, Chevin Road, Belper, Derbyshire DE56 2UN

Carl & Joan Postles
☎ 01773 822328
SC From £80–£295
Sleeps 4/6

Commended

Enjoy a holiday in one of our five attractive cottages of character overlooking picturesque countryside. The cottages with original beams are fully equipped to a high standard. Lounge, fully fitted kitchen, bathroom, 2 or 3 bedrooms, one is specially adapted for the disabled. Ideally situated for all places of interest, Alton Towers, Dales, Peak District and 6 stately homes. Open all year.

15 The Chop House, Windle Hill Farm, Sutton-on-the-hill, Ashbourne, Derbyshire DE6 5JH

K E & J Lennard
☎ 01283 732377
SC From £130–£350
Sleeps 6/8

Commended

The Chop House was originally built in 1858 as the farm corn shed, recently converted to offer comfortable, well-equipped accommodation. centrally heated, fully insulated, ideal for winter or summer lets. 3 twin bedrooms, kitchen/dining room, separate living room. Pleasant garden. Set amidst tranquil countryside south of Ashbourne, ideal base for touring Derbyshire and the Peak District. Open all year.

16 Hall Farm Bungalow, c/o Shirley Hall Farm, Shirley, Ashbourne, Derbyshire DE6 3AS
New House Farm & The Saddlery,

Mrs Sylvia Foster
☎ 01335 360346
SC From £120–£350
Sleeps 4/8

Up to Commended

Three superb properties at separate locations in unspoilt countryside 4 miles from Ashbourne. Bungalow near Shirley village, has 3 bedrooms, large garden, lovely views. Peacefully situated 18th century farmhouse at Mercaston has 4 bedrooms. The Saddlery is self-contained 1st floor barn conversion on our farm. All very well appointed. Private coarse fishing. Open all year.

Honeysuckle Cottage, c/o Park View Farm, Weston Underwood, Ashbourne, Derbyshire DE6 4PA (17)

Mrs Linda Adams
☎ **01335 360352**
SC **From £90–£350**
Sleeps 6 +cot
☼ ▪
✿ ✿ ✿ ✿ *Commended*

This is a truly delightful country cottage set in its own secluded garden with wonderful views over the Derbyshire countryside. Full of character and charm, furnished to a very high standard, with beamed sitting room, antique furnishings and pretty four poster bed. Accommodation for 6 persons in 3 bedrooms. Linen provided. Colour TV, automatic washing machine, tumble dryer and microwave

---

PRICES
Prices include VAT and service charge (if any) and are:
B&B per person per night
EM per person
SC per unit per week
Tents and caravans per pitch per night

GOOD
FOOD

Nearly all Bureau members now hold a certificate in Essential Food Hygiene.

FOLLOW THE COUNTRY CODE

Leave nothing but footprints,
Take nothing but photographs,
Kill nothing but time!

England's Heartland

Sherwood Forest/ Nottinghamshire

Group Contacts: 📠 *Sally Herrick* ☎ *01949 81733*
🆂🅲 *Janet Carr* ☎ *01623 861088*

Sherwood Forest is much smaller than it used to be, but near Edwinstowe you can still find Robin Hood, at the Sherwood Forest Visitor Centre where his story is told in a walk-through exhibition. There are also films, guided forest walks and other activities. Edwinstowe church is where Robin Hood is said to have married Maid Marion.

Worksop is a pleasant market town with a fine priory and 14th-century gatehouse. Retford has a small museum and some interesting Georgian buildings around its market square. The open-air markets at Newark and Mansfield are popular with visitors and each town has its local museums. Newark's parish church has a fine spire and interesting treasury but the nearby Minster at Southwell is on a larger scale even though Southwell, home of the Bramley apple, is hardly more than a village.

In Nottingham, Robin Hood's statue stands outside the castle which houses the city's fine arts museum, and there's a small Robin Hood exhibition at the gatehouse. At the foot of Castle Rock, beside the ancient Trip to Jerusalem Inn, is the Brewhouse Yard Museum illustrating the city's social history, while nearby the Canal Museum and the Museum of Costume and Textile show other aspects of the city's heritage. The Lace Centre, in an attractive timbered building, shows off a range of Nottingham's finest work, which you can buy as a souvenir.

BED AND BREAKFAST
(and evening meal)

Blue Barn Farm, Langwith, Mansfield, Nottinghamshire NG20 9JD

June Ibbotson
☎ 01623 742248
BB From £18–£20
Sleeps 6 cot
Commended

Welcome to our family-run 450-acre farm in peaceful surroundings on the edge of Sherwood Forest in Robin Hood country, 5 miles from M1 (J30) off A616. Many interesting places catering for all tastes only a short car journey away. Suitable for the business traveller, a place to unwind. 1 double, 1 twin en suite, 1 family, all with tea/coffee-making facilities and washbasins. Cot available. Dining room, lounge, TV. Open all year (closed Christmas Day & New Year).

Far Baulker Farm, Oxton, Nottinghamshire NG25 0RQ

Janette Esam
☎ 01623 882375
BB From £14–£18
Sleeps 6
Listed Commended

Far Baulker Farm is a 300-acre arable/livestock farm set in the heart of Sherwood Forest 10 miles north of Nottingham on the A614. One double en suite, one double with washbasin, one twin, tea/coffee-making facilities in all rooms. Visitors lounge with TV/video. A welcome awaits you in our family home. Open all year.

Forest Farm, Mansfield Road, Papplewick, Nottinghamshire NG15 8FL

Mrs E J Stubbs
☎ 0115 9632310
BB From £15–£18.50
Sleeps 5
Listed Commended

Forest Farm is located on the A60 standing well back up the farm road away from traffic noise. Pleasant views from south-facing rooms, 1 double en suite, 1 single, 1 twin, all with tea-making facilities. TV in lounge/dining room. Midway between Mansfield and Nottingham, and ideal touring or business base. Open all year (closed Dec).

Hall Farm House, Gonalston, Nottinghamshire NG14 7JA

Mr & Mrs R C Smith
☎ 0115 9663112
Fax 0115 9664844
BB From £20–£25
EM From £15
Sleeps 6
Commended

Charming 18th century farmhouse in one of Nottinghamshire's prettiest villages. Near the minster town of Southwell. Comfortable bedrooms overlook a lovely garden. Heated swimming pool, tennis court and games room; also aviary of exotic birds and flock of pedigree Suffolk sheep. By arrangement, Rosie your hostess will give you a generous dinner. No smoking in bedrooms. No pets. Open all year (closed Christmas & New Year).

Jerico Farm, Fosse Way, Nr Cotgrave, Nottinghamshire NG12 3HG

Mrs Sally Herrick
☎/Fax 01949 81733
BB From £16–£22
Sleeps 6
(5)
Commended

Jerico Farm offers warm, comfortable accommodation, surrounded by our own attractive farmland. Good firm beds and tea/coffee/chocolate-making facilities in all bedrooms, one en suite. Guests' own sitting room. Good pub food available nearby. Excellent location for visiting Nottingham, its universities, sports venues and tourist sites. Located down farm drive off A46, 1 mile north of A46/A606 junction, south of Cotgrave village. Open all year (closed Christmas).

---

6 Manor Farm, Moorhouse Road, Laxton, Newark, Nottinghamshire NG22 0NU

Mrs Pat Haigh
☎ 01777 870417
BB From £15–17
EM From £8
Sleeps 6
🐕 ♻ 🎎
Listed *Commended*

Manor Farm is a family-run dairy and arable farm of 137 acres, in the historic medieval village of Laxton, situated 10 miles north of Newark, and on the verge of the popular tourist area of Sherwood Forest in Nottinghamshire. 2 family rooms, 1 double room, tea/coffee-making facilities available. Visitors' lounge and dining room. Access to rooms at all times. Open all year (closed Christmas & New Year).

7 Norton Grange Farm, Norton, Cuckney, Mansfield, Nottinghamshire NG20 9LP

Fernie Palmer
☎ 01623 842666
BB From £16–£17
Sleeps 4
🐕 🎎 ♻ 🎎
☞ *Commended*

Norton Grange is a Grade II listed farmhouse set in the heart of the Welbeck Estate, part of the world-famous Sherwood Forest. Ideally situated for overnight stops or touring the very beautiful countryside and the many attractions, in Nottinghamshire and Derbyshire. One double room and one twin room, both with washbasin and tea/coffee-making facilities. Open all year except Christmas & New Year.

SELF-CATERING

8 Blue Barn Cottage, c/o Blue Barn Farm, Langwith, Mansfield, Nottinghamshire NG20 9JD

June Ibbotson
☎ 01623 742248
SC From £350–£375
Sleeps 8
🐕 🎎 💼
♻ ♻ ♻ ♻ *Commended*

Do come and relax in peace and comfort on our family-run farm in Robin Hood country. Visit quiet villages, stately homes rich in history, ramble through country parks or hunt bargains in thriving market towns. Blue Barn is off the A616 near Cuckney. 4 bedrooms, bathroom, breakfast kitchen, dining room, lounge, TV, washing machine and dryer. CH and linen included. Open all year.

9 Foliat Cottages, c/o Jordan Castle Farm, Wellow, Newark, Nottinghamshire NG22 0EL

Mrs Janet Carr
☎/Fax 01623 861088
SC From £180–£295
Sleeps 6 + cot
🐕 ✂ 💼
♻ ♻ ♻ ♻ *Commended*

Situated on the edge of Sherwood Forest, our recently renovated Edwardian cottages have beautiful pastoral views across our working family farm. Peaceful and cosy, with central heating, colour TV and washer/dryer. Each has 1 double and 2 twin bedrooms, with cot and highchair available. Enclosed south-facing gardens with patios. Linen provided. Brochure available. Open all year.

10 Honeysuckle Cottage, c/o Forest Farm, Mansfield Road, Papplewick, Nottinghamshire NG15 8FL

Mrs E J Stubbs
☎ 0115 9632310
SC From £200–£275
Sleeps 4/5
🐕 ✂
♻ ♻ ♻ *Approved*

400-acre arable farm near Mansfield, Nottingham and Sherwood Forest. Double room, twin room, extra fold up bed, bathroom, toilet upstairs; toilet, utility room, washing machine downstairs. Lounge with TV, dining room, fitted kitchen with microwave. Central heating, electricity, bed linen included. Regret no pets, no smoking. Open all year.

The Loft House, Criftin Farm, Epperstone, Nottingham, Nottinghamshire NG14 6AT

Jenny Esam
☎ **01159 652039**
🆂 **From £245–£285**
Sleeps 4
🛏 🍴 🔌 🐾
🔑 🔑 🔑 🔑 *Highly Commended*

17th century granary situated in the heart of Robin Hood Country, close to the historic towns of Southwell and Nottingham and all the stately homes around. Woodland walks behind farm, 4 golf courses and water sports centre close by. Central heating, colour TV, washer/dryer. Two twin bedded rooms, each with own bathroom. Heated swimming pool May–Sept, snooker room, barbecue all in a walled garden. Open all year.

Top House Farm, Lamins Lane, Mansfield Road, Arnold, Nottingham, Nottinghamshire NG5 8PH   ⑫

Mrs Ann Lamin
☎ **0115 9268330**
🆂 **From £200–£250**
Sleeps 3/4
🐾 🍴 🐕
Applied

Charming granary flat with beams, open fireplace, CH. Lounge has colour TV, patio doors onto garden. Kitchen has electric and microwave ovens, use of automatic washer and dryer. Within easy reach of Nottingham, Newstead Abbey, Southwell Minster, the Dukeries, Sherwood Forest, Derbyshire and the National Watersports Centre. Open all year.

FINDING YOUR ACCOMMODATION

The Group contacts at the beginning of each section can always help you find a vacancy in your chosen area.

CONFIRM BOOKINGS

Disappointments can arise from misunderstandings over the telephone.
Please write to confirm your booking.

England's Heartland
Shrewsbury, Ironbridge & Shropshire

Group Contacts: *Mrs Janet Jones* ☎ *01939 220223*

Shropshire with its wealth of Historic Houses, Castles and Abbeys, is the largest landbound county. Medieval Shrewsbury the county town, and up to date Telford are the principle town. With attractive market towns scattered around, leaving miles of unspoilt countryside to explore.

Don't miss Shrewsbury with it's historic buildings, passages and Castle. Famous for books and TV series about a medieval monk by Ellis Peters.

Ironbridge Gorge Museums and the world famous Iron Bridge, make this World Heritage site a must.

Hawkstone Park with its woodland fantasy of castles, cliffs and caves restored and open to the public for the first time in over 100 years.

Being so large the county caters for every need, with its own lake district at Ellesmere, hill country of South Shropshire. The Llangollen canal winding its way along and the Severn Valley Steam Railway at Bridgnorth to name but a few.

For the sports people: famous golf courses, fishing, horse riding and gliding.

Shropshire offers so much for everyone, seeing is believing!!!

BED AND BREAKFAST
(and evening meal)

Bradeley Green Farm, Tarporley Road, Whitchurch, Shropshire SY13 4HD

Ruth Mulliner
☎ **01948 663442**
[BB] **From £18–£21**
EM From £8.50
Sleeps 6
🦮 🐓 ⚰ 🎠 ⬛
♨ ♨ ♨ *Commended*

Our 180-acre family-run dairy farm is located on a main north/south route (A49) set across Shropshire/Cheshire border and only 2 miles from Wales. Wild waterfowl breeding centre with extensive water gardens and many varieties of ducks and geese for you to enjoy. Our spacious farmhouse offers very comfortable accommodation. CH, open fires and en suite facilities. Open all year (closed Christmas and New Year).

Church Farm, Wrockwardine, Wellington, Telford, Shropshire TF6 5DG

Mrs Jo Savage
☎ **01952 244917**
[BB] **From £20–£25**
EM From £15
Sleeps 8
🐓 🦮(10) ♿ 🈳 🎠 ⬛
♨ ♨ ♨ *Highly Commended*

Sit back and relax in our Georgian village farmhouse with oak beams and log fires. Built on the site of 12th century manor with sandstone foundations revealed in the attractive garden. We have lovely bedrooms with colour TVs and tea/coffee/chocolate trays. Delicious breakfasts, traditional dinners and puds! Near Shrewsbury and Ironbridge, 1 mile A5 and M54. Brochure available. Open all year.

Grove Farm, Preston Brockhurst, Shrewsbury, Shropshire SY4 5QA

Mrs Janet Jones
☎ **01939 220223**
[BB] **From £16–£20**
Sleeps 5
⚰ 🦮
♨ *Commended*

Step into Shropshire and enjoy quality accommodation and fine home cooking using local produce. Our 322-acre farm is set in a small village 7 miles north of Shrewsbury on the A49. The 17th Century house is traditionally furnished and offers warmth and comfort after the day's activities. Ideally situated for Ironbridge Heritage, Shrewsbury, Chester, Potteries and Wales. Brochures available. Open Jan–Nov.

Lane End Farm, Chetwynd, Newport, Shropshire TF10 8BN

Mrs Janice Park
☎ **01952 550337**
[BB] **From £18–£20**
EM from £9.50
Sleeps 4
🦮 🐓 ⬛
♨ ♨ *Commended*

Be sure of a warm welcome at our interesting period farmhouse set amidst lovely countryside. Bedrooms with en suite facilities. Good woodland walks nearby. Located on A41 just 2 miles North of Newport; ideal touring location for visiting Ironbridge, Weston Park, Cosford, The Wrekin, Potteries, Chester, etc. We keep pedigree Suffolk and Rouge sheep – see the lambs in spring! Open all year.

Mickley House, Faulsgreen, Tern Hill, Market Drayton, Shropshire TF9 3QW

Mrs Pauline Williamson
☎ **01630 638505**
[BB] **From £18–£25**
Sleeps 6
🦮 ⚰ ♿ ☕ 🐓 ♨ ⬛
♨ ♨ *Highly Commended*

When visiting Ironbridge, Shrewsbury, Chester, enjoy the comfort of this tastefully refurbished Victorian farmhouse with its oak beams, doors, interesting fire places. Pretty garden with birds singing as you meander through pergolas to pools and trickling waterfall. Spacious en suite bedrooms, all facilities, some ground floor. Master bedroom with Louis XIV king-size bed. Closed Christmas.

---

6 **Mill House,** Higher Wych, Malpas, Cheshire SY14 7JR

Chris & Angela Smith
☎ 01948 780362
Fax 01948 780566
▣ From £16
EM From £8
Sleeps 4
⊛ ☇ ℀

☙☙☙ *Highly Commended*

Modernised Mill House on the Cheshire/Clwyd border in a quiet valley, convenient for visiting Chester, Shrewsbury and North Wales. The house is centrally heated and has an open log fire in the lounge. Bedrooms have washbasins, radios and tea-making facilities. 1 bedroom has an en suite shower and WC. Reductions for children and senior citizens. Open Jan–Nov.

---

7 **Oulton House Farm,** Norbury, Nr Stafford, Staffordshire ST20 0PG

Mrs Judy Palmer
☎ 01785 284264
▣ From £18.50
Sleeps 6
☇ ℀ ▦

☙☙ *Highly Commended*

A 300-acre dairy farm situated on the Shropshire/Staffordshire border. Our large Victorian farmhouse offers warm, comfortable and well appointed en suite bedrooms, all with tea tray and TV. From your peaceful, rural base discover our many local attractions from the heritage of Ironbridge Gorge, the splendours of Shugborough to the bargains of the Potteries factory shops. Many local pubs and restaurants. Peace and quiet guaranteed. Open all year.

---

8 **Red House Farm,** Longdon on Tern, Wellington, Telford, Shropshire TF6 6LE

Mrs Mary Jones
☎ 01952 770245
▣ From £17
Sleeps 6
☇ ℀

☙☙ *Commended*

Our Victorian farmhouse is on a mixed farm. 2 double bedrooms have private facilities within 1 family room with separate bathroom, all large and comfortable. Excellent breakfast. Farm easily located, leave M54 (J6), follow A442, take B5063. Central for historic Shrewsbury, Ironbridge Gorge museums or modern Telford. Several local eating places. Open all year.

---

9 **The Sett Village Farm,** Stanton-upon-Hine Heath, Shrewsbury, Shropshire SY4 4LR

Brenda & Jim Grundey
☎ 01939 250391
▣ From £22
EM From £14
Sleeps 6
℀ ⅍ ☇ ▦ ℀ ▪

☙☙☙ *Highly Commended*

Full of dried flowers, our lovely farmhouse offers a warm and friendly welcome for your stay in Shropshire. Step into the countryside, relax and enjoy the delights of Shrewsbury, Hawkstone Park Follies, Ironbridge, The Potteries, Chester, Wales and so much more. Go on enjoy yourselves! 3 double rooms en suite, Tea and coffee. Full central heating. P.S. Smiles will be returned. Open all year (closed Christmas and New Year).

---

10 **Soulton Hall,** near Wem, Shropshire SY4 5RS

Ann Ashton
☎ 01939 232786
Fax 01939 234097
▣ From £23.50–£29.50
EM From £15
Sleeps 10
☇ ℀ ⅍ ⅍ ℀ ▪ ℀

☙☙☙ *Commended*

Sample English country life in an Elizabethan manor house offering very relaxing holiday. Bird watching, fishing, riding. Good food, home produce where possible, super meals. Walled garden. Licensed bar. Direct dial telephones. We welcome you. Open all year.

---

11 **Stoke Manor,** Stoke-on-Tern, Market Drayton, Shropshire TF9 2DU

Mike & Julia Thomas
☎ 01630 685222
Fax 01630 685666
▣ From £20–£25
Sleeps 6
☇(5) ℀ ℀ ▪

☙☙ *Highly Commended*

Come and experience the peace and quiet of the countryside. We offer quality accommodation, all bedrooms having bathrooms, hospitality trays and colour TV. No smoking in bedrooms. Comfortable drawing room and cellar bar for relaxing in the evening. Ideal for visiting Shropshire's many attractions, the Wedgwood Museum and Chester. Abundance of good eating places nearby. AA QQQQ. Open Jan–Nov.

Upper Brompton Farm, Cross Houses, Shrewsbury, Shropshire SY5 6LE

Mrs Christine Roberts
☎ **01743 761629**
BB **From £22**
EM from £15
Sleeps 6
ᗌ ★ ⅍ ☞
🐝 🐝 *Commended*

Elegant Georgian farmhouse set in 315 acres. Relaxed, friendly atmosphere, comfortable accommodation, delicious home cooking and a haven of peace and tranquillity. Spacious four-poster bedrooms with en suite have beverage trays and colour TV's. Large guests lounge with log fire on cool evenings. 400 yards from River Severn – fishing permits available. Shrewsbury 4 miles, Ironbridge 9 miles. Open all year except Christmas.

Willow House, Shrewsbury Road, Tern Hill, Market Drayton, Shropshire TF9 3PX

Mrs Moira Roberts
☎ **01630 638326**
BB **From £15–£16**
Sleeps 4
ᗌ ★ ⅍
Listed *Commended*

A warm and friendly welcome awaits you at our modern farmhouse with 1 double, 1 twin room and guests' own bathroom/shower. Both rooms have hot drink facilities. Guests have a separate lounge with colour TV. A good base for touring Shropshire, Cheshire, Staffordshire and local attractions of Ironbridge, Hodnet gardens, Hawkstone Follies and the Potteries. Open all year.

SELF-CATERING

Bradeley Green Cottage, Tarporley Road, Whitchurch, Shropshire SY13 4HD

Ruth Mulliner
☎ **01948 663442**
SC **From £90–£160**
Sleeps 4
ᗌ ★ ♨ ▟
ᕱ ᕱ ᕱ *Commended*

One of two cottages in country lane with lovely views. Good parking. Kitchen, diner, electric cooker and fridge, comfortable sitting room with colour TV and open fire. Logs provided (when available). Two bedrooms (twin & double), all bedding, towels are provided. Electricity by 50p meter. Bathroom with bath and shower. Ten minute walk for pub grub at the Willey Moor Lock on canal, set in open fields. Open all year.

The Granary, c/o Mill House, Higher Wych, Malpas, Cheshire SY14 7JR

Chris & Angela Smith
☎ **01948 780362**
Fax 01948 780566
SC **From £75–£145**
Sleeps 4/5 + cot
ᗌ ⅍
ᕱ ᕱ ᕱ *Commended*

The Granary is a self-contained bungalow adjacent to Mill House. Sleeps 4/5 in 2 double bedrooms, kitchen/living area, shower and WC. TV. CH. Cot and babysitting available. Situated in a quiet valley with a small stream in the garden. Convenient for visiting Chester, Shrewsbury and North Wales. Open all year.

Swallows Nest, Oulton House Farm, Norbury, Nr Stafford, Staffordshire ST20 0PG

Mrs Judy Palmer
☎ **01785 284264**
SC **From £100–£210**
Sleeps 4 + cot
ᗌ ♨ ▟
Applied

Swallows Nest has been designed with the comfort of our guests in mind. We think it is special. It is self-contained, fully equipped and all inclusive. An ideal base for a relaxing holiday: patchwork quilts, pine, pot pourri, peace and quite – perfect. See why the swallows return! Open all year.

England's Heartland

South Shropshire

Group Contact: *Mrs C Price* ☎ *01547 530249*

In an area of outstanding natural beauty, South Shropshire is full of contrasts; secluded and peaceful with rolling hills, high moorland and wooded valleys.

Shrewsbury lies in a loop of the River Severn and is entered by the English bridge or Welsh bridge and holds the keys to the mysteries of Brother Cadfael, benedictine monk of Shrewsbury Abbey.

Ironbridge, birthplace of the Industrial Revolution has six separate museums including the famous Blists Hill Open Air Museum where craftsmen link bygone times to the present day.

The river flows South, passing through Bridgnorth. Here the Severn Valley Railway steams 16 miles along the valley through Bewdley and onto Kidderminster.

Ludlow, premier town of the Marches is the perfect historic town and the large ruined castle stands high above the River Teme and is the venue for an open air Shakespearian play each year. Along the Marches are many fortifications of which Stokesay Castle is a unique example of a fortified manor house.

South East Shropshire is dominated by the Limestone ridge of the Wenlock Edge described by the poet A E housman in 'A Shropshire Lad'. Beneath this ridge the rich valley of Corvedale leads to the small market towns of Craven Arms and Church Stretton. Sheep farming country lies to the West with spectacular scenery on the Long Mynd Hills. Further west are the rugged outcrops of the Stiperstones and beyond them Bishops Castle and the hills of Clun Forest. Here Offa's Dyke, an ancient earthwork divides England from Wales.

With this varied landscape seek out the wild places of South Shropshire. It's reputation as excellent walking country is growing and will suit all abilities – from gentle strolling to a full days ramble.

BED AND BREAKFAST
(and evening meal)

Acton Scott Farm, Church Stretton, Shropshire SY6 6QN

Mary Jones
☎ **01694 781260**
🛏 **From £14–£22**
Sleeps 6
🖫 ⛺ ⅄ 🐾 🔥
⚘ ⚘ *Commended*

Situated in an area of outstanding natural beauty, the lovely old farmhouse has comfortable and spacious bedrooms, all with H & C, en suite available. There is a popular Working Farm Museum in Acton Scott. The spectacular Long Mynd Hills and the valleys of Church Stretton are nearby. Central for visiting Shrewsbury, Ludlow and Ironbridge. We look forward to welcoming you. Open mid Feb – mid Nov.

Billingsley Hall Farm, Covert Lane, Billingsley, Bridgnorth, Shropshire WV16 6PJ

Mrs Helen Sedgley
☎ **01746 861877**
🛏 **From £15–£18**
Sleeps 6 + cot
🖫 ⛺ ⅄ 🧍 🐾 🔥 ⚒
Listed *Commended*

We welcome you to spacious accommodation on a 260-acre working farm with sheep, suckler cows and arable crops. We offer 2 double/family bedrooms, 1 twin room with guests' bathroom. Lounge with log fire, dining room. Guests can follow the many walks around the woods and farmland. Situated 6 miles from Bridgnorth on B4363 to Cleobury Mortimer road, ideal base for local attractions. Also luxury self-catering. Open all year.

Castle Farm, Cheney Longville, Craven Arms, Shropshire SY7 8DR

Mrs Varny Jones
☎ **01588 673255**
🛏 **From £15**
Sleeps 5
🖫 ⛺ 🔥
Listed *Applied*

Castle Farm is steeped in history. First built in the 9th century, and rebuilt in the 13th century, it stands in its own courtyard surrounded by many ancient buildings. Close to Stokesay, Ludlow and Powys Castle, our farm is ideal for a walking holiday over Offa's Dyke or the Long Mynd. One family and one double room. Peace and quiet in abundance. Open Mar–Nov.

Court Farm, Gretton, Church Stretton, Shropshire SY6 7HU

Mrs Barbara Norris
☎ **01694 771219**
🛏 **From £19–£24**
EM £12
Sleeps 6
⅄ 🔥
⚘ ⚘ ⚘
Highly Commended

Stone Tudor farmhouse on 325-acre arable stock farm in peaceful countryside, 1 mile off B4371, equal distance to Ludlow, Shrewsbury, Bridgnorth, Ironbridge. Spacious rooms, inglenook fireplace, full CH. 2 twin rooms, 1 double, all en suite with TV, shaving points and tea/coffee. Furnished to high standard. Warm welcome and high quality cuisine using home produce whenever possible. Midweek breaks available. Open all year.

The Hall, Bucknell, Shropshire SY7 0AA

Mrs Christine Price
☎ **01547 530249**
🛏 **From £16**
EM £9
Sleeps 6
⅄ 🐾(7)
⚘ ⚘ *Commended*

The Hall is a working farm with spacious Georgian farmhouse and peaceful garden to relax in, after a day walking or exploring the Welsh Borderland with its historic towns and castles, also the black and white villages of North Herefordshire. Guest lounge, 1 twin en suite, 2 double with washbasins, shaving points. Colour TV and tea-making facilities. Open Mar–Nov.

---

6 Hurst Mill Farm, Clun, Craven Arms, Shropshire SY7 0JA

Joyce Williams
☎ 01588 640224
[BB] From £16–£17
EM From £7
Sleeps 6
🛏🧍🅿♿🚲🐕🍴
🐾 *Applied*

Winner of "Shropshire Farm Breakfast Challenge". A warm welcome to this working farm where the "kettle's always on". Well appointed bedrooms, double en suite. Riverside farmhouse and spacious gardens. Nestling in the delightful Clun Valley, between historic Clun and Clunton. Woodland and hills on either side. Two quiet riding ponies, kingfishers and herons. Pets welcome. Log fires. Also 2 luxury cottages. AA QQQ recommended. Open all year.

7 Llanhedric, Clun, Craven Arms, Shropshire SY7 8NG

Mrs Mary Jones
☎ 01588 640203
[BB] From £15–£17
EM From £7.50
Sleeps 6
🛏🚭🍴
Listed *Commended*

A friendly atmosphere and good food await you in this characteristic old farmhouse with spacious accommodation. Large gardens and lawns overlook the picturesque Clun Valley, surrounded by its hills. Near the Welsh border and Offa's Dyke. Ideal for walking or exploring the many places of historical interest, including Ludlow and Shrewsbury. Guest lounge with inglenook fireplace and oak beams. Tea/coffee facilities. Open Mar–Nov.

8 Lowe Farm, Alveley, Nr Bridgnorth, Shropshire WV15 6HX

Patricia Lawley
☎ 01299 861206
[BB] From £14–15
EM From £8
Sleeps 6
🛏🧍🅿🐕🍴
Listed *Commended*

Lowe Farm is a peaceful, friendly working farm situated just off the Bridgnorth-Kidderminster A442 road. The farmhouse is Victorian. Guests have their own dining room and lounge with colour TV, log fires and central heating. Ideal for Severn Valley Railway and Ironbridge Museums. 1 family, 1 twin bedded room (both with washbasins). Open all year.

9 New House Farm, Clun, Shropshire SY7 8NJ

Miriam Ellison
☎ 01588 638314
[BB] From £18–£21
EM From £9.50
Sleeps 6
🧍🛏🚭🅿🍴
🐾🐾 *Highly Commended*

Peaceful isolated 18th century farmhouse high in Clun hills near Welsh border. Walks from doorstep include Offa's Dyke and Shropshire Way. Large bedrooms furnished to high standard with scenic views. Tea/coffee-making, TV. Home cooking. 'New House Farm provides a family welcome and a standard of comfort which a grand hotel would find difficult to match' *Birmingham Evening Post*. Open March–Nov.

10 Seifton Court Farm, Culmington, Ludlow, Shropshire SY8 2DG

Mrs Valerie Humphreys
☎ 01584 861214
[BB] From £18–£25
EM From £12
Sleeps 6
🧍🛏🅿
🐾🐾 *Commended*

We invite you to relax in the warm, friendly atmosphere of Seifton Court situated in the Corvedale near Ironbridge. Excellent centre for touring South Shropshire and the Welsh borders. Nearby amenities include Ludlow golf course and racecourse, fishing, cycling and walking. All rooms en suite. Residents' lounge, licensed. Open all year.

11 Strefford Hall Farm, Strefford, Craven Arms, Shropshire SY7 8DE

Mrs Caroline Morgan
☎ 01588 672383
[BB] From £17–£19
Sleeps 6
🚭🛏🍴
🐾🐾 *Commended*

Set in an Area of Outstanding Natural Beauty in the quiet hamlet of Strefford, against the wooded backdrop of the Wenlock Edge and with uninterrupted views of the Long Mynd and Church Stretton hills. Spacious accommodation in 2 doubles, 1 twin (all with private bathrooms) with tea/coffee and colour TV. Full English breakfast, special diets catered for. Non smoking household. Closed Christmas and New Year.

SELF-CATERING

Billingsley Hall Farm, Covert Lane, Billingsley, Bridgnorth, Shropshire WV16 6PJ

Mrs Helen Sedgley
☎ 01746 861877
🆂🅲 From £150–£220
Sleeps 6
🛏 🐎 ⚒ 🏕 🚗 🐕 🎣
🐾 🐾 🐾 🐾
Highly Commended

The Granary provides luxury accommodation for 4/5 people in spacious oak beamed rooms – a central feature of main bedroom. Fully carpeted and heated throughout. Modern fitted kitchen including washing machine. Guests can follow walks around the farm. Pets welcome. Children catered for. Within easy reach many local attractions. Open all year.

DISABLED VISITORS

Many members offer a welcome to disabled/less able visitors. Please do check the extent of the facilities before booking.

THE 1000+ BUREAU MEMBERS OFFER A UNIQUE LINK TO CUSTOMERS ACROSS THE UK

All Bureau members belong to a local Group. Each member can refer you to an equally high quality member within his Group… or across the UK: England, Northern Ireland, Scotland, Wales.

THOSE LITTLE EXTRAS

For advice on farms that can offer 'extras' such as four-poster beds, special diets, farm trails, fishing rights – even stabling and trekking arrangements if you are bringing your own horse – ring the Farm Holiday Bureau on (01203) 696909.

England's Heartland
Herefordshire

Group Contacts: BB *Elizabeth Godsall* ☎ *01531 670408*
SC *Judy Wells* ☎ *01568 797347*

Herefordshire is a land of red earth, green meadows, quiet woods, streams and pretty black and white villages. This is the home of the world famous red and white Herefordshire cattle and a well-known centre for cidermaking. In the south are the spectacular gorges of the River Wye and the lovely woodland trails of the Forest of Dean; westward lies the tranquil Golden Valley leading into Offa's Dyke. To the east, Elgar country rises to the Malvern Hills with the finest ridge walk in England.

Herefordshire is rich in history and within reasonable travelling distance of the Black Mountains, Brecon Beacons and Elan Valley in Wales and the Clee Hills, Carding Mill Valley, Long Mynd and Wenlock Edge in South Shropshire. The county itself has a range of sights that span every period in British history from Iron Age hill forts, Roman remains, Norman castles and mediaeval manor houses to stately homes and their gardens and heritage museums. In the village of Kilpeck there are renowned 12th-century Herefordshire carvings and pagan Celtic figures.

You may also like to wander through the many street markets of the county. Hay-on-Wye is famous for its secondhand bookshops and Hereford is the home of a very large cattle market on Wednesdays.

BED AND BREAKFAST

(and evening meal)

Aberhall Farm, St Owens Cross, Ross-on-Wye, Hereford, Herefordshire HR2 8LL

Freda Davies
☎ 01989 730256
BB From £16.50–£17.50
Sleeps 6
⌇ ☙(10) ⚘ ◎
♨ *Commended*

A quiet, secluded spot 200 yards off B4521. Relax in our 17th century farmhouse with lovely views of rolling countryside. We offer 1 twin, 1 double (en suite), 1 single, vanity units, tea/coffee-making facilities, CH, guests' own bathroom and toilet, lounge and dining room. Games room, tennis court. Excellent cuisine. 'Home from home'. Large garden. AA Rec. Open all year (closed Christmas).

The Barn Farm, Leinthall Starkes, Ludlow, Shropshire SY8 2HP

Sylvia Price
☎ 01568 770388
BB From £16–£19
EM £12.50
Sleeps 6
☙ ♈
♨ *Applied*

A warm welcome, comfort and a relaxed atmosphere await you. Our traditional mixed farm is 5 miles west of Ludlow. Cosy bedrooms, 2 double en suite, tea trays. Meals served in our conservatory dining room. Special diets. Guests' own sitting room.

Grafton Villa Farm, Grafton, Hereford, Herefordshire HR2 8ED

Jennie Layton
☎ 01432 268689
BB From £17–£19
Sleeps 6
♈ ☙ ⌇ ⚘
♨ *Highly Commended*

A farmhouse of great character and warmth set in an acre of beautiful lawns and gardens amidst the picturesque Wye Valley. Beautiful fabrics and antiques throughout, charming, peaceful en suite bedrooms with, TV and drinks tray. Guests' private bathroom or en suite. We offer our guests a relaxing holiday on a 'real farm', enjoying a sumptuous breakfast with farmhouse portions. Open Feb–Nov.

Haynall Villa, Little Hereford, Nr Ludlow, Shropshire SY8 4BG

Mrs Rachel Edwards
☎ 01584 711589
BB From £16–£22
EM From £12
Sleeps 6
♈ ☙(6) ⌇ ▪
♨ *Commended*

1820s farmhouse nestling in Teme Valley 6m from historic Ludlow, ¾ from A456. Spacious bedrooms (1 en suite) offer comfort, views to 3 counties, vanity units, tea/coffee-making facilities. Guests' bathroom. Delicious farmhouse fayre (vegetarian and special diets). Relax in lounge with TV or attractive garden. Featured in Daily Telegraph. Open all year except Christmas.

The Hills Farm, Leysters, Leominster, Herefordshire HR6 0HP

Jane Conolly
☎ 01568 750205
BB From £20–£23
EM £15
Sleeps 10
♈ ⌇ ⊞
♨ *Highly Commended*

Escape to tranquillity. Breathtaking views from lovely old house. Scrumptious food including vegetarian. Delightful en suite bedrooms, one a gem of a barn conversion. Every comfort. All this for your delectation amidst superb countryside. Brochure. Open Feb–Nov.

6 **Hill Top Farm,** Wormsley, Hereford, Herefordshire HR4 8LZ

Mr & Mrs P Jennings
☎ 01981 590246
BB From £15–£17.50
Sleeps 5
🐕 🐈 ⅍ 🧍 🐎 🌳
🌼 *Commended*

A working farm offering real peace and relaxation. Glorious views in all directions. The character farmhouse is fully modernised with rooms en suite or with private bathroom. Tea/coffee facilities. An abundance of flora and fauna and many walks and sports facilities locally, including golf. Our friendly welcome and personal attention will make your stay a delight. Open all year except Christmas.

7 **Holgate Farm,** Kingsland, Leominster, Herefordshire HR6 9QS

Mrs Jenny Davies
☎ 01568 708275
BB From £15–£17
EM From £10 (optional)
Sleeps 4
⅍ 🐕 🌳
Listed *Commended*

Set amidst the beautiful North Herefordshire countryside on a family-run stock and arable farm, this attractive 17th century farmhouse offers a warm, friendly welcome. Within easy reach of the Welsh border country, Hereford, Leominster and Ludlow. Spaciously appointed bedrooms with tea and coffee trays. Guests' own bathroom and sitting room. Open all year except Christmas.

8 **Home Farm,** Bircher, Nr Leominster, Herefordshire HR6 0AX

Doreen Cadwallader
☎ 01568 780525
BB From £16–£20
Sleeps 6
🐕 🐓 ⅍ 🧍 🐎
🌼 *Commended*

We welcome you to a traditional livestock farm offering you excellent service and accommodation. Set in a peaceful, secluded area on the Welsh Border, it's 4 miles north of Leominster, 7 miles south of Ludlow, and close to Croft Castle, Berrington Hall and other attractions. All rooms have tea/coffee-making facilities. TV and washbasins. Light evening meals by request. Open Feb–Nov.

9 **Knockerhill Farm,** Callow, Herefordshire HR2 8BP

Beryl Davies
☎ 01432 268460
BB From £16.50–£18
Sleeps 4
🐕(8) ⅍ 🌳
🌼🌼 *Commended*

Situated 3 miles from Hereford, 1,000 yds off A49. The house is of great charm with tasteful antiques and impressive entrance hall, set in beautiful gardens with large croquet lawn. Double en suite, twin with private adjoining bathroom. Both fitted with basins tea/coffee making facilities, colour TV, etc. A welcome awaits with a pot of tea served in lounge or sun room. We also have an antique farm kitchen which visitors may view by request. No smoking. Open all year.

10 **Moor Court Farm,** Stretton Grandison, Nr Ledbury, Herefordshire HR8 2TR

Elizabeth Godsall
☎ 01531 670408
BB From £16
EM From £12.50
Sleeps 6
🐕 ⅍ 🌳 🐎
🌼🌼🌼 *Applied*

Relax and enjoy our beautiful 15th century timber-framed farmhouse with adjoining oast houses in a peaceful location. It's a traditional working Herefordshire hop and livestock farm, in scenic countryside central to the major market towns. Easy access to the Malverns, Wye Valley and Welsh borders. Spacious bedrooms, en suite or private bathroom, tea/coffee-making facilities. Oak beamed lounge and dining room. Open all year.

11 **New House Farm,** Much Marcle, Ledbury, Herefordshire HR8 2PH

Mrs Anne Jordan
☎ 01531 660604
BB From £15
EM From £10
Sleeps 4
🐕(6) 🐓 🐎 🐎
🌼 *Approved*

A friendly welcome awaits you at our delightful farmhouse enjoying panoramic views over Herefordshire, Worcestershire and Gloucestershire. Relax by a log fire on chilly evenings, or enjoy a swim in our outdoor pool during summer. We also welcome horses, for which a full livery service is provided. Open all year.

Old Court Farm, Bredwardine, Herefordshire HR3 6BT   12

Sue Whittall
☎ 01981 500375
Mobile 0421 424575
[BB] From £18–£22
EM From £13.50
Sleeps 4
🐴 ⅍ 🐕 🎠 ▪ 🎾
🛶 *Applied*

Old Court is a 14th century mediaeval manor situated on the banks of the River Wye. Ideal for the Wye Valley Walk. It has been carefully restored to preserve a wealth of beams and a 15ft fireplace. Gardens enjoy beautiful views to the river. There are 2 four-poster bedrooms, 2 en suite. Teamakers provided. Also evening meals and picnics. Phone for opening times.

Sink Green Farm, Rotherwas, Hereford HR2 6LE   13

David Jones
☎ 01432 870223
[BB] From £18–£23
Sleeps 6
🐴 ⅍ 🐕 ▪
🛶🛶 *Commended*

Sink Green awaits you with a warm, friendly welcome to its 16th century farmhouse overlooking the River Wye and picturesque Herefordshire countryside yet only 3 miles from the cathedral city of Hereford. Comfortable bedrooms, one with four-poster bed, all en suite, tea/coffee making facilities and colour TV. Large oak-beamed lounge and traditional farmhouse fare. Children welcome, pets by arrangement. AA listed. Open all year.

The Vauld House Farm, Marden, Herefordshire HR1 3HA   14

Mrs Judith Wells
☎ 01568 797347
Fax 01568 797366
[BB] From £18–£20
EM From £13.50
Sleeps 5
🐴 🐎 👤 ⚲ ♿ 🎠 ▪
🛶🛶🛶 *Commended*

Situated 6 miles north of Hereford in beautiful countryside, this 17th century farmhouse offers traditionally furnished, comfortable en suite accommodation with guests' own lounge and dining room. Open log fires. All home cooking to a very high standard using fresh local produce. Guests may enjoy relaxing in the wooded and lawned gardens with carp ponds. Open all year except Christmas.

SELF-CATERING

Anvil Cottage, Grafton Villa, Grafton, Hereford, Herefordshire HR2 8ED   15

Jennie Layton
☎ 01432 268689
[SC] From £120
Sleeps 4
🐴 ⅍ 👤 ⚲ ♿ 🎾
Applied

Beams, natural wood and beautiful fabrics make our recently converted wainhouse into a very well equipped cottage for the discerning visitor. Comfortable, spacious twin and double bedded rooms, each en suite. Lovely open plan lounge leading to a sheltered patio. Suitable for disabled and wheelchair guests. Linen and electricity included. Open all year.

Bankside, Dilwyn, Hereford, Herefordshire HR4 8HD   16

Mrs Anna Wellings
☎ 01544 318329
[SC] From £195–£240
Sleeps 7 + cot
🐴 🐎 🎠
🐾 🐾 🐾 🐾 *Commended*

Spacious family house, overlooking unspoilt farmland with panoramic views of Black Mountains. Famous for black and white village trail. Two double bedded rooms, 1 twin, nursery with cot, bathroom, 2 WCs. Large lounge, dining room, modern kitchen, shower room, secluded gardens with patio furniture. Linen included. Open all year.

---

17 Brooklyn, c/o Marlbrook Hall, Elton, Ludlow, Shropshire SY8 2HR

Mrs Valerie Morgan
☎ 01568 770230
SC From £150–£250
Sleeps 6
🐕 🐈 🛏 🎁
🔑 🔑 🔑 🔑 *Commended*

Situated on the Herefordshire/Shropshire border, ideal for exploring the market town of Ludlow, Mortimer Forest and Welsh Borders. Spacious accommodation consists of three bedroomed house with garden and garage. Fitted carpets and tastefully decorated. Colour TV, microwave oven, washing machine, tumble dryer, linen and towels included in price. Open all year.

---

18 Mill House Flat, Woonton Court Farm, Leysters, Leominster, Herefordshire HR6 0HL

Mrs Elizabeth Thomas
☎ 01568 750232
SC From £150
Sleeps 3/4 + cot
🐕 🐈 🛏 🎁 ⊙
🔑 🔑 🔑 🔑 *Commended*

Half-timbered brick and stone detached mill, recently converted to provide comfortable first floor self-contained accommodation. Open plan kitchen/dining room/spacious sitting room, electric fire, colour TV. Night store heating and fitted carpets throughout. Linen/electricity included. Telephone. Sunny patio, parking, freedom to walk on the farm and enjoy a wealth of nature. Own farm produce. Short breaks. Open all year.

---

19 Moody Farm Cottage, Moody Farm, Longtown, Herefordshire HR2 0LW

Judy Stone
☎ 01873 860685
SC From £125–£290
Sleeps 4/5 + cot
🐕 ✂ 🎁 🎿
🔑 🔑 🔑 *Commended*

Swans on the lake, woodpeckers in the wood! Wonderful views and setting at foot of Black Mountains. Comfortable, very well equipped cottage, part of barn conversion. River, own lake, fishing and boating. Ideal for children. Walking, birdwatching and exploring castles. One double, one single, one single/twin. Open all year.

---

20 Old Forge Cottage, Lyston Smithy, Wormelow, Nr Hereford HR2 8EL

Shirley Wheeler
☎ 01981 540625
SC From £150–£314
Sleeps 4
🐕 🛏 🎁 🕭 ⊙ 🍷
🔑 🔑 🔑 🔑 *Commended*

The Forge cottage is all on one level and retains many original features. Large open plan living room, fully equipped kitchenette, one twin en suite, one double bedroom and bathroom. CH, telephone and TV. Linen included. 14 acres of gardens and grounds. 3 day breaks Nov–Mar. Open all year.

---

21 The Vauld House Farm, Marden, Hereford, Herefordshire HR1 3HA

Judith Wells
☎ 01568 797347
Fax 01568 797366
SC From £165–£250
EM From £13.50
Sleeps 2/5 + cot
🛏 🐕 🛏 🎁 🕭 🎿 🍷
🔑 🔑 🔑 🔑 *Commended*

Set amidst beautiful countryside on family stock farm midway between Hereford and Leominster, this skilfully converted Victorian hop kiln is spacious and well-equipped. Sleeps 5 + cot. Recently renovated 17th century Cider House, retaining character and charm. Ground floor sleeps 2. Lawned and wooded gardens with moat and ponds extend to over an acre. Open all year.

---

22 No 1 Wilden Cottage, c/o Wilden Farm, St Michaels, Tenbury Wells, Worcestershire WR15 8PL

Mrs Margaret Jones
☎ 01568 750255
SC From £145–£215
Sleeps 5
🐕 🛏 🎁
🔑 🔑 🔑 *Approved*

Semi-detached cottage in own lawned garden, bordered by wooded brook and orchard. Idyllic setting for birdwatchers, naturalists and walkers, and exploring Herefordshire, Worcestershire and Shropshire. Conservation methods used on farm. Sleeps 5 in double, twin and single bedrooms. Sitting room with colour TV, open fire. Children and pets welcome. Open all year.

England's Heartland

Worcestershire

Group Contacts: BB *Mrs Pauline Grainger* ☎ *01299 404027*
SC *Mr R Goodman* ☎ *01299 896500*

Worcestershire still has that flavour of Old England with flowering hedges, grazing pastures, rolling hills and bluebelled woodland, winding lanes and sleepy villages. To the north the Georgian town of Bewdley straddles the River Severn, fringed by the Wyre Forest where wild deer wander. Bromsgrove with its Georgian buildings and gabled houses and Droitwich Spa with the High Street of timber framed shops.

Follow the gentle flow of the Severn, Teme and Avon as they make their way through the county passing through Evesham, Pershore and Upton-on-Severn. Climb the rolling hills of Malvern, Abberley, Woodbury and Clee. Discover the market town of Tenbury Wells and Malvern with its Priory and famous drinking water flowing freely at St Annes Well and Holy Well. At the south-east tip of our county lies Broadway, the picturesque Cotswold village.

Worcestershire is steeped in history and where better to discover this than Worcester itself, the heart of our county. Dominated by its grand and beautiful cathedral, the city has many interesting museums, the Commandery with its Civil War connections, the Royal Worcester Porcelain factory and the Guild Hall.

The area offers great variety and you will be sure of a warm welcome.

A483 A488 A49 Kidderminster M5
Ludlow Bewdley 9 M54
Knighton Stourport-on-Severn Bromsgrove
Tenbury 4 1 8 Redditch
A44 Wells 15 A443 5 Droitwich
Presteigne Leominster 3 11 13 A441
Llandrindod Wells A44 A44 Worcester 10 A422
A470 A4112 A49 A417 2 Pershore 6 14
Builth-Wells A4103 M5 A44 Evesham
A438 A438 Great Malvern 12
Hereford A438 A4104 7 16 A435
A465 A49 M50 A417 Broadway
Brecon Ross-on-Wye Tewkesbury
A40 A470 Gloucester Cheltenham
Abergavenny A40 M5
Monmouth A48 A417 A429
Tredegar Blaenavon
Rymney Abertillery Abersychan Cirencester

BED AND BREAKFAST
(and evening meal)

---

(1) Bullockhurst Farm, Rock, Nr Bewdley, Worcestershire DY14 9SE

Margaret Nott
☎ 01299 832 305
🅱 From £17
Sleeps 4
☼
🐾🐾 *Highly Commended*

Come and savour the peace and tranquility of our Georgian farmhouse set in large gardens and beautiful undulating countryside. En suite facilities. Well situated for exploring the Wyre Forest, Bewdley with its Severn Railway and enjoying the panoramic views over the Worcestershire and Shropshire countryside. Excellent meals available in village. Children welcome. 1½ miles off A456.

---

(2) Chirkenhill, Leigh Sinton, Malvern, Worcestershire WR13 5DE

Mrs Sarah Wenden
☎ 01886 832205
🅱 From £17
Sleeps 6
☼🐾🛏
🐾🐾 *Commended*

We welcome guests to our attractive farmhouse conveniently situated 4 miles from Malvern and 5 from Worcester. Its elevated position commands lovely views of the Malvern Hills and surrounding countryside and its rural location ensures a peaceful break. Excellent country walks or drive the Elgar Route. Dogs/horses can be housed by arrangement. Open all year.

---

(3) Church House Farm, Shelsley Beauchamp, Nr Worcester, Worcestershire WR6 6RA

Gill & Arthur Moore
☎ 01886 812393
🅱 From £16
EM From £9.50
Sleeps 4
🛏☼🏕
🐾🐾 *Approved*

A warm welcome awaits you on our 200-acre family run cattle and sheep farm in the Teme Valley. Country cooking is our speciality with meat and vegetables home or locally produced. All bedrooms have bathrooms en suite. Guests can relax in a large sitting room with colour TV after visits to the Welsh Borders, Shakespeare Country, the Malverns and many local attractions. Open March–Oct.

---

(4) Clay Farm, Clows Top, Nr Bewdley, Worcestershire DY14 9NN

Mike & Ella Grinnall
☎ 01299 832421
🅱 From £17
Sleeps 6
☼ (1) 🏕 🐾 🛏
🐾🐾 *Highly Commended*

Fully centrally heated farmhouse with log fires in winter. Friendly atmosphere, homemade cakes and tea on arrival. En suite bedrooms with tea making facilities. Full English breakfast. TV lounge. Fly and coarse fishing pools. Close proximity to Ludlow, Severn Valley Railway. On the borders of Worcestershire and Shropshire on the B4202 Cleobury Mortimer Road. Open all year.

---

(5) Eden Farm, Ombersley, Nr Droitwich, Worcester WR9 0JX

Mrs Ann Yardley
☎ 01905 620244
🅱 From £18–£20
Sleeps 5
🏕☼✂🐾
🐾🐾 *Commended*

Come and enjoy our listed 17th century home with its lovely garden and fishing on the Severn. It's just off the A449 and the Wychavon Way, a wonderful centre for exploring the heart of England, with Worcester 7 miles, Droitwich 6 miles. Bedrooms are tastefully decorated, with bathrooms en suite, tea/coffee-making facilities. Homemade produce and preserves. Open all year except Christmas.

Hill Barn Orchard, Evesham Road, Church Lench, Evesham, Worcestershire WR11 4UB

Marlene Badger
☎ 01386 871035
⒝⒝ From £15–£25
Sleeps 6
🐎 🛏 🐓 �️ 🧺 🍴 🍷 🏛 ♨
Applied

Attractive, comfortably furnished house 4 miles from historic Evesham. On edge of village in quiet orchard setting. Views, lakes wildlife, trout fishing. Spring blossom trail, Elgar route, Cotswolds, Stratford, Ragley Hall. Ideal restful or touring holiday. Stratford 10 miles, Tewkesbury 12 miles, Broadway 12 miles. Also let for self-catering during some of the summer months.

Home Farm, Bredons Norton, Tewkesbury, Gloucestershire GL20 7HA

Mick & Anne Meadows
☎ 01684 772322
⒝⒝ From £18–£20
EM From £12
Sleeps 6
🐓 🛏 �️ 🍷
🍃🍃 Commended

Mixed 150-acre family-run farm with sheep, cattle and poultry. Situated in an extremely quiet, unspoilt little village nestling under Bredon Hill. Superb position for walking, an excellent base for touring or relaxing. The 18th century farmhouse is very comfortably furnished. All bedrooms have en suite bathrooms. Gas CH. Good home cooking, evening meal by arrangement. Lounge, TV. Children welcome. Open mid Jan–mid Dec.

Hunt House Farm, Frith Common, between Tenbury Wells and Bewdley, Worcestershire WR15 8JY

Chris & Jane Keel
☎ 01299 832277
⒝⒝ From £17
Sleeps 6
🛏(8) 🐓 🍷
🍃🍃 Highly Commended

16th century timber framed farmhouse surrounded by breathtaking views. Our 180-acre farm is arable/sheep, and we offer comfort, peace and hospitality in a relaxing, friendly atmosphere. All bedrooms en suite with tea trays. Visitors welcomed with tea and homemade cake in guest sitting room. Excellent local eating houses. Convenient for Worcester, Shropshire, Hereford, NEC, Ironbridge, Wales. Open all year (closed Christmas).

Lightmarsh Farm, Crundalls Lane, Bewdley, Worcestershire DY12 1NE

Mrs Pauline Grainger
☎ 01299 404027
⒝⒝ From £18
Sleeps 4
🛏(10) 🍷 🏛
🍃🍃 Highly Commended

A small, pasture farm in an elevated position with fine views. Ideal location for walking, wildlife and exploring Heart of England. The house is approx 200 years old, full central heating, offers comfortable accommodation; TV lounge with inglenook fireplace. Both rooms have private facilities. Truly rural setting, only 1 mile from Bewdley's shops and restaurants, Severn Valley Railway and West Midland Safari Park. Brochure on request. Open all year.

Old House Farm, Tibberton, Droitwich, Worcestershire WR9 7NP

Pat Chilman
☎ 01905 345247
⒝⒝ From £18–£20
Sleeps 4
�️ 🛏 🐓 🍷 🏛
🍃 Commended

Family run 100-acre dairy farm set off A4538, in peaceful village of Tibberton but only 1 mile from M5, J6. The farmhouse is tastefully furnished for comfort and relaxation with large garden and splendid views of Malvern Hills. Central for the Heart of England including Worcestershire, Herefordshire, Warwickshire, Gloucestershire and the Cotswolds. Washbasins en suite. Open all year.

Phepson Farm, Himbleton, Droitwich, Worcestershire WR9 7JZ

David & Tricia Havard
☎ 01905 391205
⒝⒝ From £18–£25
Sleeps 8
🐓 🛏 🍷 🏛
🍃🍃 Commended

In our 17th century oak beamed farmhouse we offer a warm welcome, good food and a relaxed and informal atmosphere. The recently converted Granary has two ground floor bedrooms whilst the farmhouse has double, and family accommodation. All rooms en suite with colour TV. Peaceful surroundings on family stock farm. Walking on Wychavon Way. Featured on 'Wish You Were Here'. Open all year except Christmas and New Year.

12 **Tiltridge Farm & Vineyard,** Upper Hook Road, Upton-on-Severn, Worcestershire WR8 0SA

Sandy Barker
☎ **01684 592906**
Fax 01684 594142
BB From £18–£25
Sleeps 6
🛏 🐴 ⅍ ▲ ⅋
🐾🐾 *Highly Commended*

Period family farmhouse lying between the Malvern Hills and the attractive riverside town of Upton–on–Severn. Set in its own vineyard, the house is fully renovated with two doubles, one family room. All rooms are en suite with TV. Warm welcome and plenty of our own wine available! Four minutes from the Three Counties Showground and a good base for touring the Cotswolds, Malverns, Wye Valley and Forest of Dean. Open all year.

SELF-CATERING

13 **The Granary,** c/o Phepson Farm, Himbleton, Droitwich, Worcestershire WR9 7JZ

David & Tricia Havard
☎ **01905 391205**
SC From £145–£220
Sleeps 2/4
🐴 🛏 🐴
⚷ ⚷ ⚷ ⚷ *Commended*

The recent conversion of the old granary is reached by an outside stone staircase. The light and airy flat is double-glazed and very comfortably furnished. Situated on working stock farm in peaceful surroundings. Entrance through stable door. Fitted kitchen, colour TV, double bedroom with en suite bathroom. Linen, electricity, night storage heating included. Open all year.

14 **Hill Barn Orchard,** Evesham Road, Church Lench, Evesham, Worcestershire WR11 4UB

Marlene Badger
☎ **01386 871035**
SC From £195–£525
Sleeps 6
🐾🐴🐕⅍▲🕹☕🐾
⚷ ⚷ ⚷ *Commended*

Attractive, comfortably furnished house 4 miles from historic Evesham. On edge of village in quiet orchard setting. Views, lakes wildlife, trout fishing. Spring blossom trail, Elgar route, Cotswolds, Stratford, Ragley Hall. Ideal restful or touring holiday. Stratford 10 miles, Tewkesbury 12 miles, Broadway 12 miles. Open Easter–end October.

15 **Old Yates Cottages,** Old Yates Farm, Abberley, Nr Worcester, Worcestershire WR6 6AT

Sarah & Richard
Goodman
☎ **01299 896500**
SC From £110–£260
Sleeps 2/4
🛏 🐴 ♿ ▲ 🕹
⚷ ⚷ ⚷ ⚷ *Commended*

Four cottages in peaceful, secluded positions with private gardens, situated on small farm between Abberley Hills and the Teme Valley. Cosy, fully equipped and heated, also log fires, colour TV. Launderette and table tennis room. 1 mile from village supermarket and garage. Many restaurants, leisure and recreational activities within easy reach. Ideal centre to explore the Midlands and Welsh Borders. Brochure available. Open all year.

16 **Stable Cottage,** Home Farm, Bredons Norton, Tewkesbury, Gloucestershire GL20 7HA

Mick & Anne Meadows
☎ **01684 772322**
SC From £120–£260
Sleeps 5
🐴 🛏 ⅍ 🕹
Applied

Delightful Cotswold stone stable/barn conversion on a mixed working family farm in a quiet and picturesque village under Bredon Hill. Very cosy and tastefully furnished. Full central heating, lots of beams, own paddock. Perfect location for touring the Cotswolds, Severn Valley and Malverns with many wonderful walks. Open all year.

England's Heartland

Warwickshire

Group Contact: *Miss Deborah Lea ☎/Fax 01295 770652*

The native county of William Shakespeare has a lot to offer. With its mediaeval castles, historic towns of Warwick, Stratford-upon-Avon, Leamington Spa, Rugby and Kenilworth and its delightful countryside.

Stratford-upon-Avon is the provincial home of the Royal Shakespeare Company who perform in the three theatres near the River Avon. There are many half-timbered buildings in the town, several of which have associations with the great bard and the shopping centre satisfies the most discerning shopper. A few miles up the River Avon lies the town of Warwick with its magnificent mediaeval castle brought to life by Madame Tussaud's vignettes.

At Kenilworth, the Castle can be seen. Close by is the Royal Showground which hosts the Royal Show every July and is a year-round agricultural centre. Royal Leamington Spa is an elegant Regency town with wide streets, crescents and fine gardens and famous for its healing waters.

There are also many pretty villages throughout the county and stately homes such as Packwood House, Ragley Hall, Charlecote Park, Baddesley Clinton and Coughton Court.

BED AND BREAKFAST

(and evening meal)

---

1 **The Byre,** Lords Hill Farm, Coalpit Lane, Wolston, Coventry CV8 3GB

Mrs Betty Gibbs
☎ 01203 542098
[BB] From £15–£20
Sleeps 6
ᴤ(5) 🐾 ⅄
🐝 *Commended*

A warm welcome awaits guests to our home set in a quiet country lane on a 200-acre sheep/arable farm. Attractive double/twin bedrooms, 1 en suite, 2 with washbasins. Dining and sitting room with colour TV and full CH. Ideally situated for visiting Rugby, Leamington, Warwick, Stratford, NEC and NAC. Numerous places nearby for evening meals. East of Fosse Way on Wolston crossroads. Non smokers only. Open all year except Christmas.

---

2 **Church Farm,** Dorsington, Stratford-upon-Avon, Warwickshire CV37 8AX

Mrs Marian J Walters
☎ 01789 720471
and 0831 504194
Fax 01789 720830
[BB] From £14–£18
Sleeps 14
🐾 ᴤ 🐕 🐈 🏛 🛍
🐝 🐝 *Commended*

A warm welcome awaits you at our mixed working farm with lakes, equestrian course and woodlands to explore. Situated on edge of quiet pretty village yet ideal for touring Stratford, Warwick, Cotswolds, NAC, NEC, Worcester and Evesham. Some bedrooms en suite with TV. Stabling and fishing available. Open all year.

---

3 **Crandon House,** Avon Dassett, Leamington Spa, Warwickshire CV33 0AA

Deborah Lea
☎/Fax 01295 770652
[BB] From £18–£25
EM From £12.50
Sleeps 6
🐾 ᴤ(8) 🅿 🏛 🛍
🐝 🐝 *Highly Commended*

A warm welcome at our farmhouse offering an exceptionally high standard accommodation and comfort. Set in 20 acres, beautiful views. Small working farm, rare breeds cattle, sheep and poultry. Own produce, excellent food. Large garden. Full CH, log fire. 3 rooms with private facilities. Colour TV, tea/coffee tray. Peaceful, quiet, easy access to Warwick, Stratford, Cotswolds. Located between M40, J11/12 (4 miles). Open all year (closed Christmas).

---

4 **Frankton Grounds,** Frankton, Nr Rugby, Warwickshire CV23 9PD

Mrs Mary Pritchard
☎ 01926 632391
[BB] From £15–£20
EM From £8.50
Sleeps 4
ᴤ 🐾
Listed *Applied*

Beautifully situated in a mixed farm of horses, sheep, pedigree and commercial cattle. A warm welcome for the visitor who enjoys peace and quiet yet, with the benefit of easy access to Warwick, Leamington and Stratford. 2½ miles M45. Full CH, log fires, excellent food. 1 double with bathroom, 1 twin.

---

5 **Glebe Farm,** Exhall, Alcester, Warwickshire B49 6EA

John & Margaret Canning
☎ 01789 772202
[BB] From £16–£18
Sleeps 6
🐾 ᴤ 🏛 🛍
🐝 *Approved*

Shakespeare named our village 'Dodging Exhall' and it has somehow 'dodged' the passing of time, so if you want a true taste of rural England, come and relax in our quaint old farmhouse – parts of it dating from Tudor times – with its log fires, four-poster bed and country hospitality. 1 double, 1 twin, 2 singles, tea/coffee trays, electric blankets. Smoking in lounge. Payphone. Laundry. Ample parking. Open all year (closed Christmas & New Year).

Hill Farm, Lewis Road, Radford Semele, Leamington Spa, Warwickshire CV31 1UX

Rebecca Gibbs
☎ 01926 337571
▣ From £15–£20
Sleeps 10
🐕 ⅍ 🚐
♨♨ Commended

Hill Farm is a comfortable, friendly farmhouse situated in 350 acres of mixed farmland. Excellent breakfasts, large garden, attractive double/twin/single bedrooms, some en suite, with CH and tea/coffee-making facilities. Comfortable TV lounge, quiet room, guests' bathroom. Children welcome. AA and Farm Holiday Guide award winner. Caravanning/Camping Club certificated site. Ideal for Shakespeare Country. Open all year (closed Christmas).

Holland Park Farm, Buckley Green, Henley in Arden, Nr Solihull, Warwickshire B95 5QF

Mrs Kathleen Connolly
☎ 01564 792625
▣ From £18–£20
Sleeps 6
🐕 🐎 🐾 🏛 ▪
♨♨ Applied

A Georgian style farmhouse, set in 300 acres of peaceful farmland, including the historic grounds of 'The Mount' and other interesting walks. Large garden with pond. Livestock includes cattle, sheep and Irish Draught horses. Ideally situated in Shakespeare's country, within easy reach of Birmingham International Airport, NEC, NAC, Stratford–upon–Avon, Warwick and the Cotswolds. Open all year.

Irelands Farm, Irelands Lane, Henley-in-Arden, Nr Solihull, Warwickshire B95 5SA

Pamela Shaw
☎ 01564 792476
▣ From £17–£20
Sleeps 6
🐎 ⅍ 🏛 ▪
♨♨ Highly Commended

If a quiet, relaxing holiday is what you are looking for, then visit our late Georgian farmhouse. Large rooms all with own bath/shower, TV, tea/coffee-making facilities, radio, CH. Set in 220 acres of peaceful farmland. Close to National Exhibition Centre, Stratford-upon-Avon, Warwick, National Agricultural Centre. Looking forward to meeting you. Open all year (closed Christmas & New Year).

Lawford Hill Farm, Lawford Heath Lane, Nr Rugby, Warwickshire CV23 9HG

Mrs Susan Moses
☎ 01788 542001
▣ From £16–£18
Sleeps 6
🐎 🐕 ⅍
♨ Applied

You will find a warm welcome at our spacious Georgian farmhouse set in an attractive garden, on a mixed family farm. Full CH, log fire, attractive double and twin bedrooms. Situated two miles from Rugby. Easy access to Warwick, Sratford, NAC and NEC. Open all year except Christmas.

Little Hill Farm, Wellesbourne, Warwick, Warwickshire CV35 9EB

Charlotte Hutsby
☎ 01789 840261
▣ From £18
EM From £7.50
Sleeps 6
🐎 🐕 🏛 🐾
♨♨ Applied

Set in 700 acres of beef/arable farmland, our rambling William & Mary farmhouse offers a warm, friendly relaxed atmosphere, with antiques and beams throughout the house. Each bedroom has private bathroom and tea-making facilities. Drawing room with colour TV. The farm is situated off A429 on Warwick Road from Wellesbourne, only 6 miles from Warwick and 6 miles from Stratford-upon-Avon. Open all year (closed Christmas & New Year).

Lower Watchbury Farm, Wasperton Lane, Barford, Warwickshire CV35 8DH ⑪

Valerie Eykyn
☎ 01926 624772
▣ From £19.50–£21.50
Sleeps 5
⅍ 🐕 🐎 ▪ 🐾
♨♨ Commended

In the heart of Shakespeare Country, we offer you a warm welcome in our luxurious accommodation with outstanding views over rural Warwickshire. 1 large twin/family en suite room with lounge area, 1 twin en suite, 1 small double with own bathroom. All have colour TV, tea/coffee-making facilities. Excellent farmhouse breakfast. Village pubs for dinners. Large garden. Warwick, Stratford, NAC, NEC and Cotswolds nearby. Open all year except Christmas.

12 **Manor Farm,** Willey, Nr Rugby, Warwickshire CV23 0SH

Mrs Helen Sharpe
☎ 01455 553143
[BB] From £17.50
Sleeps 6
⚹ ▮
♨ ♨ *Commended*

Attention to detail, centralisation for Midlands motorways, accessibility to all points of the compass, makes this the perfect venue for travellers or businessmen alike. Emphasis placed on cleanliness and efficient service. Food Hygiene Certificate holder. Peace and tranquillity guaranteed. Our repeat bookings are our testimony. No smoking. No children. Open all year except Christmas.

13 **Maxstoke Hall Farm,** Fillongley Road, Maxstoke, Nr Coleshill, Birmingham, Warwickshire B46 2QT

Mrs Heather Green
☎/Fax 01675 463237
[BB] From £22–£25
Sleeps 5
🐴 ⚹ 🖉 ♔ ▮
♨ ♨ *Commended*

Elegant farmhouse, built in 1632, and set in beautiful countryside. Bedrooms have en suite facilities, TV, hostess tray. Comfortable oak-beamed dining and sitting rooms for use by guests. Evening meals (from £13) by prior notice. Situated 3 miles from Coleshill, 5 mins from M6 and M42. 15 mins from National Exhibition Centre, Birmingham Airport and International Railway Station. Open all year (closed Christmas & New Year).

14 **Packington Lane Farm,** Coleshill, Warwickshire B46 3JJ

Vera Harcourt
☎/Fax 01675 462228
[BB] From £18
Sleeps 6
🏹 ⚹ 🖉 ▮
♨ *Applied*

250-acre mixed farm with a charming, traditional farmhouse. Beamed TV room. TV, radio, tea/coffee in rooms. 3 miles National Exhibition Centre, Birmingham International Railway and Airport, 1 mile motorway network M6 J4, 3 miles M42 J6 and J9.

15 **The Poplars,** Mansell Farm, Newbold on Stour, Stratford on Avon, Warwickshire CV37 8BZ

Judith Spencer
☎ 01789 450540
[BB] From £15–£16.50
Sleeps 6
🐴 🐓 ▮
Listed *Applied*

A warm welcome awaits you on our working dairy farm. Enjoy the views of the Cotswolds from our modern farmhouse which is in easy reach of Sratford, Warwick, Oxford and NEC. 1 family and 1 twin, both en suite with TV and 1 single with washbasin. All have tea trays and CH. Good food or walk to local hostelry. Open all year except Christmas and New Year.

16 **Shrewley Pools Farm,** Haseley, Warwickshire CV35 7HB

Mrs Cathy Dodd
☎ 01926 484315
[BB] From £18–£25
EM From £9
Sleeps 6
🐴 ⚹ ♔ ▮
Listed *Commended*

Why not sample the delights of staying in a beautiful 17th century traditional farmhouse? Set in an acre of landscaped garden with 4-acre pool. Shrewley Pools has many interesting features, including timbered barn, huge fireplaces, and beamed ceilings. 2 bedrooms, 1 en suite, 1 private, 1 shower room, with tea/coffee tray. As featured in *The Times*. Close to Warwick, Stratford-upon-Avon, the NEC and NAC. Open all year (closed Christmas).

17 **Snowford Hall Farm,** Hunningham, Nr Royal Leamington Spa, Warwickshire CV33 9ES

Rudi Hancock
☎ 01926 632297
[BB] From £17–£19
Sleeps 6
🐴 ▮ 🎋
♨ ♨ *Commended*

A warm welcome and peaceful surroundings in 18th century farmhouse on 200-acre mixed working farm in rolling countryside. Near the Roman Fosse Way, ideal for visiting Stratford, Warwick, Leamington, Cotswolds, NAC and NEC. 1 double room with washbasin/WC 1 twin room with shower/basin/WC; 1 twin room with shower/basin. Singles extra. CH, good home cooking. Open all year (closed Christmas & New Year).

Tibbits Farm, Nethercote, Flecknoe, Nr Rugby, Warwickshire CV23 8AS

Alison Mills
☎ 01788 890239
⌷ From £19
Sleeps 4
🦮 🐕 🏃 🐄 ☕ 🔥
♨ ♨ *Applied*

Retreat from the trials of life to the seclusion and tranquillity of our 17th farmhouse idyllically situated within acres of rolling countryside, where we offer luxurious bed and breakfast accommodation. The pretty bedrooms have en suite or private bathrooms, colour TVs, tea/coffee making facilities. Tibbits is ideally situated for exploring the many places of historic, scenic and cultural interest in the area.

Walcote Farm, Walcote, Haselor, Alcester, Warwickshire B49 6LY

Prim & John Finnemore
☎ 01789 488264
⌷ From £17–£22
Sleeps 4
🦮 🐕 🏃 ☕ 🔥
♨ ♨ *Commended*

Stratford–upon–Avon is only 5 miles from a tranquil, picturesque hamlet and our attractive oak–beamed farmhouse with a friendly welcome and comfort assured. En suite for one double and one twin room, both with lovely views. Full central heating with log fires in winter. For local history, we have a large collection of old photographs and documents, including the Earl of Warwick's accounts for 1782–1786. Open all year.

Whitchurch Farm, Wimpstone, Stratford-upon-Avon, Warwickshire CV37 8NS

Mrs Joan James
☎ 01789 450275
⌷ From £17
EM From £9.50
Sleeps 6
🦮 🍴
♨ ♨ *Approved*

Lovely Georgian farmhouse set in park–like surroundings in peaceful Stour Valley 4½ miles from Stratford. Very convenient for Warwick Castle and Shakespeare properties. Ideal for touring the Cotswolds by car or rambling. The bedrooms are large and well furnished, all with en suite bathrooms, CH and tea/coffee-making facilities. Separate dining room and sitting room for guests. Open all year (closed Christmas Day).

Yew Tree Farm, Wootton Wawen, Solihull, West Midlands B95 6BY

Mrs Janet Haimes
☎ 01564 792701
⌷ From £18–£22.50
Sleeps 4 + cot
🦮 🏃 🐄 ☕ 🔥
♨ ♨ *Commended*

Georgian farmhouse situated on A3400 in village of Wootton Wawen, 2 miles south of Henley-in-Arden, 6 miles north of Stratford-upon-Avon. Easy reach of Warwick Castle, Royal Showground, NEC, and Cotswolds. 700-acre dairy/arable farm with lake and woodland walks. 2 large double bedrooms, CH, en suite, tea/coffee-making facilities. Cot available. Visitors' lounge with colour TV. Excellent pubs and restaurants nearby. Open all year (closed Christmas & New Year).

SELF-CATERING

Broadlane Cottage, Spernal Lane, Gt. Alne, Alcester, Warwickshire B49 6JD 22

Mrs Anne Stevens
☎/Fax 01789 488218
⌷ From £130–£260
Sleeps 6
🦮 🔥
🔑 🔑 🔑 *Approved*

A quiet, detached country cottage fully equipped for 6 people, with large, pretty garden. Very convenient for the Cotswolds, Warwick and Stratford-upon-Avon. Open all year.

23 **Furzen Hill Farm Cottages,** c/o Furzen Hill Farm, Cubbington Heath, Leamington Spa, Warks CV32 6QZ

Mrs Christine Whitfield
☎/Fax 01926 424791
⌂ From £100–£300
Sleeps 4/7
🐕 🛏 🍴
🔑 🔑 🔑 *Commended*

Furzen Hill is a mixed farm. The cottage is part of 17th century farmhouse with a large shared garden. Sleeping 7. The Barn and Dairy Cottages, both recently converted, each sleeps 4. Dairy Cottage has its own small garden. The Barn shares the Cottage garden. All have the use of tennis court. Situated within easy reach of NAC, NEC, Warwick and Stratford. Open all year.

24 **The Granary,** c/o Glebe Farm, Kinwarton, Alcester, Warwickshire B49 6HB

Susan Kinnersley
☎/Fax 01789 762554
⌂ From £80–£140
Sleeps 2 + cot
🍴 🛏 🍴 🍴
🔑 🔑 🔑 *Commended*

Off the beaten track, yet near the small market town of Alcester, this cottage retains many interesting features of the original granary combined with modern standards of warmth and comfort. The farm is bounded by the River Alne and there are a variety of attractive country walks in the area. Linen provided, colour TV. Cot available. Car space. Short breaks by arrangement. Open all year.

25 **Hipsley Farm Cottages,** Hipsley Lane, Hurley, Atherstone, Warwickshire CV9 2LR

Mrs Ann Prosser
☎/Fax 01827 872437
⌂ From £215–£325
Sleeps 18 + cots
🛏 🐕 🍴 🍴 ⚓ 👤
🔑 🔑 🔑 – 🔑 🔑 🔑 🔑 🔑
Highly Commended

Hipsley Farm is situated in beautiful rolling countryside only 3 miles from junction 10, M42/A5, so ideal for NEC, Birmingham, Warwick, Leicester. The barns and cowshed have been carefully converted into 6 comfortable, individually furnished cottages. Fully equipped including CH, colour TV, bed linen and towels, laundry, payphone, putting green, ample parking on site. One cottage suitable for disabled. ETB Highly Commended. Open all year.

26 **Irelands Farm,** Irelands Lane, Henley in Arden, Warwickshire B95 5SA

Pamela Shaw
☎ 01564 792476
⌂ From £100–£300
Sleeps 2/4
🐕 👤 🛏 🍴
🔑 🔑 🔑 🔑 *Highly Commended*

Four attractively converted oak-beamed cottages in courtyard on 220-acre working farm. Very quiet location yet within 3 miles of M42/M40 junction. All cottages centrally heated and tastefully furnished, and equipped to a high standard. Linen provided. Private patios. Open all year.

27 **Little Biggin,** c/o Broadwell House Farm, Broadwell, Rugby, Warwickshire CV23 8HF

Mrs Linda Denham
☎/Fax 01926 812347
⌂ From £150–£250
Sleeps 4
🛏(12) 🍴 🍴 🍴
🔑 🔑 🔑 🔑 *Commended*

Attractive small beamed stone cottage with quaint features and central heating, converted from 19th century farm building. Well equipped and furnished. Quiet location, ideal base for Leamington Spa, Rugby, NAC and NEC. Many glorious countryside walks. Open all year.

28 **Snowford Hall Farm Cottage,** c/o Snowford Hall Farm, Hunningham, Leamington Spa, Warwicks CV33 9ES

Rudi Hancock
☎ 01926 632297
⌂ From £120–£270
Sleeps 5
🐕 🍴
🔑 🔑 🔑 *Approved*

Fully centrally heated spacious 2–bedroomed cottage on a quiet country road surrounded by well maintained lawns and farmland. Capable of sleeping 5 people. A comfortable lounge with TV and fitted kitchen makes this cottage an ideal base for touring the Cotswolds, Shakespeare Country and exploring Warwick, Kenilworth and Oxford. The NAC is 5 miles and NEC 15 miles away. Open all year.

England's Heartland

Cotswolds and Royal Forest of Dean

Group Contacts: *Anne Meadows* ☎ *01684 772322*

The villages and scenic beauty of the Cotswolds are famed throughout the world. The many honey-coloured villages include Bibury, Broadway, Painswick and Lower Slaughter while some of the finest churches in the country are at Northleach, Fairford and Winchcombe which also has Sudeley Castle. Along the River Severn the villages have black and white half-timbered cottages and cattle graze peacefully in the orchards and meadows. Gloucester with its cathedral, the elegant Regency town of Cheltenham and picturesque Tewkesbury with its 12th century abbey are in the Severn Vale. There are numerous visitor attractions in the main towns and villages while further afield are Berkeley Castle and Sir Peter Scott's Wildfowl Trust at Slimbridge.

Bordered by two rivers, the Severn and the Wye, is the beautiful and romantic Forest of Dean, ancient hunting grounds of kings and still covered by oak woodlands.

Scattered through the Forest are mining towns such as Cinderford, Coleford and Lydney. Below Symonds Yat, the River Wye meanders dramatically in a most attractive wooded gorge.

BED AND BREAKFAST

(and evening meal)

---

(1) Abbots Court, Church End, Twyning, Tewkesbury, Gloucestershire GL20 6DA

Bernie Williams
☎/Fax 01684 292515
📠 From £14.50–£16.50
Sleeps 15
🐎 🐕 ♿ 🚴 ☂
♨ Commended

Lovely, quiet farmhouse in 350 acres between Cotswolds and Malverns. All bedrooms have colour TV, most en suite, tea-making facilities. Large lounge, separate dining room, excellent home cooked food. Licensed bar. 3 games rooms with pool table, table tennis, children's TV room, grass tennis court, bowling green, children's play area on lawn. Superb touring area. Open all year (except Christmas and New Year).

---

(2) Avenue Farm, Knockdown, Tetbury, Gloucestershire GL8 8QY

Sonja King
☎/Fax 01454 238207
📠 From £15–£20
Sleeps 6
🐕 ✗ ☂ 💼
Applied

Our home is over 300 years old and is on the edge of the Cotswold Hills in the heart of the Duke of Beaufort's hunt. The farm adjoins Westonbirt Arboretum where you can walk in 600 acres of beautiful woodland planted around 1830 by Sir George Holford. We are close to the Roman Towns of Cirencester and Bath. Open all year.

---

(3) Bould Farm, Bould, Nr Idbury, Chipping Norton, Oxfordshire OX7 6RT

Mrs Lynne Meyrick
☎ 01608 658850
📠 From £20–£25
Sleeps 6
🐕 ✗ ☂
Listed *Commended*

Bould Farm is a 17th century Cotswold farmhouse on a 300-acre family farm set in beautiful countryside, 10 minutes' drive from Stow-on-the-Wold and Bourton-on-the-Water and Burford. Within easy reach of Blenheim Palace and the Cotswold Wildlife Park. Children welcome. Spacious rooms with TV, tea/coffee-making facilities. Large garden. Good local pubs.

---

(4) Brawn Farm, Sandhurst, Gloucester, Gloucestershire GL2 9NR

Sally Williams
☎ 01452 731010
Mobile 0973 313418
📠 From £18
Sleeps 4
🐕 🐎 🐈 🚴 ☂
Listed *Applied*

Working dairy/corn farm with a 15th century listed farmhouse and large garden in an extremely quiet setting. Delightful footpaths through the farm and woods. Two very spacious bedrooms, comfortable sitting room with TV, separate dining room offering excellent breakfasts. Good local pubs. Open all year.

---

(5) Butlers Hill Farm, Cockleford, Cowley, Cheltenham, Gloucestershire GL53 9NW

Bridget Brickell
☎/Fax 01242 870455
📠 From £15
EM From £7
Sleeps 4
🐕(6) 🚴
♨ Approved

A warm welcome awaits you on this mixed working farm between Cheltenham and Cirencester. Relax in this modern spacious farmhouse, in a quiet part of the Churn Valley with attractive walks and an ideal centre for exploring the cotswolds. All rooms have H & C and tea/coffee-making facilities, separate guests' sitting room with colour TV and separate dining room. Open all year (closed Christmas and New Year).

The Coach House, Middle Duntisbourne, Cirencester, Gloucestershire GL7 7AR   6

Mrs June Barton
☎ 01285 653058
[BB] From £16–£20
Sleeps 4
⌂(12) ⌖ ⌖ ⌖ ⌖
🌢🌢 *Approved*

A warm welcome at the 17th century coachhouse by the River Dunt. Centrally situated in 400-acre arable and beef farm with lovely walks and ideal for visits to Bath, Oxford, Stratford and many pretty villages in and around Cirencester area. Pretty garden with country views. TV, tea/coffee-making facilities in bedrooms. Pleasant lounge with CTV. Always a choice of breakfast including English farmhouse breakfast. Open all year except Christmas.

Dix's Barn, Duntisbourne Abbots, Cirencester, Gloucestershire GL7 7JN   7

Mrs Rosemary Wilcox
☎ 01285 821249
[BB] From £16–£17
Sleeps 4
⌖ ⌂
🌢🌢 *Applied*

Dix's Barn is situated in an Area of Outstanding Natural Beauty. It has breathtaking views of the Cotswolds and one can take lovely walks in any direction. Ideally placed for touring by car. The farm is family run, being a mixture of arable, beef and sheep. Open all year.

Elms Farm, Gretton, nr Winchcombe, Cheltenham, Gloucestershire GL54 5HQ   8

Rosemary Quilter
☎ 01242 620150
Mobile 0374 461107
[BB] From £17.50–£20
EM From £12.50
Sleeps 4
⌂ ⌖ ⌖ ⌖ ⌖ ⌖
🌢🌢 *Commended*

New farmhouse situated on the outskirts of Gretton village enjoying picturesque views of the surrounding countryside. Visitors are welcome to walk around the farm which joins up with footpaths in the area. Ideally situated for most areas of the Cotswolds. Open all year.

Gilbert's, Gilbert's Lane, Brookthorpe, Nr Gloucester, Gloucestershire GL4 0UH   9

Jenny Beer
☎/Fax 01452 812364
[BB] From £23
Sleeps 6
⌂ ⌖
🌢🌢 *Highly Commended*

Gilbert's which nestles beneath the Cotswolds close to Gloucester may have been Whaddon Manor 400 years ago. It is listed as an architectural gem. Whilst each room has modern comforts – private bathroom, TV, radio, telephone, etc. – the atmosphere is in keeping with the unpretentious nature of the house and organic smallholding, echoing a long history of living with this environment. Open all year.

Hartpury Farm, Chedworth, Nr Cheltenham, Gloucestershire GL54 4AL   10

Peter & Peggy Booth
☎ 01285 720350
[BB] From £15–£16
EM From £8
Sleeps 6
⌖ ⌂ ⌖
Listed *Applied*

Hartpury, lying centrally in the Cotswolds and in a quiet village, provides views across the valley. Good walking. Farm produce, provided by Jersey cows and organic gardening, cooked to traditional recipes. The beamed sitting room, vintage 1650, leads onto the garden where we often serve coffee. When we can, we help with excursions and local history. Open Apr–Oct.

Home Farm, Bredons Norton, Tewkesbury, Gloucestershire GL20 7HA   11

Mick & Anne Meadows
☎ 01684 772322
[BB] From £18–£20
EM From £12
Sleeps 6
⌖ ⌂ ⌖ ⌖
🌢🌢 *Commended*

Mixed 150-acre family-run farm with sheep, cattle and poultry. Situated in an extremely quiet, unspoilt little village nestling under Bredon Hill. Superb position for walking, an excellent base for touring or relaxing. The 18th century farmhouse is very comfortably furnished. All bedrooms have en suite bathrooms. Gas CH. Good home cooking, evening meal by arrangement. Lounge, TV. Children welcome. Open mid Jan–mid Dec.

⑫ Hunting Butts Farm, Swindon Lane, Cheltenham, Gloucestershire GL50 4NZ

Jane Hanks
☎ 01242 524982
[BB] From £16–£18.50
EM From £9
Sleeps 16
🐎 🕭 🐕 ⅍ 🎇 ▪
☙☙ *Commended*

Hunting Butts is a working 200-acre beef and arable farm on the edge of beautiful countryside overlooking the historic town of Cheltenham Spa, just 1½ miles from the town centre. Cheltenham Leisure Centre is a short walk away with swimming pools, squash courts, softland, etc. Children's playground, tennis courts, boating lake and golf course are again within easy walking distance. Open all year.

⑬ Kilmorie Guest House, Gloucester Road, Snigs End, Corse, Staunton, Nr Gloucester, Gloucs GL19 3RQ

Sheila Barnfield
☎ 01452 840224
[BB] From £13.50
EM From £6.50
Sleeps 11
🐎(5) 🐎 Å 🐦 🐖 🎇 ▪
☙☙ *Applied*

Built in 1848 by the Chartists, Kilmorie is a Grade 2 listed smallholding keeping sheep, ponies, goats, ducks and hens. Children may help with animals. All accommodation on ground floor, tea/coffee trays, colour TVs and washbasins in all bedrooms, CH, large garden. Good home cooking, full English breakfast, 3 course evening meal. Some private facilities. Ideal for Cotswolds, Malverns, Forest of Dean, and places of natural and historic interest. Fire certificate. Fishing nearby. Open all year (closed Christmas & New Year).

⑭ Lydes Farm, Toddington, Cheltenham, Gloucestershire GL54 5DP

Mrs R Sharpley
☎ 01242 621229
[BB] From £16–£18
Sleeps 5
🐎(5) 🐎 🎇 🐕
☙ *Commended*

Comfortable farmhouse between Broadway and Winchcombe with panoramic views from every room. TV in bedrooms, separate dining room, garden. Dogs taken by arrangement. A grass farm grazed by cattle and horses; visitors are welcome to walk round. Ideal centre for exploring the North Cotswolds. Golf and riding nearby. Open Jan–Nov.

⑮ Manor Farm, Weston Sub-Edge, Chipping Campden, Gloucestershire GL55 6QH

Lucy Robbins
☎ 01386 840390
[BB] From £20–£25
Sleeps 6
🐎 🐎 🎇 ▪
☙☙ *Commended*

Traditional 17th century farmhouse on a 600-acre mixed farm, an excellent base for touring the Cotswolds, Shakespeare Country and Hidcote Manor Gardens. Warm, friendly atmosphere with big hearty breakfasts. Beautiful walled garden. All rooms are en suite with tea/coffee making facilities, TV/radio. 1½ miles from Chipping Campden. Lots of excellent walks around beautiful countryside. Open all year.

⑯ Manor Farm, Greet, Winchcombe, Cheltenham, Gloucestershire GL54 5BJ

Richard & Janet Day
☎ 01242 602423
[BB] From £20
Sleeps 4
🐎 Å 🐦 🎇 ▪
☙☙ *Applied*

Luxuriously restored 16th century cotswold manor on mixed family farm, excellent views, near Sudeley Castle and steam railway. Convenient to Broadway, Cheltenham, Evesham, Tewkesbury and M5. 1½ miles from Cotswold Way and Wychavon Way. Large garden, croquet lawn, children welcome, horses can be accommodated. Open Jan–Nov.

⑰ Nastend Farm, Nastend, Nr Stonehouse, Gloucestershire GL10 3RS

Jackie Guilding
☎ 01453 822300
[BB] From £16–£18
EM From £10
Sleeps 6
🐎 ⅍ 🐕
☙☙ *Commended*

Enjoy that well-earned break in the friendly atmosphere of our small dairy farm set in pleasant surroundings. Watch (or help!) the daily running of our farm. For the more energetic, walk the 1½ mile farm trail. The spacious listed farmhouse boasts many modern conveniences, including en suite, CH, all blending in nicely with the traditional flavour of the oak-beamed residence, large garden with swimming pool. Open Feb–Oct.

New House Farm, Barrell Lane, Longhope, Gloucestershire GL17 0LS

Mrs Elizabeth Beddows
☎ 01452 830484
BB From £17–£20
EM From £10
Sleeps 6
🐕 🏊 🛦 🛦
♨♨ *Applied*

Clive and Betty Beddows give you a warm welcome to their Georgian farmhouse set in 80 acres of farmland with many lovely walks. All bedrooms have private bathrooms or en suite, radio/alarms, satellite TV, electric blankets and tea/coffee-making facilities. Five golf courses within ten mile radius. Open all year.

Oakwood Farm, Upper Minety, Malmesbury, Wiltshire SN16 9PY

Mrs Katie Gallop
☎ 01666 860286
BB From £14
EM From £8
Sleeps 6
🐕 🏊 🛦
Listed *Commended*

A friendly farming couple welcome you to their working dairy farm close to the quiet village of Upper Minety. Situated off the B4040, overlooks Minety church on the edge of the Cotswolds. Ideal for touring the Cotswolds and surrounding National Trust properties. 2 double rooms and 1 twin. Guests' lounge/dining room with colour TV. Also tea/coffee-making facilities. Open all year.

Oldends Farm, Oldends Lane, Stonehouse, Gloucestershire GL10 3RL

Mrs J A Nicholls
☎ 01453 822135
BB From £14
Sleeps 6
🐕 🏊 🛦 🛦
♨♨ *Applied*

Two miles from M5, junction 13 and within walking distance of Stonehouse. Comfortable accommodation in a · Grade II listed farmhouse surrounded by orchards and open fields. A working farm supporting suckler cows, beef cattle and Welsh pony mares and foals. Family and twin rooms with en suites. Good pub food – 100 yards. Open all year except Christmas.

Postlip Hall Farm, Postlip, Winchcombe, Cheltenham, Gloucestershire GL54 5AQ

Mrs Valerie Albutt
☎ 01242 603351
BB From £18–£25
Sleeps 6
🐕 🏊 🛦 🛦 🛦 🛦
♨♨ *Highly Commended*

Superbly set in idyllic corner of Cotswolds. Postlip Hall farm offers a relaxing haven for that perfect holiday. Set off B4632 on side Cleeve Hill, 1 mile Winchcombe. Great base for Stratford, Bath, Warwick Castle, Malverns, Oxford. Wonderful walking. Golf nearby. En suite and private facilities, TV's and beverages in all bedrooms. Great atmosphere on this family working farm. Open all year except Christmas.

Saul Farm, Saul, Gloucestershire GL2 7JB

Mrs Wendy Watts
☎ 01452 740384
BB From £18–£20
EM From £10
Sleeps 6
🏊 🐕 🛦 🛦 🛦
Applied

Take a break and relax in the comfort and homely atmosphere of our 17th century house overlooking a lake. Guests are welcome to lend a hand around the farm, which is situated between the River Severn and the Berkeley Canal. Many interesting places to visit nearby. TV lounge with open fire, spacious bedrooms with en suite and home cooking are waiting for you and your family. 2 miles from M5 (jct. 13). Open all year.

Sudeley Hill Farm, Winchcombe, Gloucestershire GL54 5JB

Barbara Scudamore
☎ 01242 602344
BB From £20
Sleeps 6
🐕 🛦
♨♨ *Highly Commended*

Delightfully situated above Sudeley Castle with panoramic views across the surrounding valley, this is a 15th century listed farmhouse with a large garden on a working mixed farm of 800 acres. Ideal centre for touring the Cotswolds. Family/twin, 1 double, 1 twin, all en suite. Comfortable lounge with TV and log fires. Separate dining room. Open all year except Christmas.

---

24 Town Street Farm, Tirley, Gloucestershire GL19 4HG

Sue Warner
☎ 01452 780442
Fax 01452 780890
[BB] From £16–£21
Sleeps 4
🐎 🐂 👤 🔌 🦮 🛁
👒👒 *Commended*

Town Street Farm is a typical working family farm close to the River Severn, within easy reach of M5 and M50. The farmhouse offers a high standard of accommodation with en suite facilities in bedrooms and a warm and friendly welcome. Breakfast is served overlooking the lawns, flowerbeds and tennis court which is available for use by guests. Open all year except Christmas.

25 Upper Farm, Clapton-on-the-Hill, Bourton-on-the-Water, Gloucestershire GL54 2LG

Mrs Helen Adams
☎ 01451 820453
[BB] From £16–£20
Sleeps 10
🛏(6) 🍴 🖐 🎋
👒👒 *Commended*

A mixed family farm of 140-acres in a peaceful, undiscovered village two miles from Bourton-on-the-Water. Our centrally heated period stone farmhouse has been tastefully restored and offers a warm, friendly welcome. Quality accommodation and hearty farmhouse fayre. We are centrally located for touring or walking and our hill position offers panoramic views over the surrounding Cotswold countryside. Open Mar–Nov.

26 Wickridge Court Farm, Folly Lane, Stroud, Gloucestershire GL6 8JT

Gloria & Peter Watkins
☎ 01453 764357
[BB] From £18
EM From £12
Sleeps 6
🐂 🐎 🦮 🎋 🛁
👒👒 *Commended*

Wickridge Court Farm is situated 1 mile from the B4070 holiday route. A farm of 250 acres with cattle and horses. The historic farmhouse is a sympathetically converted Cotswold stone barn offering all en suite rooms. It is a peaceful suntrap set in a fold of the beautiful Slad Valley offering excellent walks through National Trust woods; Stroud Leisure Centre with its heated pool is 1 mile, many places of interest within easy reach. Open all year.

27 Windrush Farm, Bourton-on-the-Water, Cheltenham, Gloucestershire GL54 3BY

David & Jenny Burrough
☎/Fax 01451 820419
[BB] From £18–£20
Sleeps 4
🍴 🔌
👒👒 *Commended*

We look forward to welcoming you to our family-run arable farm in a delightful setting. 1½ miles from Bourton-on-the-Water. The Cotswold stone house has a lovely garden and panoramic views. Enjoy the beauty of the area, with its rolling hills, picturesque villages and places of interest. Our local 17th century pub is a stroll across the fields for evening meals. Open Mar–Dec.

SELF-CATERING

28 Bangrove Farm, Teddington, Tewkesbury, Gloucestershire GL20 8JB

Pat Hitchman
☎ 01242 620223
[SC] From £240–£300
Sleeps 2/8
🐎
🐾 🐾 🐾 🐾 *Commended*

An attractive self-contained property part of 17th century oak-beamed farmhouse on arable/livestock farm in quiet rural setting near Cheltenham. Ideal for walking and touring Cotswolds. Comfortably furnished, fitted carpets throughout. 3 double bedrooms (1 with washbasin), large bathroom. Downstairs cloakroom, kitchen/diner, microwave, large lounge, TV. Linen/electricity/use of washing machine included. Children welcome. Garden, hard tennis court, barbecue. Golf/riding available. Open Apr–Oct.

Court Close Farm, Manor Road, Eckington, Pershore, Worcestershire WR10 3BH

Eileen Fincher
☎ 01386 750297
SC From £160–£240
Sleeps 4/6
🐕 🏵 ♥ 🎪
♟ ♟ ♟ *Approved*

A self-contained wing of our lovely 18th century farmhouse and garden on village edge, bordering Gloucestershire. Outstanding views of Bredon Hill. Attractive set dairy farm with meadows sloping to the Avon. Fishing by arrangement. Central for Shakespeare, Malvern and Cotswold jaunts. Convenient kitchen/diner and comfortable sitting room with TV, storage heat and electric fire. 3 bedrooms, linen provided.Closed Chrismas.

Folly Farm Cottages, Malmesbury Road, Tetbury, Gloucestershire GL8 8XA

Julian Benton
☎ 01666 502475
Fax 01666 502358
SC From £75–£640
Sleeps 2–10
🐕 🐴 ♿ ♣ 🎪
♟ ♟–♟ ♟ ♟
Upto Commended

Close to Royal Tetbury, 10 superior 18th century cottages. Well furnished, fully equipped throughout. CH, CTV, microwave, linen provided. Some log fires. Games room, laundry, large gardens, barbecue and play area. Fishing, golf, riding, windsurfing nearby. Pubs 2 minutes walk. Resident host. Ideal for disabled and family reunions. Civilised pets and children welcome! Close to M4/M5. Open all year.

Manor Farm Cottages, Greet, Winchcombe, Cheltenham, Gloucestershire GL54 5BJ

Richard & Janet Day
☎ 01242 602423
SC From £150–£520
Sleeps 3/7
🐕 🐴 ♥ 🎪 ♣
Applied

Beautifully restored 15th century tithe house (pictured) and newly restored 'Shuck's Cottage' and 'Boot Hole Cottage', on family farm. Central for Tewkesbury, Broadway, Evesham, Cheltenham. Sleep 3–7, cot and high-chair available. Horses accommodated. Croquet lawn. Close to Cotswold Way and Wychavon Way, in sight of steam railway. Full central heating, every modern convenience. Open all year.

New House Farm Cottages, New House Farm, Barrell Lane, Longhope, Gloucestershire GL17 0LS

Mrs Elizabeth Beddows
☎ 01452 830484
SC From £155–£320
EM From £10
Sleeps 4–5
🐕 🐴 🎪 🕯
♟ ♟ *Commended*

Newly converted cottages in peaceful surroundings. Well equipped with dishwashers, microwaves, satellite TV, gas central heating, linen and electric all inclusive. Beautiful walking country. Evening meal available. Open all year.

Old Mill Farm, nr Cirencester, c/o Ermin House Farm, Syde, Cheltenham, Gloucestershire GL53 9PN

Mrs Catherine Hazell
☎ 01285 821255
SC From £135–£450
Sleeps 16
🐕 🐴
♟ ♟ ♟ ♟ *Commended*

Four superior barn conversions featuring Cotswold stone pillars and beams. Situated 4 miles from Cirencester on mixed farm beside River Thames and Cotswold Water Park for walking, birdwatching, fishing, sailing and jet skiing. Trains to London 1¼ hrs. Prices include full central heating, electricity, bed-linen, colour TV. Separate laundry room with pay-phone. Convenient for Stratford-upon-Avon, Oxford, Stonehenge, Bath and Tetbury. Open all year.

Shap House Farm Cottages, Shap House Lane, Yorkley, Gloucestershire GL15 4TY

Mrs Terry Capon
☎ 01594 562219
Fax 01594 564576
SC From £110–£210
Sleeps 20
🐴 🐕
♟ ♟ ♟–♟ ♟ ♟ ♟
Commended

Six well-equipped one and two-bedroomed cottages in a rural courtyard setting together with the owners' farm house. Perfectly placed for exploring the Forest of Dean with its many places of historic interest. Unlimited walking and wildlife, outdoor sports activities, pubs and restaurants. Within easy reach of Lydney, Chepstow, Monmouth, Ross-on-Wye, Gloucester and Bath. Open all year.

35 **Stable Cottage,** Home farm, Bredons Norton, Tewksbury, Gloucestershire GL20 7HA

Mick and Anne
Meadows
☎ 01684 772322
SC From £120–£260
Sleeps 5
🐕 🐎 ⅍ 🎄
Applied

Delightful Cotswold stone stable/barn conversion on a mixed working family farm in a quiet and pictuesque village under Bredon Hill. Very cosy and tastefully furnished. Full central heating, lots of beams, own paddock. Perfect location for touring the Cotswolds, Severn Valley and Malverns with many wonderful walks. Open all year.

36 **Warrens Gorse Cottages,** Home Farm, Warrens Gorse, Cirencester, Gloucestershire GL7 7JD

John & Nanette Randall
☎ 01285 831261
SC From £120–£180
Sleeps 3–5
🐎 🐕 ⅍
🐾 🐾 🐾 Approved

2½ miles from Cirencester between Daglingworth and Perrotts Brook, these attractive whitewashed cottages are ideally situated for touring the Cotswolds. The cottages are personally attended by the owners and are comfortably furnished and well equipped. 100-acre sheep, cattle and corn farm. Pottery workshop for visitors' use. Golf club nearby. Water sports 5 miles. Open Mar–Nov.

37 **Westley Farm,** Chalford, Stroud, Gloucestershire GL6 8HP

Julian Usborne
☎ 01285 760262
SC From £120–£280
Sleeps 2/5
🐕 🐎 🐎 🅰 🎄 🎄
🐾 🐾 – 🐾 🐾 🐾
Approved

Steep meadows of wild flowers and beech woods are the setting for this old fashioned 80-acre hill farm with breathtaking panoramic views over the Golden Valley. Children especially enjoy the donkey, calves, lambs and foals. Adults may prefer the complete tranquillity and abundant wildlife. Nearby horseriding, golf, gliding, watersports. Midway Cirencester – Stroud. Four cottages, two flats. Brochure available. Open Apr–Oct.

FARM HOLIDAY BUREAU

DISABLED VISITORS

Many members offer a welcome to disabled/less able visitors. Please do check the extent of the facilities before booking.

FARM HOLIDAY BUREAU

THOSE LITTLE EXTRAS

For advice on farms that can offer 'extras' such as four-poster beds, special diets, farm trails, fishing rights – even stabling and trekking arrangements if you are bringing your own horse – ring the Farm Holiday Bureau on (01203) 696909.

England's Heartland

Lincolnshire

Group Contact: *Mrs Stephanie Smith* ☎ *01507 363704*

A frequent comment of first-time visitors to Lincolnshire is "I never realised there was so much to see and do". This doesn't surprise us for we know that Lincolnshire is a large unspoilt county, full of variety and contrast waiting to be discovered.

There are some attractions that you will not want to miss: for instance, Lincoln with its magnificent cathedral, castle and Museum of Lincolnshire Life; Belton House near Grantham; Stamford, a near perfect stone town or its brick-built equivalent, Louth; Elizabethan houses such as Doddington Hall and Burghley House.

The best way to enjoy the county is to get in your car and see it for yourself. Take your time though – slow down your pace of life to match that of Lincolnshire. Drive into the countryside where you will have miles of road to yourself. Try the twisting hidden lanes of Tennyson Country where villages have names such as Bag Enderby and Ashby Puerorum. Tennyson Country forms the southern part of the Lincolnshire Wolds, designated as an Area of Outstanding Natural Beauty. Visit one of the unspoilt market towns, or go for a walk along part of the Viking Way.

Then there is Boston and its Stump, the nearby Memorial marking the spot where the Pilgrim Fathers tried to leave England ... sorry no more space – you'll just have to come and see for yourself!

Sheffield · Maltby · A1(M) · A631 · A159 · A63 · A15 · A46 · A16 · Dronfield · A57 · Gainsborough · Market Rasen · 14 · Worksop · A1 · A46 · 4 · 2 · Louth · Staveley · 10 · Chesterfield · Bolsover · 13 · 11 · Mablethorpe · Clay Cross · Warsop · A158 · Lincoln · 6 · Matlock · Mansfield · A46 · 7 · 12 · A158 · Wirksworth · Kirkby in Ashfield · A617 · Newark- · A15 · 1 · Skegness · Alfreton · A6097 · on-Trent · A153 · A61 · Belper · Ripley · M1 · A46 · Sleaford · A16 · A52 · Nottingham · Bingham · A1 · 5 · Derby · Radcliffe- · A52 · A17 · Boston · A6 · on-Trent · Grantham · Hunstanton · A607 · Ashby-De- · 9 · A15 · 3 · La-Zouch · Spalding · Holbeach · Coalville · A6 · Melton-Mowbray · Bourne · A17 · Kings · A148 · M1 · A606 · Rutland · A16 · Lynn · Leicester · Oakham · Water · Market · Wisbech · A47 · Deeping · Downham · Uppingham · 8 · Stamford · Peterborough · Market

BED AND BREAKFAST

(and evening meal)

---

① Beechwood Barn, North Moor Farm, Linwood Road, Martin, Lincoln LN4 3RA

Isobel Fletcher
☎ 01526 378339
🅱 From £15–£19
Sleeps 4
🐎 🐕 ♞ ♟ ✗
Listed *Commended*

We enjoy welcoming our guests to our delightful converted barn, still with its large open beams and memories of yesteryear. Right in the middle of Lincolnshire, ideal for touring. Cosy rooms, one double en suite and one twin bedroom with washbasin adjacent to the bathroom. Choice of generous breakfasts. Open all year.

---

② Bleasby House, Legsby, Market Rasen, Lincolnshire LN8 3QN

Janet Dring
☎ 01673 842383
🅱 From £18–£20
EM From £10–£12
Sleeps 5
🐎 ✂ ♥ ♞ ♟ ✗ ◎
🏵🏵 *Highly Commended*

Enjoy a peaceful break in welcoming farmhouse at foot of Lincolnshire Wolds. Spacious en suite rooms with colour TV. Flower-filled sun lounge and large garden. Ideal for touring beautiful countryside, historic Lincoln, Cadwell Park. Fly fishing and hard tennis court on farm. Evening meals by arrangement. Open all year.

---

③ Cackle Hill House, Cackle Hill Lane, Holbeach, Lincolnshire PE12 8BS

Maureen Biggadike
☎ 01406 426721
🅱 From £16–£19
EM From £12
Sleeps 6
🐎(10) ♞ ✂
🏵🏵 *Highly Commended*

We welcome you to our farm situated in rural position just off the A17. Comfortable accommodation (1 twin en suite, 1 double, 1 twin with washbasins and sharing guest bathroom) and traditional farmhouse fare. Farm walks, large patio and gardens. Close to the shores of the Wash with its marshes, trails and mature reserves, Spalding, Boston, Norfolk and Cambridgeshire. Open all year.

---

④ East Farm House, Middle Rasen Road, Buslingthorpe, Market Rasen, Lincolnshire LN3 5AQ

Mrs Gill Grant
☎ 01673 842283
🅱 From £18
EM From £12
Sleeps 4
🐎 ♞ ✂ ♟ ♟ ✗
🏵🏵 *Highly Commended*

Peace and relaxation await you in beamed 18th century listed farmhouse on 410 acre conservation award-winning farm with farm trail overlooking unspoilt countryside. Situated 4 miles SW of Market Rasen, ideal for rambling, touring beautiful Lincolnshire Wolds, coast, historic Lincoln and market towns. Wholesome farmhouse food, spacious bedrooms, TV and tea/coffee makers. 1 double en suite, 1 twin with private facilities. Guests' lounge. Business people welcome. Open all year.

---

⑤ Gelston Grange Farm, Nr Marston, Grantham, Lincolnshire NG32 2AQ

Janet Sharman
☎ 01400 250281
🅱 From £16–£20
Sleeps 6
🐎(5) ✂
🏵🏵 *Applied*

We are known for our welcome and homely atmosphere. Comfortable beds, 1 four poster en suite room, 1 double, 1 twin, all with HC, tea/coffee trays, TV, CH and tastefully decorated. Full English breakfast. Large garden. Lots of places to visit – Belton House, Lincoln, Newark, Boston and the coast, Robin Hood country. Northward on A1 take first right turn for Marston (after Grantham roundabout). Open all year except Christmas.

Greenfield Farm, Minting, near Horncastle, Lincolnshire LN9 5RX

Judy Bankes Price
☎ **01507 578457**
🆎 **From £18**
Sleeps 6
🛏 🕇 🚓 🗲 🛠 🛆 🌱 ◉
👑👑 *Highly Commended*

Judy and Hugh welcome you to their comfortable farmhouse set in a very quiet location yet centrally placed for all the major Lincolnshire attractions. Large garden pond, forest walks border the farm. Guests have their own sitting room with colour TV and woodburning stove, pretty en suite shower rooms, heated towel rails, radios, tea/coffee-making facilities, central heating. Excellent pub with traditional country cooking within 1 mile. AA Selected QQQQ

The Manor House, Manor Farm, Sleaford Road, Bracebridge Heath, Lincoln, Lincolnshire LN4 2HW

Mrs Jill Scoley
☎ **01522 520825**
Fax 01522 542418
🆎 **From £18**
Sleeps 6
🐕(10) 🗲 ◉
👑 *Highly Commended*

Welcome to Lincolnshire. Stay in a lovely Georgian Farmhouse situated in large walled garden. 3 miles south of Lincoln. Comfortable bedrooms with washbasins, radio, tea/coffee facilities. Large lounge with log fire for cooler evenings. Open all year (closed Christmas and New Year).

Midstone Farmhouse, Southorpe, Stamford, Lincolnshire PE9 3BX

Mr & Mrs C Harrison-Smith
☎/Fax **01780 740136**
🆎 **From £17.50–£20**
EM From £10
Sleeps 6
🐕 🕇 🛆
Listed *Commended*

A warm welcome awaits you at Midstone Farmhouse where adults and children alike will enjoy meeting Dexter cattle ponies, rabbits, ducks and George, the potbellied pig. Stamford with its fine Elizabethan Burghley House, the cathedral city of Peterborough, Rutland Water and the Nene Valley Steam Railway (with Thomas the Tank Engine) are all close by.

Sycamore Farm, Bassingthorpe, Grantham, Lincs NG33 4ED   ⑨

Mrs Sue Robinson
☎ **01476 585274**
🆎 **From £17.50**
EM From £10
Sleeps 6
🐕(6) 🗲
👑👑 *Highly Commended*

Relax and unwind in rural South Lincolnshire. Sycamore Farm stands amid beautiful peaceful surroundings yet perfectly situated for the A1 (4 miles), Grantham, Stamford, Lincoln, historic Belton and Burghley. 3 spacious attractively furnished bedrooms (2 en suite) all with colour TV, radio alarms, tea trays and lovely unspoilt views. Guests' sitting room with comfy sofas and armchairs, log fires on chilly evenings, board games, local guide books and maps. Open all year.

SELF-CATERING

East Farm Cottage, c/o East Farm, Buslingthorpe, Market Rasen, Lincolnshire LN3 5AQ

Mrs Gill Grant
☎ **01673 842283**
🆑 **From £160–£210**
Sleeps 4 +cot
🐕 🕇 🚓 🛆 🌱
🐾 🐾 🐾 *Commended*

This newly refurbished cosy farm cottage with enclosed garden, surrounded by cornfields, nestles at the foot of the scenic Wolds. Lovely, peaceful location on our 400-acre arable farm, 4 miles SW Market Rasen. Central for touring and walking in Lincolnshire. Fully equipped, 1 double, 1 twin, linen provided, CH and log fire, TV. Short breaks available. Open all year.

---

11 **Mill Lodge,** Benniworth House Farm, Donington on Bain, Louth, Lincs LN11 9RD

Mrs Pamela M. Cade
☎ 01507 343265
SC From £100–£220
Sleeps 6

Commended

Ezra and Pamela Cade welcome you to a delightful cottage on a traditional farm/Nature reserve in the beautiful Bain valley. Spacious grounds with conservatory, patio, lawn, flowering shrubs and lock up garage. Lovely walks with well maintained footpaths. Many species, some rare. Children welcome. Open all year.

---

12 **Pantiles Cottage,** c/o The Old Hall, Church Lane, Potterhanworth, Lincoln, Lincolnshire LN4 2DS

Mrs Susan Battle
☎ 01522 791338
Fax 01522 794888
SC From £180–£250
Sleeps 5

Commended

A bottle of wine welcomes you to Pantiles. It is a charming oak-beamed cottage which has been tastefully decorated and furnished to accommodate 5 people. Its quiet garden and patio overlook fields and a duckpond. Situated 7 miles from Lincoln, it is within reach of many places of interest. Linen is provided and there is central heating, a log fire and TV. Open all year.

---

13 **Pingles Cottage,** c/o Grange Farm, Broxholme, Nr Saxilby, Lincoln, Lincolnshire LN1 2NG

Pat Sutcliffe
☎ 01522 702441
SC From £180–£215
Sleeps 4

Commended

A 19th century farm cottage with its own lawn and garden, surrounded by sheep and corn fields, in the hamlet of Broxholme 6 miles from historic Lincoln. Pingles is comfortable and well-equipped for 4 people . Plenty of interesting things to do and see in the area or relax on the river bank and enjoy your own ½ mile of coarse fishing. Open all year.

---

14 **Waingrove Farm,** Fulstow, Louth, Lincolnshire LN11 0XQ

Stephanie Smith
☎ 01507 363704
SC From £175
Sleeps 2–6 + cots

Highly Commended

A tea tray with Lincolnshire plum bread and Poacher cheese, a bottle of wine, fresh flowers, newspaper and magazines welcome guests to our cottages. The farmhouse is spacious (even a nursery) combining traditional charm with excellent facilities. Bramble and Hawthorn are single storey and overlook a 'courtyard' of restored farm buildings. Open all year.

LET THE TELEPHONE RING!

Some farmhouses are big places. Let the telephone ring long enough to give the owner time to answer it.

England's Heartland

Northamptonshire

Group Contact: *Mrs A M Singlehurst* ☎ *01832 205222*

Northamptonshire, the county of 'squires and spires', has houses, monuments and fine churches too numerous to mention. There's Sulgrave Manor, home of George Washington's ancestors; Rockingham Castle which was 'Arnescote Castle' in the BBC TV series 'By the Sword Divided'; Boughton House, modelled on Versailles; and Althorp, the home of Earl Spencer, brother of the Princess of Wales.

At the castle remains, by the river in picturesque Fotheringhay, you may ponder upon the execution of Mary, Queen of Scots and the birth there of Richard III, and the Battle and Farm Museum will give you a taste of that decisive Civil War battle in 1645. A firm hold has been kept on our heritage and at Brixworth and Earls Barton you will be able to see possibly the country's finest examples of a Saxon church and tower. Many of the county's villages and towns have splendid churches dating from Norman times through to the 15th century.

Traditional methods of transport and entertainment are well preserved. The Waterways Museum at Stoke Bruerne gives you a fascinating insight into life on the canals, and there are boat trips along the Grand Union Canal. On the Nene Valley Steam Railway you can take a nostalgic trip down the line and study steam trains and rolling stock from all over the world.

BED AND BREAKFAST

(and evening meal)

---

① Castle Farm Guest House, Fotheringhay, Peterborough PE8 5HZ

Stephanie Gould
☎ 01832 226200
BB From £24–£30
EM From £9.50
Sleeps 11
♿ ⅙ ⛯ ☆
👑👑 *Applied*

Beautifully situated Victorian farmhouse on banks of the River Nene. Superb accommodation provided in rooms converted to highest standard. Private facilities, TV, etc plus guests' sitting and dining rooms. Excellent pub within strolling distance through village steeped in history. Open all year.

---

② Dairy Farm, Cranford St Andrew, Kettering, Northamptonshire NN14 4AQ

Audrey Clarke
☎ 01536 330273
BB From £18–£25
EM From £11
Sleeps 6
🐴 🐕 ⛯ ☆ ♿
👑👑👑 *Commended*

Enjoy a holiday in a comfortable 17th century farmhouse with oak beams and inglenook fireplaces. Four poster bed now available. Peaceful surroundings, large garden containing ancient circular dovecote. Dairy Farm is a working farm situated in a beautiful Northamptonshire village just off the A14 within easy reach of many places of interest or ideal for a restful holiday. Good farmhouse food and friendly atmosphere. Open all year.

---

③ Drayton Lodge, Daventry, Northamptonshire NN11 4NL

Ann Spicer
☎ 01327 702449
Fax 01327 72110
BB From £20–£25
EM From £12
Sleeps 8
🐴 🐕 ☆
👑👑👑 *Applied*

Drayton Lodge is a secluded 18th century farmhouse set on the edge of Daventry to one side and rolling Northamptonshire countryside to the other. A warm, friendly welcome awaits you. Beautiful centrally heated bedrooms with en suite bathrooms and TVs. Championship golf course within ½ mile. Historical places of interest to visit. Full traditional English breakfast served. Open all year.

---

④ The Elms, Kislingbury, Northampton NN7 4AH

Mrs Sanders
☎ 01604 830326
BB From £17.50
Sleeps 5
♿ ⅙ ☆ ♿
Listed *Applied*

A warm welcome awaits you in our Victorian farmhouse with views over the farm. Situated 2 miles from M1 Junction 16 and 4 miles from Northampton. Convenient for business stopovers and touring Cotswolds, Stratford, Oxford and Cambridge. Nene Way Walk passes through the farm. Open all year.

---

⑤ Green Farm, Weedon Lois, Towcester, Northamptonshire NN12 8PL

Mrs Paddy Elkington
☎ 01327 860249
BB From £17.50–£20
EM From £10
Sleeps 6
♿ ⛄ ⛯ ♿
Listed *Commended*

Green Farm is a comfortable 18th century farmhouse set in rolling countryside on a 550-acre mixed farm. You can enjoy private coarse fishing or visit the many local attractions, including Sulgrave Manor, Canons Ashby, and Silverstone Grand Prix circuit to name but a few! The M1 and M40 are both within 10 miles. Open all year.

Home Farm, Spratton, Northamptonshire NN6 8HW

Sue Roberts
☎ **01604 847303**
Fax **01604 820539**
🅱🅱 From £15–£16
Sleeps 4
🌣 ⛾ ✂ ♨
Listed *Applied*

Mike and Sue Roberts welcome you to their 18th century thatched farmhouse offering comfortable accommodation and traditional English breakfast. A pleasant and spacious garden can be used by guests to sit and relax. Spratton, on A50 8mN Northampton, is conveniently situated for visits to Cottesbrooke Hall, Althorp, Lamport Hall, Holdenby House Gardens and Coton Manor Gardens. Local churches of special interest. Open all year.

Lilford Lodge Farm, Barnwell, Oundle, Peterborough, Northamptonshire PE8 5SA

Trudy Dijksterhuis
☎ **01832 272230**
🅱🅱 From £18–£21
Sleeps 5
🌣 ⛾ ♨ 🌿
♨ ♨ *Commended*

Mixed farm set in the attractive Nene Valley situated on the A605, 3 miles south of Oundle and 5 miles north of the A14. Peterborough and Stamford are within easy reach. Guests stay in the recently converted original 19th century farmhouse. All bedrooms have en suite bathrooms, CH, radio and tea/coffee-making facilities. Comfortable lounge with satellite TV and separate dining room. Coarse fishing available.

Manor Farm, Adstone, Towcester, Northamptonshire NN12 8DT

Elisabeth Paton
☎ **01327 860284**
🅱🅱 From £15–£18
EM From £9 (by arrangement only)
Sleeps 6
⛾ 🌣 🧍 ♨ ■ 🌿
♨ ♨ *Commended*

Peace and quiet but plenty to see and do at this 430-acre farm. The farmhouse, built by an ancestor of George Washington in 1656, stands on the edge of a tiny village. Enjoy woodland walks, ponds, wildlife and flowers or explore nearby historic houses, the Cotswolds, Stratford-upon-Avon, Silverstone. Try our clay pigeon shooting instruction, fun for all the family. Open all year.

Murcott Mill, Long Buckby, Northamptonshire NN6 7QR

Carrie & Brian Hart
☎ **01327 842236**
🅱🅱 From £17.50–£20
EM From £7.50
Sleeps 6
🌣 🌣 ♨ 🧍 ♨ ♨
♨ ♨ *Commended*

Murcott Mill is an imposing Georgian mill house set within a working farm. It has a large garden and lovely outlook over open countryside. All rooms are en suite with colour TV. Central heating throughout and visitors have their own lounge and dining room with open log fires. An ideal stopover, close to M1 and good location for touring the area. Open all year.

Pear Tree Farm, Main Street, Aldwincle, Nr Kettering, Northamptonshire NN14 3EL

Mavis Hankins
☎ **01832 720614**
🅱🅱 From £18
EM From £10
Sleeps 4
🌣(10) ♨ 🧍 ♨
♨ ♨ ♨ *Commended*

Pear Tree Farm is a mixed 400-acre farm consisting of cattle, sheep, poultry and arable. Comfortably furnished with relaxed family atmosphere and good home cooking. Four bedrooms. Excellent for walking, birdwatching, fishing. Large garden for relaxing. Open all year except Christmas (camping Feb–Sept).

Quinton Green Farm, Quinton, Northamptonshire NN7 2EG

Mrs Margaret Turney
☎ **01604 863685**
Fax **01604 862230**
🅱🅱 From £18–£20
Sleeps 5
⛾ 🌣 ♨
♨ ♨ *Applied*

The Turney family look forward to welcoming you to their comfortable, rambling 17th century farmhouse, only 10 mins from Northampton, yet overlooking lovely rolling countryside. We are close to Salcey Forest, with its wonderful facilities for walking. M1 (Jct. 15) is just 5 mins away; central Milton Keynes 20 mins. Open all year.

(12) Spinney Lodge Farm, Hanslope, Milton Keynes, Buckinghamshire MK19 7DE

Mrs Christine Payne
☎ 01908 510267
🛏 From £18–£20
Sleeps 4
🐕(12) ⚇ ♛ ♨
☛ Applied

Spinney Lodge is a arable, beef and sheep farm. The lovely Victorian farmhouse with its large garden and rose pergola has en suite bedrooms with colour TV and tea–making facilities. Evening meal by arrangement. M1 Junc 15, 8 minutes, 12 minutes Northampton, 15 minutes Milton Keynes. Many historical houses and gardens to visit in the area. Open all year.

(13) Walltree House Farm, Steane, Brackley, Northamptonshire NN13 5NS

Richard & Pauline Harrison
☎ 01295 811235
Fax 01295 811147
🛏 From £20–£30
EM From £10
Sleeps 16
🐕 ⚇ ⛨ ♛ ♨ ⚜ ☯
☛☛☛ Applied

Our home is in the middle of nowhere but at the centre of everything. Badger woods to explore, lovely walks. Historic places to visit. Individual ground floor rooms in the courtyard now with four new additional luxury rooms, others in the adjacent licensed Victorian farmhouse. Most rooms en suite. Nearby shopping, fishing, golf, gliding, Silverstone Circuit and leisure centres. Open all year except Christmas & New Year.

(14) West End Farm, 5 West End, Welford, Northamptonshire NN6 6HJ

Mrs Susie Bevin
☎ 01858 575226
🛏 From £16–£20
Sleeps 4
🐕 ⚇ ☯
☛ Commended

This comfortable 1848 farmhouse is set in beautiful countryside. Twin and double rooms both have washbasins and tea–making facilities, double with en suite WC. Guests' sitting room with woodburner and TV. In a quiet village street with 4 local pubs. Near A50/A14 access, M1/J20. Convenient for Stanford, Lamport, Althorp and Cottesbrook, Naseby Battlefield, Cold Ashby and S. Kilworth Golf. On the Jurassic Way. Good holiday or business base. Open all year.

(15) West Lodge Farm, Pipewell Road, Desborough, Northamptonshire NN14 2SH

Margaret Dee
☎ 01536 760552
🛏 From £20–£24
Sleeps 4
⚘ 🐕 ♛ ♨ ☯
☛☛ Highly Commended

This conservation prize-winning farm has friendly, comfortable accommodation in the William IV farmhouse. Woodland walks and farm animal centre supply recreation plus all local attractions. Rare breeds of pig and sheep and delightful fancy chickens within easy access of farmhouse. Peaceful country location far from town stress. Open all year.

(16) Wold Farm, Old, Northampton, Northamptonshire NN6 9RJ

Anne Engler
☎ 01604 781258
🛏 From £20–£22
EM From £12
Sleeps 10
⚘ 🐕 ♨ ☯
☛☛☛ Applied

A friendly, informal atmosphere is offered at this 18th century farmhouse on 250-acre beef/arable farm. Main farmhouse offers attractive bedrooms. Hearty breakfast is served in oak-beamed dining room with inglenook fireplace. Relax by log fire or at snooker table. Recently converted barn provides en suite rooms overlooking pretty garden with colourful Pergola. Snacks or four course evening meals on request. Open all year.

FARM HOLIDAY BUREAU

Please mention **Stay on a Farm** when booking

SELF-CATERING

Cranford Farm, Cranford Hall, Cranford, Kettering, Northamptonshire NN14 4AL

Gayle Robinson
☎ 01536 330248
SC £235
Sleeps 5
🐎 🎠 🛡 🌾
🐾 🐾 🐾 *Commended*

Lovely Georgian mansion in the heart of a traditional estate village which is set in parkland amidst fine gardens. Many attractive walks and drives to be taken, together with historic spots to visit and a great range of cultural activities. The Villiers Suite is a stylish, self–contained apartment within the Hall.

Granary Cottage, Brook Farm, Lower Benefield, Peterborough PE8 5AE

Mrs J Singlehurst
☎ 01832 205215
SC From £150–£250
Sleeps 4
🗁(4)
🐾 🐾 🐾 *Commended*

At the beginning of a gated road we offer peace and tranquillity with picturesque walks. Granary Cottage is warm, cosy and well equipped with linen provided. Close by are the historic market towns of Oundle and Stamford and the pretty village of Rockingham. Sorry no pets. Open all year.

Papley Farm Cottages, Papley Farm, Warmington, Peterborough PE8 6UU

Joyce Lane
☎ 01832 272583
SC From £100–£340
Sleeps 2/5
🐎 🎠 🛡 ◉
🐾 🐾 🐾 🐾 *Highly Commended*

A warm welcome, peace and comfort await you deep in the heart of our large mixed farm above the Nene Valley. Choose a modern bungalow or one of four beautifully restored cottages where beams and inglenooks from 16th Century combine with today's luxuries in a large sunny garden – safe for children. All are warm, well equipped and carefully prepared especially for you. Near Oundle and Stamford. 5 miles from A1. Free brochure. Open all year.

Rye Hill Farm, Holdenby Road, East Haddon, Northamptonshire NN6 8DH

Michael & Margaret Widdowson
☎ 01604 770990
Fax 01604 770237
SC From £125–£360
Sleeps 2/6
🐎 🦌 ♿ 🎠 🛡 🌾 ◉
🐾 🐾 🐾 🐾 *Highly Commended*

Children are most welcome on our delightful, peaceful smallholding. They may search for eggs, feed the lambs, pigs, goats, chickens, ducks and geese or play in our games room. Our 4 cottages are maintained to a very high standard. They have every modern convenience combined with beams, open fires or log burning stoves. Many places of interest for the family. Open all year.

LET THE TELEPHONE RING!

Some farmhouses are big places. Let the telephone ring long enough to give the owner time to answer it.

England's Heartland

Leicestershire

Group Contact: *Ruth Lovett* ☎ *01530 270465*

Leicestershire is a land of transquil beauty spread with reminders of a turbulent history ... and it begins at every turn-off from any main road.

To find the true Leicestershire just travel over high horizons and narrow farm tracks, explore vast Rutland Water and the lazy green banks of the Grand Union Canal, take a nostalgic trip on our wealth of steam railways, walks in historic Bradgate Park or 'do battle' in Bosworth Field. Explore the counties curious customs which take place annually, such as Bottle Kicking and the Hare Pie Scramble between Hallata and Medbourne, or visit our castles and museums, timber framed cottages and grand mansions, theatres and theme parks.

Fun for the youngsters down on the farm – lambing Sundays and rare breeds; always wanted to touch the animals? – here you can. Spoil yourselves in our tea rooms, browse in the specialist shops and museums – all this and more in this green and undulating county.

BED AND BREAKFAST
(and evening meal)

Measham House Farm, Gallows Lane, Measham, Nr Swadlincote, Leicestershire DE12 7HD

Ruth Lovett
☎ 01530 270465
[BB] From £17.50–£19
Sleeps 6
�־ ⼎ ⼈ ⼤ ⼫
♛♛ *Highly Commended*

A warm welcome awaits you from John and Ruth Lovett and family, at their Georgian farmhouse, a Grade II listed building, on a 500-acre working farm. Situated on the Derbys/Leics/Staffs/Warks borders. Ideal for visiting a wealth of fascinating places. Within easy reach of Birmingham, Nottingham and Leicester and the NEC, Birmingham International Airport and East Midlands Airport.

Three Ways Farm, Melton Road, Queniborough, Leicester LE7 3FN

Mrs Janet S. Clarke
☎ 0116 2600472
[BB] From £15–£20
Sleeps 6
�־ ⼎ ⼙ ⼧ ⼒
Listed *Commended*

It's hard to believe you're only 6 miles north of Leicester in lovely Queniborough with its ancient church, thatched cottages and two good pubs. You'll be welcomed at the Clarke's bungalow in peaceful fields. All bedrooms have colour TV, tea/coffee facilities. West of Melton Road, ¼ m A607 Queniborough roundabout, connects with Leicester western bypass. Nottingham and Birmingham NEC 40 mins. Open all year except Christmas.

SELF-CATERING

Brook Meadow Holiday Chalets, Welford Road, Sibbertoft, Market Harborough, Leicestershire LE16 9UJ

Mary and Jasper Hart
☎/Fax 01858 880886
[SC] From £120–£220
Sleeps 8
�־ ⼎ ⼈ ⼫ ⼒
⼀⼀ *Commended*

We are centrally placed being near to the borders of Northamptonshire, Leicestershire and Warwickshire. Two Norwegian spruce chalets beside a peaceful 5 acre carp fishing lake in the middle of our 600 acre farm. Both chalets are furnished to a high standard, equipped with shower, microwave, colour TV and all linen. Brochure available. Open all year.

NO ANSWER?
Farmers are mostly out and about during the day.
Try to telephone before 9.30am or after 4pm.

England's Heartland
Bedfordshire

Group Contacts: ⒷⒷ *Mrs Janet Must* ☎ *01234 870234*
ⓈⒸ *Mrs Angela Little* ☎ *01525 712978*

We invite you to spend some time in the County of Bedfordshire in the rural heartland of England, ideally situated between Oxford and Cambridge. The Great Ouse, with its quiet backwaters together with the Lakes at Stewartby, Wyboston and Grafham make ideal venues for the fisherman and the watersports enthusiast. Cyclists will appreciate the ease with which they can travel throughout the area, while walkers will find the Greensand Ridge Walk provides many routes. Golfers also have a wide choice of courses.

Stately homes include Woburn Abbey and Luton Hoo, plus pretty villages with thatched cottages and beamed Tudor buildings. The National Trust owns the extraordinary 16th-century stone dovecote and stables at Willington, plus 50 acres of hill country at Dunstable Downs.

Bedford Museum and John Bunyan Museum are well worth a visit. The Cecil Higgins Art Gallery enjoys an international reputation for the quality of its collections. Luton Museum and Art Gallery exhibit local and natural history, archaeology and lace, while Stockwood Park Craft Museum has exhibits relating to rural life and crafts.

Visit the Shuttleworth Collection of historic aeroplanes and road vehicles, or for garden enthusiasts there is the Swiss Garden and Wrest Park Gardens.

For the naturalist there is the RSPB nature reserve and headquarters at Sandy. For something more exotic, visit Whipsnade Zoo or the Wild Animal Kingdom at Woburn. Whatever your interests you'll enjoy your stay in Bedfordshire.

BED AND BREAKFAST
(and evening meal)

Church Farm, High Street, Roxton, Bedford, Bedfordshire MK44 3EB

Janet Must
☎ 01234 870234
Fax 01234 871576
[BB] From £16–£19
Sleeps 6
🐓 🐕 ✄ ♞ ▪
☙ *Commended*

An attractive old farmhouse with a comfortable self-contained guest wing overlooking the garden and small orchard. Situated in a quiet village ½ mile from A1. Large bedrooms with tea and coffee-making facilities. Guests' lounge. Full English breakfast served in 16th century dining room. We offer double, single and family accommodation. Open all year.

Firs Farm, Stagsden, Bedfordshire MK43 8TB

Mrs Pam Hutcheon
☎ 01234 822344
[BB] From £15–£20
Sleeps 6
🐕 🐓 ♞ ▪
☙ ☙ *Commended*

Firs Farm is a family run arable farm, set in quiet surroundings ¼ mile south of A422. The farmhouse is timber framed and set in a large garden with swimming pool. Accommodation consists of double or twin (1 en suite) rooms with tea/coffee making facilities and guests' lounge with colour TV. Many local tourist attractions. Open all year.

Highfield Farm, Great North Road, Sandy, Bedfordshire SG19 2AQ

Margaret Codd
☎ 01767 682332
[BB] From £16–£25
Sleeps 8
🐕 🐓 ✄
☙ ☙ *Highly Commended*

Tom and Margaret Codd welcome guests to their comfortable farmhouse. Just 1 mile north of Sandy on the A1, Highfield Farm is excellently situated for visiting Cambridge, Shuttleworth, the RSPB, Grafham Water and for taking the Greensand Ridge Walk. Family, double and single bedrooms, most with en suite bathroom. Guests' sitting room with log fire and colour TV. Open all year.

Model Farm, Little Gransden, Sandy, Bedfordshire SG19 3EA

Mrs S Barlow
☎ 01767 677361
[BB] From £14–£17
Sleeps 4
🐕 🐓 ✄ ☜
Listed *Applied*

A warm welcome awaits visitors to this traditional farmhouse set in open countryside between the villages of Lt. Gransden and Longstowe. Ideally situated for visiting or working in the Cambridge or Bedford area. The National Trust property Wimpole Hall is 10 minutes' drive away. Duxford, the Shuttleworth Collection and the RSPB are within easy reach.

LET THE TELEPHONE RING!
Some farmhouses are big places. Let the telephone ring
long enough to give the owner time to answer it.

FARM HOLIDAY BUREAU

SELF-CATERING

---

⑤ 'The Old Stone Barn', c/o Home Farm, Warrington, Olney, Buckinghamshire MK46 4HN

Mr & Mrs G. Pibworth
☎ 01234 711655
Fax 01234 711855
🆂🅲 From £140–£320
Sleep 1/6

Highly Commended

A charming combination of old character and modern facilities, the Old Stone Barn is 3 ground floor and 3 first floor spacious self-contained apartments peacefully positioned on an arable farm 1½ miles north of Olney. Relax in the gardens, make use of the outdoor heated swimming pool or take day trips to Oxford, Cambridge, London or the Cotswolds. Open all year.

---

⑥ Priestley Farm, Church Road, off Temple Way, Flitwick, Bedfordshire MK45 5AN

Mrs Angela Little
☎ 01525 712978
🆂🅲 From £150–£180
Sleeps 6

Approved

The Georgian farmhouse set in open countryside offers 3 double bedrooms (one twin bedded), bathroom, lounge, kitchen/diner. Central heating. Linen provided. A working family dairy farm with 90 Jersey cows and young stock. Visitors are welcome to watch the milking and other seasonal activities. Shopping facilities and main railway station etc 2 miles, M1, 4 miles. Plenty of footpaths to enjoy the Bedfordshire countryside. Open all year.

THE 1000+ BUREAU MEMBERS OFFER A UNIQUE LINK TO CUSTOMERS ACROSS THE UK

All Bureau members belong to a local Group. Each member can refer you to an equally high quality member within his Group… or across the UK: England, Northern Ireland, Scotland, Wales.

LET THE TELEPHONE RING!

Some farmhouses are big places. Let the telephone ring long enough to give the owner time to answer it.

England's Heartland

Hertfordshire & East Buckinghamshire

Group Contacts: [BB] *Mrs A Knowles* ☎ *01442 866541*
[SC] *Mr M Buisman* ☎ *01438 718641*

Hertfordshire, a county of contrasts, is in the unique situation of being at the hub of the country's transport network whilst offering some truly unspoilt and varied rural landscapes. It well deserves the title it is often given:

'England's Best Kept Secret'.

Our area is rich in historical heritage with some important Roman sites: St Albans was the Roman town Verulamium, first recorded in 54BC. Those interested in history will enjoy many other sites including the Old Palace and House in Hatfield Park and Knebworth House.

Come and enjoy the Chiltern landscape including many picturesque villages such as Aldbury, Frithesden and The Lee. The 4,000 acres of ancient woodland of the National Trust's Ashridge Estate offer a wealth of wildlife including herds of wild deer.

Our farms can also offer the businessman or woman the chance to unwind in a homely atmosphere as little as half an hour by train from central London and close to the M1, M25 and four southern airports. A welcome change from the less individual hospitality of large hotels.

BED AND BREAKFAST

(and evening meal)

① Broadway Farm, Berkhamsted, Hertfordshire HP4 2RR

Mrs Alison Knowles
☎/Fax 01442 866541
🆎 From £19–£27
Sleeps 6
🐕 🛇 🌀 🚭 🕭 🎣 🛢
🌺🌺 *Applied*

A warm welcome is guaranteed at Broadway, a working arable farm with own fishing lake. 3 comfortable en suite rooms in recently converted buildings adjacent to farmhouse. Tea/coffee-making facilities, colour TV, CH. Everything for the leisure or business guest – the relaxation of farm life in an attractive rural setting, yet easy access to London, airports, motorways and mainline rail services. Open all year (closed Christmas).

② Church Farm, Ardeley, Stevenage, Hertfordshire SG2 7AH

Roger and Wendy Waygood
☎ 01438 861260
🆎 From £21.50
Sleeps 4
🚭 🌀
🌺🌺 *Applied*

Relax and enjoy the peace of our quiet rural village in NE Herts midway between A1 (M) Stevenage and A10 Buntingford. The newly converted luxury en suite bedrooms with TV and tea/coffee facilities overlook our tranquil water garden. Convenient for Luton and Stansted Airports. No smoking. Regret no children or pets. Open all year except Christmas and Easter.

③ Middle Farm, Throcking, Buntingford, Hertfordshire SG9 9RN

Sally Smyth
☎ 01763 281204
🆎 From £18.50–£25
Sleeps 5
🐕 🚶 📺 🌀 🛢
Applied

Victorian farmhouse with wonderful views over the open countryside. Ideally sited for Knebworth Park, Wimpole Hall, Duxford or Cambridge. One beamed double bedroom with en suite and small lobby for child's bed and one twin bedroom. All rooms have tea/coffee facilities and remote controlled colour TV. Lovely walks and good restaurants nearby. No pets. Holiday cottages also available. Open all year.

SELF-CATERING

④ Bluntswood Hall Cottages, Middle Farm, Throcking, Buntingford, Hertfordshire SG9 9RN

Sally Smyth
☎ 01763 281204
🆑 From £150–£250
Sleeps 4
🐕 🚶 🌀 🛢
🎣 🎣 🎣 🎣 *Commended*

Stables recently converted into 2 cottages with lovely views over the countryside. Ideally situated for Cambridge, Duxford, Wimpole Hall or Knebworth Park. Each beamed cottage has double bedroom, bunk bedroom or single bed, bathroom, fitted kitchen and sitting room. R/C colour TV, CH. Linen and towels included in price. Children welcome. No pets. Open all year.

Gamekeeper's Lodge, Lockley Farm, Welwyn, Hertfordshire AL6 0BL ⑤

Marinus G T Buisman
☎ 01438 718641
Fax 01438 714238
⌧ From £225–£400
Sleeps 6 + cot
⊟ ✕ ⚊ ◼ ⚓
⚓ ⚓ ⚓ *Commended*

Situated in fenced garden against woodland with superb view from furnished terrace with built-in BBQ. facing south. Double bedroom, bedroom with two bunkbeds, bathroom, shower, lounge, kitchen/dining room, utility, WC/shower. Storage heating, open fire, CTV, wash/tumble dryer, fridge/ freezer, microwave/oven dishwasher, payphone. Linen included, not electricity. Golf, riding, swimming nearby. Sorry no pets. London 25 miles. Open all year.

FOLLOW THE COUNTRY CODE

Leave nothing but footprints,

Take nothing but photographs,

Kill nothing but time!

BUREAU ACCOMMODATION MEANS QUALITY

All Bureau members are inspected and quality graded by the National Tourist Board each year, as well as by fellow members.

THOSE LITTLE EXTRAS

For advice on farms that can offer 'extras' such as four-poster beds, special diets, farm trails, fishing rights – even stabling and trekking arrangements if you are bringing your own horse – ring the Farm Holiday Bureau on (01203) 696909.

England's Heartland

Cambridgeshire

Group Contact: *Mrs Hilary Nix* ☎ *01353 778369*

Cambridgeshire is a county of contrasts, a county of quiet waterways, gentle hills, lanes, busy towns, attractions great and small, all presented with a friendly welcome for the visitor.

Best known is Cambridge itself, one of Britain's oldest university cities where the colleges in their architectural splendour rest near tranquil rivers overhung with willows, the city that inspired Brooke and Byron.

As well as Cambridge the county has many other attractions. North of Cambridge lies the strikingly flat landscape of the Fens. This once barren marshland was home to the 'Fen Tigers' who lived by cutting reeds and catching eels. Today, the landscape is crisscrossed with dykes which have vastly improved the drainage of this peaty area and made the land a valuable asset for farming.

For contrast there is the hustle and bustle of the modern city of Peterborough with its excellent shopping or the stately grandeur of Ely Cathedral, so called 'Ship of the Fens'.

Wherever you go in Cambridgeshire it is a beautiful county to explore with large towns and small villages, cathedrals and tiny churches and cricket on the village green.

Market Deeping · Wisbech · Downham Market · Rutland Water · Oakham · Stamford · A47 · A134 · A47 · Whittlesey · March · Uppingham · Peterborough · A10 · A1065 · A43 · A605 · Chatteris · Market Harborough · Corby · Oundle · Ramsey · 4 · A1 · 2 · Ely · A11 · Desborough · Kettering · A142 · A142 · Rothwell · A14 · Huntingdon · A141 · A1123 · A10 · A14 · A508 · Raunds · St. Ives · 3 · A43 · A45 · Higham Ferrars · Godmanchester · A14 · A14 · Rushden · A428 · 14 · Cambridge · Northampton · A6 · A428 · 1 · 13 · A1198 · 12 · A11 · A428 · A1 · 11 · 15 · A428 · 10 · Bedford · Biggleswade · 9 · A5 · Newport · A6 · Royston · Saffron Walden · Milton Keynes · 14 · Pagnell · A505

BED AND BREAKFAST

(and evening meal)

Gransden Lodge Farm, Little Gransden, Sandy, Bedfordshire SG19 3EB

Mrs Mary Cox
☎ **01767 677365**
Fax 01767 677647
[BB] **From £14.50–£18**
Sleeps 6
🐴 🐕 🍴 ⛺ 💼
🐾🐾 *Highly Commended*

A warm and friendly atmosphere awaits you at Gransden Lodge, where we have double, twin and single rooms with TV, clock-radio and tea/coffee-making facilities. Ample bathrooms and WCs. Dining room, also large lounge with TV. A.A. QQQ. Many local pubs and restaurants for evening meals. Situated on the B1046, west of Cambridge. London 50 miles. Also convenient for Stansted Airport (M11, jct. 12). Open all year.

Hill House Farm, 9 Main Street, Coveney, Ely, Cambridgeshire CB6 2DJ

Hilary Nix
☎ **01353 778369**
[BB] **From £18**
Sleeps 6
🍴 🐕 🐴(12)
🐾🐾 *Highly Commended*

A warm welcome awaits you at this spacious Victorian farmhouse. Situated in quiet fenland village, 3 miles west of the historic cathedral city of Ely. Open views of the surrounding countryside. Easy access to Cambridge, Newmarket & Huntingdon. Wicken Fen and Welney Wildfowl Trust are nearby. 3 tastefully furnished and decorated bedrooms, all en suite (1 on ground floor). All have own entrance, colour TV, etc full CH. Open all year.

Spinney Abbey, Wicken, Ely, Cambridgeshire CB7 5XQ

Mrs Valerie Fuller
☎ **01353 720971**
[BB] **From £18**
Sleeps 6
🐴(5)
🐾🐾 *Applied*

Spacious Georgian farmhouse, standing in a large garden with tennis court on our dairy farm which borders the National Trust nature reserve Wicken Fen. Two en suite double rooms and twin with private bathroom. Central heating and electric blankets for colder months. All with TV and tea/coffee tray. Guests' sitting room. Open all year except Christmas.

SELF-CATERING

Hill House Farm Cottage, 9 Main Street, Coveney, Ely, Cambs CB6 2DJ

Hilary Nix
☎ **01353 778369**
[SC] **From £180–£300**
Sleeps 6
🐴(8) 🍴
🔑🔑🔑 *Highly Commended*

A tasteful barn conversion on our farm is now a comfortable cottage. Furnished and decorated to a high standard. Set in a quiet village location 3 miles west of Ely with open views of Ely Cathedral and the surrounding countryside. Ideally situated for touring Norfolk, Suffolk and Cambridgeshire. Easy access to Cambridge, Newmarket and Huntingdon. Access form A142 or A10. Regret no smoking, no pets. Open all year.

England's Heartland
Norfolk and Suffolk

Group Contacts: 🅱🅱 *Mrs Rosemary Bryce* ☎/Fax 01473 652253
🆂🅲 *Mrs Margaret Langton* ☎/Fax 01473 652210

For the visitor in search of something a little different, this part of East Anglia has many delights to offer. One of the driest and sunniest parts of England, it is quiet and peaceful with traffic-free roads which enables one really to appreciate the beauty of this truly rural area. The small towns and villages with their medieval churches (and pubs!) are full of interest, the obvious example, Lavenham, being unrivalled anywhere in the country.

The Broads offer a haven for wildlife with many opportunities for birdwatching, notably at Minsmere and Titchwell bird sanctuaries (RSPB).

In the west, the Fens have their own special character and are famed for their dramatic skies and spectacular sunsets; and although very different, the gentler countryside of South Suffolk is as much a part of the East Anglian scene, and is much loved by painters today as it was by Gainsborough and Constable.

No visitor to East Anglia should miss Norwich with its beautiful cathedral, many other fine buildings and its large and colourful market.

BED AND BREAKFAST
(and evening meal)

Birds Place Farm, Back Lane, Buxton, Norwich NR10 5HD

Bill and Jenny Catchpole
☎ **01603 279585**
[BB] **From £17.50–£25**
EM From £10.50
Sleeps 6
☺(5) ⚲ 🐴 ▪
🌸🌸 *Commended*

Small family farm in the Bure Valley in beautiful Norfolk Broadland countryside. Our 17th century farmhouse has oak beams and inglenook fireplace. We are licensed and offer excellent cuisine. The two en suite rooms have TV and tea/coffee making facilities. We have riding stables at the farm. Public footpaths and fishing nearby. Open all year.

Brighthouse Farm, Melford Road, Lawshall, near Bury St Edmunds, Suffolk IP29 4PX

Mr & Mrs Truin
☎ **01284 830385**
[BB] **From £17–£25**
Sleeps 6
☺ 🐕 ⚲ ⚔ 🐴 🏇
🌸🌸 *Commended*

Timbered Georgian farmhouse, set in beautiful surroundings of the Suffolk countryside, 3 acres of picturesque gardens. We offer homely accommodation. Centrally heated throughout, log fires in TV room in winter. Two double rooms, one twin, all with en suite facilities. Historic Bury St. Edmunds/Lavenham close by. Good restaurants locally. Open all year.

Broad Oak Farm, Bramfield, Halesworth, Suffolk IP19 9AB

Mrs Patricia Kemsley
☎ **01986 784232**
[BB] **From £14–£16**
EM From £9
Sleeps 6
☺ 🐕 🐴 🏇
🌸🌸 *Commended*

A dairy farm with a spacious 16th century farmhouse, carefully modernised. Surrounded by meadowland and attractive gardens with tennis court. 3 double bedrooms with H&C, (two en suite). Separate guest bathroom. Sitting room with colour TV, dining room where good home cooking is served (evening meal by arrangement). A warm welcome is always given. Bramfield is 2 miles north west of the A12 on the A144. Southwold 7 miles. Open all year.

Church Farm, Corton, Nr Lowestoft, Suffolk NR32 5HX

Elisabeth Edwards
☎/Fax **01502 730359**
[BB] **From £18**
Sleeps 6
⚲ ⚔ 🏇
Listed *Highly Commended*

Arable farm near rural beach in quiet part of the Suffolk coastline north of Lowestoft. Beautiful Broadland Minsmere area and Norwich within easy reach. Three double rooms all with their own WC and shower, colour TV, tea making facilities. Traditional English breakfast, special diets gladly catered for. Ample parking, quiet garden. A very warm welcome awaits you at Church Farm in our clean and comfortable accommodation. Open Mar–Nov.

College Farm, Hintlesham, Ipswich, Suffolk IP8 3NT

Mrs Rosemary Bryce
☎/Fax **01473 652253**
[BB] **From £17–£22**
Sleeps 6
☺(8) 🐴 ⚲ ▪
🌸🌸 *Highly Commended*

Stay at our 15th century farmhouse (Grade II listed) on a 600-acre arable/beef farm. Comfortable accommodation in 1 double en suite; 1 twin/family and 1 single with basins share a guests' bathroom. Tea/coffee trays, CH and radio alarm clocks. Guests' lounge with TV and log fire. Close to "Constable Country" and Lavenham. Good restaurants locally. Riding and fishing nearby. Sorry no pets or smoking. Open mid Jan–mid Dec.

---

6   **Earsham Park Farm,** Harleston Road, Earsham, Bungay, Suffolk NR35 2AQ

Mrs Bobbie Watchorn
☎/Fax 01986 892180
🛏 From £18.50–£25
EM £13.50
Sleeps 6
✗ 🐴 🛢 ⚒
🌺 🌺 *Highly Commended*

Stay with every comfort in our outstanding Victorian farmhouse with beautiful views over our 600-acre farm. Elegantly furnished bedrooms (1 with four poster) have all facilities including en suites, CH. Large gardens and a collection of unusual farm animals. Easy access coast/Norwich, many local attractions. Sorry no dogs or smoking. Open all year.

---

7   **East Farm,** Euston Road, Barnham, Thetford, Norfolk IP24 2PB

Margaret Heading
☎ 01842 890231
Fax 01842 890457
🛏 From £20–£23
Sleeps 6
🐕 ✗
🌺 *Applied*

Relax and enjoy the comfort and warm welcome at East Farm in the village of Barnham. We're a 1,000-acre arable farm with beef and sheep on the edge of Breckland on Norfolk/Suffolk border between Thetford and Bury St Edmunds. A grey flint-faced house in peaceful surroundings with superb views. Spacious heated rooms with en suite bathrooms. Full English breakfast from local produce. Open all year.

---

8   **Elm Lodge Farm,** Chippenhall Green, Fressingfield, Eye, Suffolk IP21 5SL

Sheila Webster
☎ 01379 586249
🛏 From £15–£19.50
EM £10
Sleeps 6
✗ 🐴 ⊞ ☎(10)
🌺 🌺 *Commended*

This 112-acre working farm with early Victorian farmhouse overlooks a large common (SSSI) where animals graze in summer – the perfect spot for an after-dinner stroll. Spacious bedrooms (one en suite), separate dining and sitting rooms, log fires and excellent food ensure that a comfortable, relaxing holiday is enjoyed by all those we warmly welcome to this attractive and peaceful corner of Suffolk. Open Mar–Nov.

---

9   **Hall Farm,** Jay Lane/Church Lane, Lound, Lowestoft, Suffolk NR32 5LJ

Judith Ashley
☎ 01502 730415
🛏 From £16–£18
Sleeps 6
🐕 🐴 ✗
Listed *Commended*

Share our peaceful, traditional Suffolk farmhouse 1½ miles from sea on 101-acre arable farm. Very clean, comfortable accommodation in two double rooms with en suite facilities and two pretty singles, tea/coffee. Excellent breakfast with our own farm eggs. Beamed lounge, colour TV and log fire. Convenient for Broads. Open Mar–Oct.

---

10   **Hempstead Hall,** Holt, Norfolk NR25 6TN

Lynda-Lee Mack
☎ 01263 712224
🛏 From £17–£24
Sleeps 6
🐕 🐴 ✗ 🐪 🌴
🌺 🌺 *Commended*

Attractive 19th century flint farmhouse peacefully set in beautiful surroundings. 300 acre arable farm with ducks, donkeys, large gardens, and country walks. Close to the Georgian town of Holt and the North Norfolk coast and its many attractions including steam train rides and boat trips to Blakeney Point Seal Sanctuary. En suite family room, double with private bathroom. Colour TV. Tea/coffee-making facilities in rooms.

---

11   **Highfield Farm,** Great Ryburgh, Fakenham, Norfolk NR21 7AL

Mrs E Savory
☎ 01328 829249
🛏 From £16–£20
EM from £9.50
Sleeps 6
☎(12) 🌴 🛢 ⚒
Listed *Commended*

Spacious and comfortable farmhouse on working farm 10 miles from the coast. Ideal for birdwatchers and country lovers, set well away from the road in 500 acres of rolling farmland. Twin with en suite, double with hand basin sharing bathroom with second twin. Guests' sitting room and dining room. Evening meals by arrangement. Clay pigeon shooting, farm walks, horse riding locally, grass tennis court. Open all year except Christmas & New Year.

Hillside Farm, Welbeck Road, Brooke, near Norwich, Norfolk NR15 1AU

Mrs Carolyn Holl
☎ 01508 550260
[BB] From £16–£18
EM From £9
Sleeps 4
Listed *Applied*

This is a 350-acre arable and stock farm. A beautiful 16th century thatched and timber-framed house situated in a pretty village, 7 miles south of Norwich, within easy reach of coast and Broads. One twin/family room, 1 double/family room, both with private facilities. Large games barn with snooker, pool and table tennis. Five acre private lake for coarse fishing. Relaxed family atmosphere. Open all year except Christmas.

Kenton Hall, Debenham, Stowmarket, Suffolk IP14 6JU

Sharon McVeigh
☎ 01728 860279
Fax 01728 861246
[BB] From £17.50–£22.50
Sleeps 6
🥢 *Commended*

Beautiful moated Tudor hall set in peaceful surroundings, rich in wildlife with pleasant country walks nearby. One double and one family room, all furnished to high standard with en suite facilities. Guests' own panelled sitting room and dining room with elegant furnishings. Central heating throughout.

Malting Farm, Blo Norton Road, South Lopham, Diss, Norfolk IP22 2HT

Cynthia Huggins
☎ 01379 687201
[BB] From £17–£20
Sleeps 6
🥢 *Applied*

Situated on Norfolk/Suffolk border amid open countryside. A working dairy farm where cows can be seen being milked, and there are farmyard pets. Farmhouse is Elizabethan timber-framed (inside) with inglenook fireplaces. Central heating. Some four poster beds, some en suite. Easy reach Norfolk Broads, Norwich, Cambridge, Bressingham Steam Museum & Gardens. Cynthia is keen craftswoman in quilting, embroidery, spinning, weaving. Closed Christmas & New Year.

Oak Farm, Market Lane, Blundeston, Lowestoft, Suffolk NR32 5AP

Julie and Keith Cooper
☎ 01502 731622
[BB] From £14.50
Sleeps 4
Listed *Commended*

125-acre mixed farm set in peaceful countryside crossed by the Waveney Way footpath and 1½ miles from the sea. This Victorian house was originally farm cottages. We take a pride in our breakfast and local pubs offer other meals. Guests' stairs lead to a double and a twin room and a guests' bathroom. Tea/coffee facilities and colour TV in rooms. Children very welcome – reductions under 14. Closed Christmas & New Year.

Old Coach House, Thursford, Fakenham, Norfolk NR21 0BD

Mrs Ann Green
☎ 01328 878273
[BB] From £16–£20
EM From £8
Sleeps 6
Listed *Commended*

Small peaceful working farm set in parkland with cows, sheep, ducks etc. Farmhouse is a converted 17th century coachhouse. Main bedroom has four-poster sharing bathroom with 1 twin-bedded room, also 1 twin-bedded room with en suite bathroom – all have washbasins and tea/coffee facilities. Farmhouse dining/kitchen, guests' own sitting room with TV and garden room. Close to Thursford Collection and within easy reach of sandy beaches. Open all year (closed Christmas).

Park Farm, Bylaugh, East Dereham, Norfolk NR20 4QE

Mrs Jenny Lake
☎ 01362 688584
[BB] From £15–£20
EM From £9
Sleeps 6
🥢 *Commended*

Charming old family farmhouse with picturesque setting in Wensum Valley, ideally situated for exploring the Norfolk countryside and visits to Norwich, the Norfolk Broads and North Norfolk coast. One large family room, one double and one twin, all en suite. Lounge with colour TV, dining room with inglenook. Children welcome, sorry no pets. Open all year.

18 Park Farm, Sibton, Saxmundham, Suffolk IP17 2LZ

Margaret Gray
☎ 01728 668324
Fax 01728 668564
BB From £15–£19
EM From £11.50
Sleeps 6
🐕 🐎 🎠 ⚘
⚘ ⚘ *Commended*

A friendly welcome, good food and comfortable accommodation await you at Park Farm. One double, and 1 twin room for guests, each with washbasin, 1 twin with shower en suite. English breakfast and 3-course dinner are prepared from our own, or very local, produce and all tastes and special diets gladly catered for. Ideally situated for enjoying the unspoiled Suffolk countryside. Open all year (closed Christmas & New Year).

---

19 Pear Tree Farm, Hartest, Bury St Edmunds, Suffolk IP29 4EQ

Mrs Rachel White
☎ 01284 830217
BB From £19–£20
Sleeps 4
🐕 ✂
⚘ ⚘ *Commended*

A warm welcome awaits you in our modern farm chalet bungalow on this arable family farm. Ideally situated for exploring Lavenham, Constable Country, and Cambridge. We have 1 double en suite, 1 twin en suite, both with TV and tea/coffee-making facilities. Guests' TV lounge. Children welcome. Open Mar–Nov.

---

20 Priory Farm, Darsham, Saxmundham, Suffolk IP17 3QD

Suzanne Bloomfield
☎ 01728 668459
Fax 01728 668744
BB From £18–£25
Sleeps 4
🐕 ✂ 🚲 ⚓ ◎
Listed *Commended*

Comfortable 17th century farmhouse situated in peaceful countryside. An ideal base for exploring the Suffolk coast and heathlands and other numerous local attractions. Excellent pubs and restaurants nearby. 1 double, 1 twin, each with private facilities, tea/coffee making in all bedrooms. Separate guests' dining room. Cycle hire available at the farm. Open Mar–Oct.

---

21 Red House Farm, Station Road, Haughley, Nr Stowmarket, Suffolk IP14 3QP

Mrs Mary Noy
☎ 01449 673323
BB From £16
Sleeps 5
🐕(8) ✂ Å
⚘ *Commended*

Red House Farm is a fruit/arable farm in mid Suffolk. The comfortable old house is surrounded by orchards which are particularly beautiful during blossom time. We offer 1 double, 1 twin and 1 single, each with H&C, tea/coffee-making facilities, CH. Guests' lounge with TV and dining room. Good restaurants locally. Over 8's welcome. No pets or smoking. Open Jan–Nov.

---

22 Rymer Farm, Barnham, Thetford, Norfolk IP24 2PP

Sarah & Nigel Rush
☎ 01842 890233
Fax 01842 890653
BB From £18–£21
Sleeps 5
🐕 ⚓ ⚓
⚘ ⚘ *Commended*

17th century flint country home on arable farm near Bury St Edmunds. Relax in superb lounge with log fire, garden room, dining room for real farmers' breakfasts. Double en suite with TV, single/en suite, twin with private bathroom. Lovely farm walks with wildlife. Flower arranger's garden, carp pond. Open all year (closed Christmas).

---

23 Salamanca Farm Guest House, 116–118 Norwich Road, Stoke Holy Cross, Norwich, Norfolk NR14 8QJ

Roy & Barbara Harrold
☎ 01508 492322
BB From £18–£21
Sleeps 8
🐕(6) ✂ ⚓ ◎
⚘ ⚘ *Commended*

"Real experience of English hospitality" – "All we could have asked for" – just two comments from our visitors' book. The Harrold family have welcomed guests to their farm for 20 years. 4 miles from the cathedral city of Norwich, the valley of the River Tas, with the mill where Colmans began producing mustard, provides an attractive holiday base. All rooms have private facilities. Open 15 Jan–15 Dec.

Shrublands Farm, Northrepps, Cromer, Norfolk NR27 0AA (24)

Mrs Ann Youngman
☎/Fax 01263 579297
BB From £19–£23
EM From £9
Sleeps 6
⌂(12) ⚭ 🕊 ⚘ ⅄ ☕ ♨ ♞
🌸🌸 *Highly Commended*

Shrublands Farm is an arable farm set in the village of Northrepps, 2½ miles SE of Cromer and 20 miles north of Norwich. The Victorian/Edwardian house has 1 twin and 1 double with private bathrooms and 1 twin en suite. Separate sitting room and dining room for guests. Full central heating, log fires in chilly weather. Sorry, no pets. Open all year (closed Christmas & New Year).

Sloley Farm, High Street, Sloley, Norwich, Norfolk NR12 8HJ (25)

Mrs Ann Jones
☎ 01692 536281
Fax 01692 535162
BB From £16–£18
EM From £8.50
Sleeps 5
⌂(4) ⅄ 🕊 ⚘ ♨
🌸🌸 *Commended*

Comfortable farmhouse on a mixed farm, 3½ miles Norfolk Broads, easy reach of Norwich and the coast. Double/twin room with en suite, family and single rooms sharing guests' bathroom, colour TV, tea/coffee-making facilities. Sitting and dining rooms for guests. Sorry no pets and no smoking. Open all year (closed Christmas & New Year).

South Acre Hall, Southacre, Kings Lynn, Norfolk PE32 2AD (26)

Mrs Charles Fountaine
☎ 01760 755406
BB From £20–£25
EM From £15
Sleeps 4
⌂ 🕊 🕊 ⟲ ♨ ♨ ♞
🌸 *Applied*

Just off A1065, 3 miles Swaffham, 30 mins coast. Beautiful listed Elizabethan house in parkland setting situated in 600 acres of working farmland, lakes, river and woodland. Private fishing, farm trails, stabling and dog kennels. Golf courses and riding stables nearby. Good home cooking, large comfortable rooms. Evening meals and packed lunches available. Open all year.

South Elmham Hall, St Cross, Harleston, Norfolk IP20 0PZ (27)

Mrs Jo Sanderson
☎ 01986 782526
Fax 01986 782203
BB From £17.50–£25
EM From £10
Sleeps 6
⌂ ⅄ ♨ ♨ ♞
Listed *Commended*

Moated former bishop's palace with large gardens. Mixed farm, peaceful location with rare cattle and farm trails in historic landscape. Tastefully furnished comfortable rooms with tea/coffee tray. Large double/family room with bath en suite, twin and single room sharing separate bathroom and WC. Guests' lounge/dining room with TV, full CH. Child reductions, early suppers, cot and baby sitting by arrangement. Open Easter–Nov.

Stratton Farm, West Drove North, Walton Highway, Norfolk PE14 7DP (28)

Derek & Sue King
☎ 01945 880162
BB From £20.70–£23
Sleeps 6
⌂(6) ⅄ ♿ ⟲ ♨ ♞
🌸🌸 *Highly Commended*

Derek and Sue King invite you to stay on their peaceful farm which supports a prize winning herd of Shorthorn cattle. All rooms are en suite, have tea/coffee-making facilities, colour TV, and central heating. One room is specifically designed for wheelchair users. Free carp fishing and use of heated swimming pool. Full English breakfast with home produced sausages, bacon, eggs and marmalade. Open all year (including Christmas).

The Toll Barn, High Stone Road, North Walsham, Norfolk NR28 0JB (29)

Annette Tofts
☎ 01692 403063
Fax 01692 406582
BB From £19–£23
Sleeps 12
⌂(8) 🕊 ⅄ ♿ ♨ ♨
Listed *Highly Commended*

Nominated for prestigious B&B award, The Toll Barn offers outstanding comfort and privacy in a relaxed, informal atmosphere. Delightful, spacious guest–lodges around courtyard gardens, each decorated in English country house style. All en suite with TV, fridge, tea/coffee. Breakfast in old beamed dining room, or enjoy room service if you prefer. Ideal for exploring North Norfolk, Broads, coast and Norwich.

30 **Woodlands Farm,** Brundish, near Woodbridge, Suffolk IP13 8BP

Jill Graham
☎ 01379 384444
From £15.50–£18
EM From £12
Sleeps 6
(10) *Highly Commended*

A friendly welcome and good home cooking assured in our comfortable, timber-framed farmhouse set in peaceful countryside near Framlingham. Within easy reach of the coast and numerous local attractions. One twin and 2 double bedrooms with en suite bathrooms, and tea/coffee facilities. Separate dining and sitting rooms with inglenooks. Centrally heated with log fires in cold weather. Open all year (closed Christmas & New Year).

Self-Catering

31 **Baylham House Annexe,** Baylham House Farm, Mill Lane, Baylham, Suffolk IP6 8LG

Ann Storer
☎ 01473 830264
From £124–£268
Sleeps 4+cot
Commended

Self-contained part of old farmhouse. Small rare breeds farm on River Gipping with sheep, cattle and pigs. Peaceful setting, good walks. Downstairs kitchen/diner, upstairs sitting room, double bedroom, twin bedroom and cot, bathroom and WC. Fishing, garden, barbecue. Colour TV, microwave, washer/drier. Linen extra, metered oil and electricity, payphone. Children welcome, sorry no pets. Open all year.

32 **The Coach House,** Kenton Hall, Debenham, Stowmarket, Suffolk IP14 6JU

Sharon McVeigh
☎ 01728 860279
Fax 01728 861246
From £125–£380
Sleeps 8
Applied

Part of beautiful moated Tudor hall set in the centre of our 460-acre arable farm. One double en suite, one bunk bedded room with bathroom and a large additional bedroom en suite to sleep up to 4. Bed linen, towels, electricity and CH all included. Well equipped kitchen/diner, comfortable sitting room, cloakroom. Centrally situated for touring Suffolk coast (½ hour drive). Sorry no pets and no smoking. Open all year.

33 **Dairy Farm Cottages,** Dilham, North Walsham, Norfolk NR28 9QA

Annabel Paterson
☎ 01692 535178 /536883
Fax 01692 536723
From £195–£390
Sleeps 24
Highly Commened

Relax at Dairy Farm in Broadland, mixed arable and stock farm. Superb walks, acres of woodland, Victorian folly – Dilham Islands. 15 minutes to coast. Top quality accommodation, sleeps 4 in 2 bedrooms, both en suite. Full kitchen facilities, laundry facilities, games room, secure play area, wheelchair access. Pets welcome. Colour brochure available.

34 **Dolphin Lodge,** Roudham Farm, Roudham, East Harling, Norfolk NR16 2RJ

Mr & Mrs T. Jolly
☎ 01953 717126
Fax 01953 718593
From £195–£320
Sleeps 5/6
Highly Commended

Pair of beautifully restored cottages on edge of Thetford Forest on a Breckland farm. Both spacious and well equipped; central heating, Aga, woodburning stove, washing machine, tumble dryer, fridge, microwave, colour TV, cot and highchair available. Each cottage sleeps 5 in two bedrooms. Many local tourist attractions. Ideal for a quiet secluded holiday or a busy sightseeing one. Open all year.

The Granary, Priory Fram, Darsham, Saxmundham, Suffolk IP17 3QD

Suzanne Bloomfield
☎ **01728 668459**
Fax 01728 668744
[SC] **From £135–£295**
Sleeps 4
🐕 🚫 🚲
🏵 🏵 🏵 *Commended*

17th century granary tastefully converted to provide comfortable accommodation. Situated in peaceful Suffolk countryside, an ideal base for touring Suffolk coast and heathlands and other local attractions. 1 double, 2 singles. Shower room, kitchen, dining room, sitting room. Storage heaters, colour TV, washing machine. Cycle hire. Sat–Sat. Weekend lets out of season. Open all year.

The Granary Suites, Brighthouse Farm, Melford Road, Lawshall, near Bury St Edmunds, Suffolk IP29 4PX

Mr & Mrs Truin
☎ **01284 830385**
[SC] **From £150–£180**
Sleeps 2
🐕 🚫 🧍 🚲 🏵 🎾
🏵 *Commended*

Granary conversion to a high standard for self catering. Set in large landscaped gardens, small but cosy, comprising double bedroom, en suite shower, washbasin, toilet, kitchen, TV, linen etc. provided. No smoking. Open all year.

Hall Farm Cottage, Church Lane, Copdock, Ipswich, Suffolk IP8 3JZ

Mrs Yvonne Carr
☎ **01473 730287**
[SC] **From £220–£325**
Sleeps 4
🐕 🐕 🏵
🏵 🏵 🏵
Highly Commended

Part of period farmhouse on a 3 miles circular walk close to Constable country with easy access to A12 and A45. Open fireplace, fuel supplied, beamed ceilings, central heating, colour TV, washing machine. Electricity extra. Cot and high chair. 1 double and 1 twin bedroom. Open Apr–Oct.

Meadow View, Park Farm, Bylaugh, East Dereham, Norfolk NR20 4QE

Mrs Jenny Lake
☎ **01362 688584**
[SC] **From £100–£250**
Sleeps 2
🐕 🚫 ☕
Applied

Attached to charming old family farmhouse with picturesque setting in Wensum Valley, Meadow View is a comfortable, well equipped one bedroom bungalow with lovely countryside views. Sleeps 2 adults and includes living room, kitchen, bathroom, colour TV and heating. Evening meals available next door served in dining room with inglenook. Children welcome, sorry no pets. Linen provided and laundry service. Open all year.

Sid's Cottage, c/o The Grange, West Rudham, Kings Lynn, Norfolk PE31 8SY

Mrs Angela Ringer
☎/Fax **01485 528229**
[SC] **From £120–£250**
Sleeps 4
🐕 🚲 ☕
🏵 🏵 🏵
Approved

Sid's Cottage is semi-detached, surrounded by grass but has no enclosed garden. Overlooks a small orchard, patio at rear. Sleeps 4 in 3 bedrooms. Linen provided. Gas CH, open fire, colour TV, auto washing machine, fridge/freezer, microwave. Cot and highchair available on request. Electricity 50p meter. Carp fishing on farm. Heated indoor swimming pool. Good base for seeing Norfolk. Sandy beach in easy reach. Sorry, no pets. Open all year.

St Peter's View, Monk Soham Hall Lodge, Woodbridge, Suffolk IP13 7EN 40

Mrs Gay Clarke
☎/Fax **01728 685358**
[SC] **From £125–£260**
Sleeps 2–4
🐕 🚫 ♿ 🏵 🎾
🏵 🏵 🏵 *Commended*

Adjacent to St Peter's church with panoramic views, these properties are ideal for those wishing to explore the delights of Suffolk. Their spacious design has been given the highest award by the Holiday Care Service and full central heating throughout the year is included in the tariff. Extensive grounds. Practice golf area. Open all year.

41 **Stable Cottages and The Granary,** Chattisham Place, Nr Ipswich, Suffolk IP8 3QD

Mrs Margaret Langton
☎/Fax 01473 652210
⅏ From £125–£325
Sleeps 2/8

Highly Commended

Restored stables and Tudor granary converted to 3 comfortable and well-equipped holiday cottages, two with wheelchair facilities. Situated in a SE facing courtyard with CH, fitted kitchen, colour TV. Linen, towels, electricity included. Games, laundry and craft room on site. Use of heated swimming pool and tennis court by arrangement. Quiet, rural village near Constable Country. Sea ½ hr, riding, fishing nearby. Open all year.

GOOD FOOD

Nearly all Bureau members now hold a certificate in Essential Food Hygiene.

PRICES

Prices include VAT and service charge (if any) and are:
B&B per person per night
EM per person
SC per unit per week
Tents and caravans per pitch per night

FINDING YOUR ACCOMMODATION

The Group contacts at the beginning of each section can always help you find a vacancy in your chosen area.

England's Heartland

Essex

Group Contact: *Joyce Withey* ☎ *01277 362695*

Essex surprises – it is still a rural county yet just a short trip east from London. It is a land of rolling countryside and river valleys, creeks and estuaries with a scattering of villages and country towns. Essex has local farm produce, wines and seafood, oak beamed country pubs serving real ale and traditionally cosy tea shops.

In the east of the county explore the past in Colchester, the oldest recorded town in England, with a Norman castle built on the foundations of what was the largest Roman temple in Northern Europe. Wander through Hatfield Forest with its woodland, pasture, lake and nature reserve and 6,000 acres of Epping Forest.

The Essex coastline is one of contrasts, from remote marshes to lively seaside resorts. In the west of the county visit Saffron Walden and beautiful surrounding villages.

Essex is highly accessible by road and rail, with the M25 and M11 motorways and regular train services from London (Liverpool Street) throughout Essex including Stansted Airport, Port of Harwich and Felixstowe.

Haverhill
A134
Hadleigh
Ipswich
Saffron Walden
Sudbury
Royston
A131
A12
Felixstowe
A10
2 3 M11
5
Harwich
A120
Halstead
Colchester
Walton-on-the-Naze
Bishop's
4
Braintree
A120
A12
Brightlingsea
Frinton-on-Sea
Stortford
8
A1060
A131
Witham
Clacton-on-Sea
A10
Ware
Sawbridgeworth
W.Mersea
M11
A130
Maldon
Harlow
7
A414
Chelmsford
Waltham
Abbey
Epping
A130
25 26 27
A12
Burnham-on-Crouch
5
Billericay
28
1
A127
Brentwood
29
Basildon
M25
Southend-on-Sea
30
LONDON
2

BED AND BREAKFAST

(and evening meal)

---

1 **Bonnydowns Farmhouse,** Doesgate Lane, Bulphan, Nr Upminster, Essex RM14 3TB

Rose Newman
☎ 01268 542129
BB From £15–£20
EM From £8
Sleeps 6
✄ ☎
Listed *Approved*

Large, comfortably furnished, pleasantly situated in large garden with lovely views. Close to Langdon Hills Country Park and Basildon New Town (modern shopping centre). Convenient for London, Southend, South East England via M25, A13, A127. Sheep/cattle kept on the farm. 2 twin, 1 family bedrooms, 1 bath with toilet/shower, 1 shower room with toilet. Tea/coffee trays. Good cooking. Open all year (closed Christmas).

---

2 **Duddenhoe End Farm,** Duddenhoe End, Nr Saffron Walden, Essex CB11 4UU

Peggy Foster
☎ 01763 838258
BB From £18–£22
Sleeps 6
✄ ☎ (12)
🐝🐝 *Commended*

A warm welcome awaits you at this comfortable 17th century farmhouse situated in quiet rural area. All bedrooms have private or en suite bathrooms, tea/coffee-making facilities and radio. Visitors' sitting room with TV. Ideally located for Cambridge, Audley End mansion, Duxford Air Museum and Stansted Airport. Central heating throughout. Non-smokers only. Open all year except Christmas.

---

3 **Rockells Farm,** Duddenhoe End, Saffron Walden, Essex CB11 4UY

Mrs Tineke Westerhuis
☎ 01763 838053
BB From £17–£20
EM From £8
Sleeps 6
🛌 ☎ ♿ 🍽 🐾 🎿
🐝🐝 *Commended*

Rockells is an arable farm in a beautiful corner of Essex. The Georgian house has a large garden with a 3-acre lake for coarse fishing. All rooms have private facilities, one room is downstairs. Evening meal by arrangement only (no meals July–Sept). On the farm are several footpaths, and beautiful villages in the area. Audley End, Duxford and Cambridge nearby. London is about 1 hour by car or train. Stansted Airport 30 mins. Open all year.

---

4 **Spicers Farm,** Rotten End, Wethersfield, Braintree, Essex CM7 4AL

Mrs Delia Douse
☎ 01371 851021
BB From £15–£18
Sleeps 6
☎ ⚓ 🚲 🍽 🛁 🎿
🐝🐝 *Highly Commended*

Attractive farmhouse with large garden in area designated of special landscape value. Quiet arable farm with pleasant walks. Convenient for Stansted, Harwich, Cambridge and Constable country. All rooms en suite with CH, tea/coffee-making facilities, colour TV, clock radio and lovely views. Open all year.

NO ANSWER?

Farmers are mostly out and about during the day.
Try to telephone before 9.30am or after 4pm.

FARM HOLIDAY BUREAU

SELF-CATERING

The Granary and The Byre, c/o Rockells Farm, Duddenhoe End, Saffron Walden, Essex CB11 4UY

Mrs Tineke Westerhuis
☎ **01763 838053**
⌗ **From £140–£250**
Sleeps 3/5
🐴 🐾 ♒ ⚘
♞ ♞ ♞ *Commended*

The Granary and The Byre are part of Rockells farmyard, an arable farm in a beautiful corner of Essex. Lounges with kitchen area have original wood panelling. The cottages are fully equipped to high standard. Garden with 3-acre lake for excellent fishing. In the area are several footpaths and beautiful villages with excellent pubs. Audley End, Duxford and Cambridge nearby. London is 1 hour by car or train. Stansted airport 30 mins by car. Open all year.

DISABLED VISITORS

Many members offer a welcome to disabled/less able visitors. Please do check the extent of the facilities before booking.

THOSE LITTLE EXTRAS

For advice on farms that can offer 'extras' such as four-poster beds, special diets, farm trails, fishing rights – even stabling and trekking arrangements if you are bringing your own horse – ring the Farm Holiday Bureau on (01203) 696909.

Please mention **Stay on a Farm** when booking

England's South and South East

Thames Valley

Group Contact: *Mrs Mary Anne Florey* ☎ *01865 300207*

The Thames Valley is at the heart of historical England. Farms and homes are situated in the area stretching from the Chiltern Hills above Henley through the rich farmland of the Vale of Aylesbury and on to the west of Oxford and the Cotswolds.

Oxford is at the centre of the region and its dreaming spires and great buildings, including mediaeval colleges and Renaissance masterpieces such as the Sheldonian Theatre, can provide great historical interest. You can take guided tours of Oxford, Windsor and Burford or enjoy browsing in antique shops and bookshops.

Woodstock has many historical associations and is the site of Blenheim Palace, the magnificent home designed by Sir John Vanbrugh for the Dukes of Marlborough. Sir Winston Churchill was born there and is buried in the nearby churchyard of Bladon. The area includes the moated castle at Broughton near Banbury and many other Tudor and 18th century manors and country houses.

Places of interest include the Cotswold Wildlife Park, Birdland, Cogges Farm Museum and a steam railway centre and activities such as boating, pony trekking and brass rubbing are available.

BED AND BREAKFAST

(and evening meal)

Ashen Copse Farm, Coleshill, Highworth, Nr Swindon, Wiltshire SN6 7PU

Pat Hoddinott
☎/Fax 01367 240175
🅱 From £18–£20
Sleeps 6
⅍ ⛺ 🏕 ⬛
🌼🌼 *Commended*

Ideal setting for peace and quiet, walking, visiting numerous attractions. 580-acre National Trust beef and arable farm in beautiful countryside. Spacious, comfortable accommodation in 17th century farmhouse (1 bedroom en suite). Small outdoor swimming pool. Meet our lambs, calves and horse. Children's toys and games available. Reduction for children sharing. Many pubs and restaurants. Near M4 (J15). Open all year (closed Christmas Day).

Bowling Green Farm, Stanford Road, Faringdon, Oxfordshire SN7 8EZ

Della Barnard
☎ 01367 240229
Fax 01367 242568
🅱 From £18
Sleeps 6
⅍ ⛺ 🐕 🎿
🌼🌼 *Applied*

Attractive 18th century period farmhouse offering 20th century comfort situated in the Vale of the White Horse, just 1 mile south of Faringdon on the A417. Easy access to M4 for Heathrow Airport. A working farm breeding cattle and horses. Large twin/family room on ground floor en suite. All bedrooms have colour TV, tea/coffee-making facilities and CH throughout. Open all year.

Fords Farm, Ewelme, Wallingford, Oxon OX10 6HU

Marlene Edwards
☎ 01491 839272
🅱 From £18.50–£22
Sleeps 4
⅍ 🏕
Listed *Highly*
Commended

500-acre mixed farm, arable beef and sheep. Attractive farmhouse set in historic part of village with famous church almshouses and school. Peaceful surroundings with good walks and good selection of pubs nearby. Easy access to Henley, Oxford, Reading, Windsor, Heathrow and London. Friendly and comfortable atmosphere. 2 twin rooms. Open May–Mar.

Hill Grove Farm, Crawley Road, Minster Lovell, Oxfordshire OX8 5NA

Mrs Katharine Brown
☎ 01993 703120
Fax 01993 700528
🅱 From £19–£22
Sleeps 4
⅍ ⛺ 🐦 🏕 ⬛ 🎿
🌼 *Highly Commended*

Hill Grove is a mixed, family-run 300-acre working farm situated in an attractive rural setting overlooking the Windrush Valley. Ideally positioned for driving to Oxford, Blenheim Palace, Witney (Farm Museum) and Burford (renowned as the Gateway to the Cotswolds and for its splendid Wildlife Park). New golf course 1 mile. Hearty breakfasts, friendly atmosphere. Children welcome. 1 double/private shower, 1 twin/double en suite. AA listed. Open all year (closed Christmas).

Little Parmoor Farm, Frieth, Henley-on-Thames, Oxfordshire RG9 6NL

Frances Emmett
☎ 01494 881600
🅱 From £20–£26
Sleeps 5
⛺ 🎿 🏕 ⬛ 🎿
Listed *Highly*
Commended

220-acre mixed farm. Retreat to the Hambledon Valley to 16th century farmhouse with oak beams and log fires. Peaceful walks in magnificent beech woods. Farmhouse breakfast including free range eggs and local honey. Good pub and restaurant food in attractive villages nearby. Open all year.

6 **Mead Close,** Forest Hill, Nr Oxford, Oxfordshire OX33 1DY

Audrey Dunkley
☎ 01865 872248
🛏 From £16.50–£20
EM From £9
Sleeps 5
🐎 ⅍ 🅰 🐴
Listed

450 acre mixed farm, dairy and cereals. Family farm, milking 80 cows. Warm and welcoming farmhouse, full CH, 5 miles to Oxford city centre, 5 minutes to Park and Ride. Easy to find from A40. Traditional English pub in village, serving food. Enjoy visiting the Cotswolds, Blenheim Palace, Waterperry Gdns, Waddesdon Manor and Windsor. Open all year.

7 **Monkton Farm,** Little Marlow, Buckinghamshire SL7 3RF

Jane & Warren Kimber
☎ 01494 521082
Fax 01494 443905
🛏 From £19–£22
Sleeps 6
⅍ 🐎(5) 🅰 🐴 🛆
Listed *Commended*

A 150-acre working dairy farm with 14th century 'Cruck' farmhouse set in the beautiful Chiltern Hills, yet only 30 miles from London and 27 miles from Oxford. Heathrow 20 mins, 1 single, 1 double and 1 family room available. English breakfast served in the farm kitchen. Large choice of pubs and restaurants nearby. Taxi service to Heathrow available. Open all year.

8 **Moor Farm,** Holyport, near Maidenhead, Berkshire SL6 2HY

Mrs G Reynolds
☎/Fax 01628 33761
🛏 From £19.50–£23
Sleeps 6
🐎 ⅍ 🐴 🎋
🐝🐝 *Highly Commended*

In the pretty village of Holyport. Moor Farm is 4 miles from Windsor. The farmhouse is a timber-framed, 700-year-old 'listed' manor in a lovely country garden with charming en suite rooms, furnished with antiques. It is well placed for touring the Thames Valley and visiting London. Also close to Heathrow. Suffolk sheep and horses kept on farm. Open all year.

9 **'Morar',** Weald Street, Bampton, Oxfordshire OX18 2HL

Janet Rouse
☎ 01993 850162
Fax 01993 851738
🛏 From £18–£22
EM From £12.50
Sleeps 6
🖭 ⅍ 🐎(6) 🛆
🐝🐝 *Highly Commended*

A non-smoking farmhouse (retired from farming) where meat, vegetables, bread are nearly all home-produced and cooked to perfection. A member of The Guild of Master Craftsmen. Pet cats, sheep and goats will love your fuss and attention. Cotswolds, Oxford, Woodstock, swimming, sailing, riding, fishing all close by. We Morris dance, bellring, garden – and laugh! 1 twin, 2 doubles en suite. Spring breaks–4 nights BB EM £190 per couple inclusive.

10 **New Farm,** Oxford Road, Oakley, Aylesbury, Buckinghamshire HP18 9UR

Binnie Pickford
☎ 01844 237360
🛏 From £17–£20
EM From £10
Sleeps 6
🐎(6) 🐾 🎋
Listed *Commended*

Friendly atmosphere in fully modernised farmhouse. Good food, comfortable bedrooms, views over 163 acres devoted to sheep, beef, arable. Situated on Oxfordshire/ Bucks boundary in peaceful surroundings. Walks in adjacent Bernwood Forest Nature Reserve. Golf course 1¼ miles. 7 miles Oxford, close to Waterperry Gardens, Waddesdon Manor, Quainton Railway Centre, Blenheim Palace and M40. Pubs and restaurants nearby. Open all year except Christmas.

11 **North Farm,** Shillingford Hill, Wallingford, Oxfordshire OX10 8NB

Hilary Warburton
☎ 01865 858406
🛏 From £20–£22.50
Sleeps 4
⅍ 🐎(8) 🐾 🎋 🐿
🐝🐝 *Highly Commended*

Spacious and comfortable farmhouse on our 500 acres of farmland with sheep and pygmy goats. Enjoy walks by the River Thames and private fishing. Ideal for Oxford and Henley and within easy reach of Windsor and London. 2 double bedrooms with private bathrooms (1 en suite), colour TV, tea/coffee-making facilities. Excellent local pubs. Open all year.

The Old Farmhouse, Station Hill, Long Hanborough, Oxfordshire OX8 8JZ

Vanessa Maundrell
☎ 01993 882097
[BB] From £19–£20.50
Sleeps 4
⊕ ✄ ⚲(12) 🎄 🐾
🌺🌺 *Highly Commended*

17th century Old Farmhouse is full of period charm and character tastefully furnished with inglenook fireplace, beams and flagstone floors. Ideally situated close to Oxford, Woodstock, Blenheim Palace and the Cotswolds. Delicious home cooking. Warm and friendly welcome assured. One double en suite, one double sharing bathroom. French, German, Spanish, Italian spoken. Open all year (closed Christmas).

Poletrees Farm, Ludgershall Road, Brill, Aylesbury, Buckinghamshire HP18 9TZ

Anita & John Cooper
☎/Fax 01844 238276
[BB] From £19–£20
Sleeps 6
✄ 🎄
Listed *Applied*

A 16th century working beef and sheep farm with house of architectural interest. 3 quiet bedrooms, 2 doubles, 1 twin, all with H&C and tea/coffee making facilities. Guests have own lounge. Many pubs and restaurants nearby. Places of interest include Waddesdon Manor, Claydon House, Stowe Gardens and Oxford and many others as seen under Thames Valley. Elizabeth Gundrey recommended. Open all year.

Rectory Farm, Northmoor, Witney, Oxfordshire OX8 1SX

Mary Anne Florey
☎ 01865 300207
[BB] From £19–£20
Sleeps 4
✄ 🐾 🎄
🌺🌺 *Highly Commended*

Rectory Farm is a 16th century farmhouse retaining all the old charm alongside modern comforts. Both rooms have en suite facilities, central heating, tea/coffee-making facilities. We are conveniently situated for Oxford, the Cotswolds, Blenheim and the Thames path. Fishing on the Thames available. We can assure you of a warm welcome and a peaceful and comfortable stay. Open 1st Feb–mid Dec.

Vicarage Farm, Kirtlington, Oxfordshire OX5 3JY

Mrs Judith Hunter
☎ 01869 350254
[BB] From £18–£20
Sleeps 6
✄ 🎄
Listed *Commended*

Situated in the middle of an 18-hole golf course, Vicarage Farm is a comfortable family farmhouse with two double rooms, one twin with basin. Oxford is 9 miles, Woodstock and Blenheim Palace 4 miles, Stratford and Warwick ½ hour and Cotswolds nearby. You are assured of a warm welcome in this quiet and peaceful location. Home cooking. Excellent restaurants and pub nearby. Open Mar–Nov.

Wallace Farm, Dinton, Nr Aylesbury, Buckinghamshire HP17 8UF

Jackie Cook
☎ 01296 748660
Fax 01296 748851
[BB] From £20–£21
Sleeps 6
⚲ 🄬 🐾 🎄 🐾
🌺🌺 *Applied*

This 16th century listed farmhouse is situated in a quiet, rural setting in the Vale of Aylesbury, yet within easy reach of London, Oxford and Heathrow. A small family farm, rearing beef cattle and sheep, plus chickens, ducks and geese. Plenty of opportunitites for country walks, coarse fishing or browsing through our extensive library. Open all year.

Weston Farm, Buscot Wick, Faringdon, Oxfordshire SN7 8DJ

Mrs Jean Woof
☎ 01367 252222
[BB] From £19
Sleeps 4
⚲(10) ✄
🌺🌺 *Highly Commended*

Come and share our idyllic 17th century Cotswold farmhouse in peaceful surroundings. Period furniture and well maintained gardens. 500-acre mixed farm. CH, tea/coffee-making facilities and own TV, one four-poster and one twin room, each with private bathroom. Guests own dining and sitting rooms, with log fires. Ideally situated to explore this beautiful area. Open all year except Christmas.

SELF-CATERING

---

(18) **Coxwell House,** Little Coxwell, Faringdon, Oxfordshire SN7 7LP

Elspeth Crossley Cooke
☎ 01367 241240
Fax 01367 240911
SC From £350–£625
Sleeps 6
🐕 🐎 🏇 🎾 🐓
🍂 🍂 🍂 🍂 *Highly Commended*

Coxwell House is the superb main 1760 part (self-contained) of a Georgian farmhouse set in an attractive, secluded walled garden. Every modern convenience. Tennis court, indoor swimming pool. Unspoilt stone walled farming village with thatched cottages and pub. Ideal for the Cotswolds, Oxford. 1½ miles Faringdon south of A420. Open all year.

---

(19) **Hill Grove Cottage,** c/o Hill Grove Farm, Crawley Road, Minster Lovell, Oxfordshire OX8 5NA

Mrs Katharine Brown
☎ 01993 703120
Fax 01993 700528
SC From £250–£330
Sleeps 6 + cot
🍴 🐕 🛏 🎾 🐓
🍂 🍂 🍂 🍂 *Commended*

Hill Grove Cottage is a large bungalow adjacent to our farmhouse. 2 double bedrooms, 1 twin, bathroom and shower, dining room, lounge, kitchen. Fridge/freezer, washing machine, tumble dryer, CH. Gardens. Situated above the Windrush Valley, excellent walks yet within driving distance of Oxford, Woodstock and Burford. New golf course 1 mile. Cot and babysitting by arrangement. Electricity included. Linen free. Open June–Oct.

---

(20) **Moor Farm,** Holyport, near Maidenhead, Berkshire SL6 2HY

Mrs G Reynolds
☎/Fax 01628 33761
SC From £200–£390
Sleeps 2/4
🐕 🍴 ♿ 🎾
🍂 🍂 🍂 🍂 *Highly Commended*

In the pretty village of Holyport, Courtyard Cottages are on the 700-year-old manor of Moor Farm and are conversions from a Georgian stable block and two small barns. They retain the charm of their original features and are furnished with antique pine. The 4 cottages are well placed for touring the Thames Valley and are 4 miles from Windsor and convenient for visiting London. Sheep and horses are on the farm.

FARM HOLIDAY BUREAU

NO ANSWER?
Farmers are mostly out and about during the day.
Try to telephone before 9.30am or after 4pm.

England's South and South East

Hampshire

Group Contact: *Mrs Melanie Bray* ☎ *01705 631597*

Hampshire is a beautiful county of contrasts ... of creeks, harbours and beaches, grand rivers and sparkling streams, forests, and lush farmland with picturesque villages and hamlets.

The main centres of the county have all played an important role in history: the Saxons made Winchester their capital; Southampton bears witness to the Norman invasion, and Portsmouth is famous for its naval heritage with Nelson's HMS Victory, Henry VIII's Mary Rose and the first ironclad warship, HMS Warrior.

Hampshire has numerous other links with the past , Jane Austen's house at Chawton or Charles Dickens' birthplace in Portsmouth, for example, or enjoy the many rich treasures on show in the museums of the county's towns and cities.

In the New Forest there are plenty of quiet picnic spots and lots of ponies. Hampshire is served by a network of footpaths and bridleways and many country parks. There are long distance walks and guided walks which can take you round the towns and cities, along the Solent coastline or inland along the famous Test Valley. The country mansions of Broadlands, Breamore, Stratfield Saye and Highclere Castle and numerous gardens are open to the public.

[Map of England's South and South East showing locations including Basingstoke, Andover, Winchester, Salisbury, Romsey, Eastleigh, Southampton, Fareham, Portsmouth, Lymington, Bournemouth, Aldershot, Fleet, Guilford, Farnham, Reigate, Crawley, Haslemere, Horsham, Billinghurst, Petersfield, Midhurst, Horndean, Havant, Chichester, Arundel, Worthing, Bognor Regis, Cowes, Ryde, Sandown, Shanklin, Ventnor, and road numbers A338, A339, A33, A34, A303, A30, M3, A31, A32, A272, A325, A3, A24, A36, A286, A29, M27.]

BED AND BREAKFAST

(and evening meal)

---

1 **Brocklands Farm,** West Meon, Petersfield, Hampshire GU32 1JN

Sue Wilson
☎ 01730 829228
▦ From £16–£17
Sleeps 6
🐕 ♿ ⚒ 🚲 ☕ 🏺 ♻ ⛺
Listed *Commended*

Brocklands Farm in the famed Meon Valley has good views of the countryside and is within easy reach of the coastal ports and also the ancient towns of Winchester, Petersfield and Chichester. The light and airy farmhouse is furnished traditionally with a homely atmosphere. An old railway line and grass headlands provide farm walks. Day sailing in the Solent. Afternoon tea available. Open all year (closed Christmas).

---

2 **Compton Farmhouse,** Compton, Nr Chichester, West Sussex PO18 9HB

Mrs Melanie Bray
☎ 01705 631597
▦ £18
Sleeps 6
🐕 ♻ ⛺
Listed *Commended*

Children are especially welcome (half-price) at our old, flint family farmhouse. We are 200 yards up a track from the village square, next door to the church and are bordered by fields and woods. Lovely walks and plenty to do in our enclosed, child-orientated garden. Own sitting/dining room with drink-making facilities, fridge, TV. Chichester and Portsmouth nearby. Open all year except Christmas.

---

3 **Moortown Farm,** Soberton, Nr Droxford, Southampton, Hampshire SO32 3QU

Rosemary Taylor
☎ 01489 877256
▦ £15–£25
Sleeps 6
🐕(5) 🐕 ⛺
Listed *Commended*

A friendly atmosphere is found at Moortown in the heart of the Meon Valley, an Area of Outstanding Natural Beauty. Crossed by the Warfarer's Walk and South Downs Way. 1 twin en suite, 1 family with private bathroom, both with TV and tea facilities. Set in a peaceful village within easy reach of Winchester, home of King Arthur's Round Table, Portsmouth, with the Mary Rose and Nelson's flagship, Chichester and the New Forest. Open all year.

---

4 **Oakdown Farm Bungalow,** c/o Oakdown Farm, Dummer, Basingstoke, Hampshire RG23 7LR

Mrs Elizabeth Hutton
☎ 01256 397218
▦ From £15
Sleeps 6
🐕(12) 🏺 ♻
🛏 *Commended*

Oakdown Farm Bungalow is on a secluded, private road, next to junction 7 on the M3, 3 miles south of Basingstoke and close to the village of Dummer. Very good road communications to London, Winchester, Southampton, Oxford, the South-West and the Midlands. Wayfarer's Walk within 200 metres. Open all year.

---

5 **Pyesmead Farm,** Plaitford, Romsey, Hampshire SO51 6EE

Mrs C Pybus
☎ 01794 323386
▦ From £13.50–£17
EM From £7.50
Sleeps 6
♻ 🐕 ♿ ➰
Listed *Applied*

Come and stay on our small, family-run stock farm bordered by the New Forest. Guests are welcome to explore the farm. Fishing is available on our own attractive lakes. Many activities locally, including horse riding, golf, swimming and forest walks. We are within easy reach of Salisbury, Winchester and the coast. Open all year except Christmas.

SELF-CATERING

Meadow Cottage, c/o Farley Farm, Braishfield, Romsey, Hampshire SO51 0QP

Mrs Wendy Graham
☎ 01794 368265/
368513
Fax 01794 367847
SC From £150–£275
Sleeps 5 + cot
🐕 🐂 ♨
🌳 🌳 🌳 🌳 *Commended*

Well equipped, semi-detached cottage on a 400-acre beef and arable farm. Outstanding views of beautiful surrounding countryside. Ideal for walking or riding (own horse welcome), or touring historic centres of Romsey, Winchester, Salisbury, New Forest and coast. Cottage has CH, log fire, colour TV, downstairs WC, washer/dryer, cot. Garden with barbecue. Phone for brochure. Open Easter–Oct.

Owl Cottage, Lye Farm, West Tytherley, Romsey, Hampshire SP5 1LA

Maxine Vine
☎ 01794 341667
SC From £180–£280
Sleeps 5
🐕 🐂 ⅙ ♨ 💼
🌳 🌳–🌳 🌳 🌳
Commended

Owl cottage has been skillfully converted from an old barn situated in one of the most beautiful parts of Hampshire. Outstanding views, close New Forest, Salisbury, Winchester. Location perfect for touring, walking, riding in southern England. Excellently equipped cottage, central heating, electric included, washer dryer, TV, cot. Peaceful and relaxing environment. Open all year.

THOSE LITTLE EXTRAS

For advice on farms that can offer 'extras' such as four-poster beds, special diets, farm trails, fishing rights – even stabling and trekking arrangements if you are bringing your own horse – ring the Farm Holiday Bureau on (01203) 696909.

LET THE TELEPHONE RING!

Some farmhouses are big places. Let the telephone ring long enough to give the owner time to answer it.

England's South and South East
Sussex and Surrey

Group Contacts: *Sussex: Brenda Gough* ☎ *01273 478680*
Surrey: Mrs Gill Hill ☎ *01306 730210*

You've probably heard of 'Sussex by the Sea' so perhaps to you Sussex means the traditional attractions of the popular seaside resorts such as Brighton, Eastbourne, Hastings, Bognor Regis, Littlehampton and Worthing. What you may not know is that just inland there is a vast area of lovely downland punctuated with tiny villages and the occasional old market town. Further north busy towns such as Horsham, Crawley and East Grinstead are surrounded by lush green countryside. There is also a rich history here – Chichester with its famous Roman cross, nearby Fishbourne with the remains of a palace once ruled by a King Cogidubnus ... really; and Hastings – 1066 and all that.

In Surrey, the North Downs provide dramatic wooded hillsides with small, attractive towns and villages nestling in the valleys. Here you can walk along the track claiming to be the Pilgrim's Way which connects Winchester to Canterbury; clamber up famous heights like Leith Hill – just short of 1,000ft – or its neighbour Box Hill, coming down via the intriguingly named Zig Zag Hill.

Yet nowhere in these counties are you ever more than a couple of hours from central London should you wish to make a day trip there.

BED AND BREAKFAST
(and evening meal)

Compton Farmhouse, Compton, Nr Chichester, West Sussex PO18 9HB

Mrs Melanie Bray
☎ **01705 631597**
BB **£18**
Sleeps 6
Listed *Commended*

Children are especially welcome (half-price) at our old, flint family farmhouse. We are 200 yards up a track from the village square, next door to the church and are bordered by fields and woods. Lovely walks and plenty to do in our enclosed, child-orientated garden. Own sitting/dining room with drink-making facilities, fridge, TV. Chichester and Portsmouth nearby. Open all year except Christmas.

Crossways Farm, Raikes Lane, Abinger Hammer, Nr Dorking, Surrey RH5 6PZ

Sheila Hughes
☎ **01306 730173**
BB **From £16–£18**
Sleeps 6
🐴 *Applied*

Welcome to our 17th century listed farmhouse (book and TV setting) amidst the oustanding beauty of the Surrey hills. Good walks. Near A25 and Dorking/Guildford bus stop. Easy reach Gatwick, Heathrow, London, S Coast, Wisley. Large, comfortable rooms, washbasins, tea/coffee-making facilities, inglenooks, log fires, beams, colour TV. Walled garden, croquet. Laundry facilities. Elizabeth Gundrey recommended. Open all year.

Goffsland Farm, Shipley, Horsham, West Sussex RH13 7BQ

Mrs Carol Liverton
☎/Fax **01403 730434**
BB **From £15–£17**
Sleeps 5
🐴 *Commended*

Listed 17th century farmhouse on a 260-acre working farm with sheep, cattle and dairy herd. Situated in the Sussex Weald central to Gatwick and the south coast. Family room has double bed and bunk beds with washbasin and tea/ coffee-making facilities. Own bathroom with WC own sitting room with TV. Open all year.

Manor Farm, Poynings, Nr Brighton, West Sussex BN45 7AG

Mrs Carol Revell
☎/Fax **01273 857371**
BB **From £19–£25**
EM **From £10.50**
Sleeps 6
🐴 *Applied*

260-acre family run sheep/arable farm with charming old manor house resting quietly in a green valley under the South Downs. An area of outstanding natural beauty, ideal for riders, walkers and country lovers. Plenty of country pubs and eating houses nearby. A23 5 mins, Hickstead 10 mins, Gatwick 30 mins, Brighton and Hove 15 mins. Evening meal by request only. Open Mar–Dec.

Moonshill Farm, The Green, Ninfield, Battle, East Sussex TN33 9LH

Mrs June Ive
☎ **01424 892645**
BB **From £15–£17.50**
Sleeps 6
🐴 🐕(4) *Applied*

In the heart of the '1066 Country' in the centre of Ninfield opposite pub. Farmhouse in 10 acres of garden, orchard, stables. Enjoy beautiful walks, golf and riding arranged. Comfortable rooms, 3 en suite, CH and electric fires, hospitality tray, TV, lounge, parking and garage, babysitting service. Every comfort in our safe, quiet and peaceful home. Reduced rates for weekly bookings. Open Jan–Nov.

---

6 **New House Farm,** Broadford Bridge Road, West Chiltington, Nr Pulborough, West Sussex RH20 2LA

Alma Steele
☎ 01798 812215
🏠 From £18–£25
Sleeps 6
🛏(10) Å ▪ ❦
💕 *Commended*

Listed 15th century farmhouse with oak beams and inglenook fireplace, in the centre of the village, close to local inns which provide good food. A new 18 hole golf course, open to non-members, is only ¼ mile away. Many places of historical interest in the area including Goodwood House, Petworth House, Parham House, Arundel Castle. Gatwick 35 minutes. En suite facilities and colour TV in bedrooms. Open all year.

7 **Ousedale House,** Offham, Lewes, East Sussex BN7 3QF

Roland & Brenda Gough
☎ 01273 478680
Fax 01273 486510
🏠 From £21–£25
EM From £12
Sleeps 6
⚓ 🛏(12) 🅮 ▪
💕 *Highly Commended*

Spacious Victorian country house with luxury accommodation. 3½ acre garden and woodland situated on a hillside plateau with panoramic views over the Ouse river valley. Country cooking, four poster bed, modern heating. Double glazed throughout. Residents' licence. Central for touring. About 1 mile from Lewes station – courtesy car. Glyndebourne hampers provided. Brighton 9 miles. Low season weekend breaks. Open all year.

8 **The Stud Farm,** Bodle Street Green, Nr Hailsham, East Sussex BN27 4RJ

Philippa & Richard Gentry
☎/Fax 01323 833201
🏠 From £17
EM From £8.50 (by arrangement)
Sleeps 6
🛏 ♿
💕 *Commended*

70 acre sheep and cattle farm situated in peaceful surroundings and beautiful countryside, ideal for walking. 8 miles from sea, Eastbourne, Hastings, South Downs in easy reach. Upstairs, family unit of double bedded room/twin bedded room, both with handbasins, and bathroom. Downstairs twin bedded room with shower, toilet, handbasin en suite. All bedrooms with colour TV and tea/coffee-making facilities. Guests' sitting room, colour TV. Sunroom. Open all year.

9 **Stud Farm House,** Telscombe Village, Lewes, East Sussex BN7 3HZ

Tim & Nina Armour
☎ 01273 302486
🏠 From £15–£20
EM From £8.50
Sleeps 6
🐴🛏Å 🪑 🐎 ❦ 🎣 ▪ ❦
Applied

300-acre sheep farm in quiet hamlet on the South Downs Way. The sea is 1½ miles away, London 50 minutes by train, 10 minutes Newhaven/Dieppe 'Sealink Ferries'. Caravan parking, horse riding, cycling, golf, fishing, sailing, walking. Treat your horse to first class stables, grazing, downland riding. Winter breaks by log fires, farmhouse cooking, or join in the action. Open all year.

10 **Sturtwood Farm,** Partridge Lane, Newdigate, Dorking, Surrey RH5 5EE

Bridget MacKinnon
☎ 01306 631308
Fax 01306 631908
🏠 From £17.50–£25
EM From £8.50
Sleeps 5
🛏 🐎 🎣 ❦
💕 *Applied*

An attractive 18th century farmhouse in lovely countryside yet within 12 mins of Gatwick Airport. Many National Trust properties and gardens nearby. Also London, Brighton and several country towns. Open all year.

SELF-CATERING

"Badgersholt" and "Foxholme", c/o Bulmer Farm, Holmbury St Mary, Dorking, Surrey RH5 6LG

Gill Hill
☎ 01306 730210
SC From £130–£280
Sleeps 2/4
⚙ ☺ ♨ ⛺ ⛴ ⚙ ■ ⚘
⚘ ⚘ ⚘ – ⚘ ⚘ ⚘ ⚘
Commended

Two delightfully cosy, single-storey cottages, sympathetically converted from a Surrey barn, forming a courtyard with the farmhouse. Fully carpeted, electric CH, colour TV and linen (beds made up). Communal laundry room, use of 2-acre farmhouse garden. Situated in picturesque, quiet valley. Ideal walking country. "Badgersholt" sleeps 2 (also suitable disabled); "Foxholme" sleeps 4 in 2 bedrooms. Open all year.

Black Cottage, c/o Newells Farm, Newells Lane, Lower Beeding, Horsham, West Sussex RH13 6LN

Vicky Storey
☎ 01403 891326
SC From £130–£195
Sleeps 4
⛺ ☺ ⚘ ⛴
⚘ ⚘ ⚘
Approved

A delightful secluded cottage in the centre of a sheep and arable farm, with views to the South Downs. Surrounded by woods and lovely walks. Sleeps 4 in comfort. Recently modernised, it is 40 mins from Brighton, 20 mins from Gatwick, with fishing, golf and beautiful Sussex, Surrey and Kent gardens within easy reach. The ideal holiday cottage. Open all year.

Boring House Farm, Vines Cross, Heathfield, East Sussex TN21 9AS

Mrs Anne Reed
☎ 01435 812285
SC From £120–£180
Sleeps 6
⛺ ☺ ⚘ ⛴
⚘ ⚘ ⚘ ⚘
Commended

Peaceful farm cottage on sheep and beef farm. Marvellous views and walks, fishing available. Traditional local, good atmosphere/food in easy walking distance. Many beautiful places to visit. Beach within 15 miles. Accommodation (portion of farmhouse) comprises utility room, hall, WC, kitchen, dining room, sitting room, 3 bedrooms, 1 with shower, 1 with washbasin, bathroom and WC. Large garden. Open Mar–Nov.

Byre Cottages, c/o Sullington Manor Farm, Storrington, West Sussex RH20 4AE

Mrs S Kittle
☎ 01903 742469/745754
Fax 01903 742469
SC From £120–£250
Sleeps 16
⛺ ☺ ⛴
Applied

Sullington Manor is a downland arable and beef farm. A short (but uphill) walk leads to the South Downs Way and beautiful views to the sea. Byre Cottages are converted stables and form part of the original farmyard looking onto a shared lawn and 17th century tithe barn. An outdoor swimming pool with springboard and children's slide may be used by guests.

---

2 High Weald Cottages, Chelwood Farm, Nutley, c/o Sheffield Park Farm, Nr Uckfield, E Sussex TN22 3QR

Mrs Nicky Howe
☎ 01825 790235/790267
Fax 01825 790151
SC From £170–£300
Sleeps 5 + cot
☺ ⚘
⚘ ⚘ ⚘ ⚘
Commended

Picturesque semi-detached farm cottage with garden on dairy farm adjacent Ashdown Forest. Comfortable accommodation comprises 1 double, 1 twin, 1 single room, bathroom, WC, sitting room (log fire, colour TV, phone), kitchen (fridge/freezer, auto washing machine, tumble dryer, electric cooker). Close Sheffield Park Gardens, Bluebell Railway. Easy reach Downs and coast. Cot/high chair available. Beds made up. No cot linen provided; towels on request. Open all year.

2 Victoria Cottage, c/o Hole and Alchorne Farm, Bell Lane, Nutley, East Sussex TN22 3PD

Pauline & Peter Graves
☎ 01825 712475
From £145–£270
Sleeps 5

Highly Commended

A warm welcome awaits you at our comfortable, well-appointed semi-detached cottage, with lovely garden on our dairy farm. Near Ashdown Forest. 3 bedrooms (1 double, 1 twin, 1 single), bathroom, separate WC, sitting room with TV & phone, dining room, kitchen with electric cooker, microwave, fridge freezer, washing machine, tumble dryer. Beds made up. Towels on request. Ideal for visiting South Downs, castles and coast. Open all year.

FOLLOW THE COUNTRY CODE

Leave nothing but footprints,
Take nothing but photographs,
Kill nothing but time!

GOOD FOOD

Nearly all Bureau members now hold a certificate in Essential Food Hygiene.

BUREAU ACCOMMODATION MEANS QUALITY

All Bureau members are inspected and quality graded by the National Tourist Board each year, as well as by fellow members.

England's South and South East

Kent

Group Contact: *Mrs Sarah Alexander* ☎ *01322 866193/Fax 01322 868600*

Kent is very much farming country, but the distinctive features are the many orchards, hop gardens and oast houses to be found in the aptly named 'Garden of England'. The hilly areas like the North Downs and the High Weald contrast with more lowlying parts such as the Low Weald and Romney Marsh. Each area has a distinct character which makes the Kent countryside very varied and attractive. Complementing the countryside are many historic towns and villages, among them the mediaeval port of Sandwich, Tenterden in the Weald with its wide tree-lined High Street, the traditional market town of West Malling, Cranbrook dominated by its splendid windmill, Rochester with its castle and cathedral and the hilltop village of Chilham built around a square and dominated by its castle.

Kent has a wealth of attractions for the visitor. Some of these, such as Dover Castle and Canterbury Cathedral, are well known. But there is much more – Roman remains, castles such as Leeds, Walmer and Deal, fortifications like the series of coastal Martello Towers built as a defence against Napoleon, historic houses like Hever Castle, where Henry VIII courted Anne Boleyn, Churchill's home at Chartwell, Penshurst Place and Knole set in a deer park on the outskirts of Sevenoaks. There are several vineyards open to the public, wildlife parks like Howletts and Port Lympne, the Whitbread Hop Farm, a working farm museum, three steam railways, numerous gardens and various country parks and picnic sites, all ideal for walks or family picnics.

BED AND BREAKFAST

(and evening meal)

---

1 **Barnfield,** Charing, Ashford, Kent TN27 0BN

Mrs Phillada Pym
☎/Fax 01233 712421
🅑 From £18.50–£20.50
EM From £12.50
Sleeps 6
🛏 🗶 🐎 🐕 🎠 🎎
Listed *Commended*

Charming Kent Hall farmhouse built in 1420 with a wealth of character amidst peaceful farmland. Convenient for the popular sights of Leeds Castle, Canterbury, Chilham, Sissinghurst and Channel ports. A warm welcome assured with good home cooking. 1 single room, 2 double, 1 twin. Open all year.

---

2 **Blackmoor Farm,** Sheephurst Lane, The Beech, Marden, Tonbridge, Kent TN12 9NS

Mrs Jean Lutener
☎ 01622 831385/832999
🅑 From £18–£20
Sleeps 4
🛏(4) 🗶 🎠
Listed *Applied*

Listed 16th century barn with interesting features and beams throughout. On 100-acre farm growing strawberries, apples and pears, come and enjoy them. Ideal centre for visiting local castles, Canterbury, London and coast. 1 hour from air and sea ports. Two twin rooms, private bath. Open all year (closed Christmas).

---

3 **Bletchenden Manor Farm,** Bletchenden, Headcorn, Kent TN27 9JB

Mrs Gill Waters
☎ 01622 890228
🅑 From £20–£24
Sleeps 6
🛏(12) 🗶 🎠 ♿
Listed *Applied*

A warm welcome for guests at our attractive 15th century farmhouse surrounded by own farmland. 2 miles south of Headcorn village, peaceful location in the Weald of Kent. Ideal base for visiting numerous National Trust properties, beautiful gardens, golf courses and excellent pubs in the area. 1 hour train journey to London. 3 twin rooms with tea/coffee-making facilities and private bathrooms. Guests' sitting room with TV and a large beamed dining room. Open all year except Christmas.

---

4 **Conghurst Farm,** Hawkhurst, Kent TN18 4RW

Mrs Rosemary Piper
☎ 01580 753331
Fax 01580 754579
🅑 From £19.50–£21.50
EM From £12
Sleeps 6
🛏(12) 🗶 🎠 🎎
🐝🐝 *Highly Commended*

In the Weald of Kent, an Area of Outstanding Natural Beauty, Conghurst Farm offers a friendly welcome and every comfort in a peaceful, secluded Georgian farmhouse. This is an excellent centre for visiting the many houses and gardens in the vicinity. Walkers will enjoy the unspoilt countryside. Our aim is to help you have a restful break. Open Feb–Nov.

---

5 **Great Cheveney Farm,** Great Cheveney, Marden, Tonbridge, Kent TN12 9LX

Mrs Diana Day
☎ 01622 831207
Fax 01622 831786
🅑 From £18
Sleeps 3
🗶 🛏(10) 🎠
Listed *Highly Commended*

We offer comfort and a friendly welcome in our 16th century farmhouse peacefully situated between Marden and Goudhurst villages on B2079. A perfect base for discovering Kent's attractive countryside, NT properties, gardens and coast. London and Le Shuttle 1 hour. Bedrooms with private facilities, guests' lounge, TV, spacious garden and parking. Open all year except Christmas & New Year.

Hallwood Farm, Hawkhurst Road, Cranbrook, Kent TN17 2SP

Ann & David Wickham
☎ 01580 713204
🅱 From £20
EM From £15
Sleeps 6
🕇 ⅗(5) ↗
Listed *Applied*

We offer peaceful and comfortable accommodation at this 15th century hall house. Spacious garden and ample parking space. Close to Cranbrook, the centre of an area rich in castles, manor houses and interesting gardens. Open April–November.

Hoads Farm, Crouch Lane, Sandhurst, Cranbrook, Kent TN18 5PA

Anne Nicholas
☎/Fax 01580 850296
🅱 From £17
EM From £11
Sleeps 6
⅗ ⚏ ▪ ↗
Listed *Applied*

Bed and breakfast available in 17th century farmhouse on hop vine and sheep farm. Comfortable furnishings, sitting room with colour TV. Good centre for the coast, Bodiam Castle, Sissinghurst Castle, Scotney Castle and other National Trust properties. Excellent train service to London from Etchingham or Staplehurst. Dinner by arrangement. Dropside cot available on request. Open all year.

Home Farm, Riverside, Eynsford, Nr Dartford, Kent DA4 0AE

Mrs Sarah Alexander
☎ 01322 866193
Fax 01322 868600
🅱 From £19.50–£29
Sleeps 6
⅙ ⅗(12) ▪ ↗ ⚏
🐾🐾 *Highly Commended*

Our 18th century farmhouse is set in the Darenth Valley, an area of outstanding natural beauty, ideal for London, Gatwick and the Channel ports, being only 2 miles from the M25/M20 junction. Leeds Castle, Brands Hatch and many NT properties within easy reach. There is a good selection of places to eat in the village. All bedrooms have en suite facilities. Open Mar–Nov.

Leaveland Court, Leaveland, Faversham, Kent ME13 0NP

Mrs Corrine Scutt
☎ 01233 740596
🅱 From £20–£25
Sleeps 6
⅗ 🕇 ⅙ ⊞ ⚏ ▪ ↗
🐾 *Highly Commended*

Captivating 15th century timbered farmhouse on 300-acre downland farm. Easy access, 3 miles south of M2 junction 6, Faversham 5 minutes, Canterbury 20 minutes. Situated in a quiet setting with attractive garden and outdoor heated swimming pool. All rooms have en suite facilities, colour TV and tea/coffee trays. Traditional farmhouse food and warm welcome assured. Brochure available. Open Feb–Nov.

Pheasant Farm, Church Road, Oare, Faversham, Kent ME13 0QB

Lorna & Neville Huxtable
☎ 01795 535366
🅱 From £19–£21
EM From £12
Sleeps 4
⅗(5) ⅙ ↗ ▪
Listed *Applied*

14th century farmhouse on 210-acre working sheep farm, next to nature reserve and Swale estuary. All rooms are en suite with colour TV, tea/coffee-making facilities. Delightful sheltered garden with heated swimming pool. Ideal for visits to the continent and London. Historic cinque port town of Faversham 1½ miles, Canterbury 8 miles. A warm relaxing home from home. Open all year except Christmas.

Sissinghurst Castle Farm, Sissinghurst, Cranbrook, Kent TN17 2AB

James & Pat Stearns
☎ 01580 712885
🅱 From £20–£25
Sleeps 10
⅗(5) ⅙ ▪
🐾🐾 *Applied*

This Victorian farmhouse with spacious rooms and beautiful views is delightfully situated within the grounds of the famous Sissinghurst Castle Gardens. Ample parking and it only takes a minute to walk to the gardens. Surrounding farm is largely arable with cattle and sheep. Guests' sitting room, lovely garden, reduction long stay. Fire certificate. Prices rise from April. Open all year.

12 Tanner House, Tanner Farm, Goudhurst Road, Marden, Tonbridge, Kent TN12 9ND

Lesley Mannington
☎ 01622 831214
Fax 01622 832472
📖 From £18–£20
EM From £12
Sleeps 6
✂ 🐾(5) ⊞ ♿ 🐕 ⛛ ♨ ■
🌸🌸🌸 *Applied*

For a restful break, holiday or stop over, we are ideally placed in the beautiful Weald countryside. Our Tudor farmhouse in the centre of our working farm offers high standards of accommodation and cuisine. All our rooms are en suite, one with a genuine four-poster bed, and have colour TV, radio, tea/coffee-making facilities. We specialise in a countryside welcome. Visa/Access/Amex. Open all year except Christmas.

13 Wingham Well Farm, Wingham, Canterbury, Kent CT3 1NW

*Hon Mrs Georgina
Maude*
☎ 01227 720253
📖 From £17.50–£25
Sleeps 4
🐴🐾✂♿⛛♨■🌾
Listed *Commended*

Kentish hall house in quiet countryside on 168-acre farm between Canterbury (Cathedral) and Sandwich (Golf). Channel ports of Ramsgate, Dover and Folkestone and Channel Tunnel half an hour's drive away. One double with en suite bathroom, one twin with washbasin, private bathroom and WC. Open all year except Christmas and New Year.

SELF-CATERING

14 Ash Place Farm, Ash, Sevenoaks, Kent TN15 7HD

Mrs J Scott
☎ 01474 872238
📟 From £150–£220
Sleeps 4 + cot
⛛ ♨ 🌾
🐾 🐾 🐾 🐾
Commended

Luxury upstairs flat in converted Victorian farmhouse on 500-acre working farm. It comprises of large sitting room, ktichen, bathroom and 2 bedrooms, 1 with double bed, 1 with twin beds. At the top of a quiet road leading only to the farm. There is a large garden and splendid views. Many varied attractions locally and only 28 miles from Central London. Pick your own produce in season. Open all year.

15 "Birdwatchers Cottage", c/o Newhouse Farm, Leysdown-on-Sea, Sheerness, Isle of Sheppey, ME12 4BA

Sally-Anne Marsh
☎ 01795 510201
Fax 01795 880379
📟 From £160–£330
Sleeps 8 + cot
✂ ♿ 🐕 ■
🐾 🐾 🐾 🐾 *Highly
Commended*

Idyllic, well-equipped, quality cottage on a cattle, sheep and arable farm for views, walks and sightseeing. Beamed cielings, four bedrooms, CH, large garden. Should suit everyone. Situated between two nature reserves. Under an hour to Canterbury, Maidstone and Rochester. About fifty miles to London. Ideal touring base and a quiet hideaway. SAE for detailed leaflet. Open all year.

16 Golding Hop Farm Cottage, c/o Golding Hop Farm, Bewley Lane, Plaxtol, Nr Sevenoaks, Kent TN15 0PS

Jacqueline Vincent
☎ 01732 885432
📟 From £125–£250
Sleeps 6
🐴✂🐕■🌾
🐾 🐾 🐾 🐾
Highly Commended

13-acre farm producing Kent cobnuts for London markets. Surrounded by orchards and close to attractive village of Plaxtol. Secluded cottage, but not isolated. Sleeps 5, 2 double and 1 single, CH, colour TV, washer dryer and fridge/freezer, payphone. Horse riding, golf nearby. Car essential. Ample parking. Local station 2 miles with frequent trains to London. Motorway 4 miles. Dogs by arrangement only. Open all year.

The Granary, Bletchenden Manor Farm, Bletchenden, Headcorn, Kent TN27 9JB

Gill Waters
☎ 01622 890228
[SC] From £200–£350
Sleeps 4–5
🐕 🛉 ♿
Applied

Beautiful converted granary in grounds of lovely farmhouse near Headcorn. Exposed beams, private sunny patio and garden. Ideal for castles, villages, coast. Large living room with colour TV, well equipped, pretty kitchen/dining room, twin bedrooms both up and downstairs, downstairs shower room, upstairs bathroom. Open all year.

Owls Nest, Kingsnoad Farm, Pye Corner, Ulcombe, Nr Maidstone, Kent ME17 1EG

David & Doreen Roe
☎/Fax 01622 858966
[SC] From £135–£295
Sleeps 6 + cot
🐎 ✗ 🐕 ♿ 🛉 ■ ❀
🐾 🐾 🐾 *Commended*

Converted Victorian milking parlour in truly secluded peaceful farm setting, ½ mile along track between grazing sheep and ripening corn. Fully equipped with continental quilts, colour TV, shower/WC, kitchen, night storage heaters for year round occupation. Cot available. Sit awhile in large, comfortable withdrawing area beneath original oak beams and in front of blazing log fire. An ideal walking/touring base. Open all year.

Pheasant Farm, Church Road, Oare, Faversham, Kent ME13 0QB

Lorna & Neville Huxtable
☎ 01795 535366
[SC] From £189–£266
EM From £12
Sleeps 2/3
🐕(5) ✗ ❀ ■
🐾 🐾 *Highly Commended*

Attractive comfortable well-equipped beamed 14th century annexe to main farmhouse, bedroom, lounge shower, WC and kitchen, all with modern equipment. 210-acre working sheep farm next to nature reserve and Swale estuary. Delightful sheltered garden with heated swimming pool. Ideal for visits to continent and London, Faversham 1½ miles, Canterbury 8 miles. A warm relaxing home from home. Open all year except Christmas.

PRICES

Prices include VAT and service charge (if any) and are:
B&B per person per night
EM per person
SC per unit per week
Tents and caravans per pitch per night

FARM HOLIDAY BUREAU

England's South and South East

Isle of Wight

Group Contact: *Mrs Judy Noyes* ☎ *01983 852582*

The Isle of Wight with its sandy beaches and small secluded coves, and the sea never more than 15 minutes from wherever you may be, has a wide variety of holiday activities. With Cowes and the Royal Yacht Squadron, an international symbol of all that is finest in yachting, the Island is famous for its seafaring activities. A climate that tops the British Isles' Sunshine League makes the island particularly attractive in Spring or Autumn for short break holidays.

For the rambler, the birdwatcher, the angler and for those who merely wish to relax beside the splendours of ancient lighthouses or towering chalk cliffs, the Isle of Wight is the ideal holiday retreat with an internationally acclaimed network of well marked footpaths. For the more adventurous, the Island is a haven for hang-gliders, windsurfers, water skiers, canoe enthusiasts and deep sea fishermen.

Attractions for both children and adults include nature reserves, Butterfly World, the IOW Rare Breeds Park, Blackgang Chine with its history of smuggling and shipwrecks, a steam railway featuring some of the earliest steam engines, Roman remains, historic manors, mills, craft centres, and vineyards open for guided tours and wine tasting.

BED AND BREAKFAST
(and evening meal)

Auld Youngwoods Farm, Whitehouse Road, Porchfield, Newport, Isle of Wight PO30 4LJ

Judith Shanks
☎ **01983 522170**
From £14–£17
Sleeps 5
✗ ⛱(8) 🏵 ▪ ✾
Listed *Commended*

A grassland farm set in open countryside. The 18th century stone farmhouse, recently renovated, retains its original character. The guest rooms are spacious and enjoy magnificent views over the West Wight (H/C in each room. CH throughout). Close to Newtown Nature Reserve, an ideal base for the naturalist. Wild flowers. Red squirrels, owls and butterflies locally. Cowes sailing centre 4 miles. Open all year.

Great Park Farm, Betty Haunt Lane, Carisbrooke, Isle of Wight PO30 4HR

Mrs Sheila Brownrigg
☎ **01983 522945**
From £16–£18
Sleeps 6
⛱(8) 🏵
👄👄 *Commended*

Come and stay on our arable farm with its lovely old Georgian farmhouse in peaceful surroundings with magnificent views over the solent and downs. Central to all main resorts and good eating places nearby. 3 bedrooms en suite, dining, sitting room for guests, colour TV, tea/coffee-making facilities. Open March–Oct.

Kern Farm, Alverstone, Nr Sandown, Isle of Wight PO36 0EY

Mrs Gaynor Oliver
☎ **01983 403721**
From £16–£20
Sleeps 4
✗ 🏵
Listed *Commended*

Quiet and secluded 16th century listed stone farmhouse nestling at the foot of the Downs on a livestock farm with wonderful views. Situated on Bembridge Trail. Sandy beaches 3 miles. Two double en suite bedrooms with tea and coffee-making facilities. Colour TV. Open all year.

Lisle Combe, Bank End Farm, Undercliff Drive, St Lawrence, Ventnor, Isle of Wight PO38 1UW

Hugh & Judy Noyes
☎ **01983 852582**
From £16–£18
Sleeps 5
⛱ ✗
👄 *Commended*

Listed Elizabethan style farmhouse overlooking English Channel, home of the late Alfred Noyes (poet and author) and his family. 5 acre coastal garden with rare waterfowl and pheasant collection (over 100 species). Surrounded by farmlands for owner's herd of pedigree Friesians, free entry to owner's rare breeds park. Superb sea views, coves and small beaches in area of outstanding natural beauty. Open all year.

Newbarn Farm, Newbarn Lane, Gatcombe, Newport, Isle of Wight PO30 3EQ

Mrs Diane Harvey
☎ **01983 721202**
From £15–£18
Sleeps 4
⛱ ✗ 🏵
👄 *Commended*

17th century farmhouse on a 240-acre arable farm in the small hamlet of Gatcombe in the centre of the island. Wonderful walking area enjoying some spectacular views over the island and south coast. Two bedrooms, one with shower en suite, one with H/C, both with tea-making facilities. Dining room and TV lounge with inglenook fireplace. Open Easter-Oct.

SELF-CATERING

⑥ **Cheverton Farm Cottage,** Cheverton Farm, Shorwell, Newport, Isle of Wight PO30 3JE

Sheila Hodgson
☎/Fax 01983 741017
SC From £120–£350
Sleeps 4/6
🐕🐴✂🐾🐎
🔑 🔑 🔑 *Commended*

Old 'character' cottage with beamed ceilings throughout attached to main farmhouse on 550-acre sheep, beef and arable farm. Large garden and car parking area. Walking straight onto downs. Clay pigeon shooting, and dogs, cats, ponies and poultry to see. Good food locally, 10 minutes in car to nearest beach. Open all year.

⑦ **Lisle Combe Cottage,** Bank End Farm, Lisle Combe, Undercliff Drive, St Lawrence, Ventnor, IOW PO38 1UW

Hugh & Judy Noyes
☎ 01983 852582
SC From £150–£250
Sleeps 5/6
🐕
🔑 🔑 *Approved*

Listed cottage overlooking English Channel. Own garden within grounds of Lisle Combe. Large pheasant and waterfowl collection, free entry to owner's rare breed park. Many small beaches and coves for swimming or sunbathing. Colour TV, everything provided except linen. Fine coastal walks in area of outstanding natural beauty. Surrounded by 180-acre family farm with pedigree Friesian herd. Open all year.

⑧ **The Stable,** Newbarn Farm, Newbarn Lane, Gatcombe, Newport, Isle of Wight PO30 3EQ

Mrs Diane Harvey
☎ 01983 721202
SC From £125–£400
Sleeps 6
🐕🐎
🔑 🔑 🔑 🔑 *Highly
Commended*

Beautiful converted stable offering high standard of accommodation for up to six people. Both bedrooms have double beds, one with 3 ft bunks, other with cot. Secluded valley setting, excellent walking. Centrally situated for island attractions. Enclosed patio and parking. Linen and electricity included. Beds made up on arrival. Open all year.

England's West Country

Bath and Wells

Group Contact: *Mrs Jane Rowe* ☎ *01761 241294*

This area has a wealth of history going back to prehistoric times. The Druid Stones near Pensford are 600 years older than Stonehenge and there's always been a touch of magic and mystery in the air around Glastonbury, the ancient town and legendary Isle of Avalon, where it is rumoured King Arthur and his queen were buried.

The visitor is within easy striking distance of the beautiful city of Bath with its Regency architecture and older vestiges of civilisation like the Roman Baths. The whole town is alive with shops and pavement cafés. Another city within easy reach is Bristol, renowned as one of the world's leading ports. With Clifton Zoo, museums, theatres and marvellous shops, it's a visitor's delight. At the famous Wookey Hole Caves you can see the Witch of Wookey and visit a cave chamber in which the acoustics are said to be near perfection. Looking from Ebbor Gorge you will see what must be one of the grandest views in the world.

Interested in wine? There are two vineyards at Pilton and North Wootton where you can taste the local brew. And, of course, if you fancy something stronger, there is always the famous Somerset cider.

With the famous gorge and caves at Cheddar, the lovely cathedral city of Wells and the Mendip Hills, you will be spoilt for choice.

Rhymney · Blaenavon · Abertillery · Abersychan · Gelligaer · Pontypool · Chepstow · Abercarn · Caerleon · Newport · Caldicot · Nailsworth · Stroud · A419 · Cirencester · A466 · A48 · A419 · A433 · A429 · Malmesbury · Swindon · M5 · M4 · Cardiff · Portishead · Bristol · Chippenham · Calne · Clevedon · Bath · Melksham · Marlborough · Weston-Super-Mare · Barry · A38 · A37 · A4 · Devizes · Bradford-on-Avon · Trowbridge · M5 · Cheddar · Midsomer Norton · Radstock · Westbury · Burnham-On-Sea · Frome · Warminster · Wells · Shepton Mallet · A361 · A36 · Glastonbury · A39 · Williton · Bridgwater · Street · A303 · A37 · A350 · Salisbury

BED AND BREAKFAST

(and evening meal)

---

① Barrow Vale Farm, Farmborough, Bath, Avon BA3 1BL

Cherilyn Langley
☎ **01761 470300**
BB From £16
Sleeps 6
🛏(3) 🍴 🐎
♛♛ *Commended*

Barrow Vale is a family-run dairy farm, situated between the historic cities of Bath and Wells. The farmhouse, which has been comfortably modernised, offers central heating, well furnished en suite bedrooms and guests lounge with TV. It is within easy reach of places of interest with local pubs and restaurants close by. Open all year (except Christmas and New Year).

---

② Icelton Farm, Wick-St-Lawrence, Weston-super-Mare, Avon BS22 0YJ

Mrs Elizabeth Parsons
☎ **01934 515704**
BB From £15–£17
Sleeps 5
🛏(2)
Listed *Applied*

Icelton is a working dairy/sheep farm, just off the M5 (jct. 21). Ideal for touring Wells, Cheddar, and Mendip Hills. This listed farmhouse offers double room with H/C, family room with H/C and shower. Tea/coffee-making facilities. Oak-beamed dining room and lounge, both with inglenook fireplaces. English breakfast. Good pubs and restaurants close at hand. No dogs. Open Mar–Nov.

---

③ The Model Farm, Norton Malreward, Pensford, Bristol, Avon BS18 4HA

Margaret Hasell
☎ **01275 832144**
BB From £16–£18
Sleeps 6
🐎
♛♛ *Commended*

The farmhouse is situated 2 miles off the A37 in a peaceful hamlet, nestling under the Dundry Hills. A working arable and beef farm in easy reach of Bristol, Bath, and many other interesting places. The accommodation consists of 1 family room en suite and 1 double room with washbasin. Guests' lounge and dining room. Open Feb–Nov.

---

④ Pantiles, Bathway, Chewton Mendip, Nr Bath, Somerset BA3 4NS

Pat Hellard
☎ **01761 241519**
BB From £16–£18
Sleeps 6
🅖🅗 🐎 🍴 🛏
♛♛ *Highly Commended*

A warm welcome awaits at Pantiles, an attractive house with views over the Mendip countryside. Only 15 miles from Bath and Bristol, 5 miles to the lovely city of Wells. Our aim is quality B&B at reasonable prices. We offer 3 bedrooms, 1 double en suite, 1 twin en suite, 1 twin with private bath, all with hospitality tray and colour TV. Open all year.

---

⑤ Purn House Farm, Bleadon, Weston-super-Mare, Avon BS24 0QE

Thelma Moore
☎/Fax **01934 812324**
BB From £16–£20
EM From £7
Sleeps 13
🛏 🎣 🍴 ♿ ☞ 🐎 💼
♛♛ *Commended*

Peaceful 17th century farmhouse set at foot of Mendips. 3 miles from Weston-super-Mare. Five family rooms, (4 en suite, 1 ground floor). Games room. Pretty garden and pets, corner. Fishing available in River Axe which flows through the dairy farm. Riding nearby. Ideal base for Cheddar Gorge, Wells and Glastonbury. Open Feb–Dec.

Redhill Farm, Emborough, Nr Bath, Somerset BA3 4SH

Jane Rowe
☎ 01761 241294
🅱🅱 From £16–£20
Sleeps 6
🐎 🅰 ⬥
Listed *Approved*

Our listed farmhouse built in Cromwellian times is situated high on the Mendips between Bath and Wells. It is the perfect centre for outdoor activities and sightseeing. We are a working smallholding with a variety of animals to delight the children. CH. Guests' private bathroom. Fresh home produce. Tea/coffee-making facilities and washbasins in bedrooms. No dogs. Bath and West show ground 7 miles. Open all year except Christmas.

Southway Farm, Polsham, Wells, Somerset BA5 1RW

Anita Frost
☎ 01749 673396
Fax 01749 670373
🅱🅱 From £17–£19
Sleeps 6
🐎 ⬥
👑👑 *Commended*

A Georgian listed farmhouse situated halfway between Wells and Glastonbury overlooking Somerset levels and cider orchard. Accommodation is 3 comfortable and attractively furnished bedrooms, 2 with private bath, 1 en suite. A delicious full English breakfast is served. Guests may relax in the cosy lounge or pretty garden. Ideal location for touring the glorious West Country. Open Feb–Nov.

Valley Farm, Sandy Lane, Stanton Drew, Nr. Bristol, Avon BS18 4EL

Mrs Doreen Keel
☎ 01275 332723
🅱🅱 From £16–£20
Sleeps 6
🐎 ⅙ ⬥ ⬥ 🗼
👑👑 *Highly Commended*

Modern farmhouse situated on the edge of an ancient village near the river Chew with Druid Stones and many footpaths to walk. Near the Chew Valley Lakes renowned for trout fishing and in easy reach of Bath, Bristol, Wells and Cheddar. Stanton Drew is off A368 Bath to Weston-super-Mare road or the B3130 road. There are 2 rooms with double beds each with wash basins and coffee/tea making facilities. 2 en suite and 1 private bathroom. Open all year (except Christmas).

Woodbarn Farm, Denny Lane, Chew Magna, Bristol, Avon BS18 8SZ

Mrs Judi Hasell
☎ 01275 332599
🅱🅱 From £17–£20
Sleeps 6
⅙ 🐎(3) ⬥
👑👑 *Applied*

Woodbarn is a working mixed farm. 5 minutes from Chew Valley Lake. Chew Magna is a large village with pretty cottages, Georgian houses and is central for touring. There are two en suite bedrooms, one double and one family, all with tea trays. Guests' lounge and dining room. Cream teas Sundays June–September. Open Mar–Dec (closed Christmas).

SELF-CATERING

Barrow Croft, Barrow Vale Farm, Farmborough, Bath, Avon BA3 1BL (10)

Mrs Cherilyn Langley
☎ 01761 470300
🆂🅲 From £180–£300
Sleeps 4/6
🐎 🗼 ⬥
🔑 🔑 🔑 🔑 *Highly Commended*

This recently refurbished modern bungalow within the farm grounds, offers a peaceful setting with lovely rural views. Full oil CH. Situated between Bath and Wells, it is an ideal base for visiting Cheddar, the Mendip Hills and the trout fishing lakes of Blagdon and Chew Valley. Pubs and restaurants close by. Winter 3 days break. Open all year.

England's West Country
Bath and Wiltshire

Group Contacts: 🅱🅱 *Mrs Marlene Nixon* ☎ *01380 828355*
⬜ *Mrs Janet Tyler* ☎ *01380 850523*

Easily accessible within 100 miles of London, the Midlands and the sea, Wiltshire offers the best of rural England, the marvellous scenery is its biggest surprise. Almost half the county is designated as an 'Area of Outstanding Natural Beauty'.

The wide peaceful downland is rich in historic interest: Stonehenge, Avebury and Silbury Hill stand out on the rolling green plain, with picturesque villages hidden away along the chalk stream valleys. Castle Combe and the National Trust village of Lacock are well known, but there are scores more waiting to be discovered. Six hundred years of building are displayed in the magnificent collection of historic homes, i.e. Longleat, Bowood House and Corsham Court and Sheldon Manor.

Walk the ancient Ridgeway Path, an important nomadic and trading route, or the Kennet and Avon Canal now restored along much of its route. Just over the county border the Romans built their city around the hot springs, and eleven centuries later Georgian architects created the elegant city of Bath. Whether you just stop for a short break or longer, the people of Wiltshire will welcome you.

BED AND BREAKFAST

(and evening meal)

Boyds Farm, Gastard, Nr Corsham, Wiltshire SN13 9PT

Dorothy Robinson
☎ 01249 713146
BB From £16–£17.50
Sleeps 6
🐎 🍴 🐎 ⚓
🦢🦢 *Commended*

Enjoy a relaxing stay on our arable farm situated in the peace and tranquillity of the unspoilt Wiltshire countryside. Our delightful 16th century farmhouse, as featured by the *Daily Express*, accommodates families, couples and individuals, CH, H/C, tea/coffee-making facilities. Guests' own lounge with woodburning stove. Easy access to M4, Bath, Lacock, Castle Combe, Stonehenge, Bradford-on-Avon. Excellent pub food close by. Open all year.

Church Farm, Steeple Ashton, Trowbridge, Wiltshire BA14 6EL

Susan Cottle
☎ 01380 870518
BB From £16.50–£17.50
🐎 🦮 🐎 🐎
Listed *Commended*

Lovely old farmhouse dating back to 16th century in centre of beautiful village. Ideally situated for Bath, Salisbury, Longleat, Stourhead, Castle Combe. Spacious rooms, homely atmosphere, use of lounge, TV. Tea and homemade cake on arrival. No smoking in bedrooms. Please ring for directions. Open all year except Christmas.

Friday Street Farm, Christian Malford, Chippenham, Wiltshire SN15 4BU

Linda Di Claudio
☎ 01249 720146
BB From £16–£20
EM From £7.50
Sleeps 4
🐎 🍴 🐎 ⚓ 🐎
🦢 *Commended*

Welcome to our 200-acre working dairy farm. Our part 17th century farmhouse offers guests a winning combination – a lovely house with country cottage cosiness, excellent decor, delicious homecooked meals and large mature gardens. Two attractive en suite bedrooms equipped with TV, radio and hospitality tray. Ideally situated midway between Bath and the Cotswolds. Open all year except Christmas.

Hatt Farm, Old Jockey, Box, Nr Bath, Wiltshire SN13 8DJ

Mrs Carol Pope
☎/Fax 01225 742989
BB From £17.50–£20
Sleeps 4
🐎 🍴
🦢🦢 *Commended*

Extremely comfortable Georgian farmhouse in peaceful surroundings. Scrumptious breakfasts served overlooking beautiful views of the countryside. What could be nicer than sitting by a log fire in winter or enjoying the garden in summer ? Lovely walks and good golfing nearby. Ideal for touring Wiltshire and the Coltswolds yet close to Bath. One twin with en suite shower, one double/family with private bathroom, both with tea/coffee. CH. Guests' lounge. Closed Christmas.

Higher Green Farm, Poulshot, Devizes, Wiltshire SN10 4RW

Marlene & Malcolm Nixon
☎ 01380 828355
BB From £15
Sleeps 6
🐎 🍴 🐎
Listed *Commended*

Listed 17th century timbered farmhouse facing south onto village green close to a traditional inn. This is a 140 acre working dairy farm situated between Bath and Salisbury, 3 miles from Devizes and within easy reach of many National Trust properties. Tea-making facilities, guests' lounge, colour TV. Double, twin and 2 single rooms, 2 bathrooms, 2 toilets. Open Mar–Nov.

---

6 Hillside Farm, Edington, Westbury, Wilts BA13 4PG

Carol Mussell
☎/Fax 01380 830437
BB From £15–£17
Sleeps 4
🦮 📷
♨ *Commended*

A warm welcome and wonderful views are yours on our small working farm nestled under the edge of Salisbury Plain. We have one double/family room and one twin room each with wash basins, colour TV and hospitaliy tray. Lovely conservatory for guests' use. Within easy reach of Bath and NT properties. Closed Christmas & January.

7 Leighfield Lodge Farm, Cricklade, Swindon, Wiltshire SN6 6RH

Mrs Claire Read
☎/Fax 01666 860241
BB From £17.50–£20
Sleeps 4
🦮 🐎 📷
Listed *Applied*

A very warm welcome awaits you at Leighfield Lodge Farm, a 100-acre mixed farm. The accommodation includes one twin room with private bathroom and a double room with en suite facilities. Tea/coffee and television in all rooms. Evening meals by arrangement.

8 Little Cotmarsh Farm, Broad Town, Wootton Bassett, Swindon, Wiltshire SN4 7RA

Mary Richards
☎ 01793 731322
or 0831 090584
BB From £15–£18
Sleeps 6
🍴 🦮
Listed *Commended*

300 year old farmhouse with lots of character, situated 4 miles south of M4 J16 in peaceful hamlet. Comfortable attractive bedrooms with washbasins, one with toilet/shower en suite. All have tea/coffee-making facilities, heating and colour TV. Equal distance from Bath, Cotswolds and Oxford. Excellent amenities for wet days in and around Swindon. Good pub food locally. Open all year.

9 Longwater Park Farm, Lower Road, Erlestoke, Nr Devizes, Wiltshire SN10 5UE

Pam Hampton
☎/Fax 01380 830095
BB From £20–£26
EM From £11
Sleeps 12
🐎🦽🌐🦮🐕
⛺ 📷
♨ ♨ ♨ *Commended*

A peaceful retreat overlooking our own lakes and parkland with 2½ acre waterbird area. 160-acre organic farm with rare sheep. Family suite, double/twin rooms all en suite, TV and tea-making facilities, CH. 2 ground floor bedrooms. Spacious lounge, large conservatory, separate dining room. Traditional farmhouse fayre using local produce. Special diets. Local wines. Coarse fishing. Erlestoke Sands Golf Course adjacent. Open all year except Christmas and New Year.

10 Lovett Farm, Little Somerford, Nr Malmesbury, Wiltshire SN15 5BP

Susan Barnes
☎ 01666 823268
BB From £15
Sleeps 4
🦮 ⛺
Listed *Commended*

Our comfortable modern farmhouse on a small working farm has delightful country views and is situated on the edge of Malmesbury, England's oldest borough. Ideal base for visiting Bath, Cotswolds, Bristol and Stonehenge. One double en suite, one twin with washbasin, tea/coffee-making facilities, radio and colour TV. Full CH, guests' lounge, dining room with traditional log fire. Open all year.

11 Lower Foxhanger Canal Farm, Rowde, Devizes, Wiltshire SN10 1SS

Cynthia & Colin Fletcher
☎/Fax 01380 828254
BB From £15.50–£18
Sleeps 6
🐎 🦮 ⛺ 🚐 (touring & static) 🛶 ⛺ 📷
♨ ♨ *Commended*

Tranquillity awaits you by the canal adorned with gaily painted narrow boats. Assist boats through locks. Scenic walks to pubs. Fish and boat to heart's desire. Twin (en suite), double/family rooms all with colour TV in 18th century farmhouse. Self-catering in orchard alongside canal. Small campsite with facilities Open Easter–Oct.

Lower Stonehill Farm, Charlton, Malmesbury, Wiltshire SN16 9DY

Mrs Edna Edwards
☎ **01666 823310**
BB **From £15–£20**
Sleeps 6
🐕 🐈
Listed *Commended*

Large old Cotswold stone house on 180-acre dairy farm in a quiet location 3 miles from Malmesbury and 8 miles from the M4. Ideal for touring – visit antique shops in market towns, stately houses and gardens, village pubs or just relax on the lawn and enjoy farm life. Three comfortable rooms available, 1 en suite. Pets and children will enjoy the relaxed, friendly atmosphere. Open all year.

Manor Farm, Corston, Malmesbury, Wiltshire SN16 0HF

Mrs Ross Eavis
☎/Fax **01666 822148**
☎ **0374 675783**
BB **From £16–£22**
Sleeps 12
🐈 ♿ 📷
👑 👑 *Commended*

A warm welcome awaits you at our 17th century Cotswold stone farmhouse on a working dairy/arable farm. Single, twin, double and family rooms, three en suite all with colour TV, hospitality tray. Guests' lounge. Large gardens. Pub food 200 yards down the road. Convenient for M4 and visiting Cotswolds, Bath, Lacock and Avebury. A winner in the 1995 West Country Farm Holiday Awards. Open all year.

Manor Farm, Wadswick, Box, Corsham, Wiltshire SN13 8JB

Carolyn Barton
☎ **01225 810700**
Fax **01225 810307**
BB **From £18–£20**
Sleeps 6
🍴 🐈 🎣 ♿
👑 👑 *Highly Commended*

Visit our arable, sheep and horse farm nestling in the quiet hamlet of Wadswick. We are only 7 miles from Bath yet close to Lacock and other beautiful villages. Our 16th century farmhouse has large, spacious rooms, en suite with tea/coffee making facilities and colour TV. Stabling and riding available. Open Mar–Nov.

Oakfield Farm, Easton Piercy Lane, Yatton Keynell, Chippenham, Wiltshire SN14 6JU

Mrs Margaret Read
☎ **01249 782355**
BB **From £16–£20**
Sleeps 6
🐈 🧒 🍴
Listed *Commended*

Friendly welcome in Cotswold stone farmhouse with fine views over open countryside. On working livestock farm in a quiet location, excellent for wildlife. One en suite double/family room, 1 double and 1 twin room. Full central heating, tea/coffee-making facilities, colour TV. Ideal base for visiting Bath, Castle Combe, Lacock and the Cotswolds. Open Mar–Nov.

Olivemead Farm, Olivemead Lane, Dauntsey, Nr Chippenham, Wiltshire SN15 4JQ

Suzanne Candy
☎ **01666 510205**
BB **From £15–£17**
Sleeps 6
🐈 🧒 🍴
👑 *Commended*

Relax and enjoy the warm, informal hospitality at our delightful 18th century farmhouse on a working dairy farm. Twin, double, family rooms, washbasins, colour TV. Tea/coffee facilities. Generous breakfasts. Oak beamed dining room/lounge for guests' exclusive use. Large garden, play area, cot, highchair. Convenient M4, Bath, Cotswolds, Salisbury.

Pickwick Lodge Farm, Goyers Lane, Corsham, Wiltshire SN13 0PS

Gill Stafford
☎ **01249 712207**
Fax **01249 701904**
BB **From £16–£20**
Sleeps 4
🐈 🍴 📷 🏇
Listed *Commended*

Our farm lies ½ mile off the A4 between Chippenham and Bath. Ideally situated for visiting NT properties, Wiltshire, White Horses, Avebury, Stonehenge. Enjoy walking the varied and interesting footpaths or relax in our peaceful garden. Our 17th century farmhouse has oak beams, open fires, CH. Two cosy double rooms, 1 en suite, 1 with private shower room, colour TV, tea/coffee-making facilities. *Daily Express* award-winning breakfast.

---

18 **Saltbox Farm,** Drewetts Mill, Box, Corsham, Wiltshire SN13 8PT

Mary Gregory
☎ **01225 742608**
🅱🅱 **From £16**
Sleeps 4
🐾 ⚒ 🐕 👞 🕿 💼
💌 *Commended*

Quietly located 1 mile off A4 6 miles from Bath and centrally situated for touring the West Country. Our listed 18th century farmhouse is set in the unspoilt Box Valley, offering scenic walks in a wildlife and conservation area. Double and twin/family bedrooms with washbasins, tea/coffee-making facilities. Beautiful views of open countryside. Guests' bathroom. Visitors lounge/diner with colour TV, CH. Reduced rates for 3/4 day breaks. Open all year except Christmas & New Year.

19 **Tockenham Court Farm,** Tockenham, Nr Swindon, Wiltshire SN4 7PH

Mrs Elizabeth Bennett
☎/Fax **01793 852315**
☎ **0831 341310**
🅱🅱 **From £18–£20**
Sleeps 6
🐕 🐕 🕿

Listed *Highly Commended*

A warm welcome will await you at our traditional Grade II listed 16th century court house. We have 2 double rooms, one twin bedded room, CH, tea/coffee-making facilities and colour TV. Separate shower room and WC, separate bathroom and WC. Guests' own sitting room.

SELF-CATERING

20 **Home Farm Barn and The Derby,** Home Farm, Heddington, Nr Calne, Wiltshire SN11 0PL

Mrs Janet Tyler
☎/Fax **01380 850523**
🆂🅲 **From £150–£340**
Sleeps 2/5
🐕 🕿
🏇 🏇 🏇 🏇 *Commended*

Home Farm is a dairy and arable farm with its own private lake, panoramic views and unbeatable downland walks in small village. Riding school and golf course adjoin farm. 17th century barn traditionally furnished sleeps 5. Also stable conversion, bungalow-style, sleeps 2. Set in paved courtyard with Victorian lamp. Quiet idyllic spot. Colour brochure.

21 **Lower Foxhangers Farm,** Rowde, Devizes, Wiltshire SN10 1SS

Cynthia & Collin Fletcher
☎/Fax **01380 828254**
🆂🅲 **From £150–£200**
Sleeps 4/5
🐕 🐕 🏕 🔌 **(touring and static)** 🕿 🕿
Tourist Board Inspected

A relaxing rural retreat awaits you in our four holiday homes situated in orchard alongside canal with patios and garden furniture. Cycle, walk, fish, boat or feed the ducks. Several pubs within easy walking distance. Easy reach World Heritage Sites of Avebury and Stonehenge, or Georgian city of Bath. Also B&B and small campsite with facilities. Open Easter–Oct.

22 **Park Farm Cottage,** Lower Road, Erlestoke, Devizes, Wiltshire SN10 5UE

Pam Hampton
☎/Fax 01380 830095
🆂🅲 **From £225–£400**
Sleeps 7
🐕 🐕 🐕 🕿
🏇 🏇 🏇 🏇 🏇
Highly Commended

A 'country retreat', adjacent to lakes. Traditionally furnished, every facility including en suite bedrooms, large gardens and garage. Meals available in farmhouse (400 yds). Ideal for walking, coarse fishing, golf or exploring Bath, Salisbury, Stonehenge, Avebury, Kennet and Avon Canal, Longleat or just relaxing! Open all year.

Stonehill Farm, Charlton, Malmesbury, Wiltshire SN16 9DY   (23)

Mrs Edna Edwards
☎ **01666 823310**
[SC] **From £150–£210**
Sleeps 2/3
🐄 🐓
🐕 🐕 🐕 *Commended*

Stonehill is a family-run dairy farm on the Wilts/Glos border, 3 miles from Malmesbury and 8 miles M4. The Cow Byre and Bull Pen are converted cowsheds, comfortably furnished with double bed, bathroom, fitted kitchen/diner and lounge. Full CH, colour TV, microwave, all power and linen included. Facing south-west with gravel patio and garden chairs. Open all year.

FARM HOLIDAY BUREAU

CONFIRM BOOKINGS

Disappointments can arise from misunderstandings over the telephone.
Please write to confirm your booking.

PRICES

Prices include VAT and service charge (if any) and are:
B&B per person per night
EM per person
SC per unit per week
Tents and caravans per pitch per night

FARM HOLIDAY BUREAU

FARM HOLIDAY BUREAU

NO ANSWER?

Farmers are mostly out and about during the day.
Try to telephone before 9.30am or after 4pm.

England's West Country

Heart of Dorset

Group Contact: *Rosemary Coleman* ☎ *01305 848252*

The Heart of Dorset Group offers you a range of holiday accommodation in the Dorset countryside. It is an area of outstanding natural beauty renowned for its beautiful villages, magnificent hills and lovely valleys.

Wherever you stay, the coast is but a short distance away with excellent swimming, sailing and fishing. For the country lover, the area has a wide choice of forest trails, coastal and inland walks, ancient monuments, historic houses and gardens. Dorset's mild climate makes it an ideal location for a holiday all year round.

Dorset's most famous son, Thomas Hardy, was born within three miles of Dorchester; his rambling cottage, Higher Bockhampton is open to the public. Most of his books were based on villages and towns in the area, many of which still retain the rural atmosphere of Hardy's Wessex.

A romantic figure of more modern times is Lawrence of Arabia, who spent a number of reclusive years in his remote and rather bleak cottage, Clouds Hill, near Bovington Camp.

Corfe Castle, Brownsea Island, Lulworth Cove, Durdle Door ... even the Tolpuddle Martyrs' Museum are all here – you'll need more than a few days to discover Dorset!

BED AND BREAKFAST

(and evening meal)

Lamperts Farmhouse, 11 Dorchester Road, Sydling St Nicholas, Dorchester, Dorset DT2 9NU

Mrs Rita Bown
☎ 01300 341790
🅱 From £18–£20
EM From £10
Sleeps 4
🛏 ☡

🏵🏵 *Applied*

Enjoy home comforts in our thatched farmhouse in the unspoilt village of Sydling St Nicholas. Ideal for walking or touring. 1 double family room, 1 twin room, both with en suite bathroom. Guests' own lounge with inglenook fireplace, colour TV, tea/coffee-making facilities. Full CH. Open all year.

Newlands Farm, West Lulworth, Wareham, Dorset BH20 5PU

Mrs Lesley Simpson
☎ 01929 400376
Fax 01929 400536
🅱 From £18–£20
Sleeps 6
☡ ✂ ♨

Listed *Commended*

Newlands was built in the early 19th century and the farm has beautiful views of the sea and the distant Purbeck Hills. The beach is within walking distance. Well placed for coastal footpaths with water sports available within 15 miles and horse riding nearby. 2 double/family rooms with tea/coffee-making facilities and colour TV. Showers and washbasins en suite. Breakfast is served in the dining room. Regret no dogs. Open all year (closed Christmas).

SELF-CATERING

Glebe Cottage, c/o Glebe House, Moreton, Dorchester, Dorset DT2 8RQ

Carol Gibbens
☎ 01929 462468
🆂🅲 From £120–£230
Sleeps 4
♿ ☡

🐾 🐾 *Approved*

Glebe Cottage is set in an old rectory garden in the peaceful farming village of Moreton, famous for its church windows engraved by Laurence Whistler and burial place of Lawrence of Arabia. It is a wildlife haven. The cottage is detached, is on one floor with 2 double bedrooms, kitchen, living room, bathroom, night storage heating and has its own garden. Open all year.

Gore Cottage, West Milton, Bridport, Dorset DT6 3SN. c/o Wingham Well Farm, Wingham, Canterbury, CT3 1NW

Hon. Mrs Georgina Maude
☎ 01227 720253
🆂🅲 From £165–£295
Sleeps 5
🛏 ☡ ♨ ▪ ✗

🐾 🐾 *Approved*

Listed Grade II detached stone-built thatched cottage in own secluded garden on the edge of the village of West Milton. 1 double, 1 twin, 1 single, sitting room, dining/kitchen, tiny bathroom, separate WC and washbasin. The sea is about 5 miles away. Among other attractions are the Swannery at Abbotsbury and the Tropical Garden, Maiden Castle, Cerne Abbas (The Giant), Athelhampton and RAF Yeovilton. Open all year.

⑤ Lamperts Farmhouse, 11 Dorchester Road, Sydling St Nicholas, Dorchester, Dorset DT2 9NU

Mrs Rita Bown
☎ **01300 341790**
SC **From £120–£200**
Sleeps 2 + cot
♉ ♟

🐾 🐾 *Approved*

16th century wing of Lamperts Farmhouse recently refurbished as a cottage for 2 people. Snugly tucked away between the hills of the beautiful Sydling Valley right in the heart of Dorset. Fitted kitchen, sitting room with French window opening onto secluded garden. Colour TV, downstairs bathroom, double bedroom, full CH. Open all year.

⑥ Old Dairy Cottage and Clyffe Dairy Cottage, c/o Clyffe Farm, Tincleton, Dorchester, Dorset DT2 8QR

Rosemary Coleman
☎ **01305 848252**
SC **From £140–£335**
Sleeps 4/6 + cot
♉ ☕

🐾 🐾 🐾 *Commended*

Two attractively furnished character cottages with beams, inglenook fireplaces and own gardens. The mixed farm has cows, calves, horses, and beautiful woodland walks. Ducks and wildlife on the pond and streams. Fishing, ideal cycling countryside, within easy reach coast, golf, trekking, leisure centre for swimming etc. Excellent value low season with OAP reductions and winter breaks. CH. Cottages within walking distance of each other. Open all year.

England's West Country

Dorset

Group Contacts: BB *Mrs Sue Diment* ☎ *01308 482630*
SC *Mrs Hilary Hoskin* ☎ *01305 262356*

Come and explore Dorset with its delightful villages in the west of the county, the dairy pastureland of Blackmore Vale in the north, scenic Cranborne Chase in the east and the Purbeck Hills around Corfe Castle in the south.

The unspoilt countryside so vividly described by the author, Thomas Hardy is still unchanged in places – rolling downland and fertile valleys with picturesque villages of mellow stone and thatched cottages.

For a day out, travel to Salisbury and Winchester Cathedrals, or the theatres and other attractions of major resorts like Bournemouth and Poole. Dartmoor lies to the west and the New Forest to the east, both within easy reach. Sea trips for fishing or pleasure can be made from many of the ports along the coast.

Summer is not the only season in which to savour this delightful area. Winters are mild on the South Coast and spring and autumn are particularly good times for a Dorset holiday. The footpath network is unsurpassed, both inland and along the coast. The Coastal Way, in particular, offers dramatic and exciting scenery, as safe and sandy beaches give way to shifting banks of shingle and rugged cliffs teeming with birds. Historic houses, famous gardens, exciting coastline – you name it, Dorset has it!

BED AND BREAKFAST

(and evening meal)

---

1 **Almshouse Farm,** Hermitage, Sherborne, Dorset DT9 6HA

Mrs Jenny Mayo
☎ **01963 210296**
BB **From £18.50**
Sleeps 6
🐴 🅰 ⚙
🐝🐝 *Highly Commended*

This charming old farmhouse – formerly a 16th century monastery – was restored in 1849. Surrounded by 160 acres, overlooking the Blackmore Vale. Accommodation in three double en suite rooms with colour TV and tea/coffee-making facilities. Dining room with inglenook fireplace, comfortable sitting room. Garden available to guests at all times. Sherborne 6 miles, Dorchester 14 miles. AA QQQQ selected. Open Feb–Dec.

---

2 **Church Farm,** Stockwood, Nr Dorchester, Dorset DT2 0NG

Mrs Ruth House
☎ **01935 83221**
BB **From £18–£20**
Sleeps 6
🐴 🕊 ✂ 🏕 ▪
🐝🐝 *Highly Commended*

Beautiful Georgian farmhouse idyllically set amongst woodlands and streams on a working farm. Ideal for touring Dorset/Somerset border. Warm, friendly welcome in family home. Comfortable en suite rooms with colour TV, tea/coffee-making facilities, CH. Traditional breakfast. Many local pubs and restaurants. Open all year.

---

3 **Colesmoor Farm,** Toller Porcorum, Dorchester, Dorset DT2 0DU

Mrs Rachael Geddes
☎ **01300 320812**
BB **From £16**
Sleeps 4
🐴 ✂ 🏕 ▪
🐝 *Commended*

Colesmoor Farm, reached by its own private track, is surrounded by peaceful countryside with extensive views. We offer a choice of breakfasts with homebaked bread. Our ground floor accommodation includes a double room with CTV, hot drink facilities and en suite bathroom and twin room with adjacent private bathroom. Excellent choice of pubs and restaurants nearby. Brochure. Closed Mar–Apr & Dec.

---

4 **Hemsworth Manor Farm,** Witchampton, Nr Wimborne, Dorset BH21 5BN

Mrs A C Tory
☎/Fax **01258 840216**
BB **From £20**
Sleeps 6
🐴 🏕
🐝🐝 *Highly Commended*

Working family farm of approx 800 acres, mainly arable, but with cattle, sheep and pigs, and situated in unspoilt countryside with only one other farmhouse in sight! Easy access to Bournemouth, Salisbury, Dorchester and the New Forest. Two double, one family room, all spacious with colour TV, tea/coffee-making facilities and washbasins en suite or private bathrooms. Excellent local pubs in the area. Open all year.

---

5 **Henbury Farm,** Dorchester Road, Sturminster Marshall, Wimborne, Dorset BH21 3RN

Sue & Jonathan Tory
☎ **01258 857306**
Fax **01258 857928**
BB **From £19–£22**
Sleeps 6
🐴 🐕 🐎 🏕
🐝🐝 *Highly Commended*

300-year-old farmhouse facing large front lawn and pond, situated on 200-acre dairy farm. Guests' lounge with colour TV. Near to New Forest and fifteen minutes from sandy beaches. Numerous local restaurants to meet your evening requirements. Many local attractions and country walks. Ideally situated for a great holiday. En-suite facilities available. Open all year except Christmas.

Higher Langdon, Beaminster, Dorset DT8 3NN

Judy Thompson
☎/Fax 01308 862537
BB From £15–£25
EM From £10
Sleeps 4

We are a happy informal family offering the best of hospitality. Set in acres of Dorset downland, 9 miles sea, ideal for walkers, on the Wessex Way. We farm sheep, cereals and geese with farmyard animals for children to enjoy. Spacious en suite bedrooms and elegant sitting room with TV. Open all year.

Commended

Holebrook Farm, Lydlinch, Sturminster Newton, Dorset DT10 2JB

Charles & Alastair Wingate-Saul
☎ 01258 817348
Fax 01258 817747
BB From £21–24
Sleeps 12

Situated in heart of Blackmore Vale and ideal as a central base for exploring Dorset, this is a family farm of 125 acres. Accommodation in 18th century farmhouse and delightfully converted stables, each with own sitting room, kitchen, shower, WC en-suite. Swimming pool, clay pigeon shooting, large games room with pool and table tennis. Comfortable, friendly atmosphere. Good home cooking, Licence. No dogs. Open all year.

Listed *Highly Commended*

Huntsbridge Farm, Leigh, Nr Sherborne, Dorset DT9 6JA

Mrs Su Read
☎ 01935 872150
BB £18.50
Sleeps 6

Attractive stone farmhouse set in open countryside in the beautiful part of Dorset Thomas Hardy chose for his novel 'The Woodlanders'. Ideally situated for either walking or touring. Golf, riding and fishing available locally. Tastefully furnished bedrooms, 2 double en suite and 1 twin en suite, all with tea/coffee facilities, colour TV, radio/alarm and CH. So why not come and relax far from the madding crowd ? Open Mar–Nov.

Highly Commended

Kitwhistle Farm, Beaminster Down, Beaminster, Dorset DT8 3SG

Mrs Ann Hasell
☎ 01308 862458
BB From £15–£20
Sleeps 5

A friendly welcome and a cup of tea await you at Kitwhistle Farm which is a working dairy farm on the peaceful Beaminster Downs. The historic town of Beaminster is just two miles away with its many eating houses. The perfect place to tour Hardy's coast and countryside. All facilities on ground floor. Open Mar–Nov.

Approved

Maiden Castle Farm, Dorchester, Dorset DT2 9PR

Hilary Hoskin
☎/Fax 01305 262356
BB From £18–£20
Sleeps 6

Our large working farm, 1 mile from Dorchester and 7 miles from Weymouth in the heart of Hardy country, enjoys magnificent views of Maiden Castle and the surrounding countryside. En-suite bedrooms with CH, TV, tea-making facilities and a telephone for guests' use combine to offer comfort, peace and quiet – ideal for the perfect holiday. Babysitting by arrangement. Open all year.

Highly Commended

New House Farm, Mangerton Lane, Bradpole, Bridport, Dorset DT6 3SF (11)

Jane Greening
☎ 01308 422884
BB From £15–£18
Sleeps 4

Modern, comfortable farmhouse set in the rural Dorset hills. Near coast (2½ miles). A warm welcome to families, children especially. Lots to do and see in this historically beautiful area.

Applied

12 Rudge Farm, Chilcombe, Bridport, Dorset DT6 4NF

Sue Diment
☎ 01308 482630
Fax 01308 482635
BB From £21
EM From £12.50
Sleeps 6
🏵 🏵 ♿
🐾 🐾 *Highly Commended*

Peacefully situated in the beautiful Bride Valley, just 2 miles from the sea. After a day spent exploring the lovely West Dorset countryside, relax in our comfortably furnished, licensed farmhouse and enjoy dinner prepared mainly from local produce, or try one of the many good local restaurants. All rooms are en-suite with TV and tea tray and have far reaching views. Open all year.

13 Watermeadow House, Bridge Farm, Hooke, Beaminster, Dorset DT8 3PD

Mrs Pauline Wallbridge
☎ 01308 862619
BB From £18–£20
Sleeps 6
🐾 ♞ 🐶 ✂ 🐱 🏵
🐾 🐾 *Applied*

Watermeadow House stands amidst beautiful countryside on the edge of the small village of Hooke. All bedrooms enjoy splendid rural views and overlook the river Hooke which meanders close by the garden where guests are welcome to sit. Breakfast is served in the sunlounge which attracts the morning sun. Perfect for those seeking peace and quiet in a friendly atmosphere. Open Mar–Oct.

14 Yalbury Park, Frome Whitfield Farm, Dorchester, Dorset DT2 7SE

Tom and Ann Bamlet
☎ 01305 250336
Fax 01305 260070
BB From £20–£22
Sleeps 6
🐾 ♞ 🐱 🏵 ■
🐾 *Highly Commended*

Stone farmhouse with large garden in parkland to River Frome. Warm and welcoming for all country lovers. All rooms en-suite have TV, tea/coffee-making facilities, fridge, hairdrier. 1 double with french windows to garden. 1 family room. Traditional farmhouse breakfasts. Ideal for walking, beaches, fishing, riding and all country pursuits. Open all year.

SELF-CATERING

15 Dairy Cottages, Holebrook Farm, Lydlinch, Sturminster Newton, Dorset DT10 2JB

Charles & Alastair Wingate-Saul
☎ 01258 817348
Fax 01258 817747
SC From £145–£400
Sleeps 2/4
🐾 ♿ 🏵 ■ 🐾
🐾 🐾 🐾 🐾 *Highly Commended*

Beautifully converted, spacious cottages in old cow byre on working farm. Peaceful, quiet, well off beaten track. Exceptionally comfortable, oil CH, all modern appliances. Help with feeding animals or sleep all day. Games room with pool/table tennis, swimming pool, clay shooting, laundry room. Large garden for relaxing. Ideal base for exploring Hardy's Dorset. Licence. No dogs. Open all year.

16 Dove Cottage & Buddens Farmhouse, c/o Buddens Farm, Twyford, Shaftesbury, Dorset SP7 0JE

Sarah Gulliford
☎/Fax 01747 811433
SC From £90–£500
Sleeps 2/6 + cot
✂ 🐾 🐖 🐱 🏵 🐾
🐾 🐾 🐾 🐾
Commended

HARRASSED? Have a real farm holiday, guests welcome to help feed pigs, sheep, chickens and goats and watch cows being milked. Pony trekking over farm. Set in rolling hills and patchwork fields. Relax in superb farmhouse and cottage accommodation. Comfortably furnished, log fires, dishwasher, colour TV, laundry room, swimming pool. Fully equipped for babies and children. Open all year.

Graston Farm Cottage, Graston Farm, Burton Bradstock, Bridport, Dorset DT6 4NG

Mrs Sylvia Bailey
☎ 01308 897603
Fax 01308 897016
⌷ From £150–£400
Sleeps 7–9

Approved

This spacious detached cottage is situated on a dairy farm in the beautiful Bride Valley one mile from Burton Bradstock and the sea. Three bedrooms (1 double, 1 double and single, 1 twin), sitting room with woodburning stove, large well equipped kitchen/dining room and a further room with bed-settee. Open all year.

Hartgrove Farm, Hartgrove, Shaftesbury, Dorset SP7 0JY

Mrs Susan Smart
☎/Fax 01747 811830
⌷ From £125–£410
Sleeps 2/5 + cot

Commended

145 acre family dairy farm in glorious country with breathtaking views. Three character cottages and farmhouse flat, beautifully furnished and equipped. Colour TV, linen, CH, laundry room, tennis court. Magnificent walking on farm or NT downland, buzzards, badgers, deer, etc. Children will enjoy the cows, calves, sheep, pony, chickens. Small farm shop. Pretty, unspoilt villages and pubs. One cottage suitable for disabled. Colour brochure. Open all year.

Higher Langdon Flat, Beaminster, Dorset DT8 3NN

Judy Thompson
☎/Fax 01308 862537
⌷ From £135–£175
Sleeps 2

Approved

On the first floor of our farmhouse, set in 400 acres of Dorset downland. The flat has sitting room/kitchen with colour TV and microwave. Linen, CH, double bedroom with bathroom en suite. Ideal for walkers – we are on the Wessex Way and 9 miles from heritage coastline. Relaxed atmosphere. Open all year.

Higher Waterston Farm Cottages, Higher Waterston Farm, Dorchester, Dorset DT2 7SW

Mrs Carol Hammick
☎ 01305 848208
Fax 01305 848894
⌷ From £175–£430
Sleeps 4/6

Commended

Four superb courtyard cottages on sheep farm, one for disabled. 3/3/2/2 bedrooms sleeping 6/6/4/4. Each has terrace, TV, video, washing machine, tumble dryer, dishwasher, microwave, etc. Telephones. Big games barn. Tennis court. large, safe central lawn. Lovely country, beautiful walks. Centre of Hardy's Wessex. Sea 8 miles, Dorchester 4. Minimum one week summer, winter breaks. Open all year.

Luccombe Farm, Milton Abbas, Blandford, Dorset DT11 0BE

Murray & Amanda Kayll
☎ 01258 880558
⌷ From £170–£360
Sleeps 2/4

Commended

Our traditional barn conversions lie in a secluded hidden valley, deep in rolling downland. Beauty, peace and history surround you. Comfortable, well equipped and sleeping 2/4, they stand around a pond in landscaped grounds. Riding, fishing, sailing, clay shooting, good walking, cycling, etc. on farm or locally. Telephone, games room, childcare, maid and laundry service all available. Open all year.

Mead Cottage, Gorwell Farm, Abbotsbury, Weymouth, Dorset DT3 4JX 22

Mrs Mary Pengelly
☎ 01305 871401
⌷ From £200–£400
Sleeps 6

Commended

Relax, unwind and enjoy the peaceful surroundings of Gorwell Farm, a family dairy and sheep farm in its own scenic valley. 2 miles Abbotsbury and Chesil Beach. Wonderful views from the cottage and the coastal path crossing the farm. Well equipped and providing comfortable family accommodation. Only 9 miles Bridport, Dorchester and Weymouth. Winter short breaks. Open all year.

23 **Rudge Farm Cottages,** Chilcombe, Bridport, Dorset DT6 4NF

Sue Diment
☎ **01308 482630**
Fax 01308 482635
🆂 **From £150–£440**
Sleeps 2–6
♿ 👪 ⛺ 🚶 🛥
🐾 🐾 🐾 🐾

Highly Commended

Peacefully situated on 108-acre farm in the beautiful Bride Valley, just 2 miles from the sea. Superbly comfortable cottages, converted from old farm buildings around cobbled farmyard, overlooking the lake. Linen supplied, CH, laundry, games room. Lovely country walks. Short winter breaks. Open all year.

24 **Yew House Cottages,** c/o Yew House Farm, Marnhull, Sturminster Newton, Dorset DT10 1PD

Gil Espley
☎ **01258 820412**
Fax 01258 821044
🆂 **From £95–£285**
Sleeps 4/5
♿ 👪(4) 🛥 🚶 🐕
🐾 🐾 *Commended*

Three timber cottages equipped to highest standard of comfort for summer or winter holidays. Situated in a secluded rural setting overlooking Blackmore Vale. Central heating, colour TV, linen inclusive. Cot available. Excellent centre for sightseeing. Coarse fishing in Stour. Many good pubs for local beer and food. One cottage designed for disabled visitors. Colour brochure. Open all year.

FARM HOLIDAY BUREAU

GOOD FOOD

Nearly all Bureau members now hold a certificate in Essential Food Hygiene.

FARM HOLIDAY BUREAU

DISABLED VISITORS

Many members offer a welcome to disabled/less able visitors. Please do check the extent of the facilities before booking.

England's West Country

Somerset

Group Contacts: [BB] *Jane Sedgman* ☎ *01458 223 237*
[SC] *Geraldine Hunt* ☎ *01278 641228*

Welcome to Somerset. We hope that your stay with us will be truly enjoyable. There's so much to see and do, walking in the Quantocks, Brendon Hills or the National Park, visiting Taunton, the scene of Judge Jeffries' Bloody Assizes in 1685, with its County Museum and well known cricket ground; there is Wells, the smallest cathedral town in England and Glastonbury with its and abbey.

Somerset offers a tremendous range of National Trust properties from Dunster, with its castle (often used in films), to Muchelney with its thatched 14th century priest house. There are also many superb gardens such as those at Hestercombe House. Somerset is also famous for the journey to the centre of the earth at Wookey Hole and Cheddar Gorge, and for the steam enthusiast there are the West Somerset and East Somerset Railways.

Two final items most certainly not to be overlooked, cider and cheese the basic items of a ploughman's lunch. Tempted? Then give us a ring and come to stay for a few days or rent a cottage and really explore Somerset.

BED AND BREAKFAST

(and evening meal)

---

1 Binham Farm, Old Cleeve, Minehead, Somerset TA24 6HX

Mrs S Bigwood
☎ 01984 640222
BB From £16–£19
Sleeps 6
♈ ✄ ☎ ☂ ⚘ 🐄
♨ ♨ *Applied*

Predominantly 17th-century Jacobean farmhouse on a working family farm in an idyllic setting close to the Exmoor National Park and Quantock Hills. A few minutes walk across our fields to Blue Anchor sea front and the West Somerset Steam Railway. Comfortably furnished bedrooms with en suite facilities available, private lounge with colour TV, mediaeval dining hall. Full CH. Open all year.

---

2 Blackmore Farm, Cannington, Bridgwater, Somerset TA5 2NE

Mrs Ann Dyer
☎/Fax 01278 653442
BB From £18–£22
Sleeps 6
✄ ☎ ☞ ⚘ ♈
♨ ♨ *Highly Commended*

A tastefully restored and furnished mediaeval manor house dating back to the 14th century, set in rolling countryside with views to the Quantock Hills. Rooms with oak bedsteads and four poster beds, all with en suite facilities. As featured in *Country Living* magazine. Within easy reach of Exmoor, West Somerset coast, Taunton, Wells and Glastonbury. A winner in the 1995 West Country Farm Holiday Awards. Open all year.

---

3 Cokerhurst Farm, 87 Wembdon Hill, Bridgwater, Somerset TA6 7QA

Derrick and Diana Chappell
☎ 01278 422330
Mobile 0850 692065
BB From £17–£22.50
Sleeps 6
☞ ✄
♨ ♨ *Commended*

A warm welcome awaits you at this farmhouse situated in quiet countryside. The peaceful garden overlooks the lake and 100-acre family run 'pick your own' soft fruit and arable farm. Good central location for exploring Somerset. Log fires, CH, tea/coffee facilities, TV, lounge, H and C all rooms, one en suite. Good pub food 1½ miles. Open all year except Christmas.

---

4 Double-Gate Farm, Godney, Nr Wells, Somerset BA5 1RZ

Mrs H Millard
☎ 01458 832217
BB From £17–£18
Sleeps 8
☞ ✄
♨ ♨ *Commended*

Situated on the banks of the River Sheppey, this lovely old Georgian farmhouse offers – comfortable guests' lounge, games room and en suite bedrooms with tea/coffee facilities, colour TVs and CH. Lovely flower garden, outdoor breakfast in summer. Ideal base for touring, cycling, birdwatching, etc. Evening meals available in nearby village inn. AA QQQ and RAC acclaimed. Open Feb–Nov.

---

5 Greenway Farm, Wiveliscombe, Taunton, Somerset TA4 2UA

Mrs M A Wollaston
☎ 01984 623359
Fax 01984 624051
BB From £15
EM From £7
Sleeps 6
☞ ♈ ☂ ⚘
♨ *Commended*

Comfort with peace and quiet. For those who prefer action, help us on the farm or take part in a country pursuit – excellent walks, rides, game or coarse fishing can be arranged and the coast is close. Good food, home-prepared menus, comfortable lounge, excellent views. Facilities for children. Open Apr–Oct.

Hill Ash Farm, Woolston, North Cadbury, Yeovil, Somerset BA22 7BL

Mrs Jane Pearse
☎ 01963 440332
[BB] From £16–£18
Sleeps 6
🐶 ⅍ Å ♨
☛ Commended

This lovely thatched house, a listed building constructed in 1766, is set in a beautiful hamlet of south Somerset. It is an ideal centre for visiting the many tourist attractions and NT gardens in Somerset and Dorset. 2 double en suite rooms and 2 singles, all with tea/coffee making facilities, full central heating. Open Mar–Nov.

Lower Farm, Kingweston, Somerton, Somerset TA11 6BA

David & Jane Sedgman
☎ 01458 223237
Fax 01458 223276
[BB] From £19.50
Sleeps 5
🐶(6) ⅍ ℀ ♿
☛ Commended

This Grade II listed farmhouse, sited in a conservation area and overlooking a wide stretch of open country, was formerly a coaching inn and retains many of its original features. The attractively furnished rooms are all en suite, with tea/coffee-making facilities, colour TV and full central heating. Wells, Glastonbury, Cheddar, Wookey, Bath and Yeovil are within easy reach. Open all year except Christmas and New Year.

Moxhill Farmhouse, Combwich, Bridgwater, Somerset TA5 2PN

Carol Venner
☎/Fax 01278 652285
[BB] From £15–£18
Sleeps 6
🐶 ⅋ ⅍
☛☛ Highly Commended

Relax in peaceful countryside in 17th century farmhouse. Excellent base for trips to the Quantock Hills and Somerset Levels. Double and family rooms, cot available and children very welcome. En suite and private bathrooms. Full farmhouse breakfast. Excellent pubs and restaurants in nearby villages. Non smokers only. We are situated 5 miles from Bridgwater just off the A39 Minehead Road. Open all year except Christmas.

New House Farm, Burtle Road, Westhay, Nr Glastonbury, Somerset BA6 9TT

Mrs M Bell
☎ 01458 860238
[BB] From £18–£20
EM From £10
Sleeps 5
🐶
☛☛ Commended

Large Victorian farmhouse on dairy farm. Central for touring Wells, Cheddar, etc. Accommodation comprises of double room and 1 family room both en suite with colour TV, tea/coffee facilities, hair drier, etc. Lounge with colour TV, separate dining room, also sun lounge, CH throughout, plenty of local fishing. Open all year.

Northwick Farm, Mark, Highbridge, Somerset TA9 4PG

Mrs Geraldine Hunt
☎ 01278 641228
[BB] From £17.50–£20
Sleeps 5
EM from £10
🐶(5) ⅋ Å ♨ ♿
☛ Commended

Large Georgian farmhouse standing in own grounds. Three comfortable bedrooms, quality furnishings. Guests' lounge with log fire, dining room with separate tables. Views across open farmland to Mendip Hills. Excellent centre for touring, walking and sporting pursuits. Near coast and within 2 miles M5 (J22). Warm and friendly welcome assured. Open all year.

Orchard Farm, Cockhill, Castle Cary, Somerset BA7 7NY

Olive Boyer
☎ 01963 350418
[BB] From £15
EM From £8.50
Sleeps 5
⅋ 🐶 ♨ Å ☂ ■
☛☛ Commended

A 170-acre beef and cattle rearing farm in area of outstanding beauty, yet only 1½ miles from Castle Cary. Centrally-heated farmhouse with 2 en suite rooms, TV lounge. Traditional farmhouse meals served in the conservatory. Bath, Taunton, Longleat, Stourhead and coasts at West Somerset and Dorset within driving distance. Open all year.

12 **Pinksmoor Millhouse,** Pinksmoor Farm, Wellington, Somerset TA21 0HD

Mrs Nancy K M Ash
☎/Fax 01823 672361
BB From £18.50
EM From £11.50
Sleeps 6
🐕 ⅍ 🌴
😃 😃 😃 *Commended*

Stroll along the old millstream, haunt of kingfisher, snipe and mallard, go badger watching or just wander where you please around this family-run dairy farm. Period millhouse with cosy lounges, log fire, spacious en suite bedrooms, tea/coffee-making facilities, CH, colour TV, farmhouse hospitality and cooking. AA QQQQ selected. Conservation awards 1991 & 1992. Close coasts and moors. 10 minutes M5 J26. Open all year (closed Christmas and New Year).

13 **Townsend Farm,** Sand, Wedmore, Somerset BS28 4XH

Sarah Willcox
☎ 01934 712342
BB From £15.50–£17.50
EM From £10.50
Sleeps 6
🐕(5) ⅍
😃😃 *Commended*

Townsend Farm is a working dairy farm, set in peaceful countryside with views of the Mendip hills, close to Wells, Cheddar and Glastonbury, 6 miles from M5 (jct 22). The spacious Victorian farmhouse offers comfortable accommodation and a friendly atmosphere, traditional English breakfast served in dining room, relaxing separate TV lounge. All bedrooms have TV, en suite available. Open all year except Christmas.

14 **Wembdon Farm,** Hollow Lane, Wembdon, Bridgwater, Somerset TA5 2BD

Mrs Mary Rowe
☎ 01278 453097
BB From £17.50–£19.50
Sleeps 4 + cot
🐕 ⅍ 🌴
😃😃 *Highly Commended*

Enjoy a carefree break at our 17th century family farmhouse. Situated near the Quantock hills, therefore an ideal base for visiting coastlines, Exmoor, Glastonbury and oustanding National Trust properties. The farmhouse is tastefully decorated, central heating throughout offering separate lounge, dining room, bedrooms are full en suite, tea/coffee-making facilities, TV. Excellent local eating places. We are also easy to find. Open all year.

SELF-CATERING

15 **The Courtyard,** c/o New House Farm, Burtle Road, Westhay, Nr Glastonbury, Somerset BA6

Mr & Mrs P Bell
☎ 01458 860238
SC From £150–£370
Sleeps 6
🐕 🐈 🐕
🔑 🔑 🔑 🔑 *Highly Commended*

The Courtyard is a converted barn which sleeps up to 4 adults and 2 children. Its situation on a dairy farm on the Somerset Levels makes it central for touring Wells, Cheddar, Bath, etc. Superbly equipped, including colour TV, washing machine, microwave, tumble dryer. Bed-linen, electricity and heating included. Good local fishing. Open all year.

16 **Hale Farm,** Cucklington, Wincanton, Somerset BA9 9PN

Mrs Pat David
☎ 01963 33342
SC From £90–£175
Sleeps 4
🐕 🐈
🔑 🔑 🔑 *Approved*

Set in a peaceful, but not isolated, position on edge of village, only 2 miles from A303. Ideal touring. Period converted former cowshed, comfortable and fully equipped. 2 twin-bedded rooms, bathroom, kitchen, sitting room. All electric (coin meter). Linen supplied. Open all year.

Orchard Farm, Cockhill, Castle Cary, Somerset BA7 7NY

Olive Boyer
☎ 01963 350418
🆂🅲 From £119–£357
Sleeps 4/6
🐺 🛏 ♿ ♨
Applied

Two attractive cottages tastefully converted from a 'Somerset' barn, one ideal for disabled. Substantial farmhouse in own lawns with three bedrooms. All fully equipped, linen and all electricity inclusive. Overlooking countryside. Yeovilton Air and Haynes Motor Museum and many NT properties nearby. Many good pubs restaurants and take-aways at Castle Carry 1½ miles. Open all year.

Pear Tree Cottage, Northwick Farm, Mark, Highbridge, Somerset TA9 4PG

Mrs G Hunt
☎ 01278 641228
🆂🅲 From £180–£325
Sleeps 4/6
🐺(5) 🛏 ♿ ⚲ 🛋
🐾 🐾 Commended

Situated on the Somerset Levels in an area of outstanding natural beauty. Recent barn conversion. Luxurious and comfortable with beautifully co-ordinated fabrics and furnishings. Perfect for a peaceful relaxing holiday and an ideal base for touring this part of the West Country. Excellent facilities nearby for golf, fishing and riding and only 4 miles from coast. Open May–Oct.

Rull Farm, Otterford, near Chard, Somerset TA20 3QJ ⑲

Mrs Pauline Wright
☎ 01460 234398
🆂🅲 From £100–£170
Sleeps 5/6
🐺 ♨ ✂
🐾 🐾 Commended

We would like to welcome you to our family farm in the beautiful Blackdown hills with splendid scenic views. This accommodation is part of the farmhouse within easy reach of 5 local towns and coastal resorts. Open all year.

NO ANSWER?
Farmers are mostly out and about during the day.
Try to telephone before 9.30am or after 4pm.

FOLLOW THE COUNTRY CODE
Leave nothing but footprints,
Take nothing but photographs,
Kill nothing but time!

FARM HOLIDAY BUREAU

England's West Country
Exmoor

Group Contacts: 🆒 *Mrs Rosemary Pile* ☎ *015987 41236*
🆒 *Mrs Ann Durbin* ☎ *01643 831255*

Exmoor National Park is situated on the north coast of Devon and Somerset. This is an area of magnificent countryside with superb contrasts.

The park offers miles of moorland which are ideal for country pursuits such as walking and riding, and also has many beautiful villages to explore. There are over 600 miles of public footpaths.

Exmoor has a spectacular coastline of high cliffs, wild heather moorland and deep wooded coombes which cradle sparkling rivers. It is famous for the herds of wild red deer, Exmoor ponies and soaring buzzards. The rivers Exe and Barle rise high on the moors, creating attractive valleys.

Inland are the famous Tarr Steps and the Doone Valley, whilst Porlock Weir, Lynton and Lynmouth are dotted along the coast.

BED AND BREAKFAST

(and evening meal)

Coombe Farm, Countisbury, Lynton, Devon EX35 6NF

Rosemary & Susan Pile
☎ 01598 741236
🛏 From £16.75–£22
Sleeps 14
🐈 🌿 🐴 🛁
🏵 🏵 Commended

Comfortable old farmhouse set on a hillside between picturesque Lynmouth and the legendary Doone Valley. Coast path runs through the farm. Riding and fishing nearby. Beamed dining room, lounge with colour TV. 2 bedrooms with shower en suite, 3 with H/C, all with hot drinks facilities. Licensed. Wholesome breakfasts. Dogs by arrangement. Weekly terms available. AA listed. Open Mar–Nov.

Cutthorne Farm, Luckwell Bridge, Wheddon Cross, Somerset TA24 7EW

Ann Durbin
☎ 01643 831255
🛏 From £20–£27
EM From £11.50
Sleeps 6
🐴 🐈 🌿 🏕 🐕 🛁 🐎
🏵 🏵 Highly
Commended

18th century yeoman farmhouse totally secluded in heart of Exmoor. A working farm, spacious and comfortable accommodation with log fires and CH. Luxury en suite bathrooms. 4-poster bed. Candlelit dinners, cosy lounge. For extra privacy – beautifully appointed mediaeval stone cottages on side of farmhouse overlooking pond and cobbled yard. We are 2½ miles from 'The Rest and Be Thankful', Wheddon Cross, travelling on the B3224 towards Exford. Open Feb–Dec.

Edgcott House, Exford, Nr Minehead, Somerset TA24 7QG

Gillian Lamble
☎ 01643 831495
🛏 From £18–£22
EM From £11
Sleeps 6
🖭 🐈 🐴
🏵 🏵 Commended

Country house of great charm and character amidst beautiful countryside in the heart of Exmoor National Park, ¼ mile from village of Exford. Peaceful and quiet. All bedrooms have basins, private bathroom available. Excellent home cooking using fresh local produce is served in the elegant 'longroom' with its unique murals. Large garden. Comfortable, friendly centre for relaxing, walking, riding and fishing. Open all year.

Greenhills Farm, Yeo Hill, West Anstey, South Molton, North Devon EX36 3NU

Mrs Gillian Carr
☎ 01398 341300
🛏 From £14–£15.50
EM From £7.50
Sleeps 4+cot
🐴 🐈 🌿 🛁
Listed Highly
Commended

Relax and enjoy the peace and comfort of our charming farmhouse. Tastefully furnished guest wing, oakbeamed lounge with inglenook fireplace, pretty bedrooms with beverage trays. Separate dining room serving hearty breakfasts and delicious dinners. In foothills of the Exmoor National Park within an environmentally sensitive area. Marvellous for hill walks or gentle strolls. Access to farm activities. Riding and fishing nearby. Open Easter–Oct.

Highercombe, Dulverton, Somerset TA22 9PT

Barbara Marchant
☎ 01398 323451
🛏 From £17–£19
Sleeps 6
🐴 🐈 🌿
🏵 🏵 Commended

Peacefully situated former hunting lodge originating from 14th century. Set in 8 acres of land with beautiful gardens. Close to open moorland. Comfortable double or twin rooms with en suite or private bathrooms, all with tea/coffee and colour TV. Four poster room. Large guests' lounge with far-reaching views. Wild deer are often seen close by. Surrounded by farmland. Stabling. Open all year.

6   **Highercombe Farm,** Dulverton, Somerset TA22 9PT

Abigail Humphrey
☎/Fax 01398 323616
🅱 From £14.50–£16
EM From £10
Sleeps 6
🐕 🐎 🐈 🛖 🎾
Listed *Commended*

A 450-acre working farm on the edge of the moor. We have spectacular 60-mile views and red deer can often be seen from the farmhouse. Pretty rooms with tea/coffee facilities and guest bathroom. Large guest lounge with inglenook and bay window where breakfast is served. A relaxed atmosphere, a friendly welcome, personal service and quality food. Open Mar–Nov.

7   **Hindon Farm,** Nr Minehead, Somerset TA24 8SH

Penny & Roger Webber
☎/Fax 01643 705244
🅱 From £18–£22
EM From £15
Sleeps 6
🐕 🐈(10) 🎿 🐈 🛖 ♨ 🎾
Listed *Commended*

Superbly situated in Exmoor valley (Minehead 3 miles, Selworthy 1 mile) find our real working farm – 500 acres and direct access to moors, wonderful walking. Featured in *Country Living*. Spotty pigs, donkey, horses, goats, poultry and many sheep, stabling/grazing-riding arranged. Relax on large lawn with stream, picnic area. Lovely 18thC farmhouse with relaxed atmosphere and big breakfasts. Pretty bedrooms, all H&C and drinks tray. Guests' bathroom and sitting room. Open March–Oct. Brochure.

8   **Larcombe Foot,** Winsford, Nr Minehead, Somerset TA24 7HS

Mrs Val Vicary
☎ 01643 851306
🅱 From £17.50
EM From £10
Sleeps 4
🐈(8) 🐕
🦆🦆 *Highly Commended*

Larcombe Foot is an attractive period house set in the beautiful, tranquil Exe Valley. Guests' comfort within a warm, happy atmosphere is paramount. A pretty garden tom relax in, superb walks on the doorstep, Larcombe Foot makes an ideal base for exploring Exmoor and the scenic North Devon coast – 12 miles. Open Mar–Nov.

9   **Little Brendon Hill,** Wheddon Cross, Nr Minehead, Somerset TA24 7DG

Mrs Shelagh Maxwell
☎ 01643 841556
🅱 From £17.50
EM From £10
Sleeps 6
🎿 🐈(8) 🐈 ♨ 🎾
🦆🦆 *Highly Commended*

Enjoy a stay with us in our beautifully appointed farmhouse set in the peace and tranquillity of the Exmoor National Park. Three lovely en suite rooms with colour television. Log fires, cosy candlelit dinners. Central heating. Short stay or long, a truly relaxing place to pursue country pastimes. You will be most welcome. Open all year.

10   **Little Quarme Farm,** Wheddon Cross, Nr Minehead, Somerset TA24 7EA

Bob Cody-Boutcher
☎/Fax 01643 841249
🅱 From £16–£19
EM From £8–£10
Sleeps 6
🎿 🐈(2) 🐈 ♨ 🛖
Listed *Highly Commended*

Lovely old farmhouse in the heart of Exmoor in an outstanding situation with panoramic views. 2 doubles, 1 twin (1 en suite), 2 bathrooms, TV lounge, tea/coffee-making facilities. Friendly family atmosphere. Many animals, pony rides, stabling. Large garden and 18 acres. We are ¼ mile past Wheddon Cross on Exford road B3224. Open Mar–Nov.

11   **Springfield Farm,** Dulverton, Somerset TA22 9QD

Tricia Vellacott
☎ 01398 323722
🅱 From £16.50–£21.50
EM From £11.50
Sleeps 6
🐕 🐈 🎿
🦆🦆 *Commended*

A warm welcome awaits you at our 270-acre working farm. Peacefully situated between Tarr Steps and Dulverton, overlooking the River Barle valley with magnificent moorland and woodland views. Comfortable accommodation and delicious farmhouse meals. All bedrooms have en suite or private facilities. Dining room with tea/coffee-making facilities, guests' sitting room with colour TV. Open Easter–Nov.

Wood Advent Farm, Roadwater, Watchet, Somerset TA23 0RR

Diana Brewer
☎/Fax 01984 640920
BB From £18.50–£25
EM £12
Sleeps 8
🐴 🐂 🏕 🎣 🎿 ⬛
🌸🌸🌸 *Commended*

Nestling at the foot of the Brendon Hills. Listed spacious farmhouse set in 340 acres of working farm. Relaxing en suite rooms with hospitality trays. Chintzed lounge with log fires, inglenook heats the licensed dining room, where wonderful country dishes can be assured. Grass tennis court, heated outdoor pool, clay pigeon and pheasant shooting all available on the farm. Open all year.

SELF-CATERING

Croft Cottage, c/o Higher Burrow Farm, Timberscombe, Minehead, Somerset TA24 7UD

Diana Rusher
☎ 01643 841427
SC From £80–£350
Sleeps 7 + cot
🐴 🐂 🐾
🐾 🐾 🐾 *Commended*

Attractive, converted, stone built cottage situated 200 yds from farm, with own garden, and lovely views. Croft is spacious with one double room, 2 twin, 1 single, cot available. Large bathroom upstairs, second WC downstairs, washing machine. Colour TV, log fire and small library. Horses or other animals accommodated by arrangement at farm. Electricity extra. Friday change-over. Open all year.

Cutthorne Farm, Luckwell Bridge, Wheddon Cross, Somerset TA24 7EW

Ann Durbin
☎ 01643 831255
SC From £95–£425
Sleeps 4
🐂 🐴 🏕 🍴 🎣 🎿 🐾
🐾 🐾 🐾 🐾
Highly Commended

Situated in the heart of glorious Exmoor, two luxuriously appointed mediaeval barn conversions on side of farmhouse. Overlooking 14th century pond and cobbled yard. Self-catering or with meals in the farmhouse. Both furnished and equipped to the highest standard with antique pine, fitted kitchens and CH. Baby listening. Inclusive of linen, towels and electricity. Open all year.

Dunsley Farm, West Anstey, South Molton, Devon EX36 3PF

Mrs Mary Robins
☎ 01398 341246
SC From £100–£350
Sleeps 5
🐴 🐂 🎿 🍴
🐾 🐾 🐾 🐾
Commended

Self-contained cottage forming part of 16th century farmhouse, overlooks meadows and woodland valley. Access off a quiet country road. 2 bedrooms (accommodate 5 people), bathroom, large lounge/diner with colour TV. Large modern equipped kitchen, electric heating (£1 meter). Linen provided, pets welcome. Coarse fishing available on farm. Dulverton 6 miles. Open all year.

Highercombe Farm, Dulverton, Somerset TA22 9PT

Abigail Humphrey
☎/Fax 01398 323616
SC From £160–£260
Sleeps 6
🐂 🐴 🐾 🎿 🐾
🐾 🐾 🐾 🐾 *Commended*

Self-contained wing of large farmhouse on 450-acre working farm next to the moor. Well furnished in cottage style. Private entrance, large gardens, spectacular views. 2 bedrooms, bathroom, large lounge/dining room with colour TV, video, CD player/radio, woodburner. Modern pine kitchen. Linen, CH, hot water, logs included. Use of washing machine/dryer. Evening meals arranged, babysitting service. Electricity pound coin meter. Open all year.

17 Landacre Farm, Withypool, Exmoor, Somerset TA24 7SD

P G Hudson
☎ **01643 831223/ 831487**
SC **From £90–£250**
Sleeps 9
🐕 🏇 🐈 ⚘ ⛺
🔑 – 🔑🔑🔑 *Approved*

Cottage, bungalow, ground floor flat situated on moorland farm overlooking River Barle. Children and dogs welcome. Colour TV, log fires, own gardens. Bungalow, flat suitable partially disabled, both with central heating.

18 Little Quarme Country Cottages, Wheddon Cross, Nr Minehead, Somerset TA24 7EA

Tammy Cody-Boutcher & family
☎/Fax **01643 841249**
SC **From £80–£450**
Sleeps 2/6
🏇 🐕 🐈 ⚘ ⛺
🔑 🔑 🔑 🔑
Up to De Luxe

Six stone cottages furnished and equipped to the highest standards in the heart of Exmoor. All have microwaves, colour TV, videos, bed linen and towels. Standing amid 18 acres and large informal gardens, direct access to footpaths and bridlepath. Traffic free tranquillity with panoramic southerly views. Ample parking, free laundry room, childrens' play area, pay phone, stabling. Brochure available.

19 Pembroke, c/o Brake Cottage, Wheddon Cross, Minehead, Somerset TA24 7EX

Mrs J. Escott
☎ **01643 841550**
SC **From £95–£350**
Sleeps 5
🐕 🍴
🔑 🔑 🔑 🔑
Commended

Situated in a peaceful position with parking, private garden and extensive south–westerly views, detached bungalow in the heart of the Exmoor National Park, 2 minutes from village of Wheddon Cross. Well equipped with microwave, automatic washing machine, tumble dryer. Linen included. Open Mar–Dec. No pets.

20 Westermill Farm, Exford, Nr Minehead, Somerset TA24 7NJ

The Edwards family
☎ **01643 831238**
Fax **01643 831660**
SC **From £140–£340**
Sleeps 4/8
🏇 🐕 🏊 🐈 ⛺ ⚘ 🎣
🔑 – 🔑 🔑 🔑
Commended

Six delightful log cabins of superior quality. Various sizes, well equipped. In small grassy paddocks on side of valley by a river. Also bright, comfortable cottage adjoining the farmhouse overlooks the river. Patio, garage. Four waymarked walks over 500-acre farm in centre of Exmoor. 2½ miles shallow river, fishing, bathing. Laundry, payphone, information centre, seasonal small shop. Cabins open Mar–Dec, cottage all year.

21 West Ilkerton Farm, Barbrook, Lynton, North Devon EX35 6QA

Chris & Victoria Eveleigh
☎ **01598 752310**
SC **From £120–£380**
Sleeps 6
🏇 ⚘ 🐕 🐈 ⛺ 🐎
🔑 🔑 🔑 🔑
Commended

Luxurious semi-detached cottage on secluded hill farm bordering open moor. Sheep, cattle, carthorses. Coast 3 miles, riding ½ mile. 3 bedrooms (2 king size, 1 twin) 2 bathrooms, living/dining room, kitchen (Rayburn, dishwasher, washing machine/tumble dryer, microwave). CH. TV, video. Baby equipment and evening babysitting. Children, dogs and horses welcome. Special winter breaks from £60. Ideal for walking, riding, family farm holidays. Open all year.

22 Whitefield Barton, Challacombe, Barnstaple, Devon EX31 4TU

Rosemarie Kingdon
☎ **01598 763271**
SC **From £100–£300**
Sleeps 6
🐕 🐈 ⛺ ▪
🔑 🔑 🔑 *Commended*

Spacious characteristic accommodation in half of 16th century farmhouse with modern luxuries. Tastefully furnished to high standard. Warm cosy lounge, well equipped kitchen, family & twin rooms, bathroom/ shower, babysitting. Ample parking, BBQ, streamed garden. Linen & electricity incl. Peaceful surroundings with scenic walks and farm animals (cows, sheep, ponies). Central for beaches, moors. Open May–Dec.

Wintershead Farm, Simonsbath, Exmoor, Somerset TA24 7LF

Jane Styles
☎ 01643 831222
ⓈⒸ From £110–£440
Sleeps 2–6
♨ 🐎
♂ ♂ – ♂ ♂ ♂ ♂
Highly Commended

4 cottages all converted to a high standard situated in a relaxing spot with panoramic views. One 3-bedroomed, two 2-bedroomed cottages and one 1-bedroomed cottage (also small flat). All have oil central heating, linen, gas cooking and colour TV etc. Children and pets welcome. Ample parking. Pay phone, games room. Use of grounds and DIY stabling. Colour brochure available. Open all year.

Yelland Cottage, c/o West Whitefield Farm, Challacombe, Barnstaple, Devon EX31 4TU

Jean Kingdon
☎ 01598 763433
ⓈⒸ From £120–£270
Sleeps 6
🐎 ♨ 🦌
♂ ♂ ♂ *Approved*

Semi-detached cosy farm cottage on working hill farm amidst beautiful countryside within easy reach of village pub and shop. Log fire, Rayburn plus electric conveniences. Relaxing lounge, colour TV. Linen provided. Friendly, relaxed atmosphere with farm animals. Spacious garden with ample parking. Ideal for beaches, walking, fishing, riding and touring North Devon. Open all year.

CAMPING AND CARAVANNING

Halse Farm, Winsford, Minehead, Somerset, TA24 7JL

FARM HOLIDAY BUREAU

Mrs Julia Brown
☎ 01643 831259
ⓈⒸ Tents From £3
(per person per night)
Caravans From £6
44 pitches
🐎 ♨ ⛺ 🚐 ♿ ❦
✓

Small, unique caravan and tent park on a working farm. Outstanding views and moorland walking within 400 yards. A brand new loo, shower and laundry block is being built for 1996 with disabled facilities. Excellent village shop and pub only one mile. An ideal setting for seeing Exmoor and all its wildlife. Open Mar–Nov.

Westermill Farm, Exford, Nr Minehead, Somerset TA24 7NJ

The Edwards family
☎ 01643 831238
Fax 01643 831660
ⓈⒸ Tents: adult £3/child £1
Car: £1
2 adults + vehicle £7
(all prices per night)
⛺ 🐎 ♨ 🍴 ❦
✓ ✓ ✓

Beautiful secluded site for 60 tents and dormobiles beside upper reaches of River Exe. Centre of Exmoor National Park. Four waymarked walks over 500-acre working farm. 2½ miles shallow river, fishing and bathing. Loo block, showers, laundry, washing up. Information centre, small shop, payphone. A site and farm to enjoy in the most natural way. Children's paradise.

FARM HOLIDAY BUREAU

LET THE TELEPHONE RING!
Some farmhouses are big places. Let the telephone ring long enough to give the owner time to answer it.

England's West Country
North Devon Coast and Country

Group Contacts: BB *Andrea Cook* ☎ *01271 850543*
SC *Ruth Ley* ☎ *01769 572337*

Welcome to Northern Devon – an area of tremendous contrasts. Miles of golden, surf-washed beaches, wide rolling hills and the valleys of the Taw and Torridge carpeted with the patchwork of our family farms. We span the land between two famous moors. Exmoor in the north with its magnificent rolling heather clad hills and steeply wooded valleys and Dartmoor in the south with its sweep of open rugged tors, grazed by the famous ponies and watered by sparkling streams.

Our land is made to slow you down. To see and remember the countryside that still has flowers, footpaths, winding roads with high banks, villages of thatch and cob with old churches and pubs with tradition. Henry Williamson wrote his famous book 'Tarka the Otter' here and 'The Tarka Trail', a long distance footpath of 180 miles now links our moors and coast and offering varied walking together with some 26 miles for cyclists (with cycle hire nearby).

We offer historic farmhouses, involvement in real farming life, superb cooking, a variety of facilities but above all we offer the friendly welcome you need. Many of us are open all year and out of season breaks are full of delight.

Whether it's the coast or the country, whether you want to gallop across the moors or fish for salmon in our rivers, spend a day searching for antiques or the children want a farm park or you a stately home or flower-filled garden it's here in North Devon – come and share it with us.

BED AND BREAKFAST

(and evening meal)

Combas Farm, Croyde, North Devon EX33 1PH

Mrs Gwen Adams
☎ 01271 890398
[BB] From £16–£20
EM From £8
Sleeps 12
🐴 🐕 🏕 ⊛
Listed *Commended*

Combas Farm, a 140-acre stock farm, nestles in its own secluded valley, just 15 mins' walk from miles of golden sands (5 mins from the village pub!). Many repeat bookings confirm claims to a warm welcome and high standard of home cooking using home produce including unusual fruit and veg. Wisteria rambles over this 17th century longhouse overlooking a lovely garden and unspoiled view. Colour brochure. Open Mar–Nov (incl).

Court Barton, Lapford, Crediton, Devon EX17 6PZ   ②

Sheila Mather
☎ 01363 83441
[BB] From £15–£18
EM From £10
Sleeps 6
✕ 🐕 🧳 ⊛
🐝🐝 *Commended*

Undulating floorboards, beams and medieval panelling. Bedrooms with en suite or private bathroom, TV and beverage facilities. Treat yourself to delicious breakfasts and tempting dinners of local fresh produce and West Country specialities. Enjoy our dairy farm and local walks – it's a different world here. Ideally central, phone for colour brochure. Reductions for children, and 3 nights or more. Open Jan–Nov.

Denham Farm, North Buckland, Braunton, North Devon EX33 1HY   ③

Mrs Jean Barnes
☎/Fax 01271 890297
[BB] From £22–£25
EM From £12
Sleeps 24
🐕 Ⓔ 🏕 🧳 ⊛
🐝🐝🐝 *Commended*

Come on down to Deb'n, me dears, and have a cuppa tay in Ma Barnes' parlour. Us 've bin yer some yers, I can tell 'ee, and knaws all the local history. Ma Barnes' cooking is well knawn too. You be bound to enjoy ya'self while you be yer. The bedrooms is real posh yer knaw, all got their awn bathroom. Tis only a short drive to the best sandy beaches in Deb'n. So bring the family. Us like a bit of fun, you'll be made right welcome. Open all year except Christmas.

Haxton Down Farm, Bratton Fleming, Barnstaple, Devon EX32 7JL   ④

Mrs Pat Burge
☎ 01598 710275
[BB] From £14–£16
EM From £8
Sleeps 6
🐕 🐴 🏕 🧳 ⊛
🐝🐝 *Commended*

Relax among leafy lanes and wonderful scenery on our working stock farm nestling in a peaceful valley. 17th century farmhouse offers warmth and comfort with private or en suite facilities, CTV, tea trays and a warm welcome to all ages. Delicious food with hearty breakfasts and tempting 4-course dinners. Close to beach and moor and attractions galore. Give North Devon a try – you'll be pleased you did. Ring for brochure please. Open Easter–Nov.

Higher Churchill Farm, East Down, Nr Barnstaple, North Devon EX31 4LT   ⑤

Mrs Andrea Cook
☎ 01271 850543
[BB] From £15–£16
EM From £10
Sleeps 6
✕ 🐕 🏕 🧳 🐎 ⊛
🐝🐝 *Commended*

C is for Character, Comfort and Charm
C is for Cooking – Country style
C is for Couples – peaceful short breaks
C is for Children – who love holidays here
C is for Countryside – wonderful walks
C is for Coast – sandy beaches and coves
C is for Cycling – along the Tarka Trail
C is for the Cooks at Churchill – where you will find all this and more! Open all year except Christmas.

---

6 **Holloford Farm,** Higher Clovelly, Bideford, Devon EX39 5SD

Mrs Joanne Wade
☎ 01237 441275
ⓑⓑ From £17
EM for £9
Sleeps 4
🐾🐓🐕
Listed *Highly Commended*

Charming Devonshire farmhouse, recently renovated to a high standard, with many original features including oak beams and open fireplaces. The pretty bedrooms have tea/coffee-making facilities and washbasins. The farm is set in beautiful, unspoilt surroundings 2 miles from Clovelly and Hartland Point. Excellent home cooking and a warm welcome await you. Open Mar–Oct.

---

7 **Home Park Farm,** Lower Blakewell, Muddiford, Barnstaple, North Devon EX31 4ET

Mrs Mari Lethaby
☎ 01271 42955
ⓑⓑ From £15–£17.50
EM From £7.50
Sleeps 6
🐾🐕🐓🛢◎
🐝🐝 *Commended*

Panoramic scenic views combined with warm hospitality, genuine farmhouse cuisine and a relaxing, tranquil atmosphere await you at Home Park. All rooms en suite, TV, hair dryer, hospitality tray. CH. Conveniently positioned for Exmoor, N. Devon coast. Many repeat bookings comfirm excellent accommodation. 2 miles north of Barnstaple. RAC acclaimed. AA.QQQQ. Open all year except Christmas.

---

8 **Huxtable Farm,** West Buckland, Barnstaple, North Devon EX32 0SR

Jackie & Antony Payne
☎/Fax 01598 760254
ⓑⓑ From £22–£23
EM £13
Sleeps 12
🛶🐾🐓🛢◎
🐝🐝🐝 *Commended*

Relax in our medieval longhouse and barn and enjoy a 4-course candlelit dinner of farm/local produce with complimentary homemade wine. Secluded sheep farm with an abundance of wildlife. Children can play safely. En suite bedrooms with TV. Winner 'Taste of Exmoor', log fires, fitness room, sauna and games room. Informative brochure. Reductions for short/long breaks out of season and for children. Open all year (closed Christmas).

---

9 **Kerscott Farm,** Ash Mill, South Molton, North Devon EX36 4QG

Mrs Theresa Sampson
☎ 01769 550262
ⓑⓑ From £15–£17
EM From £7
Sleeps 6
🐕(8) ✄
🐝🐝 *Highly Commended*

Peaceful, olde worlde 16th century farmhouse mentioned in Domesday Book. Furnished throughout with English country antiques, pictures and china. A beautiful, comfortable and fascinating family home. The pretty bedrooms have luxury en suite or have separate guests' bathroom. Central heating, tea/coffee-making facilities and superb views. Scrumptious, hearty country cooking from Aga. Non smokers only. Open all year except Christmas.

---

10 **Meadow Farm,** East Buckland, Barnstaple, North Devon EX32 0TB

Yvonne Hopkins
☎ 01598 760375
ⓑⓑ From £16
EM From £10
Sleeps 4
✄◎
🐝🐝 *Highly Commended*

A friendly welcome awaits guests to our beautifully furnished, warm bungalow and lovely garden. Peacefully situated on edge of hamlet with far-reaching views. 2 double bedrooms, 1 en suite, 1 with magnificent half-tester bed and private bathroom. Delicious, traditional home cooking using fresh local produce. Good parking. 3 miles M5 link, 30 minutes' easy drive coast. Convenient Exmoor on Tarka Trail. Brochure. Open all year.

---

11 **Waytown Farm,** Shirwell, Barnstaple, North Devon EX31 4JN

Hazel Kingdon
☎ 01271 850396
ⓑⓑ From £16.50–£19.50
EM From £8
Sleeps 9
🐾🐓🛢◎
🐝🐝 *Commended*

A warm welcome awaits you on our family run beef and sheep farm set in beautiful countryside about 3 miles north of Barnstaple. Our 17th century farmhouse offers a warm and comfortable atmosphere with traditional farmhouse cooking. Double and family en suite bedrooms, twin and single bedrooms, all with colour TV and beverage facilities. Brochure. Weekly terms available. Open all year except Christmas.

SELF-CATERING

Ashdown, Down Farm, King's Nympton, Umberleigh, Devon EX37 9TF

Norma Latham
☎ 01769 572463
SC From £250
Sleeps 4/9

Commended

A warm welcome awaits you at Ashdown situated on 400 acre family run farm. South Molton 4 miles. South facing, wonderful views of the wooded valley and hills from all windows. Spacious property tastefully furnished. CH. 1st floor 3 bedrooms, bathroom. Ground floor 1 bedroom, bathroom, cloakroom, well equipped kitchen, dining room. Lounge, TV, table tennis. Enclosed garden, swing, barbecue. Fishing, riding nearby. Ring for brochure. Open all year.

The Barleycorn, Cleave Farm, Weare, Giffard, Nr Bideford, North Devon EX39 4QX

Elizabeth Moore
☎ 01805 623671
Fax 01805 623235
SC From £250–£500
Sleeps 5/6

Commended

Visit the heart of 'Tarka Country' on our working dairy farm. Luxury accommodation, en suite facilities. Enjoy William, our retired pony, golf nearby, fishing on River Torridge. Lovely walks near beaches and Exmoor. Stay in our peaceful, panoramic surroundings and bring your bike with you. Telephone now for details.

Barley Cottage & Old Granary, c/o Denham Farm, North Buckland, Braunton, North Devon EX33 1HY

Jean Barnes
☎/Fax 01271 890297
SC £160–£590
Sleeps 4/8

Commended

Friendly folk required to fill our cottages with fun and laughter. We will provide the rest. Everything you need for an enjoyable break. Warmth and comfort. Peaceful setting surrounded by open fields, country lanes yet only a short drive to the sandy beaches of Putsborough and Woolacombe. Have a meal in our farmhouse, drink in our bar. Come to Denham for a holiday to remember. Open all year.

Beechgrove, East Westacott, Riddlecombe, Chulmleigh, Devon EX18 7PF

Thomas & Joyce Middleton
☎ 01769 520210
SC From £145
Sleeps 5/7 + cot

Commended

Delightful bungalow with lovely views of peaceful countryside, in Area of Outstanding Natural Beauty. Lovingly cared for, a real 'home from home'. Superbly equipped for all seasons. Our guests return many times to barbecue in our pretty garden, have fun in the large games room, or relax by a cosy log fire. Children love Rosie, our adoring collie, collecting eggs, feeding time for lambs and calves and riding our trikes and bikes. Lovely sandy beaches 30–40 minutes. Open all year.

The Cottage, Lutworthy Farm, Worlington, Crediton, Devon EX17 4SW

Mrs Janet Bemrose
☎ 01884 860348
SC From £140–£200
Sleeps 5 + cot

Commended

Self-contained cottage wing of Devon longhouse on family run sheep and beef farm. An ideal area for touring, easy access to beaches and moors with country activities available locally. Cosy lounge with colour TV and open fire, well equipped kitchen. 2 bedrooms and bathroom. Brochure available. Open Mar–Dec.

17 **Drewstone Farm,** South Molton, North Devon EX36 3EF

Ruth Ley
☎ 01769 572337
SC From £130
Sleeps 6–8
🐴 🐎 ⅕ ☕
🐾 🐾 🐾 🐾 – 🐾 🐾 🐾 🐾
Commended

Escape to farm tranquillity on edge of Exmoor, 16th century luxury cottage and converted barn with beams, woodburner, colour TV, fitted carpets, washing machine. 3 and 4 bedrooms, bath-shower room. Fully equipped oak kitchen/diner and lounge enjoy panoramic country views. Enclosed lawn, children's facilities, games room, animals to see, freedom to explore the farm. Country walks, clay-pigeon shooting, trout lake. Open all year.

18 **Hollacombe Barton,** Hollacombe, Chulmleigh, Devon EX18 7QG

Christine Stevens
☎ 01837 83385
Fax 01837 83002
SC From £195
EM £5
Sleeps 2/8
🐴 🐎 🐃 ☕ 🎪 ◎
🐾 🐾 🐾 🐾 *Commended*

Children can roam and play in safety whilst parents relax in comfort in the conservatory while their evening meal is prepared. What more could you wish for? How about a superbly equipped farmhouse only 18 miles from the sea. Enjoy woodland walks, barbecues, quad bikes and pony rides. Watch the milking, make friends with our tame sheep, chickens, goats, calves and Miss Piggy! Versatile accommodation and prices for couples or families. Suits all ages and interests. Brochure.

19 **Manor Farm,** Riddlecombe, Chulmleigh, North Devon EX18 7NX

Eveline Gay
☎ 01769 520335
SC From £150
Sleeps 7/8 + cot
🐴 🐎 🧺 ◎
🐾 🐾 🐾 🐾 *Commended*

A friendly welcome awaits you at Manor Farmhouse, which has a very cosy self catering wing with lovely views. A dairy and sheep farm where children can bottlefeed baby lambs, watch the milking, make friends with Poppy our tame sheep, collect eggs, etc. 3 bedrooms, gas-fired woodburner, heating throughout, cleanliness guaranteed. Superb games room – includes play cottage, ride-on toys, snooker, table tennis, Fisher Price kitchen and much more.

20 **Nethercott Manor Farm,** Rose Ash, South Molton, North Devon EX36 4RE

Carol Woollacott
☎ 01769 550483
SC From £100–£350
Sleeps 4 and 8
🐴 🐎 ⅕ 🐃 ☕ 🎪 🧺 ◎
🐾 🐾 🐾 *Approved*

Denis and Carol assure a warm welcome at Nethercott, a 17th century thatched house on a 200-acre working farm. Three comfortable self-contained wings sleeping 4 and 8. Pleasant views overlooking woods and trout pond. Pony rides, extensive games room and laundry. Also barbecuing facilities. 6 miles from the market town of South Molton, ideal for touring Exmoor and coast. Open all year.

21 **Northcott Barton Farm,** Ashreigney, Chulmleigh, Devon EX18 7PR

Mrs Sandra Gay
☎ 01769 520259
SC From £130
Sleeps 7/8 + cot
🐴 🐎 🎪
🐾 🐾 🐾 *Commended*

Come and explore the farm, meet the animals and enjoy our beautiful countryside, children especially welcome 'help' feed lambs, calves, hens, collect eggs and watch milking. 3 bedroomed farmhouse wing offers 'home from home' comfort cosy oak-beamed lounge, log fire, heating throughout, automatic washing machine and linen provided. Large south facing garden, riding, fishing, golf nearby, warm welcome assured.

22 **Pickwell Barton Holiday Cottages,** Pickwell Barton, Georgeham, Braunton, North Devon EX33 1LA

Mrs Sheila Cook
☎ 01271 890987
SC From £120–£360
Sleeps 7/8
🐴 🐎 🎪
🐾 🐾 *Up to Commended*

Sunnyside and Pickwell Barton cottages are two spacious, well equipped farm holiday cottages on a beef, sheep and arable farm. Pickwell is a small hamlet close to Putsborough and Woolacombe's golden sandy beach. Ideal for surfing and gorgeous coastal walks across our farm with breathtaking views of the sunset over Lundy Island. Golf, horse-riding, fishing nearby. Solid fuel (Park-ray and storage heaters) available. Open all year.

Stable Cottage, Pitt Farm, North Molton, North Devon EX36 3JR

Mrs Gladys Ayre
☎ 01598 740285
[SC] From £140–£330
Sleeps 5/6
🐕 🛏 🎠
🐎 🐎 🐎 🐎 *Commended*

Enjoy peaceful surroundings at our charming cottage, set in unspoilt Exmoor countryside, 1 mile from village shops, pubs, garage, equipped to high standard with night storage heating throughout. 3 bedrooms. Bath/shower/ beamed lounge with woodburner. Colour TV, oak fitted kitchen/diner. Autowasher, fridge, microwave, etc. Own patio. Barbecue. Pond with ducks and geese. Freedom to explore our 230 acre sheep farm. Open all year.

Willesleigh Farm, Goodleigh, Barnstaple, North Devon EX32 7NA

Charles and Anne
Esmond-Cole
☎ 01271 43763
[SC] From £145–£595
Sleeps 6
🐕 ♿ ✂ 🛏 ⊚
🐎 🐎 🐎 🐎 *Highly Commended*

Try upside down living in The Gatehouse with its huge beamed sitting room; or traditional wing of our farmhouse, The Cottage, French windows to walled garden. Enclosed heated swimming pool May–Oct. Meet the crazy family, farming all hours, in all weathers, kept sane by our herd of beautiful Jersey cows and calves. Open all year.

CAMPING AND CARAVANNING

Welcombe Farm, Charles, Nr Barnstaple, North Devon EX32 7PU   25

Mrs Margaret Faulkner
☎ 01598 710440
[SC] From £100–£250
Sleeps 4/5 + cot
🐕 🛏 ✂ 🚐
Tourist Board Inspected

Imaginative private setting for a luxury caravan holiday. Comfortable and peaceful, with full facilities, two bedrooms and heating throughout. Small, family run farm with dairy cows and sheep, on the foothills of Exmoor. Panoramic views of hills and valleys from enclosed garden. Close to Tarka Trail and easy reach of sandy beaches, moors and gardens. Wildlife in abundance. Open Apr–Oct.

FARM HOLIDAY
BUREAU

DEVON FARMS
Availability of farms in Devon can be easily discovered by ringing 01548 550055.

England's West Country
Heart of Devon

Group Contacts: 🅱️ *Mrs Barbara Pugsley* ☎ *01884 253352*
            🆂🅲 *Mrs Sally Maynard* ☎ *01392 881530*

If you are undecided about which part of Devon to take your holiday, why not opt for the heart of the county … you can then tour and explore in all directions to get a taste of all that's best.

The Heart of Devon with its thatched cottages, lush meadows, steeply wooded valleys, rivers and streams, is unspoilt and rather special.

This is an area of traditional sheep and cattle farming. A visit to one of the local towns on market day will give you the chance to get the full flavour of the occasion, plus the opportunity to sample the produce itself … cheese, smoked trout, clotted cream and farmhouse cider.

As always in Devon there is much to see and do. There is a hint of nostalgia as well. Take Tiverton for example: the town's museum is one of the best folk museums in the West Country with its large railway gallery complete with restored GWR loco. The Great Western Canal, 11 miles long, offers trips by horse-drawn barge.

There is, of course, much more – and all within easy reach: Exmoor, Dartmoor, the south coast resorts and dramatic seascapes of the north.

BED AND BREAKFAST

(and evening meal)

Brindiwell Farm, Cheriton Fitzpaine, Crediton, Devon EX17 4HR

Doreen Lock
☎ 01363 866357
⬚ From £13.50–£15
EM From £8
Sleeps 5
⛺ ♞ ☞
Listed *Approved*

Delightful old farmhouse with oak beams and panelling. Tea/coffee-making facilities in all rooms. Situated between Tiverton and Crediton, and midway between north and south coasts and moors. Outstanding views to Dartmoor. 120-acre sheep farm with two doubles and one single. AA listed. Open all year.

Great Bradley Farm, Withleigh, Tiverton, Devon EX16 8JL

Mrs Sylvia Hann
☎ 01884 256946
⬚ From £17.50–£19.50
EM From £10
Sleeps 4
⚷ ⛺(10) ⑳
♨ *Highly Commended*

Tucked away in the Devonshire countryside, you will find comfort, peace and quiet in our beautiful 16th century farmhouse. Attractive bedrooms with central heating, washbasins, tea/coffee trays and private bathrooms. The guests' lounge, with TV overlooks the garden and beautiful views beyond. Delicious home cooking is served in a happy relaxed atmosphere. Non smokers only please. Brochure available. Open Mar–Oct.

Harton Farm, Oakford, Tiverton, Devon EX16 9HH

Mrs Lindy Head
☎ 01398 351209
⬚ From £13–£16
EM From £6
Sleeps 6
♞ ⛺(4) ⚲ ✿
♨ *Applied*

Welcome to our comfortable stone-built farmhouse dating from 17th century, situated in secluded but accessible position near Exmoor. 1 family, 1 twin room with washbasins. Hearty, traditional home baking using additive-free home-produced meat and organically grown vegetables. Vegetarian menu on request. Tea-making facilities, home-spun wool available. Farm walk with nature notes, friendly animals. Reduction for children. Open all year (closed Christmas & New Year).

Hele Barton, Black Dog, Crediton, Devon EX17 4QJ

Mrs Gillian Gillbard
☎ 01884 860278
⬚ From £15
EM From £8.50
Sleeps 6
⛺ ⚷ ⬛ ⑳
♨ ♨ *Commended*

Relax in peaceful surroundings with lovely views from our listed 17th century thatched farmhouse on family-run 236-acre mixed farm, 2 miles off Tiverton – South Molton Road nr Witheridge. Double or twin rooms (1 en suite), all with H and C, tea/coffee, night storage heating, 1 guest bathroom, guests' dining room and lounge with colour TV, evening meal by arrangement. Brochure. Open all year (closed Christmas).

Hornhill Farm, Exeter Hill, Tiverton, Devon EX16 4PL

Barbara Pugsley
☎ 01884 253352
⬚ From £17–£19.50
EM From £10
Sleeps 6
⛺(12) ⚷ ⑳
♨ ♨ *Highly Commended*

Overlooking beautiful Exe Valley, Hornhill is the perfect place to stay and relax. Explore our lovely county, return to comfort, warmth, delicious home cooking and a happy atmosphere. Peaceful bedrooms, one ground floor double, one with Victorian 4-poster, private, en suite bathrooms, tea/coffee-making facilities. Attractive drawing room with log fires. Large garden. Ample parking. AA 5Q Premier Selected. Open all year.

---

6 **Lower Collipriest Farm,** Tiverton, Devon EX16 4PT

Mrs Linda Olive
☎ 01884 252321
BB From £18.50
EM From £11
Sleeps 4
✄ ⛄ ⬥ ◉
♨♨♨ *Highly Commended*

Come and relax and enjoy the beauty of the Exe Valley in our 17th century thatched farmhouse. Comfortable lounge with inglenook fireplace and oak beams. Colour TV. Central heating throughout. Twin/single rooms with bathroom en suite, tea/coffee-making facilities. Delicious, traditional fresh cooking with our/local produce. Lovely walks over 220-acre dairy farm, conservation pond/ woodland area. An AA award-winning farm. Open Feb–Nov. Brochure available.

7 **Marchweeke Farm,** Thelbridge, Witheridge, Tiverton, Devon EX16 8NY

Ann Webber
☎ 01884 860418
BB From £15
EM From £8
Sleeps 4
☌(3) ⛄ ◉
♨♨ *Commended*

We warmly welcome you to come and enjoy the peace and quiet of our lovely Devon longhouse with its beautiful views. One double en suite, one twin with private bathroom both with tea/coffee-making facilities. Separate dining room with inglenook and beams. Lounge with CTV. Delicious home cooking using own and local produce. Access at all times. Brochure available. Children welcome with reduced rates for 12 years and under. Open Feb–Nov.

8 **Newhouse Farm,** Oakford, Tiverton, Devon EX16 9JE

Mrs Anne Boldry
☎ 01398 351347
BB From £16–£19
EM From £10
Sleeps 6
☌(10) ⬥ ⛄ ⬥ ▪ ◉
♨♨ *Commended*

A perfect base for discovering Devon, our livestock farm is close to Exmoor. A 400-year-old longhouse, tastefully and comfortably furnished featuring oak beams and inglenook. Bedrooms have CH, tea trays, en suite available. We aim to provide the best of farmhouse cooking – original recipes, 13 varieties of marmalade, home-baked bread, delicious puddings our speciality. AA QQQQ. Detailed brochure. Open all year (closed Christmas).

9 **Quoit-at-Cross Farm,** Stoodleigh, Tiverton, Devon EX16 9PJ

Mrs Linda Hill
☎/Fax 01398 351280
BB From £17.50
EM From £9.50
Sleeps 6
☌ ✄ ▪ ⬥
♨♨♨ *Commended*

Charming 17th century farmhouse in conservation village. Excellent accommodation, twin/double rooms, en suite, colour TV and tea/coffee-making facilities, delightful inglenook dining room and relaxing lounge. Full English breakfast. Superb dinners, Heartbeat Award meals. Large garden, ample parking. Easy reach National Trust properties, beaches, etc. A361 2½ miles. Open from April.

10 **Wishay Farm,** Trinity, Cullompton, Devon EX15 1PE

Mrs Sylvia Baker
☎ 01884 33223
BB From £14–£16
EM From £8
Sleeps 6
☌ ◉
♨♨ *Commended*

Comfortable and spacious 17th century farmhouse, set amid the peace and seclusion of the countryside. Ideal base for touring. Comfortable lounge with colour TV. Central heating. 1 family room with en suite bathroom, double with separate guests' bathroom, both with colour TV, fridge and tea/coffee-making facilities. Children welcome. Golf and indoor bowls rink nearby. Open all year.

FARM HOLIDAY BUREAU

DEVON FARMS

Availability of farms in Devon can be easily discovered by ringing 01548 550055.

SELF-CATERING

Brindiwell Farm, Cheriton Fitzpaine, Crediton, Devon EX17 4HR

Doreen Margaret Lock
☎ **01363 866357**
sc From £150–£200
Sleeps 4
☞ ☜

ℱ ℱ ℱ *Approved*

Self-contained wing of delightful old farmhouse in peaceful countryside with outstanding views. One double, one single bedroom and Z bed. Colour TV. Midway between north and south coasts and moors. Close Dartmoor and Exmoor. Open all year.

Cider Cottage, c/o Great Bradley Farm, Withleigh, Tiverton, Devon EX16 8JL

Mrs Sylvia Hann
☎ **01884 256946**
sc From £135–£325
Sleeps 5 + cot
☞ ◉

ℱ ℱ ℱ ℱ *Highly Commended*

Charming cottage, originally 17th century cider barn, on 155-acre dairy farm. Beautiful views, spacious accommodation for 5. 3 pretty bedrooms. Bed linen included. Comfortable oak-beamed lounge, superb new kitchen with dining area. Washing machine available. All tastefully furnished and equipped to provide a high standard of comfort and convenience. Large garden with picnic table. Walk our country lanes. Explore moors and coasts, or stay and enjoy the farm. Open all year.

Hele Barton, Black Dog, Crediton, Devon EX17 4QJ

Mrs Gillian Gillbard
☎ **01884 860278**
sc From £100–£320
Sleeps 6
☞ ⅍ ■ ☜ ◉

ℱ ℱ ℱ ℱ *Commended*

Pretty thatched cottage with large lawn adjoining open fields. 3 bedrooms, NS heaters, linen provided, well equipped kitchen, woodburner. Ideal for touring or just relaxing. Brochure. (Also for 1996, 2 bedroom (en suite) barn conversion, suitable for disabled, with own garden.) Open all year.

Hele Payne Farm, Hele, Exeter, Devon EX5 4PH

Irene and Sally Maynard
☎ **01392 881530/ 881356**
sc From £90–£330
Sleeps 3/5/6
☞ ☜ ⚞ ⚘ ■
ℱ ℱ ℱ ℱ *Up to Highly Commended*

Relax in our heated swimming pool. Let your children explore the farm by helping to feed the baby calves or by playing in the beautiful gardens. Fishing. All three cottages (Honeysuckle Cottage, The Wheat Loft and Horseshoe Lodge) are furnished, cleaned and decorated to a high standard and have colour TV, bed linen, laundry room, cot, highchair and central heating. Open all year.

Wonham Barton, Bampton, Tiverton, Devon EX16 9JZ

Anne McLean Williams
☎ **01398 331312**
sc From £120–£255
Sleeps 4/6
⚞ ☞ ⅍ ⚞ ■ ⚘
ℱ ℱ ℱ *Commended*

In the beautiful Exe Valley near Exmoor, our generously equipped, fully heated, self-contained farmhouse wing enjoys panoramic views and its own garden. Children welcome, cot and highchair available, dogs by arrangement. Visitors can enjoy a working farm and 300 acres of pasture and woodland with cattle, sheep, wildflowers, birds and deer. Riding, fishing, swimming, golf nearby. Village 2 miles. Open part of year only.

England's West Country

East Devon

Group Contact: *Jill Balkwill* ☎ *01548 550055/Fax 01548 550312*

East Devon has picturesque villages and miles of sandy and pebble beaches. This is the country of the old sea dogs of Elizabethan times, such as Sir Francis Drake and Sir Walter Raleigh. East Devon Farm and Country Holiday members offer a choice of farmhouse bed and breakfast and self-catering accommodation all of a high standard.

Wherever you stay you are not far from the coast where you can enjoy peaceful clifftop walks and spectacular seascapes. Inland a little way you can wander over moors and common land or down winding country lanes. For the more active there's swimming, riding, sailing, fishing and windsurfing.

If it's places of interest you want, East Devon won't let you down – there are craft centres, churches, markets and museums. Exeter alone boasts a cathedral with a 300ft nave – the longest span of unbroken Gothic vaulting in the world, plus priceless manuscripts; a Maritime Museum with more than 100 craft from all over the world, and the Royal Albert Memorial collection of lace, glass and china.

If all that leaves you hungry, you can choose to take meals in village inns, thatched cottage cafés or seaside restaurants. Whatever your choice you will find excellent fare ... at very fair prices.

BED AND BREAKFAST

(and evening meal)

Aller Barton Farm, Cullompton, Devon EX15 1QQ

Sally Cooke
☎ **01884 32275**
Fax 01884 35837
[BB] **From £15.50**
EM From £7.50
Sleeps 5
🐓 🐴 🐖 ▪
👑👑 *Approved*

Delightful, spacious farmhouse set in 250 acres of its own land. Large sitting/dining room with colour TV. Two en suite bedrooms each with tea/coffee facilities. Central heating. Warm welcome, generous home cooking. Ideal touring centre for coast, moors and many local attractions – something for everyone. Relax in garden or, for the more energetic, tennis court and games room. 1 mile M5. Brochure. Open all year.

Barn Park Farm, Nr Cotleigh, Stockland Hill, Honiton, Devon EX14 9JA

Pamela Boyland
☎ **01404 861297**
[BB] **From £15–£16**
EM From £8.50
Sleeps 4
🐓 🐴 🍴 🌾 ▪ ◎
👑 *Commended*

Barn Park Farm, a working dairy farm situated near the A30/A303 junction, is set in picturesque countryside within reach of many beauty spots and the coast. The farmhouse is full of character having a homely atmosphere. Traditional English breakfasts using eggs from our free range hens. Evening meal available. Open all year.

Claypitts Farm, East Hill, Ottery St Mary, Devon EX11 1QD

Jayne Burrow
☎ **01404 814599**
[BB] **From £15–£18.00**
Sleeps 6
🍴 🐴(3) 🌾 ▪ ◎
👑👑 *Commended*

Relax on our sheep/arable farm in the beautiful Otter Valley. Lovely walks and many attractions nearby, including Sidmouth 4½ miles. Double en-suite, twin and double with washbasins, guests' toilets/bathroom, tea/coffee facilities. Excellent comfortable accommodation, beamed ceilings, CH, large lounge, log burner, dining room. Good farmhouse cooking. Large garden, children's play area, many small animals (chickens, ducks and geese). Open Easter–Nov.

Godford Farm, Awliscombe, Honiton, Devon EX14 0PW

Sally Lawrence
☎ **01404 42825**
[BB] **From £15–£18**
EM £10.50
Sleeps 6
🐴 🌾 ▪ ◎
👑👑 *Commended*

We invite you to stay on this family-run dairy farm, set in a beautiful river valley. Listed farmhouse with large sitting and dining rooms. Colour TV. Central heating. Drinks facilities in bedrooms. Large garden, play area, games barn for all ages. Delightful area for walking. Cots and highchairs provided. Family and twin rooms, private bathrooms. Children reduced rates. Brochure. Open Easter–Oct.

Great Houndbeare Farm, Aylesbeare, Exeter, Devon EX5 2DB

Hazel Bale
☎/Fax 01404 822771
[BB] **From £18–£26**
EM From £8
Sleeps 10
🐴 🐓 👤 🦆 🐖 🍴 ▪ 🎿 ◎
👑👑 *Commended*

Unwind and relax in tranquil surroundings amid a small arable farm with woodland and a lake. We offer coarse fishing, bicycle and barbecue hire. All rooms are en suite with colour TV, tea and coffee facilities, etc. Guests' lounge with separate dining room. Full central heating. Brochure available. Closed Christmas and New Year.

6 **Higher Coombe Farm,** Tipton St John, Sidmouth, Devon EX10 0AX

Kerstin Farmer
☎ 01404 813385
▣ From £18
Sleeps 10
♨ ⚘ 🏕 ◉
🐾 *Commended*

The Farmer family welcome you to a relaxing stay on their sheep and beef farm, peacefully situated in the beautiful Otter Valley yet only 4 miles from Sidmouth seafront. Family, double, single rooms all have washbasins, tea/coffee-making facilities, colour TV. (No smoking in bedrooms.) Lounge with colour TV, separate dining room. Children welcome. Generous farmhouse breakfast. Open most of the year.

7 **Higher Weston Farm,** Weston, Nr Sidmouth, Devon EX10 0PH

Sandy MacFadyen
☎ 01395 513741
▣ From £16–£20
Sleeps 6
♨ 🐎 ✂ 🐕 ♿ ← 🏕 ⚘
🐾🐾 *Commended*

Enjoy a relaxed, comfortable holiday in superb heritage coast location, 3 miles from Sidmouth. Fully equipped en suite rooms, comfortable lounge. Breakfast menu includes vegetarian. Lovely garden, croquet, badminton, stabling available. Conservation award winning, working farm. Fields extend to coastal footpath, superb views of Lyme Bay, and to unspoilt Combe and beach. Open Feb–Nov .

8 **Lane End Farm,** Broadhembury, Honiton, Devon EX14 0LU

Mrs Molly Bennett
☎ 01404 841563
▣ From £16–£18
EM From £9
Sleeps 6
♨ 🐎 🏕 🏕 ♿ ◉
🐾🐾 *Commended*

At Lane End Farm you will enjoy delicious home cooking in glorious surroundings. Panoramic views of the Blackdown Hills, an Area of Outstanding Natural Beauty. With cattle and sheep grazing, floral gardens all within walking distance of the unspoilt thatched village of Broadhembury. Tea/ coffee facilities in bedrooms (1 en suite). CH, colour TV. Colour brochure. Children reduced rates. Evening meals optional. Open all year.

9 **Lower Pinn Farm,** Peak Hill, Sidmouth, Devon EX10 0NN

Elizabeth Tancock
☎ 01395 513733
▣ From £16–£19
Sleeps 6
🐾 ♨ ⚘ 🏕 ◉
🐾🐾 *Commended*

A friendly welcome and comfortable, spacious rooms await you at Lower Pinn. 2 miles west of the coastal resort of Sidmouth. Many coastal and country walks. Two double/twin en suite, one double with washbasin. All rooms have colour TV, hot drink facilities. CH. Access at all times. Guests' lounge, dining room with separate tables. Good hearty breakfasts. Ample parking. Several local pubs and restaurants. Open most of the year.

10 **Newcourt Barton,** Langford, Cullompton, Devon EX15 1SE

Mrs Sheila A Hitt
☎ 01884 277326
▣ From £15.50–£16.50
Sleeps 6
✂ ♨(11) 🏕 ⚘ ← ◉
Listed *Applied*

Newcourt Barton is an ideal base for touring the Devon coast and countryside. It is a working farm with sheep. The red brick farmhouse is surrounded by a large garden with grass tennis court. Situated in a quiet position 4 miles Cullompton, M5 J28. Coarse fishing on farm. 1 twin, 1 double, 1 family, H/C, toilet and shower. Tea/coffee-making facilities, TV, lounge, dining room, full English breakfast. Local inn and restaurants for evening meal.

11 **Pippinfield Farm,** Harepath Hill, Colyford, Seaton, Devon EX12 2TD

Anne Spanton
☎ 01297 21521
▣ From £20–£21
EM From £8.50
Sleeps 6
♨(9) 🐎 ✂ ⚘ 🏕
🐾🐾 *Commended*

Ideal base for touring the Devon coast. The front of the house is south facing with panoramic views of the Axe estuary. Beyond is the pretty village of Axmouth, also the sea at Seaton which is approx 2 miles. Easy reach of Lyme Regis, Charmouth, Beer, Sidmouth, Budleigh Salterton, Exeter. We offer every comfort, en suite rooms, friendly atmosphere. Senior citizens welcome. Open most of year.

Pitt Farm, Fairmile, Ottery St Mary, Devon EX11 1NL   12

Susan Hansford
☎ 01404 812439
BB From £16–£20
EM From £9
🦌 ⊛
🐾🐾 *Commended*

A warm family atmosphere awaits you at this 16th century thatched farmhouse which nestles in the picturesque Otter Valley ½ mile from A30 on B3176. Within easy reach of all East Devon resorts and pleasure facilities. Good home cooking using fresh local/own produce. A working beef/ arable farm surrounded by lovely countryside and rural walks. Family, double and twin rooms. Lounge with colour TV. Fire certificate. Closed Christmas & New Year.

Rydon Farm, Woodbury, Exeter, Devon EX5 1LB   13

Sally Glanvill
☎ 01395 232341
BB From £17–£22
Sleeps 6
🐎🦌 ♿
🐾🐾 *Commended*

Come and enjoy the peaceful tranquillity of our 16th century Devon longhouse on a working dairy farm. Exposed beams and inglenook fireplace. Bedrooms with tea/coffee facilities, hairdryers, full CH, private or en suite bathrooms. Romantic four-poster. Full English breakfast with free range eggs. Several local pubs and restaurants. Featured in the Daily Mail. QQQQ AA Selected. Open all year.

Skinners Ash Farm, Fenny Bridges, Honiton, Devon EX14 0BH   14

Mrs Jill Godfrey
☎ 01404 850231
BB £15.50
EM £7
Sleeps 6
🦌🐎✂🦌🎪♿ ⊛
Listed *Commended*

Enjoy a relaxing holiday on a family-run rare breeds farm. Two large family rooms with tea/coffee facilities, TV, private bathroom. Farmhouse cooking, cream teas. Farm walk, pony rides, egg collections. Lovely views. Near local beaches. Walk to two local inns. Please send for brochure. Open all year.

Smallicombe Farm, Northleigh, Colyton, Devon EX13 6BU   15

Maggie Todd
☎ 01404 831310
BB From £17.50–£19.50
EM From £9
Sleeps 6
🦌✂♿🐣🦌 🎪 ⊛
🐾🐾 *Commended*

Children are welcome at our small farm set in an area of outstanding natural beauty, but convenient for all East Devon coastal resorts. Help collect your own eggs for breakfast, feed our friendly pigs, goats, sheep and cows. Family suite and ground floor twin/double room. All en suite with tea/coffee and colour TVs. Cots, highchairs and baby sitting provided. Play area, games room and laundry. Reductions children and weekly. Open all year.

Wiscombe Linhaye Farm, Southleigh, Colyton, Devon EX13 6JF   16

Sheila Rabjohns
☎ 01404 871342
BB From £15–£18
EM From £7
Sleeps 6
♿🦌🦌(5) 🎪 ⊛
🐾🐾 *Commended*

A small working farm in the quiet countryside of East Devon but in reach of Sidmouth and Lyme Regis. A friendly atmosphere on this family farm with good home cooking from home/local produce. Two ground floor bedrooms with private bathroom, one en suite. Drink facilities, TV and hair dryers in all bedrooms. Colour TV in lounge and separate dining tables. Three double rooms. Open Easter–Oct.

SELF-CATERING

---

17   **Bertie's Barn,** Skinners Ash Farm, Fenny Bridges, Honiton, Devon EX14 0BH

Mrs J. S. Godfrey
☎ **01404 850231**
[SC] From £150–£250
EM £7
Sleeps 6
Commended

Enjoy a relaxing holiday on a family-run rare breeds farm in a luxury flat in a converted barn. Enjoy pony rides, farm walks, egg collections, Devonshire cream teas. Near local beaches and tourist attractions. On A30 Honiton to Exeter road. Please send for brochure. Open all year.

---

18   **Bodmiscombe Farm,** Blackborough, Cullompton, Devon EX15 2HR

Mrs Brenda Northam
☎ **01884 266315**
[SC] From £110–£265
Sleeps 4 + cot
Commended

A warm, friendly welcome assured on our family farm set in an Area of Outstanding Natural Beauty. Wonderful views from listed 17th century Devon longhouse with beamed ceilings. Private coarse fishing, 20-acre woodland trail. Central for coast and moorland or stay around farm and watch us at work. Electricity not metered. Short breaks. Brochure. Open all year.

---

19   **Court Brook Farm,** Clyst St George, Exeter, Devon EX3 0NT

Jenny Broom
☎ **01392 877710**
Fax 01392 873378
[SC] From £150–£265
Sleeps 2/5 + cot
Approved

Relax in our comfortably furnished cottage in the small village of Clyst St. George. An ideal touring base only 5 miles from Exmouth and 5 miles to Exeter's Cathedral City. In easy reach of Dartmoor. Well equipped kitchen/diner, lounge with colour TV, bathroom with bath/shower. 3 bedrooms, 1 twin, 1 double, 1 single. Garden with picnic furniture and ample parking, full details available. Open Mar–Nov.

---

20   **Lemprice Farm,** Yettington, Budleigh Salterton, Devon EX9 7BW

Mrs Hanneke Coates
☎ **01395 567037**
Fax 01395 567585
[SC] From £160–£475
Sleeps 4–7
Up to Highly Commended

Four south-facing stone barn cottages suitable for disabled. Exceptional walking area of outstanding natural beauty and scientific interest. Home of the rare barn owl. All cottage gardens overlook small lake and marshes abundant with wildlife, hills and open countryside beyond. All linen and electricity included. Dogs by arrangement only. Three miles to beach. Brochure. Winter short breaks.

---

21   **Mill Cottage,** Aylesbeare, Exeter, Devon EX5 2DB

Hazel Bale
☎/Fax 01404 822771
[SC] From £250–£750
Commended

Luxury cottage overlooking lake, lawns and woodland. Safe for children and peaceful for adults. Central heating, log fire and satellite TV. Kitchen fitted with dishwasher, washing machine, microwave and fridge freezer. Linen and towels available, all beds have duvets. Three bathrooms. M5 5 miles. Brochure available. Open all year.

Oak Cottage, Aller Barton Farm, Cullompton, Devon EX15 1QQ   (22)

Sally Cooke
☎ **01884 32275**
Fax 01884 35837
SC **From £120–£420**

Commended

Ideal centre to experience glorious Devon. Large, spacious, comfortably furnished farmhouse situated in farm surroundings. Five bedrooms plus nursery (bedlinen included). Two bathrooms, one en suite. Spacious dining room, separate sitting room. Kitchen with fridge/freezer, dishwasher, microwave. Laundry room and payphone. Garden, play area, tennis court, games room. 1 mile M5. Brochure. Open all year.

Otter Holt and Owl Hayes, c/o Godford Farm, Awliscombe, Honiton, Devon EX14 0PW   (23)

Sally Lawrence
☎ **01404 42825**
SC **From £100–£295**
Sleeps 4 + cot

Commended

Come and see where the hayracks are in our beautiful barn cottages, one of the many features that make them unique. Each cottage comprises beamed lounge with colour TV, pine kitchen/diner with washer/dryer, microwave, fridge/ freezer. CH. 2 bedrooms (linen included). Walkers' paradise. Relax in the garden and games barn, or watch the cows being milked. Children welcome, large play area. Cot available. Brochure. Open all year.

Smallicombe Farm, Northleigh, Colyton, Devon EX13 6BU   (24)

Maggie Todd
☎ **01404 831310**
SC **From £95–£555**
Sleeps 2–8

Commended

Small farm in superb rural setting yet close to coast. Help collect your own eggs for breakfast, feed our friendly pigs, goats, sheep and cows. Children's play area, large games room, laundry. Recently converted barns retaining original features but with all modern conveniences. Sleep 2, 4, 5 and 8. One specially designed for wheelchair users. Cots and highchairs available. Open all year.

DISABLED VISITORS

Many members offer a welcome to disabled/less able visitors. Please do check the extent of the facilities before booking.

FOLLOW THE COUNTRY CODE

Leave nothing but footprints,
Take nothing but photographs,
Kill nothing but time!

England's West Country

Dartmoor and South Devon

Group Contacts: 🅱 *Janet Hooper* ☎ *01803 862326*
🆂🅲 *Mrs Angela Bell* ☎ *01364 621391*

If you enjoy the outdoor life, this area offers unlimited opportunities in the 365 square miles of Dartmoor National Park with its contrasting open moorland and wooded valleys. The coast, walking, horseriding, climbing, birdwatching and golf, or alternatively coarse, game and sea-fishing, sailing and windsurfing, are all within approximately half an hour's drive.

Also easily accessible are many places of interest. Dartington Hall, centre of culture and the arts, Buckfast Abbey, the Dart Valley Steam Railway and the Shire Horse Centre. You may also visit historical sites from the Bronze Age onwards, country mansions, busy markets, antique and craft shops, country parks, National Trust properties, museums and resorts of all kinds from bustling Torquay to tranquil villages and the historic Elizabethan town of Totnes.

Food and drink can be a special delight in this part of the world. No visit would be complete without sampling a traditional cream tea. Then there's the local cider!

And for appetites of a different kind you can spend your evenings enjoying the theatre, concert and show life on offer in Torquay, Paignton, Plymouth and Exeter.

BED AND BREAKFAST
(and evening meal)

Adams Hele Farm, Ashburton, South Devon TQ13 7NW

Dorothy Dent
☎ 01364 652525
BB From £15–£17
EM From £7
Sleeps 6
🐓 🐕 🏌
🌸🌸 *Approved*

This 16th century listed farmhouse with oak beams and log fires nestles on a south facing hill overlooking the Dart valley and moors. It is a comfortable base from which to explore Dartmoor and the South Devon coast. 90 acres stocked with ponies, cattle and sheep. Peace, comfort and good home cooking with farm and local produce. 3 spacious double rooms, 2 with private shower and toilet, all with H/C, tea/coffee-making facilities. Open Feb–Nov.

Berry Farm, Berry Pomeroy, Totnes, Devon TQ9 6LG

Mrs Geraldine Nicholls
☎ 01803 863231
BB From £14.50
EM From £8.50
Sleeps 6
🍴 🐕(3) 🐓 🏌 🏕 🏌
Listed *Commended*

Large mixed working farm surrounded by lovely old cider orchards in village 1½ miles from Totnes town. Spacious rooms, tastefully decorated, with tea/coffee facilities, washbasins – 1 family, 1 double, 1 twin. Bathroom, shower, separate toilet. Guests' lounge, TV. Good local eating places, evening meal by arrangement. Parking. Ideal base for touring coast/moors. Open all year.

Budleigh Farm, Moretonhampstead, Devon TQ13 8SB

Mrs Judith Harvey
☎ 01647 440835
Fax 01647 440436
BB From £14–£18.50
Sleeps 5
🐕 🏕 🏌 🎿 🏊
🌸 *Commended*

Lovely old thatched farmhouse, a listed building, set in the Wray Valley, part of the Dartmoor National Park, ½ mile from Moretonhampstead. Just off the A382 which makes Budleigh easy to find and a good base for exploring the area. Pretty garden. Fishing, riding and golf nearby. Outdoor heated swimming pool. Open Mar–Nov.

Charford Farm, Avonwick, Totnes, Devon TQ9 7LT

Anne Barons
☎ 01364 73263
BB From £15–£20
EM From £9
Sleeps 6
🐕 🐓 🍴 🏌
🌸🌸 *Commended*

A friendly working farm with cows, calves, horses, etc. Ideal for touring the area. Lovely old farmhouse, peacefully situated and offering every comfort. Spacious family and double rooms with bathrooms en suite, double/twin with washbasin, all with tea-making facilities and colour TV. Evening meals with plenty of good farmhouse cooking. Brochure available. Open Mar–Nov.

Crannacombe Farm, Hazlewood, Loddiswell, Nr Kingsbridge, South Devon TQ7 4DX

Shirley & Stephen Bradley
☎ 01548 550256
BB From £16–£16.50
EM £9
Sleeps 8
🍴 🐕 🏌 🎿
🌸🌸 *Commended*

In an area of outstanding natural beauty near Kingsbridge. Working farm, Georgian farmhouse, comfortable, informal, absolutely peaceful. We have family/double bedrooms with private bathrooms and TV, hot drink facilities and a separate children's room sleeping 2. Lovely walks, stunning views and a clean river to paddle, play and picnic by. Excellent food, prize winning cider, delicious juice.

---

6 Dodbrooke Farm, Michelcombe, Holne, Nr Ashburton, Devon TQ13 7SP

Judy Henderson
☎ 01364 631461
BB From £14.50–£16.50
EM From £6
Sleeps 6
ħ ♋ ℀
Listed *Approved*

Dodbrooke Farm is a listed 17th century former longhouse in an idyllic valley at the foot of Dartmoor. Food is home produced and the rooms are warm and comfortable. There are sheep and goats on the farm and a lovely garden for guests to explore. Come and enjoy a friendly atmosphere with local walking, riding and carriage driving. Open all year (closed Christmas).

---

7 Foales Leigh, Harberton, Totnes, Devon TQ9 7SS

Carol Chudley
☎ 01803 862365
BB From £15–£20
Sleeps 6
♋(5) ⅍ Ā ℀ ▟
♨ ♨ *Commended*

A charming 16th century farmhouse in traditional courtyard setting. This family farm is situated in peaceful, unspoilt countryside within easy reach of beaches, moors and towns. Comfortable accommodation includes large oak-beamed lounge and 3 spacious bedrooms: 1 double/family and 1 double, both en suite and 1 twin, all with TV, CH and beverage trays. Delicious Aga-cooked breakfast. Closed Christmas & New Year.

---

8 Frost Farm, Hennock, Bovey Tracey, South Devon TQ13 9PP

Linda Harvey
☎ 01626 833266
Fax 01626 835758
BB From £17–£19
EM From £9.50
Sleeps 6
♋ ⅍ ♿
♨ *Commended*

A pretty, pink-washed, thatched old farmhouse on working part organic farm in our green valley. Lovely for walking, bird watching, NT houses, gardens. Explore Dartmoor or seaside. Good farmhouse food, fresh meats, vegetables, fruits, local cream/ice creams. Large, spacious bedrooms en suite with tea/coffee facilities, colour TV, CH. Ground floor bedroom. Cosy, relaxed atmosphere. Closed Christmas.

---

9 Great Court Farm, Weston Lane, Totnes, Devon TQ9 6LB

Janet Hooper
☎ 01803 862326
BB From £14–£16
EM From £8.50
Sleeps 6
⅍ ♋ ▟
♨ *Highly Commended*

A warm welcome, views of Totnes and comfortable, friendly accommodation await you at our 400-acre dairy farm running down to the River Dart. Colour co-ordinated spacious bedrooms with tea/coffee making facilities, colour TV's, washbasins, central heating, 1 family/twin, 2 doubles, 2 bathrooms/shower, separate toilet. Guest lounge with colour TV. Dining room to enjoy good food. Evening meal by arrangement. Playroom, garden, swimming pool. Plenty of inns and restaurants nearby. Open all year.

---

10 Great Sloncombe Farm, Moretonhampstead, Newton Abbot, Devon TQ13 8QF

Mrs Trudie Merchant
☎ 01647 440595
BB From £19–£20
EM From £10.50
Sleeps 6
ħ ♋(8) ⅍ ▟
♨ ♨ ♨ *Highly Commended*

Share the magic of Dartmoor all year round whilst staying in our lovely 13th century farmhouse. A working dairy farm set amongst meadows and woodland, abundant in wild flowers and animals. A welcoming place to relax and explore Devon. Comfortable double and twin rooms all en suite with central heating, TV. Plenty of delicious home-cooked Devonshire food. Open all year.

---

11 Greenwell Farm, Nr Meavy, Yelverton, Plymouth, Devon PL20 6PY

Bridget Cole
☎/Fax 01822 853563
BB From £19–£22
EM From £11.50
Sleeps 6
♋ ▟
♨ ♨ ♨ *Commended*

Fresh country air, breathtaking views and scrumptious farmhouse cuisine. This busy farming family welcomes you to share the countryside and wildlife. A period farmhouse located in Dartmoor National Park, ideal for walking. En suite facilities, heating, hospitality trays in our spacious, comfortable rooms. Licensed, brochure available. Open all year (closed Christmas).

Higher Venton Farm, Widecombe-in-the-Moor, Newton Abbot, South Devon TQ13 7TF

Mrs Betty Hicks
☎ 01364 621235
[BB] From £15–£19
Sleeps 6
🐕 🐈(5)
Listed *Approved*

A friendly welcome awaits you at Higher Venton Farm, a 16th century thatched farmhouse and working farm. Peaceful and relaxing, ideal for touring Dartmoor. Riding stables nearby. Coast 16 miles, ½ mile from Widecombe village. Good local eating places recommended. 1 double en suite, 1 double and 1 twin with washbasins. CH, tea/coffee-making facilities, lounge with colour TV. Open all year except Christmas.

Hillhead Farm, Ugborough, Ivybridge, Devon PL21 0HQ

Mrs J Johns
☎ 01752 892674
[BB] From £14–£16
EM From £9
Sleeps 6
🐈 🐕 🖈 🎋 🐎
🌸 *Commended*

Comfortable, welcoming family farmhouse. Guests' sitting room with TV and woodburner. 1 twin room, 2 double rooms both with TV and all with tea/coffee facilities and H&C. Guests' private bathroom, also separate toilet. Full CH, open log fire in dining room. Good, home cooked and largely home produced food. Open all year except Christmas.

Lower Southway Farm, Widecombe-in-the-Moor, Newton Abbot, Devon TQ13 7TF

Dawn Nosworthy
☎ 01364 621277
[BB] From £14
Sleeps 6
♿ 🐈 🖃 🎋 🐎 🍴
Listed *Approved*

Situated in the lovely valley of Widecombe-in-the-Moor within the Dartmoor National Park with superb views. Ideal for walking, riding or touring Dartmoor. Excellent farmhouse food. 2 doubles, 1 twin, each with H/C, tea/coffee-making facilities and heating. Lounge with colour TV. Open all year except Christmas.

Lower Thornton Farm, Kenn, Exeter, Devon EX6 7XH

Mrs Alison Clack
☎ 01392 833434
[BB] From £17
Sleeps 4
🐈 🖈 🎋 🍴
🌸🌸 *Commended*

Come and relax at our secluded family farm with panoramic views. Just 2 miles from A38. Ideal base to visit Exeter, Torquay, Dartmoor, coast and racecourse. Our ground floor bedrooms are spacious and comfortable. One room en suite opening onto patio and garden, other has private bathroom. Both with tea/coffee facilities. Guests' lounge, colour TV, CH throughout. Child reductions. Open Jan–Nov.

Mill Farm, Kenton, Exeter, Devon EX6 8JR

Delia Lambert
☎ 01392 832471
[BB] From £14–£17.50
🐈 🍴
🌸🌸 *Commended*

Mill Farm – a charming farmhouse with all modern comforts lovely en suite rooms with colour TV available. Also reasonably priced standard rooms. Ideal Powderham Castle, beaches, bird watching, forest walks, racecourses. Dartmoor 20 minutes. Lovely rural setting. Good parking. Very easy to find. Don't miss out. Send for a brochure now!

Mill Leat Farm, Holne, Ashburton, Newton Abbot, Devon TQ13 7RZ

Dawn Cleave
☎ 01364 631283
[BB] From £15.50–£18
EM From £7.50
Sleeps 6
🐈 🐕 🎋 🐎
Listed *Approved*

120-acre hill farm situated on the edge of Dartmoor, an ideal place for touring Devon's beautiful countryside, moorland or beaches. Comfortable accommodation in 18th century farmhouse with large spacious bedrooms, en suite available, with tea/coffee facilities. Very peaceful surroundings, just right for relaxing. Closed Christmas.

18 New Cott Farm, Poundsgate, Newton Abbot, Devon TQ13 7PD

Margaret Phipps
☎ 01364 631421
Fax 01364 631338
🅱🅱 From £17–£18
EM From £9.50
Sleeps 6
👤 ✂ 🐕(3) ☞ 🌾 💼
🏵🏵 *Commended*

A friendly welcome, beautiful views, pleasing accommodation await you at New Cott in the Dartmoor National Park. Enjoy the freedom and peace of open moorland and the Dart Valley. Trout fishing, farm trail, birds and animals on the farm. Riding, golf, leisure centre a short distance. Bedrooms en suite, tea/coffee. Central heating. Lots of lovely homemade food. Weekly reductions. Suitable for less able guests. Open all year except Christmas.

19 Peek Hill Farm, Dousland, Yelverton, Devon PL20 6PD

Justine Colton
☎ 01822 852908
🅱🅱 From £15–£18
Sleeps 6
🐎 🐕 ✂ Å 🌾
🏵🏵 *Commended*

"Come up where the buzzards fly, the air is clean, the water clear". Situated on the southern slopes of Dartmoor with sweeping views to Cornwall and adjacent to wooded Burrator Lake. Comfortable, sunny bedrooms, with private bathrooms. Log fire in lounge and much more. We are friendly and informal and are easily located off B3212. Open Jan–Nov.

20 Smallacombe Farm, Aller Valley, Dawlish, Devon EX7 0PS

Mrs Alison Thomson
☎ 01626 862536
🅱🅱 From £15–£17
EM From £8.50
Sleeps 6
🐕 🐎 🐈 🌾 🍴
🏵🏵 *Commended*

Off the beaten track, yet only two miles from Dawlish and the beach. Enjoy the best of both worlds, 'country and coast'. Children play freely with no fear of busy roads. Meet our 3 friendly dogs. Relax in the peaceful surroundings and homely atmosphere. 2 double rooms, 1 twin room, family unit available, en suite. Reductions for children, weekly discounts. Ring or write for brochure. Open all year.

21 Strashleigh Farm, Ivybridge, Devon PL21 9JP

Mrs Paula Salter
☎ 01752 892226
🅱🅱 From £15–£17
Sleeps 6
✂ 🐕(5) 💼
Listed *Commended*

A comfortable bed and a delicious, farmhouse breakfast awaits you. Strashleigh is a working farm, situated on the A38 near Ivybridge. The house provides an interesting history and wide views of beautiful Devonshire countryside. Perfect base for touring, beaches. City entertainment, sports facilities and tourist attractions. 2 double rooms, 1 twin, all with H&C and tea-making facilities and lounge with CTV. Open April–Sept.

22 Venn Farm, Ugborough, Ivybridge, Devon PL21 0PE

Pat Stephens
☎ 01364 73240
🅱🅱 £17
EM £10
Sleeps 12
🐎 🐕 💼
🏵🏵 *Commended*

Working farm amid peaceful scenery in the South Hams on edge of Dartmoor. Children encouraged to take an interest in farm life. The speciality of the house is 'carve your own roasts' and the atmosphere is friendly and relaxed. Accommodation comprises 2 family en suite rooms and separate garden cottage with 2 bedrooms, bathroom and picnic patio. Open Jan–Nov.

23 Wellpritton Farm, Holne, Ashburton, South Devon TQ13 7RX

Sue Gifford
☎ 01364 631273
🅱🅱 From £17
EM From £8
Sleeps 11
🐎 👤 🐕 💼 🍴
🏵🏵 *Highly Commended*

A beautiful farmhouse on the edge of Dartmoor, where goats, horses, rabbits and chickens are kept and sometimes sheep and cattle. Only ½ hour drive from Exeter, Plymouth and Torbay with riding, fishing, walking, sailing and golf nearby. Modernised to high standard – most rooms en suite, games room and swimming pool. Caring personal attention. Farm produced food. Weekly rates B&B & EM from £161. Open all year including Christmas.

Whitemoor Farm, Doddiscombsleigh, Nr Exeter, Devon EX6 7PU

Mrs Barbara Lacey
☎ 01647 252423
🆎 From £16.50–£17.50
EM From £8
Sleeps 6
🐕 🐈 ⚥ ⚘ 🛏 ♨ ▪
☙ *Approved*

Listed 16th century thatched farmhouse, set in seclusion of its own garden and farmland within easy reach of Exeter, coast, Dartmoor and forest walks. The Cobb House has exposed beams, log fires. Home made preserves. Good meals at local inn. Evening meal on request. Children and pets welcome. Swimming pool available. Open all year.

Wooston Farm, Moretonhampstead, Newton Abbot, Devon TQ13 8QA

Mary Cuming
☎/Fax 01647 440367
🆎 From £17–£20
EM From £10
Sleeps 6
🐕 🐈 (10)
☙☙☙ *Highly Commended*

Wooston Farm is situated above the Teign Valley in the Dartmoor National Park with views over open moorland. The farmhouse is surrounded by a delightful garden. There are plenty of walks on the moor and wooded Teign Valley adjoining farm. Good home cooking and cosy log fires await you at Wooston. 2 double en suite, 1 with four-poster, 1 twin room. Also mountain bikes available. Open all year except Christmas. AA listed.

SELF-CATERING

Budleigh Farm, Moretonhampstead, Devon TQ13 8SB

Mrs Judith Harvey
☎ 01647 440835
Fax 01647 440436
🆂🄲 From £84–£320
Sleeps 6
🐈 🐕 🛏 ⚘ ♿ ☂ ☃ ▪
🏠 🏠 – 🏠 🏠 🏠
Commended

Seven cottages and flats, converted from barns, each with its own character, on a farm tucked into the end of the Wray Valley ½ mile from Moretonhampstead. Outdoor heated swimming pool, barbecue; table tennis and darts. Small campsite. Excellent centre for exploring the area. Open Jan–Dec.

Longmeadow Farm, Coombe Road, Ringmore, Shaldon, Teignmouth, Devon TQ14 0EX

Mrs Anne Mann
☎ 01626 872732
Fax 01626 872323
🆂🄲 £140–£285
Sleeps 4
🐈 🛏 ⚘
🏠 🏠 🏠 *Approved*

Enjoy the best of both worlds on our South Devon farm set in lovely countryside but less than a mile from the beach and Shaldon village. Comfortable accommodation (in two units each sleeping 4) adjoining traditional style farmhouse overlooking estuary. Garden, patio, barbecue. Ideal location for touring coast, moors. Walks, fishing, riding nearby. Ample parking. Brochure available. Open all year.

Narramore Farm Cottages, Narramore Farm, Moretonhampstead, Devon TQ13 8QT

Narramore Farm Cottages, Narramore Farm, Moretonhampstead, Devon TQ13 8QT

Sue Horn
☎/Fax 01647 440455
🆂🄲 From £100–£450
Sleeps 2/5
🐈 🛏 🐕 ♿ ☂
🏠 🏠 🏠 🏠 *Highly Commended*

Narramore is a 107-acre stud/deer farm situated in glorious countryside. Five comfortable, fully equipped character cottages surround a heated pool and hot spa. Woodburners, satellite TV, games/laundry room, payphone. Play area, small animals, fishing lake, boat, barbecue. Nature walks plus the opportunity to badgerwatch make this a magical place to stay. Colour brochure available. Open all year.

29 **Shippen and Dairy Cottages,** c/o Lookweep Farm, Liverton, Newton Abbot, Devon TQ12 6HT

Averil Corrick
☎ 01626 833277
SC From £130–£370
Sleeps 4/5 + cot
🏠 ⏱

🗝 🗝 🗝 – 🗝 🗝 🗝 🗝
Commended

Come and relax in the peace and tranquillity of these two delightful barn converted cottages. Set within the Dartmoor National Park with easy access to the coast, golf, riding, walking and fishing locally. Sleeps 4/5, fully equipped and well furnished throughout. Own gardens with beautiful views. Ample parking. Use of outdoor heated swimming pool. High chairs, cots and linen available. Open all year.

30 **Strashleigh Farm,** Ivybridge, Devon PL21 9JP

Mrs Paula Salter
☎ 01752 892226
SC From £160–£240
Sleeps 2 + cot
⏱

🗝 🗝 🗝 *Approved*

Peacefully set with views of Dartmoor, Strashleigh Annex is a 1 level self-contained wing of the farmhouse. Double bedroom with en suite bathroom, newly fitted kitchen with dishwasher and a cosy open plan living area with a beautiful granite mullion window, woodburner and colour TV. Being near A38, its a perfect base for many attractions and activities. Brochure available. Open Apr–Sept.

31 **Wooder Manor,** Widecombe-in-the-Moor, Newton Abbot, Devon TQ13 7TR

Mrs Angela Bell
☎ 01364 621391
SC From £90–£600
Sleeps 2/16
♿ 🏠 ⏱ ♨

🗝 🗝 🗝 🗝 *Commended*

Cottages and converted coachhouse on 108-acre family farm, nestled in picturesque valley surrounded by unspoilt woodland, moors and granite tors. Central for touring Devon and exploring Dartmoor by foot or on horseback. Clean and fully equipped. Colour TVs, laundry facilities, microwaves, central heating. Gardens, courtyard for easy parking. Good food at local inn (½ mile). Choose a property to suit you from our brochure. Open all year.

FARM HOLIDAY BUREAU

DEVON FARMS

Availability of farms in Devon can be easily discovered by ringing 01548 550055.

FARM HOLIDAY BUREAU

THOSE LITTLE EXTRAS

For advice on farms that can offer 'extras' such as four-poster beds, special diets, farm trails, fishing rights – even stabling and trekking arrangements if you are bringing your own horse – ring the Farm Holiday Bureau on (01203) 696909.

England's West Country

Moor to Shore in Devon

Group Contact: *Mrs Jill Balkwill* ☎ *01548 550055/Fax 01548 550312*

The South Hams in South Devon is a unique part of the West Country, catering for a wide variety of tastes. The area lies between Plymouth and Torbay, is easily accessible from the A38 and is renowned for its beauty and variety of countryside. Not just the countryside either – it has such towns as Elizabethan Totnes with its castle, or the historic seaport of Dartmouth scattered around the Dart estuary and plenty of attractive villages.

The coastline, which is truly spectacular, has sheltered harbours and estuaries at Yealm, Salcombe and Dartmouth and a host of sandy beaches, ideal for bathing.

Fishing, riding and golf can be enjoyed in many places and if you could ever possibly tire of the area, turn north and the Dartmoor National Park is just a stone's throw away. The mild climate of the area makes it particularly attractive for out-of-season visits.

The area also includes wildlife and country parks, a Shire Horse Centre at Dunstone near Yealmpton and a wide variety of interesting museums. For those fans of steam, the area boasts two steam railways on the Dart Valley Railway, one of which connects with Totnes main line.

BED AND BREAKFAST
(and evening meal)

---

① Burton Farm, Galmpton, Kingsbridge, South Devon TQ7 3EY

Anne Rossiter
☎ 01548 561210
[BB] From £19–£22
EM From £9.50
Sleeps 22
✂ ☎ ☂ ☄ ☃
☙ *Highly Commended*

Working dairy and sheep farm situated in the valley running towards Hope Cove. 3 miles from famous sailing haunt of Salcombe. Walking, beaches, sailing, windsurfing, bathing, diving, fishing. Guests welcome to enjoy the farm's activities according to season. Traditional farmhouse cooking, home produce (clotted cream, etc). 4 course dinner. Access to rooms at all times. En suite available and washbasins. Tea-making facilities. Closed Christmas.

---

② Coombe Farm, Kingsbridge, South Devon TQ7 4AB

Beni & Johnathan Robinson
☎ 01548 852038
[BB] From £18.50–£20
Sleeps 6
☎(12) ✂ ☂ ☄ ☃ ☙
☙ *Commended*

Come and enjoy the peace and beauty of Devon in our lovely 16th century farmhouse. Wonderful breakfast, large elegant rooms each with own bathroom, colour TV, hot drink facilities. Artists have use of an art studio, and fisherman the well known Coombe Water fishery. Open all year except Christmas.

---

③ Court Barton Farmhouse, Aveton Gifford, Kingsbridge, Devon TQ7 4LE

John & Jill Balkwill
☎ 01548 550312
[BB] From £16–£24
Sleeps 18
☎ ☄ ☂ ☃ ◎
☙ *Commended*

Delightful 16th century listed manor farmhouse situated in 40-acre farm. Accommodation in 7 bedrooms, mostly en suite, tea/coffee-making facilities. Comfortable TV lounge with lots of books, sunny breakfast room to enjoy delicious country farmhouse breakfasts. Full central heating and log fires in colder weather. Close to moorland, beaches, ideal centre for walking, sailing, fishing, birdwatching. Open all year except Christmas. Welcome Host.

---

④ Gabber Farm, Down Thomas, Plymouth, Devon PL9 0AW

Margaret MacBean
☎ 01752 862269
[BB] From £15.50–£17.50
EM From £8
Sleeps 12
☎ ☂ ☃
☙ *Commended*

A warm welcome is assured on this working dairy farm in an area of outstanding natural beauty. Situated on the coast near Plymouth with lovely walks and within easy reach of the beaches. Good home cooking, hot drinks facilities in all rooms, double and family with en suite showers. Open all year except Christmas.

---

⑤ Helliers Farm, Ashford, Aveton Gifford, Kingsbridge, Devon TQ7 4ND

Christine Lancaster
☎/Fax 01548 550689
[BB] From £16
Sleeps 9
✂ ☎
☙ *Highly Commended*

A small sheep farm set on a hill overlooking a lovely valley in the heart of the South Hams, an ideal centre for touring the coasts, moors and Plymouth. Recently modernised accommodation comprises family, double, twin and single rooms, all with washbasins and tea/coffee facilities. Double or family en suite. 2 bathrooms, lounge, TV, games room. Fish pond. Hearty breakfasts with local produce. Fire certificate. Open all year except Christmas.

Higher Kellaton Farm, Kellaton, Kingsbridge, Devon TQ7 2ES

Mrs Angela Foale
☎ **01548 511514**
🛏 **From £13.50–£17.50**
Sleeps 6
🛇 🛉 ⅍ 🏛
Applied

Relax in our peaceful old farmhouse and spacious garden close to good beaches, coastal walks and family attractions or enjoy our mixed 350-acre family worked farm. 2 doubles and 1 twin, all with washbasins and tea/coffee-making facilities. Guests' own bathroom and sitting room with TV. Children and pets welcome. Non-smoking. Dinner by arrangement. Open Apr–Oct.

Little Orcheton Farm, Modbury, Ivybridge, South Devon PL21 0TF

Mrs Mary Doidge
☎ **01548 830515**
🛏 **From £15**
EM From £8
Sleeps 6
🛇 ⅍ 🏛
Listed *Applied*

A quiet and peaceful working sheep farm set in the Erme Valley, offering a friendly welcome and excellent farmhouse food. 2 miles from beach, 6 miles from moors. Two double bedrooms, 1 twin and 1 family room. Open Easter–Oct.

Slade Barn, Netton Farm, Noss Mayo, Nr Plymouth, Devon PL8 1HB   ⑧

Sandy Cherrington
☎/Fax **01752 872235**
🛏 **From £16.50–£18.50**
EM From £8
Sleeps 6
🛇(10) 🏛 ⬛
Listed *Commended*

Coastal South Devon beside the beautiful Yealm estuary. Lovely barn conversion. Indoor pool, games room, tennis court, gardens. Fabulous NT cliff walks, nearby sandy beaches. Double and 1 twin shared bathroom, CH, TV/ radio, tea/coffee on request. Open all year.

SELF-CATERING

Burton Farm Cottages, Burton Farm, Galmpton, Kingsbridge, South Devon TQ7 3EY   ⑨

Anne Rossiter
☎ **01548 561210**
🆂🅲 **From £75–£425**
Sleeps 4/5 + cot
🛇 🛉 🏛
🐾 🐾 🐾 🐾
Approved

Situated in a pretty hamlet adjoining open farmland, these cob and slate cottages are 5 miles from Kingsbridge with good shopping facilities, 3 miles from the sailing haunt of Salcombe and 1 mile from lovely beaches of Hope Cove and Thurlestone. Decorated and furnished, many original features with stone-built fireplaces and electric heating. Guests welcome to enjoy farm activities. Meals (from £8.50) available on request. Open all year.

Coombe Farm, Wembury Road, Plymstock, Plymouth, Devon PL9 0DE   ⑩

Rodney and Suzanne MacBean
☎ **01752 401730**
🆂🅲 **From £100–£340**
Sleeps 5/6
🛇 🛉
🐾 🐾 🐾 *Approved*

Coombe Farm dates back to the 14th century and is situated in a peaceful valley on the outskirts of Plymouth. An ideal centre for touring and within easy reach of moors and coast. The cottage is well equipped with two bedrooms, lounge, kitchen/diner, bathroom. Linen and electric included. Safe parking. Open all year.

11 **Ledstone Farm,** Ledstone, Kingsbridge, South Devon TQ7 2HQ

Ann Lidstone
☎ **01548 852662**
SC **From £100–£200**
Sleeps 3
♿ ½ ☕ ☂
♤ ♤ ♤ ♤
Highly Commended

Convenience and contentment guaranteed. One-level accommodation, formerly a fodder loft, with picturesque views. Adjacent parking. Quiet hamlet location twixt Totnes, Dartmouth and Salcombe. Open all year.

---

12 **Netton Farm Holiday Cottages,** Netton Farm, Noss Mayo, Nr Plymouth, Devon PL8 1HB

Sandy Cherrington
☎/Fax **01752 872235**
SC **From £150–£1,200**
Sleeps 2–12
♿ ☇ ☂ ▪
♤ ♤ *Commended*

Nestled into one of the most beautiful stretches of South Devon coastline, this small complex is ideally situated to cater for all tastes. Attractive, comfortable accommodation and warm, friendly atmosphere. Cottages sleep 2 to12. Use of lovely indoor pool, games room, tennis court, gardens. Rural and peaceful, superb coastal walks and nearby sandy beaches. SAE for colour brochure. Open Apr–Sept.

---

13 **Oldaport Farm Cottages,** Modbury, Ivybridge, Devon PL21 0TG

Miss C Evans
☎ **01548 830842**
Fax **01548 830998**
SC **From £136–£383**
Sleep 2/6
♿ ☇
♤ ♤ ♤ – ♤ ♤ ♤ ♤
Highly Commended

Oldaport is a small sheep farm of 60 acres, lying in the Erme Valley, and offering lovely views of the countryside. The four cottages, which sleep 2/6, were redundant stone barns which have been carefully converted into comfortable holiday homes. All fully equipped, heating in all rooms. Sandy beaches nearby, Dartmoor 8 miles. Excellent birdwatching. Brochure available. Open all year.

---

14 **Traine Farm,** Wembury, Plymouth, Devon PL9 0EW

Sheila Rowland
☎ **01752 862264**
SC **From £95–£350**
Sleeps 5 (+ 2) + cot
♿ ☇ ☂ ☀ ▪
♤ ♤ *Commended*

Spacious, character wing of attractive Georgian farmhouse on a dairy farm overlooking village of Wembury and heritage coast. Ideal location for family holidays, close to beaches, moors and good centre for walking, sailing, diving, golf. 7 miles from Plymouth city centre. CH, colour TV, large garden. Open all year.

---

15 **Withymore Cottage,** Withymore Farm, Malborough, Kingsbridge, South Devon TQ7 3ED

Mrs Jo Hocking
☎/Fax **01548 561275**
SC **From £130–£350**
Sleeps 6 + cot
☂ ♿ ☕ ☂
♤ ♤ ♤ ♤ *Commended*

Recently modernised cottage nestling in a peaceful valley on a family-run dairy farm within a short distance of Salcombe. Very comfortable and furnished to a high standard throughout. Colour TV, bed linen, CH. Well equipped kitchen. Large enclosed garden. Ideal centre for family holiday with many beaches, sailing, fishing, golf, horse riding and spectacular coastal walks. Open all year.

FARM HOLIDAY BUREAU

DEVON FARMS

Availability of farms in Devon can be easily discovered by ringing 01548 550055.

England's West Country

West Devon Welcome

Group Contact: *Mrs Jane Pyle* ☎ *01363 82510*

West Devon, with its sheltered valleys, rugged hills and picturesque villages, offers you a chance not just to visit the countryside but to be a part of it ... on our working beef, sheep and dairy farms. A chance to enjoy a real family holiday, enjoying the peace of the countryside, joining in the local activities, travelling out to enjoy the beautiful beaches, entertainments, sights and attractions. A year-round delight.

There are many varieties of animals, birds and wild flowers for you to see. Walks and trails have been established in many forests and around a number of reservoirs. More active pursuits include riding and fishing or the more leisurely crafts of pottery, spinning or jewellery-making to learn.

For those interested in history or literature there are many ancient churches, Bronze Age settlements and the home of Sir Francis Drake plus the setting for the 'Hound of the Baskervilles'. Morwellham Quay and other National Trust properties are within easy reach .

Resist, if you can, the locally made cheese, yoghurt, chocolate, fudge, cider or the famous Devon Cream Tea. West Devon has so much to offer ... why not come and share a little bit of "our heaven down in Devon".

Bideford
South Molton
A361
Wellington
26
A39
A386
Tiverton
27
A303
Chard
A377
Stratton
A3072
3
2
Crediton
M5
A35
Honiton
Bude
Holsworthy
1
Okehampton
A30
A30
A388
Exeter
29
30
5 6
Moretonhampstead
31
Sidmouth
Seaton
Launceston
A386
Budleigh Salterton
Exmouth
A30
Dawlish
A380
A38
Newton Abbot
Teignmouth
4 7
Tavistock
Torquay
Buckfastleigh
Liskeard
Torbay
Saltash
Plymouth
Totnes
Brixham
Looe
Torpoint
Dartmouth
Kingsbridge

BED AND BREAKFAST

(and evening meal)

---

①   **Higher Cadham Farm,** Jacobstowe, Okehampton, Devon EX20 3RB

John & Jenny King
☎ **01837 851647**
Fax **01837 851410**
🛏 **From £16.50–£22.50**
EM From £8
Sleeps 17
🐎 🕷 ⊡ 🔥 🌿
🏵 *Commended*

Superb farmhouse accommodation, tasty home cooking, and breathtaking Devon scenery, that's the appetising recipe on offer at Higher Cadham in the heart of Tarka Country. Facilities for the less agile, en suite, flexible meal times, riverside walks and lots more! Ring for a brochure and details of our special offers. Open all year except Christmas.

---

②   **Lower Nichols Nymet Farm,** North Tawton, Devon EX20 2BW

Mrs Jane Pyle
☎ **01363 82510**
🛏 **From £17**
EM From £11
Sleeps 6
🍴 🐏 🐈 🌿 🔥
🏵🏵 *Highly Commended*

We offer a haven of comfort and rest on a modern working dairy farm and provide the perfect base for exploring the beauties of the West Country. Residents' lounge, colour TV. All rooms en suite, plus tea/coffee-making facilities. An ideal holiday centre – beaches, golf, good walks, riding, fishing, fine houses and gardens nearby to visit. Open Easter–Oct (incl).

---

③   **Oaklands Farm,** North Tawton, Devon EX20 2BQ

Winifred Headon
☎ **01837 82340**
🛏 **From £15–£16**
EM From £8
Sleeps 5
🕷 🐏 🍴
🏵 *Applied*

A warm welcome awaits you at Oaklands, a 130-acre farm in the centre of Devon. Easy to find on a level drive from a good road. Traditional farmhouse cooking with ample of everything. Heating and electric blankets in bedrooms. Lounge with colour TV. Pleasant gardens. Reductions for children. Open all year except Christmas.

---

④   **Rubbytown Farm,** Gulworthy, Tavistock, Devon PL19 8PA

Mary Steer
☎ **01822 832493**
🛏 **From £18**
EM From £12
Sleeps 6
🍴 🐏 **(5)** 🌿 🔥
🏵🏵 *Highly Commended*

Stay in our lovely old farmhouse and sleep in four-poster beds. Enjoy woodland walks. There is abundant wildlife, you may see deer if you are lucky and at dusk the foxes and badgers at play. Help with feeding the calves. Good farmhouse cooking with evening meals served by candlelight. St Mellion Golf and Country Club nearby. Upholstery classes are held locally. 2 double, 4 posters, en suite, 1 twin with private bathroom, games room. Evening meal served by candlelight by prior arrangement. Closed Christmas.

---

⑤   **Week Farm,** Bridestowe, Okehampton, Devon EX20 4HZ

Margaret Hockridge
☎ **01837 861221**
🛏 **From £20–£22**
EM From £10
Sleeps 12
🕷 ⅙ 🐏 🔥
🏵🏵 *Commended*

Guests return annually to our 17th century farmhouse. Set in rolling countryside ¾ mile from old A30. Good home cooking and every comfort. Central for Dartmoor and coast, 8 miles Cornwall. Lounge with colour TV and log fires. 3 doubles, 2 family rooms all en suite (1 ground floor). Tea/coffee-making facilities, night storage heaters, colour TV. Heated outdoor swimming pool. Birthdays, anniversaries catered for. Come and spoil yourselves. Fire certificate held. Open all year (closed Christmas).

SELF-CATERING

The Granary and Little Week Barns, Week Farm, Bridestowe, Okehampton, Devon EX20 4HZ

Margaret Hockridge
☎ **01837 861221**
🆂🅲 **From £180–£595**
Sleeps 5/8 + cot
🐕 ♿ 🐎 ▪
🔑 🔑 🔑 🔑
*Up to Highly
Commended*

A cream tea awaits you at these semi-detached barn conversions situated in a pretty part of Devon countryside where scenery, moorland and wildlife are magnificent. Near A30, ideal touring base for both coasts, Cornwall, Dartmoor and numerous attractions. Attractive garden with patio, BBQ, heated outdoor swimming pool. Well fitted kitchen, (washing machine, microwave, dish-washer, fridge freezer), lounge, colour TV. Open all year.

Rubbytown Farm, Gulworthy, Tavistock, Devon PL19 8PA

Mary Steer
☎ **01822 832493**
🆂🅲 **From £150–£350**
🐎 ✂ 🐾
🔑 🔑 🔑 🔑 *Commended*

Recently converted old granite barns retaining original features. Beautifully furnished, fully equipped kitchens, wonderful views with gardens and orchard. Come and relax in this beautiful countryside, and see foxes and badgers at play and much more wildlife. Everyone welcome, we aim to make your holiday one to remember. Open all year.

England's West Country

Upper Tamar, North West Devon

Group Contact: *Marlene Heard* ☎ *01409 253339*

This area covers the North Cornwall/Devon border area with its glorious coastline and miles of sandy beaches, sheltered coves and rugged cliffs, friendly resorts and quiet villages, country market towns and wide open spaces peacefully set in undulating countryside.

The coastline from Hartland to Crackington Haven is as dramatic as it is beautiful. Bude, once described by the late Sir John Betjeman as 'the least rowdy resort in the country' has retained its atmosphere of easy-going charm while catering for the most discerning of modern day tourists. Another resort which tourists are advised to visit is Clovelly with its steeply cobbled streets. Holsworthy and Launceston have weekly cattle and pannier markets. Both have a golf course and sports hall and Launceston also has a heated swimming pool. There are several pony trekking centres in the area and facilities for fishing at sea, on the lake or by the river.

This area has been recommended as a restful, comfortable base for touring the whole of Devon and Cornwall. There are many tourist attractions including the moors, National Trust properties, steam railways, leisure parks, museums and the cities of Exeter, Plymouth and Truro all within easy driving distance.

Northam
Bideford
South Molton
A361
Wellington
A39
Tiverton
27
A386
A377
28
Stratton
A3072
Honiton
Bude
M5
A30
Holsworthy
Crediton
Okehampton
A30
A388
29
Exeter
30
Sidmouth
Launceston
31
A386
Budleigh Salterton
A39
A30
A380
Dawlish
Tavistock
A38
Newton Abbot
Teignmouth
Bodmin
Torquay
Liskeard
Buckfastleigh
Torbay
Saltash
Plymouth
Totnes
Brixham
Lostwithiel
Looe
Torpoint
Dartmouth

BED AND BREAKFAST

(and evening meal)

Cornakey Farm, Morwenstow, Bude, Cornwall EX23 9SS

Mrs Monica Heywood
☎ **01288 331260**
🅱 **From £15–£16**
EM From £7
Sleeps 6
🐕 🍽 ■
🍲 *Applied*

This is a 220–acre mixed coastal farm with extensive views of sea and Lundy island from bedrooms and bathroom. Good touring centre with easy reach of quiet beaches. The farmhouse offers one family room en suite and one double room. Bathroom, toilet, lounge (colour TV), dining room, games room. Children welcome at reduced rates. Cot, highchair, babysitting. Good home cooking with fresh vegetables. Open all year except Christmas.

Elm Park, Bridgerule, Holsworthy, Devon EX22 7EL

Sylvia Lucas
☎ **01288 381231**
🅱 **From £14.50–£16.50**
EM £7
Sleeps 12
🐓 🐕 🍽 ■
🍲🍲 *Approved*

Elm Park is 6 miles from Cornish surfing beaches at Bude and ideal for touring both Devon and Cornwall. Children are especially welcomed with pony and tractor and trailer rides. Twin and family rooms with en suite, colour TV and tea/coffee making facilities. Ample 4-course dinners with freshly produced fare and delicious sweets. Big weekly reductions and everyone made most welcome and comfortable. Games room. Open Mar–Nov.

THOSE LITTLE EXTRAS

For advice on farms that can offer 'extras' such as four-poster beds, special diets, farm trails, fishing rights – even stabling and trekking arrangements if you are bringing your own horse – ring the Farm Holiday Bureau on (01203) 696909.

DEVON FARMS

Availability of farms in Devon can be easily discovered by ringing 01548 550055.

England's West Country
Cream of Cornwall

Group Contacts: BB *Pamela Treleaven* ☎/Fax 01726 75819
SC *Evelyn Julian* ☎/Fax 01503 262855

Cornwall has a coastline of 326 miles with its unique coastal footpath. It is a county of amazing contrasts with wonderful stretches of firm golden sands and soaring cliffs on the north coast, to tiny coves, picturesque fishing villages and sheltered, wooded estuaries on the south coast. Beaches from Bude to St Ives are famous for the wonderful Atlantic surf, whereas south coast resorts, such as Looe, Fowey, Mevagissey and Falmouth are ideal centres for sailing, fishing and windsurfing, with numerous safe bathing beaches spread all along this coast.

However, Cornwall has more than just the coastline to tempt you – there is a wealth of potteries and art galleries throughout the county (notably the Tate Gallery at St Ives). A wide choice of famous gardens and National Trust properties such as St Michael's Mount and Lanhydrock are open to the public. The atmospheric Bodmin Moor with mystical standing stones, Tintagel with King Arthur's Castle and the Iron Age village, Chysanster are just some of the fascinating places waiting for you to explore.

BED AND BREAKFAST
(and evening meal)

Arrallas, Ladock, Truro, Cornwall TR2 4NP ①

Mrs Barbara Holt
☎ **01872 510379**
Fax 01872 510200
BB From £18–£20
EM From £9.50–£12.50
Sleeps 6
🐴 🎇 ■ 🐾
👑👑👑 *Highly Commended*

Arrallas is part of the Duchy of Cornwall enjoying a "heart of the country" peaceful atmosphere. We are adjacent to 400 acres of Duchy woodlands, offering wonderful walks and superb views from the house. 15 minutes drive from the North coast. Centrally situated for touring. All bedrooms en suite (2 double, 1 twin) with TVs. Quality menus. Choice of 2, 3 or 4 courses. Full central heating. Parking. Beverage facilities. Phone for directions. Open Feb–Nov.

Bokiddick Farm, Lanivet, Bodmin, Cornwall PL30 5HP ②

Gill Hugo
☎ **01208 831481**
BB From £18–£21
Sleeps 5
🐴(3)
👑👑 *Commended*

The warmest of welcomes awaits you. Relax in our friendly farmhouse and enjoy delicious farmhouse cooking. Two pretty bedrooms, both en suite with colour TV. Explore our dairy farm, watch the milking. Central location for both north and south coasts, good touring base, close to National Trust Lanhydrock House. Wonderful views. Open Easter–Oct.

Bucklawren Farm, St Martin-by-Looe, Cornwall PL13 1NZ ③

Mrs Jean Henly
☎ **01503 240738**
Fax 01503 240481
BB From £17–£19
EM From £9.50
Sleeps 12
🐴 🗗 🐶 🎇 ■
👑👑👑 *Highly Commended*

Bucklawren is situated deep in unspoilt countryside yet only 1 mile from the beach, 2½ miles from Looe. It is a large working farm with a spacious, comfortable farmhouse which enjoys beautiful sea views and a large garden. We offer excellent accommodation with family and en suite rooms. Farmhouse cooking in a friendly and relaxed atmosphere. Winner 1995 West Country Farm Holiday Award. Open Mar–Nov (incl).

Caduscott, East Taphouse, Liskeard, Cornwall PL14 4NG ④

Lindsay Pendray
☎/Fax **01579 320262**
BB From £15–£18
EM From £8.50
Sleeps 4/5
🥢 🐴 ■
Listed *Approved*

Down the lane wild flowers nod in passing; relax and unwind in attractive 17th century listed farmhouse peeping over the valley where streams converge to journey to the sea at Looe. Double room (en suite, toilet/shower), adjoining twin bedded room. Personal attention, facilities for children. Meals all prepared/served in traditional style. Open Apr–Sept incl. Easter. Out of season advanced bookings taken.

Carglonnon Farm, Duloe, Liskeard, Cornwall PL14 4QA ⑤

Mrs Ann Bray
☎ **01579 320210**
BB From £15–£16
Sleeps 6
🐴 🎇
👑👑 *Commended*

A lovely 18th century Georgian farmhouse which is part of the Duchy of Cornwall Estate. A working mixed farm of 230 acres, situated 4½ miles from fishing port of Looe. Forestry walks from farm. Golf, horse-riding, Theme Park, coastal walking, moors all nearby. Two doubles en suite. One twin with private bathroom. Tea/coffee-making facilities, central heating. Open Jan–Dec.

6   **Degembris Farmhouse,** St Newlyn East, Newquay, Cornwall TR8 5HY

Kathy Woodley
☎ 01872 510555
Fax 01872 510230
BB From £18
EM From £10
Sleeps 12
♿ ☂ ▪
🐾🐾🐾 *Highly Commended*

Degembris nestles in a south facing hillside overlooking a beautiful wooded valley. Its low beams and log fires make this listed 18th century farmhouse a delight. Come inside (mind your head!) and enjoy the charming Georgian surroundings, complete with creaky floorboards! Take a stroll along our farm trail which wanders through woodland and fields of corn. Open all year except Christmas.

---

7   **Ennys,** St Hilary, Penzance, Cornwall TR20 9BZ

Sue White
☎/Fax 01736 740262
BB From £20–£26
EM From £16
Sleeps 10
♿(5) ☞ ☂ ▪ �ూ
🐾🐾🐾 *Highly Commended*

Beautiful 16th century manor farm in idyllically peaceful wooded surroundings. Excellent suppers by candlelight. Bread baked daily. Log fires. Romantic four-poster overlooking walled gardens, tennis court and swimming pool. Self-contained family suite. Near to beaches, St Michael's Mount and St Ives Tate Gallery. Weekend winter breaks. Featured in *Country Living, The Daily Telegraph, Sunday Times* and *Traveller.* Open all year (closed Christmas).

---

8   **Hendra Farm,** Polbathic, Torpoint, Cornwall PL11 3DT

Mrs A Hoskin
☎ 01503 250225
BB From £14–£17
Sleeps 5
⚥ ♿
🐾🐾 *Commended*

Hendra is a working farm situated in an area of outstanding natural beauty. The fishing port of Looe is 6 miles, and safe bathing beaches of Downderry and Seaton only 2 miles. The main shopping centre of Plymouth is within ½ hours travelling. TV lounge. Family room with en suite shower and WC. Babysitting. Open Mar–Nov.

---

9   **Higher Kergilliack Farm,** Budock, Falmouth, Cornwall TR11 5PB

Jean Pengelly
☎ 01326 372271
BB From £15–£17.50
EM From £8
Sleeps 6
♿ 🐕 ☂
🐾🐾 *Commended*

18th century Georgian listed farmhouse on 130-acre dairy farm, former residence of Bishop of Exeter. Poppy our friendly dog will show you round the farm and garden. Overlooks Falmouth Bay near the seal sanctuary and Trebah and Glendurgan Gardens. 1 double with en suite WC and shower, 1 twin/family with en suite WC and bath. Take 2nd right on A39 at Hillhead roundabout. Open all year.

---

10   **Higher Trevurvas Farm,** Ashton, Helston, Cornwall TR13 9TZ

Kate Jenkin
☎ 01736 763613
BB From £17–£18.50
EM £11
Sleeps 8
♿(10) ⚥ ☂ ▪
🐾🐾 *Commended*

Traditional hospitality, modern creature comforts, peace and quiet, wonderful walking country, farmhouse breakfasts, excellent dinners (optional) – all this available at Trevurvas, a small beef and sheep farm overlooking Mounts Bay. Three doubles and one twin room, all with en suite or private facilities. Colour brochure available. Open Jan–Nov.

---

11   **Kerryanna Country House,** Treleaven Farm, Mevagissey, Cornwall PL26 6RZ

Linda Hennah
☎ 01726 843558
BB From £18–£24
EM From £10
Sleeps 12
♿(5) ▪
🐾🐾🐾 *Commended*

Surrounded by farmland, wildlife and flowers, the farm is only 8 minutes' walk from the centre of Mevagissey. Romantic en suite bedrooms with TV and beverage tray. Beautiful gardens with heated outdoor pool and stunning views. Games barn, putting green. Hearty breakfasts and delicious suppers. A warm welcome assured. Mentioned in the *Daily Telegraph* and Gill Charlton's *A Week in Cornwall.* Open Mar–Oct.

Longstone Farm, Trenear, Helston, Cornwall TR13 0HG   (12)

Gillian Lawrance
☎ **01326 572483**
BB **From £16–£18**
EM From £8
Sleeps 14
🐎 ♿ 🐄
🍵 *Commended*

A warm welcome awaits you at Longstone Farm, situated in the centre of West Cornwall's peaceful countryside. Ideal for touring both coasts and holiday attractions including Flambards. Traditional farmhouse fare served and leisure facilities nearby. All bedrooms en suite or private facilities. Ample room to relax and make yourself at home in our TV lounge and sunlounge/play area. Open Feb–Nov.

Loskeyle Farm, St Tudy, Bodmin, Cornwall PL30 3PW   (13)

Mrs Sandra Menhinick
☎ **01208 851005**
BB **From £14–£15**
EM From £8
Sleeps 6
🐎
🍵 *Commended*

Loskeyle is a working dairy farm in the Duchy of Cornwall where a warm welcome awaits you. Relax and enjoy the peace and tranquillity of farm life. Chidlren especially welcome, free babysitting by arrangement. Delicious farmhouse cooking using local produce. Watch milking, feed hens. Ideal base for north and south coasts. Golf, camel trail nearby, also pony trekking over moors only a stone's throw away. Open Mar–Nov.

Manuels Farm, Quintrell Downs, Newquay, Cornwall TR8 4NY   (14)

Mrs Jean Wilson
☎ **01637 873577**
BB **From £19**
EM £12
Sleeps 10
🐎 ✂ 🐄 🐎 🎪 🧺
🍵🍵 *Highly Commended*

A listed 17th century farmhouse situated in a sheltered valley, 2 miles from Newquay's magnificent beaches. Relax in peaceful countryside in this traditional Cornish farmhouse. Beautifully furnished, delicious plentiful farmhouse cooking. Log fires. Award winning garden. Children especially welcome. Nursery teas, free babysitting, play area, pony rides. Meet a whole variety of pets and farm animals on this friendly working farm. Open all year (closed Christmas).

Polhormon Farm, Polhormon Lane, Mullion, Helston, Cornwall TR12 7JE   (15)

Alice Harry
☎ **01326 240304**
BB **From £15–£18**
Sleeps 8
🐎 🐄 🎪 🌱
🍵 *Commended*

We're "proper Cornish" down on Polhormon Farm. Come and enjoy a relaxing holiday in our Georgian home set high and above Poldhu beach on unspoilt Lizard Peninsula. A great place for beaching and cliff walks. Children very welcome at reduced rates and free babysitting. Comfortable, well furnished rooms, family atmosphere and personal attention. Spoil yourselves. Open Easter–Nov.

Polsue Manor Farm, Tresillian, Truro, Cornwall TR2 4BP   (16)

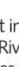

Geraldine Holliday
☎ **01872 520234**
BB **From £15.50–£17.50**
EM From £8.50
Sleeps 14
🐎 🐄 🧺 🌱
🍵 *Approved*

The farmhouse on this 190-acre working farm, set in glorious countryside, overlooks the tidal Tresillian River and one of the prettiest parts of Cornwall. Only minutes from the beautiful cathedral city of Truro. Centrally situated between north and south coasts, ideal centre for touring the county. Delightful country walks. All bedrooms have H/C. Traditional home cooking, comfortable, relaxed friendly atmosphere. Open most of year.

Poltarrow Farm, St Mewan, St Austell, Cornwall PL26 7DR   (17)

Judith Nancarrow
☎ **01726 67111**
BB **From £18–£20**
EM From £10
Sleeps 12
🐄 🍵 🎣 🍵 🎪 🧺
🍵🍵 *Highly Commended*

Poltarrow is a delightful farmhouse, set in 45 acres between Fowey and Mevagissey. The bedrooms have views across rolling countryside and are individually decorated with bathrooms, TV and tea/coffee. The dining room serves traditional farmhouse fare using local meat, fish and vegetables cooked by the Aga. Relax beside a log fire and plan your day exploring Cornwall from this central location. Open all year except Christmas and New Year.

---

18   **Rose Farm,** Chyanhal, Drift, Penzance, Cornwall TR19 6AN

Mrs Penny Lally
☎ 01736 731808
BB From £17.50–£19
Sleeps 8
🐎 ☂
☙❧ *Commended*

Rose Farm is a small working farm in a little hamlet close to the picturesque fishing villages of Mousehole and Newlyn and 7 miles from Lands End. The 200-year-old granite farmhouse is cosy with pretty, en suite rooms. 1 double, 1 family suite and a romantic 15th century four poster room in barn annexe. We have all manner of animals, from pedigree cattle to pot-bellied pigs! Open all year (closed Christmas).

---

19   **Treffry Farm,** Lanhydrock, Bodmin, Cornwall PL30 5AF

Pat Smith
☎/Fax 01208 74405
BB From £19
Sleeps 6
✂ 🐎(6) 🐓 ➳ ☂ 🐎 ▪
☙❧❧ *Highly Commended*

Historic, listed Georgian farmhouse (1720) on 200 acre dairy farm adjoining National Trust Lanhydrock. Three pretty bedrooms with colour TV and en suite facilities, one with four-poster bed. Ideal location for touring Cornwall within easy reach of many beaches. Special activity breaks including golf, fishing, cycling and walking can be arranged. Warm welcome guaranteed. Open all year except Christmas and New Year.

---

20   **Tregaddra Farm,** Cury, Cross Lanes, Helston, Cornwall TR12 7BB

June Lugg
☎/Fax 01326 240235
BB From £18.50
EM From £8
Sleeps 14
✂ 🐎 ▪
☙❧❧ *Highly Commended*

Unwind in this beautifully furnished 18th century farmhouse with en suite bedrooms, two with balconies. Heated swimming pool, lovely garden and views of peaceful countryside for a 15m radius. Beaches, coastal walks, golf, horse riding, sailing and tourist attractions nearby. Children love the calves, barn owls, tractors, games room and farmhouse fare. Open all year.

---

21   **Tregaswith Farmhouse,** Tregaswith, near Newquay, Cornwall TR8 4HY

John & Jacqui Elsom
☎ 01637 881181
BB From £20–£22
EM From £10
Sleeps 6
🐎(10) 🐓 ✂ 🐓 ▪
☙❧❧ *Highly Commended*

Tregaswith is a small hamlet just outside Newquay, 5 minutes' drive to beaches and several National Trust properties near. The farmhouse built over 250 years ago, now a smallholding breeding rare poultry and horses. Pony rides and an introduction to carriage driving can be arranged. We have a reputation for delicious food. 3 beautiful bedrooms, all en suite. Antiques and oak beams throughout. Open all year.

---

22   **Tregidgeo,** Grampound, Truro, Cornwall TR2 4SP

Mrs Sally Wade
☎/Fax 01726 882450
BB From £18–£20
EM From £9.50
Sleeps 6
🐎(10) ➳ ▪
☙❧ *Commended*

Tregidgeo is a mixed farm of 216 acres. The elegant farmhouse is found in a beautifully secluded and peaceful setting overlooking lovely gardens, lake and countryside. Excellent spacious accomodation. Bedrooms all en suite with TV, beverage facilities and CH. Luxury four-poster. Delicious home cooking with fresh farm and local produce. Private coarse fishing. A very relaxing holiday. Open Mar–Nov.

---

23   **Treglisson,** Hayle, Cornwall TR27 5JT

Carole Runnalls
☎ 01736 753141
BB From £18.50–£23.50
Sleeps 15
🐎 🅰 🛏 ▪ ☂
☙❧ *Highly Commended*

Treglisson is a listed Grade II 18th century farmhouse set in peaceful, rural surroundings yet only 1 mile from the A30. Comfortable beds, antique furniture and fresh flowers. Hearty breakfasts served in the conservatory. We also have a heated indoor swimming pool. Close to 3 mile-long golden sandy beach. An ideal base for touring West Cornwall. Open Feb–Oct.

Tregonan, Tregony, Truro, Cornwall TR2 5SN (24)

Sandra Collins
☎ 01872 530249
🆙 From £14
Sleeps 6
🎠 ▪
👄 *Commended*

Discover Tregonan, tucked away down half–mile private lane. Comfortable, spacious farmhouse set in secluded garden, at centre of 300 acre arable and sheep farm. 6 miles west of Mevagissey, on threshold of renowned Roseland Peninsula. 2 beaches within 3 miles. All bedrooms H/C, beverage-making facilities, radio. Good selection of eating places locally. Open Mar–Oct.

Tregondale Farm, Menheniot, Liskeard, Cornwall PL14 3RG (25)

Stephanie Rowe
☎/Fax 01579 342407
🆙 From £17.50–£19.50
EM From £9
Sleeps 6
🍴 🎠 ♞ ▪
👄👄
Highly Commended

Come and join our family with the peace of the countryside near the coast. Explore our woodland farm trail amidst wildlife, flowers and birds singing on a 200-acre mixed farm. Pedigree animals naturally reared, tennis court and play area. The characteristic farmhouse with all en suite bedrooms with TV and tea/coffee, is beautifully set in original walled garden, home grown produce our speciality. Idyllic for discovering Cornwall. Open all year.

Trehane Farm, Trevalga, Boscastle, Cornwall PL35 0EB (26)

Mrs Sarah James
☎ 01840 250510
🆙 From £16–£18.50
EM From £10
Sleeps 6
🐕 🍴 🎠 ♞ ▪ ✾
Applied

Welcome to Trehane, a dairy farm on the spectacular North Cornwall heritage coast. Farmhouse set in magnificent position overlooking sea, superb coastal views. We offer a comfortable friendly atmosphere and wholesome nourishing food using fresh farm produce and home baked bread. Enjoy fine walks along the coast or inland on to Bodmin Moor. Learn to spin. Open all year.

Trenderway Farm, Pelynt, Polperro, Cornwall PL13 2LY (27)

Mrs Lynne Tuckett
☎ 01503 272214
🆙 From £22–£28
Sleeps 8
🍴
👄👄 *Highly Commended*

Built in the late 16th century, Trenderway is set in beautiful countryside yet only 5 minutes from Polperro. Bedrooms here are truly superb, decorated with the flair of a professional interior designer. A hearty farmhouse breakfast is served in the sunny conservatory. Although an evening meal is not provided, excellent nearby restaurants can be recommended. Open all year except Christmas.

Treveria Farm, Widegates, Looe, Cornwall PL13 1QR (28)

Mrs J. Kitto
☎/Fax 01503 240237
🆙 From £18–£20
Sleeps 6
🎠 🐾 🍴 📺 ♞ ▪
👄 👄 *Commended*

Treveria is a delightful manor house set in a large garden overlooking the farm and surrounding countryside. A high standard of accommodation is offered with beautifully decorated en suite rooms, one with four-poster. All rooms have colour TV and beverage facilities. Looe and Polperro with their quaint harbours and excellent restaurants are only a short drive away. Open Mar–Nov.

Trewellard Manor Farm, Pendeen, Penzance, Cornwall TR19 7SU (29)

Mrs Marion Bailey
☎/Fax 01736 788526
🆙 From £16
Sleeps 6
🎠
👄 👄 *Commended*

The farm is situated in a superb coastal position between Lands End and St Ives. We offer a friendly, relaxed atmosphere with seasonal fires and CH. 3 bedrooms (1 en suite) all with tea/coffee facilities. Use of swimming pool (June–Sept) with good beaches within easy reach. Golf and coarse fishing available nearby. This is an outstanding area for walking, either inland or on the coast path. Open all year (closed Christmas).

30 **Wheatley Farm,** Maxworthy, Launceston, Cornwall PL15 8LY

Valerie Griffin
☎/Fax 01566 781232
BB From £16–£23
EM From £11.50
Sleeps 9
♿ ⚥

♨ ♨ ♨ *Highly Commended*

Beautifully situated close to Crackington Haven and the spectacular North Cornwall coast, Wheatley Farm is the ideal place to escape and unwind. Lovely old farmhouse on working farm. Delightful bedrooms, all en suite, one with 4-poster bed. Friendly atmosphere, personal attention at all times. Our speciality is our excellent, carefully prepared food which brings guests back time and again. Open Easter–Sept.

SELF-CATERING

31 **Beechleigh Cottage,** Tregondale Farm, Meheniot, Liskeard, Cornwall PL14 3RG

Stephanie Rowe
☎/Fax 01579 342407
SC From £90–£395
Sleeps 4 (+ cot)
♿ ⚥ ⚘

⚘ ⚘ ⚘ ⚘ *Highly Commended*

In the leigh of our farmhouse beech tree, this peaceful, attractive character cottage nestles. Warm and cosy in winter, barbecue on the patio in summer, play tennis, explore the woodland farm trail, hear birds singing, enjoy wild flowers and lambs in Spring. See South Devon cattle. A warm welcome awaits you all the year. Come and discover the beauty of Cornwall. Open all year.

32 **Bokiddick Farm,** Lanivet, Bodmin, Cornwall PL30 5HP

Gill Hugo
☎ 01208 831481
SC From £90–£330
Sleeps 4
♿ ⚘

⚘ ⚘ ⚘ *Approved*

Beautifully situated twixt coast and moors lies Bokiddick, our pretty two bedroomed-bungalow enjoying magnificent views. Peaceful location, central for both north and south coasts, good touring base. Explore our dairy farm, watch the milking or just relax in the garden. The warmest of welcomes awaits you. Close to Lanhydrock House. Open all year.

33 **Bucklawren Farm,** St Martin-by-Looe, Cornwall PL13 1NZ

Mrs Jean Henly
☎ 01503 240738
Fax 01503 240481
SC From £100–£420
Sleeps 2/6
⚘ ♿ ⚥ ♨ ⚘

⚘ ⚘ ⚘ ⚘ *Highly Commended*

Three attractive stone cottages recently tastefully converted from farm buildings, furnished to high standard, and set in a large garden. Bucklawren is situated in the countryside by the sea and only three miles from the fishing village of Looe. Ideal position for coastal paths, National Trust properties, fishing trips, beaches and Plymouth. Winner 1995 West Country Farm Holiday Award. Open Mar–Jan.

34 **Cadson Manor Farm,** Callington, Cornwall PL17 7HW

Brenda Crago
☎/Fax 01579 383969
SC From £150–£380
Sleeps 4 + cot
♿ ⚘ ⚘

⚘ ⚘ ⚘ *Highly Commended*

The friendliest welcome awaits you at Cadson, true Cornish hospitality guaranteed to make your stay extra special. Traditional furnishings tastefully blended with modern conveniences, sitting peacefully beneath Cadson Bury, affording unspoilt views of this ancient monument set in the beautiful Lynher Valley. Secluded, yet close to all main towns, riding, golf, beaches all within easy reach. Farm & river walks.

The Coach House, c/o Lantallack Farm, Landrake, Nr Saltash, Cornwall PL12 5AE   **35**

Nichola Walker
☎ 01752 851281
SC From £185–£450
Sleeps 6/7
🎠 🛏 🐴 🎾 🐕 🏃 💼
🐾 🐾 🐾 🐾
Commended

Georgian farm coach house, extremely comfortable with oustanding views across undulating countryside and wooded valleys. The perfect retreat for a relaxing holiday. Ponies, sheep, ducks, hens and a friendly ram called Donald. Weekly art classes in Barn Studio. Golf at St Mellion, 10 mins. away. Close to sea and moors. 2 bathrooms, log fire, CH, phone, microwave, dishwasher and games room. Linen/electricity inclusive. Open Mar–Nov.

Glynn Barton Farm Cottages, Glynn Barton, Cardinham, Bodmin, Cornwall PL30 4AX   **36**

Diana Mindel
☎ 01208 821375
SC From £120–£455
Sleeps 2/6
🎠 ♿ 💼
🐾 🐾 🐾 🐾
Commended

Peaceful, picturesque hamlet amidst breathtaking valley views, surrounded by forestry and farmland. Splendid woodland walks on your doorstep. Relax by landscaped, secluded heated pool, or rest in attractive four poster bed. Friendly donkeys, goats, chickens and pony in nearby paddock. Centrally positioned for exploring the many mysteries and beauties of captivating Cornwall. Open all year.

Hendra Farm, Rose, Truro, Cornwall TR4 9PS   **37**

Janet Symons
☎ 01872 572273
SC From £180–£450
Sleeps 7
🎠 🐴 🎾 🐕 🔫 🐑
🐾 🐾 🐾 🐾 Commended

Spacious old farmhouse with pretty garden, two bathrooms and good firm beds. Explore our 160-acre dairy and sheep farm, sunbathe or fish by secluded private lake, or follow the footpath to the coastal path and glorious beaches. Tariff includes central heating, log fire, linen, pet. Babysitting usually available. Open all year.

Hilltown Farm, St Neot, Liskeard, Cornwall PL14 6PT   **38**

Julia Holden-White
☎ 01579 320565
SC From £100–£325
Sleeps 4/5
🎠 🐴 🐕
🐾 🐾 🐾 Commended

Close to the moors, our farm's comfortably converted old stone barn with its peaceful atmosphere makes two cosy holiday homes. Excellent location for walking, cycling, fishing and entertaining children. Easy drive to north and south coast. Included: pony rides/drives, river fishing, barbecue, sandpit, log fires, games room. Highly recommended for all ages. Open all year.

Lodge Barton Farm, Liskeard, Cornwall PL14 4JX   **39**

Rosanne Hodin
☎ 01579 344432
SC From £100–£380
Sleeps 2/5 + cot
🔫 🎠 🐕 🔫 🐑
🐾 🐾 🐾 🐾
Commended

Lodge Barton is set in a beautiful river valley flanked by woodland. We keep a milking herd of goats and also have calves, ducks, hens and geese. Everyone can help milk, feed and collect eggs. Our character cottages are luxuriously equipped including heating, woodburners, video, linen, laundry room, private gardens and playground. We are close to sea, moors, sailing, windsurfing, riding, fishing, golf. Open all year.

Lower Trengale Farm, Liskeard, Cornwall PL14 6HF   **40**

Louise Kidd
☎ 01579 321019
Fax 01579 321432
SC From £100–£395
Sleeps 4/5
🔫 🎠 🏃 🐟 🐑
🐾 🐾 🐾 🐾 Commended

A small farm, set in beautiful countryside, offering three comfortable and well equipped cottages which have been carefully converted from a stone barn. Children love helping with the cows, sheep, pigs, hens and their young. There is a pony to ride, a sandpit, swings and table tennis. Lovely views from the garden. All linen supplied, laundry and babysitting available. Open all year.

41   **Manuels Farm,** Quintrell Downs, Newquay, Cornwall TR8 4NY

Alan & Jean Wilson
☎ 01637 873577
ⓈⒸ From £100–£430
Sleeps 2/5 + cot
🐕 🐎 🐈 ⛺ ▪
🔑 🔑 🔑 *Commended*

Imagine a family holiday close to Newquay's magnificent beaches but tucked away in your own quiet valley. Secluded from the crowd but perfectly placed for touring, walking and riding. Your own character cottage in the country, on the farm, with gardens, flowers, pets and farm animals around you. The children will enjoy the calves, tractor and ponies while you relax. Electricity and linen included. Open all year.

42   **Old Newham Farm,** Otterham, Camelford, Cornwall PL32 9SR

Mrs Mary Purdue
☎ 01840 230470
ⓈⒸ From £100–£460
Sleeps 2/4/6
🐎 🐕 🐈 ⛺
🔑 🔑 🔑 🔑 *Approved*

Three individual stone and slate cottages around an old farmyard dating back to medieval times, at the end of a quiet country lane. Our 30-acre farm is managed in a traditional way with cattle, sheep and other small animals for the children. Here you can find the peace of the Cornish countryside yet be only 3 miles from the most spectacular coastline in the area. Cottages with character, open fire, CH. Open all year.

43   **Pencarrow Cottage,** Trevissick Farm, Trenarren, St Austell, Cornwall PL26 6BQ

Mrs Pamela Treleaven
☎/Fax 01726 75819
ⓈⒸ From £120–£350
Sleeps 6
🐎 🐕 🐈 ⛺
🔑 🔑 🔑 – 🔑 🔑 🔑 🔑
Commended

Stay 'far from the madding crowd' in our 18th century cottage in solitary seclusion or 'to the manor born' in a family apartment in the east wing of the manor farmhouse enjoying spectacular views of sea and countryside. Boasting 3 miles of coastline, Trevissick is situated between St Austell and Mevagissey Bays. Golf and driving range 1 mile. Excellent walking and birdwatching. Open all year.

44   **Poltarrow Farm ,** St Mewan, St Austell, Cornwall PL26 7DR

Judith Nancarrow
☎ 01726 67111
ⓈⒸ From £125–£430
Sleeps 2/6
🐕 🐎 🖥 🦽 🐴 🐈 ⛺ ▪
🔑 🔑 🔑 🔑
Commended

Charming, cosy cottages set in 45 acres of peaceful farmland on the south coast between Fowey and Mevagissey. Excellent central location for touring Cornwall's coast and countryside. Each cottage is individual, featuring wood beams, stone walls, log fires, four-poster, chintz and roses round the door. Everyone enjoys the freedom of the farm, meeting the animals and a ride on Taffy the pony. Open all year.

45   **Rescorla Farm Cottages,** Rescorla, St Austell, Cornwall PL26 8YT

Judith Clemo
☎/Fax 01726 850168
ⓈⒸ From £160–£400
Sleeps 5
🐕 🐎 🎪 🖥
🔑 🔑 🔑 – 🔑 🔑 🔑 🔑
Commended

Relax in your own rural retreat. Peaceful hamlet location, perfect for touring coast and countryside. Friendly farm, pets for the children, eggs to collect while you relax by a log fire or visit the nearby trout fishery. Tariff includes linen, towels and electricity. Open all year.

46   **Rooke Farm Cottages,** Rooke Farm, Chapel Amble, Wadebridge, Cornwall PL27 6ES

Mrs Gill Reskelly
☎ 01208 880368
Fax 01208 880600
ⓈⒸ From £190–£630
Sleeps 2–7 (+ cot)
🐎 🐕 ⛺
🔑 🔑 🔑 🔑 🔑 *Highly*
Commended

Something special – luxury country cottages set in 235 acres of Duchy of Cornwall farmland. On outskirts of the pretty Chapel Amble close to many golden beaches. Exclusively furnished and equipped with all that's required for a relaxing holiday. Pretty en suite bedrooms, log fires, dishwasher, satellite TV, hi fi and phone. Electricity heating, quality linen and towels inclusive. Each has private enclosed garden with barbecue. Brochure. Open all year.

Tredethick Farm Cottages, The Guildhouse, Lostwithiel, Cornwall PL22 0LE

Tim & Nicky Reed
☎/Fax 01208 873618
⌗ From £130–£440
Sleeps 28
🐂🐕♿🏹🐎🛥️🏺🎾 ⊚
🌳🌳🌳🌳 *Highly Commended*

Exceptional character cottages set amongst beautiful countryside. Walk from your door through meadows and woods to the River Fowey and on to the quiet creekside village of Lerryn – the inspiration behind *The Wind in the Willows*. Tredethick makes an ideal touring base for exploring the delights of coast and countryside or simply relaxing and enjoying the rural idyll. Winners of 4 awards. Open all year.

Tredinnick Farm, Duloe, Liskeard, Cornwall PL14 4PJ

Mrs Angela Barrett
☎ 01503 262997
Fax 01503 265554
⌗ From £125–£475
Sleeps 2/10 (+ cot)
🐕🐎
🌳🌳🌳🌳 *Commended*

Welcome to our 470-acre Duchy of Cornwall farm. The fully equipped, spacious half of farmhouse is designed to make sure your holiday is enjoyable. Log fires, electric blankets, CH when required, colour TV, dishwasher, microwave, bedlinen, laundry room, own garden. Ideal position for fishing villages of Looe and Polperro, beaches, NT properties, riding, golf, local pubs serving good food. Open Mar–Oct and Christmas.

Treffry Farm Cottages, Treffry Farm, Lanhydrock, Bodmin, Cornwall PL30 5AF

Pat Smith
☎/Fax 01208 74405
⌗ From £85–£550
Sleeps 2/8
🐂🐕🐎🐈🎾🏺🎾
🌳🌳🌳🌳 –
🌳🌳🌳🌳🌳 *Highly Commended*

Imagine country cottages, rambling roses, chintzy sofas, rocking chairs, pot pourri, log fires on winter days, barbecues on summer nights – they're here at Treffry. Our dairy farm adjoins the National Trust at Lanhydrock where you can walk for miles in glorious parkland. Central for exploring all Cornwall. Relax and meet our farm animals and pony. Special golf, fishing, walking and cycling breaks. A warm welcome awaits you. Open all year.

Tregevis Farm, St Martin, Helston, Cornwall TR12 6DN

Julie Bray
☎ 01326 231265
⌗ From £170–£400
Sleeps 7 + cot
🐖🐕
🌳🌳🌳🌳 *Commended*

Come and relax at Tregevis, a working dairy farm in the picturesque Helford River area, just ½ mile from the little village of St. Martin and 5 miles from sandy beaches. The accommodation is a self-contained, spacious part of the farmhouse, very comfortable, well equipped and with a games room. The large lawn area with swings will prove popular with children, as will our farm animals. Open Easter–Oct.

Treharrock Farm Cottages, Treharrock Farm, Pendoggett, Port Isaac, Cornwall PL29 3TA 51

Linda Leigh-Firbank
☎ 01208 880517
⌗ From £150–£395
Sleeps 6
🐕🏹🏺
🌳🌳🌳🌳 *Highly Commended*

A relaxing break awaits you in one of our two cosy cottages with breathtaking views of countryside and coastline. Superbly equipped with open fire for those chilly evenings. Electricity and linen included. Treharrock is a family-run dairy farm which offers you a chance to see our way of life. Everyone welcome. Open all year.

Treleaven Farm Cottages, Treleaven Farm, Mevagissey, Cornwall PL26 6RZ 52

Mrs Linda Hennah
☎ 01726 843558
⌗ From £150–£525
Sleeps 4–6
🐕
🌳🌳🌳🌳 *Highly Commended*

Surrounded by rambling countryside, wildlife and flowers, the farm is only 8 minutes' walk from the centre of Mevagissey. Each cottage has luxury pine fitted kitchen with dishwasher, microwave, fridge/freezer and cooker. Lovely bathroom with shower, cosy lounge with TV, some en suite bedrooms. CH included in winter. Linen and electricity inclusive. Laundry room. Ample parking. Games barn. Next to Heligan Gardens and central for touring. Open all year.

53   **Tremadart Farm,** Duloe, Liskeard, Cornwall PL14 4PE

Evelyn Julian
☎/Fax 015032 62855
🆂🅲 From £130–£495
Sleeps 12
🐎 ■
🔑 🔑 🔑 🔑
Commended

We welcome you to Tremadart Farm, a mixed farm which is part of the Duchy of Cornwall. Set in large secluded garden close to village of Duloe and three miles from Looe. Four bedrooms, bathroom, shower room, 2 toilets. Golf, fishing, sailing, horse riding, coastal and country walks close by. Open all year.

54   **Trevalgan Farm,** St Ives, Cornwall TR26 3BJ

Jean Osborne
☎ 01736 796433
🆂🅲 From £150–£400
Sleeps 2/6
🐎 🎲 🐎 ■
🔑 🔑 🔑 – 🔑 🔑 🔑 🔑
Commended

Trevalgan is a coastal stock-rearing farm surrounded by magnificent scenery, just 2 miles from St Ives. Enjoy walking our farm trail to the cliffs overlooking the sea, a paradise for nature lovers. Traditional granite barns have been carefully converted into 7 lovely holiday homes around an attractive courtyard. Land's End, St Michael's Mount, Mousehole and Lamorna within easy reach by car. Open all year (closed Feb).

55   **Trewalla Farm Cottages,** Trewalla Farm, Minions, Liskeard, Cornwall PL14 6ED

Cheryl van der Salm
☎ 01579 342385
🆂🅲 From £150–£360
Sleeps 2/4 (+ cot)
🐎 🐎 🐎
🔑 🔑 🔑 *Commended*

Our small, traditionally-run farm on Bodmin Moor has rare breed pigs, hand milked sheep, hens and geese, all free-range and very friendly. Our three cottages are beautifully furnished and very well equipped. Their moorland setting offers perfect peace, wonderful views, ideal walking country and a good base for exploring – if you can tear yourself away! Open Mar–Dec.

56   **Trewithen Country Lodges,** Trewithen Farm, Laneast, Launceston, Cornwall PL15 8PW

Mrs Margaret Colwill
☎ 01566 86343
🆂🅲 From £150–£350
Sleeps 6
🐎 🛏 🎲
🔑 🔑 🔑 *Commended*

Enjoy that well-earned break amidst peace and tranquillity in Scandinavian style lodges. Just two situated in a large garden with panoramic views of the surrounding Bodmin Moor. While you relax on the verandah the children will enjoy the swings, pet pony and farm animals. The cosy accommodation is tastefully furnished with well equipped kitchen, microwave, washer/dryer. Bedlinen provided. Open Mar–Jan.

57   **Wheatley Farm Cottages,** Maxworthy, Launceston, Cornwall PL15 8LY

Valerie Griffin
☎/Fax 01566 781232
🆂🅲 From £140–£470
Sleeps 2/7
🐎
🔑 🔑 🔑 🔑
Highly Commended

Beautifully situated close to Crackington Haven and the spectacular North Cornwall coast, Wheatley Farm is the ideal place to relax and unwind in one of our two tastefully restored country cottages. Each set in its own garden offering seclusion and privacy. Absolute comfort. Working farm. Come and meet the animals, pony rides, play area for children. A warm welcome awaits you – do come. Open all year.

CAMPING AND CARAVANNING

Nancolleth Farm Caravan Gardens, Newquay, Cornwall TR8 4PN

Joan Luckraft
☎**01872 510236**
🆂 **From £115–£275**
Sleeps 4/6
🛇 ⚡
✓ ✓ ✓ ✓ ✓
Rose Award

Nancolleth a 250-acre farm, 5 miles from Newquay. Central for touring Cornwall. Secluded caravan park with 6 deluxe 6 berth caravans in garden setting, well spaced, on hard standings with parking. Each caravan has 2 bedrooms, shower room with toilet, colour TV, fridge, spacious lounge, dining and kitchen areas. Laundry. Phone. Country Trail. Families and couples welcomed. ETB Rose Award Caravan Holiday Park Award 1996. Open May–Oct.

NO ANSWER?
Farmers are mostly out and about during the day.
Try to telephone before 9.30am or after 4pm.

FINDING YOUR ACCOMMODATION

The Group contacts at the beginning of each section can always help you find a vacancy in your chosen area.

CONFIRM BOOKINGS

Disappointments can arise from misunderstandings over the telephone.
Please write to confirm your booking.

THOSE LITTLE EXTRAS

For advice on farms that can offer 'extras' such as four-poster beds, special diets, farm trails, fishing rights – even stabling and trekking arrangements if you are bringing your own horse – ring the Farm Holiday Bureau on (01203) 696909.

DISABLED VISITORS

Many members offer a welcome to disabled/less able visitors. Please do check the extent of the facilities before booking.

THE 1000+ BUREAU MEMBERS OFFER A UNIQUE LINK TO CUSTOMERS ACROSS THE UK

All Bureau members belong to a local Group. Each member can refer you to an equally high quality member within his Group… or across the UK: England, Northern Ireland, Scotland, Wales.

FOLLOW THE COUNTRY CODE

Leave nothing but footprints,
Take nothing but photographs,
Kill nothing but time!

BUREAU ACCOMMODATION MEANS QUALITY

All Bureau members are inspected and quality graded by the National Tourist Board each year, as well as by fellow members.

North Wales

Llŷn Peninsula

Group Contact: *Mrs R. D. Wynne-Finch* ☎ *01758 770209*

With more than 70 miles of coastline, backed by the dramatic mountains of Snowdonia, this is an Area of Outstanding Natural Beauty where the warm waters of the Gulf Stream give a mild climate all year round. The Welsh language and way of life still flourish here and while you struggle with the seemingly impossible Celtic names, you will appreciate the very Welshness of it all.

It is also an area compact enough to travel around and get to know – and one that you will want to come back to time and time again.

No-one comes to this part of Wales without setting foot on mighty Mount Snowdon; and even if you only clamber for a relatively short distance you will be rewarded with views the like of which you will never have seen before. And you could always walk one way and take the famous narrow gauge railway the other!

Right at the foot of the Peninsula lies Bardsey Island – a bird sanctuary, place of pilgrimage and the legendary resting place of 20,000 saints.

Nestling on its own wooded peninsula you will find Portmeirion, the Italianate extravaganza created by the late Sir Clough Williams Ellis, full of delightful surprises in the shape of statues, follies and fake facades.

Amlwch

Prestatyn

Holyhead

Llandudno Colwyn Rhyl

A5 Llangefni Beaumaris Conwy Bay

Abergele A55

Menai Bangor Penmaenmawr

Bridge Llanfairfechan

Bethesda

A470 A543

Caenarfon A5 Llanrwst

Ruthin

Betws-y-Coed

A494

A499 A487 A498 A470 A5

Blaenau Ffestiniog A5

Criccieth Porthmadog Ffestiniog

7 4 A497

3 1 A4212 Bala

2 Pwllheli

5 6 Harlech A494

A470 Lake Vyrnwy

Llanfyllin

Dolgellau

Barmouth

BED AND BREAKFAST

(and evening meal)

---

1 **Mathan Uchaf Farm,** Boduan, Pwllheli, Gwynedd LL53 8TU

Mrs Jean Coker
☎ 01758 720487
Fax 01758 720020
🏨 From £15–£17
EM From £8
Sleeps 6
🐕 🐈 🐎
♥ Commended

A 190-acre dairy farm, situated off the main Pwllheli to Nefyn road. Centrally positioned for northern and southern beaches of peninsula. Guests can participate in farm activities. Large garden provides safe play area. We have 2 dogs who play ball and a Shetland pony. 1 double room, 1 family room with washbasins, 1 twin bedded room. Dining room, sitting room with colour TV. Good food and friendly atmosphere are our aim. Open Mar–Nov.

SELF-CATERING

---

2 **Castellmarch,** Abersoch, Pwllheli, Gwynedd LL53 7UE

Mrs H M Jones
☎ 01758 712242
🆂🅲 From £90–£300
Sleeps 2–5 (+ cot)
🐈 🐕
🏵 🏵 🏵 – 🏵 🏵 🏵

Castellmarch, a traditional family run beef and sheep farm, 1 mile from the yachting village of Abersoch, and minutes walk from sandy beach. Listed 16th century farmhouse. This was once the home of fabled March Ap Meirchion – a man with horse's ears. Cegin-isa (wing of farmhouse) sleeps 4. All rooms have exposed beams. The Granary sleeps 5. A chalet set on elevated position sleeps 5. All enjoy sea and countryside views. B&B available in farmhouse. Brochure. Open Mar–Nov.

---

3 **Cefnamwlch,** Tudweiliog, Pwllheli, Gwynedd LL53 8AX

Mrs R. Wynne-Finch
☎ 01758 770209
🆂🅲 From £100–£245
Sleeps 4/6 + cot
🐎 🏵
🏵 🏵 🏵

Houses 1 & 2 sleep 6 in 3 double bedrooms. Cot available. Converted from wing of owner's 17th century manor farmhouse on ancient Welsh estate. Situated in beautiful woodland setting 1 mile from village of Tudweiliog, along rhododendron drive. Easy reach sandy beaches, golf course. Ideal touring centre. Colour TV, tumble dryer and spindryer. Play area. Electric 50p meter. Ty Thimble Cottage sleeps 4 in 2 double bedrooms. Open Easter–end Oct.

---

4 **Gwynfryn Farm,** Gwynfryn, Pwllheli, Gwynedd LL53 5UF

Sian B Ellis
☎ 01758 612536
Fax 01758 614324
🆂🅲 From £94–£480
Sleeps 2/8
🐕 🐈 ♿ 🎣 Å 📺 ●
🏵 🏵 🏵 🏵 – 🏵 🏵 🏵 🏵 🏵

Our **organic** dairy farm is a haven for nature lovers, away from the madding crowd, yet only 1½ miles from Pwllheli. Cottages for romantic couples/houses 4–8 persons, all personally supervised, WTB 4–5 dragons – quality assured. Snowdon 25 miles, sea 2 miles – vary your activity to suit the weather or your mood. Beds made up, storage/central heating. Mini breaks Oct–Mar. Sample our hospitality. Gold Award Welcome Host. Send for colour brochure. Open all year.

Rhydolion, Llangian, Abersoch, Pwllheli, Gwynedd LL53 7LR

Catherine Morris
☎ **01758 712342**
SC **From £105–£350**
Sleeps 6–8

🐕 🐾 ♿ ☺ ♨ 🍴 🚶 🚲

✽ ✽ ✽ ✽ ✽

Charming 16th century farmhouse wing and a ground floor cottage (suitable for wheelchair users), both with 3 bedrooms, providing interesting blend of 'olde worlde' charm and modern comfort. Beams, inglenook fireplace, four poster (farmhouse only), microwave, dishwasher, etc. Laundry room. Situated in a delightful, peaceful setting, beach only ¾ mile. Ideal sailing, surfing, cycling and good walks area or join in farm activities. Open Mar–Nov.

Tai Gwyliau Tyndon Holiday Cottages, c/o Penlan, Rhos Isaf, Caernarfon, Gwynedd LL54 7NG   ⑥

Mrs Elisabeth Evans
☎ **01286 831184**
SC **From £99–£390**
Sleeps 5/7

🐕 🐾

✽ ✽ ✽

120 acre sheep farm on the beautiful Lleyn heritage coast. Peaceful and relaxing self-contained cottages and bungalows. 1 mile from Llanengan with its country pub and 6th century church. Boating resort of Abersoch only 2 miles away, beautiful sandy beach of Porthneigwl within 200 yards (with private access). Most cottages have glorious views of the bay. Ideal family holiday. Personal supervision. Free brochure. Short breaks. Open all year.

Towyn Farm, Tudweiliog, Pwllheli, Gwynedd LL53 8PD   ⑦

Iona Wynne Owen
☎ **01758 770230**
SC **From £150–£350**
Sleeps 6/7 + cot

🐕 ♿ 🐾 🍴 ♨ ☺ 🎣

✽ ✽ ✽ ✽ ✽

Enjoy a relaxing holiday in unspoilt area of outstanding natural beauty. 200 yds from Towyn beach. Ideal fishing, surfing, boating. Nefyn golf course 5 miles. A 300-year-old modernised farmhouse, carpeted throughout, colour TV, 4 bedrooms, duvets and heaters. Open fire in autumn/winter. Bathroom with bath and shower. Fitted kitchen, washing machine, tumble dryer, microwave oven. Sheltered lawn garden with barbeque. Free babysitting. Cot and high chair. Also ground level cottage sleeping 6. Brochure.

FOLLOW THE COUNTRY CODE

Leave nothing but footprints,
Take nothing but photographs,
Kill nothing but time!

FARM HOLIDAY BUREAU

BUREAU ACCOMMODATION MEANS QUALITY

FARM HOLIDAY BUREAU

All Bureau members are inspected and quality graded by the National Tourist Board each year, as well as by fellow members.

North Wales

Snowdonia

Group Contact: *Mrs Jane Llewelyn Pierce* ☎ *01248 670147*

In Snowdonia those interested in history have a wealth of locations to visit, from the early 12th century Welsh fortresses at Dolbadarn and Dolwyddelan to the magnificent castles of Edward 1st at Caernarfon, Beaumaris, Harlech and Conwy. The National Trust's historic houses include Plas Newydd on Anglesey and Penrhyn Castle near Bangor. Segontium Fort at Caernarfon is witness to the four hundred years of Roman occupation and there is an interesting museum nearby.

Take a boat trip along the Menai Strait, a ride on a steam train into the mountains with the Talyllyn or Ffestiniog Railways, alongside Llanberis Lake or even up Mount Snowdon itself. Visit the heart of a Welsh slate cavern, take a trip to the theatre at Bangor or Harlech, or see craftsmen at work – some of the many choices available.

Add to this the Sports Council's excellent centres near Caernarfon and Capel Curig, heated swimming pools at Caernarfon, Bangor and Harlech, golf at one of the many courses with superb sea views, some really excellent restaurants and pubs and walks in the mountains or forests, and often a week is all too short a time to stay with us.

Most of us are Welsh speaking as Snowdonia is the heartland of the Welsh language and we will be very happy to teach you a few Welsh greetings or tell you more about our ancient language.

BED AND BREAKFAST

(and evening meal)

Drws-y-Coed, Llannerch-y-Medd, Isle of Anglesey LL71 8AD

Mrs Jane Bown
☎ **01248 470473**
BB **From £18–£20**
EM From £12
Sleeps 6
🐎 ⚏ 🐴
🏵 🏵 🏵 *De Luxe*

Enjoy peace, wonderful panoramic views of Snowdonia at this beautifully appointed farmhouse. Comfortable en suite bedrooms with all facilities. Spacious lounge with log fire, dining room with separate tables. Excellent food. Games room, pony rides. Historical farmstead. Visitors return year after year to enjoy the warm hospitality and lovely private walks. Open all year except Christmas.

Gwrach Ynys, Talsarnau, Nr Harlech, Gwynedd LL47 6TS

Mrs Deborah Williams
☎ **01766 780742**
Fax 01766 780742
BB **From £17.50–£20**
EM From £10
Sleeps 15
🐎 🐕
🏵 🏵 🏵 *De Luxe*

Relax in the peace and comfort of our secluded Edwardian House. Conveniently located, close to sea and mountains with many tourist attractions nearby. Ideal golfing, rambling, birdwatching area. En suite bedrooms with TV, telephone, beverage facilities. Meals lovingly prepared using fresh local produce. Children free accommodation if sharing with two adults on weekly lets. WTB Farmhouse Award. AA Selected. Open all year except Christmas.

Llwydiarth Fawr, Llanerchymedd, Isle of Anglesey, Gwynedd LL71 8DF

Mrs Margaret Hughes
☎ **01248 470321/**
470540
BB **From £22.50–£25**
EM From £12.50
Sleeps 6
🐎 ⚏ 🖼 ☕ 🎾 💼
🏵 🏵 🏵 *De Luxe*

Secluded Georgian mansion set in 850 acres of woodland and farmland. Ideal touring base for island's coastline, Snowdonia and North Wales coast. Nearby is Llyn Alaw for trout fishing. Reputation for excellent food using farm and local produce. En suite bedrooms. TV, CH, log fires. Walks and private fishing. Winner of the BBC 'Welsh Farm housewife of the Year' competition. Member of Taste of Wales. Warmest Welcome Award 1993. Closed Christmas.

Pengwern, Saron, Llanwnda, Caernarfon, Gwynedd LL54 5UH

G & J Lloyd Rowlands
☎/**Fax 01286 831500**
Mobile 0378 411780
BB **From £20–£25**
EM From £12
Sleeps 6
⚏ 🐎 🎾
🏵 🏵 🏵 *De Luxe*

Charming, spacious farmhouse of character, situated between mountains and sea. Unobstructed views of Snowdonia. Well appointed bedrooms, all with en suite bathrooms. Set in 130 acres of land which runs down to Foryd Bay. Jane has a cookery diploma and provides the excellent meals with farmhouse fresh food, including home-produced beef and lamb. Excellent access. Open Feb–Nov.

Plas Cichle, Beaumaris, Anglesey LL58 8PS

Eirwen Roberts
☎ **01248 810488**
BB **From £19–£21**
Sleeps 6
🐎(5) 🎾
🏵 🏵 *Highly Commended*

This beautiful period farmhouse offers accommodation in spacious double or family rooms, most en suite, all with TV and beverage tray. Close to historic town of Beaumaris, ideal base to enjoy the many local attractions and activities, or just to relax and enjoy the panoramic views. Start your day with a hearty Welsh breakfast, and in the evening, relax in our comfortable guest lounge. Brochure. Open Feb–Nov.

---

6   **Plas Tirion Farm,** Llanrug, Caernarfon, Gwynedd LL55 4PY

C H Mackinnon
☎ 01286 673190
[BB] From £18–£20
EM From £12
Sleeps 6
🐾
🌣🌣 *De Luxe*

Welcome to our working dairy farm with comfortable, heated accommodation. All en suite bedrooms with beverage facilities, TV and panoramic views. Recommended for breakfast and dinners using fresh produce. Special diets available; residential licence; packed lunches. Rough shooting. 4 miles Llanberis and Caernarfon, 10 miles Anglesey, 8 miles beach. Wales Farmhouse Award; Open May–Sept.

---

7   **Plas Trefarthen,** Brynsiencyn, Anglesey, Gwynedd LL61 6SZ

Marian Roberts
☎ 01248 430379
[BB] From £17.50–£20
Sleeps 12
🐾 [£]
🌣🌣 *Highly Commended*

Secluded Georgian house in 200 acres of land on the shore of the Menai Straits. Uninterrupted views of mighty Snowdon and Caernarfon Castle. Ideal base for touring Anglesey and Snowdonia, walking, birdwatching and visiting local National Trust properties. Most bedrooms en suite bathrooms, all with beverage facilities, colour TV. Full size snooker table. Warm Welsh welcome. Croeso. Open all year.

---

8   **Tre'rddôl Farm,** Llanerchymedd, Isle of Anglesey, Gwynedd LL71 7AR

Ann Astley
☎ 01248 470278
Fax 01248 470276
[BB] From £18–£20
EM From £11
Sleeps 6
🐎🐴🏃🎯💼
🌣🌣 *Highly Commended*

If you are looking for freedom and relaxation this 200-acre family farm on B5109 can oblige. Its historic 17th century house and country antiques add to the mystery and character of the past. Ornithologists' paradise, fishing at Llyn Alaw. Spacious en suite bedrooms with TV, beverage facilities. Guests' comfort a priority and food a speciality. Children enjoy pony rides and participate in farm activities. Wales Farmhouse Award. SAE for brochure. Open Jan–Nov.

---

9   **Ty Mawr Farm,** Llanddeiniolen, Caernarfon, Gwynedd LL55 3AD

Mrs Jane Llewelyn Pierce
☎ 01248 670147
[BB] From £15–£20
EM From £12.50
Sleeps 6
🐾🎯💼
🌣🌣🌣 *Applied*

Charming, warm country farmhouse on 100-acre farm with superb views of Snowdonia mountain range. Ideal for touring North Wales and Anglesey. Caernarfon only 5 miles. All rooms have en suite bathrooms, TV and tea and coffee facilities. Two lounges with wood fires and a separate dining room. Good home cooking. Ample parking area. Open all year.

---

10   **Ystumgwern, Hall Farm,** Dyffryn Ardudwy, Gwynedd LL44 2DD

Jane E Williams
☎ 01341 247249
Fax 01341 247171
[BB] From £18–£20
Sleeps 6
🐾🎯♿☂🏃✈💼🎾
🌣🌣 *De Luxe*

For a Welsh farm holiday Ystumgwern is ideal, set in Snowdonia National Park. Pony trekking, bird watching, golf, rivers, lakes, sandy beaches, steam trains, a castle and a wealth of eating places, all within 6 miles. The 16th century farmhouse is full of character with two dining rooms, one with inglenook fireplace. All bedrooms have en suite, and a private lounge. Reputation for high standards. Reduced rates for children. Open all year.

FARM HOLIDAY BUREAU

NO ANSWER?

Farmers are mostly out and about during the day.
Try to telephone before 9.30am or after 4pm.

SELF-CATERING

Bryn Beddau, Bontnewydd, Caernarfon, Gwynedd LL54 7YE

Eleri Carrog
☎ 01286 830117/
673795
Fax 01286 675664
🆂🅲 From £100–£320
Sleeps 5

Cosy stone–built stable cottage with views of mountains and sea. Excellent centre for walks, touring, lovely beaches and Snowdonia. Secluded setting yet only 3 miles from Caernarfon. Lovely gallery bedroom with graceful arch windows, twin room, cot. Ideal for families or that romantic break. Spacious beamed lounge of great character and many books. Patio, barbecue. "Croeso Cymreig". Open all year.

Chwilog Fawr, Chwilog, Pwllheli, Gwynedd LL53 6SW

Catherine Jones
☎/Fax 01766 810506
🆂🅲 From £100–£380

Situated in an elevated position with panoramic views of Llyn and Snowdonia. Secluded and peaceful yet convenient for beach, fishing, golfing and lovely country walks. Superior 3 bedroom farmhouse, 2 or 3 bedroom chalets or luxury caravans. Exceptionally well appointed with extensive range of facilities. Open Mar–Nov.

Hafod & Hendre, c/o Ty Mawr Farm, Llanddeiniolen, Caernarfon, Gwynedd LL55 3AD

Mrs Jane Llewelyn Pierce
☎ 01248 670147
🆂🅲 From £100–£300
EM From £12.50
Sleeps4/6

Two luxurious, self-catering converted granaries situated in a private courtyard on our working farm. Hafod sleeps 2 and Hendre 4. Camp beds are available for extra children. Both are centrally heated and have wood burning stoves. CH, electricity, towels and full bedding included in price. Caernarfon 5 miles, Snowdon 4 miles. Brochures available. Open all year.

Llwydiarth Fawr Farm Cottages, Llanerchymedd, Isle of Anglesey, Gwynedd LL71 8DF

Mrs Margaret Hughes
☎ 01248 470321/
470540
🆂🅲 From £100–£550
Sleeps 4–9

Superbly furnished and equipped, beautifully positioned in the centre of Anglesey and surrounded by owner's farmland. Snowdonia and the coast within easy driving distance. Nearby is Llyn Alaw, excellent for trout fishing. In winter the cottages are warm and welcoming with log fires and CH. Well equipped kitchens have microwave, tumbledryer, washing machine, dishwasher. A warm Welsh welcome to guests who will enjoy our walks and private fishing. Open all year.

Llys Bennar, Dyffryn Ardudwy, Gwynedd LL44 2RX

Catrin Rutherford
☎/Fax 01341 247316
🆂🅲 From £176–£364
Sleeps 4/7

Attractive 18th century farm buildings converted into charming cottages, within a courtyard setting. They have retained the original charm of the oak beams, one with inglenook fireplace. Both have nightstore heating. Laundry facility available. Ten minutes to village or to sandy beach. One mile from station. In Snowdonia National Park. Many attractions in the area. Open all year.

---

16 Pen-y-Bryn, Chwilog, Pwllheli, Gwynedd LL53 6SX

Mrs Sulwen Edwards
☎ 01766 810208
Fax 01766 810064
SC From £100–£425
Sleeps 2–8

We offer a choice of luxury accommodation for the discerning. Enjoy a memorable holiday in our tastefully restored farmhouse or bungalow. Both are set in their own garden with permanent barbecue and enjoy panoramic views of Cardigan Bay and Snowdonia. Here you will find peace and tranquillity yet be within easy reach of towns, beaches, tourist attractions, fishing and shooting, children's play area. Open all year.

17 Ynys, Ystumgwern, Dyffryn Ardudwy, Gwynedd LL44 2DD

Jane & John Williams
☎ 01341 247249
Fax 01341 247171
SC From £140–£440
Sleeps 2/8

A taste of luxury with a cosy, relaxed atmosphere in quiet setting, 1 mile from sandy beach, shops and station. Kitchen/diner with dishwasher, microwave, Aga, oak beams. Lounge has electric or open fire in inglenook fireplace. Each bedroom is tastefully furnished and heated. Laundry room. Barbecue and picnic tables. Ample parking via private drive. Warm welcome to all. Colour brochure available. Open all year.

THOSE LITTLE EXTRAS

For advice on farms that can offer 'extras' such as four-poster beds, special diets, farm trails, fishing rights – even stabling and trekking arrangements if you are bringing your own horse – ring the Farm Holiday Bureau on (01203) 696909.

DISABLED VISITORS

Many members offer a welcome to disabled/less able visitors. Please do check the extent of the facilities before booking.

North Wales

Heart of Snowdonia

Group Contacts: *Paula Williams* ☎/Fax 01766 590281
Olwen Davies ☎/Fax 01678 520456

A choice of quality, traditional Welsh farmhouses, ALL located in the Snowdonia National Park, an ideal base for exploring the whole of North Wales. Most have en suite bedrooms, tea trays, colour TVs, CH and provide full farmhouse breakfasts with optional evening meals.

There are numerous attractions within this area including the spectacular Ffestiniog Railway, Bala Lake Railway and the Welsh Highland Railway at Porthmadog. Slate is the theme at Blaenau Ffestiniog, where the Llechwedd Slate Caverns and Gloddfa Ganol Mountain Centre welcome thousands of visitors journeying into Victorian working conditions. Stroll through the unique Italianate village of Portmeirion. Try dry slope skiing at Trawsfynydd or pony trekking nearby. Bala Lake is renowned for its watersports, sailing and windsurfing, close to the white water canoe centre. Keen fishermen can fish at Bala Lake, Llyn Celyn and Trawsfynydd. Bodnant Garden in the Conwy valley is world acclaimed. There are many National Trust properties to visit as well as a great choice of historic and Roman ruins.

All this plus the mountains, lakes, waterfalls and fine beaches await you. Hear our language, listen to local choirs practising, above all relax, find peace and tranquillity in the resplendent beauty that surrounds you.

BED AND BREAKFAST

(and evening meal)

---

① Bryn Celynog Farm, Cwm Prysor, Trawsfynydd, Gwynedd LL41 4TR

Mrs G E Hughes
☎/Fax 01766 540378
BB From £16
EM From £9.50
Sleeps 6
☺ ⛄ 🐄 🛉 ⛄ ⛄ ●
⚘ ⚘ *Highly Commended*

Set amidst beautiful mountains a working farm 3 miles from Trawsfynydd village. Modernised farmhouse, twin, double and family bedrooms, one en suite, all with washbasins, tea/coffee facilities. Lounge with colour TV, log fire. Reputation for excellent food and friendliness. Optional evening meal. Wales Farmhouse Award. Open all year.

---

② Cwm Hwylfod, Cefn–Ddwysarn, Bala, Gwynedd LL23 7LN

Joan Best
☎ 01678 530310
BB From £13–£15
EM From £9.50
Sleeps 6
☺ 🛉 ⛄ ⛄ ●
⚘ *Commended*

Set in hills near Bala, our 400–year–old farmhouse is warm and welcoming. The views are spectacular. Animals abound and everyone, especially children, can take part in farm activities. Bedrooms have washbasins and tea making facilities. The guest lounge has TV, books and games. Full central heating. For our home–cooked evening meals we use the best of local produce. All diets catered for. Taste of Wales. Open all year except Christmas.

---

③ Fferm Fron-Gôch, Frongoch, Bala, Gwynedd LL23 7NT

Carys Davies
☎/Fax 01678 520483
BB From £15
EM From £8
Sleeps 6
☺(6) ⛄ ●
⚘ ⚘ *Highly Commended*

Enjoy a relaxed, friendly stay in our old, historic farmhouse. Traditionally furnished, log fires, oak beams. All bedrooms en suite, private facilities, TV, radio, tea/coffee. Perfect for unwinding or exploring Snowdonia and its magnificent countryside. Walks, fishing, water sports, leisure centre, cinema close by. Excellent home cooking. Welcome Host, Farmhouse Award. Brochure. Open all year.

---

④ Old Mill Farmhouse, Fron Oleu Farm, Trawsfynydd, Gwynedd LL41 4UN

Carol Bain
☎/Fax 01766 540397
BB From £17.50–£19
EM From £8.50
☺ ⛄ 🐄 ♿ 🛉 ⛄ ⛄ ⛄ ●
⚘ ⚘ *Applied*

Relaxing friendly welcome and atmosphere at our restored farmhouse (circa. 1700), overlooking the lake and mountains. Cottage-style level access bedrooms in adjacent stonebuilt courtyard. All en suite with TV, CH, tea/coffee. Ample portions of fresh wholesome food. Huge inglenook log fires. Child reductions, pets' corner. Winner Holiday Care Award, Welcome Host, wheelchair friendly. Ideal touring location. Open all year.

---

⑤ Rhydydefaid Farm, Frongoch, Bala, Gwynedd LL23 7NT

Olwen Davies
☎/Fax 01678 520456
BB From £14.50–£17
Sleeps 6
☺ ⛄ ✂ ⛄ ⛄ ⛄ ●
⚘ ⚘ *Highly Commended*

A true Welsh welcome awaits you at our traditional Welsh stone farmhouse. 3 miles from Bala near A4212 road. 100-acre working farm. Oak beamed lounge with inglenook fireplace. 1 oak beamed en suite, family bedroom, twin/single bedrooms with wash basin. All with tea/coffee-making facilities. Ideal for touring Snowdonia. Open all year except Christmas & New Year.

Tyddyn Du Farm, (b), Gellilydan, Ffestiniog, Gwynedd LL41 4RB

Paula Williams
☎/Fax 01766 590281
BB From £16–£20
EM From £10
Sleeps 8
🐎 🐓 🐖 🛏 🎋 ⊙
🐾🐾🐾 *Highly Commended*

Located amidst spectacular scenery, guests are very welcome to enjoy the old world charm of our 400yr old farmhouse (WTB Farmhouse Award). Excellent central location. Most bedrooms en suite, one superb private cottage suite, all have remote control TV and beverage facilities. CH with log fires. Delicious candle light dinners. Working farm with pony, ducks and bottle fed lambs. Weekly dinner B&B from £160–£185. Stamp please for brochure. Open all year.

Tyddyn Iolyn, Pentrefelin, Nr Criccieth, Gwynedd LL52 0RB

Maurice & Charlotte Lowe
☎ 01766 522509
BB From £14–£18
EM From £9
Sleeps 12
🐎 🐓 ✂ 🐖 🛏 🎋 ⊙
🐾 🐾 *Highly Commended*

Lovingly restored, secluded 16th century oak-beamed farmhouse, set in idyllic farmland. Breathtaking views of Snowdonia and coastline. Perfect base for exploring Portmeirion, Snowdonia, Llyn Peninsula. 2 family en suites, 4 poster en suite, twin and double with basins, beverage trays. Traditional cooking/vegetarian. Abundance of books/local information. Cats, chickens, pony. Mountain bike hire. Farm Tourism Award. Open all year.

SELF-CATERING

Caerwych Farmhouse, Llandecwyn, Near Harlech, Gwynedd LL47 6YT

Richard Williams-Ellis
☎ 01766 770913/
771270
SC From £150–£400
Sleeps 9/10
🐎 🐓 🐖 🍴 🛏 🎋 ⊙
🐾 🐾 🐾

Secluded and set in marvellous scenic countryside with stupendous views to the sea. We are a typically traditional sheep farm but also breed horses and are replanting ancient woodlands. The stone farmhouse is old, large and handsome. Central heating throughout. Five bedrooms. Perfection for walkers. Accompanied trail riding in the mountains. Open all year.

North Wales
Warm Welsh Welcome Clywd

Group Contacts: *Mrs Anwen Roberts* ☎ *01745 730627*
Mrs Helen Parry ☎ *01745 550276*

Clwyd – its northern boundary strung with seaside resorts – comes up with some surprising contrasts, from the sandcastle and holiday atmosphere of the coast to the fortresses left behind from mediaeval times. It is a beautiful county with a necklace of seaside towns and unspoilt inland scenery.

St Asaph, at the head of the Vale of Clwyd, might be just a large village, but it is also a cathedral city. The cathedral may be the smallest in the country but it is also one of the oldest in Wales, dating back to the 15th century. It houses some rare treasures like the original copy of William Morgan's Welsh translation of the Bible.

Further into the county lies Ruthin Boasting a wealth of history including a castle which provides a very popular mediaeval banquet . Also there is the 'Maen Huail' stone where King Arthur is said to have beheaded his rival in love. The craft centre is well worth a visit, as are the ones at Nannerch and Llanasa. Crafts of a different nature are to be found in Llangollen where horse-drawn barges glide along the Shropshire Union Canal. Llangollen also hosts the International Musical Eisteddfod in early July.

BED AND BREAKFAST

(and evening meal)

Bach-y-Graig, Tremeirchion, St Asaph, Clwyd LL17 0UH

Anwen Roberts
☎ 01745 730627
[BB] From £19
EM From £10.50
Sleeps 6
✄ 🐕 ☕ ♨
♛ ♛ ♛ *De Luxe*

A 16th century listed farmhouse nestling at the foot of the Clwydian Range with beautiful views of the surrounding countryside. Highest standard of traditional furnishings and decor, en suite, TVs, tea/coffee-making facilities in bedrooms, full CH, beamed inglenook fireplace with log fires. Central for North Wales, Chester, coast 9 miles. Games room. 40 acre woodland trail. WTB Farmhouse Award. AA selected award. RAC acclaimed. Closed Christmas/New Year.

Bodangharad, Llanfwrog, Ruthin, Clwyd LL15 2AH

Enid Jones
☎ 01824 702370
[BB] From £13.50
Sleeps 6 (+ cot)
🐕 🐕 ♨ 🐕
Listed *Applied*

Bodangharad is a 100-acre dairy/sheep farm in unspoilt countryside, with a wealth of wild flowers and hedgerows. Panoramic views of Vale of Clwyd. We are a few minutes' drive from historic market town of Ruthin, with easy access to Chester, coast and Snowdonia. House with interesting interior with exposed beams, open fires and spacious rooms for guests. It offers peace and tranquillity and plenty of farmhouse fresh food. Open Easter–Nov.

College Farm, Peniel, Denbigh, Clwyd LL16 4TT

Helen Parry
☎ 01745 550276
[BB] From £16–£17
EM From £7.50
Sleeps 5
🐕 ♿ ✄ 🐕 ♨
♛ *Highly Commended*

We warmly welcome you to College Farm, situated in a beautiful and quiet area just 3 miles from Denbigh with its ancient castle, wide high street and colonnades. Central for the coast, Snowdonia and Chester. Bedrooms have washbasins, CH and hospitality trays. Spacious lounge with log fire. Good food, free range eggs and vegetables from our organic garden. WTB farmhouse Award, Welcome Host. Open Mar–Nov.

Pentre Bach, Llandyrnog, Clwyd LL16 4LA

Marie Carrington-Sykes
☎ /Fax 01824 790725
[BB] From £16.50–£25
Sleeps 4
🐕(5) 🐕
♛ ♛ *Applied*

Pentre Bach is situated near the village of Llandyrnog in the beautiful Vale of Clwyd. Built in 1745, this red brick farmhouse is a peaceful setting for the country lover. Two guest bedrooms, each with private/en suite bathrooms and beverage facilities. Within easy reach of Snowdonia, Chester and N. Wales coast. Open all year.

LET THE TELEPHONE RING!

Some farmhouses are big places. Let the telephone ring long enough to give the owner time to answer it.

FARM HOLIDAY BUREAU

SELF-CATERING

5 Bach-y-Graig, Tremeirchion, St Asaph, Clwyd LL17 0UH

Anwen Roberts
☎ 01745 730627
SC From £110–£325
Sleeps 6 + cot

Stay on a working dairy farm in this 16th century farmhouse, retaining the charm but offering comforts and convenience of modern living in high standard accommodation. Dark oak, fully equipped kitchen. 3 bedrooms, 1 four-poster bed. Bathroom with shower/bath. Downstairs toilet, CTV heating. Log fires. Linen provided. Games room, large garden with swings/slide. Central for Chester, Snowdonia and coastal resorts. No pets. Open all year.

6 Tyddyn Isaf, Rhewl, Ruthin, Clwyd LL15 1UH

Elsie Jones
☎ 01824 703142/
703367
SC From £90–£240
Sleeps 2/6 + cot

Enjoy a holiday in our self-contained part of farmhouse or recently converted granary in picturesque Vale of Clwyd. Both fully equipped to high standard. Farmhouse has lounge/diner, 2 bedrooms sleeping 4/6, bathroom, separate toilet. Granary has 1 bedroom with vanity unit, sofa bed in lounge, sleeps 2/4, shower room. 3 miles from Ruthin and within easy reach of Chester, the coast and Snowdonia. Bedlinen provided. No pets.

FARM HOLIDAY BUREAU

GOOD FOOD

Nearly all Bureau members now hold a certificate in Essential Food Hygiene.

FARM HOLIDAY BUREAU

CONFIRM BOOKINGS

Disappointments can arise from misunderstandings over the telephone.
Please write to confirm your booking.

76

North Wales

Llangollen

Group Contact: *Mrs Shelagh Roberts* ☎ *01978 823403*

A romantic town on the salmon-filled Dee. It is hard to imagine a more idyllic location. The discerning visitor can browse around the shops, St Collens Church, and the European Centre for Traditional and Regional Cultures, cross the 14th century bridge which is on of the seven wonders of Wales, take a horse-drawn boat along the canal or a steam train ride through the Vale. Plas Newydd – home of the Ladies of Llangollen, Valle Crucis Abbey, The Pillar of Eliseg and the Horseshoe pass are all within a short distance

In the eighth century Offa, King of Mercia, built Offa's Dyke. Part of this legendary dyke runs parallel to the river Dee beneath the Eglwseg rocks past Castell Dinas Bran, which is well worth the climb far a spectacular view of the town. You can also enjoy the Panoramic Walks down to Trevor and Thomas Telford's famous aqueduct, crossing high above the Dee.

In early July the surrounding hills really do come alive to the sound of music when the International Music Eisteddfod welcomes singers and dancers from all over the world. This was first held in 1947 to heal wounds of war, and the same welcome continues throughout the year.

BED AND BREAKFAST

(and evening meal)

---

① Cefn Y Fedw Farm, Garth, Llangollen, Clwyd LL14 1UA

Mrs Shelagh Roberts
☎/Fax 01978 823403
🛏 From £16–£18
EM From £8
Sleeps 6
🐄 ⅋ 🛉 🐎 ♨ 💼
🌸🌸 *Commended*

Cefn Y Fedw stands high above Garth village in the hills behind Llangollen in an area of outstanding beauty, close to the Offas Dyke Path and National Trust properties. A working farm offering good food (Taste of Wales member), comfortable accommodation in spacious rooms. Private guest bathrooms. 1992 Wales Tourist Board Warmest Welcome Award. Closed April. Off the A593.

SELF-CATERING

---

② Fawnog Rydd, Derwen, Corwen, Clwyd LL21 9RN

Mrs Margaret E Jones &
M Jones
☎ 01824 750660/
750219
🏠 £90–£230
Sleeps 6
🐄 🎣 🔟
🏵 🏵 🏵 🏵

Detached farmhouse on working farm, surrounded by rolling farmland. 5 miles from Ruthin and close to lake Brenig and Clocaenog Forest. Fine walking countryside, ideal for coast, Snowdonia and Chester. Lounge with beamed ceiling, dining kitchen, bathroom, 2 double bedrooms, 1 twin on ground floor well equipped and heated. Open all year.

PRICES

Prices include VAT and service charge (if any) and are:
B&B per person per night
EM per person
SC per unit per week
Tents and caravans per pitch per night

FARM HOLIDAY
BUREAU

77

Mid Wales

Croeso Cader Idris

Group Contact: *Mrs Deilwen Breese* ☎ *01654 791235*

A true Welsh welcome 'croeso' is offered by the farming families around Cader Idris, one of the highest peaks in Wales; from the farms you can explore the coast and the countryside of this lovely area of Wales.

A vast area of green valleys and mountains criss-crossed by long distance footpaths, old drover's lanes and mountain paths which provide some of the finest hill walking country in Britain. For the explorer and adventurer, fishing, golfing, riding, pony trekking, climbing, canoeing and a mountain bike safari ensure a wealth of activity.

Dolgellau, beneath the majestic peak of Cader Idris, and Fairbourne, with its beautiful beach, combined with a visit to a real gold mine at Ganllwyd is a day out to remember. The working demonstrations of wind, water and solar power at the National Centre for Alternative Technology near Machynlleth. At Machynlleth experience the mysterious and magical World of the Celts, a unique attraction telling the story of the Celtic people.

An exciting area of contrasts, from the golden beaches of the coast to the high mountains of the National Park, there is something for everyone, from craft workshops to forest visitor centres, towering castles to deep slate caverns.

The Welsh language is heard frequently, the farmers of Cader Idris have roots deep in the area. A warm welcome is extended to visitors to share the language, history, culture and hospitality of one of the loveliest areas of Wales.

BED AND BREAKFAST
(and evening meal)

---

(1) Gogarth Hall Farm, Pennal, Machynlleth, Gwynedd SY20 9LB

E D Breese
☎/Fax 01654 791235
[BB] £13.50–£17
EM From £7.50
Sleeps 6
🐴 🐾

💐💐💐 *Highly Commended*

It's always a pleasure to welcome guests to our farm. Walk the hills, birdwatch, enjoy home cooking, see the animals or just relax. Central for touring, Centre for Alternative Technology and Celtica nearby. Aberdovey beach 4 miles. En suite facilities, guests' sitting and dining rooms, pool table. Spectacular views of Dovey estuary out to Cardigan Bay. Brochure. Open all year.

SELF-CATERING

---

(2) Carn y Gadell Uchaf, c/o Henblas, Llwyngwril, Gwynedd LL37 2QA

Mrs Swancott Pugh
☎/Fax 01341 250350
[SC] From £125–£450
Sleeps 6
🐾

💐 💐 💐 💐 💐

An historic 16th century farmhouse situated 1 mile from A493, a perfect retreat with panoramic views of Cardigan Bay. Stone spiral staircase, inglenook fireplace with log fire, 3 bedrooms, 2 bathrooms, colour TV, video, dishwasher, washing machine, fridge/freezer, microwave, games room, drying room. Excellent accommodation, ideal for exploring Snowdonia National Park. Welsh speaking family. Brochure. Open all year.

BUREAU ACCOMMODATION MEANS QUALITY

FARM HOLIDAY BUREAU

All Bureau members are inspected and quality graded by the National Tourist Board each year, as well as by fellow members.

Mid Wales

Montgomeryshire/ Heart of Wales

Group Contact: *Mrs Gwyneth Williams* ☎ *01686 430285*

The Heart of Wales has unspoilt villages, bustling little towns, and marvellous scenery – hills and mountains, sparkling streams, superb woodlands, tranquil lakes and reservoirs.

It is also surprisingly compact, with plenty to do and see without travelling far from your base. Roads are relative traffic free and none of the properties is much more than one hour's drive from the sandy beaches and rugged cliffs of the coast. There are plenty of country pubs for a lunchtime snack and the food we serve is largely fresh local produce, often from our own gardens. English is understood everywhere, but you will hear Welsh spoken, particularly in the north and west. You will soon become accustomed to the seemingly difficult sounds of our place names and personal names (we are all used to advising guests on pronunciation!) We also make a point of having information in our houses about events and places of interest, to help you enjoy your stay.

There are reminders of border struggles years ago; and the 8th century rampart built by King Offa is now a 170-mile public footpath. Among other man-made attractions, the area is renowned for its unique black-and-white buildings, including cruck houses, box-framed houses and their many variations.

BED AND BREAKFAST

(and evening meal)

---

(1) Cilthriew, Pentre, Kerry, Nr.Newtown, Powys SY16 4PF

Gary or Margaret Barbee
☎ 01686 670667
[BB] From £18–£21
Sleeps 6
🐕🐎♿🐾🐈🍼
🌼🌼🌼 *Highly Commended*

Chilthriew is an enchanting 16th century farmhouse set in the beautiful unspoilt Vale of Kerry where a warm and genuine welcome awaits you. Heavily beamed interior lounge with inglenook log fire. Imaginative country cooking is served in the candlelit dining room. Three en suite bedrooms, one on the ground floor. Guests may relax in the gardens or fish in the private carp pools. Open all year.

---

(2) Cwmllwynog, Llanfair Caereinion,Welshpool, Powys SY21 0HF

Joyce Cornes
☎ 01938 810791
[BB] From £16–£18
EM From £8
Sleeps 4
🐕🐈
🌼🌼🌼 *Highly Commended*

Built in the early 17th century Cwmllwynog is a traditional long farmhouse of character on a working dairy farm. We have a spacious garden with a stream at the bottom and a lot of unusual plants. All bedrooms have colour TV and drink making facilities. Double room en suite, twin with hot and cold and private bathroom. Delicious home-cooked meals cooked. Just for you! We can help you with routes. Open Mar–Nov.

---

(3) The Drewin Farm, Churchstoke, Montgomery, Powys SY15 6TW

Mrs Ceinwen Richards
☎ 01588 620325
[BB] From £15–£17
EM From £8
Sleeps 6
🐈🍴🐕🏃🎿⛺🍼
🌼🌼🌼 *Highly Commended*

Relax in our friendly family run and beautifully furnished 17th century farmhouse with panoramic views. Bedrooms have TV, hairdryer and drinks facilities, (en suite available). Games room with snooker table, dining room with large inglenook fireplace, separate lounge, full CH. Good home cooking, vegetarian by request. Offa's Dyke footpath runs through our mixed farm. Featured on BBC Travel Show 1993. Warm Welsh welcome. AA Selected. WTB Farmhouse Award. Open Mar–Nov.

---

(4) Little Brompton Farm, Montgomery, Powys SY15 6HY

Gaynor Bright
☎ 01686 668371
[BB] From £16–£18
EM From £9
Sleeps 6
🐈🍴🐕🏃🐾🍼⛺●
🌼🌼🌼 *Highly Commended*

A true oasis of tranquillity in beautiful scenery and this 17th C stone farmhouse is offering friendly hospitality. Pretty rooms enhanced by quality furnishings and antiques, all amenities, en suites available. Traditional farmhouse cooking. Offa's Dyke footpath runs through farm. WTB Farmhouse Award. AA selected. Welcome Host. Situated 2 miles east of Montgomery on B4385. Open all year.

---

(5) Llettyderyn, Mochdre, Newtown, Powys SY16 4JY

Mrs Margaret Jandrell
☎ 01686 626131
[BB] From £16–£19
EM From £8
Sleeps 4
🐈🐕
🌼🌼🌼 *Highly Commended*

Llettyderyn – a restored 18th century farmhouse with exposed beams, inglenook fireplace and traditional parlour. A working farm rearing sheep and beef. 2 miles from Newtown; an ideal base for touring Mid-Wales. Excellent farmhouse cooking, with home-made bread. Vegetarians catered for. Double and twin-bedded rooms both en suite, tea-making facilities and TV. Full central heating. Ample parking. Open all year.

Lower Gwerneirin Farm, Llandinam, Powys SY17 5DD

Mrs A Brown
☎ **01686 688286**
⊞ **From £15–£18**
EM From £8
Sleeps 6
🐾 ⌣
👑👑👑 *Highly Commended*

Beautifully situated in the Severn Valley, the farmhouse is a spacious Victorian dwelling offering comfortable accommodation. All rooms have CH and drinks facilities. Double and twin en suite, 1 double own bathroom. Guests lounge with log fire. Fishing in own trout pool. We have a wealth of wildlife. Ideally located for exploring Mid Wales. Large garden with beautiful views. Superb home cooking. Open all year.

Lower Gwestydd, Llanllwchaiarn, Newtown, Powys SY16 3AY

Iris Jarman
☎ **01686 626718**
⊞ **From £16.50–£17**
EM From £9
Sleeps 4
🐾 ♟
👑👑 *Highly Commended*

Lower Gwestydd is a listed half-timbered farmhouse set on a quiet hillside 2 miles north of Newtown just off the B4568 road. Guests have own lounge and dining room. All rooms centrally heated, 2 bedrooms en suite, all have beverage trays. WTB Farmhouse Award, hygiene certificate, Hostess Award. Finalist in the Best British Breakfast 1991 competition. Large garden with beautiful views, own produce. Open all year.

Moat Farm, Welshpool, Powys SY21 8SE

Gwyneth Jones
☎ **01938 553179**
⊞ **From £17–£19**
EM From £10
Sleeps 6
🐾 ♟
👑👑 *Highly Commended*

Moat Farm is a 260-acre dairy farm set in the beautiful Severn Valley. The 17th century farmhouse offers warm and comfortable accommodation with good home cooking served in a fine timbered dining room, traditionally furnished with Welsh dresser. All rooms en suite with tea/ coffee facilities and colour TV. Quiet lounge, pool table and spacious garden. Good touring centre. Near Powis Castle. Golf, riding and fishing nearby. Open Mar–Nov.

Trewythen Farm, Trewythen, Llandinam, Powys SY17 5BQ ⑨

Ceinwen & Ann Davies
☎/Fax **01686 688444**
⊞ **From £17–£19**
EM From £8
Sleeps 6
🐾 🐕 ✄
👑👑 *Highly Commended*

Enjoy the peace and tranquillity of Trewythen which is set in beautiful countryside on this mixed working farm. Superbly furnished with luxury en suite rooms, centrally heated. Lounge with oak beams offers log fires for the cooler evenings and colour TV. Separate dining room. Ideal for touring Mid Wales and walking. WTB Farmhouse Award and hygiene certificate. Open Apr–Nov.

SELF-CATERING

Cwm Y Gath, Trewythen, Llandinam, Powys SY17 5BQ ⑩

Ceinwen & Ann Davies
☎/Fax **01686 688444**
⊞ **From £90–£250**
Sleeps 4
🐾 🐕
🌼 🌼 🌼 🌼

Enjoy a welcome on the hillside at the old and cosy shepherd's cottage overlooking a working beef and sheep farm with magnificent views in peaceful surroundings. Refurbished to a high standard with a wealth of oak beams and inglenook fireplace. The cottage has one double and one twin bedroom (H&C). An ideal spot for nature lovers and walkers. Golfing, fishing, ponytrekking and lakes nearby. Enquiries welcome. Open all year.

Gungrog Cottage, c/o Gungrog House, Rhallt, Welshpool, Powys SY21 9HS

Mrs Eira Jones
☎ 01938 553381
🆂 From £120–£180
Sleeps 6
☂ ✂ 🎄 ⚕
Applied

Off the A483 opposite its junction with the A458, just east of Welshpool, Gungrog Cottage is located at a place called Rhallt, standing in an elevated position giving magnificent views of the Severn Valley. Set in 21 acres of farmland, the cottage is fully centrally heated and well-equipped. Kitchen/diner, bathroom with shower. The cottage was converted from a 16th century barn and retains much of its original charm and character. Open all year.

 Red House, Trefeglwys, Nr Caersws, Powys SY17 5PN

Gwyneth Williams
☎ 01686 430285
🆂 From £80–£230
Sleeps 5 + cot
☂ 🏕 ⚕
🌼 🌼 🌼 🌼

A highly furnished, self–contained part of the farmhouse, situated on a mixed working family farm. Panoramic views, unspoilt scenery and the tranquillity of the Trannon Valley. Ideal base for touring Mid Wales. Llanidloes 6 miles. Guests' comfort is the priority. Log fire, oak beams, garden furniture, ample parking and wildlife. Open all year.

Mid Wales

Radnor

Group Contact: *Mrs Ann Edwards* ☎ *01597 810211*

Mid-Wales is an area of outstanding natural beauty; with rugged mountain scenery, lakes, gentle hills and beautiful valleys.

It is an area abounding in wildlife and natural history, providing a habitat for rare birds and flowers. It is still possible to see the Red Kite in its last stronghold in Wales.

This breathtaking scenery is perfect for walkers; from gentle rambles to exploring the long distance footpaths of Glyndwr's Way and the Upper Wye Valley; for the more experienced and adventurous, the remote areas of the vast Elan Valley watershed.

The area is steeped in history and includes Roman encampments, castles, caves, old mine workings, churches and monuments. It also offers practically every sport or pastime that requires an outdoor or country environment. This is a place to come to relax, to enjoy the peace, tranquillity and solitude of George Borrow's 'Wild Wales' and the place to recharge your batteries.

337

BED AND BREAKFAST

(and evening meal)

---

1 Beili Neuadd, Rhayader, Powys LD6 5NS

Mrs Ann Edwards
☎ 01597 810211
BB From £17–£19
EM From £9
Sleeps 6
🛏 🐾(8) 🐕 🍴 🐎
♥♥♥ *Highly Commended*

An attractive 16th century stone-built farmhouse set amidst beautiful countryside in a quiet, secluded position approx. 2 miles from small market town of Rhayader. Guests are assured of every comfort with CH, log fires and well appointed accommodation in single, double and twin bedded rooms, all with private facilities. WTB Farmhouse Award winner, good food and comfortable surroundings. Open all year (closed Christmas).

---

2 Bwlch Farm, Llananno, Llandrindod, Wells, Powys LD1 6TT

Dorothy Taylor
☎ 01597 840366
BB From £17.50–£19
Sleeps 6
🛏 🐾 🍴 🐎
♥♥ *Highly Commended*

Come to the Bwlch and spend a peaceful holiday in our beautiful 15th century farmhouse. Go walking, birdwatching or touring or just laze and admire the magnificent views. You will be made welcome. We're ½ mile from A483 and 12 miles north of Llandrindod Wells. Open all year except Christmas.

---

3 Cefnsuran, Llangunllo, Knighton, Powys LD7 1SL

Gill Morgan
☎ 01547 550219
BB From £16–£17.50
EM From £9.50
Sleeps 6
✂ 🐾(10) 🏕 🚗 🐕 🐴 🍴
🚲
♥♥ *Highly Commended*

15th/16th century accommodation on working farm. Ideal for a relaxing holiday. Good walking area. (Offa's Dyke, Glyndwr's Way), superb views, abundant wildlife. Fishing, riding, boating, games room, snooker table, table tennis. Ideal biking country. Excellent food, traditional farmhouse fayre, vegetarian and special diets catered for by prior arrangement. Open all year.

---

4 Cwmgilla, Knighton, Powys LD7 1PG

Margaret Davies
☎ 01547 528387
BB From £16–£17
Sleeps 5
🐾(10) 🏕 🐕
♥ *Highly Commended*

Cwmgilla is a 600-acre mixed farm set in secluded valley with beautiful views of surrounding hills and woods. Ideal base for walking, touring or relaxing. Comfortable, modern farmhouse, all rooms with H&C, tea/coffee-making facilities. TV lounge and separate dining room. Excellent breakfasts. Fishing. 1½ miles from Knighton. Open Mar–Nov.

---

5 Highbury Farm, Llanyre, Llandrindod Wells, Powys LD1 6EA

Shirley Evans
☎ 01597 822716
BB From £15–£18
EM From £8.50
Sleeps 6
🐾 🐕 🏕 🍴
♥♥ *Highly Commended*

A warm welcome awaits you at our smallholding one mile from the spa town of Llandrindod Wells. Comfortable, spacious bedrooms with beverage trays. Double and family/twin room, one double en suite. Full CH. TV lounge, separate dining room, snooker table. Evening meal by arrangement. WTB Farmhouse Award. Brochure available. Ideally situated for touring heart of Wales. Open Mar–Nov.

Pilleth Court, Whitton, Knighton, Powys LD7 1NP   6

Mrs Heather Hood
☎ **01547 560272**
🅱 **From £17–£20**
Sleeps 6
🛏(9) ✳ 🐾 ⟲ 🏕
🏵 🏵 *Highly Commended*

A listed Elizabethan house, tastefully furnished to retain its character and atmosphere, on a large working farm set in marvellous, unspoilt countryside. All guest rooms have panoramic views. One room is en suite and has TV and all rooms have tea/coffee-making facilities. A wonderful centre for walking and touring. Open all year except Christmas.

DISABLED VISITORS

Many members offer a welcome to disabled/less able visitors. Please do check the extent of the facilities before booking.

FOLLOW THE COUNTRY CODE

Leave nothing but footprints,
Take nothing but photographs,
Kill nothing but time!

BUREAU ACCOMMODATION MEANS QUALITY

All Bureau members are inspected and quality graded by the National Tourist Board each year, as well as by fellow members.

Mid Wales

Ceredigion

Group Contact: *Mrs Beti Davies* ☎ *01570 422447*

Through the ages travellers have come to Ceredigion. Eight centuries ago Gerald Cambrensis wrote of its kindly people; somewhat later the Victorians passed long summers by its fine beaches. Today's visitors can rediscover the old hospitality that is so warmly given.

The 'Cardis', as the district's native inhabitants are known, have guarded their heritage well – many still speak Welsh, Europe's oldest living language.

Ceredigion's 52-mile coastline, much now owned by the National Trust, looks out on the expanse of Cardigan Bay. Yachts and dinghies sail from small harbours like Aberaeron and New Quay, and the many sandy beaches, among them Aberporth and Llangrannog, are a haven for sunbathers and swimmers.

Inland, around Tregaron you might spot rare birds like the red kite, whilst the River Teifi produces some fine catches of salmon and sewin. Between the mountains and sea is an unspoilt patchwork of farmland; small market towns have market days well worth experiencing.

Machynlleth

Tywyn

A487

Aberystwyth A44

Aberaeron

New Quay A482 ② A485

③

A487 A486 ① Lampeter Llanwrtyd-Wells

A475

Cardigan A483

Newcastle Emlyn

Fishguard A484 Llandovery

A487 A40 A40

A478 Llandeilo

BED AND BREAKFAST

(and evening meal)

Bryncastell Farm, Llanfair Road, Lampeter, Dyfed SA48 8JY

E A Beti Davies
☎ 01570 422447
[BB] From £16–£18
EM From £10
Sleeps 6
👦☺🍽✗🏕🏠☕🛖
💼
🐝🐝 *Highly Commended*

'Croeso' to our 140-acre family farm commanding panoramic views over the Teifi Valley. All modern facilities with unrivalled hospitality and excellent cuisine. Access to farm activities, hillside walks or gentle strolls along the river bank in an area of unspoilt natural beauty. ¾ mile fishing and shooting, 1 mile from university market town of Lampeter. WTB Farmhouse Award. Open all year.

Brynog Mansion, Felinfach, Lampeter, Dyfed SA48 8AQ

Eleanor Davies
☎ 01570 470266
[BB] From £16.50–£18
Sleeps 6
🐦(6) 🅰☕
🐝🐝 *Highly Commended*

Secluded spacious 250 year old country mansion and 170-acre grazing farm, approached by ¾ mile rhododendron-lined drive off the A482 main road. 15 mins by car. Lampeter University town and seaside resort of Aberaeron and coast. Full Welsh breakfast in the grand old dining room. Rough shooting, birdwatching, riverside walks. Brochure available. Open all year except Christmas & New Year.

Dremddu Fawr, Creuddyn Bridge, Lampeter, Dyfed SA48 8BL

Mrs M A Williams-Jones
☎ 01570 470394
[BB] From £17.50–£20
EM From £12.50
Sleeps 4
🐦✗🛖💼
🐝🐝🐝 *Highly Commended*

Come to us for a genuine taste of Welsh farming life. Small farmhouse on 163-acre cattle and sheep farm set in rolling countryside between Lampeter and the Cardigan Bay coast. Guest bedrooms have pine furniture, tapestry bedspreads and little 'extras' such as mineral water and chocolates – all made in Wales! 'All Wales Top Cook ' award – mouthwatering food. Open all year.

FOLLOW THE COUNTRY CODE

Leave nothing but footprints,
Take nothing but photographs,
Kill nothing but time!

Mid Wales

Heart of Cardiganshire

Group Contact: *Carole Jacobs ☎ 01239 851261*

The magic of Cardiganshire will enchant you with its gentle mountains and unspoiled coastline encircling pastureland threaded with rivers famous for sewin and salmon.

This undiscovered part of West Wales, free of traffic and crowds, is home to the Red Kite. Otters have returned to the rivers; dolphins and seals play in Cardigan Bay; butterflies shelter among wild flowers. Here is the heartland of Welsh Cob breeding. Monthly horse sales are held in Llanybydder, trotting races at Tregaron and Synod Inn and pony trekking can be enjoyed in the mountains or along the coast.

Cardiganshire's 52 mile coastline has safe, sandy beaches and spectacular walks. It stretches from Cardigan to Aberystwyth, a university town and home to Wales' National Library and the thriving Arts Centre. The county's main river, the Teifi, is shared by fisherman, canoeists and the famous coracle men of Cenarth. These are well-stocked lakes to satisfy the angler. Here, in the ancient kingdom of Ceredig, a rural way of life persists in the small farms and villages where Welsh is still the first language. Woollen mills, potteries and Celtic crafts reflect the traditional image of Cardiganshire.

Come and join us, the food is fresh, the beds are comfortable and the hearth is warm.

BED AND BREAKFAST

(and evening meal)

Broniwan, Rhydlewis, Llandysul, Cardiganshire SA44 5PF

Carole Jacobs
☎ 01239 851261
BB From £16.50
EM From £8.50
Sleeps 4
🐕 ✄ 🏇(6) 🧍 🏛 🎋 🎍
🌺🌺 *Highly Commended*

Unwind in the peace of our ivy-clad farmhouse sheltered by pine trees, 10 minutes from National Trust beaches and coastal walks. Enjoy fishing and otter watching on River Teifi near Cardigan. Plenty of our own farm-produced food including vegetarian. En suite/private facilities. Quiet pets welcome. Reduced weekly terms. WTB Farmhouse Award.

Pant-Teg, Llanfair Clydogau, Lampeter, Dyfed SA48 8LL

Mrs Pat Brown
☎ 01570 493416
BB From £16–£18
EM From £7
Sleeps 6
🐕 ✄ 🏛 🎋
🌺🌺🌺 *Highly Commended*

Welcome to Pant-Teg! Once an old stone hill farm, now a peaceful country home, it rests on the gentle mountainside with magnificent views. Red kites wheel overhead and wildlife surrounds us. Beautiful lawned gardens, pond, meandering brook. Enticing meals, vegetarian if preferred, served in our charming conservatory. Cosy woodburner and en suite facilities complete your comfort. Come and join us! Open all year.

Pantycelyn, Blaencwrt, Llanwnnen, Lampeter, Dyfed SA48 7LW

Mrs Ann Jenkins
☎ 01570 434455
BB From £15–£18
EM From £8.50
Sleeps 4
🐕 🏇
🌺🌺 *Highly Commended*

Relax at Pantycelyn, a comfortable farmhouse in peaceful countryside within easy reach of Cardigan Bay and Cambrian Mountains. Ideal base for enjoying Cardiganshire's attractions: birdwatching, fishing, riding, local markets, horse sales, trotting races, craft centres, potteries. En suite bedrooms, genuine home cooking, ample local information and our own Welsh Cobs and foals. Open all year except Christmas.

FARM HOLIDAY
BUREAU

THOSE LITTLE EXTRAS

For advice on farms that can offer 'extras' such as four-poster beds, special diets, farm trails, fishing rights – even stabling and trekking arrangements if you are bringing your own horse – ring the Farm Holiday Bureau on (01203) 696909.

South Wales

Brecon

Group Contact: *Mrs Mary Adams* ☎ *01874 636505*

The Brecon Beacons welcome you to the great outdoors. This unspoilt countryside of mountains and forests, hills and valleys with rivers and lakes, caves and waterfalls, offers a great variety of country pursuits.

Enjoy watersports on Llangorse Lake, visit Dan-yr-Ogof show caves, take a trip on the Monmouth to Brecon canal or Brecon Mountain Railway. The hills delight climbers, walkers and pony trekkers. Fish in the rivers Wye and Usk or the many reservoirs. Guided walks start from the National Park Visitor Centre and Craig-y-Nos Country Park.

There are craft centres to visit, castles and historic sites. Browse around museums and secondhand bookshops and listen to the local choirs.

Sample home cooking at its best, and wherever you go you will be greeted by friendly, helpful people.

[Map of South Wales showing towns including Knighton, Presteigne, Aberaeron, New Quay, Llandrindod-Wells, Lampeter, Llanwrtyd-Wells, Builth-Wells, Newcastle Emlyn, Llyswen, Hay on Wye, Llandovery, Brecon, Talgarth, Sennybridge, Llandeilo, Ammanford, Abergavenny, Kidwelly, Merthyr Tydfil, Rhymney, Brynmawr, Tredegar, Blaenavon, Abertillery, Abersychan, Burry Port, Llanelli, Gorseinon, Neath, Aberdare, Gelligaer, Pontypool, Caerleon, Rhondda, Abercarn, Swansea. Roads labelled A487, A483, A40, A48, A44, A438, A470, A4067, A465, A485.]

BED AND BREAKFAST

(and evening meal)

Brynfedwen Farm, Trallong Common, Sennybridge, Brecon, Powys LD3 8HW

Mrs Mary Adams
☎ 01874 636505
[BB] From £17
EM From £9
Sleeps 6
♿ ☞ ⚡
♛♛♛ *Highly Commended*

Brynfedwen, situated between Brecon and Sennybridge, is a hill livestock farm with lovely views over the Brecon Beacons and Usk River Valley. Excellent facilities for walking and all country pursuits. Traditional stone farmhouse. Central heating. TV lounge with log fire. 2 family rooms and 1 twin bedded flat (equipped for disabled), all en suite. Personal attention and good home cooking. Children welcome. Farmhouse Award. AA selected. Open all year.

Cwmcamlais Uchaf, Cwmcamlais, Sennybridge, Brecon, Powys LD3 8TD

Mrs Jean Phillips
☎ 01874 636376
[BB] From £16–£17
EM From £9.50
Sleeps 6
☞(8) ☞ ⚡ ⚘
♛♛♛ *Highly Commended*

Cwmcamlais Uchaf is a working farm situated in the Brecon Beacons National Park. 1 mile off the A40 between Brecon and Sennybirdge. Our spacious 16th century farmhouse has exposed beams, log fires and 3 tastefully decorated bedrooms, 1 double en suite, 1 double and 1 twin with private bathrooms. Tea/coffee-making facilities. The River Camlais with its waterfalls, flows through the farm land. Open all year.

Lodge Farm, Talgarth, Brecon, Powys LD3 0DP

Mrs Marion Meredith
☎ 01874 711244
[BB] From £16
EM From £10
Sleeps 6
☞ ☞ ⚡ ☂ ⚘
♛♛♛ *Commended*

Enjoy the peace and tranquillity on this working farm, nestling in the Black Mountains in eastern part of the National Park yet only 1½ miles from Talgarth off A479. Attractively furnished bedrooms, tea-making facilities, all en suite, 1 family, 1 double, 1 twin. Varied menu, including vegetarian, of freshly prepared real food. A warm welcome of prime importance. Central base, walking, touring, pony trekking. Hay-on-Wye, Brecon 8 miles. Open all year.

Trehenry Farm, Felinfach, Llandefalle, Brecon, Powys LD3 0UN

Mrs Theresa Jones
☎ 01874 754312
[BB] From £18–£19
EM From £9.50
Sleeps 6
☞ ⚑
♛♛♛ *De Luxe*

Trehenry is a 200 acre mixed farm situated east of Brecon, 1 mile off A470. The impressive 18th century farmhouse with breathtaking views, inglenook fireplaces and exposed beams offers comfortable accommodation, good food and cosy rooms. TV lounge, separate dining tables, central heating, tea-making facilities, all rooms en suite. Brochure on request. Farmhouse Award winner. Open all year except Christmas.

LET THE TELEPHONE RING!

Some farmhouses are big places. Let the telephone ring long enough to give the owner time to answer it.

SELF-CATERING

5 **Trehenry Farm,** Felinfach, Llandefalle, Brecon, Powys LD3 0UN

Mrs Theresa Jones
☎ **01874 754312**
SC **From £250–£400**
Sleeps 8
🐕 🐈 🖼 🏕 💼
🌼 🌼 🌼 🌼 🌼

For a holiday to remember then come to Trehenry 200 acre working farm. Tranquillity surrounded by breathtaking views. 17th century farmhouse modernised to a high standard with oak beams, inglenook fireplace. 3 bedrooms, 2 en suite, 1 private. Bed settee in second lounge. Very well equipped kitchen, lounge with TV, video, CH, wood stove. Price includes linen, electric, heating. Brochure. Open all year.

DISABLED VISITORS

Many members offer a welcome to disabled/less able visitors. Please do check the extent of the facilities before booking.

THOSE LITTLE EXTRAS

For advice on farms that can offer 'extras' such as four-poster beds, special diets, farm trails, fishing rights – even stabling and trekking arrangements if you are bringing your own horse – ring the Farm Holiday Bureau on (01203) 696909.

Please mention **Stay on a Farm** when booking

South Wales

Gwent

Group Contact: *Mrs Ann Ball* ☎ *01873 821236*

To the north of the county are the Black Mountains and the Brecon Beacons with majestic peaks and deep sheltered valleys. This area contains part of the Brecon Beacons National Park which provides opportunities for pony trekking, walking and many other activities.

Eastern Gwent is very different – the countryside is pastoral with undulating, wooded hills and the river valleys of the Usk and Wye. Ancient market towns and picturesque villages are dotted throughout this part of the county. Part of the Welsh Marches falls within this region and there are a number of strategically placed castles, including Raglan and Chepstow, reminders of less peaceful times. Tintern Abbey, immortalised by Wordsworth, shows a more tranquil face of the county.

Western Gwent can boast bracing, beautiful mountainsides, spectacular views and lovely walking country. It also has a rich industrial heritage with a wealth of attractions for those fascinated by the way we used to live.

Gwent is also an ideal base for exploring the interesting country and attractions in the South Wales and Border areas. Brecon Beacons National Park, the Forest of Dean, the Mendip Hills, the Cotswolds, Bristol and Bath ... are all within 60 miles.

BED AND BREAKFAST

(and evening meal)

---

① Chapel Farm, Blaina, Gwent NP3 3DJ

Mrs Betty Hancocks
☎ 01495 290888
🆎 From £17–£19
EM From £7
Sleeps 6
�ే(4) 🕱
🐾 *Commended*

You will find traditional Welsh hospitality at Chapel Farm, a working sheep farm with panoramic views overlooking the towns of Blaina, Nantyglo and Brynmawr. The 15th century cruck farmhouse has been renovated to provide modern comfort yet keeping its old world charm. Home cooking, evening meals (pre-booked). Children welcome. Open all year except Christmas.

---

② Little Treadam, Llantilio, Crossenny, Abergavenny, Gwent NP7 8TA

Beryl Ford
☎ 01600 780326
🆎 From £18–£21
EM From £10
Sleeps 6
🐓 🕱
🐾🐾🐾 *Highly Commended*

Relax and enjoy comfort and peace in our 16th century beamed farmhouse. Delicious food. Restaurant licence. Centrally situated for Brecon National Park, Wye Valley and Black Mountains. Offa's Dyke Path long distance walk passes through the farm with White Castle a 2 mile walk away. All rooms en suite with radio and colour TV. WTB Farmhouse Award. Open Mar–Nov.

---

③ Parsons Grove, Earlswood, Nr Chepstow, Gwent NP6 6RD

Gloria Powell
☎/Fax 01291 641382
🆎 From £17–£19
Sleeps 6
🔴 🐓 ఈ ☍
🐾🐾 *Highly Commended*

On edge of Wye Valley, peaceful and traffic-free, yet only 15 minutes Chepstow and M4. Large, centrally heated, country house, beamed lounge, log burner. Sunny conservatory in which to enjoy breakfast, overlooks swimming pool, and 2-acre vineyard. Magnificent views of Wentwood Forest and Earlswood Valley. All rooms en suite, tea/coffee-making facilities, radio and colour TV. Access at all times. Open Jan–Nov.

---

④ Pentre-Tai Farm, Rhiwderin, Newport, Gwent NP1 9RQ

Susan Proctor
☎ 01633 893284
🆎 From £16–£21
Sleeps 6
ఈ 🕱 ✂ 🖐 🏕 ⌨ 🕱 📱 🌾
Highly Commended

Gateway to Wales. A warm welcome awaits you at our peaceful sheep farm located in the countryside yet only 3 miles from M4. Most rooms en suite, all with TV and beverage facilities. Children welcome at reduced rates. Ideal base for Wye Valley, Brecon Beacons, Cardiff, Welsh Folk Museum and magnficient Welsh castles. Open Feb–Nov.

---

⑤ Pentwyn Farm, Little Mill, Pontypool, Gwent NP4 0HQ

Stuart & Ann Bradley
☎/Fax 01495 785249
🆎 From £15–£18.50
EM From £11
Sleeps 6
ే(4) 🕱 📱 🌾
🐾🐾🐾 *Highly Commended*

A 125-acre stock farm on the edge of the Brecon Beacons National Park where good food and hospitality are of prime importance. The 16th century Welsh longhouse with 20th century comforts has a beamed dining room and sitting room with log fires. Swimming pool. 3 bedrooms (2 en suite) with tea-making facilities. Restaurant licence. Rough shooting. WTB Farmhouse Award. Open Jan–Nov.

Tŷ-Gwyn Farm, Gwehelog, Usk, Gwent NP5 1RT

Jean Arnett
☎ 01291 672878
[BB] From £15–£19
EM From £10.50
Sleeps 6
✕ ☎(5) ♞ ▪
☙☙☙ Highly
Commended

Wake up and sit up to magnificent views of Brecon Beacons National Park from all 3 bedrooms (2 bath en suite with colour TV and hospitality tray). Hearty breakfasts and meals served in spacious dining room or conservatory overlooking secluded lawns. Mountains, castles, golf, fishing all nearby. Quality meals, vegetarians and own wine welcome. WTB Farmhouse Award. Brochure available. Open all year.

Ty Shon Jacob Farm, Coch-y-North Lane, Tranch, Nr Pontypool NP4 6BP

Mrs Agneta Harris
☎ 01495 757536
Fax 01495 769882
[BB] From £15–£16
EM From £6.50
Sleeps 6
☎ ♞ ♞ ☎ ▪ ☂
☙☙ Applied

Splendid views! Get away from it all to this small stud farm, a quiet retreat close to the Welsh National Park. Open all year.

The Wenallt Farm, Gilwern, near Abergavenny, Gwent NP7 0HP

Janice Harris
☎ 01873 830694
[BB] From £15–£18
EM From £10.50
Sleeps 8
☎ ♞ Å ♿ ▪ ☎ ☂
☙☙☙ Commended

A 16th century Welsh longhouse set in 50 acres of farmland in the Brecon Beacons National Park commanding magnificent views over the Usk Valley. Retaining all its old charm with oak beams, inglenook fireplace, yet offering a high standard with en suite bedrooms, good food and a warm welcome. An ideal base from which to see Wales and the surrounding areas. Licensed. AA listed. Brochure available. Open all year.

SELF-CATERING

Granary & Coach House, Upper Cwm Farm, Llantilio Crossenny, Abergavenny, Gwent NP7 8TG

Ann Ball
☎ 01873 821236
[SC] From £175–£330
Sleeps 12
☎ ♞ ☎
❀❀❀❀

Holidays and short breaks in beautifully converted old barn on working sheep farm. Family accommodation with CH, TV, electricity, bed linen, towels included. Peaceful superb views, ideal for walking, birdwatching, exploring Welsh castles, Brecon Beacons, Wye and Usk Valleys. The Granary (upper) and Coach House (ground) each have 1 double and 2 twin bedrooms, lounge/dining/kitchen, bathroom with shower. Brochure. Open all year.

Parsons Grove, Earlswood, Nr Chepstow, Gwent NP6 6RD 10

Gloria Powell
☎/Fax 01291 641382
[SC] From £90–£330
Sleeps 4/6
♞ ♿ ☎
❀❀❀❀ – ❀❀❀❀❀

Close to Wye Valley, set in 20 acres of peaceful countryside with heated swimming pool. Three cottages, furnished to very high standard. Fully carpeted with colour TV, fitted kitchen, refrigerator, cooker and microwave. All linen (duvets) included. Overlooking vineyard with panoramic views of beautiful valley and Wentwood Forest. Riding nearby. 10 minutes St Pierre Golf Club. Open all year.

11 **Pentwyn Stable Cottages,** Pentwyn Farm, Little Mill, Pontypool, Gwent NP4 0HQ

Stuart & Ann Bradley
☎/Fax 01495 785249
SC From £160–£230
EM From £11
Sleeps 4/5
🐕 🐴 🎋 🛍
🏵 🏵 🏵 🏵

Relax in rural tranquillity in our delightfully converted stable cottages. Enjoy the castles, museums and water sports. Walk in the Black Mountains or along the canal bank. Each cottage has 2 bedrooms, a fully fitted kitchen and a large beamed sitting room with wood burner and wonderful views over the large garden with swimming pool and barbecue. Linen and electricity included in price. Meals available in farmhouse. Open all year.

12 **Worcester House,** Castle Farm, Raglan, Gwent NP5 2BT

Mrs Vivien Jones
☎ 01291 690492
SC From £125–£275
Sleeps 6/7
🐕 🐴 🎋 🛍
🏵 🏵 🏵

Part of a 17th century manor house. The oldest brick building in Gwent. Easy access to Wye Valley, Brecon Beacons and Forest of Dean. Many castles and golf courses nearby. Raglan Castle 20 yards, overlooking picturesque village of Raglan. A 200-acre working dairy/arable farm with 3 bedrooms bathroom and separate shower room with WC. Living/dining room with french windows leading to large lawn, modern kitchen. Open most of year.

FARM HOLIDAY
BUREAU

THE 1000+ BUREAU MEMBERS OFFER A UNIQUE LINK TO CUSTOMERS ACROSS THE UK

All Bureau members belong to a local Group. Each member can refer you to an equally high quality member within his Group… or across the UK: England, Northern Ireland, Scotland, Wales.

FARM HOLIDAY
BUREAU

FOLLOW THE COUNTRY CODE

Leave nothing but footprints,
Take nothing but photographs,
Kill nothing but time!

South Wales

Carmarthenshire

Group Contact: *Marian Lewis* ☎ *01550 720410/Fax 01550 720262*

Carmarthenshire is a county of contrasts from the Black Mountain through the tranquil Towy Valley, to the picturesque coastal villages and golden sands of Carmarthen Bay.

It is at the heart of West Wales which means you can enjoy a different route every day to many and varied locations. Welsh is spoken throughout the county adding to the special Celtic atmosphere. Find the traditional markets and hear the farmers talk about the ups and downs of agricultural life.

All the main towns are steeped in history and many have their own castles, see especially Kidwelly and Llanstephan near the coast and Carreg Cennen in the hills.

For walking, choose coastal paths or cliffs, the magnificent scenery of the Towy, Teifi and Taf valleys, Brechfa forest, Brecon Beacons National Park or the Llyn Brianne reservoir with maybe the chance of sighting a rare Red Kite.

Every sport is catered for with excellent leisure centres, superb fishing and all country pursuits. Add to that the country parks, steam railway, crafts, antiques, agricultural shows, choirs and music festivals and soak up the warm Welsh welcome in our homes.

Croeso i Sir Gaerfyrddin.

BED AND BREAKFAST
(and evening meal)

---

(1) Capel Dewi Uchaf Farm, Capel Dewi, Carmarthen, Dyfed SA32 8AY

Fredena Burns
☎ 01267 290799
Fax 01267 290003
BB From £23.50
Sleeps 6
🐎 ⅄ 🐴 🐈 🐕 ⌂
🐑🐑 *Highly
Commended*

Our beautifully restored 500 year-old award-winning farmhouse offers our guests complete comfort and relaxation. Renowned home cooked cuisine, log fires. Nestled in the undulating Towy Valley, ideal for all kinds of leisure pursuits year round. See our magnificent herd of deer. For latest brochure contact Fredena Burns. Open all year except Christmas.

---

(2) Cwmgwyn Farm, Llangadog Road, Llandovery, Carmarthenshire SA20 0EQ

Marian Lewis
☎ 01550 720410
Fax 01550 720262
BB From £19–£20
Sleeps 6
🐎
🐑🐑 *Highly Commended*

Welcome to the country on our livestock farm with superb views overlooking the River Towy, 2 miles from Llandovery on A4069. The 17th century farmhouse is full of charm and character with inglenook fireplace, exposed stonework and beams. 3 spacious luxury en suite bedrooms with bath/shower, hairdryer, TV, tea/coffee. Enjoy tranquil riverside setting from garden or picnic area. Ideal for touring mid/South Wales. Open Easter–Oct.

---

(3) Llanerchindda Farm, Cynghordy, Llandovery, Dyfed SA20 0NB

Nick Bointon
☎ 01550 750274
Fax 01550 750300
BB From £21
EM From £9
Sleeps 21
⅄ ⚲ ♨ 👤 👍 ♟
🐑🐑 *Commended*

Nestled into the southern slopes of the Cambrian Mountains, Llanerchindda has spectacular views over the Towy Valley and Brecon Brecons. We have 9 comfortable en suite rooms (TV/tea), residents' lounge, dining room, library. Underfloor heating, log fires, licensed, disabled facilities. We serve delicious homemade food and have much of our own produce. A wonderful, quiet location. Open Apr–Oct.

---

(4) Plas Farm, Llangynog, Carmarthen, Dyfed SA33 5DB

Mrs Margaret Thomas
☎ 01267 211492
BB From £15
Sleeps 6
🐎 🐓 👤 ♟
🐑🐑 *Applied*

Plas is a family-run working dairy farm situated 5 miles west of Carmarthen in quiet countryside yet an ideal base for touring the unspoilt coastline and numerous historical places and Welsh craft shops inland. Good golf course nearby. Homely atmosphere and warm welcome assured. All rooms have colour TV, tea/coffee facilities, en suite available. Choice evening meals at local inns. Closed Christmas & New Year.

---

(5) Trebersed Farm, St Peters Travellers Rest, Carmarthen, Dyfed SA31 3RR

Mrs Rosemary Jones
☎ 01267 238182
Fax 01267 223633
BB From £16–£18
Sleeps 6
🐎 🐓 ⅄ 🎋
🐑🐑 *Highly Commended*

A warm welcome awaits you at our working dairy farm. Wellingtons available! Excellent touring base overlooking thriving market town of Carmarthen, just off main A40. Three comfortable rooms, one family, all en suite, with tea/coffee tray, central heating, radio alarm and colour TV.

South Wales

Pembrokeshire

Group Contact: *Mrs Betty Devonald* ☎ *01348 881277*

Pembrokeshire is the south western corner of Wales. A large portion being covered by the Pembrokeshire Coast National Park, including most of the coastal strip and Preseli Hills. The countryside is unspoilt with an abundance and variety of wild flowers everywhere from the coast to the banks that skirt the miles of narrow country lanes.

The beaches vary from long sandy stretches to small rocky coves – but you could see them all if you walked the coastal footpath from St. Dogmael's in the north to Amroth in the south – 180 miles! You would also see the islands off the coast including Skomer and Skokholm which are nature reserves; and Caldy, inhabited by Cistercian monks. Some of these islands can be visited and you may see seals here or indeed off any part of the coastline.

The variable terrain from coast to hill, moorland to marsh provides an agreeable habitat for a wide variety of birds, insects and animals. The area is full of historical relics from ancient to modern, with Iron Age settlement remains, cromlechs and standing stones right up to those of more recent times with many castles and, of course, the fine cathedral of St. David's.

Aberaeron
New Quay
A487
Lampeter
Cardigan
Newport
A487
Egwyswrw
Newcastle Emlyn
A485
Llandovery
A483
Fishgaurd
1 9
6
4 8 7
A40
A478
St.Davids
2
Carmarthen
A48
Llandeilo
Haverfordwest
5
3 A40
Whitland
A40
Narberth
Ammanford
Templeton
A477
Kidwelly
19
Neyland
18
Burry Port
Llanelli
Pembroke
Tenby
Gorseinon
17
16 15 14
Neath
Swansea
41

BED AND BREAKFAST

(and evening meal)

---

① Gilfach Goch Farmhouse, Fishguard, Pembrokeshire, Dyfed SA65 9SR

June Devonald
☎/Fax 01348 873871
🛏 From £18–£24
EM £12
Sleeps 12
✕ 🐕

🌑🌑🌑 *Highly Commended*

Charming farmhouse with attractive grounds in National Park for people who want somewhere relaxing, peaceful and very comfortable. Oak beams, stone walls, inglenook, pretty bedrooms (en suite), magnificent views to the sea. Small holding with friendly animals and friendly Welsh people too! Superb meals – own produce giving variety, quality and quantity. Residential licence, fire certificate, pay phone. Farmhouse Award. Open Easter–Nov.

---

② Lochmeyler Farm, Llandeloy, Pen-y-Cwm, Nr Solva, Haverfordwest, Dyfed SA62 6LL

Mrs Morfydd Jones
☎ 01348 837724
Fax 01348 837622
🛏 From £15–£20
EM From £5
Sleeps 24
🛏 ♿ 🐕(10) ⊞ ♠
🌑🌑🌑🌑 *De Luxe*

Lochmeyler is a 220-acre dairy farm in the centre of St David's Peninsula, 4 miles from Solva Harbour. Twelve en suite bedrooms (no smoking in bedrooms), TV. 4-poster beds available. Two lounges, 1 non-smokers. Choice of menus, traditional and vegetarian. RAC highly acclaimed, AA selected. Member of Taste of Wales, WTB Farmhouse Award. RAC Guesthouse of the Year '93. Licensed, credit cards accepted. Open all year.

---

③ Lower Haythog, Spittal, Haverfordwest, Pembrokeshire SA62 5QL

Nesta Thomas
☎/Fax 01437 731279
🛏 From £17.50
EM From £10
Sleeps 10–12
🛏 🐕 ✕ 🐎 ⚘ ♠ 🦜
🌑🌑🌑 *Highly Commended*

For a taste of Wales and real country life join us on our farm 5 miles north of Haverfordwest. Charming combination of old character and modern facilities in 300 year old farmhouse. Oak beams, inglenook, CH, log fires, comfortable lounge for relaxing. Peaceful, entertaining with superb home cooking – we recommend it! Well appointed bedroom facilities. Pretty gardens, imaginatively designed. Trout fishing, pony rides. Fire and basic food hygiene certificates. Open all year.

---

④ Penygraig Farm, Puncheston, Haverfordwest, Pembrokeshire SA62 5RJ

Betty Devonald
☎/Fax 01348 881277
🛏 From £15–£17.50
EM From £8
Sleeps 6
🐕 🛏 ⚘
🌑🌑 *Highly Commended*

A warm welcome awaits you at Penygraig, a working farm, situated near the picturesque Preseli Hills, with plenty of walks, natural trails and places of unspoilt beauty to be enjoyed. The rugged coastline of North Pembrokeshire being not far away. In the spacious dining room good wholesome cooking is served. There is 1 double room en suite, 1 family room. All rooms have tea trays, reductions for children sharing. Open Apr–Oct.

---

⑤ Spittal Cross Farm, Spittal Cross, Haverfordwest, Dyfed SA62 5DB

Mrs Susan Evans
☎ 01437 741206
🛏 From £15
EM From £8
Sleeps 4
🐕 🛏
🌑 *Applied*

A family run 200-acre dairy farm in the heart of the beautiful Pembrokeshire countryside, making it a convenient touring base for the many local activities, beaches and places of historical interest. We offer hearty breakfast, imaginative dinners and comfortable accommodation. Reduced rates for children. Dining/sitting room with colour TV, games and books available. Central heating throughout. Food hygiene certificate. Open Apr–Oct.

Trepant Farm, Morvil, Maenclochog, Pembrokeshire SA66 7RE

Marilyn Salmon
☎ 01437 532491
BB From £15.50–£18.50
EM From £9
Sleeps 4
🐎
👄👄 *Highly Commended*

A warm Welsh welcome on our mixed dairy farm in the beautiful Preseli hills, sandy beaches and hidden coves. Pony trekking, fishing are all nearby. Relax in the evening with excellent home cuisine using best local produce. Vegetarians welcome. One room with en suite facilities. Open Mar–Oct.

Yethen Isaf, Mynachlogddu, Clynderwen, Pembrokeshire SA66 7SN

Mrs Ann Barney
☎ 01437 532256
BB From £17–£20.50
EM From £9.50
Sleeps 6
🐎 ♞ 🛁 🎏 ⬤
👄👄 *Commended*

Yethen Isaf sits right in the midst of the Preseli Hills, offering superb walking, yet only 10 miles from the coast. The farm is approx 200 acres, breeding pedigree Welsh Black cattle and Beulah Speckleface sheep. The 250-year-old farmhouse offers superb, comfortable accommodation with home cooking, central heating and log fires. One room with en suite facilities. Visits and activities arranged. Welcome Host. Taste of Wales member. Open all year.

SELF-CATERING

Garden Farm, Tufton, Haverfordwest, c/o Yethen Isaf, Mynachlogddu, Clynderwen, Pembs SA66 7SN

Mrs Ann Barney
☎ 01437 532256
SC From £130–£400
Sleeps 4–7
🐎 ♿ 🐾 ♞ 🎏 ⬤
🏠🏠🏠🏠 – 🏠🏠🏠🏠🏠

Situated in Preseli Hills only 9 miles from coast at Fishguard and 9 miles from Haverfordwest. A tranquil working beef and sheep farm. Attractively restored Victorian farmhouse and superbly converted granary. Warm and comfortable with heating, TV etc, modern kitchen facilities. Bed linen provided. Sorry no pets. Stabling and facilities available for horses. Visits and activities can be arranged. Welcome Host. Open all year.

Gilfach Goch Farmhouse Cottages, Gilfach Goch, Fishguard, Pembrokeshire SA65 9SR

June Devonald
☎/Fax 01348 873871
SC From £160–£500
Sleeps 5/6
🐎 🐾 🍴 ⬤
🏠🏠🏠🏠🏠

Choose from the 200 year old stone walls, beamed ceiling and inglenook of Garn Madog, or Edwardian elegance, vivid colours and style of Brynawelon, two outstanding renovations in quiet, sheltered location. Panoramic landscape of sea/hills. National Park. Each house has secluded private patio, lawns, parking, woodburner, elec heating, microwave, dishwasher, washing machine. Open all year.

South Wales

Pride of Pembrokeshire

Group Contact: *Mrs Vivienne Lockton* ☎ *01994 419327*

Pembrokeshire and its borderlands are renowned for their flora and fauna,
unrivalled sandy beaches, spectacular coastal scenery and gentle heaths and
moorlands of the Preseli Hills. The sunshine record, contrary to popular belief, equals
the best in the UK.

There are castles and forts from Norman to Victorian times, Dylan Thomas's Boat
House at Laugharne and many more modern attractions like Oakwood Leisure Park,
Wales' premier farm-based attraction at Folly Farm and Pemberton's Chocolate
Factory to name but a few.

The area has excellent safe sailing and windsurfing facilities, fishing in sea, river
and pond, pony trekking, etc. Visit the many offshore islands, some of which have
nature reserves, walk the coastal path, estuaries of the Cleddau rivers, the ancient
Preseli Hills and the old pilgrims' routes of the Landsker Borderlands.

Those of us who live in this area readily share our treasures with our visitors.
Come and see us – soon.

BED AND BREAKFAST

(and evening meal)

The Bower Farm, Little Haven, Haverfordwest, Pembrokeshire SA62 3TY

John Birt-Llewellin
☎ 01437 781554
BB From £18–£25
EM £15
Sleeps 6
🐕 🐎 ♿ 🚲 🐈 🏕 ⚓

🌺🌺🌺 *Highly Commended*

An extensively modernised traditional farmhouse on working sheep farm offering peace, warmth, comfort and friendliness to the casual or longer stay visitor. Dogs, horses (livery available) and children welcome. Walking distance of Broadhaven beach and coast path. Impressive sea views over St Brides Bay and islands. All rooms en suite. Open all year except Christmas.

Brunant Farm, Whitland, Dyfed SA34 0LX

Mrs O. Ebsworth
☎ 01994 240421
BB From £18–£20
EM From £10
Sleeps 6
🐕 🐎 ⚓

🌺🌺🌺 *Commended*

'Never enough time to enjoy this to the full, never enough words to say how splendid it was': John Carter, Thames TV (Wish You Were Here). Welcome to our 200 year old farmhouse centrally situated for touring, beaches, walking, golf or just relaxing. Comfortable, spacious bedrooms, all en suite, tea/coffee, TV, hairdriers. Good home cooking. Comfortable lounge, separate tables in dining room. Licence applied for.

Castell Pigyn, Llanboidy, Whitland, Dyfed SA34 0LJ

Marian Davies
☎ 01994 448391
Fax 01994 448755
BB From £18–£19
EM From £9
Sleeps 6
🐕 ⚓

🌺🌺🌺 *Highly Commended*

Castell Pigyn is situated 4 miles north of Whitland in a peaceful area with fabulous views of undulating farmland. Accommodation with en suite bedrooms. Lounge with TV, dining room with family tables, good home cooking. CH throughout, ample parking. (Also self catering cottage sleeping 4 in 1 double and 1 twin bedded room with washbasins. Bathroom with bath and shower. CH, TV. Garden.) Brochure available. Open Jan–Nov.

Croft Farm, Croft, Nr Cardigan, Pembs, Dyfed SA43 3NT

Andrew & Sylvie Gow
☎/Fax 01239 615179
BB From £15
EM From £10
Sleeps 6
🐕 🐎

🌺🌺🌺 *Highly Commended*

Croft is situated in the North Pembs countryside near beaches, National Park and stunning cliff paths. The farmhouse has two double en suite rooms and one twin with private facilities each with colour TV and tea/coffee. Relax by the fire on darker evenings. Home cooked evening meals are available. Guests may use the garden, patio, barbecue and play park. Children may help feed all our farm animals. Open all year.

Dolau Isaf Farm, Mynachlog-ddu, Clunderwen, Pembrokeshire SA66 7SB

Mrs V. C. Lockton
☎ 01994 419327
BB From £15
EM From £7.50
Sleeps 4
🐕 🐎 🏕 🚗 ⚫

🌺 *Commended*

We welcome you to our 70-acre farm situated in the Preseli Hills where you can see grazing amongst our sheep and cattle angora goats for this is the home of Preseli Mohair. We offer personal service and make every effort to provide for your comfort in this unspoilt setting. Walking, riding and fishing available locally. Lounge, TV and home cooking. Welcome Host Award. Open all year.

6 **Knowles Farm,** Lawrenny, Kilgetty, Pembrokeshire SA68 0PX

Mrs *Virginia Lort-Phillips*
☎ 01834 891221
Fax 01834 891344
BB From £15–£18
EM From £10
Sleeps 6
🕭 🕱 🖊 🛉 🎠 🐾 🏺 ♟
🐝 🐝 *Highly Commended*

With land sloping down to the shores of the Upper Cleddau river, we provide the perfect base for boating, birdwatching, walking or fishing. Bedrooms all face south and are cosy and bright. All have tea/coffee-making facilities and are either en suite or with private bathroom. Relax and unwind in total tranquillity.

---

7 **Lower End Town House,** Lampeter Velfrey, Narberth, Dyfed SA67 8UJ

Judy Smith
☎ 01834 831738
BB From £16.50
EM From £7
Sleeps 4 + cot
🕭 🐎 🕱 🖊
🐝 🐝 *Applied*

Beef and sheep farm owned and run by a young couple. Recent total refurbishment of the farmhouse has been aimed at recalling the peace and tranquillity of a bygone age whilst incorporating the comforts of a modern one. Easily accessible from the A40. Ideal for touring, walking or just unwinding. Evening meals by arrangement. Babies, dogs, and horses welcome. Open all year except Christmas & New Year.

---

8 **Plas-y-Brodyr,** Rhydwilym, Llandissilio, Clynderwen, Dyfed SA66 7QH

Mrs *Janet Pogson*
☎ 01437 563771
BB From £15–£18
EM From £10
Sleeps 6
🖊 🕭 🐾 🏺 🏺 ●
🐝 🐝 *De Luxe*

Plas-y-Brodyr is a small farm in the hidden valley of Rhydwilym with many local walks, abundant wildlife, fishing and only a short drive to many beautiful beaches. Our beamed farmhouse is comfortably furnished; pretty bedrooms (1 en suite) have tea/coffee, H/C, CH, hairdryer. Relax by log fires in inglenook sitting room after good home cooking. Colour brochure. Open all year including Christmas.

---

9 **Point Farm,** Dale, Haverfordwest, Pembrokeshire SA62 3RD

Mrs *Elizabeth Webber*
☎ 01646 636254
BB From £15–£20
Sleeps 5
🕭(8) 🐾 🐾 🏺
🐝 🐝 *Highly Commended*

Beautifully situated period farmhouse in the Pembrokeshire National Park in an unrivalled position overlooking the sea. Comfortable en suite double/single accommodation with full facilities. On coastal path near lovely beaches and offshore islands. We can arrange sailing, windsurfing, fishing, riding and even flying for the enthusiastic. Wonderfully relaxed evenings. Open Jan–Nov.

---

10 **Skerryback,** Sandy Haven, St. Ishmaels, Haverfordwest, Dyfed SA62 3DN

Mrs *Margaret Williams*
☎ 01646 636598
BB From £15
EM From £10
Sleeps 4
🕭 🖊 🐾 🏺 🏺 ●
🐝 *Highly Commended*

Warm Pembrokeshire welcome on coastal farm. A haven for walkers and bird lovers, near Sandy Heaven and ideal for visiting the bird sanctuaries of Skomer and Skokholm. Drying facilities, open fire in cold weather. TV lounge. Double and twin rooms with H/C and tea-making facilities.

---

11 **Ty Newydd Farm,** Llanycefn, Clynderwen, Dyfed SA66 7XT

Mrs *Miriam Dunn*
☎ 01437 532717
BB From £12–£14
EM From £8
Sleeps 2
🕭(10) 🕱 🛉 🎠 ♿ 🐾 🏺
🐝 *Applied*

Welcome to our farm. Home cooking, vegetarians catered for. Livery available and equine courses by BHS qualified staff. We also have an animal sanctuary which has been featured in magazines and you are welcome to help or just mix with the animals. Open all year.

Whitegates, Little Haven, Haverfordwest, Pembs SA62 3LA (12)

Richard Llewellin
☎/Fax 01437 781552
BB From £18.50-£22
EM From £14
Sleeps 6
🐕 ⛺ 🅿 🧍 🚶 ⛵ 🛥
♣♣♣ Commended

Character country house-style accommodation with panoramic views of beautiful fishing village and St Brides Bay. Most rooms en suite, all with tea/coffee facilities. Heated swimming pool and TV lounge. Visit our own ostrich farm or walk the coastal path and lovely sandy beaches. Also golf, fishing and windsurfing all available. Special out of season breaks. Open all year.

SELF-CATERING

Castell Pigyn, Llanboidy, Whitland, Dyfed SA34 0LJ (13)

Marian Davies
☎ 01994 448391
Fax 01994 448755
SC From £100-£220
Sleeps 4
🐕

♣♣♣♣

Situated 4 miles north of Whitland in a peaceful area with views of undulating farmland, semi-detached to our farmhouse, the cottage is completely self-contained with 1 double and 1 twin bedded room, each with washbasins and shaver points. Bathroom with bath and shower. Pine kitchen units and dining room furniture. Three piece suite, colour TV, fitted carpets. Secluded garden, ample parking. Open all year.

Croft Farm Cottages, Croft, Nr Cardigan, Pembs, Dyfed SA43 3NT (14)

Andrew & Sylvie Gow
☎/Fax 01239 615179
SC From £105-£395
Sleeps 25
🐕 ⛺

♣♣♣♣♣

The farm is situated in North Pembs countryside near beaches, National Park and stunning cliff paths. The slate cottages are furnished, equipped, cleaned to high standards. Flowers, tea tray, Welsh water and wine welcome you. Guests may use the garden, patio, barbecue and play park. Children may help feed calves, pig, sheep, ducks, rabbits, chickens, pheasant, etc. Featured in Holiday Which? Farm Holidays 1995. Open all year.

Dove Cottage, Dyffryn Isaf, Llandissilio, Dyfed SA66 7QD (15)

Mrs Pamela Morgan
☎/Fax 01437 563657
SC From £160-£225
Sleeps 4
🐕 ⛺ 🍴 🛥

♣♣♣♣

A well equipped, stone-built cottage, sleeps 4, in tranquil valley setting on 20-acre smallholding. Abundant flora and fauna. Good walking country with Preseli Mountains nearby. Brochure available. Open Apr-Nov.

Gwarmacwydd, Llanfallteg, Whitland, Dyfed SA34 0XH (16)

Mrs A Colledge
☎ 01437 563260
Fax 01437 563839
SC From £100–£398
Sleeps 22
🐕 ⛺ 🍴 ⛵ 🛥

♣♣♣♣

Gwarmacwydd is a country estate of over 450 acres including two miles of river bank. Five character stone cottages, all nicely furnished and equipped with all modern conveniences and heating. Working farm with cows, calves, lambs. Colour brochure available. Open all year.

Haven Cottages, Whitegates, Little Haven, Haverfordwest, Pembs SA62 3LA

Richard Llewellin
☎/Fax 01437 781552
SC From £95–£360
Sleeps 2–12
🐕 🐎 ⊡ 🐟 🥾 🏕 💼
🌼 🌼 🌼 🌼

Character holiday cottages within 200 yards of sandy beach in the coastal National Park and with easy access to all bird islands. Also golf, riding, fishing, windsurfing, or walking. Linen and heating provided, also TV. All with walled garden, on edge of village alongside our ostrich farm. Pets welcome. Brochure. Open all year.

 Point Farm, Dale, Haverfordwest, Pembrokeshire SA62 3RD

Mrs Elizabeth Webber
☎ 01646 636254
SC From £180–£300
Sleeps 5
🐕 🐎 🐟 🥾 🏕
🌼 🌼 🌼 🌼

Comfortable stone-built cottage, sleeps 5, with outstanding views over the bay. On coastal path adjacent to lovely beaches and offshore islands. All water sports can be arranged and fishing and even flying. Wonderfully relaxed atmosphere with lots to do. Open all year.

NO ANSWER?

Farmers are mostly out and about during the day.
Try to telephone before 9.30am or after 4pm.

CONFIRM BOOKINGS

Disappointments can arise from misunderstandings over the telephone.
Please write to confirm your booking.

GOOD FOOD

Nearly all Bureau members now hold a certificate in Essential Food Hygiene.

Northern Ireland

County Londonderry

Group Contact: *Mrs Margaret Moore* ☎ *01265 868229*

This is a fertile agricultural county with small farms scattered across the broad sweeping land and long Atlantic beaches.

The city of Londonderry (also known as Derry) is best known for its massive ring of fortified walls and singing pubs. In the county's north-east corner is Coleraine (with one of the main campuses of the University of Ulster), conveniently close to the seaside resorts of Portstewart and Castlerock for sea angling, golf and children's amusements. For rewarding scenic drives the Sperrin Mountains are best approached from Limavady and the beautiful Roe Valley Country Park. The Bann river is noted for trout and salmon.

BED AND BREAKFAST

(and evening meal)

---

① Ballycarton Farmhouse, 239 Seacoast Road, Bellarena, Limavady, Co Londonderry BT49 0HZ

Mrs Emma Craig
☎ 015047 50216
[BB] From £14
EM From £7
Sleeps 7
🐕 🐂
Registered

Farmhouse (central heating) on 50 acre farm amid coastal and mountain scenery. Gliding, climbing, fishing. 1 single, 1 double, 1 twin, 2 family rooms (3 H/C). Dogs allowed outside. On coast road, near sandy beaches. Coleraine 14 miles, Limavady 5 miles. Open all year.

---

② Ballyhenry House, 172 Seacoast Road, LImavady, Co Londondery BT49 9EF

Mrs Rosemary Kane
☎ 015047 22657
[BB] From £15–£17
🐂 🐕 🐎 🍴 🎾 🛁
Registered

Why not get away from it all at Ballyhenry House and be pampered in a very comfortable farmhouse situated in the beautiful River Roe valley? You can relax and enjoy the clean air, peace and quiet of the country. Alternatively golf, hang-gliding, horse riding, water skiing, walking, hill climbing are all within 5 miles. Open all year except Christmas.

---

③ Bealach Speirin, Coolcoscreaghan, 75 Glen Road, Garvagh, Coleraine BT51 5DF

Jerry & Celilia Mullan
☎ 012665 58696
[BB] From £12
EM From £9
Sleeps 6
🐂 🍴 🎾
Registered

Quiet family farmhouse, scenic countryside in ESA, hill walking, shooting and fishing on the head waters of the famous Agivey river. Forest walks, pony riding, golf and leisure nearby. 2 double rooms (1 en suite, 1 H&C), 1 twin. Home baking/cooking a speciality. Open all year.

---

④ Bellevue Country House, 43 Greenhill Road, Blackhill, Coleraine, Co Londonderry BT51 4EU

Elizabeth Morrison
☎ 01265 868797
[BB] From £16
EM From £9
Sleeps 6
🐂 ✂ 🍴 🐎 🛁
Registered

Listed country house with magnificent views of North Antrim Hills and Bann Valley. Salmon river fishing on farm. Tea-making facilities, colour TV. Family room, double H/C. twin H/C. Garvagh 3 miles. 7 miles on A29 from Coleraine and then B66 Ballymoney. Convenient to Portrush and Giants Causeway. A warm welcome awaits you. Open Mar–Oct.

---

⑤ Braehead House, 22 Braehead Road, Londonderry BT48 9XE

Mrs Maureen McKean
☎ 01504 263195
[BB] From £14–£15
Sleeps 6
🐂(3) ✂ 🛁
Registered

Georgian farmhouse on mixed farm on main Letterkenny road to Donegal town. Overlooking River Foyle and golf course. Ideal for touring North West and Donegal. 1 family, 1 twin, 1 single room, all with H&C. Open Mar–Nov.

Brown's Country House, 174 Ballybogey Road, Coleraine, Co Londonderry BT52 2LP

Mrs Jean Brown
☎/Fax 012657
31627/32777
BB From £18
EM From £11
Sleeps 16
Registered

A chalet bungalow with spacious lawns. Central heating. Home baking. On Ballymoney – Portrush road (B62). Safari Park 4 miles. 2 double bedrooms, 4 twin rooms, 1 family room, 3 ground floor, 1 single, all en suite. Tea/coffee in all rooms. Small dinner parties welcome. Babysitter. Dogs allowed (outside). Bushmills 4 miles, Coleraine and Portrush 5 miles. Open all year.

Elagh Hall, Buncrana Road, Londonderry BT48 8LU

Elizabeth Buchanan
☎ 01504 263116
BB From £15–£16
Sleeps 10
Registered

Listed historic country house with spacious gardens, own spring water, views of Grianan Castle and Donegal Hills. 2 en suite family rooms, 1 twin with H&C. ½ mile from Donegal border. Beaches, golf, fishing, riding nearby. 1 mile sports complex. Londonderry 2 miles, from Derry take Buncrana Road, turn right at check point. Open Mar–Oct.

Greenhill House, 24 Greenhill Road, Aghadowey, Coleraine, Co Londonderry BT51 4EU

Mrs Elizabeth Hegarty
☎ 01265 868241
BB From £22–£27
EM From £15
Sleeps 14
Registered

Georgian country guest house (with central heating). Good views across wooded countryside in the Bann Valley and the Antrim hills. Convenient to North coast. Fishing and golf nearby. 3 double, 2 twin, 2 family all H/C, 6 rooms with private bath/shower and toilet. Garvagh 3 miles. 7 miles on A29 from Coleraine and then B66 (Ballymoney). Recommended in international guides and recipient of awards. Open Mar–Oct.

Groarty House, 62 Groarty Road, Londonderry BT48 0JY

Margaret Hyndman
☎ 01504 261403
BB From £13.50
Sleeps 6
Registered

Farmhouse set in the peace and tranquillity of the countryside yet just 3 miles from city centre, with beautiful views overlooking town and Foyle estuary. Golf course, riding and fishing nearby. 2 miles sports complex. 1 double, 1 twin and 1 family room all with H&C. Central heating. From Londonderry take Buncrana Road (A2) past Templemore Sports Complex, turn left after Texaco petrol station. Open all year.

Heathfield House, 31 Drumcroone Road, Garvagh, Coleraine, Co Londonderry BT51 4EB

Mrs Heather Torrens
☎ 012665 58245
BB From £16–£18
EM From £10
Sleeps 6
Registered

Comfortable, spacious 17th century farmhouse on working beef and sheep farm, set in large garden in lovely countryside. Ideal base for touring north coast. Golf and horse riding nearby, fishing on River Agivey. Walk our country lanes. Central heating, TV lounge with piano, log fires. Good farmhouse cooking. 1 double/twin en suite, 1 twin H&C, with TV, tea/coffee facilities. On A29 Garvagh-Coleraine road. Open all year.

Inchadoghill House, 196 Agivey Road, Aghadowey, Coleraine, Co Londonderry BT51 4AD

Mamie & Ann McIlroy
☎ 01265 868250/
868232
BB From £13
Sleeps 6
Registered

Georgian farmhouse with central heating. Situated on 150 acre mixed farm, colour TV. Home cooking. River fishing on farm, golf nearby. 1 single, 1 double and 1 family room, all with H/C. Babysitting available. Dogs allowed outside. Farm off A54, Coleraine 9 miles, Ballymoney 6 miles, Kilrea 5 miles. Open all year.

---

⑫ Killeague Farm, 156 Drumcroon Road, Blackhill, Coleraine, Co Londonderry BT51 4HJ

Margaret Moore
☎ 01265 868229
🛏 From £16–£18
EM From £10
Sleeps 6
🌾 🐴 🕿 🏇 🐕
Registered

Georgian farmhouse built 1783. Central heating, tea-making facilities, colour TV. On dairy farm, stabling available. Outdoor riding arena. Riding instruction given by arrangement. Fishing in river on farm. 1 double en suite, 1 double H/C, 1 family en suite. On A29. Garvagh 5 miles, Coleraine 6½ miles. Convenient to golf courses, Giant's Causeway and Bushmills Distillery. Good food, good fellowship is our motto. Open all year.

---

⑬ Killenan House, 40 Killenan Road, Drumahoe, Co Londonderry BT47 3NG

Mrs Averil Campbell
☎ 01504 301710
🛏 From £12–£13
🐴(5) 🕿
Registered

Farmhouse on 70-acre farm in rural setting close to historic city, north coast, Donegal. Fishing, golf, flying club nearby. Babysitter. Dogs allowed outside. 1 twin, 1 double, 1 family room, all with H&C. Central heating. A6 Claudy direction from Londonderry, 5m B118 (Eglinton) 1½m left Killenan Road, first right. Open all year.

---

⑭ Sperrin View Farmhouse, 110A Drumbole Road, Upperlands Maghera, Co Londonderry BT46 5UX

Barbara Crockett
☎ 01266 822374
🛏 From £15
EM From £7.50
Sleeps 6
🐴 🕿 🍽 🍴 🏇
Registered

Farmhouse in Bann Valley with views of Sperrins, Antrim Hills. Just off several main routes. Central base for touring, golf, fishing, walking, riding or tracing your roots. Port of entry collection service. 2 double, 2 single rooms, all with CH, TV and telephone. Dogs allowed outside.

---

⑮ Tullan's Farm, 46 Newmills Road, Coleraine BT52 2JB

Mrs Diana McClelland
☎ 01265 42309
🛏 From £12.50
Sleeps 5
🐴
Registered

1 double room en suite, 1 family room with H&C. Farmhouse (central heating) 1 mile from Coleraine. Nearby fishing, swimming pool, bowling, ice-skating, horse riding and birdwatching. Babysitter. Dogs allowed outside. Portstewart/Portrush 5 miles. Golf and sandy beaches 5 miles. Turn off A29 Coleraine bypass (Cookstown–Portrush), ½ mile past roundabout (junction A26) into Newmills Road. Open all year.

Northern Ireland

County Antrim

Group Contact: *Irene Adair* ☎ *016937 63012*

To the south east of the county, Belfast provides six-day shopping and city entertainment while to the north west lies the Causeway Coast, a playground of holiday resorts, with the Giant's Causeway the dominant feature. Between lie the nine glens of Antrim and their quaint waterfoot villages, the spectacular coast road, Carrickfergus Castle, and inland towns like Antrim with its ancient round tower and splendid park. There's a lakeside steam railway at Shane's Castle, pony trekking near Ballycastle, golf at Royal Portrush, as well as bathing, boating and fishing along the hundred miles of shore.

BED AND BREAKFAST

(and evening meal)

---

① Bannside Farmhouse, 268 Gortgole Road, Portglenone, Ballymena, Co Antrim BT44 8AT

Misses E & A Lowry
☎ **01266 821262**
▦ **From £12.50–£14**
Sleeps 5
🐕
Registered

Farmhouse in peaceful, rural location convenient to the River Bann, which is popular with anglers. Portglenone 3½ miles, Ballymena 12 miles. Forest park and picnic area nearby. Central for touring beauty spots of Counties Antrim and Londonderry. One hour from Larne harbour, and city and international airports. Open all year.

---

② Beechgrove, 412 Upper Road, Trooperslane, Carrickfergus, Co Antrim BT38 8PW

Betta Barron
☎ **01960 36604**
▦ **From £15–£17**
EM From £8
Sleeps 15
🐕 🐎 ♿ 🐱 ⛺ 💼
Registered

A warm welcome awaits you at Beechgrove farmhouse (central heating) on 16 acre mixed farm near sea. Fishing, golf, riding. Knochagh monument, Belfast zoo, leisure centre nearby. 3 single, 1 double, 2 family rooms, 1 twin (all H/C). Babysitter. Dogs allowed (outside). Off A2, 1 mile south of Carrickfergus. Larne 10 miles. Belfast 10 miles. Carrickfergus 3 miles. Open all year.

---

③ Breezemount, 27 Ballylig Road, Dunloy, Cloughmills, Ballymena BT44 9DS

Mrs May O'Mullan
☎ **01265 638468**
▦ **From £16**
Sleeps 4
🚭 ☕
Registered

Modern country bungalow (central heating) with separate dining room and TV lounge. 1 double, 1 twin en suite. 10 miles Ballymena on Coleraine road A26, 8 miles Ballymoney, 16 miles Ballycastle. Close to Logan's Fashions. Scenic drives through Glens of Antrim. Fishing locally. Bedtime cup of tea/coffee served. Non-smokers preferred. Open all year.

---

④ Caldhame Lodge, 102 Moira Road, Nutts Corner, Crumlin, Co Antrim BT29 4HG

Mrs Ann McKavanagh
☎ **01849 423099**
▦ **From £16**
EM From £8.50
☕
Registered

Guest house situated on a large dairy farm minutes from Belfast International Airport. Close to Dunadry, Lisburn, Ulster Grand Prix Circuit. All rooms en suite, 3 with bath and shower, colour TV, tea/coffee making facilities, trouser press. TV guest lounge. Local amenities include fishing, golf, shooting, leisure complex.

---

⑤ Carnside Farm Guest House, 23 Causeway Road, Giant's Causeway, Bushmills, Co Antrim BT57 8SU

Frances Lynch
☎ **012657 31337**
▦ **From £14**
EM From £8
Sleeps 15
🐕 🐈 ♿
Registered

Farmhouse (central heating) on 200-acre dairy farm. Magnificent coastal view. Fishing, golf, water sports. Old Bushmills Distillery 2 miles has weekday tours. 1 single, 3 double (1 en suite), 1 twin, 3 family rooms (1 en suite), 2 on ground floor, all H&C. Babysitter. Dogs allowed (outside). Bushmills 2 miles, Ballycastle 12 miles, Giant's Causeway ¼ mile. Open Mar–Oct.

Carrick Dhu Guest House, 6 Ballyreagh Road, Portrush, Co Antrium BT56 8LP

Mrs H McClay
☎ 01265 823666
▣ From £18
EM From £10
Sleeps 18
♿ ✄ ♿
Registered

Seven bedroomed guest house with 2 double, 2 twin, 3 family, all en suite. Colour TV, tea/coffee-making facilities, electric blankets in all rooms. Sea views, private car parking. Adjacent to golf course and other amenities. Winner of many awards. Child discounts, self catering available June–Aug. Suitable for families. Open all year except Christmas & New Year.

Clearsprings Farm, 9 Belfast Road, Nutts Corner, Crumlin, Co Antrim BT29 4TQ

Eileen P Duncan
☎ 01232 825275
▣ From £15
Sleeps 6
♿ ✄
Registered

Spacious, modernised house with 1 double en suite, 2 twin with H&C. Beautiful mature garden, ample parking. Rural setting, home from home atmosphere. All home cooking. Tea-coffee making facilities, electric blankets. 400 yards from Nutts Corner roundabout, 2nd house on right, A52 Belfast Road. 5 minutes Belfast International Airport. Pick-up service. Open all year.

Country Guest House, 41 Kirk Road, Ballymoney, Co Antrim BT53 8HB

Dorothy Brown
☎ 01265 662620
▣ From £15–£17
EM From £8
Sleeps 10
🕒 ♞ ♿ ♿ ♞ 🏕 💼
Registered

Modern bungalow in 1 acre garden, featured on TV for relaxing atmosphere. All rooms en suite with phone, tea and coffee-making facilities. TV lounge and dining room for guests. Your own door keys to come and go as you please. Causeway coast, Antrim Glens, Giant's Causeway all within 15 miles, recreation centre 1 mile. Brochure on request. Open all year.

Craig's Farm, 90 Hillhead Road, Ballycarry, Carrickfergus, Co Antrium BT38 9JF

Mrs J Craig
☎ 01960 353769
▣ From £15
Sleeps 6
♿ ♞ ♿ ♿ ♞
Registered

3 rooms, 1 twin with H&C, 1 family and 1 double both en suite, all with tea/coffee. Centrally heated farmhouse located in quiet rural surrounds. Convenient for golf, fishing, horse riding, walking. TV lounge. Babysitter. Dogs allowed outside. From Lame take the A2 towards Carrickfergus. Take 2nd right when you come through Glynn village. Signposted Ballycarry. Open all year.

Cullentra House, 16 Cloghs Road (off Gaults Road), Cushendall, Co Antrim BT44 0SP

Olive McAuley
☎ 012667 71762
▣ From £14–£16
Sleeps 6/8
♿ ✄ ♿ 💼
Registered

Country house nestling amid breathtaking scenery of Glenballyeamon and Glenaan, overlooking Sea of Moyle. Golf course, Ballycastle and Giant's Causeway nearby. 1 family, 1 double and 1 twin. TV, tea/coffee-making facilities. Homely atmosphere and warm welcome extended to all guests. Open all year except Christmas.

Dieskirt Farm, 104 Glen Road, Glenariff, Co Antrim BT44 0RG

Kathleen McHenry
☎/Fax 012667 71308
☎ 012667 71796
▣ From £12.50–£16
EM From £6.50
Sleeps 6
♿ ♞ ♿ ♞ 🏕
Registered

Modern farmhouse (CH) on a hill sheep farm in the Glens of Antrim. Panoramic views of Antrim coast and Scottish hills. Conveniently situated to numerous amenities: Ulster Way, golf, horse riding and tourist attractions: Glenariff Forest Park 5 minutes, Giants Causeway, Bushmills Distillery, etc. Open May–Oct.

12 **Hill Vale Farm,** 11 Largy Road, Crumlin, Co Antrim BT29 4AH

Mrs Janet E Duncan
☎ **01849 422768**
BB **From £14**
Sleeps 6
☒ ☒ ⚲ ☚ ▪
Registered

Farmhouse (central heating) on 100-acre farm, situated minutes from Belfast International Airport. Convenient to Crumlin, Nutts Corner, Antrim and Lisburn. 1 twin, 2 double rooms, all with H&C. Dogs allowed outside. At Nutts Corner roundabout take sign for Crumlin, turn right after 2 miles onto Manse Road, go to end, straight over crossroads onto Largy Road ½ mile on right. Open all year.

13 **Hill View,** 30 Middle Road, Islandmagee, Larne, Co Antrim BT40 3SL

Mrs Maureen Reid
☎ **01960 372581**
BB **From £14–£16**
Sleeps 6
☒
Registered

Country bungalow (central heating) near sea with panoramic views. Conservatory. Tea/coffee-making facilities. 1 twin en suite, 1 double, 1 family, all ground floor with TV. Dogs allowed (outside). Horse riding, sea fishing, golf, open farm nearby. Off A2, 7 miles south of Larne. Take B90 to Islandmagee. Carrickfergus 7 miles. Open all year.

14 **Islay-View,** 36 Leeke Road, off Ballymagarry Road, Portrush, Co Antrim BT56 8NH

Eileen Smith
☎ **01265 823220**
BB **From £14**
Sleeps 6–8
☒ ♿
Registered

3 rooms, 1 double en suite, 1 family, 1twin. Bungalow on 60-acre mixed farm with view of Giant's Causeway. TV lounge, tea/coffee-making facilities. House baking, farm produce, central heating, electric blankets, wheelchair ramp. Babysitter. Dogs allowed outside. Off Ballymoney/Portrush road (B62). Portrush 2½ miles, Coleraine 6 miles. Open Easter–Sept.

15 **Kenbaan,** 55 Bayhead Road, Portballintrae, Co Antrim BT57 8SA

Mrs Elizabeth Morgan
☎ **012657 31534**
BB **From £15**
Sleeps 6
CH ☒ ☒ ☒ ☒ ☒
Registered

Situated in pretty harbour village of Portballintrae near Dunluce Castle, Bushmills Distillery, Giant's Causeway. Panoramic views of North Antrim coast. 1 twin, 2 double rooms, all with H&C, satellite TV and tea and coffee-making facilities. Large, comfortable guests' lounge. Private car parking. Play golf on world-famous Royal Portrush which is only a few minutes' drive. Bushmills 1½ miles, Portrush 4 miles. Open Jan–Nov.

16 **Loguestown Farm House,** 58 Loguestown Road, Portrush, Co Antrim BT56 8NY

Mrs Mary K Adams
☎ **01265 822742**
BB **From £12–£14**
Sleeps 6
☒ ☒
Registered

Modernised farmhouse (central heating) located on 28 acre mixed farm. Close to amenities of the Causeway Coast. 1 twin room, 1 double with shower, 2 singles, all with H&C. Tea/coffee making facilities. Dogs allowed. Off A29, Portrush 1 mile, Coleraine 4 miles. Open all year.

17 **Maddybenny Farm House & Mews Cottages,** 18 Maddybenny Park, Portrush, Co Antrim BT52 2PT

Rosemary White
☎/Fax **01265 823394**
BB **£20–£25**
SC **From £150–£400**
Sleeps 6
☒ ☒ ☒ ☚
Registered

Award-winning house 2 miles from Portrush, Portstewart, university, 7 golf courses, beaches. Ideal base for touring Causeway, coast and glens of Antrim. Three en suite rooms. Own riding centre, BHS Approved. Cordon bleu cooking. A29 Portrush to Coleraine road, signs for riding centre. Advance booking is essential. Also 3 star self-catering cottages. Open all year.

Neelsgrove Farm, 51 Carnearney Road, Ahoghill, Ballymena, Co Antrim BT42 2PL

Mrs Margaret Neely
☎ 01266 871225
BB From £15–£18.50
EM From £9
Sleeps 6
⊛ ♿(2) ⚊ ♞
Registered

Country house (central heating) in 1 acre of grounds on mixed farm. Home baking. Water skiing 2 miles. Sports complex 5 miles. 6 miles from Ballymena, 15 miles from International Airport. Convenient to Glens of Antrim and River Bann. Fishermen welcome, tackle space available. 1 double en suite, 1 double, 1 twin room with H/C. Dogs allowed outside. Open all year.

Sprucebank, 41 Ballymacombs Road, Portglenone, Co Antrim BT44 8NR

Mrs Thomasena Sibbett
☎ 01266 822150
BB From £14.50–£16.50
Sleeps 8
♿ ♞ ⚊
Registered

Highly recommended farmhouse accomodation in spacious garden. 1½ miles from Portglenone on A54. Tea/coffee-making facilities in all rooms. Convenient to Glens of Antrim, Causeway coast, Sperrin mountains, fishing on River Bann. Fishermen welcome – tackle space available. Dogs welcome outside. Open all year.

Valley View, 6a Ballyclough Road, Bushmills, Co Antrim BT57 8TU

Valerie McFall
☎ 012657 41608/41319
BB From £12–£15
Sleeps 14
♿ ♿
Registered

Family-run with homely atmosphere and very comfortable accommodation. Convenient to all the North Antrim coastal attractions including Giant's Causeway. Beautiful views of mountains and Bush river valley. 4 new rooms all en suite, 1 disabled, each with coffee/tea-making facilities. Home cooking, tea on arrival. No smoking. Families very welcome. Open all year.

The Villa Farmhouse, 185 Torr Road, Cushendun, Co Antrim BT44 0PU

Mrs C Scally
☎ 012667 61252
BB From £18
EM From £8.50
Sleeps 5
♿
Registered

Tudor style farmhouse, with panoramic views of Antrim Coast and Glens of Antrim overlooking the Cornish style village of Cushendun. 1 double and 1 family room, both en suite, 1 twin with H&C. Tea and coffee making facilities. Golf, fishing, sightseeing, pony trekking. Giant's Causeway close by. Home cooking, baking a speciality. Open Mar–Nov.

White Gables, 83 Dunluce Road, Bushmills, Co Antrim BT57 8SJ

Mrs Ria Johnston
☎ 012657 31611
BB From £19.50–£22
EM From £12.50
Sleeps 6
⊛ ♿ ♞ ⚊
Registered

Country house on A2 coast road near Dunluce Castle and Giant's Causeway (4 miles). Panoramic views of North Antrim coast. All bedrooms en suite. Tea/coffee-making facilities. Home cooking at its best. Awards include All Ireland Galtee Breakfast and Taste of Ulster. Ample car parking space. AA selected QQQQ. Open Mar–Nov.

Northern Ireland

County Tyrone

Group Contact: *Irene Adair* ☎ *016937 63012*

Between the Sperrins in the north and the green Clogher Valley with its village cathedral in the south lies this region of great historical interest. The county's associations with the USA are recalled at the Ulster-American Folk Park near Omagh and Gray's old printing shop in Strabane still contains its 18th century presses. A mysterious ceremonial site of stone circles and cairns near Davagh Forest has recently been uncovered and there are other Stone Age and Bronze Age remains in the area. There are forest parks, Gortin Glen and Drum Manor, for driving or rambling, excellent trout and salmon waters near Newtownstewart, and market towns for shopping and recreation. Dungannon is notable for its fine glassware, Tyrone Crystal.

BED AND BREAKFAST

(and evening meal)

Charlemont House, 4 The Square, Moy, Co Tyrone BT71 7SG

Mrs Margaret McNeice
☎ **01868 784895**
🅱 **From £15**
Sleeps 7
🐕
Registered

Beautiful Georgian house set in the square of historical Moy on the main route between Armagh City and Dungannon. Convenient to the M1 motorway and ideally located for fishing, riding and sightseeing. 1 family, 1 double, 1 twin room. Evening meal by arrangement. Open all year.

Greenmount Lodge, 58 Greenmount Road, Gortaclare, Omagh, Co Tyrone BT79 0YE

Mrs F Louie Reid
☎ **01662 841325**
Fax 01662 840019
🅱 **From £17–£20**
EM From £12
Sleeps 22
🐕 🐎 ✂ ♿ 🎣 🍴 🛄
Registered

Farm guest house on 150-acre farm. Superb accommodation, excellent cuisine. Central for sightseeing Fermanagh, Lakeland, the Sperrin Mountains. A5 from Ballygawley to Omagh, left before Traveller's Rest at Fintona sign 1 mile. Open all year.

Tannaghlane House, Caledon, Co Tyrone BT68 4XU

Mrs Ella Reid
☎ **018681 568247**
🅱 **From £15**
EM From £8.50
Sleeps 2
Registered

Georgian farmhouse set in open countryside on large farm. One twin room en suite. Electric blankets, TV, tea making facilities. Dogs allowed outside. Adjacent to farmhouse is Ireland's only school of cake artistry known as 'Ella's Barn' – courses and demonstrations most of the year. Just ½ mile off B45 Dungannon-Caledon road 2 miles out of Caledon village. Open all year.

FARM HOLIDAY BUREAU

GOOD FOOD

Nearly all Bureau members now hold a certificate in Essential Food Hygiene.

Northern Ireland

County Fermanagh

Group Contact: *Mrs Mary Fawcett* ☎ *01365 322725*

Ulster's Lakeland spreads its web of waterways, islands, forest and glen, castles and abbey ruins right across the county. Enniskillen, county town and shopping centre, strides the narrows between upper and lower Lough Erne. From here pleasure boats run daily cruises in summer. Golf, sailing, water-skiing and even pleasure flying are available nearby. Fishermen need no reminder that these are the waters where record catches are made. Two of Ulster's finest houses in National Trust care, Florence Court and Castle Coole, are in Fermanagh, too and there is an underground boat trip at Marble Arch Caves. Visitors to the old pottery at Belleek can watch craftsmen at work on fine porcelain.

Strabane

Newtownstewart
A5

A505

Omagh
Cookstown

Lower
Lough Erne
2
A32
A5
A29
Lough
Neagh

Belleek   A46
9 Irvinestown
Dungannon
6 7

5
Aughnacloy
14
15
13
12
11

A4
Enniskillen
Portadown

A4
A28
A3

Drumcard
Armagh
Upper
Mullan
4 Lough Erne

A509
Newtownbutler

BED AND BREAKFAST

(and evening meal)

Al-Di-Gwyn Lodge, 101 Clabby Road, Fivemiletown, Co. Fermanagh BT75 0QY

Mrs V Gilmore
☎ 013655 21298
[BB] From £14–£17
Sleeps 10
Registered

Country house (central heating). Modern in character, 4 twin rooms, 1 double, all en suite. Guest comforts a high priority. Residents' lounge. National Trust properties, monuments, lakes, fishing, golf, cruises nearby. Home baking. Fire Authority certificate. Fivemiletown 1½ miles on B107 (Tempo Road). Enniskillen 14 miles. Open all year.

Ardess House, Kesh, Co Fermanagh BT93 1NX

Dorothy Pendry
☎ 013656 31267
[BB] From £22.50
EM From £12.50
Sleeps 6
🛏 🛌 ✄ ▪
Registered

A warm welcome to Ulster's Lakeland. Relax in the tranquil atmosphere of Ardess House, a restored Georgian rectory with modern comforts. Traditional and vegetarian cookery using produce from the organic kitchen garden. Jacob sheep in the paddocks, peacocks in the garden and a wealth of bird life. Guests can join in activities in the craft centre. Open Jan–Nov.

Bayview Guest House, Tully Churchill, Enniskillen, Co Fermanagh BT93 6HP

Dorothy Hassard
☎ 013656 41250
[BB] From £14–£17
EM From £6.50
Sleeps 10
🛏 🛌 ☞
Registered

Centrally heated farmhouse on a working dairy farm overlooking Tully Bay, Lower Lough Erne. Near Tully Castle, Lower Lough Navar Forest Park & Belleek Pottery, Marble Arch caves, National Trust properties and golf course. 1 twin en suite, 2 doubles (1 en suite), 1 family with H&C. On A46 road form Enniskillen to Belleek. 11 miles Enniskillen. 3 miles Derrygonnelly. Open Mar–Nov.

Broadmeadows Guest House, Cleenish Island Road, Bellanaleck, Enniskillen, Co Fermanagh BT92 2AL

Liliann McKibbin
☎ 01365 348395
[BB] From £15
EM From £10
Sleeps 6
Ⓖ 🛌 ♿ ✄ 🛏 ⚓
Registered

Chalet bungalow (central heating). Close to Lough Erne. Angling, sailing, near Florence Court (National Trust) and Marble Arch Caves. 1 single, 1 double, 1 twin, all ground floor with H&C. Suitable for elderly or disabled visitors. Babysitter. Personal attention to special needs. Owner qualified nurse. Dogs allowed outside. 1½ miles east of Bellanaleck on road to Cleenish Island. Enniskillen 6 miles. Open all year.

Lackaboy Farm Guest House, Tempo Road, Enniskillen, Co Fermanagh BT74 6EB

Mrs Derick Noble
☎ 01365 322488
[BB] From £15
EM From £10
Sleeps 18
🛌 ✄
Registered

Centrally heated farmhouse on 60-acre dairy farm next to Castle Coole (NT). Opposite Fermanagh Agricultural Centre. Lakes, fishing, golfing, scenic drives nearby. 1 twin, 1 family, 2 double rooms all en suite, 3 singles and 3 doubles all with H&C. Babysitter. No smoking. Enniskillen 1 mile. B80 from Enniskillen, turn left after ¼ mile. Open all year.

---

6   Lakeview Guest House, Drumcrow, Blaney, Enniskillen, Co Fermanagh BT93 7EY

Mrs Jason Hassard
☎ 013656 41263
▣ From £14
EM From £7.50
Sleeps 11
Registered

Grade A farm guesthouse (CH) adjoining Lower Erne with a lovely panoramic view of Islands and miles of waterway. Situated on A46 road 10 miles from Enniskillen, 23 miles from Atlantic beaches, near places of historical interest and Lough Navar Forest Park. 1 double, 1 twin and 2 family rooms, 1 en suite on ground floor. All H&C. Separate dining tables. Fire certificate. Hospitality Award winner. Homely atmosphere. Dogs allowed outside. Open Mar–Nov.

7   The Olde School House, Tully, Killadeas, Enniskillen, Co Fermanagh BT92 1FN

Mrs Joan Moore
☎ 013656 21688
▣ From £16–£18.50
EM From £10
Sleeps 18
Registered

Renovated school building of unusual character, set in heart of Fermanagh Lakes. Beside Castle Archdale Country Park, St Angelo Airport, Necarne Equestrian Centre. NT properties, Marble Arch Caves, Belleek Pottery 30 minutes drive. Comfortable, relaxed surroundings. Home baking, personal supervision, tea-making facilities. Warm welcome at all times. No smoking. Open all year.

8   Riverside Farm Guest House, Gortadrehid Culkey Post Office, Enniskillen, Co Fermanagh BT92 2FN

Mrs Mary Isobel Fawcett
☎ 01365 322725
▣ From £15–£17
EM From £8
Registered

Farmhouse (central heating) on 65-acre livestock farm. NT properties, fishing, shooting, scenic drives, golfing nearby. 2 family rooms (1 en suite), 3 twin, 1 double, 1 single, all H&C. Babysitter. Dogs allowed outside. Fire certificate. Small parties catered for (max 25). Self-catering bungalow. From Enniskillen take A4 for 1½ miles, left (A509) for 1½ miles. Enniskillen 3 miles. Open all year.

9   Rossgweer House, 274 Killadeas Road, Lisnarick, Co Fermanagh BT94 1PE

Mrs M Hemphill
☎ 01365 621924
▣ From £16
EM From £8
Sleeps 16
Registered

Guest house on small 30-acre farm convenient to Castlearchdale Country Park. 5 miles from Lakeland Airport where collection service can be arranged. Peaceful surroundings. A warm welcome awaits you at all times. 3 doubles, 1 twin, 1 single, all en suite, 1 double with H&C, 1 family, 1 twin. Two rooms on ground floor. TV in rooms. Dogs allowed outside. Open all year.

BUREAU ACCOMMODATION MEANS QUALITY

FARM HOLIDAY
BUREAU

All Bureau members are inspected and quality graded by the National Tourist Board each year, as well as by fellow members.

Northern Ireland

County Armagh

Group Contact: *Irene Adair* ☎ *016937 63012*

Northern Ireland's smallest county rises gently from Lough Neagh's banks, southward through apple orchards, farmland and hill forest to the rock summit of Slieve Gullion, mountain of Cuchulain. But the crown of Armagh is the city itself, a religious capital older than Canterbury, with two cathedrals, the Georgian Mall and a Planetarium and Observatory. Craigavon has a leisure centre and ski-slope, with lakes for water sports, and there is sailing on Lough Neagh and angling and canoeing on the Blackwater river.

A505
A29
A31
Ballyclare
A8
Antrim
Carrickfergus
Cookstown
Lough Neagh
A29
Belfast
Bangor
Holywood
Donaghdee
Newtownards
A5
Dungannon
A29
14
15
13
12
M2
Lisburn
Aughnacloy
A3
Lurgan
9
Saintfield
A28
Portadown
A1
A7
Armagh
A3
Banbridge
A24
A28
A27
A50
Downpatrick
A1
A25
Dundrum
Newry
Newcastle
Warrenpoint
Kilkeel

BED AND BREAKFAST

(and evening meal)

---

① Deans Hill, College Hill, Armagh, Co Armagh BT61 9DF

Mrs Jill Armstrong
☎ **01861 524923**
🅱 **From £20**
Sleeps 5
Registered

Listed Georgian family home (CH) set in wooded grounds. 1 twin, 1 double, both en suite, 1 single with H&C. All have tea/coffee-making facilities. Guests' sitting room with open fire. Full Irish breakfast. Tennis, croquet, petanque. 10 mins walk from historic Armagh City including Planetarium, museums, St Patrick's Trail, restaurants, shops, NT properties nearby. Dogs allowed outside. First stone gateway on left after Planetarium. Open all year.

---

② Heimat, 6 Polnagh Road, Killylea, Co Armagh BT60 3AY

Rodney & Doris McLoughlin
☎ **01861 568661**
🅱 **From £12.50**
Sleeps 5
❧ ♞
Registered

Chalet bungalow on mixed farm overlooking Killylea village. Fishing at Benburb, clay pigeon shooting. 2 doubles, 1 single room, all on ground floor. Babysitter. Dogs allowed outside. Home cooking. Navan Fort 3 miles. Armagh City 6 miles. Open all year.

---

③ Ivanhoe, 10 Valley Lane, Waringstown, Craigavon, Co Armagh BT66 7SR

Mrs Frances Dewart
☎ **01762 881287**
🅱 **From £12–£15**
Sleeps 6
❧ ♞
Registered

Georgian farmhouse close to fishing, boating, golf, Craigavon lakes and leisure centre. 1 mile from Waringstown off Clare Road. 1 twin, 2 double rooms. Open all year.

FARM HOLIDAY BUREAU

FOLLOW THE COUNTRY CODE

Leave nothing but footprints,
Take nothing but photographs,
Kill nothing but time!

Northern Ireland
County Down

Group Contact: *Mrs Cissie Annett* ☎ *013967 22740*

This area includes the populous dormitory fringe along Belfast Lough (do not miss the Folk Museum at Cultra) and the ancient shrines of St. Patrick's Country round the cathedral hill at Downpatrick; the flat golden beaches of the Ards Peninsula and the mountainous Kingdom of Mourne; lively Newcastle with its seaside festival, and stately homes like Mount Stewart and Castle Ward open to visitors.

Horseriding, sailing, angling and golf are everywhere within reach, and there is motor racing at Kirkistown and sea angling in Strangford Lough.

A505
A29
A31
A29
A5
A29
A28
A3
A3
A28
A27
A1
A29
A50
A25
A8
A2
A21
A7
A24
M2

Ballyclare
Antrim
Carrickfergus
Cookstown
Bangor
Donaghdee
Lough Neagh
Belfast
Holywood
Newtownards
Dungannon
Lisburn
Ballywalter
Aughnacloy
Lurgan
Greyabbey
Portadown
Saintfield
Armagh
Dromore
Ballynahinch
Crossgar
Banbridge
Downpatrick
Dundrum
Ardglass
Newry
Newcastle
Warrenpoint
Annalong
Kilkeel

BED AND BREAKFAST

(and evening meal)

1 Ballycastle House, 20 Mountstewart Road, Newtownards, Co Down BT22 2AL

Margaret Deering
☎ 012477 88357
BB From £18
SC From £160–£200
Sleeps 6
ħ ⅍ ♋
Registered

Ballycastle House is situated in a peaceful country setting overlooking Strangford Lough. Convenient to fishing, sailing, golfing, flying club, National Trust properties. Beside Mountstewart House and Gardens. Every comfort, hospitality assured. Winner of 3 tourism Awards. 3 double rooms all en suite. Dogs allowed (outside). Vintage engine collection. Newtownards – A20 south 4 miles, Ballywalter signpost left 800 metres farmhouse left. Open all year.

2 Beechhill Farm, 10 Loughries Road, Newtownards, Co Down BT23 3RN

Mrs Joan McKee
☎ 01247 818404
Fax 01247 812820
BB From £15–£17
EM From £10
Sleeps 6
ħ ♋ Å ♞ ☞ ♣
Registered

Farmhouse on the Ards peninsula on a working farm. 1 double, 1 single, 1 family room (all H/C). Dogs allowed outside. A20 south from Newtownards, 2 miles left at Millisle signpost, right at T junction, left at Loughries School. Newtownards 4 miles, Bangor 8 miles. Open all year except Christmas.

3 Bushymead Country House, 86 Drumaness Road, Ballynahinch, Co Down BT24 8LT

Mrs Sally Murphy
☎ 01238 561171
BB From £12–£18
EM From £5
Sleeps 21
♋ ħ ⅍ ♞ ☞ ♣ ▪
Registered

Country house situated on main Ballynahinch to Newcastle road (A24) on doorstep of Newcastle and the Mourne Mountains in the heart of Down. Close to all tourist attractions, golf, fishing, horse riding, forest parks, museums, NT properties, etc. Large bedrooms, most en suite with TV, all with tea/coffee facilities. Open for all meals. Food hygiene certificate. Separate guests' lounge. Open all year.

4 Carrig-Gorm, 27 Bridge Road, Helen's Bay, Bangor, Co Down BT19 1TS

Mrs Elizabeth Eves
☎ 01247 853680
BB From £20–£25
Sleeps 6
☺ ♋
Registered

Part Victorian, part 18th century house (central heating) in secluded gardens ½ mile from sea. Seven golf courses within 5 miles. Coastal walks, fishing. 1 twin, 1 family room en suite. A2 from Belfast, 8 miles, Helen's Bay turn left 1¼ mile turn right, 4th house on left. Train ¼ mile. Open all year except Christmas.

FARM HOLIDAY BUREAU

NO ANSWER?

Farmers are mostly out and about during the day.
Try to telephone before 9.30am or after 4pm.

Drumgooland House, 29 Dunnanew Road, Seaforde, Co Down BT30 8PJ

Alice McLeigh
☎ 01396 811956
Fax 01396 811265
[BB] **From £16.50–£20.50**
Sleeps 6
🦮 🐴 🎣 ⛵ ♨ ⛺ 🎿
Registered

Drumgooland House is a large, modernised country house close to the Mourne Mountains, situated on 60 acres of land with small lake stocked with trout. We have horses and ponies for trekking, hunting and cross country riding. Ideally situated for golfing, mountain climbing and water sports. Each room has colour TV, tea-making facilities, central heating, double glazing. Ten minutes from Newcastle. Open Jan–Nov.

Edenvale Country House, 130 Portaferry Road, Newtownards, Co Down BT22 2AH

Diane Whyte
☎ 01247 814881
[BB] **From £20–£25**
Sleeps 6
🦮 🐴
Registered

Beautifully restored Georgian country house, just 2 miles from Newtownards in a delightfully secluded area. Extensive views of the Mournes over Strangford Lough and National Trust wildfowl refuge. Sailboarding, birdwatching, golf and horse riding within easy reach. All rooms en suite. Stabling for horses and dogs.

Ernsdale, 120 Mountstewart Road, Carrowdore, Newtownards, Co Down BT22 2ES

Dot McCullagh
☎ 01247 861208
[BB] **From £13.50–£14**
Sleeps 7
🦮 🐴
Registered

Farmhouse (central heating) on 52 acres. Convenient to North Down resorts, pony trekking, National Trust properties, sailing. 1 twin, 1 double, 1 family room, all with H&C. Guests' bathroom, separate shower room. Babysitter, dogs allowed outside. From Newtownards A20 (4 miles). Left at Ballywater/Carrowdore sign, 2½ miles. Open Mar–Nov.

Fair Haven, 16 Moneydarragh Road, Annalong, Co Down BT34 4TY

Mrs Iris Jardine
☎ 013967 68153
[BB] **From £13–£14**
EM From £6.50
Sleeps 6
🦮 🐴 🍴 ♨
Registered

Modern, spacious bungalow situated between the Mourne Mountains and the Irish Sea. Just metres off main road. Large garden and ample parking. Hill walking, golf, fishing, tennis and horse riding nearby. Silent Valley 3 miles. 1 double room en suite, 1 family room. Home baking, TV lounge, warm welcome. Open all year.

Four Winds, 237 Kilkeel Road, Annalong, Co Down BT39 4TW

Dorothy Stevenson
☎ 013967 68345
[BB] **From £15.50**
🐴 ♿
Registered

Modern farmhouse (central heating) on elevated site with panoramic views of Mourne Mountains and Irish Sea. Two en suite and one downstairs for disabled. Home baking. Bowls, tennis and fishing nearby. Dogs allowed. 4 miles from Silent Valley, 1 minute walk to beach.

Greenacres, 5 Manse Road, Newtownards, Co Down BT23 4TP

Dorothy Long
☎ 01247 816193
[BB] **From £16–£20**
EM From £10
Sleeps 4
🦮 🐴
Registered

Stone-built country house in landscape gardens. Taste of Ulster award winner. National Trust properties, flying club, fishing, golf nearby. Situated within walking distance of Newtownards, bus stop nearby. All rooms have TV, tea-making facilities. Hairdryer available. Open all year.

---

(12) Greenlea Farm, 48 Dunover Road, Ballywalter, Newtownards, Co Down BT22 2LE

Evelyn McIvor
☎ 012477 58218
BB From £14
EM From £6.50
Sleeps 12 (+ cot)
☺(12) ♠ ⚱
Registered

Come feel at home in our friendly little home with the big welcome. 5 bedrooms, all with H&C. CH. Large dining room, guests' own sitting room with piano and TV. We provide good food, enjoy people and will make your stay memorable. ½ mile off A2. Yachting, fishing, golf, flying club, racing (Kirkiston), NT properties nearby. Bangor 10 miles, Portaferry 14 miles, Belfast City Airport 20 miles. Open all year.

(13) Havine Farm, 51 Ballydonnell Road, Downpatrick, Co Down BT30 8EP

Mrs Murtle Macauley
☎ 01396 851242
BB From £13
EM From £6.50
Sleeps 6
☺ ♠
Registered

A modernised 18th century farmhouse situated on 125 acre working farm in the heart of St Patrick's country, with central heating, H/C running water in all 3 bedrooms. Home cooking, homely atmosphere. Mournes Tyrella beach, horse riding nearby. AA award winner. Open all year.

(14) Morne Abbey Guest House, 16 Greencastle Road, Kilkeel, Co Down BT34 4DE

Mrs Annabel Shannon
☎ 016937 62426
BB From £15.50
EM From £9
Sleeps 10
Registered

Country house on mixed farm in magnificent setting. A warm welcome assured, home cooking a speciality. Fishing, riding, tennis, bowls, golf nearby. 1 single, 2 twin, 1 double, 1 family room. All with H&C, 2 en suite. Sea 1 mile, Silent Valley 4 miles. Kilkeel ½ mile. Open Apr–Sept.

(15) Mountain Pass, 49 Sandbank Road, Hilltown, Co Down BT34 5XU

Mrs Clare Devlin
☎ 018206 38002
BB From £14
EM From £10
Sleeps 6
Registered

Modern bungalow, situated in the heart of the Mourne Mountains, 3 minute walk to mountain paths. Ideal location for relaxing holiday to incorporate rock climbing and mountaineering or just to relax and enjoy the peaceful scenery. 3 miles outside Hilltown heading for Spelga Dam. Turn right at first crossroads. 1 twin and 1 double room, both en suite, 1 double with H&C. Dogs allowed outside. Open all year.

(16) Mountpleasant, 38 Banbridge Road, Gilford, Co Down BT63 6OJ

Mrs M Buller
☎ 01762 831522
☺ ♠ ⚱ ♞ ⛄ ☂
Registered

Listed Georgian house in superb countryside with 5 bedrooms, tastefully decorated. Central for touring any part of N. Ireland. Choice of breakfast. Health and hygiene certificate. Excellent restaurants nearby. We offer good food, friendly service and a warm welcome to all our guests. Tea making facilities and H&C in all bedrooms. 1 mile from Gilford on Banbridge Road. Open all year.

(17) Mourneview, 32 Drumnascamph Road, Laurencetown, Gilford, Co Down BT63 6DU

Esther & Nettie Kerr
☎ 01820 626270/
24251
BB From £15–£16
Sleeps 15
☺ ✂ ♿ ☂ ☂
Registered

Superbly appointed bungalow beautifully designed on 200 acre farm providing a welcoming homely atmosphere. Guests TV lounge, dining room, tea/coffee-making facilities, payphone. Health/hygiene and fire certificates. Good base for touring. Linen. Homelands and participating in the full range of leisure activities nearby. 4 en suite rooms which are also suitable for disabled guests. Also 3 rooms with H&C. Open all year.

Old Town Farm, 25 Corrigs Road, Newcastle, Co Down BT33 0JZ

Mrs W M Annett
☎ **013967 22740**
🛏 **From £15**
Sleeps 6
🛇 🐴 🐕
Registered

Farmhouse with central heating on 88-acre dairy farm in quiet surroundings with panoramic view of Mournes. Near Forest Park and golf. Three double rooms, one en suite. Fishing and pony on farm. Babysitter. From Newcastle take A50 (Castlewellan road), 1½ miles, 1st right past caravan site. Open Apr–Sept.

Sharon Farmhouse, 6 Ballykeel Road, Ballymartin, Kilkeel, Co Down BT34 4PL

M. Bingham
☎ **016937 62521**
🛏 **From £14–£16**
Sleeps 6
🐴 🚲 🛇 🚶 ✂
Registered

Farm bungalow – 1 family, 1 twin, 1 single, all with H/C and central heating. Guest bathroom/shower. With excellent sea and mountain views. Situated ideally for mountaineering and 10 minutes from beach. 2 miles from Kilkeel town and fishing port. The area is rich in varied birdlife. Good wholesome home cooked food served in abundance. A warm and welcoming atmosphere. Your comfort is our pleasure. Open all year.

The Sycamores, 52 Majors Hill, Annalong, Co Down BT34 4QR

Ann McKee
☎ **013967 68279**
🛏 **From £15–£16**
EM From £9
Sleeps 9
🛇 🍽 📺 🚲
Registered

Traditional farmhouse accommodation with CH and open fires. Situated in outstanding beauty of the countryside with panoramic view of Mourne Mountains and overlooking Irish Sea. Activities such as tennis, bowls, fishing, riding, golf all close by. Very central for touring. Bedrooms en suite with colour TV, tea/coffee-making facilities and electric blankets on all beds. Open all year.

Trench Farm, 35 Ringcreevy Road, Comber, Newtownards, Co Down BT23 5JR

Maureen Hamilton
☎ **01247 872558**
🛏 **From £15**
EM From £10
Sleeps 6
🛇 🍽 🚶 🚗
Registered

Farmhouse (central heating) on 100-acre horticultural farm overlooking Lough Scrabo Tower and Forest Park. National Trust properties. Golf, driving ponies kept as hobby. 1 twin room (H/C), 1 single, 1 family. Electric blankets. Babysitter. TV lounge, home cooking. A21 Newtownards Road from Comber first road on right. Comber 3 miles, Newtownards 4 miles. Open all year except Christmas.

Wyncrest, 30 Main Road, Ballymartin, Kilkeel, Co Down BT34 4NU

Robert & Irene Adair
☎/Fax **016937 63012**
🛏 **£19.50**
EM £13
Sleeps 11
🖝 🛇 🍴
Registered

BTA Commended country farm guesthouse with 'Taste of Ulster' and All Ireland Galtee Best Breakfast Awards. Two double, 4 twin (4 en suite). Electric blankets, tea/coffee facilities in all rooms, colour TV in en suite rooms. On main Newcastle/ Kilkeel road (A2), Kilkeel 3 miles, Newcastle 10 miles. Reductions for extended bookings. Open Apr–Sept.

Please mention **Stay on a Farm** when booking

For information on farm holidays in various countries in Europe please contact the following:

GERMANY

Arbeitsgemeinschaft für Urlaub auf dem Bauernhof in der Bundesrepublik Deutschland e.V.
Godesberger Allee 142-148
53175 BONN
☎ [49] 228 81 98 220
Fax [49] 228 81 98 231

Deutsche Landwirtschafts gesellschaft
Eschborner Landstraße 122
60489 FRANKFURT
☎ [49] 69 247 880
Fax [49] 69 247 88 110

BELGIUM

Gîtes de Wallonie
Rue de Millénaire, 53
6941 VILLERS SAINTE GERTRUDE
☎ [32] 86 49 95 31
Fax [32] 86 49 94 07

FINLAND

Lomarengas
Malminkaari 23
00700 HELSINKI
☎ [358] 0 351 61 321
Fax [358] 0 351 61 370

FRANCE

Fédération Nationale des Gîtes de France
56, rue Saint Lazare
75009 PARIS
☎ [1] 49 70 75 75
Fax [1] 49 70 75 76

Agriculture et Tourisme
Assemblée Permanente des Chambres d'Agriculture
9, avenue George V
75008 PARIS
☎ [1] 47 23 55 40
Fax [1] 47 23 84 97

HUNGARY

Association of Village Farm Houses
Szoboszalai u. 2-4
1126 BUDAPEST
☎ [36] 1 155 533 312
Fax [36] 1 155 18 57

Hungarian Federation of Rural Tourism
Klauzal Ter 5
1072 BUDAPEST
☎/Fax [36] 1 268 05 92

ICELAND

Icelandic Farm Holidays
Hotel Saga – Hagatorg
107 REYKJAVIK
☎ [354] 5 623 640
Fax [354] 5 623 644

IRELAND

Irish Farm Holidays
2 Michael Street
LIMERICK
☎ [353] 61 400 700
☎ [353] 61 400 707
Fax [353] 61 400 771

Irish Country Holidays
Rural Development Centre
ATHENRY CO GALWAY
☎ [353] 91 44 473
Fax [353] 91 44 296

ITALY

Agriturist
C. SO Vittorio Emmanuelle, 101
00186 ROMA
☎ [39] 66 85 23 42
Fax [39] 66 85 24 24

LUXEMBOURG

Association pour la Promotion du Tourisme
Rural au Grand-Duché du Luxembourg
c/o Centrale Paysanne
2980 LUXEMBOURG
☎ [352] 48 81 61
Fax [352] 40 03 75

PORTUGAL

Privetur
Nucleo Regional Do Minho E Litoral Norte
Largo das Pereiras
4990 PONTE DE LIMA
☎/Fax [351] 58 741 493

ROMANIA

Antrec
National Association of Rural, Ecological, Cultural, Tourism
B. P. 22-559
BUCAREST
☎/Fax [40] 1 222 83 22

Bran Imex
Bran Jud. Brasov
Str. dr. A. Stoian 395
☎ [40] 68 23 66 42
☎ [40] 1 666 59 48
Fax [40] 68 15 25 98

SLOVAKIA

Slovensky Zväz Vidieckej Turistiky A Agroturistiky
Trencianska 55
82101 BRATISLAVA
☎ [42] 7 215 800/209
Fax [42] 7 214 903

SPAIN

Red Andaluza de Alojamientos Rurales
Apartado Correos 2035
04080 ALMERIA
☎ [34] 50 26 50 18
Fax [34] 50 27 04 31

SWEDEN

The Sweddish University of Agricultural Sciences
Ala Box 7013
75007 UPPSALA
☎ [46] 18 67 19 12
Fax [46] 18 67 19 80

SWITZERLAND

Verein "Ferien auf dem Bauernhof"
Feierlenhof
8595 ALTNAU
☎/Fax [41] 72 65 23 72

Index

To farms offering a welcome to disabled visitors, business people,
and/or providing camping and caravanning facilities

County		Farm	Page no.	Disabled facilities	Tents	Touring caravans	Static caravans	Business people welcome	Meeting room (capacity)
Cornwall (continued)	B&B	Manuels Farm	305					✔	
		Polsue Manor Farm	305					✔	✔ (12)
		Poltarrow Farm	305					✔	
		Treffry Farm	306					✔	
		Tregaddra Farm	306					✔	
		Tregaswith Farmhouse	306					✔	✔ (8)
		Tregidgeo	306					✔	
		Treglisson	306		✔	✔		✔	✔ (24)
		Tregonan	307					✔	✔ (20)
		Tregondale Farm	307					✔	
		Trehane Farm	307					✔	
		Treveria Farm	307					✔	
	SC	Bucklawren Farm	308					✔	✔ (20)
		The Coach House	309		✔			✔	✔ (30)
		Glynn Barton Farm Cottages	309	✔				✔	
		Lower Trengale Farm	309		✔				
		Manuels Farm	310					✔	
		Nancolleth Farm Caravan Gardens	313				✔		
		Poltarrow Farm	310	✔				✔	
		Tredethick Farm Cottages	311	✔				✔	
		Treffry Farm Cottages	311					✔	
		Treharrock Farm Cottages	311					✔	
		Tremadart Farm	312					✔	
		Trevalgan Farm	312					✔	
Cumbria	B&B	Bessiestown Farm	69					✔	✔ (10)
		Cracrop Farm	66					✔	✔ (6)
		Craigburn Farm	69	✔					
		Garnett House Farm	97					✔	
		Gateside Farm	97					✔	
		Hornby Hall	88					✔	✔ (30)
		Howard House Farm	66		✔			✔	✔ (12)
		Keskadale Farm	92				✔	✔	
		Meaburn Hill Farm	88		✔	✔			
		Middle Bayles Farm	85					✔	
		New Pallyards	66	✔				✔	✔ (12)
		Stanger Farm	94					✔	✔ (6)
		Streethead Farm	89					✔	
		Tranthwaite Hall	97		✔				
		Tymparon Hall	92			✔		✔	
	SC	Birchbank Cottage	98		✔	✔			
		Burn and Meadow View	67	✔				✔	✔ (20)
		Green View Lodges & Well Cottage	89	✔				✔	

County		Farm	Page no.	Disabled facilities	Tents	Touring caravans	Static caravans	Business people welcome	Meeting room (capacity)
Cumbria (continued)		Grey Croft	86					✔	
		Preston Patrick Hall Cottage	98					✔	✔ (30)
		Skirwith Hall Cottage	89					✔	
		Smithy Cottage	89					✔	
		Stanger Farm	95					✔	
Derbyshire	B&B	Beechenhill Farm	144					✔	✔ (6)
		The Beeches Farmhouse	150					✔	✔ (12)
		Chevin Green Farm	150			✔			
		Cote Bank Farm	144					✔	
		Dannah Farm	150	✔				✔	✔ (25)
		Henmore Grange	144	✔				✔	✔ (14)
		Lane End Farm	144			✔			
		Mercaston Hall	151		✔	✔		✔	✔ (8)
		Middlehills Farm	145		✔	✔	✔	✔	
		New Park Farm	151	✔				✔	
		The Old Bake and Brewhouse	145		✔	✔			
		Park View Farm	151					✔	
	SC	Archway Cottage	146			✔			
		Briar, Bluebell & Primrose Cottages	152					✔	
		Chevin Green Farm	152	✔		✔			
		Cruck Cottage	146					✔	
		Hall Farm Bungalow	152	✔					
		The Hayloft	146		✔	✔			
		Honeysuckle Cottage	153					✔	
		Honeysuckle & Jasmine Cottages	147		✔	✔	✔	✔	
		Old House Farm Cottage	147					✔	
		The Old Stables	147	✔	✔	✔			
		Shatton Hall Farm Cottages	148					✔	
Devon	B&B	Adams Hele Farm	287					✔	
		Aller Barton Farm	281					✔	✔ (15)
		Barn Park Farm	281					✔	
		Berry Farm	287					✔	
		Budleigh Farm	287		✔	✔		✔	✔ (25)
		Burton Farm	294					✔	✔ (25)
		Claypitts Farm	281					✔	
		Combas Farm	271		✔				
		Coombe Farm	294		✔	✔		✔	✔ (6)
		Court Barton	271					✔	

County		Farm	Page no.	Disabled facilities	Tents	Touring caravans	Static caravans	Business people welcome	Meeting room (capacity)
Devon (continued)	B&B	Court Barton Farmhouse	294					✔	✔ (25)
		Denham Farm	271					✔	✔ (30)
		Elm Park	301					✔	
		Foales Leigh	288		✔			✔	
		Frost Farm	288	✔					
		Godford Farm	281					✔	✔ (8)
		Great Court Farm	288					✔	✔ (6)
		Great Houndbeare Farm	281		✔	✔		✔	
		Great Sloncombe Farm	288					✔	
		Greenwell Farm	288					✔	✔ (16)
		Haxton Down Farm	271					✔	
		Hele Barton	277					✔	✔ (8)
		Higher Cadham Farm	298	✔					
		Higher Churchill Farm	271					✔	✔ (6)
		Higher Coombe Farm	282					✔	
		Higher Weston Farm	282			✔		✔	✔ (6)
		Hillhead Farm	289		✔				
		Home Park Farm	272					✔	
		Huxtable Farm	272		✔			✔	✔ (10)
		Lane End Farm	282	✔				✔	
		Lower Nichols Nymet Farm	298					✔	✔ (12)
		Lower Pinn Farm	282					✔	
		Lower Southway Farm	289	✔	✔			✔	
		Lower Thornton Farm	289					✔	
		Mill Farm	289					✔	
		Mill Leat Farm	289		✔				
		New Cott Farm	290	✔				✔	✔ (12)
		Newcourt Barton	282		✔	✔			
		Newhouse Farm	278					✔	
		Peek Hill Farm	290		✔				
		Pippinfield Farm	282		✔	✔			
		Quoit-at-Cross Farm	278					✔	✔ (15)
		Rydon Farm	283					✔	✔ (10)
		Skinners Ash Farm	283					✔	✔ (25)
		Slade Barn	295					✔	
		Smallicombe Farm	283	✔				✔	✔ (20)
		Strashleigh Farm	290					✔	
		Venn Farm	290					✔	
		Waytown Farm	272					✔	
		Week Farm	298	✔				✔	✔ (12)
		Wellpritton Farm	290	✔				✔	
		Whitemoor Farm	291		✔			✔	

County		Farm	Page no.	Disabled facilities	Tents	Touring caravans	Static caravans	Business people welcome	Meeting room (capacity)
Devon (continued)	B&B	Wiscombe Linhaye Farm	283	✔					
	SC	Ashdown	273	✔				✔	
		The Barleycorn	273	✔				✔	
		Beechgrove	273	✔				✔	
		Bertie's Barn	284					✔	✔ (25)
		Bodmiscombe Farm	284	✔				✔	
		Budleigh Farm	291	✔	✔	✔		✔	✔ (25)
		The Cottage	273					✔	
		Drewstone Farm	274	✔					
		The Granary & Little Week Barns	299	✔				✔	✔ (12)
		Hele Barton	279					✔	
		Hele Payne Farm	279					✔	
		Lemprice Farm	284	✔					
		Longmeadow Farm	291		✔	✔			
		Manor Farm	274					✔	
		Mill Cottage	284		✔	✔		✔	
		Narramore Farm Cottages	291	✔	✔				
		Nethercott Manor Farm	274	✔				✔	
		Netton Farm Holiday Cottages	296					✔	
		Smallicombe Farm	285	✔				✔	✔ (20)
		Traine Farm	296					✔	
		Welcombe Farm	275				✔		
		West Ilkerton Farm	268		✔				
		Whitefield Barton	268					✔	✔ (12)
		Willesleigh Farm	275	✔					
		Wonham Barton	279					✔	✔ (12)
		Wooder Manor	292	✔				✔	
Dorset	B&B	Almshouse Farm	254		✔	✔			
		Church Farm	254					✔	✔ (18)
		Colesmoor Farm	254					✔	
		Higher Langdon	255		✔	✔		✔	✔ (20)
		Holebrook Farm	255	✔				✔	✔ (80)
		Maiden Castle Farm	255		✔			✔	
		Rudge Farm	256					✔	
		Yalbury Park	256					✔	✔ (10)
	SC	Dairy Cottages	256	✔				✔	✔ (60)
		Glebe Cottage	251	✔					
		Gore Cottage	251					✔	
		Hartgrove Farm	257	✔	✔			✔	
		Higher Langdon Flat	257		✔	✔		✔	✔ (20)

County		Farm	Page no.	Disabled facilities	Tents	Touring caravans	Static caravans	Business people welcome	Meeting room (capacity)
Dorset (continued)	SC	Higher Waterston Farm Cottages	257	✔					
		Luccombe Farm	257	✔	✔	✔		✔	✔ (12)
		Mead Cottage	257		✔	✔			
		Rudge Farm Cottages	258	✔				✔	
		Yew House Cottages	258	✔				✔	
Co. Durham	B&B	Bee Cottage Farm	76					✔	✔ (12)
		East Mellwaters Farm	81		✔	✔		✔	✔ (20)
		Greenwell Farm	77	✔				✔	✔ (12)
		Low Cornriggs Farm	85					✔	✔ (10)
		Mount Escob Farm	77					✔	
		Wythes Hill Farm	81		✔				
	SC	Bradley Burn Holiday Cottages	78	✔	✔	✔		✔	
		Greenwell Hill Stables and Byre	78	✔				✔	✔ (12)
		Papermill Cottages	79					✔	✔ (8)
East Sussex	B&B	Moonshill Farm	229	✔	✔	✔		✔	
		Ousedale House	230					✔	✔ (25)
		The Stud Farm	230	✔					
		Stud Farm House	230		✔	✔		✔	✔ (50)
	SC	2 Victoria Cottage	232					✔	
Essex	B&B	Rockells Farm	218	✔					
		Spicers Farm	218		✔	✔		✔	✔ (10)
Gloucestershire	B&B	Abbots Court	182	✔					
		Avenue Farm	182					✔	
		Elms Farm	183		✔	✔			
		Gilbert's	183					✔	✔ (8)
		Hunting Butts Farm	184	✔				✔	✔ (12)
		Kilmorie Guest House	184		✔	✔		✔	✔ (12)
		Manor Farm, Weston-Sub-Edge	184					✔	
		Manor Farm, Winchcombe	184		✔	✔		✔	✔ (10)
		New House Farm	185		✔				
		Oldends Farm	185					✔	
		Postlip Hall Farm	185					✔	
		Town Street Farm	186		✔	✔		✔	
		Upper Farm	186	✔					
		Wickridge Court Farm	186					✔	✔
		Windrush Farm	186			✔			
	SC	Folly Farm Cottages	187	✔				✔	✔ (200)
		Manor Farm Cottages	187		✔	✔		✔	✔ (10)
		New House Farm Cottages	187		✔				

County		Farm	Page no.	Disabled facilities	Tents	Touring caravans	Static caravans	Business people welcome	Meeting room (capacity)
Gloucestershire	SC	Westley Farm	188	✔	✔				
Greater Manchester	B&B	Globe Farm	135		✔	✔		✔	
	SC	Dove Cottage	133					✔	
Hampshire	B&B	Brocklands Farm	226	✔		✔		✔	✔ (12)
		Oakdown Farm Bungalow	226					✔	
	SC	Owl Cottage	227	✔				✔	
Herefordshire	B&B	Hill Top Farm	168		✔	✔			
		Home Farm	168		✔	✔			
		Old Court Farm	169					✔	✔ (30)
		Sink Green Farm	169					✔	✔ (8)
		The Vauld House Farm	169	✔	✔	✔		✔	
	SC	Anvil Cottage	169	✔	✔	✔			
		Mill House Flat	170		✔	✔			
		Old Forge Cottage	170	✔	✔	✔		✔	
		The Vauld House Farm	170	✔	✔	✔		✔	
Hertfordshire	B&B	Broadway Farm	204	✔				✔	✔ (12)
		Middle Farm	204		✔	✔		✔	✔(100)
	SC	Bluntswood Hall Cottages	204		✔	✔		✔	✔(100)
		Gamekeeper's Lodge	205					✔	
Humberside	B&B	The Grange	115		✔	✔			
		High Belthorpe	119		✔	✔			
		High Catton Grange	119					✔	✔ (8)
		Kelleythorpe Farm	119					✔	✔ (10)
	SC	The Cottage	120					✔	
Isle of Wight	B&B	Auld Youngwoods Farm	239					✔	✔ (10)
Kent	B&B	Bletchenden Manor Farm	234					✔	
		Hoads Farm	235					✔	
		Home Farm	235					✔	
		Leaveland Court	235					✔	
		Pheasant Farm	235					✔	
		Sissinghurst Castle Farm	235					✔	✔ (25)
		Tanner House	236		✔	✔		✔	✔ (25)
		Wingham Well Farm	236		✔	✔		✔	
	SC	Birdwatchers Cottage	236	✔				✔	
		Golding Hop Farm Cottage	236					✔	
		The Granary	237	✔					
		Owls Nest	237	✔				✔	
		Pheasant Farm	237					✔	
Lancashire	B&B	Brandreth Barn	130	✔				✔	✔ (40)
		Eaves Barn Farm	132					✔	

County		Farm	Page no.	Disabled facilities	Tents	Touring caravans	Static caravans	Business people welcome	Meeting room (capacity)
Lancashire (continued)	B&B	Higher Wanless Farm	132			✔			
		Pasture Bottom Farm	133	✔	✔	✔		✔	
		Sandy Brook Farm	130	✔					
		Stirzakers Farm	128					✔	
	SC	Brackenthwaite Cottages	126		✔	✔		✔	
		Martin Lane Farmhouse Cottages	130		✔	✔			
Leicestershire	B&B	Measham House Farm	199		✔	✔			
		Three Ways Farm	199	✔				✔	✔ (10)
	SC	Brook Meadow Holiday Chalets	199		✔	✔		✔	✔ (10)
Lincolnshire	B&B	Beechwood Barn	190					✔	
		Bleasby House	190					✔	
		East Farm House	190					✔	
		Greenfield Farm	191					✔	
		Midstone Farmhouse	191					✔	
	SC	East Farm Cottage	191					✔	
		Waingrove Farm	192	✔				✔	
Norfolk	B&B	Birds Place Farm	209					✔	
		Hempstead Hall	210			✔			
		Highfield Farm	210					✔	✔ (8)
		Old Coach House	211		✔	✔		✔	
		Rymer Farm	212					✔	✔ (20)
		Salamanca Farm Guest House	212					✔	✔ (14)
		Shrublands Farm	213		✔	✔		✔	
		Sloley Farm	213		✔	✔		✔	✔ (8)
		South Acre Hall	213		✔			✔	✔ (14)
		South Elmham Hall	213					✔	
		Stratton Farm	213	✔				✔	✔ (10)
		The Toll Barn	213	✔				✔	✔ (10)
	SC	Dairy Farm Cottages	214	✔				✔	✔ (10)
		Sid's Cottage	215				✔		
North Yorkshire	B&B	Ainderby Myers Farm	107		✔				
		Barn Close Farm	112	✔				✔	
		Bay Tree Farm	107	✔					
		Bowes Green Farm	104					✔	
		Carr House Farm	107					✔	✔ (16)
		Church Farm	119					✔	
		Clough House Farm	104					✔	
		Elmfield Country House	107	✔				✔	✔ (30)
		Haregill Lodge	108					✔	
		Hatton House Farm	104					✔	
		Hill End Farm	112					✔	
		Island Farm	115					✔	✔ (8)

County	Farm	Page no.	Disabled facilities	Tents	Touring caravans	Static caravans	Business people welcome	Meeting room (capacity)
North Yorkshire (continued) B&B	Knabbs Ash	104					✔	
	Lamb Hill Farm	108					✔	
	Lane House Farm	126		✔	✔	✔	✔	
	Laskill Farm	108	✔	✔	✔		✔	✔ (20)
	Lovesome Hill Farm	108	✔	✔	✔			
	Lund Farm	120			✔		✔	
	Mill Close Farm	108					✔	
	Mount Grace Farm	112					✔	✔ (20)
	Mount Pleasant Farm	109	✔				✔	
	Newgate Foot	115		✔			✔	✔ (20)
	North Pasture Farm	105		✔			✔	
	Plane Tree Cottage Farm	116		✔				
	Rains Farm	116	✔		✔			
	Valley View Farm	113	✔	✔	✔		✔	
	Wenningber Farm	101		✔	✔			
	Wilson House	81	✔	✔				
	Winifred Farm	120		✔				
SC	Blackmires Farm	116		✔				
	Cawder Hall Cottages	101	✔				✔	✔ (12)
	Clematis Cottage & Well Cottage	110			✔			
	Clough House Farm	105					✔	
	1&2 Dove Cottages	120					✔	
	Lund Farm Cottage	121			✔		✔	
	Pond Farm	117				✔		
	Rains Farm	117	✔		✔			
	Stanhow Farm Bungalow	110	✔				✔	
	Valley View Farm	113	✔	✔	✔		✔	
Northamptonshire B&B	Dairy Farm	194					✔	✔ (10)
	The Elms	194					✔	
	Green Farm	194					✔	
	Manor Farm	195		✔	✔		✔	✔ (20)
	Murcott Mill	195			✔			
	Pear Tree Farm	195		✔	✔			
	Walltree House Farm	196	✔				✔	✔ (10)
	West Lodge Farm	196					✔	✔ (60)
	Wold Farm	196					✔	✔ (10)
SC	Cranford Farm	197					✔	✔ (80)
	Papley Farm Cottages	197					✔	
	Rye Hill Farm	197	✔				✔	✔ (12)
Northumberland B&B	Ald White Craig Farm	66					✔	
	Burton Hall	71	✔					
	Doxford Farmhouse	71		✔	✔		✔	✔ (25)
	Earle Hill Head Farm	71		✔			✔	✔ (10)
	Elford Farmhouse	71					✔	

County		Farm	Page no.	Disabled facilities	Tents	Touring caravans	Static caravans	Business people welcome	Meeting room (capacity)
Northumberland	B&B	Gairshield Farm	76		✔				
(continued)	SC	The Old Smithy	74	✔					
		Rye Hill Farm	77		✔	✔		✔	✔ (10)
		No. 2 and 3 Cottages	74	✔				✔	
Nottinghamshire	B&B	Blue Barn Farm	155					✔	
		Far Baulker Farm	155		✔	✔		✔	
		Forest Farm	155					✔	
		Hall Farm House	155					✔	✔ (20)
		Jerico Farm	155					✔	✔ (6)
	SC	Blue Barn Cottage	156					✔	✔ (12)
		Foliat Cottages	156					✔	✔ (8)
		Honeysuckle Cottage	156					✔	
		The Loft House	157			✔			
Oxfordshire	B&B	Hill Grove Farm	221			✔		✔	✔ (10)
		Little Parmoor Farm	221					✔	✔ (10)
		Mead Close	222		✔	✔			
		Morar	222					✔	
	SC	Hill Grove Cottage	224			✔			
Shropshire	B&B	Acton Scott Farm	163			✔			
		Billingsley Hall Farm	163		✔	✔		✔	✔ (12)
		Bradeley Green Farm	159					✔	
		Church Farm (Wrockwardine)	159	✔				✔	✔ (12)
		Haynall Villa	167					✔	✔ (8)
		Hurst Mill Farm	164	✔	✔	✔		✔	
		Lane End Farm	159					✔	
		Lowe Farm	164			✔			
		Mickley House	159	✔				✔	
		New House Farm	164		✔				
		Seifton Court Farm	164		✔	✔			
		The Sett Village Farm	160					✔	✔ (12)
		Soulton Hall	160					✔	✔ (25)
		Stoke Manor	160					✔	
		Strefford Hall Farm	164					✔	✔ (15)
	SC	Billingsley Hall Farm	165		✔	✔			
		Bradeley Green Cottage	161					✔	
Somerset	B&B	Binham Farm	260		✔	✔			
		Blackmore Farm	260					✔	✔ (30)
		Cutthorne Farm	265		✔	✔			
		Greenway Farm	260					✔	✔ (8)
		Hill Ash Farm	261		✔	✔			
		Hindon Farm	266					✔	✔ (15)
		Little Brendon Hill	266					✔	
		Little Quarme Farm	266					✔	✔ (30)
		Lower Farm	261	✔					

County		Farm	Page no.	Disabled facilities	Tents	Touring caravans	Static caravans	Business people welcome	Meeting room (capacity)
Somerset (continued)	B&B	Northwick Farm	261	✔	✔	✔			
		Orchard Farm	261		✔	✔		✔	
		Redhill Farm	243		✔	✔			
		Southway Farm	243					✔	
		Wood Advent Farm	267		✔			✔	✔ (20)
	SC	Cutthorne Farm	267		✔	✔			
		Landacre Farm	268	✔	✔	✔			
		Orchard Farm	263	✔	✔	✔			
		Pear Tree Cottage	263	✔	✔	✔			
		Westermill Farm	268		✔			✔	
	CC	Halse Farm	269	✔	✔	✔			
		Westermill Farm	269		✔				
Staffordshire	B&B	Manor House Farm	151					✔	
		Oulton House Farm	160					✔	
	SC	Lower Berkhamsytch Farm	147	✔				✔	
		Swallows Nest	161					✔	
Suffolk	B&B	Brighthouse Farm	209		✔	✔			
		Church Farm	209		✔	✔			
		College Farm	209					✔	✔ (10)
		Earsham Park Farm	210					✔	
		Kenton Hall	211					✔	
		Priory Farm	212			✔		✔	
		Red House Farm	212		✔				
		Woodlands Farm	214					✔	
	SC	The Coach House	214					✔	
		The Granary	215			✔			
		The Granary Suites	215		✔	✔			
		St Peter's View	215	✔					
		Stable Cottages and The Granary	216	✔					
Surrey	SC	Badgersholt and Foxholme	231	✔		✔		✔	✔ (12)
Warwickshire	B&B	Church Farm	176	✔				✔	✔ (12)
		Crandon House	176					✔	✔ (12)
		Glebe Farm	176					✔	
		Hill Farm	177			✔			
		Holland Park Farm	177					✔	
		Irelands Farm	177					✔	
		Lower Watchbury Farm	177					✔	✔ (8)
		Manor Farm	178					✔	
		Maxstoke Hall Farm	178			✔		✔	✔ (10)
		Packington Lane Farm	178			✔		✔	
		The Poplars	178					✔	
		Shrewley Pools Farm	178					✔	✔ (6)

County		Farm	Page no.	Disabled facilities	Tents	Touring caravans	Static caravans	Business people welcome	Meeting room (capacity)
Warwickshire (continued)	B&B	Snowford Hall Farm	178					✔	
		Tibbits Farm	179		✔	✔			
		Whitchurch Farm	179					✔	✔ (12)
		Yew Tree Farm	179		✔				
	SC	Hipsley Farm Cottages	180	✔				✔	
		Irelands Farm	180	✔					
West Sussex	B&B	Goffsland Farm	229		✔	✔		✔	
		Manor Farm	229		✔	✔		✔	
		New House Farm	230		✔			✔	
West Yorkshire	B&B	Birch Laithes Farm	123					✔	✔ (10)
		Brow Top Farm	100					✔	
		Scaife Hall Farm	105					✔	✔ (6)
	SC	Bottoms Farm Cottages	101					✔	✔ (12)
		Westfield Farm Cottages	102	✔				✔	
Wiltshire	B&B	Ashen Copse Farm	221					✔	
		Boyds Farm	245					✔	✔ (10)
		Friday Street Farm	245					✔	
		Hillside Farm	246					✔	
		Leighfield Lodge Farm	246					✔	
		Longwater Park Farm	246	✔				✔	
		Lower Foxhanger Canal Farm	246		✔	✔	✔	✔	✔ (12)
		Manor Farm, Corston	247					✔	✔ (10)
		Oakwood Farm	185					✔	
		Pickwick Lodge Farm	247					✔	
		Saltbox Farm	248					✔	
	SC	Lower Foxhangers Farm	248		✔	✔	✔		
Worcestershire	B&B	Chirkenhill	172					✔	✔ (12)
		Clay Farm	172		✔	✔		✔	✔ (50)
		Hill Barn Orchard	173		✔	✔		✔	✔ (20)
		Lightmarsh Farm	173					✔	
		Old House Farm	173					✔	
		Phepson Farm	173					✔	
		Tiltridge Farm	174					✔	✔ (10)
	SC	Hill Barn Orchard	174		✔	✔		✔	✔ (12)
		Old Yates Cottages	174	✔				✔	
SCOTLAND									
Angus	B&B	Purgavie Farm	39		✔	✔		✔	✔ (10)
		Wemyss Farm	39					✔	✔ (20)
	SC	Purgavie Farm	40		✔	✔		✔	✔ (10)
Borders	B&B	Cliftonhall Farm	62					✔	✔ (6)
		Lyne Farm	62					✔	✔ (10)
		Morebattle Tofts	62		✔	✔		✔	
		Overlangshaw Farm	62	✔	✔				
		Wiltonburn Farm	63		✔			✔	✔ (6)

Region		Farm	Page no.	Disabled facilities	Tents	Touring caravans	Static caravans	Business people welcome	Meeting room (capacity)
Borders (continued)	SC	Bailey Mill	63	✔				✔	✔ (30)
		Cherry Tree Cottage & Rowan Tree Cottage	63					✔	
		Craggs Cottage	63					✔	
		Little Swinton Cottages	64	✔					
Clyde Valley	B&B	Dunsyre Mains	53		✔				
		Walston Mansion Farmhouse	53					✔	✔ (10)
	SC	Carmichael Country Cottages	53	✔		✔		✔	✔ (50)
Dumfriesshire	B&B	Ericstane	58		✔				
East Lothian	B&B	Barney Mains	60					✔	✔ (10)
		Eaglescairnie Mains	60					✔	✔ (10)
		Rowan Park	60					✔	✔ (10)
Fife	B&B	Ardchoille Farmhouse	45					✔	
		Cambo House	45					✔	✔ (30)
		Dunbog Farm	45					✔	
	SC	Cambo House	46					✔	✔ (30)
		Mountquhanie Holiday Homes	46	✔				✔	✔ (12)
Heart of Scotland	B&B	Allanfauld Farm	48		✔			✔	✔
		Belsyde Farm	48					✔	✔ (12)
		Easter Glentore Farm	48					✔	✔ (8)
		Lower Tarr Farm	49					✔	✔ (8)
		Monachyle Mhor	49	✔				✔	✔ (20)
		Overshiel Farm	49					✔	✔ (8)
		The Topps	50	✔				✔	✔ (20)
		West Plean	50					✔	✔ (12)
	SC	Crosswoodhill	51	✔				✔	✔ (8)
Highlands	B&B	Daviot Mains Farm	34					✔	
		Glen Cloy Farmhouse	34					✔	
		Thistle-Doo	35	✔	✔	✔			
	SC	Borlum Farm Cottage	35	✔	✔	✔			
		Lochletter Lodges	36	✔				✔	✔ (10)
		Mains of Aigas	36					✔	
		Strone Cottage	36	✔					
Perthshire	B&B	Pitmurthly	42		✔	✔			
	SC	Wester Riechip	43					✔	
WALES									
Clwyd	B&B	Bodangharad	327					✔	
		Cefn-y-Fedw Farm	330		✔	✔		✔	✔ (10)
		College Farm	327	✔				✔	
Dyfed	B&B	The Bower Farm	357					✔	✔ (8)
		Broniwan	343		✔			✔	✔ (18)

Region		Farm	Page no.	Disabled facilities	Tents	Touring caravans	Static caravans	Business people welcome	Meeting room (capacity)
Dyfed (continued)	B&B	Brunant Farm	357					✔	✔ (20)
		Bryncastell Farm	341	✔	✔		✔	✔	
		Capel Dewi Uchaf Farm	352					✔	
		Castell Pigyn	357					✔	
		Dolau Isaf Farm	357		✔	✔			
		Dremddu Fawr	341					✔	
		Knowles Farm	358		✔	✔		✔	✔ (10)
		Llanerchindda Farm	352	✔	✔	✔		✔	
		Lochmeyler Farm	354	✔				✔	✔ (40)
		Lower Haythog	354					✔	
		Pant-Teg	343					✔	
		Plas Farm	352					✔	✔ (12)
		Plas-y-Brodyr	358					✔	
		Skerryback	358					✔	
		Ty Newydd Farm	358	✔	✔	✔		✔	
		Whitegates	359		✔			✔	✔ (20)
	SC	Dove Cottage	359					✔	
		Garden Farm	355	✔					
		Gwarmacwydd	359					✔	
		Haven Cottages	360					✔	
Gwent	B&B	Parsons Grove	348	✔					
		Pentre-Tai Farm	348		✔	✔		✔	
		Pentwyn Farm	348					✔	✔ (14)
		Tŷ-Gwyn Farm	349					✔	
		Ty Shon Jacob Farm	349					✔	✔ (12)
		The Wenallt Farm	349	✔	✔			✔	✔ (20)
	SC	Parsons Grove	349	✔					
		Pentwyn Stable Cottages	350					✔	✔ (20)
		Worcester House	350					✔	
Gwynedd	B&B	Bryn Celynog Farm	324		✔				
		Cwm Hwylfod	324		✔				
		Llwydiarth Fawr	319					✔	✔ (10)
		Old Mill Farmhouse	324	✔				✔	✔ (12)
		Rhydydefaid Farm	324				✔		
		Tre'rddôl Farm	320		✔			✔	
		Tyddyn Du Farm	325					✔	
		Tyddyn Iolyn	325					✔	
		Ty Mawr Farm	320					✔	✔ (10)
		Ystumgwern	320	✔	✔	✔		✔	
	SC	Bryn Beddau	321					✔	
		Caerwych Farmhouse	325					✔	
		Chwilog Fawr	321			✔	✔		
		Gwynfryn Farm	316	✔	✔	✔		✔	
		Hafod and Hendre	321					✔	✔ (10)

Region		Farm	Page no.	Disabled facilities	Tents	Touring caravans	Static caravans	Business people welcome	Meeting room (capacity)
Gwynedd (continued)		Llwydiarth Fawr Farm Cottages	321	✔	✔		✔	✔	
		Llys Bennar	321	✔	✔	✔			
		Pen-y-Bryn	322		✔	✔			
		Rhydolion	317	✔	✔	✔			
		Towyn Farm	317	✔	✔	✔			
		Ynys	322	✔	✔	✔		✔	
Powys	B&B	Brynfedwen Farm	345	✔					
		Cefnsuran	338		✔	✔		✔	✔ (15)
		Cilthriew	334	✔	✔			✔	✔ (12)
		Cwmgilla	338		✔				
		The Drewin Farm	334		✔			✔	✔ (8)
		Highbury Farm	338		✔				
		Little Brompton Farm	334		✔	✔		✔	
		Lower Gwestydd	335					✔	
		Trehenry Farm	345					✔	
	SC	Red House	336					✔	
		Trehenry Farm	346		✔			✔	
NORTHERN IRELAND									
Antrim	B&B	Beechgrove	366		✔	✔		✔	
		Carnside Farm Guest House	366		✔				
		Carrick-Dhu Guest House	367	✔					
		Country Guest House	367					✔	✔ (16)
		Craig's Farm	367		✔	✔			
		Cullentra House	367	✔				✔	
		Dieskirt Farm	367		✔				
		Hill Vale Farm	368					✔	✔ (8)
		Islay-View	368	✔					
		Valley View	369	✔					
Down	B&B	Beechhill Farm	378		✔				
		Bushymead Country House	378					✔	✔ (40)
		Drumgooland House	379					✔	✔ (15)
		Fair Haven	379					✔	
		Four Winds	379	✔					
		Greenlea Farm	380					✔	
		Mountpleasant	380		✔				
		Mourneview	380	✔					
		Sharon Farmhouse	381	✔	✔				
		The Sycamores	381	✔				✔	✔ (10)
		Trench Farm	381		✔	✔		✔	
		Wyncrest	381					✔	

County		Farm	Page no.	Disabled facilities	Tents	Touring caravans	Static caravans	Business people welcome	Meeting room (capacity)
Fermanagh	B&B	Ardess House	373					✔	✔ (18)
		Broadmeadows House	373	✔	✔				
		The Olde Schoolhouse	374	✔	✔			✔	✔ (20)
		Riverside Farm Guest House	374	✔	✔	✔			
		Rossgweer House	374	✔					
Londonderry	B&B	Ballyhenry House	362					✔	✔ (20)
		Bellevue Country House	362					✔	
		Braehead House	362					✔	
		Brown's Country House	363	✔				✔	✔ (10)
		Elagh Hall	363		✔	✔		✔	✔ (12)
		Greenhill House	363					✔	✔ (14)
		Groarty House	363					✔	
		Heathfield House	363					✔	✔ (15)
		Killeague Farm	364		✔				
		Sperrin View Farm House	364					✔	
Tyrone	B&B	Greenmount Lodge	371	✔				✔	✔ (70)